W9-BXA-497

THIRD EDITION

John Braheny

The Craft and Business of
Songwriting

a practical guide to creating and marketing
artistically and commercially successful songs

WRITER'S DIGEST BOOKS

writersdigestbooks.com
Cincinnati, Ohio

The Craft and Business of Songwriting, third edition© 2006 by John Braheny. Manufactured in the United States of America. All rights reserved. No part of this book may be reproduced in any form or by any electronic or mechanical means including information storage and retrieval systems without permission in writing from the publisher, except by a reviewer, who may quote brief passages in a review. Published by Writer's Digest Books, an imprint of F+W Publications, Inc., 4700 East Galbraith Road, Cincinnati, OH 45236. (800) 289-0963. Third edition.

Visit our Web site at www.writersdigest.com for information on more resources for writers.

To receive a free weekly e-mail newsletter delivering tips and updates about writing and about Writer's Digest products, register directly at our Web site at http://newsletters.fwpublications.com.

10 09 08 07 06   5 4 3 2 1

Distributed in Canada by Fraser Direct
100 Armstrong Avenue
Georgetown, ON, Canada L7G 5S4
Tel: (905) 877-4411
Distributed in the U.K. and Europe by David & Charles
Brunel House, Newton Abbot, Devon, TQ12 4PU, England
Tel: (+44) 1626 323200, Fax: (+44) 1626 323319
E-mail: postmaster@davidandcharles.co.uk
Distributed in Australia by Capricorn Link
P.O. Box 704, Windsor, NSW 2756 Australia
Tel: (02) 4577-3555

Library of Congress Cataloging-in-Publication Data
Braheny, John, 1938-
  The craft and business of songwriting, third edition / by John Braheny.
     p. cm.
  Includes bibliographical references and index.
  ISBN-10: 1-58297-466-7
  ISBN-13: 978-1-58297-466-8 (pbk. : alk. paper)
  1. Popular music--Writing and publishing. I. Title.
  MT67.B65 2007
  782.42164'13--dc22

                    2006015554

Edited by Ian Bessler and Michelle Ehrhard
Designed by Claudean Wheeler
Production coordinated by Robin Richie

fw

F+W PUBLICATIONS, INC.

PERMISSIONS

SHE'S IN LOVE WITH THE BOY Words and Music by Jon Ims © 1991. Warner/Chappell Music Inc. and Rites of Passage Music (BMI). All Rights Reserved. Used by Permission.

DON'T LAUGH AT ME Words and Music by Steve Seskin and Allen Shamblin © 1997. Sony Music Publishing/ David Aaron Music (ASCAP) and Built on Rock Music (ASCAP) All Rights Reserved. Used by Permission.

Excerpt (Ringtone Deals in the U.S.) from "Taking a Glance at New Media Deals in the Music Industry" by Dina LaPolt (www.LaPoltLaw.com) , Esq. August 2005 from MusicBizAcademy.com.

5th edition of *Music, Money, and Success: The Insider's Guide to Making Money in the Music Business* written by Jeffrey Brabec and Todd Brabec (published by Schirmer Trade Books/Music Sales). By permission © 2006 Jeff Brabec, Todd Brabec. Also see www.musicandmoney.com.

Acknowledgments for the Original Edition

There are many people who, both directly and indirectly, helped to write this book. It's impossible to put them in any order of rank, so I'll do it in a roughly chronological order.

My late parents, William and Cecilia, who always encouraged me to do my best at whatever I did; my brothers, Dan and Kevin, and my sister, Mary, who did the same; and my friend, Len Chandler, with whom I've been growing and learning and dreaming since we started the Los Angeles Songwriters Showcase in 1971. Without his support and his taking on an extra workload while I worked on the first edition (and his reminders that my sentences are too long), this couldn't have been written. Also, I must thank the LASS office staff, and Joy Wildin in particular, who shared that extra load with great patience.

The LASS sponsor, BMI, and in particular the late Ron Anton, whose support for eighteen years allowed us to create new ways to help songwriters. *Music Connection* magazine publishers, Michael Dolan and Eric Bettelli, who asked me to write a column for their new magazine in '77 and Mandi Martin-Fox, who convinced me I could do it.

My wife, JoAnn, whose love and support allowed her to put up with a home in which every available surface was covered with "the book," vacations dreamed of but not taken, weekend plans canceled, and other inconveniences too numerous to mention. Thank God she has a great sense of humor. Her good ideas and critiques and countless hours of typing also helped shape this book.

My friend and agent for this book, Ronny Schiff, who persistently pursued getting it published and contributed her expertise on the print music business. My original editor at Writer's Digest Books, Julie Whaley, who believed in this project. Her relentless encouragement, critiques, and suggestions pushed me to make this a much better book than it otherwise would have been.

Many friends have read various parts of this book and contributed information and critiques. They include hit songwriter Alan O'Day, publisher Dude McLean, A&R exec (now NARAS head) Neil Portnow, music business consultant Thomas A. White, attorneys Michael Fletcher, Jeffrey Graubart, Kent Klavens, Al Schlesinger, Jack Whitley, and Gary Wishik. Literally hundreds of other music industry pros have contributed to my understanding of the craft and business of songwriting and the ability to teach it. I also want to thank thousands of hopeful and successful songwriters whose songs continue to enrich my life. This is a kind of payback and, I hope, an investment in encouraging you to give us all more great songs.

David "Cat" Cohen, whose "Theoretically Speaking" column I had admired so much when he was a fellow *Music Connection* writer, that I asked him to contribute the "Writing Music" chapter. He continues to grow as a teacher. And Chris Blake, whose "The Imagination of the Listener" provides such valuable information on how lyrics are effectively communicated.

Acknowledgments for The Third Edition

I still owe the same debt, after all these years, to the people thanked above.

Much has happened because of this book since the first and second editions were released. It brought me new friends all over the world. It presented me with opportunities to pursue my love of teaching at The Musicians Institute in Hollywood, the L.A. Recording School, The National Guitar Summer Workshops in Nashville and L.A., and to be a guest speaker at Berklee College of Music in Boston, UCLA, and the University of Colorado, among others. It let me hang out with, interview, learn from and share many a panel at events with my songwriting heroes. It has introduced me to some amazingly talented new writers who found me because they read the book. In fact, it spawns a continuing series of adventures with my wife and soulmate, JoAnn, as we travel together doing seminars for songwriters' organizations and events around the country. Her experience in the entertainment industry and, in particular, her expertise in the creative process has not only contributed immeasurably to my own education but helped her be my best critic. She continues to enrich my life with her love and wisdom. I'm a lucky guy.

I'm very pleased by the comments from so many readers, who have said they found this book inspiring and enlightening. It has helped them pursue their dreams, armed with the information they needed. Hit writers like John Ims ("She's In Love With The Boy") and Jason Blume (who has written wonderful songwriting books of his own) have told me how much they appreciated it. It has put me in the company of great songwriting teachers too numerous to mention (and, besides, whom do I leave out?) from whom I've learned so much about both the topic itself and how to teach it. They're all in this new edition in many ways.

Special thanks for their expertise in this edition goes to: David "Cat" Cohen; *Music Connection* magazine and its publishers, Michael Dolan and Eric Bettelli; Michael Laskow and the great staff at TAXI; marketing consultant Tim Sweeney; songwriter/producer Hank Linderman; author Dan Kimpel; attorneys Steve Winogradsky, Ken Helmer, Ben McLane, Dina LaPolt and Andrea Brauer; tax accountant Mark Rothstein; songwriters and teachers, K.A. Parker, Pat Pattison, and Michael Silversher; our computer tech guru, Douglas E. Welch; Writer's Digest editors Ian Bessler and Michelle Ehrhard; friends and indie music pioneers Derek Sivers, Brian Austin Whitney, and Diane Rapaport; to the many songwriting teachers who use this book as a text; Ronny Schiff and Disc Marketing who made it possible for me to interview legendary songwriters for United Airlines Inflight Entertainment's Salute to Songwriter Channel; and my son, Mike Toth, who teaches me in many ways and with whom I share the joys of music and technology. Many others are mentioned throughout the book in introductions to their valuable contributions.

About the Author

John Braheny is a music industry consultant and mentor/coach for songwriters and performers. His clients are individuals as well as companies and include TAXI (the independent A&R service), songwriter organizations, and Web site services. John has been a musician, songwriter/performer, recording artist, film composer, commercial jingles producer, and music publisher. He and Len Chandler cofounded and directed the legendary BMI-sponsored Los Angeles Songwriters Showcase (LASS), a national non-profit service organization for songwriters, from 1971 until joining forces with the Songwriters Guild of America in 1999. He coproduced twenty-two annual Songwriters Expo international education and discovery conferences. John has contributed articles to national songwriting publications and Web sites and was a columnist for *Music Connection* and *Music Biz* magazines. He has taught classes on songwriting and the music business at UCLA, Musicians Institute, and Grove School of Music and is a guest speaker and teacher at universities and songwriter organizations throughout the U.S and Canada. He is past president of the California Copyright conference, an organization for entertainment attorneys and music publishers, and has served several terms on the board of the Recording Academy (the GRAMMY organization). For several years he co-hosted "Samm Brown's For the Record," a weekly music industry talk show on KPFK (Pacifica Radio Network) in Los Angeles. John has conducted 55 interviews with hit songwriters and producers for United Airlines In-flight (audio) Entertainment. For more information, visit his very informative Web site at www.johnbraheny.com.

Table of Contents

Introduction

Welcome to my book. Before I start showing you around the place, I think it's only right that I tell you why I brought you here. The reason is that I know you're out there slaving over a cold piece of paper and a hot guitar, keyboard, or computer. You have dreams of writing hit songs, becoming a recording artist, a producer, or anything that will bring you recognition and/or money (or at least buy you a tuna fish sandwich) for doing what you love to do. You care enough about doing it well that you're willing to invest some time in research and development to make sure you're not missing any tricks that helped others be successful. And you also want to make sure you don't make some dumb business move that could blow all your progress.

So I thought that, instead of giving you that information one-on-one for the next few years—which I wouldn't mind, really—it would be much smarter for me to bring you all here at once. (It also will help me buy my own tuna fish sandwich.)

How did I know you were out there? Easy. You've been calling and e-mailing me with your problems, questions, fears, and dreams for years, and I think I've returned most of your calls and e-mails by now.

How Did I Learn What I Know?

How do you know I'm giving you good information? Trust me! (This is the last time you should accept that answer.) But seriously, the question deserves a serious answer, so if you'll come with me for about two minutes I'll give you some background on how this "music information junkie" has fed his habit and can help to feed yours.

My back story starts with eight years of classical violin, a B.A. in Theatre with minors in Psychology and English, six years on the road as a solo folksinger, a year in a blues band, a record deal in '68, recordings of my songs, commercial jingle production, and finally the ideal gig that I never could have imagined, but that used every skill I'd learned just because I'd loved it.

The Craft and Business of Songwriting

The Los Angeles Songwriters Showcase (LASS), which Len Chandler and I founded in 1971, filled a need by providing a focus for songwriting activities and information. Sponsored by Broadcast Music Inc. (BMI) for eighteen years, the Showcase drew the song-hungry music industry pros to a weekly gathering of the best new songwriting and writer/performer talent around. Stevie Nicks and Lindsey Buckingham, Stephen Bishop, Karla Bonoff, Wendy Waldman, Warren Zevon, R. C. Bannon, Kieren Kane, Chick Rains, Oingo Boingo, Alan O'Day, Jules Shear, Janis Ian, Robbie Nevil, and the world's most successful songwriter, Diane Warren, are among the thousands of writers and writer/artists we showcased back then.

We auditioned hundreds of songs a week and showcased the best writers and songs we heard. We found that many of the writers we auditioned exhibited raw talent but little understanding of songwriting craft that could make their songs more commercially viable and/or appealing to their listeners. (Commercial success is not proof of great art, but you already know that.) Those writers whose songs we rejected wanted to know why. To offer them some constructive help, we looked for ways to explain those basic principles that seem to be the common denominators of artistically and commercially successful songs. We also needed information about the music business so we could counsel the writers who were on the brink of making major career decisions. Several circumstances helped us to develop the information we needed.

In 1972, the Los Angeles Songwriters Showcase (then called the Alternative Chorus Songwriters Showcase) began a weekly music industry interview session. It gave us an ongoing opportunity to question hundreds of industry pros including hit songwriters and producers, attorneys, publishers, record company executives, recording artists, managers, record promoters, radio personalities and program directors, club owners, and others. Largely because of this experience, publishers Michael Dolan and Eric Bettelli asked me to write a songwriting column for their new biweekly, *Music Connection* magazine, in 1977. The magazine has subsequently developed into one of the country's best music publications.

During the next six years, I wrote more than 150 "Songmine" columns on all aspects of the art, craft, and business of songwriting. It was a golden opportunity to consolidate and focus the information derived from this unique vantage point.

In 1979, we created "Cassette Roulette" at the Showcase, in which a different guest-publisher was invited to critique songs each week. "Pitch-A-Thon," an extension of that idea, brought in a different producer or record company A&R (artist and repertoire) representative each week to screen songs for specific recording projects. These weekly events gave us and our audiences the opportunity to observe the critical processes of hundreds of publishers, producers, artists, and record company representatives. In addition, our friends in the industry, who believe there is no such thing as a dumb question, generously shared their information with us whenever we asked.

After LASS joined forces with the National Academy of Songwriters (NAS) in 1996, I ran the West Coast office of Wynnward Music, a publishing and production company, for two years. It gave me the opportunity to get valuable experience from "the other side of the desk."

Since then, I've been a consultant for hundreds of writers and writer artists on their songs and careers. I have interviewed scores of my songwriting heroes for United Airlines' United Entertainment Network as a consultant for Disc Marketing's In-flight division. For about five years I interviewed music industry pros as co-host of the talk show, *Samm Brown's For The Record* at KPFK (90.7FM) in L.A. I've also been (and remain) a consultant for Taxi.com, JPFolks.com, and several new publishing companies. I also continue to learn from those of you who attend my songwriting and music marketing classes throughout the country. All these situations keep me connected to and fascinated by this industry.

So there's my background, at least since 1971. As you might imagine, for an information glutton it's an endless banquet. Because this industry continues to grow and change, so does the information. That's why you and I will never stop learning about it. But at least this book will give you a good start.

Songwriting Principles

There are no absolute rules or formulas for songwriting. For every "rule," you'll find a song that broke that rule and succeeded. The music industry has many "right" ways to do anything, including writing great songs.

If you want to write successful songs, instead of learning "rules," you need to be aware of principles, the freedoms and restrictions of the medium for which you want to write, and to have at your command a wide range of options with which to solve each creative problem.

This book will provide you with these options. In most cases you'll find that you already know them instinctively but have never seen them in writing. In recognizing them you'll commit them more strongly to memory and use them more often and more effectively.

Writing a great song is only part of being a successful songwriter. Unsung thousands possess the talent and craft to write great songs, but without understanding the business and the knowledge of how to protect your creations and get them heard by those who can make them successful, those songs are like orphans. And I'm guessing you have a few great orphan songs.

This book explains in plain language how the music industry works, relative to you, the songwriter, whether you write for yourself or your band or for other artists. It will hopefully demystify and humanize what can often feel to a newcomer like a cold, monolithic, and impersonal industry.

Success in the music/entertainment industry requires a combination of talent, love for the art and craft, hard work, a tremendous amount of persistence, and a good dose of dumb luck. To capitalize on dumb luck, you need to be ready when opportunity drops out of the sky. To be ready for your big break, you have to pull your craft and business together. By reading this book (and others recommended in this book), by listening and analyzing all forms of popular music, especially the music you love, by using Internet to its full advantage and by meeting as many people in the business as your can, you'll maximize your chances for success.

Can Songwriting Be Taught?

Can you learn to write songs from a book? Are songwriting classes a waste of time? Critics of songwriter education say it's a waste, that, "You're born with it, and if you're not, there's nothing you can do to get it." Since classes in the craft of songwriting are usually accompanied by some business information, there may be a few among the critics who fear education because they can no longer take advantage of writers' ignorance. But for the most part, music industry pros recognize that they actually benefit from informed writers who understand the business and how to approach it in a professional manner.

In terms of craft, I do believe that, though you may have been born with a predisposition to music and language skills, it's more important to have been raised in an environment where you were encouraged to explore, read, and express yourself verbally and musically and were given positive strokes for it. Some people with the natural talent and drive will pick up what they need to know about the craft by trial and error as they go. Many others with as much talent need to be in a supportive environment and be provided with a base of information by way of classes, books, and workshops to help their creativity bloom.

Though the "trial and error" method is a great teacher and will never be replaced by classes and books, the time you can waste in the "school of hard knocks" may also be devastating to your ego and your will to persevere. "If I knew then what I know now" has been a sad commentary on too many wasted careers. So, getting as much information as early as possible about both craft and business can save you years. Assuming that you're starting with some talent, imagination, and a love for music and/or language, there are basic principles involved in being a good and commercially successful songwriter that *can* be taught. Primarily, you'll be organizing material that you already know instinctively and putting it in a context that helps you remember it when you need it. All types of artists need a knowledge of the media in which they work, their limitations, freedoms, and properties. Painters need to know about the properties of acrylics, oil paints, and watercolors, the types of brushes and canvas, the mechanics of visual perspective. They need to train their eyes.

As songwriters, you need to train your ears. For you, it's important to know, for instance, that Top 40 radio, musical theater, and film all have different requirements for the way songs are written. It's important to have the choice of many different ways to achieve dynamics in a song, and to know why an artistic choice would work in one situation and not in another. Awareness is a tool that can save time and get you what you want much faster. Knowledge serves your inspiration. Craft serves your imagination.

You can't be taught inspiration or imagination. You *can* be taught ways to get in touch with what you have to say and how to communicate it effectively. It's sad to hear songs on the radio with great form and zero substance. It's sadder for me to know that you're out there with something to say that could make me laugh, cry, think about something in a new way, and otherwise enrich my life, but don't know how to do it. This book's for you!

What's New in This Edition?

Very little changes in the craft of songwriting—the same song structures and basic principles still work, though creative writers and producers continue to find new ways to use them. But the industry has changed considerably. Audiences have changed too in that they expect much more access to their favorite artists. E-mail, artist blogs, and podcasts have made that possible. Rather than to look at major label deals as the biggest goals in their careers, many artists have instead become entrepreneurs. Because of that, a wealth of online tools has been created to assist in their DIY efforts.

The business has also changed with the increase of visual media and easier access to decision-makers in that realm, so music libraries and film and TV song placement companies are now playing a more prominent role in the mix of opportunities for songwriters and bands. This edition addresses all those changes.

I've included:

New information on:

>Sources of new Digital Royalties

>Contemporary radio formats

>Podcasting, Webcasting, and Blogging

>Film/TV music contracts and cue-sheets

>Cellphone ringtones

Expanded sections on marketing your music:

>Production music libraries

>Music for video games

>Children's music

>Musical Theatre

>Music for commercials

>Online song-pitching services and marketing strategies

>Web sites for a range of services from online rhyming dictionaries to the Copyright Office

Find Ongoing Updates to This Book at www.johnbraheny.com

Because the industry changes quickly, some of the information you get here may be dated by the time you read it. That's a big problem with music industry books. However, because my Mac and I are avid Web surfers and information-collecting partners and because my fellow information junkies are always sharing new discoveries with me, I can update you via my Web site (www.johnbraheny.com) where you'll be able to locate the new information you need. Sign up for my e-mail newsletter at the site. Look for my songwriting info Blog and Podcast soon too. You'll also find:

- **updated examples of songs** that demonstrate principles, forms, etc. where they're used in the book

- **links to current articles of interest** on craft and current copyright challenges

- **links to organizations and services**

- **interviews with hit songwriters**, film composers, and industry professionals

- **my own experiences and opinions**

- **a way for you to ask specific questions and get answers**

Funny how, not that long ago, books and direct contact were the only ways we could keep up to date and connected. Now we have the advantage of access to an almost infinite amount of information on the Internet whenever we need it. Who knows how we'll get our information ten years from now? There's one thing we can be sure of, though is that regardless of the medium, we'll always look to music to make a powerful human connection. That's where you come in!

PART 1
The Craft

1 Creativity and Inspiration

Creativity: What Is It and Do You Have It?

Writing songs is at heart a creative endeavor. We songwriters must first understand what creativity is in order to harness it. Creativity is the ability to create something original. It is inspiration and imagination.

Because we are so dependent on the muse, it is essential that we know where creativity comes from, and to make some attempt to control it. Stimulating creativity and keeping it flowing past the dreaded specter of writer's block are very real battles, particularly for those whose livelihoods depend on constant creative output. Hence, there have been many studies and theories put forth on how creativity works, and on who is creative, and who is not.

Psychologists who study creativity have found that there are several qualities shared by most creative people. See how many of these apply to you. Don't be discouraged if you don't possess all of them. This is a broad generalization.

- You're a risk-taker. You don't play it safe. You take intellectual and emotional risks (like submitting your songs for criticism).

- You have a talent in a particular area, and since you're reading this book, we'll assume it's in language or music.

- You think for yourself and make up your own mind about things. You feel that *you*, not fate, luck, or society are in control of your life.

- You're a nonconformist. You often go against the grain.

- You're playful. You like to try new things or find new ways of looking at or doing things just for fun.

- You have a sense of humor. You tend to see the humor in novel or incongruous situations that others may not see.

- You find it easy to entertain yourself and seldom get bored.

- You're a daydreamer with a rich fantasy life. You can get totally lost in a fantasy and be oblivious to everything else.

- You can function in a state of confusion. You can tolerate ambiguity. This quality can help you look at more than one side of a problem. You find yourself saying, "It could be this way, but on the other hand . . ." You can be comfortable in either structured or unstructured situations in which there are no clear directions or guidelines.

- You enjoy complexity. It's intriguing and challenging. You have the ability to see complex relationships between seemingly unrelated situations or ideas.

- You're flexible. You can usually figure out a variety of novel solutions for any problem.

- You're self-motivated, persevering, and passionate about what you do. You work at something until you finish it.

Creative people also have the ability to absorb, digest, and organize external stimuli, reshape them into something original, and re-communicate them in an art form. To a noncreative person, telephone tones are just sounds he hears when he makes a call. To a creative person, they may become the basis of a melody that can eventually become a full-blown composition. For a creative person, a combination of words overheard in an elevator unlocks the memory of an old love affair: The lover stepped into an elevator after a last traumatic goodbye. The conversation produces not only a memory but also a song title, "Going Down for the Last Time." The songwriting process gives the writer a therapeutic way to deal with that experience. To an uncreative person, it was just another conversation.

Dr. Roland Jefferson, a psychiatrist, novelist, and screenwriter, believes that there are three categories of creativity: those who have genetic predispositions to visual creativity, such as painters, photographers, sculptors, and architects; those who have inherited the ability to use words, such as lyricists, poets, novelists, and journalists; and those with the ability to internalize and manipulate auditory stimuli, including musicians, composers, and sound engineers. According to Dr. Jefferson, it is not uncommon for creative people to possess combinations of these talents, such as in the case of a composer/lyricist or a composer who can visualize his music. Novelists, screenwriters, actors, and filmmakers obviously use a visual/auditory and verbal combination.

Then there is the broadly held belief that creativity is an essential part of being human, that it is not necessary to produce a work of art to prove that one is creative. Choosing a gift for a friend, picking out what to wear to a party, or deciding what to eat at a restaurant are fundamentally creative acts that all of us do regularly.

Most studies of the characteristics of "creative" people are done only on those who have demonstrably contributed to the arts and sciences, who we all would agree are creative. While there is certainly a value in noting those characteristics, these studies neglect to note the creative characteristics of everyone. We all have the capacity for creativity. Buying into an "us and them" mindset where you think, "those people are creative and I'm not," begets a self-defeating attitude that inhibits your creative potential.

Developing Your Creativity

Since you're reading this book, you're searching for ways to make the most of the talent and creativity you already have. Psychologists have been working for eons to gather the information you need. Here are some of the highlights.

Dr. George Gamez is a psychologist and songwriter, and the author of *Creativity: How to Catch Lightning in a Bottle*. He specializes in helping people develop their creativity through self-hypnosis and visualization techniques. Self-hypnosis, or auto-suggestion, emphasizes achieving a "state of receptivity" to suggestions that you give yourself. Visualization involves picturing yourself being who you want to be and doing what you want to do, the way you want to do it. Both techniques have been used successfully to help develop positive self-concepts, which are, in turn, related to our self-expectations and consequent behavior. Statements like "I'm not a very good songwriter," "I'll never be that good," or "I just don't think commercially," become self-fulfilling because they both reflect and reinforce a negative and limiting self-image. Developing a positive self-image can help you, not only in writing songs, but in effectively dealing with the industry—something that involves perseverance and overcoming the fear of rejection.

STAGES IN THE CREATIVE PROCESS

Psychologists who specialize in creativity generally agree that the creative process goes through four stages. As they relate to songwriting, they are:

1. **Preparation:** the gathering of the physical tools and the establishment of form, theme, and style. In a broader sense, preparation involves your music education, life experiences, and the development of your unique viewpoint and style.

2. **Incubation:** the unconscious process leading to creation in which, given the theme or problem, the subconscious works on a solution. We've all had the experience of trying to remember someone's name, only to have it pop into our heads later, after we've stopped trying. The period when we weren't trying is called incubation.

3. **Illumination:** the outward stage at which words and music are initially created, written down, or recorded. This is also described as the "Aha!" or "Eureka!" phase. During this phase we should suspend the inner critic, be spontaneous, and allow a free flow of ideas. Too often we stop the flow by being too self-critical, by working on a detail of rhyme or meter. Ideas flow from each other, and a tangent idea may be better than the original—so we shouldn't stop ourselves before we can get to that tangent.

4. **Verification:** the stage at which we need to be critical, looking at the song as a product in an objective and detached way, rewriting, polishing, looking for the right meter and rhyme. Separation of the illumination and verification stages is crucial, though occasionally in this phase you'll get another "Aha!" moment.

Motivation: Overcoming the Barriers

To become more creative, it's important not only to know how to enhance creativity but to be aware of what can kill it. Psychologist Teresa Amabile, writer of *The Social Psychology of Creativity* and *Growing Up Creative*, has conducted many tests to find out the following, which I've adapted to songwriting situations.

Dr. Amabile tested the "intrinsic motivation principle" of creativity, and found that people will be most creative when they feel motivated primarily by the interest, enjoyment, satisfaction, and challenge of the work itself, not by external pressures.

Among the creativity killers she discovered are:

1. **Evaluation.** Concern with what someone else will think of your work can hinder your own creative impulses. We all need love and approval, and it's easy to allow that need to become your motivation. If you learn your craft in a classroom situation or through individual lessons, your teachers will evaluate your skills as part of the learning process. But that is for the process of learning. You need to shut out that concern for outside approval while you're creating.

2. **Surveillance.** Knowing that someone is literally watching you work can kill creativity. As in the case of evaluation, you want to please the other person instead of yourself. Even imagining that someone is listening or watching can be inhibiting. But surveillance can enhance your performance as well. When you're performing live, the audience can inspire you. That's obviously different, however, from someone standing over you while you're working something out.

3. **Reward.** When you focus entirely on a goal or reward—the gold record, the recording contract, the hit single, or the money—something dangerous can happen. Once you get the reward, you may be robbed of your internal motivation. You may also write in a way that takes minimal exploration to get to the next reward. On the other hand, giving yourself a treat for work that you feel good about is positive, because the motivation and reward remain internal.

4. **Competition.** The creative process is easier when you don't feel like you're competing. If you're focused on competition, you'll tend to let someone else's reaction determine whether you should be satisfied with your own work.

5. **Restricted choice.** Limiting your options to achieving your goal will hinder your creativity because you'll tend to internalize the restrictions rather than the freedoms. In songwriting, focus on the parameters rather than on the many options within the parameters.

AVOID BURNOUT

If you get to a point where you can no longer enjoy the process and you're overwhelmed by the external pressure (thinking, for example, "This song *needs* to be a hit," or "If I don't get this recorded, I'm worthless"), then you have "creative burnout." You're no longer writing for yourself, but are doing it for all the wrong reasons. If you're a professional writer, you're probably in a situation in which you *must* please someone else as well as yourself. Even then, there will be times when your publisher will say, "That's good, but could you change this verse?" and you may have to reply, "No, this is for me and I don't care if it doesn't get recorded." Sometimes, writing with that kind of freedom, writing from your heart and your emotional core, becomes the very thing that will make your song appealing to another artist and an audience.

In order to operate at peak performance during the creative process, you should be motivated internally by the spirit of play and exploration and forget about what anybody else might think. You'll have plenty of time to worry about others' opinions later.

Craft vs. Inspiration

Your craft is at the service of your inspiration, giving you confidence and a dependable vehicle for communicating those inspirations in a way that an audience can easily understand and enjoy. I've asked many hit songwriters whether they write from craft or from inspiration. Some view writing as a profession, a job, pure craft. They're very disciplined about it and never refer to the cosmos as a source of inspiration. They actively look for song ideas in everything they read, watch, listen to, and experience. They give little credit to inspiration and approach songwriting as they would an enjoyable 9-to-5 job. They describe the craft of songwriting as a game of organizing ideas, a kind of word-engineering and problem-solving experience, like a jigsaw puzzle in which the pieces come from rhyming dictionaries, thesauruses, and real life, and in which there are several right ways to put the pieces together. Their knowledge of the most effective construction principles provides goals and methods for assembling a clear picture.

Most amateur writers and many writer/artists fall into another general category. I'll call them inspiration writers—which, I should add, doesn't mean that those in the first category never get inspired. Rather, it means that those in this category *rely* on inspiration rather than craft. My impression of hard-core inspiration writers is that they will write only when inspired and won't rewrite, feeling that the remarkable revelation they got from the Creator and put on paper is sacred. This attitude will stand in the way of success for these writers, regardless of how wonderful their inspirations are.

It's risky for industry pros to work with this type of writer. Many inspiration writer/artists have had short careers because their first album contained the best of their songs to date. They had ten years to write the first album, but when they needed to turn out ten more songs for their second album, they faced the dreaded "sophomore slump." They discovered that it's too hard to be inspired during a six-month road trip, and when it came time to get back in the studio, they no longer had the luxury of waiting for inspiration. Without discipline and command of their craft, they were in trouble.

Songwriters who sit down and write a hit song in ten minutes usually have the craft down so well that they don't think about it. It's automatic. They get the idea, focus on exactly what they want to say, and the rest of it comes easily. "If you think of a great title, the song writes itself" is a typical statement from craft practitioners. On the other hand, most professional writers (even ones who *have* written a hit in ten minutes) typically write many pages to get one great line, or will write several mediocre-to-good songs for every song they consider great. There are also writers who find it difficult to discuss their creative processes and downplay the craft involved in their work. They deny making conscious craft decisions, but the songs nonetheless show organized thought processes and good command of the craft.

I believe that many successful writers have acquired their craftsmanship unconsciously, by osmosis. They've been emotionally affected by so many great songs for so long that they instinctively know, for instance, when there needs to be a chorus or bridge, or when a lyric line could be stronger. They go by feel, but behind it there's a subconsciously developed analytical process. In contrast, when a writer plays me a twelve-verse song with nine lines per verse, a chorus that occurs only once, and no rhymes at all, I know I'm not listening to the work of a natural writer who has unconsciously learned the craft. I'm prompted to ask whether the writer has ever listened to the radio.

There are dangers inherent in both extremes. I've heard writers who are trying so hard to write a well-crafted, formulaic hit that they forget about imagination and originality and end up with songs that remind me of science-fiction cyborgs: They look great on the outside but have nothing inside but machinery. On the other hand, I've heard writers with great ideas but no discipline or knowledge of how to communicate them, so all that good inspiration goes to waste.

In contrasting craft and inspiration writers, I have depicted two extremes. Ideally, the inspiration is recognized as only part of the songwriting process. Your craft allows you to maximize the impact of your inspiration.

Developing a Songwriter's Consciousness

Regardless of which songwriting philosophy you subscribe to, it's helpful to learn how craft and inspiration work together when we create. That's because, regardless of your mastery of craft, if you haven't found a concept that's fresh or a unique way of viewing your world, your songs are much less likely to attract anyone's attention. To find that gold nugget of a concept, you need to launch a mining operation by developing a songwriter's consciousness. (See chapter four, "Titles" on page 62.)

Songwriter's consciousness is the readiness to recognize what could be a good song idea. If you have it, you'll start to find ideas everywhere. Songwriter's consciousness filters everything through a network of "idea inspectors" who sit on duty, watching for a big juicy idea to come down the road. They've already been trained to see the signs, so they start getting excited when they see one coming. Sometimes an idea is so low key and subtle that they don't see if right away. Sometimes it's one they're already familiar with, so it doesn't seem exciting anymore. Some ideas may have been around so often that an inspector may miss an aspect that's still worthwhile. But to those juicy ideas that are fresh and original, the inspector will say: "Wait a minute, Juicy, I'm not letting you by 'til we can play a while and check out your potential. You may be just the one we're looking for!"

One useful strategy for developing this songwriter's consciousness is based on a popular theory with which I agree: The human mind is a complex computer that responds only according to the way it's been programmed. The problems occur when we give the computer conflicting messages, like: "I'd love to write a hit song!" and "I'm not a good enough musician to be a songwriter" or "I don't know how." Your mind just sits there and says: "Let me know when you decide." Giving yourself a positive "I am a songwriter" program is very important to the songwriter's consciousness. Once you grasp some of the basic principles of what makes songs work, you'll know what to do with the endless supply of ideas the world provides.

> When I asked Dewayne Blackwell about writing the Garth Brooks hit "Friends in Low Places," he said he was having a drink one night with his friend Earl "Bud" Lee. "That wasn't my title. That was Bud Lee, my co-writer on that," says Blackwell. "When I heard him say, 'Who's going to pay for these drinks if I have friends in low places?' I said, 'Is that a title?! Is that a song?' And he said, 'Not yet!'"

HARNESSING THE SUBCONSCIOUS

Since you never know when and where inspiration will strike, the only thing you can control is your readiness to catch it. Imagine the following scenario:

You're lying in bed, half asleep in that twilight zone where ideas just seem to pop into your head. You've got one! It rolls out like a movie in your mind: A great concept, exciting lines, you see it all. You've had a hard day at work and your body doesn't want to move to get a pen and paper. "It's such a good idea," you say to yourself. "No way I'll forget this one."

The next sound you hear is the alarm clock. You're up, showered, breakfasted, and on the job. About noontime you remember that you had an idea for a song last night but you can't quite recall what it was. Another great idea down the tubes. That could have been the hit that paid the rent for the rest of your life!

Do you think now it would have been worth it to keep a pencil and paper by your bed? Or easier yet, a cassette or portable digital recorder? (The obvious advantage of the recorder is that you can also capture melody and phrasing.) Have one or the other with you always. Have an extra pad and pencil in your car for those freeway daydreams, too. Driving time, and those times between being asleep and awake, seem to be when the brain allows the best communication between the conscious and subconscious. That's fertile, creative territory. Protect it! Keith Richards says he wrote "(I Can't Get No) Satisfaction" from a guitar riff heard in a dream. He woke up long enough to turn on a cassette recorder, sang the riff and went back to sleep.

Here are two other strategies that can help.

Keep an Idea Notebook. Every writer I know has some kind of book or other place to store those little pieces of paper they collect with lines or fragments of ideas. You should have one, too. When you get a chance to write, you've got lots of ideas in front of you. It's a good idea to transfer them periodically from those scraps of paper into a notebook or computer. In the process, you reinforce your memory of them and make it easier to link them with other ideas or phrases with which they'll fit.

The Tubes' Fee Waybill showed me his notebook once. It was thick with very meticulously laid out individual lines, as well as pages of finished songs. The lines were all numbered, with some crossed out. He said he did that because he came up with a lot of interesting one-liners, so whenever he got stuck for a line for a song he was working on, he'd go back through the book. If he found a line he could use, he'd put a line through it so he wouldn't accidentally use it in another song. He's probably got them all catalogued in his computer now.

Develop a Personal Shorthand. Sometimes you may want to write about the person you're with at the time. That's when it's beneficial to have a personal brand of shorthand. I know one writer who developed a whole code of geometric symbols that only he could understand. Many writers are very candid in writing about their personal relationships and have difficulty expressing negative feelings a lover is not yet aware of. If you find yourself having to explain something you wrote, you could say: "This isn't really about us, it's just something I'm creating from the memory of another relationship," or "It's about a friend's romance," or "Don't get paranoid. I'm a songwriter and I make this stuff up! I don't want to have to worry that every time I write something you're going to think it's about us." Of course, depending on the circumstances and what you wrote, any of those approaches could sound utterly ridiculous, so don't quote me.

There also will be times when you'll get an idea in a situation where it won't be socially acceptable to whip out your pen and start writing. In those situations, like at formal social gatherings or in mid-conversation, you can use what Len Chandler calls "The Weak Bladder Syndrome" and head for the restroom to work in private.

Finding Your Own Creative Process

Every writer eventually finds her own process (or more than one) for creating. Though it's a good idea to explore many, your own unique personality will determine an approach that's comfortable and productive for you.

It's important not to put yourself down for having a creative process that's different from someone else's. Don't worry about which process works for someone else unless you want to collaborate with that person, in which case your process should be compatible. Here are some of the more typical processes:

"Deadline" writer. You're part of a very large breed. You've got a lot going on in your life and need an external force to make you put this song on the front burner. Someone says, "I need this by tomorrow morning. The music supervisor needs it at 10 A.M." Your adrenaline starts pumping and every synapse in your brain is working full out. The ability to write and rewrite well under deadline pressure is extremely valuable, since those opportunities happen constantly in the music business. If you get a reputation for being able to deliver, you get the jobs. If you're the type of person who needs deadlines to get things done, but don't happen to have any external deadlines, find a way to trick yourself into one. Making an appointment to show a publisher or producer a new song or booking studio time to record a demo are great ways to create your own deadlines.

"Total focus" writer. You like to sit down with a project and devote your total attention to it until it's finished. No other projects. No diversions or distractions. Just straight-ahead concentration from start to finish, no matter how long it takes. You polish each line as you go.

"Scattered" writer. You may have several songs going at once, get bored or burned out with one and work on another, and go back to the first later, maybe with fresh ideas generated by working on the others. You're the kind of writer who has difficulty sustaining interest. You'll work for a while, look for inspiration in the refrigerator, make a sandwich, watch TV, go back to work, stop, make some phone calls, take out the garbage, go back to work, stop, read a magazine, go back to work again. You may feel guilty for not keeping at it but, in fact, the song is incubating in your subconscious as you do all those other things.

"Project" writer. You work best within some kind of framework with an established goal or motivation ("I'll pay you a thousand dollars to write a theme for a play in two weeks"). You have a direction, a framework, and a motive. You may be very creative within that type of situation but otherwise you're not very productive. Recognizing that, you need to search for projects or create them. People with your approach frequently write for TV series, films, and commercials.

Your approach may incorporate elements of more than one of those listed here, and it may also change with time and experience, but it's important for you to realize that whatever works for *you* is right.

DEVELOP A CREATIVE RITUAL

Getting ready to "commit" to writing may involve a common process that Len Chandler calls "sharpening pencils." You seem to be doing everything but writing. You clean the house, prepare the writing space, and actually sharpen pencils. You make sure you have your "sure-fire hit" songwriting pencil and paper and maybe your "great idea" hat. This kind of ritual is valuable because it gets you ready and primes your creative pump. While you're doing it you're probably working on the song without realizing it.

You may think you must be the only writer in the world who goes through this craziness, or that if you were a real pro you wouldn't have to. Wrong! Yours may be a unique ritual, but most writers have one or more.

INDIVIDUAL PREFERENCES AND COLLABORATION

Some writers can write only when they're alone. Some can write in a room full of people with the radio and TV going at the same time. Some need silence. Some, though they might be equally adept at writing words and music, are more productive in a collaboration.

Sheila Davis, in *The Songwriters Idea Book*, relates creative styles with your personality type as determined by the Myers-Briggs Type Indicator, which is based on the work of psychologist Carl Jung. Sheila has developed her own version of the profile, and I feel it's a valuable tool not only for getting better acquainted with your own individual process, but for understanding those of collaborators. I highly recommend you read it.

My wife, JoAnn, covers this in her "Goosing Your Muse" creative process seminars on how to stimulate and maintain your productivity. Another area she has found particularly helpful is exploring how we process information. Understanding that each of us, based on our individual preferences, values a different aspect of the project can alleviate conflicts. She refers to our different approaches or modes as being auditory, visual or kinesthetic. Some people simply respond to the creative process with an attitude of "I don't know how I know, but I know." We usually refer to that as intuition. Going beyond that, these modes help us to clarify the "aha" when an idea surfaces. Most of us experience a combination of modes, but favor one. What shape does the experience of getting an idea take for you? Our preference is usually revealed in the way we express ourselves. When someone says, "I can *see* how . . ." or "It *looks* to me like . . ." that person is revealing a *visual* preference. Those who are more *auditory* will say, "It *sounds* to me as if . . ." or "I *hear* what you mean . . ." and those who are more *kinesthetic* might respond with, "It *feels* to me as if . . ." or "I *get* what you mean . . ."

It's helpful to realize which preferences we have, so that we can:

1. recognize the difference between ourselves and our collaborators

2. work less judgmentally and more amicably with our collaborators

3. use this information as a powerful tool to move past our creative blocks

How we *look* (clothes and hair, the image the band projects), how we *sound* (production, performance) or the overall *feel* of the project may be valued differently by different members of the group.

For a quick way to find which modality may apply to you, notice how the following exercises affect you. (Remember, we tend to combine some of our preferences, like auditory/kinesthetic or visual/kinesthetic.) The scientific study of these modes is called neurolinguistics.

1. Record a TV program that has plenty of action, like car chases. When you play it back, turn the volume off. Try to create a musical or rhythm track that fits the action segment. If you can watch something and respond to it easily with your own soundtrack, then your modality may be *auditory*. Or go to an art gallery, and after you've viewed the various works of art, notice if you have a melody or lyrics developing in your head. You are responding to what you see by *hearing* something in your head.

2. Listen to some recordings of symphonic, new age, or other instrumental music. Notice whether you tend to see pictures in your mind. Sometimes you may see only colors or patterns, but this could indicate that you are predominantly *visual* in how you receive information.

3. Think about your favorite places and experiences. As you describe them to yourself, notice whether you think mostly in terms of how you *feel*. People who tend to perceive kinesthetically seem to be more affected by atmosphere, mood, and ambiance, or rhythm, movement, and dance. They can be repulsed by or enamored of a combination of sensory input. These people might avoid a restaurant because it just doesn't "feel right" to them.

Breaking Writer's Block

You're sitting in front of a blank piece of paper or computer screen, just *knowing* that you've come up with all the ideas you'll ever come up with and that anything you *do* think of has already been written. You try your brand new pen with the easy glide point, but can't convince it to write anything. You go through all your customary rituals but still nothing happens.

At this point, you've landed where nearly every other writer has been at one time or another: The Planet of the Dry. It is comforting, in a way, to know you're not the only writer in the world who has ever felt totally stupid and useless.

Writer and psychotherapist Lynne Bernfield says, "Being blocked doesn't mean that you don't want to produce, are self-destructive or lazy, have dried up or been deserted by the muse. It is a coded message from your unconscious telling you that something must be attended to, and, as such, is a blessing in disguise." She believes that one of the things to be attended to is "unfinished business" in other areas of our lives. We won't allow ourselves to start new business until we've finished that old business. So try to identify it and deal with it. You *will* get through this!

Though there are those who deny there's any such thing as writer's block, to deny it is to acknowledge that it exists. For some people, denial is the best way to deal with it. Whatever works! Here are some of the other ways to dealt with this problem.

1. Try a different mode. Find out which modality is yours (visual/auditory/kinesthetic). Then, when you experience a creative block, try to switch to a mode that is unusual for you. Do what does *not* come naturally to you, even if it's just for an hour.

Say you're an auditory type of person, and you have reached a lull in your songwriting. Spend the afternoon painting or coloring (visual), or take a long walk (kinesthetic). New ideas will appear more quickly than if you simply stay in your rut, hammering at your piano or guitar, trying to force them out.

If you are blocked and you are more visual, then it might be helpful to listen to music while sitting in a dark room. Indulge in a massage. Or listen to a good novel on tape. Pictures will form in your mind's eye.

If you are more kinesthetic, sitting through a lecture or class, concentrating on the presenter and the material, may help you get past a block. Most kinesthetic people want to move when they know they can't. In fact, they reveal their preference by pacing when they think or talk, and they tend to gesture with their hands or their whole body. Keep a journal (written or on tape) of experiences that "move" you. Describe the various elements of the events in as much detail as you can; for example, "When I squatted down to meet the puppy, his warm, wet tongue on my face tickled me." Lyric ideas can develop from feelings such as these.

2. Just start writing—anything. Make a grocery list, write a letter to the editor—anything to jumpstart your creative engine and get something on the blank page. Julia Cameron (author of *The Artist's Way*) prescribes doing "morning pages" in which you write three pages of anything and everything that comes into your head without stopping, censoring, or editing. Pat Pattison (author of *Writing Better Lyrics*) has a related morning exercise he calls "object writing," in which you select an object in the room to write about, freely associating whatever memories come up but using a maximum of sensory images to describe the sights, sounds, taste, and feelings. Limit yourself to ten minutes so you'll know that you always have time to do it. The beauty of these exercises is that you create something every day and don't get hung up on needing it to be a "work of art."

3. Psych yourself out of the pressure to produce a hit or great work of art. Focus on having fun. Remind yourself that nobody else will ever see your bad work. I frequently hear successful writers say things like, "If I get one in ten to twenty songs that I think is viable, I figure I'm doing great," or "I had to write a hundred bad songs before I started getting to the good stuff." And these are people with multiple hits! I used to think, naively, that once a writer figured out how to write a hit, she could pretty much nail it every time. Wrong! So stop beating yourself up!

4. Create an atmosphere. Listen to your favorite artist's records. Listen to music that puts you in a mood, and savor it.

5. Find other places to write. Try the beach, the woods, a mountain, a car, a bus station, a noisy restaurant, a dance club. Try writing at a different time of day.

6. Just forget about writing altogether. Relax, have some fun, go to a movie, go bowling, go bicycling, whatever.

7. Try stream-of-consciousness or problem-solving techniques. See the explanation of these starting at the bottom of this page.

8. If you're a musician, play what you don't usually play. Play scales you don't usually play, play a CD you don't normally listen to, or learn a solo written for an instrument you don't normally play. If you're a guitarist, for instance, learn a Bach violin solo. Maybe try playing it back at half-speed. Or learn a jazz sax solo.

9. Write with someone you haven't written with before. One of the best things about a new collaborator is that they can get you out of your comfort zone with a fresh point of view and new ideas.

It's possible that none of the above will work. At that point it may be useful to dig a little deeper. Two other effective methods merit more of an in-depth explanation. Even if you don't feel blocked, they're great ways to get started.

Stream of Consciousness

One further approach is the *stream-of-consciousness* technique. It's used in what was described earlier as the *illumination phase* of the creative process, during which spontaneity is encouraged and the "inner critic" is ignored. It's a great way to generate ideas. This is a technique used by many successful writers.

In an interview by Theresa Ann Nixon, **Paul McCartney** discussed a prose piece he'd been working on: "So when my hand didn't know what to put on the paper, my head just said to my hand, 'Write! Put it down. It doesn't matter what you say, just put it down. Even if it's all mistakes. Just put it down.' I got this method of just forcing my hand to write, no matter what it was. And later I talked with Quincy Jones about this when we were doing "The Girl Is Mine" with Michael Jackson. He said he had gotten this book twenty years ago that had changed his life, where the fellow explained that there were two aspects to a creative act. One was just to create it, just do it. The other was judicial, checking everything. He said the biggest mistake everyone makes is to try to do the two at once. And suddenly *ding!* that's exactly what my problem is. In all those years with essays in school, you know, I was trying to get that wonderful opening.... When you try to do everything at once, there's just no time. Your brain can't cope. You'll kill all your enthusiasm and creative spirit by checking your spelling and going to see, 'Is this the right word, is it clever enough? Will the L.A. Times critic like it if I say *hobgoblin*? Yes, there is a better word. Or shall I just say, *demon*? No. *Hobgoblin*. No, *demon*.' And you've just spent half a bloody hour."

STREAM-OF-CONSCIOUSNESS EXERCISE

You hear a friend use an interesting phrase and you write it on a notepad, napkin, your hand—or you memorize it. Later on, you're noodling on your piano, guitar, or whatever is handy, turn on your recorder and forget it's there. Next, you grab some chords, maybe just play a bass line, get a nice groove going with your feet, get an attitude going: sad, bittersweet, mad, haughty, playful, loving, romantic. Picture yourself with that attitude talking to someone, and just say out loud everything you can think of that relates to the situation that you're remembering or creating.

It's strange to hear yourself talking out loud when you're alone, but the more you do it, the less strange it becomes. You want to rhyme this line? If it doesn't just appear, forget it. Keep going. Don't stop the flow; you'll fix it up later. Just get all the ideas out there for now. Babble on a while. None of it has to make much sense or have any continuity at this stage. You can influence the direction of the flow by describing a scene, a setting, or a feeling. If there is another person in this setting, consider your relationship to him. What motivates that person and dictates your attitude toward him? What does he say? What do you say? What happened before and what happened after? If you get off on a tangent, that's okay because the tangent may take you to a better place. Don't worry, just keep it going.

All talked out? Play back the recording and listen. Yes, you'll think some of it is total nonsense, but did you really think everything you said would be profound? Some of the stupid stuff may be a bridge to something better. This line could have smoother meter, a better flow, if you changed a couple of words.

Now you're into the *verification phase* of the process. Be critical. Pull out all the good lines and ideas. Write them down, leaving plenty of room to rewrite and add other lines that you think of. Now is the time to pay more attention to form, continuity, rhyme schemes, meter. You may find that most of those were established during that free-form session and now they just need to be rethought and examined more closely. You may discover that what you thought was the chorus works better as a verse, or vice versa. Perhaps what you thought was the first verse should be the last. Maybe the first phrase you wrote down that triggered this whole process is no longer nearly as good as other ideas the process produced.

What happens during the stream-of-consciousness process is that you pull out a lot of ideas and make a lot of creative hookups and links that you might not ordinarily make when you're trying too hard. You also avoid getting hung up trying to make something rhyme or make your meter tight at the expense of flow and focus. Once you've filled a few pages, you'll have a better concept of how to structure the idea and you'll also have come up with some great lines, some rhythms that those lines may suggest, and some good rhymes that will feel natural because you'll be writing closer to the way you think and speak. At that point, you can start a new page with the best lines you've come up with.

Keep in mind, while you're in the critical phase, that nothing is sacred. Don't get married to a line that's great by itself but doesn't fit the rest. Put it away in your collection of great lines and use it to trigger another session. As a matter of fact, don't throw anything away. If you're working on paper, don't erase. Draw a single line through the reject. If you work with a word processor, cut or copy sections you don't want to another area, or create a different file for the new version, but save your old drafts. If you're working on tape, always save your tapes. Not only can you return to them for musical ideas (much easier with digital recording), but if you're ever involved in an infringement case, they may be helpful to show the process by which you arrived at your finished song.

Problem Solving

Another creative springboard is the *problem-solving* technique in which you make up arbitrary "problems" to solve creatively. The fact is that a substantial amount of the creative process involves problem solving anyway. Like putting together a crossword puzzle, it's word and music architecture and design.

In a way, writing a good title before you write the song is an exercise in problem solving. This is a pretty typical approach for country writers, since the success of a country song depends (much more than other styles) on finding a strong *concept* embodied by the title. The problem is to find a great way to set up the title and make it pay off. Maybe the title suggests a mood and the "problem" is to maintain and heighten the mood. Maybe the title suggests a story to develop. There is more about writing from titles in chapter four.

The following Problem-Solving Exercise will give you some ideas to build on. If you ever run into trouble getting started, just pick one of your premises at random and link it with a lyric idea from your collection. Remember that trying to make the puzzle work is a great exercise of your creativity and will force you into solutions you may not have come up with otherwise. At the same time, remember that creativity is a fluid process and if the exercise only serves to get you started it has done its job.

PROBLEM-SOLVING EXERCISE

In the absence of a "real world" creative problem, simulate one or come up with an arbitrary premise or set of parameters, using these attributes:

1. Form (number and length of sections, bars per section)

2. Tempo

3. Time signature(s)

4. Key

5. Melodic mode

6. Number of chords per section or song

7. Number of instrumental tracks

8. Density of instrumental parts

9. Mood

10. Rhyme scheme

11. Lyric density

For example:

An eight-bar verse with a nine-bar chorus. A 120 tempo. The bass with a maximum of four notes every two bars. Rapid-fire sixteenth-note lyric in the verse, half-note lyric in the chorus.

A ten-bar verse (two five-bar sections), eight-bar chorus. A maximum of five chords.

A 28½-second jingle for a teddy bear, conveying warmth, playfulness. (You'll have to name the bear.) A 10-second "donut" (a hole in the lyric for dialogue), 15 seconds from the start. Write the jingle for a female vocalist.

Remember, too, that many musical and lyrical innovations have resulted from *creative accidents* in which the artist had the presence of mind to recognize a good idea when he accidentally stumbled across it on his way to something else. Taking advantage of those situations requires that you maintain an open mind and stay flexible.

Developing Good Work Habits

Not everyone can form consistent writing habits. Many of the most successful writers have schedules that allow for very little consistency. Developing a regular pattern or schedule for your writing, however, can have valuable advantages. Say you make a commitment to yourself—or, even better, to a collaborator—that you're going to meet every Saturday to write from 9 A.M. until noon. First, you'll feel better that you're no longer procrastinating. Second, getting something accomplished every week will do a lot for your self-confidence, and third, it activates a psychological phenomenon that's very productive.

When your subconscious knows that next Saturday at 9 A.M. it has to develop some new ideas or solve a creative problem from last week, it works on it while you do other things.

There are writers who set aside a specific amount of time each day just to write, even though there are days they feel that they haven't been productive. They may set a goal to just learn one new chord progression. They may come up with a germ of an idea to work on the next day.

Hit songwriter and composer Tom Snow ("He's So Shy," "You Should Hear How She Talks About You") likes to get an idea started at the end of a writing session but saves developing the idea till the next session. He says it keeps him excited about working on the idea so that by the time he gets into it, his brain is already cooking. The technique is one of Snow's personal methods of manipulating his creative juices. You'll learn to develop techniques that suit your own personality.

2 Subject Matter

Finding Ideas

Your subject is the raw material of songwriting. Coming up with that fresh sounding "hook" phrase, or an idea that hasn't been stated in quite the same way before, is important if you want to be viewed as a creative writer. You'll need to develop your ability to recognize and generate lyric ideas from a variety of everyday sources. This chapter will explore some specific places to look for ideas and a few general subject areas with hints on how to approach them effectively.

Sources for song ideas are everywhere. Here are a few that are endlessly productive:

News and human-interest talk shows on radio and TV. These are extremely popular and elicit an incredible array of emotional problems and conflicts from their callers and in-studio audiences. Each day's topic usually deals with current news events or ethical problems. These shows involve the general public in passionate interchanges that reflect human conflicts. Check to see if there are any shows in your area hosted by psychologists discussing personal problems. These are particularly juicy, especially on radio, where the callers are anonymous. They provide a tremendous education in human behavior as well. As you listen, remember it's not just the subjects you're listening for, but also the language with which people express themselves.

The networks present special, in-depth programs on a variety of informative and controversial topics. You'll find yourself agreeing or disagreeing and, in the process, distilling your own point of view, which will work its way into your songs.

Soap operas and prime-time dramas. The writers of these shows are also listening to talk shows for ideas.

Listening to music on the radio. This is really stimulating, especially while driving on the freeway when your left brain is occupied with driving, leaving your right brain to daydream. At times I've half-heard lines of songs on the radio and said to myself, "What a great line!" But when I heard it again later, I discovered—to my pleasure—that it wasn't really the line I thought I'd heard after all. By some strange approximation of vowel sounds it had triggered a new line that I could use.

It can be a productive exercise to ignore the song you're hearing and use the rhythm section or mood as a foundation for your own song. Perhaps it'll help you come up with an interesting phrasing of lines that you may not have thought of otherwise. It's also important to listen to the radio to maintain a sense of what's happening in the marketplace and to get familiar with the new artists who have developed devoted followings and critical praise. Who *do* you like and why? Who *don't* you like and why?

Poetry and books with great colloquial dialogue. These can inspire and trigger new ideas. Language-oriented Web sites and reference books, such as *McGraw-Hill's Dictionary of American Slang and Colloquial Expressions* (see bibliography) contain a wealth of ideas. And because hip-hop/urban music is so popular, an ongoing, updated site devoted to the evolution of hip-hop slang is essential to keep up with its constant changes. (Search "hip-hop slang" in an Internet search engine or go to www.rapdict.org and http://en.wikipedia.org/wiki/Hip_hop_slang.)

Note: Wikipedia is an online encyclopedia that can be very useful for researching pretty much anything. However, since the Web site is updated by its users, you can't always trust its accuracy. In most cases, though, it lists additional research sources and direct links.

Conversations with friends or discussions you overhear. These will provide some great titles, especially if the language is particularly distinctive or colorful. Most of the great lyricists I've interviewed tell me they're "conversation voyeurs."

EXERCISE

Give yourself the challenge of finding one good line, idea, or title in a five-minute slice of conversation from any source. It's a great way to demonstrate to yourself what a wealth of material is available almost anywhere.

Examine your own life experiences. Think about your feelings toward your lover or romantic situations—positive or negative, past or present—and turn those feelings into actual dialogue or a story. Some writers write only from personal experience. Don't forget that, like a novelist, you're a creator; so if you hear someone else's story and it moves you, chances are it'll move others, too. You can also change, embellish, or totally fabricate a story that will move or entertain people just as much. That's called "poetic license," not dishonesty.

Once you program your subconscious to look for ideas, it'll automatically do it. But you have to help, by getting ideas down on paper or computer or tape recorder as soon as possible or your subconscious won't believe you're serious. The "idea inspectors" will say, "We pick up on these great ideas but the turkey never does anything with them. Why should we bother?"

The Commerciality of Subject Matter: Mass Appeal

At some point before, during, or after the writing of a song, it behooves a writer to decide whether the song idea itself is commercial. Now don't get defensive! I'm not saying that every song you write must appeal to a mass audience. At the risk of repeating this message too many times, I'll say again that you should write everything and anything your creative impulses trigger. At some point, though, if you want to make a living at songwriting, you've got to develop some perspective on your songs. The one you wrote about your second-cousin's appendicitis may be important to you personally, but everybody else will say, "So what?" You need to decide which of your songs are going to be meaningful in some way to a mass audience before shopping them to publishers or producers. Many different kinds of songs can work.

UNIVERSAL THEMES

Occasionally a monster hit will emerge with far more than the basic ingredients. One of the classics was "I Will Survive," the number-one hit that Freddie Perren and Dino Fekaris wrote for Gloria Gaynor in 1979. Along with the great groove and production, the song had a lyric idea that made its popularity continue long after that groove and production would have burned out by repetition. The lyric was an anthem for women, something positive from someone who sounded like she knew what she was talking about, with a story that sounded familiar. The message was positive: that no matter how her lover had treated her before, she didn't have to take it anymore because she had found a new self-respect. The song is still popular more than twenty-five years later.

One of the most important functions of a song is to give people a vehicle to express hopes, dreams, and inner conflicts that they might otherwise keep inside.

Songs have a way of uniting us by defining those common strings that bind us together. Mark D. Sanders and Tia Sillers's hit, "I Hope You Dance," expresses a universal theme that everyone can relate to. Philosophy handed down from a parent who wants her child to experience all life has to offer will always be relevant. The Madonna hit, "Papa Don't Preach," explored one of the sad choices of a pregnant teenager. Often the more commercial songs are the ones that not only express more personal situations and feelings, but also do it in a way that everyone else can easily understand and identify with.

BEING BELIEVABLE

The values and experiences reflected in your songs should be those you feel comfortable with or that reflect your own situation. If you're a writer/artist, a major part of your appeal will be that people will identify with your point of view. Don't take a different point of view on every record; people will never really learn who you are. Also, as an artist, be leery of recording a song that you're not completely comfortable with. You may be doomed to playing it for years. If you write but don't perform, you're not as restricted; you can write either for the market or from the point of view of the artist.

CLEVERNESS

Beyond the considerations we've just discussed, there are some stylistic concerns that affect the commerciality of a song. One of those is *cleverness*. Country music has always been the home of clever wordplay, the new twist on an old cliché, and the lyrical turnaround. Some examples include "Lying Time Again," "Yippi Cry Yi," "Nothing Sure Looked Good On You," and "Wishful Drinkin'." The old pop tune, "I Had Too Much to Dream Last Night," is another example of the kind of cleverness designed to stick in the listener's mind. The human-interest story song with a surprise ending has wide appeal. The John Michael Montgomery hit, "The Little Girl" (Harley Allen), the Clay Walker hit, "The Chain of Love" (written by Rory Lee Feek/Jonnie Barnett), and Jamey Johnson's "The Dollar" are great examples.

To pure "heart" writers, songs built around cleverness may seem contrived. "Punch line" songs run the risk of wearing out their welcome quickly, like a joke you've heard too many times. The only thing that makes a song like these worth hearing again is a great storyteller and an interesting story (or stories) leading up to the punch line. Toby Keith's "As Good as I Once Was" is a good example.

The more conversational and natural the lyric feels and the more vivid the visual imagery, the less contrived the song will seem. In other words, the trip should be as rewarding as the destination. "The Gambler," the classic by Don Schlitz, is a very cleverly concocted story. Even though the use of a deck of cards as an analogy for life isn't a new idea, the song's natural, colloquial, rhymed language and movie-like imagery make it a wonderful piece of work.

CROSSOVER RECORDS

If you're concerned about selling records, you must appeal to a large section of the record-buying population. Consistently at the top of the best-seller and most-played lists are *crossovers*, which you'll hear a lot about in the recording industry.

A crossover record is one that can be played on more than one radio format. Crossover artists include Mariah Carey, Babyface, Toni Braxton, and Madonna, whose records regularly get played on R&B/hip-hop and adult contemporary radio stations, and country artists LeAnn Rimes, Trisha Yearwood, Faith Hill, Tim McGraw, Martina McBride, and Lonestar, who may cross over to adult contemporary and Top 40 charts.

Modern rock artists like Limp Bizkit and mainstream rock artists like the Offspring and Metallica seldom cross over. Though artists such as Aerosmith, Maroon 5, Coldplay, and 3 Doors Down will, with certain singles, cross to pop and adult contemporary formats. Crossover potential, in fact, is based more on the record than the artist. Record companies frequently promote different songs on an album in different radio formats. The principle of crossover is that the more radio formats that air the record, the more people will hear it and be motivated to buy it. Video and film exposure are still other avenues that can further contribute to the power of a crossover song, record, or artist. Savvy Internet marketing via artist's and record company Web sites and Web radio can also introduce music to potential fans who may not, as a habit, listen to (or have available to them) certain radio formats.

LOVE THEMES

Of all possible song themes, love is the most popular. No other subject is as universal, no other human need so emotionally rich, provocative, and potentially traumatic. A quick survey of the top singles in any category of the trade charts will show that over 75 percent of their subject matter pertains to love or lust. We spend most of our lives looking for it, exulting in it, or losing it.

To illustrate, I've broken the subject down into several categories based on the span of a relationship, with a variety of samples for each.

Feeling the need. The longing to love and be loved has inspired some classics, such as "Lookin' for Love," "When Will I Be Loved," "Dream Lover," "Looking for Another Pure Love," "You Can't Hurry Love," "I Would Do Anything For Love (But I Won't Do That)," "Again," and "Boulevard of Broken Dreams."

I think I've just found her (or him). This is the point where you've just seen someone, you think you might be in love already, and you're scoping out the situation. Examples include "I'm Into Something Good," "I Saw Her Standing There," "Like to Get to Know You," "I've Just Seen a Face," "Oh Pretty Woman," "Sharing the Night Together," "Somebody's Baby," and "Love Or Something Like It."

The big come-on. A formidable category, since so many love and lust games are played out to a background of popular music. It encompasses both the bold and tender. Think of "Let's Spend the Night Together," "Kiss You All Over," "I'm in the Mood for Love," "Feel Like Makin' Love," "Lay, Lady, Lay," "Sexual Healing," "I'm Ready," "Tonight's the Night," "Temptation," "Come On Over"—and thousands more, including about 75 percent of all hip-hop and rap songs.

This is it, I'm in love. For better or worse, you've passed the point of no return. This is one of the biggest categories of love songs, with "Fooled Around and Fell in Love," "Can't Help Falling in Love," "It's So Easy," "Truly," "Baby, I Love You," "Your Song," "My Girl," "My Own True Love," "True Blue," "Nothing's Gonna Stop Us Now," "Thank You," "The Way You Love Me," "Head Over Feet," and "This Kiss."

The honeymoon is over. Or: "The Thrill Is Gone," "Don't Be Cruel," "Cold as Ice," "Suspicious Minds," "We Can Work It Out," "This Masquerade," "You've Lost That Lovin' Feeling," "You Don't Bring Me Flowers," "Love on the Rocks," "You Keep Me Hanging On," "Say My Name," "Smoke Rings in the Dark," and "My Give a Damn's Busted."

Cheating. Songs of infidelity, guilt, suspicion, and jealousy are popular despite their negativity, because everyone can identify with those feelings and experiences—and they're great drama. These include "Lying Eyes," "(If Loving You Is Wrong) I Don't Want to Be Right," "Me and Mrs. Jones," "Your Cheatin' Heart," "You Belong to Me," "Who's Cheatin' Who," "What She Don't Know Won't Hurt Her," "The Thunder Rolls," "Whose Bed Have Your Boots Been Under?"—and songs about *not* cheating like "When I Think About Cheating."

Leaving. Along with cheating, the trauma of good-bye is an emotional minefield, with heavy pathos. Listen for it in "I'd Rather Leave While I'm in Love," "For the Good Times," "By the Time I Get to Phoenix," "Bye Bye Love," "Don't Think Twice, It's All Right," "Breaking Up Is Hard to Do," "If You Leave Me Now," "I've Been Loving You Too Long," "I Will Survive," "Fifty Ways to Leave Your Lover," "I Can't Make You Love Me," "If You're Gone," "Behind These Hazel Eyes," and "Big Blue Note."

Remembering how it used to be. After the breakup and the passage of time, the more positive among us tend to fondly remember the good times and forget the bad. If we've been on the losing end, there's a profound sense of loss and longing that has created some classics, such as "I Can't Stop Loving You," "As Tears Go By," "Tears on My Pillow," "Hello Walls," "Funny How Time Slips Away," "San Francisco Bay Blues," "I'm Sorry," "She's Gone," "Same Old Lang Syne," "Yesterday," "I'll Be Over You," "Best I Ever Had," and "Like We Never Loved at All."

Philosophy. It's also human nature to aid the recovery process by trying to provide a rationale and perspective for it all. The attempt has been made in "All in Love Is Fair," "Only Love Can Break Your Heart," "The Things We Do for Love," "It's All in the Game," "The Rose," and "Please Remember Me."

SEX SELLS

Sex sells just about everything. It is a universal preoccupation, particularly for those in the prime record-buying age groups. A look at any week's *Billboard* Hot 100 singles chart shows that outright sex themes are still prime song lyric topics.

Radio wasn't always as tolerant as it is now. If writers wanted to get that powerful, money-making airplay they had to avoid the subject of sex, or be very clever about it. In the early 1950s, even songs like "Teach Me Tonight"—as tame as it sounds today—were considered risqué. See how jaded we've become?

Throughout history there's been a wealth of bawdy balladry. During the 1960s folk revival, Oscar Brand ("Bawdy Songs and Backroom Ballads"), Ed McCurdy ("When Dalliance Was in Flower") and others resurrected and recorded volumes of it. Most of these songs never got airplay, but enjoyed underground success. A strong division had always existed between what could be sold on record and what was considered fare fit for the air, but in the past few years that division seems to have disappeared. If a song isn't getting airplay, it's more likely because it doesn't sound like a hit than because it's offensive. There are rock stations that would have been shut down fifteen years ago for playing songs that seem commonplace today. Record companies release both "dirty" and "clean" versions of singles, the latter complete with bleeps where the words have been censored. Public attitudes are always in a state of change, however, and a songwriter must always be aware of those changes. If you're going to write about sex, the next big question is, "How?" Songwriters will always reflect their own personal attitudes about the subject, no matter how self-indulgent, sexist, debauched, or immature they may be.

Those of you who have more positive attitudes about sex should get your songs out there, too. Songwriters must make sure there are more wholesome philosophies and values offered to impressionable minds to balance all the edgier songs about sex, or we invite censorship. For instance, female artists in all genres today have managed to counter male artists who demonstrate disrespect of women in their songs. In the process, they're gaining legions of young fans.

The treatment of sex in a song may be subtle or explicit. Explicitness gets old fast and ultimately is not as stimulating as a song that is more clever, subtle, and sensuous, using double entendre. It's been said that the mind is the most sensitive erogenous zone. Use your imagination and creativity to stimulate it.

The Censorship Issue

Sex-oriented lyrics of varying degrees of explicitness can be found in all styles of music. Those in rock, R&B, hip-hop and rap are increasingly under fire from self-appointed guardians of our national morality. These elements have raised the specter of music censorship, which, if they materialize, would constitute a major barrier to self-expression. It's apparent that placing warning stickers on CDs has helped artists sell those albums more than it's hurt their sales.

Perhaps the focus on content also has made us aware of the power lyricists wield. Songwriters, who spend a substantial part of their careers attempting to gain some acceptance by the industry, are unaccustomed to imagining a ten-year-old kid singing their lyrics. That reality (assuming the song is a hit) has caused many writers to reassess their responsibility to the listener. I wish more writers would think about it while they're writing the songs. Whether or not you allow this pressure to influence your creative choices, the responsibility should not be taken lightly.

Sex is not only a powerful human drive but a major topic on TV, in novels and in our own conversations. It can't be ignored and won't ever go away. To censor sex as a song topic would be like asking songwriters not to write about love. Having said that, I *am* concerned about the effect of explicitly sexual, misogynous and violent lyrics coming from talented and successful artists on the kids who look up to them, especially when such songs are heavily promoted by record companies whose primary concern is their bottom line. Maybe the best we can hope for is parents who care enough to discuss these songs and the notions they convey with their kids and to model the attitudes they want their kids to learn.

Writing From Emotion

Most songwriters, particularly in the early stages of their development, seem motivated primarily by the need to express some kind of emotional turmoil. Most often it's "my baby left me," or "I'm so lonely," or "he/she's cheatin' on me"—all negative scenarios. We may think our experience is unique, that only we can feel such pain. But intellectually, we know how common this situation really is. In times of extreme stress, our ability to think rationally is temporarily on vacation. Consequently, when the professional songwriter in us looks back on those songs after we've chilled out, we're amazed at how trite and unimaginative those "agony" songs are. Not that agony or another strong emotion doesn't occasionally spawn something profound; but most often, it just spawns self-indulgence. There's nothing wrong with writing songs during these periods—as therapy. Just don't get the idea that because you wrote something in a distressed emotional state, it's *automatically* going to produce a fantastic song.

When I asked one of my favorite writer/artists, Dave Alvin (formerly of the Blasters), about writing close to emotional situations, he said he liked to get a little distance between the situation and the song.

> Songs I *have* written close to something emotional tend to suffer from all the problems of an amateur songwriter. You've got to blow the clichés out. Every time I sit down to write a song it's as if I've never written a song before and I start with "the moon in June is shining on the spoon" and it takes me a while to say "hey that's been done before." Sometimes when you write from emotion you just have to get it out so you just say "I love you, pleeeease come back!" over and over again. So it's best, at least for me, to let it gestate for a while and build up a little wisdom behind it.

On the other hand, when I interviewed Melissa Etheridge about her CD, *Skin*, for United Airlines' in-flight audio, she told me that she had written all the songs for the project within two weeks, in the middle of a very emotional breakup. She feels she writes best while the emotions are still raw. It's her way of dealing with the stress, a kind of therapy. She said she's used songwriting that way since she started writing at thirteen.

> I believe that when I get the closest to my own truth about what I'm going through—the more singular in my experience I get, the more universal the music is and the more people say "I know what you mean and I know how you feel," and that means so much to me.

Both of these writers are masters of their craft, whose long experience enables them to recognize at what point in their emotional process they're capable of writing at their peak. This is something you will discover for yourself, but it's important that your emotions serve your own individual truth.

The Craft and Business of Songwriting

34

Message Songs

Another song genre that grows out of a strong emotional state, though often a more positive one, is the "message" song. Even though it's positive, it can have the same drawbacks as the "agony" song unless you're careful. Here's an example:

You've just had a religious experience and must tell the world about your revelation. The spirits have laid a great truth on you and, as a musician, and songwriter, you're uniquely qualified to spread the word. So you dash off a song. After all, you have a vital message to share, so you don't want to bother with all those crass commercial techniques like rhyme and meter. They seem so unimportant next to the innate power of the message. You just know that when you sing it, everyone within earshot will automatically share your feelings.

Wrong! Suddenly, as you play the song for a publisher, or even for someone on the street, reality becomes a new revelation. You realize this person (a) doesn't care, or (b) has heard it all before and doesn't think it makes any more sense now than it ever did, or (c) already shares your belief and is bored by the way you stated it. You've told it the way you felt it, but failed to communicate it to someone who needs the message, or failed to move someone who already knows it by not presenting it in a fresh, new way.

Very few message songs actually communicate their message. If the lyric is weak, the music has to be doubly strong to make up for it. The Beatles' "All You Need Is Love" is, on paper, one of the most trite lyrics ever written—but it works, thanks to an interesting melody, a 7/4 time signature, strong production, and the Beatles' fame. Without a powerful musical vehicle, the words of a message song have to be good enough to stand on their own.

When we were auditioning singer/songwriters in the early days of the Los Angeles Songwriters Showcase, Len Chandler and I had a phrase, "man on the mountain," for an artist with a particularly preachy kind of stance. It translates to: "I, at my tender age, have gone to the mountaintop and learned the secret of the universe. And now, from this lofty perch, I'm going to tell all you unfortunate, unenlightened people how to live your lives."

As a listener, I have one demand: Don't preach to me! If I want to be preached at, I'll go to church. If I need guidance, I'll look for someone with credentials.

I'm not anti-message songs. On the contrary, I don't think there are enough effective ones around. I'd just like writers to take their messages seriously enough to devote some time and craft to ensuring I receive them effectively.

Now that I've told you what doesn't work, what does?

Some people might respond to the preachy approach, which often depends on phrases like "You've got to," "You'd better," and "Don't ever,"—phrases that have all the subtlety of a sledgehammer. More of us, however, would rather be led gently than driven to enlightenment with a whip.

One of my favorite message songs of 2002 was the Black Eyed Peas/Justin Timberlake hit, "Where Is the Love?" I considered it the new equivalent of Marvin Gaye's classic, "What's Going On." Both songs come from the standpoint of someone who's baffled by the injustices and inequities of our time—a great approach that avoids being preachy.

The most effective songs are the ones that involve me in a scene I'm already a part of, or one I feel is cut so realistically from the fabric of life that I *could be* part of. Jesus, Buddha, and all the great religious leaders used parables to get their messages to masses of people, to relate those messages to people's everyday lives. The Good Samaritan was one of Jesus' greatest hits. Wouldn't you feel great it you wrote a song that, two thousand years later, still taught the same message as strongly as it did when it was written?

A classic example of a beautifully delivered message is Steve Seskin and Allen Shamblin's "Don't Laugh at Me," a hit for country artist Mark Wills. The song about tolerance was also recorded by Peter, Paul and Mary; the group's Peter Yarrow set up a project for Operation Respect called "Don't Laugh at Me," a curriculum designed to teach tolerance in schools. This program has already been implemented in more than 20,000 schools across the country. Steve Seskin now enjoys performing at school assemblies in support of this program. The song is also available as a children's book, *Don't Laugh at Me*, which was featured on PBS's *Reading Rainbow* in September 2002. (In addition, this song is a great example of one written in first-person universal. Another example of this approach was Michael Jackson and Lionel Richie's "We Are the World.")

Don't Laugh at Me
by Steve Seskin/Allen Shamblin

Vs   I'm a little boy with glasses
The one they call a geek
A little girl who never smiles
'Cause I have braces on my teeth
And I know how it feels to cry myself to sleep

Vs   I'm that kid on every playground
Who's always chosen last
A single teenage mother
Tryin' to overcome my past
You don't have to be my friend
But is it too much to ask

Cho Don't laugh at me
Don't call me names
Don't get your pleasure from my pain
In God's eyes we're all the same
Someday we'll all have perfect wings
Don't laugh at me

Vs   I'm the beggar on the corner
You've passed me on the street
And I wouldn't be out here beggin'
If I had enough to eat
And don't think I don't notice
That our eyes never meet

Vs I lost my wife and little boy when
Someone crossed that yellow line
The day we laid them in the ground
Is the day I lost my mind
And right now I'm down to holdin'
This little cardboard sign . . . so

Cho Don't laugh at me
Don't call me names
Don't get your pleasure from my pain
In God's eyes we're all the same
Someday we'll all have perfect wings
Don't laugh at me

Br I'm fat, I'm thin, I'm short, I'm tall
I'm deaf, I'm blind, hey, aren't we all

Cho Don't laugh at me
Don't call me names
Don't get your pleasure from my pain
In God's eyes we're all the same
Someday we'll all have perfect wings
Don't laugh at me

Steve writes (and co-writes) compassionate social commentary songs. Though he's had a ton of country hits, I don't consider them archetypal country songs. He writes songs about what moves him personally, songs that appeal to the heart. They aren't necessarily written in a country style or specifically to be hits, and artists looking for those qualities love his honesty (for more information, check out www.steveseskin.com).

In previous editions I used Harry and Sandy Chapin's classic "Cat's in the Cradle" as an example of a great message song. The Chapins didn't give us any "shoulds" in this song, not even in a concluding moral saying, "So we should all make more time for our kids and our parents." They didn't have to. They held a mirror up to life that made listeners think about their relationships with their parents, and did it with real-life dialogue and situations we've all been in. They also did it from a first-person point of view.

Your choice of a point of view—whether to write in first, second, or third person—is critical in a message song. Often, it's effective to describe a situation in terms of your own personal involvement (for more about point of view, see chapter four, page 75). When you offer a message, you're actually trying to sell something. Testimonials are always very effective sales devices. A good approach is to let people in on your own discovery: the insight that got you so excited, you wanted to tell us about it. Your enthusiasm will motivate us without your having to preach to us. Assuming that you put the song together in a way that makes people want to sing along, the first-person point of view allows your audience to internalize the message by saying *I* or *we* along with you. "Don't Laugh at Me" and Michael Jackson and Lionel Richie's "We Are the World" are written in a universal first-person point of view, where the message involves all of us. Another effective point of view is that of the seemingly uninvolved storyteller. This type of song doesn't moralize because, if the story is told well, there's no need for moralizing. One of the most powerful examples is Bob Dylan's "Ballad of Hollis Brown," a song about a man who kills his family and himself rather than see them starve to death because he can't find a job. Dylan wrote many effective songs in this way. "The Way It Is" by Bruce Hornsby, and Rory Lee and Jonnie Barnett's Clay Walker hit, "The Chain of Love," are other good examples.

I don't mean to imply that there are only a few approaches to writing effective message songs. What I'm focusing on here are ways to write for mass audiences who don't necessarily share your point of view. You can use a sledgehammer approach for a song designed to rally people who are already on your side. Toby Keith's "Courtesy of the Red, White, and Blue (The Angry American)" worked well for him, uniting his core audience as much as it alienated liberals. You can use humor, satire—anything that works. And don't forget that the *music* is also important in helping people to hear the message—*and* remember it.

Message writers often choose not to collaborate, perhaps for fear their message will somehow become compromised. But they may be compromising their ability to get that song to a wide audience. If you can write a powerful lyric but are a little shaky in the music department, look for someone who composes well in a contemporary style. The music can be such a powerful vehicle for delivering the message that it shouldn't be taken lightly. Social and political message songs occasionally become hits, and a controversial message may help a song gain notoriety, but it's still the power of the performance, the music, and the production that makes a radio station play it. Your message deserves the best of *all* ingredients.

Novelty Songs

Every writer seems to have at least one crazy, off-the-wall novelty song that he writes just for fun. The spirit can be as much fun for an audience to hear as it is for the writer to write.

Novelty songs, however, are extremely difficult to place with a recording artist. Aside from a few artists such as Ray Stevens ("The Streak," "People's Court"), Jim Stafford ("Spiders and Snakes"), Ross Bagdassarian (a.k.a. Dave Seville) (The Chipmunks), "Weird Al" Yankovic ("Eat It"), and Pinkard & Bowden, who built careers on novelty records, most artists and their producers and record companies view novelty records, particularly for new artists, as career killers. If an artist gets a hit on a novelty record, it's next to impossible to get radio to accept any kind of serious music from the artist after that. If you feel you've got a terrific novelty song, forget pitching it to publishers. Instead, pitch it directly to the few artists who do them, their managers or producers. It's a long shot, but one that might work.

The Dr. Demento Show is a nationally syndicated radio program featuring novelty material from unknown writers. "Weird Al" got his start there, and Dr. Demento still plays his songs. Contact the show at: Dr. Demento, c/o The Demento Society, P.O. Box 884, Culver City, CA 90232, or go to his Web site: www.drdemento.com. The Internet offers loads of other sites that feature novelty songs. Just search "novelty songs" in your browser. Web radio providers like www.live365.com also feature radio stations that have novelty playlists. Just type "novelty" into the search box that asks what style you're looking for. Then contact the DJ who programs it and ask if you can submit your song.

Another approach is to pitch your song to a non-novelty artist who might use it in a live performance. Most artists like to lighten up their stage act by inserting a funny song. They'll often hire writers to create such special material for the act, to be based on the personality of the artist and the function the material needs to fulfill in the show. Contact the artist's manager. If they like it and use it in the act, chances are they won't record it, so charge them a usage fee.

Be careful, though, if you write parodies of well-known songs. Though this may be considered a "fair use" area, you could still be subject to a lawsuit. The safest approach is to get permission from the publisher first (see chapter eight, "Copyright Infringement" on page 161).

Lifestyle Songs

This category of songs encompasses a wide range of topics and is most prevalent in hip-hop, rap and country. Topics might include:

- Drinking and drugging

- Mama's (Daddy's, Grandpa's) advice

- This city life is bad and I long for the simple, peaceful life of my small-town childhood

- I can't wait to get out of this simple, boring small town

- She pursues her dream in the city while he stays in the country (or vice-versa)

- Motorcycles (usually Harleys) and the carefree life on the road

- Violence, women, money, braggadocio (prevalent in hip-hop and rap)

- I was raised on the Bayou (in the projects, on the farm); this type of song seeks to establish the artist as "authentic"

My friend Kevin Johnston from Nashville is a songwriter, publisher, and producer who, for ten years, wrote an annual "Nashville Cliché Commission" report" for *Music Row* magazine that spoofed the most frequently used lyric and video clichés of the previous year.

Kevin regularly pitches songs in Nashville and says,

> In terms of pitching songs to a major artist, lifestyle songs are the most dangerous song a new writer can write. There are two reasons most lifestyle songs get rejected. The first is that they're not the lifestyle of that particular artist, and the second is, "So what?" The latter refers to songs that describe a lifestyle, but there's no real point to it, no story, no moral, just a description. So though it might bring back some pleasant memories for a listener, it's not a compelling lyric in itself and has no appeal at all to anyone who doesn't share the lifestyle. Regarding the first, a common fantasy for new writers is that there is a universal country lifestyle and they assume that a mass country audience and at least most country artists have the same memories. Beware of stereotypes!
>
> There is also a common misperception that, if an artist generally likes a song that has specific references (my son, my job at the foundry, my home on the lake, my favorite horse) that don't apply to him or her, the artist will just ask for a rewrite of those references to personalize them. The reality is that the song will be rejected. This is one of the advantages of writing *with* the artist, or writing in third person.

Lifestyle songs can work for an artist but you have to do lots of research on that *specific* artist to increase your odds. But then you must harbor no illusions that the same song will work for anyone else.

Christmas Songs

Every year I receive a few Christmas songs to critique by mail. A lot of them are on lead sheets (lyrics with musical notation), which tells me these people are novices, as lead sheets went out of style years ago for pitching songs. Maybe they figure that if they could just write one good Christmas song, like "White Christmas," they'd be set for life. It's rare to find a Christmas song that manages to avoid clichés. But let's assume someone did manage to skate past the frosty snowman in the silent night, past the chipmunks and the reindeer, to sit by the cozy fireside and roast chestnuts as their kids ask when Santa's coming and ponder why it can't be this way all year 'round . . . and decided to write a song about it.

What does the Christmas song market look like?

I spoke with publishers and other industry folks and the consensus is that it's an even bigger long shot than trying to get a hit record. Obviously, the first barrier is that the song is seasonal, not the kind people will buy year 'round. The real barrier, though, is that a record needs airplay to become a hit, and few radio stations allot that much time for Christmas music.

Right after Thanksgiving (about the same time retailers start hyping sales of holiday gifts), the radio rotation of Christmas songs begins, escalating until most stations have maybe a few days' worth of increased Christmas fare up to Christmas Eve and Day. The airplay of these songs is encouraged by the stations' ad salespeople to stimulate Christmas shopping activity for their accounts.

They figure their audience isn't tuning in to hear Christmas music. Unless major artists record Christmas CDs, it's seldom worth it for a record company to ship records for a short period of time, then pay to have the leftovers shipped back. The retailers would rather use their stockroom space for records that sell year 'round. In the 2005 holiday season, however, more than twenty-five major artists released Christmas CDs, and though many of these were re-releases, others were debut albums that undoubtedly will be released again in the future. Holiday compilations are also very popular. If the song fits a contemporary rock or other mass-appeal radio format, it's more likely to get played on those stations than something like "White Christmas," but it would still help if you had a contemporary superstar to perform it.

There are more opportunities on Web radio during the holidays. And with the slow demise of brick-and-mortar retail outlets and the rapid rise of online music purchases, the retail space problems mentioned above won't be much of a factor in the future.

One publisher who specializes in holiday songs is Justin Wilde. His company, Songcastle Music, can be contacted via his Web site: www.christmassongs.com.

PRINT MUSIC

Ronny Schiff, an expert in the field of print music, says that she knows of several Christmas and Hanukkah songs, old and new, that have become successful in the educational market by virtue of having great choral arrangements. These were popularized mainly by word of mouth among choral directors and presented in annual school and church pageants. One of the best examples is "Caroling Caroling?" by Albert Burt. Another is the Ukrainian folk song, "Carol of the Bells," which was popular as a choral piece for generations before someone added English lyrics and recorded a pop Christmas arrangement. "So, often this 'back door' method is a good introduction to the public for this type of song," says Schiff.

Recently, there have been some newer Christmas songs recorded as well as some older songs revitalized or remixed. The 'tween, New Age, country, and rock markets have been fertile areas for new holiday songs. Schiff adds that Christmas songs sell best in books and not in individual sheet music. This, I suspect, reflects the fact that people will buy a book of standards, but it takes continued popularity of an individual song before it starts being included in the books.

TELEVISION

Every year major artists perform on TV Christmas specials. With some ingenuity, good timing and contacts, or a good publisher, your song may have a shot at getting on one. Otherwise the new song that's needed for the special is written "for hire" by musical directors who work for the show.

CONTEMPORARY CHRISTIAN AND GOSPEL

This part of the industry is very popular and may be more receptive than pop radio to Christmas songs with a religious message. Look at *Billboard* magazine's Contemporary Christian chart for artists and labels that specialize in this area. There is a wide range of musical styles within this category, from traditional to contemporary, and a plethora of Christian radio stations. (See chapter three, "Radio Formats" on page 46.)

If you're a long-shot player and an excellent writer, if you're willing to start pitching your songs in July and to work for years to develop a standard, you may be one of the few who gets a big royalty check for Christmas. My friend Nadine McKinnor and Donny Hathaway wrote a Christmas song, "This Christmas," recorded many years ago, and it continues to be recorded annually by both new and established artists. It *can* happen!

3 The Media and Listeners

The Media

Let's assume you're a songwriter who ultimately wants your songs to reach the public. As much as you'd like to just wave that magic wand and have everyone automatically hear them, the reality is that before that happens, your song must be approved by a whole series of people. Publishers, producers, record company A&R (artists & repertoire) representatives, record promoters, radio program directors, and club owners all, in their own ways, decide in which medium your music belongs or whether your music is appropriate for their particular medium.

When we attend a classical music concert, we expect to hear long compositions with several different movements. In a film, we expect to hear music that creates a mood that enhances and heightens the action and drama.

When we turn on a pop, country, R&B, rock, or other contemporary music station, we know we'll hear songs that will hold our attention with excellent production and arrangements, and that have frequent, regularly recurring changes in lyrical, musical, and rhythmic texture, and a fairly predictable form.

In musical theater, the songs reveal the characters' personalities and help tell the story. When a character sings a song, the lyric and music must feel natural to that character. However, since theater is a *visual* medium, the songs don't need to be structured like radio songs, unless they're also intended for airplay. The visual aspect will help hold our attention, so the songs aren't as dependent on the type of "reach out and grab you" dynamics that radio needs.

The point is that every medium has both restrictions and freedoms that are created by the function of that medium, the needs of the industry, and the expectations of the audience. The more we understand the medium in which we want to work, its principles and forms, the better we can manipulate it.

A Poem Is Not a Lyric

In the print medium, we have an exceptional legacy of poetry in all languages. Much of that poetry also lends itself to recitation and, in fact, may be written specifically to be recited. It is one of a poet's creative options, and if he chooses it, he knows that there are certain words or syllables that won't flow comfortably in speech but will work fine on paper. On the other hand, some words that can conjure pictures when spoken passionately don't have nearly as much impact on paper. Dylan Thomas's poetry, though it does work on paper, clearly was written to be recited, and recordings of Thomas or Brendan Behan reciting it can bring tears to the eyes. The point is that poetry lives in the media of both print and speech. Lyrics, on the other hand, live elsewhere.

A common misconception is that songs are simply poetry put to music. It is true that an immense number of treasured lyrics do work as well on the printed page as in a musical context. The written and vocal styles of writer/artists such as Jackson Browne, Joni Mitchell, Bob Dylan, and Tom Waits are so well integrated that an unusually poetic phrase that feels right at home in their music may not work comfortably for another artist. Very few Joni Mitchell songs can be performed by another artist without imitating her style.

Performers such as these are considered "album artists." In other words, we buy their albums not because they include a hit single, but because we like their style and the people we perceive them to be. We're likely to read their lyrics on the CD inserts and allow them a little more "poetic license," a little more abstraction, and a few more obscure references that we're challenged to figure out. We don't mind because we're already fans.

The point is that in most cases, a good poem does not necessarily make a good lyric. The obvious difference is that a lyric must function with music. It must be sung. A poem written for the printed page alone can use graphic style and unusual placement of words on the page to emphasize subtleties in meaning. It's not expected to rhyme. It can use identities (*board/bored*) and sight rhymes (*love/move*). It can indulge in abstractions, because if the words aren't readily understood, our eyes and minds can stop for as long as we need to let them sink in or bounce around in the brain.

Much of what is referred to as "poetry" is actually *verse*. The distinction involves substance and form, imagination and craft. Verse is really anything that conforms to accepted metrical rules and structure. Anyone can write good verse with decent rhymes and accurate meter, but if it's devoid of substance and imagination, it's not poetry.

Good lyrics need to have all those attributes and more (and less). In an interview with Oscar-winning lyricist Dean Pitchford ("Footloose"), I asked what he felt was the difference between poetry and lyric, since he had been a poet prior to becoming a lyricist:

> I think poetry, in its final form, is on the page. Maybe when it's read, it achieves something else, but poetry is on the page. Lyric is only 50 percent of the work of a song, and it's spare. It can't be very full or fleshed out. Otherwise you don't leave much room for the music to do anything, or for the interpretation of the singer, which is why I learned very early on that you don't read lyrics to people who aren't in the music industry. It doesn't read, it doesn't speak, and a musician could maybe hear it like the song it could become, but a lyric is not a finished thing. You also have to resist the temptation to fill all the corners, to expand to fill your space. People hand me these typewritten sheets saying, "What do you think?" and it looks like the Gettysburg Address—long extended lines and they're very erudite and smart and there's lots of thought and inner rhymes and alliteration, but there's no space for the music.

The lyric, like a poem, seeks to express an idea or emotion imaginatively in a condensed, yet powerful way. Music helps it do that. In his classes, film composer and teacher Eddy Lawrence Manson asks a student to walk across the room the same way several times. Each time, he plays different music, each selection expressing a different mood. The music gives a different impression of what that person is feeling, where he or she is going. You can use music to do that to a lyrical phrase, too. The right—or wrong—music can give that spare and lean phrase exactly the right or wrong meaning. Beginning lyricists have a tendency to minimize the importance of music as a vehicle to deliver their message.

Unlike in poetry, the words in a lyric must easily lend themselves to singing. Words like *orange* are not only impossible to rhyme, but difficult to sing. A lyricist needs to be able to imagine someone singing the words.

In writing lyrics for radio songs, we need to remember that listeners don't have the same amount of time to wonder what the words really mean as they do when they read poetry. They have only a quick three to four minutes.

A Song Is Not a Record

Making a record is a craft in its own right. Today, the craft of making a recording involves the combined skills of singers, musicians, arrangers, producers, and recording engineers. Their creativity and command of the technology involved can transform a mediocre song into a wonderful sonic experience. But they can't make it a great song. A great song has a life of its own. It will move you even if it's sung *a cappella*. No matter who sings it, in any era or in any style, it will still be a great song. Many writers voice the complaint, "My song is better than a lot of stuff I hear on the radio, so why doesn't anyone want it?" They may be right, but what they've failed to recognize is the difference between a hit *record* and a hit *song*.

The appeal of the *record* may be based primarily on any combination of ingredients aside from words and melody: a powerful vocal performance, an artist or group with a unique identity or sound, a great arrangement, or business considerations such as timing or promotion. There are a lot of hit *records* that don't have a memorable melody or lyrics; perhaps we just remember the hook line. We may even find ourselves humming the bass line. Those aren't songs—they're records.

I've bought CDs—records—solely because I loved their sound, even though I couldn't hum the melodies or understand the lyrics. I enjoyed them simply as a listening experience. However, if there had been great lyrics to go with that experience, I would have had a much greater level of enjoyment. Those of you who record your own material will, I hope, remember that the more you approach your art and craft with a desire to communicate and a commitment to excellence, the more powerfully an audience will experience it.

Most of us can't write a *record* because we're not in control of the recording situation as producers or artists—though we *can* put together a demo that suggests the ingredients that give the producer a blueprint to work from. Some producers and artists strive for the best product possible by seeking out the best songs available, whether they write them themselves or go for "outside" (other writers') songs. Others—the ones more concerned about collecting royalties than turning out a quality product—would rather record a mediocre song of their own than look for a great song by someone else. It's up to the record buyers whether they'll continue to subsidize mediocrity.

Now that songs can be bought individually from online sites, it becomes crucial for companies to release the best songs regardless of who wrote them.

Writing for Radio

Even with the proliferation of new outlets for exposing music on the Internet, radio remains the dominant outlet for mass marketing music. The dominance of commercial radio will weaken in the future as more listeners choose commercial-free satellite radio and use music subscription services for previewing, buying, and downloading songs to their digital players from artists' Web sites and online retailers like iTunes.

Regardless of our disenchantment with the consolidation of radio and the homogenized playlists that are alienating an increasing number of listeners, radio will remain a major force for some time to come because it appeals to passive listeners. As songwriters, we have to realize that although it's human nature to assume that everyone else must enjoy the same music we enjoy, we're more discriminating than most listeners. I have to keep reminding myself that, in a way, I live in a bubble. I associate with songwriters, musicians, and industry people. I seek out good music on the Internet. I have broadband Internet access, an iPod, and I listen to Web radio. Though broadband Internet use is increasing dramatically, I can't assume that everybody else is savvy and connected yet. I do know, however, that whatever medium we use to receive our music, the qualities that make us enjoy the best songs on radio are the same ones that make us like music, regardless of how we hear it. So the information here about writing for radio applies across the board.

One thing we need to remember is that radio isn't in the music business—or in the business, necessarily, of giving us the best music available. Radio stations are in the *advertising* business. They'll play or do whatever will attract the largest possible listening audience (and, need I mention, whoever pays them to play it). The bigger the audience, the more money advertisers will pay to sell everything from zit cream to retirement homes. The approaches vary widely, from high-energy Top 40 (or 20) stations with hard-sell styles, to instrumental Muzak-type stations, where the commercials register almost subliminally. Some stations seek to reach a wide variety of listeners and age groups, with music that's interesting and not too high energy. This used to be called MOR ("middle of the road") or "easy listening," but is now classified as AC (adult contemporary). Others attempt to pinpoint a specific market with a specific style of music. (See "Radio Formats" on the next page.) Personally, I think the best new music I'm consistently hearing is on National Public Radio.

The competition between radio stations is fierce, particularly between those with similar formats. They're obsessed with preventing "dial outs." Once they have you tuned in, they don't want you to go away. Consequently, one of the most important requirements for music on the radio is that it holds the listener's attention. While it's true that holding someone's attention on the radio is accomplished by a combination of song, artist, and production, you need to start with a song that lends itself well to radio. The following chapters will help you create that type of song.

Song Length

The greatest percentage of hit radio songs used to be approximately three minutes long. Today they average more than four minutes. You rarely hear them much longer than five minutes because radio wants to play more songs while maintaining plenty of space for commercials. Knowing this, few publishers, producers, and record companies want to buck the system by signing, producing, or recording a longer song. They also know that exceptionally long songs aren't as likely to get maximum "rotation," that is, the number of times per hour or day a song gets played. They'd rather have a short song that gets played once an hour than a long one that's played every three hours. With a higher frequency of airplay for your song, you, as a writer, will make more money from BMI, ASCAP or SESAC, the performing rights organizations (see chapter nine, "Performance Royalties" on page 175). It's interesting to note that when radio was much tougher about keeping songs down to three minutes, record companies were known to put 2:59 on the label of a single that really ran maybe 3:04, just for that extra edge!

> A great story is told about country music legend Buck Owens ("Act Naturally"), who had worked in radio before his career as a recording artist. Knowing that DJs frequently found themselves with less than three minutes to go before a newsbreak or commercial—too short for a three-minute record but too long to fill with idle chatter—he fashioned his first releases to two minutes or under and let the DJs know it. Consequently, he got lots of airplay in those awkward time slots.

Radio personnel will play a longer song if there is such an incredible public demand for it that they might lose listeners to another station. However, that song had better be able to hold an audience's attention from beginning to end and make them want to hear it again.

Major artists can get away with long songs on hit radio because everyone wants to hear these artists. A common practice is to edit a record for different functions: a short version for the radio single and longer versions and special mixes for specialty radio shows and the dance-club market.

Something else to consider in the length of the song is the *introduction*. Intro lengths vary, but most people feel that approximately ten seconds of introduction is optimum for a slow song. For an upbeat dance tune, twenty seconds or more can work because, if it grabs your body, you'll keep listening. Even though these general time guidelines are important, it's more important that the intro be easily identifiable and *musically interesting*. It should involve changing textures, adding instruments, or other arrangement devices to keep it developing. Nothing induces boredom faster than an intro that goes nowhere.

A unique, identifiable introduction will make a radio station's program director pay attention. If you've caught *his* attention, he'll figure that his audience is likely to pay attention, too. DJs love to talk over intros. Many people find it irritating, but it gets back to radio trying to save more time for commercials. Some DJs just get excited about having sound tracks behind their own voices as they introduce a song. It's a good idea to include the duration of your intro on the DJ's promotional copy so she'll know how long to talk, although it's easy these days for DJs and programmers to quickly get those timings on the CD (or digital) player (see chapter twelve, "Intros in Demos" on page 258).

RADIO FORMATS

Here's a list of the major new-music (as opposed to "oldies") radio formats in the U.S. and Canada, courtesy of independent radio airplay promoter Bryan Farrish (www.radio-media.com). The list includes his comments on each format. Obviously, the number of stations in these categories is subject to change.

I checked with Bryan to see if there were any major changes for this edition. It had seemed to me there were more R&B, hip-hop stations now. He replied, "Actually, the totals are not that different. There are a lot of grey areas within each one. Urban can be CHR or CHR rhythmic, depending on who you ask, and that can add or subtract 100 all by itself."

46

Country

2,300 stations. Country is the real "Top 40" of the U.S., because of its popularity. "Young country" and "hot country" appeal to younger listeners, using newer artists, younger DJs, and a more energetic approach. The whole "new" approach really took hold about the time Garth Brooks started gaining popularity. More traditional country stations (sometimes known as "heritage" stations) are sort of the oldies of country radio, but they also are specific in which new artists they play.

One special subcategory of country is the "Americana" format. It is a cross between rock and country, with about a hundred stations, most of which are small. Americana is an interesting format, with some really eclectic artists and new labels.

Religious

1,900 stations. Includes various Christian music styles, gospel, and many stations with a large amount of teaching content. Although its a big format, hundreds of religious stations offer fewer opportunities for new music because so much of their airtime is devoted to talk, satellite programming, and older songs.

There is no set number of religious stations that play new music and any particular station may play anywhere from one to twenty-four hours of new music daily.

Adult Contemporary

1,500 stations. Includes "mainstream" AC, "modern" AC, "hot" AC and "soft" AC. AC is similar to religious in that hundreds of its stations have limited capacity for new music because of the talk, satellite or sports programming they carry.

Nevertheless, there are enough small AC stations that play new music for a new artist to stand a chance—if promoted correctly.

Rock

800 stations. Includes modern, alternative, and straight rock. These are usually very high-profile stations, but it is tougher for independent artists to get played on them. However, specialty shows and mixshows offer more opportunities for airplay. They are one- or two-hour programs on a commercial station usually broadcast late at night, often on weekends, that feature music that the station normally does not play.

Spanish

600 stations. All variations included.

Top 40

400 stations. Includes "rhythmic crossover" stations; that is, Top 40 with a beat. This is a very difficult format for indie artists. But again, specialty shows and mixshows save the day.

Urban

300 stations. Includes urban, R&B, hip-hop, and urban AC. Also very difficult for new artists, but thankfully it also offers mixshow support.

Classical

150 stations.

> **Jazz**
>
> 150 stations. Includes "straight" jazz (that is, traditional), and "smooth" jazz. Straight jazz is a viable format for an indie artist. Smooth, however, will be very difficult to break into.
>
> **Kids**
>
> 50 stations. These are mostly the Radio Disney stations, all of which are programmed from the home office.

Singles, Albums, Live Performances, Video

The ability to distinguish between the requirements of these four different media and art forms can eliminate a lot of confusion for a writer or writer/performer.

LIVE PERFORMANCES: MY AUDIENCE LOVES IT—WHY DON'T YOU?

Welcome to the disconnection between live performance and recording. Let's say you're primarily a live performer who is used to getting an enthusiastic response from an audience. You think, "I'm ready to do a CD of my songs and see if I can get a record deal" (or a publishing deal, a manager, film and TV placement, good reviews, better gigs, etc.). So you save up your cash and record those songs—the ones your club audiences love, with the arrangements they love. Then you start sending them out and get comments like, "I like your style but you need better songs," "Good singer but I don't hear any hits," "I suggest you find better songs," "Nothing here of interest but let me know when you have some more songs." You can't believe it! Your audiences go wild for these songs. They even request them. After all, aren't these the people who're gonna buy your records anyway? Why can't these so-called music professionals hear how great these songs are?

Audiences almost always respond to a high-energy, enthusiastic performance, to a heartfelt delivery, and to a performer with conviction and personal charisma, especially one who has spent some time honing those live-performance skills. But the positive response a writer/artist/band gets from a live performance can be very misleading when he/she/they don't separate the *performance* from the *song*.

As a writer/performer, you may take your excellent performing ability for granted. Chances are, though, that you're connected to what you've written in a very personal way. In your mind, the songs are the focus, so you assume that people are applauding the songs rather than the presentation.

When people go to a club, pay a cover charge, and spend another $20 or more on drinks and food, they're willing to go more than halfway to be entertained. If you're a good performer, you may easily satisfy that customer. But when you take a demo with those same songs to a hard-nosed publisher or a record company A&R rep who's separating the performance from the song and looking for a hit, it's a whole new situation. Since they can't see your facial expressions and body language, and can't be moved by your charismatic presentation, the song has to stand on its own.

A lot of music works in clubs that would never work as a hit single. A ten-minute vamp will work for a dancing crowd and a ten-minute guitar or drum solo can bring a club or concert crowd to frenzy, but put it on the radio and even the same person who loved it in concert may change the station. What about jam bands like Phish, Dave Matthews Band, and Widespread Panic who sell tons of records of their performances? The fact is that most of their CDs are sold to those concertgoers who relive the concert experience through the recording, not because the group has a hit single.

An interesting side note is that when Dave Matthews got together with hit producer Glen Ballard to write the *Everyday* album (and that hit single), he had to learn a whole new process for writing songs. They had to design each song to ensure tightness and the maximum dynamics and structure needed to make it work on radio, instead of letting the song develop organically, as it would in a live performance. Also, solos that, in live performance, could last several minutes had to be restricted in the recorded arrangements to a few choice bars.

Unless you're a jam band with a mega following, a music industry pro must rely on the million-dollar gamble that people who have never seen you perform live will be captivated by the song and its recorded presentation when they hear it on the radio.

"But," you say, "I'm not looking for a hit record. I'm just trying to sell my own records and give people who buy them a great experience. What do I need to know that will make my recorded songs better?" Several factors that may not be necessary for songs performed live are more critical for successful recorded versions.

Structure

Producers often complain that the biggest problem in producing artists and bands who have created their songs for a live-performance context is that the songs often need to be restructured. Good structure is a major selling point for listeners (and industry professionals). In live performance, however, it's more important to generate energy, so in the effort to keep a performance amped up, there's a natural tendency—particularly for bands—to set up a great groove and just lean on it instead of going into a couple of new sections to break it up.

A live performer may also do a long instrumental section that stretches a song to ten minutes (something the bands I have performed in would frequently do when we didn't have enough material). Without the visual aspect of the band or the vibe of a roomful of people to enhance the experience, however, a recorded song has to depend on the dynamics of tension and release, or surprise vs. predictability. A verse/chorus, verse/chorus setup gives us the predictability factor, then the surprise element of a totally different bridge, then back home to a chorus and out. This is a time-tested structure that, given enough contrast in each section, will hold an audience's attention almost by itself. But there are lots of effective structures (see chapter five, "Song Form" on page 82).

Dynamics

A change in dynamics is an effective way to keep the listener interested in a song. A melody, set of chord changes, groove or lyric meter that is totally different in your chorus than in your verse can be a powerful attention-getter, whether the song is heard live or on CD. More subtle contrasts, such as a different rhyme scheme in the chorus, will work better on CD than live. That great, dynamic two-bar phrase or four-bar pre-chorus that telegraphs the arrival of the chorus will not only bring a live audience to its feet, but also will work well on CD. But unless you think of making it part of your song when you write it, you'll never know what it *could* do if it were written differently. Without those dynamic sections you may still be able to get by (and please your live crowd) with all the other attributes you've got going for you, but it won't necessarily work as well on the CD. (See chapter five, "Song Dynamics" on page 96.)

Lyric

In a club, particularly with rock and hip-hop (because they depend largely on intensity, energy, and attitude), we rarely hear all or any of the words. We're captivated by the lights and sounds. We're "spoken to" with body language and facial expressions, so even though we may not hear the exact lyric, we get the drift. Maybe we'll pick up a catchphrase that we can hook our own meaning on. On a CD, on the other hand, we may be able to hear most or all of the words. If we're hearing them for the first time, without all the flash and excitement of a club, the lyric needs to captivate and delight us all by itself.

ALBUMS

Albums are another medium altogether. Generally speaking, albums allow more creative latitude, particularly for self-contained bands and writer/artists. An artist's hit single may produce a completely different listening experience from her concerts or albums. Both of the latter can be much more spontaneous and unpredictable. They can stretch the forms and create tremendous tension with long repetitive vamps that would never work in the limited time-frame of a single. Longer, more dramatic songs are possible, often resembling those of musical theater. Most great performing artists present an audience with quite a different experience in concert than on record, even when they deliver the hits that made them famous.

Sound and style are among the selling points for album artists. Sting and Radiohead are good examples of artists with unique and popular sounds and styles. People buy albums by New Age artists like Jim Brickman, George Winston, and Yanni because they create a *mood* that's comforting. The appeal of other album artists such as Tom Waits, Joni Mitchell, Dar Williams, and a rapidly expanding list of independent artists, is their personal point of view. We read the liner notes, follow the lyrics, and generally pay attention to their songs in a way not far removed from the way we pay attention at a concert. We get to know the artists and relate to them in an intimate way, coming to feel like they are old friends. Consequently, their songs don't have to *demand* our attention as a hit single would. They already have us.

Nevertheless, the album has an obligation not to betray the buyer's trust. No one likes being seduced by a hit single, only to be profoundly disappointed by a mediocre album with forgettable songs and mundane performances. Personally, I'll forgive an artist for being adventurous on an album, even if it falls short of my expectations, but I can't forgive one who cops out by giving me empty filler just to have an album to sell.

With the introduction of iTunes and other sites that allow us to purchase single songs, we've almost come back around to the days of the hit single. The benefit for fans is that we're able to buy those few songs that we love without having to buy the whole album. It puts music publishers and record companies in a bind, however, because the traditional strategy is to use the singles to sell the album, where most of their income is generated. Consequently, many artists and record companies won't release single songs for online purchase, forcing us to buy the whole album. This, in turn, drives fans to illegal downloads—a vicious cycle.

VIDEO

Somewhere between recordings and live performance is video, which can deliver some of the excitement of a live show and allow artists tremendous exposure over established outlets like Black Entertainment Television and Country Music Television, as well as individual specialty shows. MTV's not giving us much music anymore, but with a growing number of broadband Internet connections, more fans will be watching videos on their computers. I don't believe video has much relevance to your songwriting craft. No matter what kind of song you write, creative video producers will find ways to make it visually appealing, often creating scenarios that bear little—if any—relationship to what the song is about.

Record companies only make videos for songs that they plan to pitch to the radio, too. Because video has so much power as a marketing tool, however, it has influenced record companies to sign artists who are great looking and visually exciting. Despite what producers say about recording being "all about the songs," the visual aspect can be a determining factor in their decisions about who gets signed and who doesn't.

With the price of high-quality digital video cameras, editing software, and media (DVD and solid-state memory) coming down with each new model, creating a video is now well within the reach of hobbyists who are learning firsthand to be directors. We're seeing more indie solo artists and bands creating their own videos and reaping the benefits of that exposure. There are also increasing numbers of outlets for international online exposure of music videos.

On an artistic level, video gives artists the opportunity to create images for their music that can stay in a listener/viewer's mind. Another factor to consider is that in video, particularly performance videos that actually show the artist singing (as opposed to "concept" videos that show almost everything *but*), it's possible for viewers to "get" the lyric faster. No matter what the video style or means of distribution is used, your craftsmanship is still extremely important.

The Listener: Know Your Audience

Most new writers give little conscious thought to who they're writing for. They may write primarily for themselves, thereby reaching an audience of their peers who share their emotional concerns, social scene, political views, colloquial language, and musical tastes. They become popular not because they're deliberately writing for a target demographic group, but because they *are* that group. Self-contained writer/artists and groups like the Rolling Stones may not only keep the audience who grew up with them, but also continue to appeal to an audience maybe thirty years younger who can still identify with their attitudes because those attitudes haven't changed that much. They're basic and universal.

If you want the creative challenge of writing songs for artists in different musical styles from the one(s) you've been most at home with, be prepared to stretch. Analyze the appeal of one artist and the characteristics of his or her audience (see chapter eleven, "Casting: The Right Song for the Right Artist" on page 221). Immerse yourself in the artist's work. Listen to the radio stations that play his or her records. Buy some of them yourself, especially recent successful ones. Then write a song in that artist's style.

Be careful not to make quick, stereotyped judgments or harbor any negative attitudes about the style you're trying to write in. It's difficult enough to come up with something worthwhile even when you know and love a style. I once counseled a writer who expressed interest in writing country songs. I asked who his favorite country artists were and he said, "I don't know. I never listen to country. In fact, I don't even like it! It just seems like it would be easier to write than pop, and more artists record songs they don't write." I told him to forget it. His motivation was all wrong.

Moreover, unless you make a thorough study of an unfamiliar style, you can easily get way off track. You have to know, for instance, that while jazz fans may love complex melodies and chord changes, they don't work in country songs. Abstract lyrics that might spark a pop or rock piece would turn off a country audience.

One of the most common problems for style-switching writers comes from inappropriate combinations of music and subject matter. For instance, a romantic lyric like "I Will Always Love You" wouldn't make it in heavy metal because rebellion, not romance, is what interests heavy metal's audience: primarily teenage white males. A hard, frantic edge in a piece of rock music needs a lyric with an attitude to match—nothing soft, mushy, or tender. On the other hand, though these artists write their own songs, Rob Thomas and 3 Doors Down appeal to both young men and women because there's room in their images for both vulnerability and harder-edged personal statements. It allows room in their repertoires for romantic ballads *and* rockers.

When writing in a style that's new to you, try to visualize the audience. A writer once played me a song about a man who was propositioning his wife's best friend. He tells her that she shouldn't think about getting too involved, however, because he's still in love with his wife. Musically, the song was a mellow pop ballad, a style that appeals primarily to women, and it was addressed to a woman. It would seem, therefore, that the writer intended women to be the target audience, and that he expected them to identify with the best friend—but that's where the writer went wrong. Think about it. Even if we assume that the friend liked the guy and was flattered by the come-on, she wouldn't appreciate hearing him say he was still in love with his wife! And what if those potential record buyers identified with the wife? They certainly would not enjoy a song in which a husband propositions her best friend. So the subject matter effectively alienated the very audience that would be most drawn to the musical style. If the writer had thought from the outset about how his audience would feel as they listened to the song, he would not have considered it pitchable.

Whether you're writing a song to perform yourself or for someone else, you must have an idea of who your audience is and how they will respond if you expect your song to sell.

THE IMAGINATION OF THE LISTENER BY CHRIS BLAKE

I interviewed songwriter Chris Blake around the time I started writing this book and discussed with him what makes songs work for an audience. I found him to be even more obsessed with the subject than I was, to the degree that he had spent a lot of time in research. I was even more pleased to see how well he articulated the results of his research, and decided that the material was important enough to be included here. Though Chris's experience is mostly in country, where lyric is king, I feel this information is extremely valuable no matter what style of music you write.

Imagination plays a large part in our perception of a song. The imagination converts words into experiences, turning songs into old friends that we want to hear again and again. The hit song lyric is one which, one way or another, gives the imagination what it needs to do that job, simply, easily, and completely.

The theater of the imagination performs twenty-four hours a day. It literally cannot *not* function, but as a mechanism it has certain characteristics—certain ways of acting and reacting—which we, as writers, need to know about.

Much remains to be learned about the human imagination and how it works, but a review of some of what has been found so far could make a difference to your work as a lyricist. I'm going to spare *you* the specific references and technical talk that is in much of the scientific literature. But for those of you who enjoy that sort of thing, see the bibliography. I do want to point out some specific characteristics of the imagination, which have been confirmed by scientific research and are totally relevant to the job of the song lyricist.

The imagination is a stimulus-response mechanism. That is, it will not act unless *acted upon*, at which point it will act (or more properly, react) totally automatically.

What stimulates the imagination is just about any *cue* that it perceives. To keep it simple, we can talk about cues as *internal* and *external.*

Internal cues are those that originate from within—from thoughts, associations, and memories. Fantasies and daydreams are good examples of the imagination responding to internal cues. While it's important to notice that the imagination itself cannot originate a stimulus, it can and does respond to its own images all the time. All of us who have ever been guilty of daydreaming (while that half-finished lyric sits unattended in front of us) have been caught up in what the people in the lab jackets call an "associative response chain"—really an instance of the imagination taking off on its own material and going on and on.

This ability of the imagination to entertain itself is one of your major concerns as a lyricist. For now, just know that it *is* a relatively weak phenomenon. It is easily interrupted by external stimuli that, because they exist in present time, appear to hold a much stronger demand for the attention of the imagination. That ringing phone, with all its potential for who might be calling, will stop a daydream every time. Sometimes, that's a shame.

External cues are just what they sound like: sights, sounds, smells, and touch sensations—the whole world we perceive outside us. We take them in and interpret them in our own experience, giving them meaning and order in our own reality. We then attempt to communicate our realities to one another using a set of mutually agreed-upon sounds we call *words.* These words, when spoken and heard, become powerful external cues to the imagination: the cues we, as lyricists, are primarily concerned with right now.

Nowhere is the stimulus-response characteristic of the imagination clearer than in the domain of words. The imagination can't resist them. Indeed, it's a good thing! Were it not for the ability of our imaginations to convert words into images, we simply could not communicate with each other. (Nor could we communicate with ourselves, for it is in our imaginations that we put the world together.) But, let's keep it simple.

It's 6:30 A.M., and Larry, fanatic that he is, is going out jogging. This morning he's trying a new running route and, as he heads out the door, his roommate, Max (who has run the new route before), yells after him to "watch out for the dog."

As Larry goes down the steps he wonders, as he always does, why he's doing this crazy thing. But not as hard as he's wondering what Max was talking about. Dog? What dog? Watch out? Why? Larry has been hooked. And his imagination is off and running (faster than Larry, probably).

Before we find out what happened, let's take a look at what went on inside Larry's head after the dog warning. It may seem a dry exercise, but as a lyricist, you had best begin practicing this way of thinking.

Larry's mind now launches into an enormous amount of activity, but let's just touch on the highlights. *"Watch out for the dog."* What does that mean? It's not just automatic. He's got to remember: what, exactly, does *watch out* mean, and what is a *dog*?

Well, Larry's no dummy. He is now somewhere in the "watch out for the dog" ballpark in his mind, with a vague kind of picture of what those words mean to him. And there he would remain if he didn't have an imagination. But he does have one, and because it's an automatic response mechanism, it reacts automatically to the words.

Now, the imagination is not a selective machine. That is, it doesn't make choices for us. It is programmed to retrieve from the files and project on our screens exactly what it's told to—no less. And what is in our files—our memory—on any given subject? *Only every experience, thought, fantasy, emotion, and impulse we've ever had that we associate, however loosely, with that subject.*

Poor Larry! All he ever did was decide to take a new running route. Let's listen in while his imagination does what it is built to do:

Dog. Yessir, coming right up. Hmm, let's see, 'dog' . . . ah, here it is: Lassie, Rin-Tin-Tin (excitement) . . . German police dogs, big, teeth (fear) . . . memory of being bitten by Mrs. Smith's Doberman (fear, pain, anger)

. . .old Fido and me playing on the front lawn (happy) . . . Fido grew old and had to be put to sleep (sad) . . . your parents bought you a new puppy, but he had to be housebroken (disgust) . . . and so on . . .

As much as all this information is, it's just a fraction of what Larry has filed away with the word *dog*. But, his roommate wasn't just talking about any dog. He was talking about a *watch out* kind of dog:

Hmm, let's see, "Watch out"—oh, yeah, it's right here . . . pain, anger . . . what Mom said just before I burned my hand on the stove (fear, pain) . . . it's what you're supposed to do because Santa Claus is coming to town (confused) . . . what that kid shouted at me just before the baseball hit me in the head (pain) . . . what a roommate would say if I were about to go running past a man-eating dog (fear, anger) . . .

So, now Larry's imagination has *watch out* and *dog* files on tap. It puts them together and begins to feed Larry the following kinds of images:

Rabid wolves chasing starving children through the Russian woods (terror) . . . Mrs. Smith's Doberman resurrected from the past and waiting for me just around the corner (fear) . . . Cujo crouched behind the next bush waiting . . . the Big Bad Wolf . . . packs of wild dogs, led by an evil-minded little mutt who looks suspiciously like Fido . . .

All this sounds a little silly, but to Larry these kinds of images don't seem silly at the time. The point is to notice the enormity and the complex variety of the information that becomes available to Larry's imagination from just a few words.

And he can't help himself. Notice that nothing about Larry's wild imagining was voluntary. Unless he particularly enjoys being afraid, we have to think that Larry probably wished he could think of something else while running. What I hoped to demonstrate is that the imagination (given appropriate cues) will do its thing, no matter what. It is a stimulus-response mechanism.

But please notice that the imagination is literally "wild" and has no discipline to it. *You*, the writer, must realize that you set off this same crazy process in the listener's head with every word you write; and it is *you* who must bring discipline to the listener's imagination. You need to impose controls on it in order to keep it somewhere in the domain in which you intend it to be.

Your tool for this job of channeling imagery is the *specificity* in your words. It's why God invented nouns and verbs and modifiers—adjectives and adverbs—tools to specify *exactly* who, what, where, when, why, and how.

As we saw with Larry, the imagination will come up with the whole crazy file unless it gets further directions. The quality of the image will be generalized and nonsensical. The tendency of the imagination is to quit the job under these conditions—for reasons we shall see—or to re-create only one particular image for arbitrary reasons, and *it may or may not be the image you want the listener to experience.*

Experiment for yourself. How intensely can you become involved with the following words?

Car

Book

Musical instrument

Not very, huh? You may have chosen to focus on one image that had personal meaning in your experience. The problem is that I meant you to *see*:

My great 1982 Porsche 928 with the broken right taillight

My paperback book with a blue cover and the words *Gifts of God* printed in gold on the front

My old white Telecaster guitar with the broken B-string and the missing volume knob

While the examples may seem arbitrary, the implications for your work are direct. You want the listener's imagination to re-create what *you* want it to; and for that, you need to be specific, or the imagination will abandon you, your words, and your song, and wander off down god-knows-what corridors of its own. It may pay more attention to other more specific and immediate information—the car ahead, the fight he had with his wife last night, or whatever. It's called "getting bored," and it is astonishing how often we simply *bore* listeners away from our songs by refusing to give them specific items to imagine. The imagination *is* a restless and highly distractible child, full of all good intentions and no self-control. If you want its attention, you'd better keep it busy with specific tasks.

But what tasks? Read on.

The imagination is an "analog information" mechanism: That is, it can create pictures only out of the information already stored in the mind's experience. Larry's "dog" emerged as a composite of many past real and imagined events, feelings, and pictures. Nothing really new was a part of that image, save possibly some new combinations of old information.

The phrase "floating in space" can be imagined only by memories of experiences we've already had—none of which, of course, include really floating in space. Maybe it's the feeling of semi-weightlessness we've had floating in water, various remembered scenes from sci-fi movies, or perhaps the sensation of room and freedom around us (because we've heard space is empty, vast, and infinite). All sorts of images, feelings, and sensations occur, but all of them are taken from experiences real and imagined that we've already had. Nothing new. The imagination literally cannot deliver to us the experience of floating in space, but it tries hard (as it's designed to do) to re-create the experience out of old bits and pieces of information available to it. Our experience of the words can only be *imaginary* because we cannot come up with the real thing.

This is the primary reason that songs must be built on universal themes. As a songwriter, you simply cannot write about things that are outside of most people's experience and expect them to be able to relate to—to become involved in—the song through their imaginations. If they cannot relate *at the level of their imaginations*, the song becomes meaningless simply because they don't have the machinery to deal with it. Their reaction, of course, is one of instant frustration and turnoff. And your song doesn't get listened to.

It's amazing how often songwriters seem to believe they can get around this one. I wish I had a dime for every song I've heard from people who want to crash into the commercial market and yet who write about such obscure items as working on the floor of the stock market, the intricacies of shifting through ten different truck gears, and the tactics employed in nineteenth-century sea battles.

It's one matter to use specific detail to contribute to a universal emotion (plot). It's another to write your song exclusively about something with which you're familiar but about which a large block of listeners would have no experience or little knowledge.

Just remember to be very careful about the ideas, metaphors, and images you use in your song and keep a ruthless eye out for the possibility that you are excluding large blocks of people from participating in your song. Among the chief villains here are songs that are totally about marriage or totally about divorce. You have to remember that lots of people have been neither married nor divorced.

Mental images are complete neurophysiological events. That is they occur in the brain and throughout the body simultaneously.

Unreal as imagined experiences are, they actually can produce the *experience* of reality. It's a testimony to how powerful the imagination truly is that we don't just *imagine* the sensation of weightlessness; we *feel* it. Indeed, we react emotionally and physically to images in our mind. Our bodies produce what scientists call "secondary sympathetic responses" to mental imagery. The word *red* causes "red" activity in the parts of our eyes that react to color; the word *ouch* causes muscle contraction. And nerve endings truly react to the phrase *the touch of your hand*.

Notice for yourself the number of song titles and lyrics that use images that suggest or involve physical action:

"With Arms Wide Open"

"Jumpin' Jumpin'"

"We Danced"

The list would be nearly endless. The usefulness of such physical action imagery is obvious when you consider the fact that we react to mental images with actual physical sensation and action. In short, lyrics that involve such demands in their imagery hook the listener not just from the standpoint of their beauty or cleverness but from a physical standpoint as well. Remember that the imagination responds automatically to words. You literally tell it what to do and it is helpless not to respond. If you give clear, simple, precise directions to it, you can produce powerful *emotional* and *physical* events in the listener.

Are you beginning to understand just how totally listeners are "hooked" by a good lyric? We don't *have* images; we *do* them. We imagine with our whole selves.

We can produce audio "images" feeling and sensation "images," and so forth. We can, in fact, "image" just about any experience we've ever had, think we've had, or imagine we've had—and you as the songwriter can direct us to do that if only you are clear in your directions and keep in mind the response characteristics of the imagination.

But you must realize some of the imagination's limits. Chief among these is its inability to re-create conceptual abstractions. An abstraction, for our purposes, is a subjective, usually very general, piece of information.

An abstraction just floats there. It's not grounded in *specificity* (who, what, where, when, or why). Because it is nonspecific, the imagination, working the way it does, doesn't know what to do with it and isn't interested. Try to imagine such external cues as *decency, belief, transcendent, wonderful, beautiful*, and so forth. Abstractions lack focus.

On the face of it, this creates an alarming problem for songwriters, for the worst abstractions of them all are the body of words that refer to the emotions, one of which is *love*.

So how do you write a song about an emotional state such as love? Your goal is to involve the listener as deeply as possible by writing words that are usable by his imagination so that he can re-create the words of the song. The very words you would think the listener wants to hear—*love, sad, sorrow, you hurt me, I need you*—are abstractions the imagination cannot process.

The key to resolving this dilemma is simple enough. First, remember that listeners want "the real thing": information accessible to their imaginations as they listen. Second, notice that abstractions are convenient for organizing and labeling our life experiences, but they are most definitely not life itself.

For the fun of it, let's look at the abstract phrase, *falling in love*. At the risk of offending the romantic poet in all of us, those words don't really refer to anything at all. They are only a kind of organizing label system, a file into which we put what for each of us have been unique and very real experiences. When I remember "falling in love" (the last time it happened to me), what I remember was:

- being able to think of nothing else except Betsy

- feeling lightheaded and slightly dizzy when I was around her

- losing my appetite

- daydreaming about us together

- making plans for our future

- wishing time would go faster so that I could be with her

- having my phone bill quadruple

- loving the smell of her perfume on my sweater

And on and on. Even that list is not too specific, but I *know* it brought you into a more real contact with my experience of "falling in love" than the phrase itself ever could. Are you beginning to get the drift?

Life is not an abstraction. It is moment to moment: real, specific, and concrete. And so it is that when the imagination re-creates life it can do so only with specific and concrete images. So, when you write lyrics, you must give the mind the kind of cues and information it needs to do its job or it won't bother with the information. **Abstractions simply do not work in the imagination.** They, in fact, serve to turn it away.

And yet it is true that songs are about abstractions. It's been said that there are seven possible "plots" to a commercial song: love, hate, loneliness, happiness, sadness, jealousy, and revenge. Every one of those words is an abstraction. Every one of them is basically unusable by the imagination. And every one of them refers to what is at the heart of universal commerciality.

Nonetheless, it does present an apparent contradiction. How does the writer write about abstract emotions in a way that engages and involves the listener so he can participate in the song? How do you give the imagination the concrete specifics it needs to kick into gear? The answer lies in those questions. *The successful lyricist writes about abstractions through the use of detailed, concrete, specific (nonabstract) information.*

Two fine examples of what I'm talking about are found in "Miss Emily's Picture" and the country classic, "The Gambler."

"Miss Emily's Picture," recorded by John Conlee, is about a man who's lonely, blue, and missing Miss Emily terribly. But notice how dry that description is. The vehicle—the medium—through which the writer, Hollis R. DeLaughter, communicates those feelings is simple, repeated descriptions of the act of looking at Miss Emily's picture. Notice that that is *a physical act* in which *you* can imagine and participate. Remember the number of times you've looked at pictures of someone very special to you. The idea is easy to re-create in your imagination. Absolutely nowhere in the song does the singer talk about missing Emily, or how he loved her, or anything else like that; and yet the impact of those emotions is profound and lasting. It is a very emotional song in which not one emotion is ever *mentioned by word.*

"The Gambler" outlines a whole philosophy of living. And if Don Schlitz, the writer, had gone at it directly, it could have been one of that year's ten worst songs. If, instead of telling us about when to "hold 'em" and when to "fold 'em," he'd said something like:

It's important to know when to persist in trying to achieve your goals, and when to give up.

You have to know when to decide to give up what you're doing gradually, and to know when to give up quickly.

You should never make a judgment about how your life is going while it's going on.

There'll be plenty of time to look back to see how it all went, after your life is over.

Those statements are an attempt at a straight, conceptual description of the philosophy in "The Gambler." It's what we all know he meant. But, obviously, the words are simply *poison* in terms of retaining our interest and involving us in the song. As ludicrous as the examples seem, many songwriters actually write their lyrics at this level of abstraction. The lyrics are accurate. They say what the songwriter wants to say. They have meter and rhyme. But they are extraordinarily uninvolving and boring.

Examine your songs rigorously to be sure you're not falling into the trap of settling for abstractions when you could *express your abstractions in a lively, imaginative way, preferably in a way that involves the listener in some form of action.* Notice that "The Gambler" got its job done by delivering the abstraction using the active metaphor of a poker game. The song also is one of a very few that goes three verses before it gets to the chorus, a tribute to the fact that *action* can hold our attention anyway.

The imagination is addicted to action. Notice the difference in your imagination between: "the red brick" and "the brick flew toward the store window."

It's not that the imagination cannot handle the idea of "the red brick." It's okay as images go. It has a color. It has a form we're all familiar with. It's concrete (so to speak). You can feel it. You can see it. You might turn it around in your imagination and examine it, and (with some encouragement) spend enough time to really get into its "brickness." But the chances are you'd get bored fast and lose interest.

That is because mental images have a rapid decay rate. Research shows that the images in our minds last less than a second and, visually speaking, are not too clear in the first place. The picture in your mind's eye is somewhat granular (something like a snowy television picture), with best definition and clarity in the center of the picture and degeneration of that image away from the center. So we "see" our images for only a very short time, and they are not too clear to start with. This is true for one image, for that one *instant in time.*

So to stay with that brick long enough to produce any involvement, one must re-create the image a number of times in succession. Re-creating the same image is not something the imagination does too eagerly; try it and you'll see. The imagination quickly gets bored with the same item over and over again. And when the imagination gets bored, it wanders (away from your song).

What keeps the imagination on target and involved is action. The reason is that action demands change in an image—usually movement—and that allows the imagination to constantly create new versions. This keeps the quality of imagery fresh and our involvement more complete. The image of the brick headed toward that store window is a cue for a whole series of images that the imagination cannot resist.

Here's another experiment. Try to remember the last blue-eyed person you saw. Notice whether or not your imagination is re-creating that person in one image or in action. Are you not remembering your blue-eyed person *doing something*? Try the image in "freeze-frame" (no action) and notice how fast it fades away.

Imagination can sustain an image only if that image includes some sort of action. This is the major problem the imagination has with abstractions: they do not involve action. Abstract concepts may suggest action, cause a desire for action, or even describe a whole series of actions, but an abstract word does not refer to action itself, nor does it describe a specific action.

Sorrow, for example, is a fairly specific abstraction, but it is not truly useful for producing an image. If the image of sorrow—the imagined *experience* of sorrow—is what you want to deliver, try "falling teardrops," "aching feeling," "breaking heart," and so forth. Such action words will produce the *experience* of sorrow, and make your lyrics come alive and seem lifelike in the listener's imagination. In a sense, because of the mental and physical effects of images, the good writer will allow the listener to *do* sorrow.

Hit writers understand this double need for action and abstraction and strive to combine the two:

- "Take Your Memory With You"

- "Stand Inside Your Love"

- "Falling Away From Me"

Each title mentions the abstraction itself but gives it action metaphorically. Memory doesn't do anything, obviously, but in "Take Your Memory With You," Vince Gill said something that the imagination can do something with, and thereby hooked the listener. Notice how much more alive that line is than: "I Don't Want to Have to Think About You Anymore" or "When You Go I'm Gonna Miss You." It's the action that hooks us.

The imagination functions at its best with simple images. This is implicit in the examples we've already seen. An image lasts in the mind for only a short time. The *field of image*—the vision of the mind's eye—resembles our true field of vision, with more clarity toward the center and decreasing resolution toward the edges. For these two reasons, the imagination, with its short memory and limited field of clear vision, engages most readily with *simple images*. It does its job best when requested to produce a single object or action that it can place right in the center of its field of vision. Notice the ease with which you can produce an image for "Lipstick on Your Collar" vs. "The Marks of Cheating Are All Over You."

While some would-be hit writer might try his hand at that second line, as an image it is overly complex. The tendency of the imagination is to abandon the task if the image is too complex and varied. One "broken white feather" stays in your imagination far longer than "a flock of many colored seabirds." Specific, simple images get more mileage in the imagination than groups of things do. It's why songs that deal with "I" or "you" (meaning a specific person), work better than "people" or —"everybody" songs. Such message songs run the risk of providing too much for the imagination to handle. ("The Gambler" got away with it mostly because both the setting—a conversation between an old man and the singer—and the main image—a poker game—were very specific.)

When imagery becomes too complex and varied, the imaging process is no longer free and experiential, but becomes more like mental work. And mental work is not what the listener has in mind when he turns on the radio.

Look through your songs to find those places where you could narrow down your images to one single item: one specific instance, one emotion, one moment in time. I know you're trying to sum up all of life in a three-minute pearl of wisdom. But believe me, your goal will elude you if you try to do it in one song. A song that tells the truth about one single moment in time can deliver the experience of living more vividly than all the writings of philosophers over the ages.

With all due deference to you poets out there, *life—moment to moment—*is outrageously simple. The imagination knows it. The listener knows it. Everybody knows it. So keep it simple. Cut narrow and cut deep.

The risk to the writer (and one of the reasons many writers avoid simplicity) is that simplicity and specificity render one vulnerable. Your simple song could turn out to be simply awful—especially if you're trying out an unusual story, theme, or plot. It's far safer to stick with tried and true banalities and abstractions that sound like other great songs you've heard.

The problem is that, while there is much to be learned from other songs, there is really no safe harbor for a songwriter. If she hides, so will the song.

So, say what you've got to say directly and take your lumps. You'll be surprised at how few lumps there are when you write straight. It's part of growing professionally.

But don't write in code. Write "user friendly" songs and remember that the users listen with their imaginations. Let them.

Enjoy.

Chris Blake has been a songwriting teacher and a professional songwriter with many credits, and has served as manager of Nashcal Music, the West Coast subsidiary of the Nashville-based Fischer Music Group, and his songs have been recorded by Moe Bandy, Joe Stampley, John Conlee, Johnny Carver, Billy "Crash" Craddock, and others. Since the first edition of this book, he has immersed himself in university research, studying the mind and the imagination.

---

4 Writing Lyrics

When we think in terms of the world's population, there are very few people who have the opportunity and talent to communicate their feelings and opinions to anyone beyond their immediate family, friends, or co-workers. Politicians use the electronic media. Actors do, too, but they're usually speaking someone else's thoughts. Novelists and journalists, when they're allowed to speak freely, may reach a large audience, but its numbers are still fairly limited. Radio, TV, films, and the Internet are the media by which most people receive information. These media share a form of communication that reaches and influences people all over the planet: music. As a skilled songwriter, you wield a tremendous power to communicate to millions of people. That realization (along with your desire to prove to your relatives that you can make a living at this) should make you want to do your best.

In this chapter, I'll discuss various techniques and principles that will help you express your ideas through lyrics as effectively as possible, so that when you get that opportunity to talk to the world, they'll love listening.

Simplicity

I asked hit producer John Ryan (Allman Bros. and Santana) what he felt was one of the most important common denominators of successful songs. It was a question I had asked many others, and the reply is almost always the same as Ryan's:

> Simplicity—in saying something that everyone experiences in his or her life, but doesn't know quite how to say. You're taking a song out of your head and giving it to an artist or performing it yourself. Then you have to try to get someone else to receive your communication. You're not doing it just for yourself. *You want someone else to feel what you feel about life, maybe challenge them.*

When hit songwriter, producer, and publisher Jack Keller was critiquing songs one night, he remarked to songwriters several times, "You've got too many ideas here. Focus on one idea, and build your song around it."

We've all read how-to manuals that say things like: "insert the strand in the elliptical aperture" when they could say: "put the thread through the hole in the needle" or simply, "thread the needle."

Applying that example to lyric writing, two common problems are saying more than you need to say, and not saying clearly what you mean. Have you ever had a friend with whom you communicated so well that you could convey a whole idea in two words that would mean absolutely nothing to anyone else who heard them? Made you feel clever, didn't it? Sorry, but you can't bring that friend with you into the songwriting game. If you expect to win, you can't set up a private conversation with an exclusive audience; instead, you must make yourself understood by as many listeners as possible.

A songwriter once played me five songs, none of which made any sense. She wanted to know why the songs didn't work for me. I read her back a few lines and asked what they meant. Some of her explanations were worth whole songs in themselves, but nowhere in what she had written could I make the connection until she told me the background. The writer was intelligent and talented, but she was playing an intellectual game with her lyrics. She seemed to be saying, "How obtuse and clever and abstract can I make this so it's challenging to listen to?" The songs were so challenging, they weren't worth bothering to figure out.

If your lyric doesn't attempt to communicate, you're operating in a vacuum—which is fine if you just want to write for yourself. You can derive some benefit from keeping a personal diary, but if you want to make a living by writing, your songs have to communicate their messages easily to others.

Focus

Another critical aspect of effective lyric writing is focus. You should be able to describe in one word the emotion or mental state that a song expresses. Happiness, sadness, love, hate, fun, jealousy, and resentment are just some of the emotions we've all felt. Any of these could be, in a broad sense, the subject of your song—provided you focus on specifics.

Beginning songwriters tend to want to settle on the first thing that comes out of their heads, whether it's focused or not. While it's a good idea to write all your thoughts down, eventually you need to zero in on a single idea. You may want to express that idea as a story or just explore different aspects of it. Many successful songs don't follow a linear story line or plot. But if you do write about a feeling, make it just one.

You should also be able to describe in a short phrase what the song is *about*. In chapter two, pages 31–32, I listed several subject areas as they relate to love relationships. Phrases such as "I think I've just found her (or him)," "Remembering how it used to be," and "Cheating," succinctly describe the subject of a song.

FOCUS EXERCISES

EXERCISE 1: Ask yourself these basic questions as you brainstorm, or to help you bring an idea into focus after that initial inspiration.

Who is singing the song? Male? Female? You? Someone else? What is the point of view? Someone who's been left? Someone who's leaving? Someone who's sad? Angry? Lonely? Happy? Who is the song being sung to? A lover? Someone you'd like to meet? The general public? A friend? God? What does the singer want to accomplish? To express love or another emotion? Give people a philosophy? Teach something? Criticize? Arouse?

As a purely commercial consideration, you should also ask: Is this a subject or attitude that an artist other than myself would be interested in expressing? For example, if you write a song with the message,

"I'm a thoroughly despicable person," you have to ask yourself how many recording artists would want to record a song like that even if they believe it about themselves. Generally speaking, artists will stay away from songs that are very depressing, (notwithstanding "Whiskey Lullaby" and a few others) or make them appear unlikable. Having said that, it *can* work to say, "I've done something terrible. Won't you please forgive me?" It's a staple of country writing, since both men and women, it seems, never get tired of hearing someone sing about how he made the biggest mistake of his life when he did her wrong.

EXERCISE 2: Listen to a few songs on the radio and write down one line for each that expresses what the song is about. Then do it with your own songs. If you have trouble condensing them, they're not focused.

Attitude

Attitude, which in a songwriting context means an aggressively stated point of view, is another factor that requires consistency and focus. Though we most commonly find songs that express a strong attitude in rock and hip-hop, attitude is very important in first-person songs (those using *I, me, my*) of any style. Alanis Morissette's songs have attitude. Listen to the attitude in Bonnie Raitt's "Something to Talk About," in most of Toby Keith's hits, including "How Do You Like Me Now?!" in Destiny's Child's "Independent Women," in Mary Chapin Carpenter's "He Thinks He'll Keep Her," in Gretchen Wilson's "Redneck Woman," and in one of my favorites, Deana Carter's "Did I Shave My Legs For This?" Attitude carries an energy and conviction that identifies artists as communicators who fearlessly speak their own truth. Whether we find ourselves agreeing or not, attitude has a power that is bound to move us as listeners.

Titles

A strong title can go a long way toward ensuring that industry people and the general public will remember your song. Generally, if you're searching (as you should be) for a way to say something in a fresh and unusual way, you're likely to arrive at an imaginative title in the process. Concept and title are so wedded that many writers, particularly in country music, don't even begin to write a song until they have a great title. It's a very common and practical way to start. Sometimes, if you have the right title, the song practically writes itself.

Of course, you don't have to have a great title to have a hit song. Look at any list of Top 10 songs and you'll see titles that are dull and ordinary, as well as titles that are imaginative and intriguing.

Pretend you're a publisher, producer, or artist with two demos in front of you: one called "I Love You" and another called "Silent Partners." Which one would you be most interested in hearing? You've already heard "I Love You" twenty times this week. You've never heard "Silent Partners," but it's an interesting concept that makes you start guessing right away what the song's about. If it's interesting to you, it might also interest a radio program director.

If you can come up with a short title phrase that embodies a concept, it's easier to focus your lyric from the beginning. Here are some hit titles that are intriguing in themselves: "She Talks to Angels," "Tears in Heaven," "Cleopatra's Cat," "Standing Outside the Fire," "Kryptonite," and "Black Horse and the Cherry Tree." Some titles stick in the mind because of unusual word combinations, such as "Mandolin Rain" and "Silent Lucidity."

Not only is the concept of the title important, but you'll increase its memorability if it sounds "catchy." A catchy title often has a combination of a pleasing meter and some poetic device like alliteration (repetition of beginning consonants): "We Can Work It Out," "I Need to Know"; or assonance (repetition of vowel sounds): "Achy Breaky Heart," "Boot Scootin' Boogie," "Show Me the Meaning of Being Lonely"; or rhyme: "Okie From Muskogee" and "Honky Tonk Badonkadonk."

Common phrases from everyday language also become more memorable in songs: "It's Always Somethin'," "Knock on Wood," "I Heard It Through the Grapevine," and "She's All That." Twists of common phrases also work: "Stop! In the Name of Love," "You Ain't Hurt Nothing Yet."

Aside from the benefits derived from a phrase that's catchy, clever, and conceptual, the real magic of the title in most successful songs comes from the way it fits with the music and is supported by the rest of the lyric. That combination can make an otherwise mundane title seem profound. Titles that include city or state names are a good case in point. Randy Newman's "I Love L.A." or Billy Joel's "New York State of Mind" could make someone feel nostalgic whether they'd been there or not. Hoagy Carmichael and Stuart Gorrell's classic, "Georgia on My Mind," does the same.

Sometimes a musical figure or the emotional intensity of the music itself suggests a title. This is a spontaneous process that resembles a sort of musical Rorschach test: "What does this chord, riff, or melody make you think of?" It's a process in which the musician shuts down that practiced intellectual approach and gets very close to his emotional core. A good groove can be hypnotic, put you in a mood, and trigger ideas and phrases that you might never come up with while you're staring at a piece of paper. This method of starting a song is very common with rock songwriters.

Place that good title in the strategic first or last line of your chorus (or verse, depending on the form), ensuring that it will be repeated several times during the song. You can then practically guarantee it will be remembered. If it's easy to remember, a potential record buyer knows what to ask for at the record store or radio request line, or what to buy from an online distributor. This is an important commercial consideration. Many potential hits may have been lost for lack of an obvious or well-placed title, unless they came from an established band. (There are always notable exceptions. For example, Nirvana already had a good head of steam before "Smells Like Teen Spirit" became a hit, and even though the title didn't appear in the song, fans were *motivated* to know the title.)

Increasingly, those looking for new songs and artists on popular Internet sites decide to listen to a song because they find the title intriguing because the title is all they can go by at that point. As a marketing strategy for artists and bands, an interesting title has proven to be very effective.

Another commercial reason to craft a unique title is that if you use a common one like "I Love You," your song may get mixed up with another one called "I Love You." Then listeners or radio programmers may choose the wrong song, Or worse, through computer or human error, someone else gets your royalties. That's a fate neither you nor the other writer deserves.

TITLE AND CONCEPT EXERCISES

In my classes, I ask my students to come up with ten titles in three minutes. Sometimes I'll make it two minutes, but the point is to give them as little time as possible to think about the process, and to download phrases from their subconscious without evaluating them. They can think about short phrases that express their emotional state, look at something in the room in a fresh way, or anything that works.

The titles don't have to be good. K.A. Parker is an inspiring lyric teacher in Los Angeles and a former staff writer with Motown's Stone Diamond Music publishing company. I asked her to contribute some of her own exercises for generating titles.

When I'm looking for a great title, I go to an event with the intention of finding a title while I'm there. I tell myself I can leave when I hear three great titles. It makes me a better listener. This technique works for any event. Try it next time you go to a movie, a bookstore, or a social gathering.

Speaking of bookstores, I find great titles among the stacks, especially the Romance section, where I never shop. It's here I see titles I would never have imagined on my own.

One of my favorite exercises is to spend a few hours with books of photography. I give titles to the pictures and use them to title my own pieces. *Time* magazine's "Year in Pictures" is a great tool for this. I have used the great photographs from the priceless *Family of Man* collections so many times, I bought the book and its equally brilliant offspring, *The Family of Woman* and *The Family of Children*.

First Lines

The first words from a singer's mouth are critical, particularly if they're the first words you've ever heard from that artist. It all goes into that first-impression evaluation you make as a listener about whether or not you like the record. So, with your writer's hat on, think about how strongly you can interest the listener with that first line or lines. When a publisher or producer hears that first line, she will also be deciding whether to keep listening or turn it off. If she isn't sold on the song, she will not be optimistic about selling it to an artist.

Your first line should set the tone for the whole song and make us want to hear what comes next. Don't fall prey to the temptation to start with "I'm just sittin' here . . ." (a) writing this song, (b) thinking about you, or (c) looking at the ___, or "Woke up this mornin' . . ." (didn't we all?), or other equally uninteresting clichés. Though these might be penciled in to get your motor running, when you get down to a rewrite they should be the first things that get crossed out.

You can set your first scene by asking several questions. Their answers will contribute to what you want your lyric to accomplish.

1. Where is it taking place? Is it important to the song? What kind of place is it? Are there evocative features? "Ten miles west of Houston," "In a dirty downtown doorway," "At home in your love," and "Halfway into heaven" are all about places, either geographical or emotional. If you allude to a particular country or city, or the mountains, the beach, or wherever, be wary of passive, "picture postcard" openers that don't imply action, flavor, attitude, or emotional charge.

2. Can the hour, day, season, or year offer a flavor that enhances the emotional impact of your song? Think of the number of songs that use *morning* or *night* to evoke a mood.

3. If the song is addressed to someone, is there something arresting you can say?

4. If the song is *about* someone, can you say something that immediately gives a picture or a quick personality sketch?

5. Is there an *active image* you can use? (See chapter three, "The Imagination of the Listener," page 52.)

6. If you're expressing an emotion, can you do it in a *poetic* or *dramatic* way? "I feel so out of place," for instance, just kind of lies there. Contrast that with George Gobel's old line, "The world's a tuxedo and I'm just a pair of brown shoes." Of course, that type of cleverness isn't always the answer; it depends on the tone you want to establish. The Brad Paisley/Alison Krause hit, "Whiskey Lullaby" (written by Jon Randall and Bill Anderson) could have started out by saying something mundane like: "The way she left was cruel enough that he never could forget." Just contrast that with their opener: "She put him out like the burning end of a midnight cigarette." *Put him out* is a metaphor we all understand. The line establishes a mood. It's visual and it doesn't just *tell*, it *shows*, whereas the mundane line is abstract and general.

A listener should have the answers to the *who, what, when,* and *where* by the end of the first verse, as well as know the song's attitude and mood. But most importantly, the listener should be persuaded to keep listening—no matter how you accomplish it, whether it's with your lyric, your music, or better, by both.

Second Verse Curse (a.k.a. Second Verse Hell)

Coming up with a second verse is an almost universal challenge for lyric writers. If you have a story to tell and know where you want it to end you won't have much of a problem. However, if you're not a particularly linear thinker, it may be a lot tougher. Here are some ways to work it out:

1. Map it out. Start from scratch and map out the whole song. Read your first verse and summarize it in one short sentence. Keep it short:

> This part is about . . .
>
> Then the next verse will be about . . .
>
> And in the last verse I'll wrap it up with . . .

Are you sure it's really the first verse, or does it just happen to be where you started? You may discover that the first verse you wrote was like a siphon—just to suck the air out of the hose. Once you get rid of that, the real juice starts to flow.

2. If the first verse has introduced a character (other than yourself as a narrator) or a situation that has piqued the listener's interest, you need to satisfy that interest in the next verse or chorus. Imagine somebody asking you:

> "And then what happens?"
>
> "Well, how did you feel about that?"
>
> "Why do you think that happened?"

Paraphrase what happens next, or use stream-of-consciousness or clustering techniques to explore any of those questions. Just write whatever you think of without editing, chasing rhymes, or keeping to a meter. You might also just try talking it through and recording it.

3. Try switching the first verse to the second verse position and writing a new first verse to create a way to get to the second.

4. If it's a relationship song—a love song—try to explore another aspect of the relationship. What has loving that person done to change your life? Be careful not to wander into cliché city here with: "Since I found you, baby, I've never been the same." (*How* have you never been the same?) Be specific, for instance, "You made me ashamed to yell at waiters!!"

5. Expand the story in the first verse. Include more information to lead you into the next verse.

6. Try making your first verse the chorus. If you already have a chorus, you may not have set it up in a way that the verses can easily lead into it. Sometimes you need to work backward from the chorus.

7. Bring in a co-writer. Some writers are great starters, while some are great finishers.

8. Bruce Springsteen says he likes to start with the personal and go to the universal in the second verse. Personally, I think it's better to go to the universal in the chorus or bridge.

9. Give it up for now and just let the idea incubate. It's amazing how the answer will come to you when you're not trying so hard. Something you'll see or hear or remember from your past will just kick in out of nowhere. In an interview I did with Hal David, he said that when he started the lyric to "What the World Needs Now Is Love," he had put a list of manmade things in the verses and just knew he didn't have it yet. Months later, as he was driving into New York City from upstate, he was noticing how beautiful the mountains were and suddenly realized he needed to talk about things *God* had made. At that point, the lyric all slipped into place: "Lord, we don't need another mountain . . ."

Rhyme

I'd guess more than 99 percent of all commercially successful songs use rhyme. Why is it so important? What is it that makes rhymes work?

There's a reason that people still remember the nursery rhymes of childhood: Their rhymes are strong and predictable, and the meter is solid and consistent. Together, rhyme and meter serve as a powerful memory trigger. How many lyrics do you think you'd remember if nothing rhymed? Rhyme has other values as well. It can create a sense of symmetry and completion, and it offers an opportunity to enhance the power of a line by establishing a pattern that creates the expectation of a resolution.

Rhyme is a tool you can't afford to ignore. To drop it deliberately just to be different, or assume it's not important, isn't a sensible attitude for someone who's trying to be a successful songwriter. Not that there aren't exceptions to the rule, but when you want the odds in your favor, you must use every tool you have.

In musical theater, rhymes are expected to be perfect—unless the character wouldn't rhyme perfectly. It's not so much a question of whether the rhymes work, but of how they're judged by critics who hold the power of life and death over a production. Musical theater boasts a long history of exceptional craftsmanship and the artists aim to keep it that way. Whenever you start to think it's too hard or impossible to come up with perfect rhymes in a context that makes them feel perfectly natural, study the masters. For instance, listen to the work of lyricists Alan and Marilyn

Bergman in their songs for the Barbra Streisand film *Yentl*. We need such standards to remind us that it's still possible to put in the extra effort and come up with perfect rhymes without sacrificing naturalness.

TYPES OF RHYME

Perfect. The stressed sounds that end the lines are *identical*, though the preceding consonants are different: *god/quad, action/fraction, variety/society*. This is without question the most powerful rhyme you can use. There is an ongoing debate among writers about whether it is the *only* form of rhyme to be used. My feeling is that you should make *every* effort to find a perfect rhyme without having to alter the meaning of the line. If you can't find one, opt for the next best.

Imperfect, near, false, slant, oblique, or half-rhyme. Approximates rhyme, as in *port/fourth, loss/wash, around/down, shaky/aching*. Some would argue strongly that it shouldn't be called *rhyme* at all, but *assonance*. Anyway, let the nitpickers argue. Sometimes you just can't find a perfect rhyme to fit your meaning, but an imperfect, near rhyme fills the bill. Imperfect rhymes are common and quite acceptable in pop music.

Masculine or "one rhyme." A single-syllable rhyme, as in *pack/rack*, or multisyllable words in which the last syllables rhyme, as in *fantasize/idolize*.

Feminine or "two rhyme." A two-syllable rhyme, with the stress on the penultimate syllable. The vowels and inner consonants must match, as in *maker/shaker, masquerading/degrading*.

Three rhyme. A rhyme in which the stress comes on the third-to-last syllable, as in *medium/tedium, facilitate/rehabilitate*.

Open rhyme. A rhyme that doesn't end in a hard consonant, as in *glow/snow* and *fly/try*. Use open rhymes whenever possible on notes that are to be held.

Closed or stopped rhyme. A rhyme that ends in a consonant that makes us close our mouths and that can't be sustained when sung (*b, d, k, p, q* and *t*). *L, m, n,* and *r* can be sustained. *F, s, v* and *z* can be sustained, but don't sound very pleasant. *S* sounds (sibilants) drive recording engineers crazy. Pay close attention to these "singability" factors as you write your lyrics.

Internal, inner, or inside rhyme. End rhyme, of course, occurs at the end of a line. Internal rhyme occurs within the line, as in "The *fate* of the *great state is now in your hands*."

The constant creative challenge is to find the best rhymes possible and still retain the flow of natural speech patterns, while at the same time not compromising content and mood. Read aloud, the lines should feel as natural as conversation. Every line presents a new challenge. It may be that, after exploring the possibilities, you'll need to choose a less-than-perfect rhyme. It's more important that you opt for naturalness, mood, or clarity of content over convenience or cleverness for its own sake.

RHYMING TIPS FROM AN EXPERT

The following is an excerpt from Pat Pattison's *Writing Better Lyrics* that offers alternatives to perfect rhyme.

Remember, lyrics are sung, not read or spoken. When you sing, you exaggerate vowels. And since rhyme is a vowel connection, lyricists can make sonic connections in ways other than perfect rhyme. Here are the most useful:

Family Rhyme

1. The syllables' vowel sounds are the same.
2. The consonant sounds after the vowels belong to the same phonetic families.
3. The sounds before the vowels are different.

Table of Family Rhymes

Here's a chart showing the three important consonant families:

	PLOSIVES	FRICATIVES	NASALS
Voiced:	b d g	v TH z zh j	rn n ng
Unvoiced:	p t k	f th S sh ch	

Each of the three boxes (plosives, fricatives, and nasals) forms a phonetic family. When a word ends in a consonant, you can use the other members of that family to find substitutes for perfect rhymes.

Rub/up/thud/putt/bug/stuck all end with members of the same family of plosives, so they are family rhymes.

Love/buzz/judge/fluff/fuss/hush/touch end with members of the fricative family, so they are family rhymes. *Strum/run/sung* rhyme as members of the nasal family.

Say you want to rhyme line two, below:

Tire tracks across my face
I'm stuck in a rut

First, look up perfect rhymes for *rut: cut, glut, gut, hut, shut.*

The trick to finding a rhyme to say what you mean is to expand your alternatives. Look at the Table of Family Rhymes above and introduce yourself to relatives of *t:*

ud	uk	ub	up	ug
blood	buck	club	hard up	bug
flood	duck	hub	makeup	jug
mud	luck	pub	cup	unplug
stud	muck	scrub		plug
thud	stuck	tub		shrug
	truck			snug
				tug

Much better. That's a lot of interesting stuff to say no to. Now, how about this:

Tire tracks across my back
There's nowhere I feel safe

First, look up perfect rhymes for safe in your rhyming dictionary. All we get is waif. Not much. Now look for family rhymes under f's family, the fricatives. We add these possibilities:

as	av	az	aj
case	behave	blaze	age
ace	brave	craze	cage
breathing-space	cave	daze	page
	grave	haze	rage
chase	shave	phrase	stage
face	slave	paraphrase	
disgrace	wave	praise	**aTH**
embrace			bathe
grace	**aTH**		
lace	faith		

Finally, nasals. The term nasals means what you think it means: all the sound comes out of your nose.

Tire tracks across my head
Pounding like a drum

Look up perfect rhymes for drum: hum, pendulum, numb, slum, strum.

Go to the Table of Family Rhymes on the previous page and introduce yourself to m's relatives:

un	ung
fun	hung
gun	flung
overrun	wrung
won	sung
jettison	
skeleton	

Finding family rhyme isn't hard, and its rewards are amazing. So there's no reason to tie yourself in knots trying to use only perfect rhyme when family rhyme sounds so close. When sung, the ear won't know the difference.

For a complete and detailed exploration of rhyme types, read Pat Pattison's *Songwriting: Essential Guide to Rhyming* (see bibliography).

RHYME SCHEMES

To make rhyme work as a memory tool, you must be consistent. Once you establish a rhyme scheme for your verses, it's best to use the same pattern in all the verses. That same verse pattern in the choruses and bridge, however, could get monotonous, so it's better to establish one rhyme scheme for the verse, one for the chorus, and yet another for the bridge. You can introduce a subtle element of surprise this way without affecting the predictability of the song. Another way to surprise the listener is to either precipitate or delay the rhyme. It can be used with any rhyme scheme and the rhyme can occur at any of the underlined positions in the last line:

Ta TUM Ta TUM Ta TUM Ta
Ta TUM Ta TUM Ta TUM
Ta TUM Ta TUM Ta TUM Ta
Ta TUM Ta TUM Ta TUM Ta TUM Ta TUM

Here are the most common rhyme schemes:

1. a *more*   (Rhyming all four lines) Usually too predictable. This gets old fast.
   a *score*
   a *floor*
   a *door*

2. a trust   (Rhyming second and fourth lines)
   b *guess*   Has flexibility and the element of predictability without the boredom.
   c hurt
   b *mess*

3. a luck   (Rhyming first and second lines, third and fourth lines)
   a stuck
   b *brave*
   b *save*

4. a *able*   (Rhyming first, third, and fourth lines)
   b still
   a *cable*
   a *stable*

5. a *making*   (Rhyming first and third, second and fourth lines)
   b *good*
   a *taking*
   b *could*

6. a *friend of mine*   (Rhyming first and second lines)
   a *send a sign*
   b try

7. a *when*   (Rhyming first, second, and third lines)
   a *then*   or
   a *men*   (First, second, and third PLUS the last lines of adjoining verses)
   c *know*
   b *stand*
   b *band*
   b *land*
   c *show*

There are other variations. These forms are often doubled, for instance. Given that one of their functions is to help us remember, rhymes in any consistent position in the lines may work. In the English language, though, there is an expectation that the *primary* rhymes come at the ends of the lines. Because they're in a powerful position, it becomes especially important that they enhance the mood and meaning of the song, or at least that they don't distract the listener.

SOME COMMON PROBLEMS WITH RHYME

A common failing among songwriters is to say what you want to say in the first two lines and then, instead of finding an equally strong statement to finish the verse, settling for a weaker line for the sake of the rhyme. Sure, you save some work, but you've also effectively weakened your song. Better to write several versions of the first two lines to come up with an end word (root) that offers more rhyming possibilities. Don't reach for the easy rhyme if it dilutes your efforts.

And beware of these possible rhyming pitfalls:

INVERSIONS

Inversions involve twisting the order of words to use a rhyme that wouldn't naturally occur at that point. It almost always feels awkward. Here's an example:

> *I never knew how much I'd missed*
> *Until your candy lips I kissed*

In this situation, I'd go for *lips* as the end rhyme, even though it lacks the perfection of *missed/kissed*. "Till I kissed your candy lips" just feels more natural. There's another practical element to avoiding inversions. If you want to be immediately understood, remember that it takes a little longer for a listener to process a line in which the object comes before the verb (as in the example above).

IDENTITIES

Identities are not rhymes. Identities include the same words, words with the same consonant preceding the same final sound (*buy/goodbye*), and homonyms, words that sound identical even though they are spelled differently (*bear/bare*, *no/know*). You won't get arrested for substituting identities for rhymes; it's just lazy writing. A common exception is the repetition of a variation of a line for emphasis: "Goin' downtown, goin' way downtown."

SLANG

Slang is a great source of new rhymes. Many hits have been based on slang words and expressions. The only drawback is that if you're trying to write a song people will record twenty years from now, the slang we use today may sound really dumb in the future. Would anybody record a song today that included *twenty-three skidoo*, or *the cat's meow*, a phrase that was popular in the 1930s? Similarly, using *groovy* would put a song squarely in the 1960s.

COLLOQUIAL PRONUNCIATION

Sometimes it's good to be able to tailor a song to a particular musical style, like country or R&B, using colloquial pronunciations common in that style (e.g., rhyming *hang* with *thang*, or *again* with *pain*). But bear in mind that colloquial pronunciations have drawbacks that are similar to those of slang. Here the problem does not involve changing fashions, but the number of artists who will be able to record the song. By creating rhymes that depend on nonstandard pronunciations, you're limiting the potential coverage of those songs to artists who are comfortable with those styles.

THE EXCEPTIONS

We hear more songs these days that don't rhyme. In most cases, they're from self-contained bands. They write their own material and are not that interested in having other artists record their songs. Because they aren't exposed to the same industry scrutiny, they have a more wide-ranging creative palette from which to paint their songs. More power to them. If you can get your message across to your audience without the use of rhyme, there's no rule that says you have to use it. Be aware though, that laziness is not a good enough reason to ignore a powerful tool.

Even in pop music, there are examples of songs that don't use rhyme. The standard "Moonlight in Vermont" is a good example; Lionel Richie's "Lady," a major hit for both him and Kenny Rogers in the 1980s, doesn't rhyme. So, why do they work? There are several possibilities: (1) They both have exceptional melodies; (2) One of rhyme's functions is to help us remember the lyric, and both of those lyrics, especially "Moonlight in Vermont," are simple enough to remember without it; (3) In the case of "Lady," the melody's metrical and rhythmic construction does not set up a *rhyme expectation*, so we never miss it.

Rap Rhyme

In rap, many pop songwriting conventions go out the window since there's much more emphasis on the flow, the rhythm, and the feeling of spontaneity. Rap will allow any kind of rhyme that works, so you'll hear lots of words with the wrong syllable emphasized to achieve a rhyme—something that is not nearly as acceptable in other styles. It's just one of those cases in which a style has its own combinations of ingredients that differ from others. That doesn't mean that the best rap doesn't adhere to standards; it's just that there's still an excitement in rap that makes it *feel* like it's created spontaneously, so we tend to make more allowances for its not being perfect.

A good book for this genre is Kevin Mitchell's *Hip-Hop Rhyming Dictionary*. Also, if you're seriously interested in the art, and its origins and history, look for *Freestyle: The Art of Rhyme* on DVD.

RHYMING DICTIONARIES AND THESAURUSES

Some writers look at rhyming dictionaries as a crutch, as though it were cheating to use one. If you've been writing for any time at all, you probably know the most natural possibilities for rhyme. But when you're really stuck, it's always good to know that there's somewhere you can go *quickly* to make sure you have the best rhyme possible for the line. I've also run across rhymes in these sources that inspired a whole new thought pattern. The human mind has such wonderful facility for connecting the dots between seemingly unrelated images and words that anything *you* feed it can become an ingredient for something new.

The Modern Rhyming Dictionary by professional lyricist Gene Lees, and *The Complete Rhyming Dictionary and Poet's Craft Book* edited by Clement Wood are both good ones.

When you're looking for a particular word and can come up only with a word that's somewhere in the neighborhood, you need a thesaurus. It will give you words or phrases that mean the same or almost the same thing (synonyms), or the opposite (antonyms), as well as words and phrases that are only remotely related. It incorporates slang and lists words by part of speech. Using a thesaurus is like a treasure hunt in which each new discovery can send you on yet another exciting journey. It's an indispensable tool. *Roget's International Thesaurus of English Words and Phrases* is my favorite. Microsoft Word and other word processing programs also contain thesauruses.

SONGWRITING SOFTWARE

Fast, efficient rhyming dictionaries and other more elaborate software programs that offer a variety of valuable features are available for songwriters who use computers. Among the best are:

> RhymeWIZARD (www.rhymewizard.com)

> A Zillion Kajillion Rhymes & Clichés (www.eccentricsoftware.com)

For overall songwriting software programs, I feel the two best are MasterWriter (www.masterwriter.com) and Lyricist (www.virtualstudiosystems.com). They offer both lyric and music capabilities that include extensive rhyming dictionaries, thesauruses, and chord charting. MasterWriter even features audio recording.

A good central place to find a selection of songwriting software is Songwriting Software Plus (www.songwriting-software.com).

Poetic Devices

Great poets throughout history have used many devices that are regularly put to work in the service of a great lyric by today's songwriters. At their best, these devices initially go unnoticed, like the subtle spices in a gourmet dish. Though you might not consciously identify them right away, you know that without them the dish wouldn't taste nearly as good. Only when the chef tells you what the spices are do you start to distinguish them in the overall taste. That's ideally how poetic devices should work. Our attention should not be pulled from the overall meaning and flow of the lyric to these devices. If they're too obvious or overused, our focus shifts. They say, "Look here, see how I did this! Clever, eh?"

The skill of contemporary writers lies in using poetic devices in a subtle way to achieve the naturalness of common speech. Such devices include:

Alliteration: the repetition of consonants, especially initial ones. This is a device that can get ridiculous if carried to extremes, but if used with taste, can be subtly effective. In "Same Old Lang Syne," Dan Fogelberg wrote "She would have *l*iked to say she *l*oved the man, but she didn't *l*ike to *l*ie."

Assonance: vowel sounds are repeated within a line, but not the subsequent consonant sounds, for example, "You w*o*n't be g*o*ing h*o*me."

Similes: comparisons using the word *as* or *like*, for example, "straight <u>as</u> an arrow," "hard <u>as</u> a rock" and "sleeping <u>like</u> a log." Don't settle for such commonplace clichés, however. If something comes to your mind that you've heard before, look for a new idea.

Metaphors: comparisons that don't depend on *like* or *as*. Paul Simon's "I Am a Rock" is an example. If he had written, "I'm Like a Rock," it would have been a simile—and not nearly as effective.

Allegory: a device that allows the writer to treat an abstract idea with concrete imagery. In other words, you can tell a story on both material and symbolic levels. Paul McCartney's "Ebony and Ivory" used the image of black-and-white piano keys working together as an allegory for racial harmony.

Personification: attributing human characteristics to inanimate objects, for example, "When the ground started rolling, I heard the buildings scream."

Hyperbole: an obvious exaggeration to drive home a point. The Beatles' "Eight Days a Week" is an example. "You're a hurricane" is both hyperbole and a metaphor.

Irony: saying the opposite of what you mean, or emphasizing the incongruities of a situation. Paul Simon's "7 O'Clock News/Silent Night" sets the Christmas classic with its refrain of "Sleep in heavenly peace" over news reports of war atrocities.

Antithesis: contrasting two opposing ideas. Michael Hazelwood and Albert Hammond's "It Never Rains in Southern California," ("it pours") uses antithesis effectively.

Characterization: the creation and representation of convincing characters. Always look for a line of dialogue or an image that gives us revealing details about the character or situation. In John Lennon and Paul McCartney's "Eleanor Rigby," we hear three beautifully concise character studies. Jerry Jeff Walker's "Mr. Bojangles" is an effective example of characterization. Janis Ian's "At Seventeen" is another masterful character study. Its revealing very personal details allow us all to experience once again the often agonizing process of growing up. Eminem's "Stan" presents a believable interaction between his character, Slim Shady, and a fan.

Pronouns

One of the most common problem areas in lyric writing is the use of pronouns. Pronouns take the place of both proper and common nouns. The words pronouns replace are referred to as *principals*. Here are five rules for the use of pronouns, all established in the interest of clarity:

1. Make it clear what the pronoun you're using is a substitute for.

2. The principal must be close by so the listener doesn't get confused about what the pronoun stands for.

3. Avoid putting two principals close by or the listener won't know which one the pronoun represents. Consider this example: *When John talked to Joe, he realized that he was getting old but not wise.* Was it John or Joe who was getting old?

4. Avoid having one pronoun represent two principals at once. Consider: *He was rich but he was poor.* Was principal one rich and principal two poor, or is there only one principal involved?

5. If possible, avoid placing the pronoun before its principal. "She heard the message he delivered but didn't believe the messenger." It takes the listener a few seconds to make the connection that "he" is the messenger.

Be very careful about the number of pronouns you use in a song. Without realizing it, you can create a maze in which only you know who's saying what to whom. Consider: *She said she thought he loved her more than she loved him, and she wouldn't recommend that he move in.* There are at least three different ways that line could be interpreted. If you can read the line at your leisure, you can probably figure them out, but when the line goes by in seven seconds in a song, you're in trouble.

Pronouns serve a valuable function when they're used properly. They can help to guide the listener away from vagueness by letting them know exactly who is saying or doing what.

POINT OF VIEW

Pronouns are important in establishing a point of view. Certain creative decisions need to be made by the songwriter. The options are:

- using first person pronouns (*I, me, we*) to relate a personal experience: "*I* was on *my* way to nowhere."

- using second person pronouns (*you*) to address another: "*You* Are So Beautiful."

- using third person pronouns (*he, him, she, her, it, they, them*) to relate an experience about something or someone else: "*He* was a high school hero in a one-horse town."

Choose a point of view and pronouns that will provide the greatest clarity and impact. For instance, it's usually very effective to deliver a strong philosophical message in the first person ("Here's what happened to me") or in the third person, in which you tell a story about someone else and we understand the message in our own way. Second-person messages ("You should . . .") may alienate listeners because they imply that the singer doesn't need the message, but "*you do.*" On the other hand, positive second-person sentiments such as "you're wonderful," or "you deserve the best," can be very powerful.

Some writers use *you* as a substitute for *I* in a rhetorical way. "What do you do when you fall in love with someone you can't have?" We read this as "What do *I* do?" The approach puts distance between the singer and a hurtful problem. There's no wrong or right here. The impact of the pronoun you choose can vary with each song. It's always a good idea to check out all the possibilities to create the most powerful emotional statement. "I can't pretend that I don't hurt" may be better than "You can't pretend that you don't hurt" because, when the listener sings along, he is singing about himself rather than about an anonymous "you."

The most commonsense rule to follow in all of this is to try to put yourself in the place of the listener, no matter how emotionally involved you may be in expressing your personal feelings. It's a difficult thing to do in the heat of passionate inspiration, so it's a good idea to put a song away for a few days to allow yourself to be more objective when you look at it again.

A commercial aspect of choice of "person" is the pitchability of the song. As I mentioned earlier (see chapter two, "Lifestyle Songs," on page 39), first-person songs have to be a perfect fit for an artist. If there is anything that doesn't reflect the attitude or experience of a specific artist, he'll reject it. However, if it's a story in third person, the artist may relate to the overall message but he can be removed from the specifics.

EXERCISE:

Look at the lyrics for your favorite song. If it's in first person, change it to second or third person. If it's in third person, change it to first or second. Think about which version seems to have the most impact for you. You'll usually discover why the writer chose to do it that way. Now do the same for your own lyrics.

For an in-depth look at psychological principles in the effectiveness of visual imagery and figurative language, see chapter three, "The Imagination of the Listener" on page 52.

Prosody and Meter

Prosody is the agreement of lyric and music. Ideally, you want the emotional tone of the music to enhance the song's message. If the lyric has an "up," positive message, it would generally be unwise to set the music in a minor key. Minor chords tend to suggest pain, longing, despair, loss, and sadness. The melody line can also be used to illustrate the lyrics. If the ascending melody for Jimmy Webb's "Up, Up, and Away" or Curtis Mayfield's "Move On Up" were written as a series of *descending* notes, the result would have sounded ludicrous. It's also possible that your message might be enhanced by doing just the opposite of what feels natural, for effect—but that should be a conscious choice, not an accident. A good example is Bertolt Brecht and Kurt Weill's "Mack the Knife," a dark, grisly lyric with a jaunty, happy melody.

Other factors can contribute to bad prosody. Watch for combinations of words that might be *heard* as entirely different phrases: *What do I know?/What a wino?*; *Let the winds take hold/Let the wind stay cold*; or *'Scuse me while I kiss the sky/'Scuse me while I kiss this guy* (which became the title of a very funny book, *'Scuse Me While I Kiss This Guy and Other Misheard Lyrics* by Gavin Edwards). A similar problem exists with adjoining words that end and begin with the same sound. Phrases like *teach children* or *strange journey* will give a good singer an anxiety attack because there's not enough space between similar consonant groups to allow the tongue to recover. Make certain that what listeners hear is what you *want* them to hear, and that the singer can easily sing what you write.

The best way to make sure your lyrics will sing well is to sing them as you write them. Sing your lyrics at the tempo they'll be performed. Some lyrics that look fine on paper and sing easily at a slow tempo may tie a singer's tongue in knots when you increase the tempo even a little. If the words feel at all awkward in your mouth or don't sing smoothly, change them.

Some words, such as *long* and *cool*, carry their own emotional meanings that may feel wrong when sung over short, choppy notes. Action words like *jump, run, crash,* and *flash* may feel out of place in a slow ballad, but right at home in a high-intensity rocker.

One of the most important elements of prosody is the metrical pattern of the lyric. You can achieve good prosody by choosing a meter that emphasizes natural speech patterns and ties them effectively to the musical pulse and melody. It should allow the words to fit comfortably with the music, without putting the accents on the wrong syllables or squeezing too many words into too little musical space.

If you were paying attention in English class instead of daydreaming about being a rock star, you would probably already know the material that follows. You just didn't think you'd ever need to use it, right?

Why do you need to know about meter? You may not need to remember the names of the patterns, but you should know that they are options to be considered and that they can be used for emotional effect and for variety. Few things are more deadly than an entire lyric in perfect iambic pentameter, and the melodies to those lyrics don't usually save them. When was the last time, by the way, that you heard someone use iambic pentameter in a conversation? So let's go back to English class again.

Regular groupings of stressed and unstressed syllables are called *metric feet*. We usually hear them in groups of two or three, though pentameter means *five feet*. Those most commonly used in poetry and lyric are:

NAME OF METRIC FOOT	EXAMPLES	ACCENT FOOT
iamb	in-**sane**, good-**bye**, to-**night** for **good**	ta **TUM**
trochee	**heal**-thy, **lov**-er, **mon**-ey	**TUM** ta
anapest	go-ing **out**, ma-king **sense**, un-der-**stand**	ta ta **TUM**
dactyl	**po**-e-try, **ul**-ti-mate, **I'm** o-kay, **you're** o-kay	**TUM** ta ta
spondee	**down-town**, **star-ship**, **head-long**	**TUM TUM**
amphibrach	be-**liev**-ing, con-**cern**-ing, I **love** it	ta **TUM** ta

The emotional impact of a song can be greatly influenced by your choice of meter. Spondees (TUM TUM) have a very deliberate feeling. Iambic pentameter (ta TUM/ta TUM/ta TUM/ta TUM/ta TUM) is the most commonly used meter and has a long history in English poetry, probably because it's *closest* to human speech. It's good for seriousness. So are dactyls (TUM ta ta).

Three-syllable meters, particularly anapests (ta ta TUM/ta ta TUM/ta ta TUM), have a lightness about them that doesn't suit them for particularly heavy subject matter.

Though overuse of the same meter can be monotonous, just enough repetition can create tension to set a listener up for a dynamic change of meter. In songwriting, you need to repeat the metric feet in a way that not only makes them fit comfortably with the musical pulse, but *emphasizes the intended meaning of the lyric.*

As an illustration, let's take a line that could have several meanings and work it to find its best setting.

I **need**/you **in**/my **life**/ (Iamb)	A duple meter (two syllables per foot) emphasizing need, in, and life. In doesn't take the emphasis particularly well because it's a weaker word.

or

I need/**you** in/**my** life/ (Trochee)	Another duple meter emphasizing I, you, and my. Feels more natural.

I need **you**/in my **life**/ (Anapest)	A triple meter (three syllables per foot) emphasizing you and life.

or

I **need** you/in **my** life/ (Amphibrach)	A triple meter emphasizing need and my.

Depending on the length of notes and rests, these versions could be done in either 4/4 or 3/4 time.

Try your own melodies with these variations. Sing them out loud. You'll find your melodies changing with each variation to *accommodate the meaning of the line and the musical meter.* This is a process that should happen regardless of whether you're writing melody to lyric, lyric to melody, or lyric alone. Once you get used to it, the process goes very fast.

Let's try a straight 4/4 with equal emphasis on each note.

4/4	1	2	3	4	1	2	3	4
	/	/	/	/	/	/	/	/
	I	need	you	in	my	life		

It feels a little stiff this way and life held this long, is a little strained. Better to make life a beat shorter and end in a rest.

How about emphasizing 1 and 3?

4/4	1	2	3	4	1	2	3	4
	/	-	/	-	/	-	/	-
	I	need	you	in	my	life		

Not bad, but it would again be awkward to hold life. You can also add to the emphasis of you by raising the melody on that word.

Still emphasizing 1 and 3, you can use a pickup, starting the lyric before the downbeat.

4/4	1	2	3	4	1	2	3	4
	/	-	/	-	/	-	/	-
I	need	you	in	my	life			

This gives you the chance to use the accents and maintain your choice of emphasis.

2/4	1	+	2	+	3	+	4	+
	/	-	/	-	-	-		
	I	need	you	in	my	life		

By using eighth notes, you can emphasize need and life. Eighth notes also give the line more urgency.

Let's try leaning on the backbeat, 2 and 4.

4/4	1	2	3	4	1	2	3	4
	-	/	-	/	-	/	-	/
	I	need	you	in	my	life		

We're still accenting the in here, but can deemphasize it by raising the melody on both need and life.

Still accenting the backbeat, you can delay the line and try an eighth note feel again.

4/4	1	+	2	+	3	+	4	+
	-	-	/	-	-	-	/	-
		I	need	you	in	my	life	

This one feels good, too.

Now let's switch to 3/4 waltz time.

3/4	1	2	3	1	2	3	
	-	-	/	-	-	/	-
	I	need	you	in	my	life	

A little stiff—too predictable.

3/4	1	2	3	1	2	3	1	2	3	A little smoother with more room for a singer to play with the words.
	-	/	-	-	/	-	-	/	-	
	I	need		you	in		my	life		

3/4	1	2	3	1	2	3	1	2	3	More interesting, less predictable.
	/	/	-	/	/	-	/	-	-	
	I	need	you	in	my		life			

or with a pickup ...

3/4	1	2	3	1	2	3	1	2	3	Again, more interesting with room for a singer to move.
	/	-	-	/	/	-	/	-	-	
	I need		you	in	my		life			

Lyric Context

Context can do so much to enhance the power of a lyric. Let's take a scenario in which a young guy takes his girlfriend home. When they get to her parents' house, he leans over to kiss her goodnight and she turns her head away. At this moment, he knows the relationship is in trouble. He may have wondered or been worried before, but *this* is the pivotal event.

Now let's change the context of this event. Instead of picturing the two of them alone together, imagine that he's standing with a group of other guys and the girl is coming down the street. As she joins the group, the guy pulls her over to kiss her, but she turns her head away. The same gesture is now much more powerful because we see him embarrassed in front of his friends. We can make more inferences from the second scenario: the fact that he wanted her to kiss him in front of his friends shows his possessiveness, and perhaps his insecurity. So the stakes, and consequently the drama of the situation, are increased. The only thing that was different was the context: the scene surrounding the event. I see many, many songs from inexperienced writers that could use that extra bit of imagination to create a more powerful context.

Let's look at the situation presented in Jon Ims's "She's in Love With the Boy" (see chapter five, "Writing and Rewriting 'She's in Love With the Boy'" on page 103). If Ims had started the song with Tommy and Katie in the drive-in, it still may have been a decent song. But by first describing Katie's boredom in the context of her isolated little town, he gives the song both a backdrop and a setup that enhance the drama of the "pivotal event." She *needs* to get away and we can't help wondering if the possibility expressed in the line "Even if they have to run away" isn't fueling her love and desire to escape an overprotective father.

Clichés

How often have you heard: *feel the pain, by my side, set me free, lost without you, broken heart, all we've been through, hold me close, my foolish pride, all night long, give you my heart, want you, need you, love you, all my love, more than friends, never let you go, more than words can say, when you walked into the room, when you came into my life, when I first saw you, dream come true, call on me, our love is forever*—and the ever popular *oh baby*? Then there are the cliché rhymes: *hold (take my) your hand/understand/be your man. Dance/take a chance/romance. Kiss you/miss you . . .* and on and on. Of course *you've* never been guilty of using any of these worn-out phrases and rhymes. But just in case you're thinking about it, I'll try to answer the questions I know you'd want to ask.

Every time I turn on the radio, to any format, I hear clichés often the same ones that are in my songs. Those songs are hits, so how can you say that clichés don't work out there in radioland?

Most of the songs you hear on radio are written by the artists who perform them. In those cases, there are few, if any, gatekeepers who are willing or able to criticize the artist's songs, particularly once the artist has become successful. Most artists are signed because they have a great sound, a great look and a vocal style that allow audiences to recognize them instantly—not because they sing great lyrics. Also remember that a lyric by itself is neither a song nor a record. If you're a lyricist, you may hear those cliché lines and disregard the other factors that have put the song on the radio. A dynamic, engaging melody and a groove ideal for the artist's style contribute to the success of the *song*, and a great arrangement and creative production contribute to the success of the *record*. No matter what A&R reps say about the songs being *the* most important factor, it ain't *necessarily* so—though in the mix of ingredients, lyrics are very important in pop ballads and country songs.

So it's more important to avoid clichés if I'm not an artist?. It's always important to avoid them, but if you're a writer submitting songs to artists who don't write (or who write but also record "outside songs" in hopes of getting a hit whether they've written it or not), you go through the gatekeepers. Your song passes the ears of publishers, producers, and A&R reps who, no matter how young, have already heard thousands of songs. They've heard all the worn-out lines and predictable rhymes mentioned above—and more. They know that, in order to compete with the songs submitted by the world's most successful writers (or songs by the artist's spouse, or songs by other writers signed to their producer's publishing company), your song has to be *better* than theirs. It has to be so unique that *they* would not have thought of it, and so compelling that they know it would become a hit for someone else if they don't record it themselves. Lyrics full of clichés are viewed as lyrics that *anyone* could write: not unique, not compelling.

How can I avoid using clichés? The best way to avoid clichés is to write with as much specific detail as possible about your own personal experiences and trust that you tap universal emotions. Also, if you've heard the line before, push yourself until you find a new way to say it.

But thirteen-year-old kids haven't heard those clichés nearly as often or for nearly as many years as the gatekeepers. So they're not clichés to them, are they? True enough. But do you want to look back years later and be embarrassed, even if your songs are successful, realizing that you missed an opportunity to have made them great songs?

Can't I use clichés in a creative way? Absolutely. How often have you heard *break my heart*? Now tell me how often you'd heard "Unbreak My Heart" before the Diane Warren song became a major hit for Toni Braxton. Warren took a cliché and did something so simple and obvious that writers all over the world are kicking themselves for not thinking of it first. Your job is to think of it first.

In this chapter, I've explored the major areas that concern you as a lyric writer. There's a *lot* more to learn. If you're serious about being a songwriter, you'll read everything you can on the subject (see the bibliography for some suggestions), but there's no better and faster way to improve than to write constantly. When you do, you'll create your own examples and encounter problems that will give a practical context to what you read.

5 Constructing a Song

Basic Principles of Commercial Songwriting

I'm not big on rules. Successful writers break them all the time. Some break them by accident and are accidentally successful. Those writers may be "one hit wonders" because they don't understand *why* it worked on the first one. Some understand why the rules were made and break them consciously, knowing the *principles* behind them. I believe that if you know some of the basic principles that make songs work, that make them communicate, you can make use of alternative techniques to compensate for the rules you break. For example, a "rule" is that you don't go more than two verses before the chorus and repeat the chorus at least three times. The Kenny Rogers hit, "The Gambler" and the Eagles' "Lyin' Eyes" both broke that rule. They compensated with compelling *lyrics that held your attention* for three verses before the chorus. The Clay Walker hit, "The Chain of Love," is AABAABA (verse-verse-chorus-verse-verse-chorus-verse) with only two choruses, ending with a verse—a triple rule-breaker by having two verses after the first chorus, only two choruses, and ending with a verse. But the *concept* and great *story line* held our attention and were ultimately more important to the success of the song than the rules it broke.

I won't talk in terms of emotional content at this point. We all know soulful "heart" songs and soulless but well-crafted songs that are just as successful. Something that speaks to *my* heart may leave *you* cold. So I'll limit this to principles that work for all songs, both hits and album cuts, though you'll have a little more latitude as an album artist if you have a distinctive and appealing *sound*.

Here are the basic, underlying principles:

Maintain a balance between predictability and surprise. If your song is too predictable, listeners get bored with it and tune out. If it's too complex, listeners don't feel comfortable and tune out.

Make it *easy* for listeners to remember your song. Easily remembered melodies, lyrics, concepts, and hooks (anything you remember after the record is over) help your song to stay in your listeners' consciousness.

Hold the attention of your audience. The tools needed to do the above include a mix of repetition, rhythm, rhyme, placement of hooks, title line, dynamics, and structure.

Does all popular music need to adhere to these principles? Not at all. Just the pop radio-oriented songs you want your audience to remember. These principles work for album-oriented songs, too, but may not need to be used in the same concentrated way because fans listen to albums differently than they listen to "hit"-oriented records. They buy albums because they're already committed to liking the artist or the artist's sound. Exceptions are dance club music, which doesn't need to rely on the same techniques and structures as pop music because it already *has* your attention in a dance club, and musical theater, which, as a visual medium, already has your attention. As I mentioned in chapter three (see page 96), hip-hop and rap today work somewhere between pop and dance music and are predominantly a producer's medium. If you're not a producer and are writing songs for someone else to record, you need to team up with a producer to make it happen.

We often listen to music on the radio while we're doing something else—driving, working, exercising—so radio hits need to break through all that to capture your attention and hold it. That's why these principles, though they're important for all styles of songs both in live performance and on recordings, work especially well for radio hits.

Words and Music Together

No matter how creative and powerful lyrics or melodies may be by themselves, they take on new life, power, and magic when they're together. The song is greater than the sum of its parts. Whether you're a specialist at words or music or a genius at both, an essential aspect of your craft is the understanding of how to make the parts fit together to create that magic. In this chapter I'll cover the elements of songwriting that relate most to words and music as a whole.

SONG FORM

The form, also called the *format* or *structure*, is a song's basic shape or organization. In this section, I'll examine and explain:

- how a song's basic components—verses, choruses, bridges and pre-choruses—work together to keep a listener's interest
- the basic forms and variations of a song and their best uses
- how to analyze form so you can keep up with contemporary trends

In the 1950s and early 1960s, hardly more than three different chord progressions (formulas) were used in popular music. If a song didn't conform to one of them, the odds were heavily against its becoming a hit, so the chord progression formulas perpetuated themselves. The 1-6m-4-5 (C Am F G) progression spawned hundreds of hits like "26 Miles (Santa Catalina)," "Silhouettes," and "Earth Angel." The twelve-bar blues format (E 4 bars/A 2 bars/E 2 bars/B7 1 bar/A 1 bar/E 2 bars) was also popular as it laid the foundations for rock and roll.

Those old progressions are familiar enough to make us feel at home when they are used in new songs and by new artists. They're predictable: the chords, the words and the tunes are different, but the basic shape of the songs is the same, so we can learn them quickly. Some basic forms and variations will continue as they have for many, many years for a simple reason: They work.

WHY SONG FORMS WORK

The underlying principle of song form as it relates to the balance of predictability and surprise is this: In order to have a surprise, you need to establish something predictable. Notice, as you study these forms, that the surprise element is established by the repetition of two predicatable, similar elements. This is true for comedy as well—the joke format with the Minister, the Priest, and the Rabbi, three blondes, the three wishes, etc. establishes two setup scenarios with the third being the payoff. With melodies (whether in verses or choruses), a repetition of two melody lines establishes an *opportunity* to have the third line be a change—a surprise. It's what keeps it interesting. If you go beyond two identical melody lines, it begins to build tension. The more tension you build, the more need for an exciting resolution. If that tension does not resolve, it can be a disappointment—too predictable.

The same principle operates with song form. And AAA form needs to resolve or pay off musically and lyrically in the last line of the verse. In an AABA, the first two verses set up the bridge. In the verse/chorus forms, a verse/chorus module (also called a "system") repeats twice and works as a setup for a bridge. Another variation: Verse/chorus forms that start with two verses can combine the above with the two-verse setup of the AABA form except that it will go first "pay off" to a chorus rather than to the bridge (as in AABA).

Though this is a guiding principle, it's not a hard and fast rule as you have a variety of elements in a song and a recording (storyline, melody, arrangement, production) that can contribute to capturing the listener's attention. However, this principle is behind what makes these song forms a very powerful tool. And knowing *why* they work will help you manipulate them in creative ways that go beyond the basic roadmaps you'll see below.

THE COMPONENTS OF FORM

Verse

The verse is the major vehicle for conveying the information of the song. Its other major function, both lyrically and musically, is to set up (or lead to) the chorus, the bridge, another verse, or a title or hook line. If it doesn't do one of those things well, it's not working.

Verses have certain basic characteristics:

- The lyric from verse to verse is different or contains substantial new information each time. It may contain elements of previous verses (such as the title line if the song has no chorus).

- The melody is essentially the same each time we hear it, although there is room for variation and some flexibility to accommodate the lyric. The reason for keeping the melody the same is that familiarity makes it easier for the listener to focus on the changing lyric.

Chorus

In contemporary songwriting, the chorus focuses the essence, emotion, and meaning of the song into a simple and easily remembered statement, like "I Can Love You Like That," "Mo Money Mo Problems" or "You Were Meant For Me." The chorus is also usually the segment of the song often referred to as the *hook*—the catchiest, most memorable part of the song. While verses usually concentrate on detail, the chorus can make a broader statement that bears more repetition.

The basic characteristics of the chorus are:

- The melody is the same each time we hear it.

- The song's title usually appears in the first or last line, and possibly more.

- The lyric is usually the same each time, although you may want to use some new lyric information in subsequent choruses to develop the story. A good example of that would be a *turnaround*: a tactic commonly used in country music, where the twist is not revealed until the last chorus.

An example of a song with a chorus that changes every time but still works well is Blessid Union of Souls' "I Wanna Be There." It has an eight-line chorus that repeats the title at the beginning of lines 1, 2, 4, 5 and 8, with the rest of the chorus lyric changing in every verse. SHeDAISY's "Little Good-Byes" is another good example. In the chorus, the title repeats four times but the list of little "reminders" to the man she's leaving is different in each chorus. A title repeated that many times guarantees that a listener has *something* to sing along with, and can easily learn. It also allows writers to change other information in the chorus without worrying about losing their listeners.

Even though there may be reasons for you to change the lyric, there is a very practical reason for you to keep at least a substantial part of it the same—you want listeners to learn your song quickly and easily. If they hear the same chorus three times during the song, they can go away singing it. If you change all or even some of the lyric and music in each chorus, you make it harder for the listener to remember the lyrics. If you have information in the verses that you want people to think about, the chorus should let a listener relax with its simplicity to allow the verse information to sink in. Be aware that, in a song, the listener's attention is divided between the lyric and the music, making it extra important to retain simplicity. So even when you feel you need to change the chorus lyric, a substantial amount of it—particularly the title line—should remain the same and be repeated every time.

Bridge

Also called the *release*, *break*, or *middle eight*, the bridge provides a variety of important functions in a song. Musically, it helps to relieve the boredom factor, and for that reason, it's usually placed about two-thirds of the way into the song (after the second chorus in a verse/chorus form), which is normally when people may begin to tire of melodic repetition. The bridge zaps the listener back to attention and helps her to refocus on the song. It can also add drama in many other ways, such as introducing contrast, change, and unpredictability to the song. The bridge can use any of the devices used to achieve contrast described in the "Song Dynamics" segment later in this chapter (see page 96).

The bridge can also be purely instrumental. The melody should sound as different as possible without sounding like it belongs in a different song. Lyrically, it offers you the opportunity to change gears. You can reiterate the philosophy of the song in a whole new way by changing the "person" (going from *they* or *you* to *I*, for example), going from specific imagery to something more abstract (or vice versa), or using it as an aside or for outside commentary.

The basic characteristics of a bridge are:

- Its melody is different from the verse and the chorus, although occasionally a portion of the verse or chorus melody may be used in the bridge.

- It usually doesn't contain the title or hook, but that's certainly not the law. That decision may depend on how many times you have repeated the title or hook in the song. If you haven't done it much, it might be smart to use it again.

- It usually occurs only once in the song, but it *can* be repeated in an extended verse/chorus form or to extend an AABA form. (In the Police classic, "Every Breath You Take," which is essentially an AABA form, Sting created a second bridge.) Three things prevent a repeated bridge from sounding like a chorus:

  1. It usually doesn't contain the title or hook.
  2. Unlike a chorus, a bridge is not a standalone melodic statement.
  3. If it is constructed correctly, its melody leads back into the verse or chorus.

- It is rarely over eight bars long. After all, it's supposed to be a diversion, not a whole piece in itself. It may be two bars or two lines or whatever is needed to fulfill the function of breaking up the song.

- It is entirely optional.

You will most want a bridge if you have a lot of melodic repetition in your verses and choruses. The more repetition, the more you risk inducing boredom, and bridges are great "boredom busters."

Pre-Chorus

Pre-choruses are melodic segments that are different from the verses, chorus, or bridge. They are known by many other names (climb, lift, channel, B-section, pre-hook, setup), all of which give you clues about their function. They're used extensively in all styles of contemporary radio music. Producers seem to favor pre-choruses to help create an additional level of interest to keep a song exciting, particularly in up-tempo or dance songs where extra length and faster tempo can make a straight verse/chorus form feel too repetitive. However, as the list below indicates, they're also used to add drama to ballads.

When you first hear a pre-chorus, it almost sounds as if it's going to be the chorus, until you hear the chorus that follows. It should increase the melodic tension to the point where there is a great sense of release going into the chorus.

The basic characteristics of pre-choruses are:

- They directly precede the chorus.

- They usually precede *each* chorus, but may be dropped after the first couple of times if you can find a way (musically) to get back to the chorus without it. In that case there's usually a bridge to perform that function between the second and third choruses.

- Lyrics can be the same each time or different. In fact, consider the option of a pre-chorus if you need more than one verse of lyric—but don't need enough lyric for two verses—to set up the chorus lyrically.

- Melodies are the same each time.

- The length varies, like the bridge, from one lyric line to four. Pre-choruses usually last no longer than eight bars.

- Their major function is melodic and dynamic—to build tension to increase the feeling of release in the chorus.

The pre-chorus melody, lyric meter and phrasing (see "Song Dynamics" on page 96) should change to enhance the feeling of anticipation going into the chorus. You can think of it as providing the same kind of anticipation that a great drum fill provides. The pre-chorus can be built in a variety of ways as demonstrated in these hit songs:

Boyz II Men's "End of the Road" (written by Kenneth "Babyface" Edmonds, Antonio Reid, Daryl Simmons); Shania Twain's "Any Man of Mine" (Robert John "Mutt" Lange, Shania Twain); All-4-One or John Michael Montgomery's "I Can Love You Like That" (Steve Diamond, Jennifer Kimball, Maribeth Derry); Sheryl Crow's "Every Day Is a Winding Road" (Sheryl Crow, Jeff Trott, Brian MacLeod); Faith Hill's "Like We Never Loved at All" (Scott Sacks, John Rich, Vicky McGehee); All-American Rejects' "Dirty Little Secrets" (Tyson Ritter, Nick Wheeler); Natasha Bedingfield's "Unwritten" (N. Beddingfield, Danielle Vrisebois, Wayne Rodrigues).

Refrains

A refrain is a repeated final title line on the ends of verses in AAA forms and sometimes AABA forms to get a repetition of the title. In contemporary radio music, we rarely hear refrains because a chorus that includes several repetitions of the title multiplied by three chorus repeats serves to drive home that title more effectively. Refrains were a staple of traditional folk music in which they needed many verses to tell the story, and choruses would have lengthened the song too much. Singer-songwriters rooted in traditional folk music like Bob Dylan ("Blowin' in the Wind") or John Denver ("Annie's Song") occasionally used refrains. Paul Simon also used a refrain in "Bridge Over Troubled Water." It was common in early commercial songwriting terminology to refer to what we now call a chorus as a refrain.

ANALYZING FORM

Before getting into the forms themselves, I'll explain how you can analyze the song forms that you hear.

To start, consider the first melodic segment you hear (not including the intro) as A. The next complete melodic section that has a melody different from A is designated B, the third C, and so on. Repeats of any melodic segment get the same letter they got the first time.

Count bars or measures starting at the downbeat as follows:

For 4/4 time: **1** - 2 - 3 - 4, **2** - 2 - 3 - 4, **3** - 2 - 3 - 4, **4** - 2 - 3 - 4, etc.

For 3/4 waltz time: **1** - 2 - 3, **2** - 2 - 3, **3** - 2 - 3, **4** - 2 - 3, etc.

When the next melodic segment starts, begin counting at bar one again. Enter the total number of bars in each segment. Be sure to include any instrumental breaks, using *inst.* or a dash or some other shorthand to designate them, along with the number of bars they run. You'll end up with a diagram that looks something like this:

A-8, A-8, B-8, A-8,
or
A A B A or A B C ins A B C
8 8 8 8   8 8 8 2 8 8 8

Here's a more graphic way to lay it out quickly so you can easily add extra bars and make notes. Each of the slash notes represents a beat (in 4/4 time).

```
INTRO   1 / / / 2 / / / 3 / / / 4 / / /
A       1 / / / 2 / / / 3 / / / 4 / / / 5 / / / 6 / / / 7 / / / 8 / / /
B       1 / / / 2 / / / 3 / / / 4 / / /
C       1 / / / 2 / / / 3 / / / 4 / / / 5 / / / 6 / / / 7 / / / 8 / / /
INS     1 / / / 2 / / /
```

Try this exercise with songs on the radio. It will give you a repertoire of basic forms and, more importantly, it will show you a wide range of variations that work, such as extra bars of music between sections. Even though you'll find the forms falling into predictable patterns, the variations often give the song the sense of surprise that makes it special and exciting.

Note how the form contributes to the memorability of a song by helping it achieve a balance between *predictability* and *surprise,* repetition and new information, all within a commercially acceptable time limit.

THE BASIC FORMS

AAA

A Title/hook in first or last line unless there is a repeated lyric chorus with the same melody, in which case the title will appear in the chorus.

A "

A "

This is an old form used commonly in traditional folk music, but rarely with good results in contemporary songs because there's no chorus or bridge to help sustain melodic interest. The title line usually appears in the first or last line. The form can have any number of verses. You might use this form if you had a lot of important lyrical content but wanted to eliminate the time spent repeating choruses. In the absence of a chorus that sums up the song, the verses usually end with a dramatic payoff line. Often they'll end in a refrain, a line that repeats a couple of times.

Examples: Johnny Cash's "I Walk the Line"; Bette Midler's "The Rose" (written by Amanda McBroom); Glen Campbell's "By the Time I Get to Phoenix" (Jimmy Webb); Bob Dylan's "The Times They Are a-Changin'"; Alan Jackson's "Remember When"; and Miranda Lambert's "Kerosene" are all AAA forms. Note that all are writer/artists except Campbell and McBroom.

Some songs follow the AAA form melodically, but contain a chorus lyric that repeats: Bruce Springsteen's "Born in ihe U.S.A."; Billy Ray Cyrus' "Achy Breaky Heart" (written by Don Von Tress); and the Goo Goo Dolls' "Iris" (written by John Rzeznik).

There are variations of this form, like Don Henley's "Dirty Laundry," which uses a short refrain between every couple of verses. It's not a standard AAA form because the refrain isn't a part of the basic melodic structure of the verse, and the refrain isn't a chorus because it's very short and does not contain the hook line (which *is* contained in the verse).

Musically, Bruce Springsteen's "Born in the U.S.A." is an AAA: Although it has a chorus, its melody is the same as the verses. That's very unusual, and if you had written this song instead of "The Boss" and you weren't already a successful artist, your publisher probably would have demanded a rewrite. Without a powerful performance and lyrics, the song would be musically uninteresting.

Another variation of the AAA form is an extension created by repeating part or all of the last line (a refrain). This special focus on that line, however, makes it important that it be the title line. A short instrumental section or melodic instrumental hook can be used to break up the potential monotony.

Caution: You need to be very careful to make the melody as interesting as possible (like "The Rose") without making it too complex to be remembered easily. This is generally accomplished with a melodic variation in the last two melodic lines of each verse. Hum any of the examples mentioned to see what I mean.

AABA

A   Title/hook in first or last line—Four eight-bar sections

A   Title/hook in first or last line

B   New melody and lyric (referred to as the bridge or middle eight)

A   Title/hook in first or last line

variations

A   As above

A

B   New melody and lyric

A

B   Repeat B section with or without new lyric or make up a totally new bridge as Sting did in "Every Breath You Take" (which would make it a C section).

A   Repeat first A or part of first and part of second A or part of first A and new lyrics.

A   Repeat second A

AABA is a classic song form with a long and popular history. At one time it was considered the ultimate song form: It's short, concise, melodically seamless and easy to remember. It is used in all styles of music and all tempos, but most frequently in slow or mid-tempo ballads, because its thirty-two bars (four eight-bar sections) make for a very short song at fast tempos. Variations have developed that can accommodate faster tempos and the need for more room to tell the story. You'll find your own as the need arises. Hook/title placement is usually in either the first or last line of the verse, but it can occur in both (like "Yesterday"). You'll hear songs in which the title will also be recapped in the B section, although the objective is to go to a totally new place in that section both musically and lyrically.

Note that, despite its illustrious history, the AABA form is not usually considered the most commercially viable, and most of the songs you'll hear that use it are written by the artists who perform them. When given a choice, most producers will choose to record a song with a repeating chorus; however, if the song has a powerful lyric and melody, it can easily overcome that hurdle.

Examples: The Beatles' "Yesterday" (John Lennon, Paul McCartney); Billy Joel's "Just the Way You Are"; Bruce Springsteen's "Fire" and "Streets of Philadelphia"; and Shania Twain's "From This Moment On."

VERSE/CHORUS FORMS

The varieties of this most popular form provide a maximum of chorus repetition and two or more verses to tell your story.

#1	#2	#3	#4	#5
A Verse	**A** Verse	**A** Chorus	**A** Verse	**A** Verse
B Chorus	**B** Chorus	**B** Verse	**A** Verse	**B** Pre-chorus
A Verse	**A** Verse	**A** Chorus	**B** Chorus	**C** Chorus
B Chorus	**B** Chorus	**B** Verse	**A** Verse	**A** Verse
A Verse	**C** Bridge	**A** Chorus	**B** Chorus	**B** Pre-chorus
B Chorus	**B** Chorus		**B** Chorus	**C** Chorus

Version #1 gives you a maximum verse and chorus repetition. A potential problem is that, if you have a lot of melodic repetition within each verse or chorus, such as an eight-bar section made up of three two-bar melodies with a slight variation in the fourth two-bar melody line, you may have too much repetition. In that case, **Version #2** features a bridge after the second chorus. You can also choose either a short instrumental section followed by a short bridge or an instrumental section by itself. **Version #3** with the chorus first can give you more repetition of the chorus in a shorter time. The choice of whether to start with a chorus depends on the lyric development of the song. If it's important to generate a dynamic opening to the song, try the chorus first unless you want the verses to build interest and suspense and set up the chorus as a payoff. Many 1960s Motown hits used variations of this form. It's always a good idea to give it a test by switching the verse and chorus positions to see which works best.

Version #4 with two verses in front is also a much used form. Its workability depends on a very strong lyric continuity between the first and second verses to offset the delay in getting to the chorus. This is more of a problem in a slow ballad than in an up-tempo song because of the additional time it takes to get to the chorus. Every word has to propel the story forward. Repetition of information is deadly. Remember, you should have a very important reason to delay the chorus. If each of your two verses cover the same information in a different way and don't depend on each other, this is not the best form to use. But if you do need to use two verses, look for some arrangement devices or write a variation of the first verse melody to help sustain musical interest in the second verse. Consider using your title in the first line of the chorus to avoid further delay in reaching the hook line. You also need to add a bridge to this form.

Variations of this form opening with three verses (AAABAB or AAABAAB) are rare, and the two examples that come to mind—the Eagles' "Lyin' Eyes" (Don Henley/Glenn Frey) and Kenny Rogers' "The Gambler" (Don Schlitz)—both have such exceptional lyric continuity that a chorus any earlier would be an unwelcome intrusion (see chapter three, "The Imagination of the Listener," on page 52).

You'll also occasionally hear an AABAABB variation, particularly on up-tempo songs. Again, those choices will be different for each song but the guiding principle is that you don't delay the chorus unless you have another good way to sustain the listener's interest. An interesting variation is the beautiful message story song "The Chain of Love" recorded by Clay Walker that has such strong lyric continuity that it was a hit as an AABAABA with only two chorus repeats.

Version #5 offers the excitement of three different melodic segments. The pre-chorus is the segment that makes the difference here. This form works great for up-tempo songs where the three segments go by quickly, but it's also been successful in ballads and mid-tempo songs. Variations are possible with this form, including repeated instrumental versions of any of the segments and instrumental breaks between segments. Here are some examples:

AABC ABC BC BC or

ABC ABCDC or

ABC ABCD BC, the **D** being a bridge with a new melody, with or without lyrics.

DANCE MUSIC

With the increase in the number of dance songs in the four-minute range on the pop and R&B/hip-hop charts, we see much more experimentation with these extended forms. Dance records are developed for pop, rock, and urban radio and as singles for the dance club market. The records are usually formatted in a way that allows the record to be re-edited or re-mixed. Originally, a longer version is recorded with more segments that can be removed to make a shorter version for radio, or can be left in for the dance club market or radio stations that like to play the long versions.

Records earmarked specifically for the dance club and rave market and not for radio can break more rules. Since there's already a captive audience, you don't need to get their attention, and tracks well over four minutes are the norm, there can be long, slow-building intros, additional sections and long instrumental breaks that would be too monotonous on radio. The major appeal of these records is having a relentlessly exciting dance groove. Beyond that, there are no rules. Aside from a few conventional arrangement tricks like dropping out and bringing in instruments or repeating loops, there is a lot of room for creativity in vocal and instrumental textures, particularly for songwriters with arranging and producing skills. Dance music is usually composed with the groove first, then other instruments, loops, and vocals are added later. DJs/MCs/producers have become the new stars of the dance scene because of new digital "turntable" technology that allows them to seamlessly keep the music going by segueing between songs with different tempos, and create their own digital loops to provide transitional grooves.

EXERCISES IN FORM

1. Write a song adhering strictly to each of the standard forms mentioned.

2. Pick one of your favorite hits and write a new lyric to its melody. This is called the "dummy melody" exercise, and it is commonly used by lyricists writing without a new melody. Try to write the lyric with the same emotional feeling as the original. You may even try to use the same rhyme scheme. Then have a collaborator create a new melody without letting him know the melody you used.

3. Analyze the forms of ten current hits. Do this exercise about once a month with ten new songs. It's a great way to stay current, and to explore new form variations and why you think they work.

4. Write songs in the standard forms using new variations of those forms.

CHOOSING A FORM

Even when your songs come to you spontaneously, you must still decide which form to use. Usually writers will come up with a single verse or chorus idea first. After that first flash of inspiration and an exploration of what you want the song to say, you need an idea of the type of form you want to use to help you say it more effectively. You may do that unconsciously, as a natural result of having listened to the radio all your life—you just feel where there ought to be a change without really making a conscious evaluation of the reasons. That approach often works just fine, but sometimes it doesn't, and you need to know enough about a variety of options to decide which form to use. Like a beginning guitar player who writes monotonous two-chord songs because he only knows two chords instead of learning more chords, what you already know or feel about form could be limiting.

Another problem in choosing form by "feel" is the songwriting equivalent of painting yourself into a corner. You might lock into a form that, by the time you've said what you wanted to say, has resulted in a five-minute song that you really wanted to be three minutes. You're now faced with a rewrite that might include a restructuring of the whole song. It's much harder to get out of a corner like that than it is to set it up better in the beginning. Even if you do have to restructure the song because the form you chose didn't quite work—or you had another idea halfway through the song—the important thing is that you make those decisions on the basis of knowing your options.

So what do you consider in your choice of form? If you're starting with the music, tempo is a major factor in dictating the form. If it's an up-tempo song, you may need a form with many sections (like ABCABCDC or AABABCB) to help you sustain musical interest. If it's a slow or mid-tempo ballad, you can use either the longer or shorter forms.

If you're starting from a lyric, the mood and subject matter will dictate the tempo of the music. "Genie in a Bottle" wouldn't work very well as a slow ballad, and the lyric to the *Titanic* theme "My Heart Will Go On" wouldn't be as effective in a fast dance song.

Tempo is also determined by the ease with which the lyrics can be sung. The problem usually arises when there are lots of words. If the tempo is too fast, you may tie knots in your tongue trying to get them all in. If you want a rapid-fire one syllable per eighth- or sixteenth-note lyric, you have to be extra careful that the words are easy to pronounce and sing together. It's a good idea to experiment with a metronome by singing the lyric against various tempo settings. Fewer words generally pose fewer problems, but the challenge is to phrase them in an interesting way against the rhythm. There are other tempo variables available, due to the fact that you can have a slow moving lyric and melody over a double-time groove.

Whichever way you choose, once you've set the tempo and determined how many lyric lines will be in each segment, you've begun to lock yourself into the form. If it takes one minute to get through a verse and chorus, and you're looking for a three-minute song, your options have already shrunk.

Also consider the amount of lyric needed to tell the story. Though it's always a good idea to condense, you must choose the form that best serves the amount of lyrics you need. The AAA form gives you the most room to stretch lyrically, even though, as I mentioned earlier, it's not a good form from a commercial standpoint. Any up-tempo three- or four-section form can give you plenty of lyric space with strong musical interest, particularly if you use pre-choruses for new lyric information each time. One-section (AAA) and two-section (ABABAB) forms at fast tempos, though they allow for a maximum of lyric information, can be melodically boring because the melodies repeat so often.

With a spare, condensed lyric, you have many options. You can lay them over either an up-tempo track or a slow ballad and in either case have plenty of room to accommodate the individual phrasing styles of different singers. You can use any form and ensure a maximum amount of both repetition and musical interest. However, a spare lyric at a slower tempo has more of an obligation to be interesting. You're making the listener wait for that lyric to unfold, and it had better be worth the wait. The same is true of the music.

Like anything else, once you've worked with these forms, they'll eventually become second nature to you. You'll also find that when you get yourself into problematic situations, you'll find creative solutions. A substantial amount of innovation in music is initiated by a need to find a graceful way out of a jam. If you already have a repertoire of solutions, you're ahead of the game.

Hooks

Hook is the term you'll hear most often in the business and craft of commercial songwriting. (Well, maybe not as much as "Sorry, we can't use your song," but it's possible that the more you hear about hooks now, the less you'll hear "we can't use it" later.)

The hook has been described as "the part(s) you remember after the song is over," "the part that reaches out and grabs you," "the part you can't stop singing—even when you hate it," and "the catchy repeated chorus." Some of the world's greatest hook crafters are commercial jingle writers: How many times have you had a jingle stick in your mind that you can't get rid of?

Here are several categories of hooks:

The Structural Hook. For songs in this category, a part of the structure of the song functions as the hook. The most common is the *hook chorus*. It repeats several times during the song, and should contain the title or *hook line*, usually the first or last line (see "Chorus Construction" on page 93). We may also consider memorable B sections, particularly in an AABA form, to be hooks, but the chorus is almost universally referred to as "the hook."

Instrumental Hooks. There are melodic phrases in songs that may not be part of the vocal melody, yet stick in our minds as though they were. In the last line of the chorus of the Beatles' "Something" after "Don't want to leave her now, you know I believe and how . . ." is George Harrison's melodic guitar figure that we think of whenever we think of the melody, though there's no lyric over it. If we heard that figure by itself, we'd be able to name that tune. The repeated riffs or loops that introduce and run beneath the Rolling Stones' "(I Can't Get No) Satisfaction," Stevie Wonder's "Superstition," Michael Jackson's "Beat It," and Jay-Z's "Can I Get a . . ." are as memorable as any other parts of the songs.

Too often, I think, songwriters tend to believe that creating those instrumental hooks is the job of the arranger, producer, or studio musicians. It should be kept in mind that if those are the hooks that sell the song to the public, they'll sell the song to the producer and artist if *you* create them first.

Story Line Hooks. Have you ever heard a song and afterward couldn't quite remember the melody or the exact words but you could remember the story? Sometimes the story itself is so powerful and evocative that it's the thing that stays in your mind longer than the exact words or melody.

Production Hooks. Production hooks aren't always possible for a songwriter, but today more writers than ever before have access to great composing and recording technology. The sounds on both demos and master recordings have become very important. Experiment with the way various instruments sound in combination. Experiment with electronic keyboard synth "pre-sets" combined with acoustic instruments or samples of natural sounds. You can digitally sample sound sources or buy them on disks, tapes or ROM cartridges and modify them yourself. MIDI (Musical Instrument Digital Interface) technology has made possible an almost infinite variety of sonic combinations.

Early recording techniques such as "phasing" and "flanging" were later incorporated into software versions that you could use at the tap of a button. Today virtually any sound modification device used in the studio has been converted to some portable digital form that you can use at home or on stage. Certain sounds will evoke certain emotional responses. Use them as artistic tools along with lyric and melody to create mood and emotion. One of the most effective hooks is a sound no one has ever heard before. Remember, however, that once you get into the technology of creating sounds, it can be so much fun that you can easily forget that the song is still the most important thing. No matter how exciting those sounds are, they won't make up for a weak song.

Hooks are essential in commercial music. They are points of reference that keep us interested and focused on the song. They are devices that help us remember, and they are an entertainment in themselves. Part of your job as a commercial writer is to be able to use as many different types of hooks as possible.

Chorus Construction

After the first couple listens, the part of the song people remember best is the chorus. Effective choruses are a magic mix of lyric, melody, and phrasing.

The majority of choruses adhere to certain guidelines. I say majority because there are songs that ignore some of the guidelines and still win by the strength of their performance, arrangement, or production.

- The title should appear in the chorus. We should know it's the title because of its placement in the chorus or its degree of repetition. If words or phrases other than the title repeat in the chorus or in strong positions, the listener won't know which is the title when they call the radio station to request it, download it, or ask for it at the music store. This is why you sometimes see songs with two titles, like "Untitled (How Does It Feel)," "Over My Head (Cable Car)," "C'mon 'N Ride It (The Train)," or "Just Might (Make Me Believe)"—that usually means that someone felt the song's title was not its strongest hook, or even that the song has two hooks and they're covering their bets by putting both in the title. Since you can't buy or request a song if you can't remember its name, these are very important commercial considerations.

- Keep the information simple enough for people to remember easily. If you're a literary genius, you may tend to think most choruses are too simple. Don't worry about it. They *need* to be simple!

- The chorus needs to distill and focus the song.

- It needs to stand repetition.

- The words of the chorus need to be easily remembered. It also helps if the melody is fun and easy to sing. And one more time—keep it simple!

- The action of the verses should not pass the action of the chorus chronologically. Meaning, you can't have a couple breaking up for good in the last verse, but trying to get together in the last chorus.

- Choruses can run from two to eight lines (depending on your definition of a line).

Here are some common lyric constructions:

Repeat the same line two or more times. This can get monotonous unless that line is fun to sing or shout (like "Take this job and shove it"), it's sung with a style that makes it interesting (like "Whoomp! There it is"), or it's musically exciting.

First and third lines are the same, second and fourth lines are different. This offers the possibility of having a strong payoff line to end the chorus. The last line in the chorus is a power position, and there are high expectations for it to be strong and satisfying. Examples: Bruce Hornsby's "The Way It Is"; Brian McKnight's "Anytime" (written by Brian McKnight/Brandon Barnes); and Paula Cole's "I Don't Want To Wait."

First and third lines are the same, second and fourth lines are the same. Provides maximum repetition of both lines and makes the chorus very easy to remember. Example: Eagle Eye Cherry's "Save Tonight."

First three lines are the same, fourth line is different. This has some of the potential monotony of the repeated construction and the payoff advantage of the second example. The repetition of the first three lines makes for a powerful setup, so the payoff needs to be strong. Example: Steve Winwood's "Higher Love."

All four lines are different. Doesn't risk monotony and doesn't set up as much of an expectation for a powerful last line as the above constructions (but give them one anyway). Examples: Bette Midler's "The Wind Beneath My Wings" (written by Larry Henley/Jeff Silbar); Dixie Chicks, "Wide Open Spaces" (Susan Gibson); Mariah Carey, "Dream Lover" (Mariah Carey/Dave Hall/David Porter); and Natalie Imbruglia, "Torn" (written by Paul Thornalley/Scott Cutter/Anne Preven).

The first or last part of each line is repeated (and is almost always the title). This is one of the oldest and most common structures. It goes back to "call and response" songs in tribal music and Gregorian chants. Examples: Irene Cara's "Fame " (written by Dean Pitchford/Michael Gore); Ace of Base's "All That She Wants"; SHeDAISY's "Little Good-Byes"; Shania Twain's "You're Still the One" (Shania Twain/Robert John "Mutt" Lange).

The first and last lines are the same, the second and third are each different. This gives you a chance to repeat the hook line at both the beginning and the end. Example: Huey Lewis, "The Heart of Rock and Roll."

These are just a few common structures. There are many more. Chorus structures are far less standardized than song forms. Pick up a contemporary songbook at your local music store or listen to a Top 40 countdown, and what you'll find is an incredible degree of diversity. In fact, a good share of hits are successful *because* their choruses are unusual—like Macy Gray's "I Try."

Melodic construction of choruses roughly follows the lyric structures; however, a tremendous variety of rhythmic and phrasing options is available. A lyricist should always keep in mind that there is great flexibility in pop music in the ways that lyrics can be stretched, spaced, and positioned relative to the music. Looking at a lyric on paper only gives us a part of the story.

Repetition

One of the most important ingredients of successful songs is repetition. Repetition is a key part of learning almost anything. So if you want someone to learn your song quickly (and you do!), you can't afford not to use it.

Several studies have been made showing that most listeners have some resistance to hearing something unfamiliar. They'd rather hear a song they already know. It may be a little disappointing to learn that most people are so unadventurous, but it's really not surprising. As writers and musicians, we are always looking for something fresh and new, and tend to forget that there's a public out there who doesn't share that need for change. They feel comfortable with the familiar, and uncomfortable with the unfamiliar.

This poses obvious problems for radio stations that would like to add a new record by a new artist, but whose audience polls tell them they should keep playing established hits instead. The more they repeat those old songs, the more comfortable people feel with them, and the more personal nostalgia they generate. Since radio stations rely more heavily on listener polls and feedback to program their music, and since listeners can't request what they haven't heard, new writer/artists are fighting an uphill battle.

If you can write songs for established artists with already familiar and easily identifiable voices and styles, you have an edge, because a new and unfamiliar song by Kelly Clarkson, Faith Hill, or Brooks and Dunn is going to get played before an unfamiliar song by an unfamiliar artist.

Whether you're writing for yourself or someone else, you need to minimize the odds against you. Since your challenge with a new song is to break through that resistance, build instant familiarity into a song with the repetition of melodic themes, choruses, or instrumental figures (riffs). Write a chorus that is totally and instantly understandable, simple, easily remembered, and that touches their hearts and their feet. By the time the song is finished and the listeners have heard it three or four times, they'll know it and want to hear it and sing it again.

The general objective is to have enough repetition without inducing boredom. It's sometimes difficult to determine how much is too much. Lyricists, in general, seem to get bored very quickly and even a very little repetition can make them feel guilty about not doing their job properly. On the other hand, a musician who's just found a great groove will tend to play it 'til the neighbors have him arrested. This supports the theory that you can get away with more repetition of a short lyric phrase if it's catchy and fun to sing, in other words, if it's "musical" by virtue of its meter, phrasing, rhythm, rhyme, assonance, and alliteration. "Chattanooga Choo Choo," "Little Latin Lupe Lu," "Getting Jiggy Wit It," "Livin' La Vida Loca," and "Honky Tonk Badonkadonk" all have those catchy qualities about them.

Obviously, the amount of repetition you use depends on the purpose of the song and what audience you're trying to reach. A ten-minute dance song can light up a dance floor but merely be annoying if you hear it on the radio while stuck in traffic.

Repetition of melody allows listeners to focus more on the lyrics. If the melody changed in each of the sections and never repeated, we'd be too distracted to follow the lyrics. One of the reasons why the melodies in traditional country music have such simple familiarity is because country music is very lyric oriented and the familiarity helps the listener concentrate on the words.

Lyric repetition also serves to let the listener's mind rest. If, as a writer, you're giving listeners information in the verses, a repeated chorus coming up says, "Okay, you'll only have to concentrate a little longer, when the chorus comes back you can rest your mind and just groove; and when it's over, you'll know just when to get ready to concentrate again." That mental preparation to pay attention is the basis of the need to have "pick-ups" before choruses and verses, intros to songs, drum fills, or chord changes, or something that telegraphs that there's going to be a change. We like those when we dance, too. They help us to choreograph ourselves.

Repetition of words or short phrases, or the first part of a familiar melody or lyric, creates tension in a song. But in order to work, it has to pay off big. Otis Redding was great at that. "You got to, got to, got to, got to" and when he finally hits "Try a Little Tenderness," it's a release and a relief and feels good.

However, too much repetition can wear out its welcome fast. We all know songs like that. Pay attention to the ones that do it to you and figure out why. A chorus made up of the same short repeated phrase throughout can be death. Ideally, a song should have a good balance of predictability and surprise without too much of either.

Song Dynamics

Among the most powerful tools you can use to make your songs more commercial and to impress industry pros with your command of the craft, is the use of contrasts and variations that I call "song dynamics." I've also observed that it's the tool most commonly overlooked and underused by amateur songwriters. In this section, we'll look at several devices you should have in your bag of tricks and why they work.

There are crucial points during a song at which the audience's attention must be dramatically and positively captured in order to make it effective on radio. I had a very valuable experience that helped to confirm my information about these factors.

Len Chandler (my partner in the Los Angeles Songwriters Showcase) and I were asked to produce demos of some strong commercial songs by a company that regularly tested records on behalf of producers and record companies. Every Saturday, four hundred young potential record buyers of several demographic groups (divided into age, sex, and racial groups) sat in a theater and turned a dial on the arm of their seats to indicate responses to a given song ranging from "don't like it" to neutral to "love it." As the song was played in the theater, lyrics were shown on the screen and, simultaneously, a computer totaling the combined responses of each demographic group drew a graph of that group's reaction so that we could see how they responded at any given moment of the song. From watching those reactions and from the director's interpretations of what we saw, we learned the following:

• Intros for ballads should be shorter in order to get the listener into the body of the song more quickly. Intros for up-tempo songs can be longer because people get involved physically almost immediately and don't need to wait. People reflect on ballad lyrics in a more passive way, which increases the need for a blockbuster chorus.

• People will try to identify the voice when it's first heard. If it's familiar, it usually generates a positive reaction. People always feel more comfortable with a voice they know than one they don't, because they have to decide whether they like an unfamiliar singer.

This phenomenon also contributes to the difficulty for an unknown artist to get exposure on the radio. A good example was an unknown male artist with a beautiful but very high voice who got a negative reaction from the audience. We concluded that the audience was turned off because they didn't know whether to identify a male or female (the lyrics didn't immediately establish a gender). The problem here wasn't the high voice in itself; it was the lack of gender identity.

• The reaction at the first sound of a voice is critical to the audience's continued reaction to the record. The longer it takes to respond positively, the harder it is to build interest through the rest of the song. In the absence of a familiar voice, the lyric content of the first line is very important to the audience's response. This is the audience's first exposure to the song and artist, and there's an automatic tendency to pay attention when someone starts to sing, just as there is when someone starts to talk. If people don't understand or hear or like what's being said, the reaction will be negative.

• The chorus is another critical place in a song. If audience interest doesn't increase perceptibly at the beginning of the chorus and increase throughout, continued positive interest in the remainder of the record is unlikely.

In television, the pros say that there should be a new camera angle or other change at least every fifteen seconds to keep the viewer's interest. (In music videos, that time is considerably shorter.) This principle has an analogy to radio. We remember only a fraction of what we hear compared to what we see, so we begin to understand why we're so easily distracted when we listen to the radio. That means that the battle for people's attention on the radio is fierce. Most of us are listening in the car, at work, or otherwise occupied, so the songs have to be very dynamic to break through and capture our attention. Now that we understand what has to be done, how can we create the excitement that solves the problem?

One of the main components of the Superlearning techniques developed by Russian educators now being used in the West is that teachers vary the tone, intensity and pitch of their voice frequently as they deliver the material. Those changes continue to stimulate the student's attention. Since this is the same effect you want to achieve in your listeners, you can use this principle by increasing and releasing tension, and thus achieve contrasts between different segments of the song. Try out some of these:

Change the groove. You could go from a straight "on the beat" feel in the verse to a more syncopated feel in the chorus or vice versa. In other words, go from emphasizing *1-2-3-4* to *1-and-2-and-3-and-4*—like a reggae beat.

Change chord progression. Initiate a whole new chord progression for the chorus and another for the bridge. Modulating up or down, or playing the same progression in a different key, are arrangement devices that can be built into your demos.

Change time. Don't change tempo or pulse if you're going for a radio or dance market record. Major artists have done it (Paul McCartney's "Live and Let Die," Queen's "We Are the Champions"), but it's a very risky business, even to start slow and break into an up-tempo dance groove. Once you've engaged a listener or dancer in the pulse of a song, it's a solid base on which you can build other dynamics. Against that solid base you can go from 4/4 time to a couple of bars of 3/4 time to increase tension as the Beatles did on "We Can Work It Out." It can make for an interesting transition between verse and chorus, for example, but be careful not to continue for more than a bar or two or you'll ruin the groove. An established artist can occasionally still pull it off. Toby Keith's "Get Drunk and Be Somebody" goes from a 4/4 shuffle to a 3/4 bridge to good effect. One more time—there are no rules, but there *are* odds.

Change melody. A melodic change in the chorus is probably the most effective song dynamic you can use to make a song memorable and commercially viable. Generally, you'll want it to "lift" out of (up from) the verse melody by starting above the last note of the verse. That's not a rule, however, and there have been rare songs that have achieved a contrast by dropping down from the verse. A change in chord progressions will automatically induce a change of melody in the chorus. It can also be effective to change the chorus melody before you work out new chords. Try playing and singing your verse melody right up to the place where your chorus is supposed to come in, then stop playing and continue *a cappella*. Record it so you can listen to it away from your instrument.

Change lyric density. The term *lyric density* refers to the number of words that must fit within a measure. You might have rapid-fire lyrics with one syllable per sixteenth note during the verse, then change to one syllable per quarter note in the chorus. Or do the opposite, all the while keeping the tempo the same. Many hit songs use that technique. The rest of the chorus continues in the same pattern, giving our minds another subconscious cue to remember the lyric and melody.

When you're analyzing the songs you hear on the radio, notice how many times this is used. Contemporary songs in all styles use this shifting of lyric density not just to contrast verses, pre-choruses, and choruses, but within those sections as well. Mariah Carey and Usher are masters of this technique, but they're not alone in the hip-hop and pop genres. It's always been a staple in rap, not only within the rap sections, but contrasting the rap verses with sung choruses that are much more spare. We're also hearing it increasingly in country.

Change the lyric meter. Changing lyric meters within a line from line-to-line or section-to-section is one of the most common techniques used in successful songs, and one of the most underused by novice songwriters. Though keeping the same meter through a verse can subtly build tension that can be released when you change it in the chorus, it risks being too predictable. You can also alternate between two different meters every other line (or within the same line). There are many options.

Here's an example of changing lyric meters within lines. Think of the melody in the first three lines of Lennon and McCartney's "Yesterday" visually:

(pattern 1)	(pattern 2)	(pattern 1)
/ - -	- - - - - -	/ - -

(pattern 2)	(pattern 1)
- - - - - -	/ - -

(pattern 3)	(pattern 1)
/ / / /	/ - -

> Tip: If you can sing your verse lyric to your chorus melody, it's a good indication that your song could benefit from a new chorus lyric meter to help generate a new melody and provide more contrast.

EXERCISE

Try this while you're listening to your favorite songs: Instead of singing along with the lyrics, pretend the words are part of the rhythm and just speak them, maybe substituting "da-da-da" for the words so you can get a sense of their meter, or rhythm.

Listen to any of Diane Warren's hits: "Unbreak My Heart," "Because You Loved Me," "I Don't Want to Miss a Thing," and many others. She's a master at changing her lyric meter and density in the middle of a line, at the choruses, or at the bridges in ways that feel natural and conversational. Rob Thomas is another writer who's great at that. Listen to the way you speak and pay attention to the natural rhythms of others. We rarely, if ever, hear people speak in iambic pentameter: "da-DUM da-DUM da-DUM da-DUM da-DUM" (five metric feet), because it feels so stiff and predictable. When you write lyrics and music together, by yourself, whether for yourself as a singer or someone else, you have an opportunity to marry lyric and music in a uniquely conversational way. Collaborations can also have a very special magic when writers are in synch with each other. As a lyricist, the ability to express your own attitudes and ideas in a way that's natural for you is one of the best ways to create a unique song or singing style.

If you're a lyricist working without a melody, you should employ changes in lyric density, meter, and rhyme scheme, particularly at choruses and bridges, so that eventually, your composer has a head start in creating musical contrasts. Writing lyrics against a metronome pulse, drum machine, or loop software (there's lots of it free and legal online these days) will help you to hear those patterns in a useful context and have fun experimenting with the phrasing.

EXERCISE

To discover your own unique speech patterns, next time you're on the phone with a friend, record your end of the conversation. When you listen back, listen for your own personal vocal cadences and patterns. Pay attention to your vocal inflections. As in the previous exercise, substitute da-da-da for the actual words but keep your vocal inflections.

Change the rhyme scheme. You can have a different rhyme scheme in your verses than in your chorus and/or your bridge. Try not to use the same end rhymes in more than one verse (see chapter four, "Rhyme Schemes" on page 69).

Change where you begin the sung lyric. You can start it as a pickup *before* beat *one*, for example on beat *three* or *four* of the previous bar or beat **three** *and* or **four** *and* of the previous bar. You can start it on *one* (the downbeat). You can start it on beat **one** *and* or *two*.

For example, on the Beatles' "We Can Work It Out," the verse vocal starts "**Try** to see it . . ." on **one** *and*, and starts both the title line, "**We** can . . ." and the bridge, "**Life** is very short . . ." on *one*.

These devices have infinite variations. It's in their imaginative use that you exercise your creative muscles. They won't all work on all songs, but they're options you can try on each song. Arrangement devices such as silence, dropping out and bringing in instruments, and changes in intensity, volume, and texture can be used to further give your songs drama. These are devices to explore when you record your demo.

Rewriting

Before recording a demo of any song, you'll want to be sure it's the best it can be. Usually the first draft of any song can use improvement. So before your ecstasy about finishing it compels you to spend your hard-earned cash on a demo, it's well worth putting your song away for a few days. Being able to look at the song more objectively may spare you the frustration of hearing a publisher or producer say, "This is really good but the second verse needs a rewrite," and knowing you'll have to spend even more money to re-record the vocal. Not that a rewrite is a guarantee that it won't happen anyway, but at least you'll know you gave it your best shot.

It's often said that writing successful songs is 10 percent writing and 90 percent rewriting. In interviews with hundreds of hit songwriters, I have rarely heard them say that their hits came out all at once in their final version. The ones who can nail it or at least get close to the finished song the first time around have been at it so long that their creative flow and critical faculties practically work in unison. Even relatively inexperienced writers will find they can occasionally write a song in fifteen minutes that's nearly in its finished form. But for most writers, those times are rare.

One of the differences between a pro and an amateur writer is that the pro usually recognizes from the beginning that he will probably be able to come up with rewrites to improve the song. The amateur tends to think that everything that comes out of the original, inspired state is wonderful and shouldn't be tampered with.

The latter attitude is the enemy of professionalism. Most writers go through this stage of development with great difficulty. The first time a publisher or producer rejects a song and suggests a rewrite, the writer usually rebels, thinking, "Who are you to criticize my work? Nobody knows better than I when it's finished or not!" I've watched many writers go through this stage, then take the suggestions, rewrite, and be forced to admit to themselves that they really liked the changes they made and felt the songs had become much stronger. Once songwriters have gone through that experience, the perspective makes them much more open to change, particularly if the end result is getting a song recorded or published. This doesn't mean that every criticism you receive is valid just because it comes from a so-called authority, but it is necessary to keep an open mind even if you eventually decide to leave the song unchanged.

Although it may be important to your livelihood that you rewrite for commercial considerations, it's most important to satisfy yourself that this is the best work you can do. Hopefully, you want to create something that will continue to be enjoyed for a long time. Five or twenty years from now, you don't want to be embarrassed to hear that song and know that if you'd just been a little harder on yourself, you'd be proud of it.

Sometimes it's valuable to imagine your toughest critic reading your lyric or hearing your song and picking it apart. This may point up some flaws that you hadn't noticed before.

Here are some areas to look at for possible rewrites:

- Make sure your lyrics and music work well together, and that you haven't placed accents on the wrong syllables or tried to fit too many words together in a short musical space. Words need to be easily sung and comprehended.

- Can you substitute an image or action or dialogue line that will condense and heighten the impact of the song? The less wordy a lyric is, the more room an artist has to phrase it in his or her style.

- Is every line important and every word necessary? If you can omit a line or a word without affecting the meaning and flow of the lyric you need to replace it with a stronger one. Every line should contribute to the overall meaning.

- Does your song contain all the dynamics necessary to hold a listener's attention? Does your chorus stand out melodically from your verses? Can you rearrange rhyme schemes or meter to enhance the difference between sections of your song? Try some alternate melody lines while imagining an appropriate singer performing them. You may find something better than your first idea.

The late, great Jack Segal, hit lyricist, super craftsman, and teacher, laid out some tools for rewriting in his lyric class that are well worth knowing: reduction, inversion, insertion, and rhyme relocation.

REDUCTION

Reduction is the shortening of sentences or lines. Specifically, making fewer syllables and fewer metric feet. Let's take a line that's seven metric feet. (˘ = unaccented ′ = accented)

> And **there** I **was** just **hang** - ing **on** to **all** those **worn** out **lines**

Take out the useless words and cut it down to five feet with a one-syllable pickup:

> I was **hang** - ing **on** to **all** those **worn** out **lines**

Always look for ways to streamline your lyrics. If the above line was locked into a musical pattern that accommodated the first version, the reduced version would lend itself to a variety of new phrasing possibilities that the first version didn't offer.

INVERSION

Inversion is a tricky form of rhyme relocation, reversing part of the line so that a new rhyme word emerges from the interior to the end position. It's important to preserve the natural, conversational flow of the line and if the inversion appears to have been done only to achieve a rhyme, it feels awkward.

> *I loved you then, I love you still,*
> *Break us up, they never will.*

That's an example of a mediocre line gone bad. *I love you still* is an acceptable inversion of *I still love you*, but the last line is one you'd never say in conversation. Obviously, the most natural line is *They'll never break us up*. You could say, "They try to break us up. They never will." You'd then have two complete thoughts. If that possibility messes up your meter, you'd have to go back to the first line and look for another end word to give you a new choice of rhymes. In doing so, you might use another form of inversion by inverting the order in the first line to "I love you still, I loved you then" giving you *then* to work with. In this case, you're also reversing the natural time order of *then/still*, which weakens the line. You could also say, "I love you now" instead of "still," though it does have a slightly different meaning—an important element for consideration in this jigsaw juggle.

Sometimes, it's better just to start over!

INSERTION

This is filling in the blanks when the desired meter, number of syllables and lyrical concept are known: You've got your verse or chorus written, your meter is established, you know what you want to say. You realize that there's a weak line in the middle that could be replaced. Now you have a real jigsaw puzzle.

Here's an example in something I wrote. The first draft:

> She drifted past the mirror but she didn't even look.
> A week ago she would have fixed her hair.
> I could see that the spark had vanished from her eyes,
> And she was too far in the ozone now to care.

I felt I needed something to replace the third line that said something about the emotional impact, the desperation the man was feeling.

> She drifted past the mirror but she didn't even look.
> A week ago she would have fixed her hair.
> I was fading from her life and trying to hold on
> But she was too far in the ozone now to care.

Even that line went through the same process, from "She was shut out of my life and I needed to break through" to "I was fading from her life and I needed to break through," which felt more vulnerable, to the final choice which felt vulnerable but also more helpless.

RHYME RELOCATION

Rhyme relocation is the flip-flopping of the rhymes to strengthen the power of the lyric and rhyme. The stronger rhyme-word of the two should come second whenever possible. Inversion is actually a form of rhyme relocation. You get more power out of placing the strongest word as the end rhyme. There are words that are obviously more powerful than others, said/dead, had/bad, dream/scream, well/hell. Obviously, the second word in each pair would evoke the strongest emotional response in the listener. If you find you've got the strongest word first, try to reverse them. It won't always work and ultimately, it's a juggle between the power of the line, the power of the word, the meaning and the flow. The principle, overall, is always to escalate toward the most powerful word, line or idea.

If you're writing a story song, save the payoff until the last verse. The last line of every section is a power position because it's where the tension is released. If you blow it with a weak line, chances are that the listener will feel let down enough to have forgotten that brilliant line in the middle of the verse.

In the case of lines, an interesting example is in George Michael's classic Wham! hit, "Careless Whisper":

> *To the heart and mind*
> *Ignorance is kind.*

If you turned the lines around, you'd get a slightly more natural, conversational feel, but you'd lose considerable impact since "Ignorance is kind" is the real payoff line.

If you're writing the lyric first, you have the luxury of performing these changes without restriction. However, if the change gives you a different meter, you'll want to follow through with the same meter in the rest of the verses, or the rest of the choruses (if that's what you're changing). If you don't, you'll give your melody writer a nervous breakdown—unless you're the melody writer, too. At times, it's actually easier to make reductions when the melody and lyrics are already married. When you're able to sing it, you'll notice the awkward little spots where you could drop a word or two and give the singer more time to hang onto a word. It's also easier to feel when an insertion might help to enhance the rhythm of the lyric. Adding a word or two in the right place could help make the song catchier.

There are obviously no hard and fast rules about this, but the general principle is that every word should perform a valuable function for the song. If it does nothing to enhance the rhythm, meaning, or sound of the lyric, it shouldn't be there.

Once you're used to working with these techniques, you'll find that you'll use them very quickly to explore the new possibilities they provide.

WRITING AND REWRITING
"SHE'S IN LOVE WITH THE BOY" BY JON IMS

Jon Ims is a superb craftsman and a wonderful teacher. His song, "She's in Love With the Boy" was the breakout hit single for a Nashville demo singer named Trisha Yearwood. It introduced her to the world and established her career. Breakout singles are the hardest to select. There's a lot of promotion money riding on them and the choice has to be a good one. The industry is littered with the broken bones of careers that, once hopeful, simply died when the first single tanked and the record company decided maybe the artist wasn't as exciting to the public as the company thought. The combination of the song and artist was inspired.

The song was a combination of inspiration and hard work. By his count, Jon rewrote the song about thirty-two times. I called him and asked if he'd contribute his writing and rewriting experiences to this chapter and he graciously agreed. Though there are many, many ways to go about writing successful songs, this is a great lesson, both in terms of a broad process and specific techniques he used to put it together, his understanding of what was needed to make it work, and the determination to continue to rewrite it 'til it was as good as it could be. Was it worth the work? It's now in the Songwriters Hall of Fame.

The song was born from the quirky first phrase "Katie's sittin' on the old front porch watchin' the chickens peck the ground." It just popped out one day while I was fishing around for song ideas. I quickly wrote it down then I sat and stared at it for a good amount of time while I fooled around on the guitar and drum machine looking for something simple and catchy that fit the phrasing.

I found a nice little guitar groove and a punchy drum setting after a while and began to explore some chord changes. Still no further lyric was presenting itself. When I got tired of staring and waiting for divine intervention to inspire me with the next line I decided to use a "clustering" technique. I took the words *Katie*, *front porch*, *chickens*, and *peck the ground*, and put each of them in the center of their own separate blank legal pad page. The idea was to splay out strings of words or phrases from the central word and take any associations that came up without prejudice. One word would lead to another and pretty soon I'd be in "the zone" where I was no longer thinking with the left brain but automatically writing the next thing that popped into my head. Just spilling it all out. I then went from one page to the other writing down whatever happened to show up.

Katie was a character, so my mind flew over every aspect of who she might be, what she might be into, and what images inhabited her world. The "Katie Zone." *Porch* was a location, so I soon found myself jotting down memories from the farm I was born on back in Pennsylvania. Soon the page was filled with smells, sounds, and pictures from my childhood. *Watchin' the chickens peck the ground* brought forth all the things on that farm that lived and moved, including Dad's *beat up Chevy truck*. I was then immersed in memories of the old Ims place on Town Line Road. In addition, *peck the ground* was a little more complex because it implied an attitude: boredom. And it recalled for me colloquial phrases that I'd grown up with. I made a long list of those, including *short end of the stick* and *he ain't worth a lick*. My writing tablet was now filled with pages of jottings held together by a very loose but common thread.

While all this was going on, pictures were forming in my head. I began to see a young female character with likes, dislikes, and motivations along with a number of vivid small town locations. And I knew she was bored. What would perk her up? Was she waiting for someone? My imagination was kicking into gear. I was getting somewhere without even having written the second line to the song.

Before long, I was developing a story and writing lines using the technique of opposites. What's the opposite of boredom? Action. Who might be the opposite of Katie? Tommy. Okay, let me introduce Tommy in an opposite of boredom, like "layin' on the horn splashin' through the mud and the muck." That'll work. My dad used to say *muck* a lot. What a word. You can almost sink your hands into it.

Next came the dilemma of plot. If this was going to be a story, which is what it felt like it was becoming, it was time to take these characters somewhere—have something happen. The plot, like all good stories, had to create tension. There had to be a conflict. Conflict is created by opposites. Can you tell my mother was an English teacher? What's the opposite of Katie and Tommy? Who could be opposed to them? Dad. So I decided to take them on a date and have her dad be less than enthusiastic about it.

At this point I realized that the form of the song had to be established before I could go any further and it was time to make a "song map." I decided that the story within the song would take place in the verses, the plot would be made evident in the lift sections, and the resolution to the plot would take place in the chorus. The music, although remaining simple, would also have to differ slightly from section to section. For example, I chose one minor chord to be placed in the verses and another to fit the chorus. Little things. The song's melodic peak would also occur at the title line. That is, assuming I would find a title.

I also decided at this point that the characters would be most effectively brought to life if I quoted them and that the narrator would let us in on what Katie's feelings were.

Soon the story was developing and moving through time, the plot was thickening, and each section had a cool little guitar riff to accompany it. The lyric, although not perfect, was shaping up and I knew that there would be time later to edit through it all and spruce up the action verbs, cut out the words that were clunking up the flow, check the rhyme schemes, make sure the melody was falling on the right words, etc.

That's when I got stuck.

I didn't have a clue as to how to resolve the plot in a way that was interesting. I liked the characters, there was definitely a clash between Katie and Tommy and Dad. But where should I go with it? Everything I could think of was a cliché—the same old same old. I was determined not to go there. This song had a great energy and I didn't want to sacrifice it to the god of mediocrity. I decided to sleep on it. Literally. I had been working all day and was fried. Just before I turned in, I stood up and looked at all those pages lying there and decided it needed more focus. What was the point of this story? What was the bottom line? It was simple. Katie was in love with Tommy. So I wrote *She's in Love With the Boy* in thick black magic marker on a piece of paper and stood it up on end like a tent in the middle of it all. I had titled my table. Then I went to bed.

At some point during my Alpha state early the next morning, I was lying in bed hearing the guitar chords and floating through a random stream of old memories when I suddenly hit upon a memory that shot me right out of bed and back to the writing table.

When I was nineteen and in college, I dated a cute blond high school senior named Lynn whose dad didn't approve of me because I was older (by two years), had long hair, and was in a rock band. Each time I'd pick her up to go out I was reminded sternly that she had a curfew and that I might look more presentable if I got my hair cut. As it happened, one night the band was playing at a huge party in a barn out in the middle of nowhere. The place was going crazy. The host kept asking for one more song, one thing led to another, and before I knew it we were about an hour late getting back. Big mistake. When we finally arrived, her dad sat me down and started reading me the riot act. I was getting an earful when suddenly slipping down the stairs in curlers and a housecoat was Lynn's mother. She began to defend me and in the course of doing so mentioned that when she and he were dating years before that her father didn't approve of him either. And that the present situation was a mirror of that experience. And could he lighten up a little and see some of himself in me. That statement took the steam out of him and led to us reconcile our differences over coffee in the kitchen.

And here I was years later realizing that was what the song was about. I had been writing it unconsciously up to this point but now the songs' pivotal moment was rushing out of this old memory. Time to get back to work.

There was a lot to cover in the last verse. First, I had to get rid of the pacing technique I had employed in the earlier verses where a line was followed by a support line that further explained the previous one (as songwriter Harlan Howard said, "Tell 'em, then tell 'em that ya told 'em"). Now, each line had to further the point. The song was picking up momentum.

I carefully crafted the last verse section using quotes in the exchanges between characters along with more of the colloquial phrases I had clustered the day before. The lift was now given to the mother and had the responsibility of turning the tables on Dad to complete the plot twist. When the final chorus kicked in it would now apply to both Katie and Tommy and Mom and Dad. The moral of the story: "Let he who hasn't sinned cast the first stone," would be shown rather than told ("show, don't tell"). I wrote and rewrote this last section for hours to find the right order of lyric unfoldment, and the right amount of syllables and stresses so it would sing well. It had to rock and make sense at the same time. Have I mentioned that I love rewriting? I also take it for granted. Nobody is a genius all at once.

After putting the song through the performance test at various gigs, I realized that I needed a grand statement at the end to encapsulate the whole story. That's when I again recalled Harlan Howard's words and decided to "tell 'em" again. This took about a weeks' worth of cocktail napkins with scribbled phrases unloaded from jeans pockets the morning after until I finally settled on "What's meant to be will always find a way."

And that statement is as true for the sentiment of the song as it is as for the song itself because it has certainly found its way and changed the lives of both Trisha Yearwood and myself in many ways. And all because of a little phrase that jumped out of my head about chickens pecking the ground.

Go figure.

She's in Love With the Boy (Jon Ims)

Vs.   Katie's sitting on the old front porch
                Watchin' the chickens peck the ground
                There ain't a whole lot goin' on tonight
                In this one-horse town.
                Over yonder, comin' up the road
                In a beat-up Chevy truck
                Her boyfriend Tommy, is layin' on the horn
                Splashin' through the mud and the muck

Pre-cho. Her daddy says, "He ain't worth a lick
                When it comes to brains, he got the short end of the stick"
                But Katie's young and man she just don't care
                She'd follow Tommy anywhere

Cho.   SHE'S IN LOVE WITH THE BOY
                SHE'S IN LOVE WITH THE BOY
                SHE'S IN LOVE WITH THE BOY
                AND EVEN IF THEY HAVE TO RUN AWAY
                SHE'S GONNA MARRY THAT BOY SOMEDAY

Vs.   Katie and Tommy at the drive-in movie
                Parked in the very last row
                They're too busy holdin' on to one another
                To even care about the show
                Later on outside the Tastee Freeze,
                Tommy slips somethin' on her hand
                He says, "My high school ring will have to do
                'Til I can buy a wedding band."

Pre-cho. Her daddy says, "He ain't worth a lick
                When it came to brains, he got the short end of the stick."
                But Katie's young and man she just don't care
                She'd follow Tommy anywhere

Cho.   SHE'S IN LOVE WITH THE BOY
                SHE'S IN LOVE WITH THE BOY
                SHE'S IN LOVE WITH THE BOY
                AND EVEN IF THEY HAVE TO RUN AWAY
                SHE'S GONNA MARRY THAT BOY SOMEDAY

Vs.   Her daddy's waitin' up till half past twelve
                 When they come sneaking up the walk
                 He says, "Young lady, get on up to your room
                 While me and junior have a talk."
                 But Mama breaks in and says, "Don't lose your temper
                 It wasn't very long ago

When you yourself was just a hay-seed plowboy
Who didn't have a row to hoe.

Pre-Cho. "My daddy said you wasn't worth a lick
When it came to brains, you got the short end of the stick
But he was wrong and honey you are too
Katie looks at Tommy like I still look at you."

Cho. SHE'S IN LOVE WITH THE BOY
SHE'S IN LOVE WITH THE BOY
SHE'S IN LOVE WITH THE BOY
WHAT'S MEANT TO BE WILL ALWAYS FIND A WAY
SHE'S IN LOVE WITH THE BOY
SHE'S IN LOVE WITH THE BOY

What's meant to be will always find a way
She's gonna marry that boy someday.

I'd like to point out a few things that make Jon's song work so beautifully.

Structure: ABC ABC ABC (verse/pre-chorus/chorus verse/pre-chorus/chorus verse/pre-chorus/chorus). He extends the chorus at the end, reiterating his "What's meant to be . . ." philosophy. He doesn't need a bridge because there's enough melodic contrast with the three sections. The song, though it's well fleshed out and clocks in at close to four minutes, has plenty of sectional contrast and doesn't seem too long, because the story holds our interest. He changed the lyric in the last pre-chorus and found a brilliant way to highlight a pivotal story change while still using nearly all the content of the previous pre-chorus' first two lines.

Chorus: Lots of hook repetition. No way to forget the title. If you remember the melody you'll recall that instead of filling the space between the hook repetitions with lyric, he used a one-bar guitar riff to fill it in and it becomes part of the song. Also note that the last line of the pre-chorus in each case changes phrasing and melody enough to telegraph that the chorus has arrived. In a story song with this much lyric it's a good idea to get as spare as you can in the chorus. Keep it simple!

The dialogue is utterly believable and brings these characters to life. The line "When it comes to brains . . ." is one that every country fan is probably familiar with. And I love the way Katie's father refers to Tommy as "junior." It's just the right tone of intimidation and depersonalization and sets up a great contrast when the mother starts to take *him* to task. And she does it in a way that only a wife who's been through these battles many times has learned to do. She's the ultimate diplomat when she says "Katie looks at Tommy like I still look at you" directly after she tells him he's wrong. A brilliant piece of dialogue that rings so true. The line "Katie looks at . . ." is also a great emotional setup for the "She's in love with the boy" hook.

There's another element here that, in fact, I learned from Jon when we co-taught a seminar in Massachusetts a few years ago. You need to maintain a "consistent level of specificity." Notice that it's not just a front porch, it's an "old" front porch. The fact that it's been there a while is important. It's not only a "beat up" truck. It's a beat up "Chevy" truck. It's not just a movie, but a "drive-in" movie, and they're not just parked, they're in the "very last row." They didn't just come home, they were "sneaking" up the walk and daddy wasn't just waiting up, he was waiting 'til "half past twelve." Consistent specific detail.

This is the kind of writing and rewriting that's worth spending the time on.

A CHECKLIST FOR YOUR SONGS

TAXI (www.taxi.com) is the world's leading independent A&R company. It provides free pre-screening services for hundreds of record companies, producers, music publishers, film and TV music supervisors, managers, and other legitimate industry professionals. In turn, it provides members with a bi-weekly listing of those companies and what they're currently looking for in songs and artists. They also provide critiques for members as part of the screening process.

Since I developed TAXI's first critique sheet (on page 109) and assisted in its ongoing changes, I thought it would be helpful to provide an explanation of the factors that went into it. Whether or not you're a TAXI member, this should be helpful to you in determining what goes behind TAXI screeners' decisions, beyond determining if the song is *appropriate* for the style and artists listed. I hope it will also serve as a guide to the viability of your own songs.

Style

On target for listing: This means that the style is appropriate for what the listing asks for but does not necessarily mean that the *song* is appropriate. For example, the musical style may be on target but the lyric may not be appropriate for the artist's image (see chapter eleven, "Casting: The Right Song for the Right Artist" on page 221).

Hard to classify: Styles are usually attached to current radio formats because the majority of the listings are looking for songs that can introduce the artist to the public via a radio hit. If you are not writing in a style that you hear on the radio, chances are this box will be checked. Oldies radio doesn't count. Even though you can hear it on the radio, no one introduces new artists or expects to get airplay with new songs on an oldies radio format. Having said that, there are times when it's a *good* thing to be unclassifiable if they're looking for Algerian influenced French hip-hop and that's what you do. (Then again, you might say that *is* a classification.)

Not close enough to what listing asked for: Simply not on target stylistically, musically or lyrically for this listing. Note that the TAXI listings at the www.taxi.com Web site are accompanied by a link at the top of each stylistic category that will take you to a list of artists named (as "a la" or "like") within the listings. Clicking on an artist's name will take you to that artist on Amazon.com where you can listen to clips of the artist's songs. Beyond that, it's a good idea to do a search on an Internet browser such as www.google.com for the lyrics to those songs. If your songs don't come close to the style of the artist or the style in general, this box will be checked.

Not "current" sounding: The song sounds stylistically dated. A style that may have been viable at one time but is no longer heard on contemporary radio. If you catch yourself only listening to oldies radio, playing your old albums, or saying any of the following—"They don't write songs today like they used to"; "I loved those songs they played when I was in high school"; "I never listen to the radio. There's nothing good on it anymore"; "I don't relate to any of the new music"—you may be writing in a dated style.

There are writers who tend to get stuck in a time period, usually that period in which they were passionate about the music and memorable events were occurring in their lives and relationships. As they get older and the peaks and valleys of their lives even out somewhat, songs don't "attach" to them as they used to. If they're not pursuing songwriting as a full-out vocation, they tend not to invest much time in analyzing current musical styles and looking for artists and songs they like. They tend to continue to listen only to those songs that had an emotional impact on them, those with nostalgia value. Consequently, they write melodies and in styles that are most accessible to their memories.

TAXI® Song and Demo Feedback

NAME   LISTING #   SONG TITLE

STYLE
- ❏ On target for this listing
- ❏ Hard to classify
- ❏ Not close enough to what listing asked for
- ❏ Not "current" sounding

MELODY
- ❏ Good music in verses
- ❏ Verses could be stronger
- ❏ Good music in choruses
- ❏ Choruses could be stronger
- ❏ Verses/Choruses sound too similar
- ❏ Memorable "hook"
- ❏ Hook not obvious enough

STRUCTURE
- ❏ Intro too long
- ❏ Well-written structure
- ❏ Good sectional contrast
- ❏ Not enough sectional contrast
- ❏ Could use a bridge

LYRIC
- ❏ First line makes me want to hear more
- ❏ Engaging
- ❏ Cohesive
- ❏ Good use of imagery
- ❏ Rhymes well
- ❏ Communicates emotion to listener
- ❏ Lacks focus
- ❏ Unique
- ❏ Too abstract
- ❏ I don't understand it
- ❏ Too predictable
- ❏ Too many cliches
- ❏ Awkward phrasing (see comments below)
- ❏ Vocal deos help to sell song
- ❏ Vocal does not help to sell song

TITLE
- ❏ Good title
- ❏ So-so title
- ❏ Can't determine title by listening
- ❏ Could appear in a more strategic place
- ❏ Doesn't repeat enough
- ❏ Repeats too often

OVERALL COMMENTS:

OVERALL RATING
These numerical scores are an indication of your relative strengths and weaknesses, and do not determine whether or not the song is forwarded

1	2	3	4	5	6	7	8	9	(10=best)	
○	○	○	○	○	○	○	○	○	○	Music
○	○	○	○	○	○	○	○	○	○	Lyrics
○	○	○	○	○	○	○	○	○	○	Marketablility
○	○	○	○	○	○	○	○	○	○	Arrangement
○	○	○	○	○	○	○	○	○	○	Production
○	○	○	○	○	○	○	○	○	○	Engineering

The main reason(s) you were not forwarded for this listing is:

NOTE: The comments and numerical scores on this sheet are meant as helpful, objective information and are not used to determine whether or not a tape should be forwarded. Each listing has unique criteria and submissions are considered with those in mind. This is just one person's opinion, albeit an informed one. There are many informed opinions on any given work. So, pro or con, don't let it change your life! © TAXI 1992, 1996, 2002.

Constructing a Song

Current sounding can also relate to the appropriate style of production, arrangement, or instrumentation.

Title

Good title: A title that is unusual (consequently, easy to remember) and makes us want to hear it. This is important, especially in country songs, because it indicates a fresh concept or angle (see chapter four, "Titles," on page 62).

So-so title: generic, clichéd and uninteresting. Yes, there are many hits with so-so titles and this is certainly not something that will keep you off the charts or keep you from getting forwarded by TAXI. But an unusual and intriguing title, more often than not, indicates that there is a unique point of view and focus of the lyric. Examples of so-so titles are: "I Love You," "Going Home," "Don't Ever Leave." Good titles: "Live Like You Were Dying," "Tequila Makes Her Clothes Fall Off," "Hate It Or Love It," or "Shake It Off."

Can't determine title by listening: By the time a song finishes playing on the radio, the listener should know what to call the radio or record store to request or an online distributor to buy. Those factors are of critical importance to whether or not the song continues to get airplay. Continuing airplay will determine how many people hear and buy it. If a listener doesn't recognize the artist and can't figure out what the title is, and if the DJ doesn't announce the title after the song is over, how can the listener request the song?

Could appear in a more strategic place: Those "strategic places" are called *power positions*. They're the places in the song where a listener is most likely to be tuned in. In an AABA form, the power position is in the first or last line of the verse (sometimes both): the first line because it's the first vocal line we hear and we're ready to pay attention, the last because the melody usually develops in such a way that it creates an expectation of a resolution or a change in melody in that last line. It's somewhat the same as a punch line in a joke that has repetitive elements. That line then become a focus of attention and the ideal place for the title. Also in an AABA form, the title is occasionally found in the bridge.

In verse/chorus forms (AABABAB, ABABAB, ABABCB, etc.), the power positions are the first and last lines of the chorus for the same reasons mentioned above. Sometimes a title will work if it's also in the first or last lines of the verse, but it's usually more effective to reserve it for the chorus.

Doesn't repeat enough: The title needs to stick in the listener's mind. You need to have enough repetition of the title for people to remember it. That's one of the advantages of the placement in power positions mentioned above. It ensures that the title is repeated every time you repeat the chorus. If you haven't placed it in one of those positions, it won't get repeated.

Repeats too often: There's nothing intrinsically wrong in repeating the title often in the chorus. In fact, in most cases it's a good thing. Rock and up-tempo pop songs and anthems; R&B and rap use repetition to great advantage. It's more of a problem in country and pop ballads where the lyric plays a more important role in the mix of ingredients. This is an individual judgment call for TAXI screeners who judge styles they're familiar with, and for you as a writer. It has more to do with how much of a continued flow of new information we've come to expect from that particular lyric. For example, if the title repetition (especially in a ballad) takes a long time and repeats the same melody, we, as listeners, get too anxious for it to move along.

Melody

Good music in verses: The melody supports the lyric. Typically, verse melodies in pop or AC ballads need to be at least as memorable as the lyric, since there's more focus on the melody. In rock, and R&B/hip-hop, elements other than melody, such as sounds (created by arrangement, production, or sound design), may be sufficient to provide a good balance between melody and lyric. Where lyric is a more important ingredient, as in country, verse melody tends to be a less important factor, unless it's on the pop side of country.

Verses could be stronger: See above.

Good music in chorus: The chorus is a crucial element in all commercial music styles since it's the section that contains the title and is the part listeners learn first and remember longest. Its melody needs to be easily remembered and not too complex. It also needs to offer a clear contrast to the verse melody, since it needs to let the listener know that it's the chorus. Ideally, the phrasing is different enough that you shouldn't be able to sing the verse lyric to the chorus melody.

Chorus could be stronger: See above.

Verses/chorus sound too similar: Though there have been successful songs with the same or similar melodies in both verse and chorus ("Achy Breaky Heart," "Born in the U.S.A."), it's a long shot. Most often this is a result of writing a lyric first and deciding later which verse should be the chorus. If your goal is to write a hit, construct a chorus melody that's as different as possible from the verse in its phrasing and energy. Lack of contrast is one of the most common shortcomings TAXI screeners note in the songs they critique. Analyze the top songs in your favorite genre, particularly those not written by the artist, and note the techniques they use to differentiate verse and chorus. Exceptions: songs written to be played at dance clubs rather than on mainstream radio and some urban styles mixed for club play.

Memorable hook: In this context, it means that there is a part that helps to identify the song by its uniqueness and repetition. This can involve title placement and repetition, memorable repeated instrumental riffs/figures, or anything a listener will remember after the song is over—a repeated line that grabs a listener's attention (see "Hooks" on page 92).

Hook is not obvious enough: See above.

Structure

Intro too long: Intros should stay short in song demos, usually no more than four bars. In artist demos you have a little more leeway but, generally speaking, keep them short in ballads. With an up-tempo track in any style, you can make it longer since the beat immediately involves the listener's body and takes the focus off waiting for the lyric to start. The longer the intro, though, the more interesting it needs to be to hold a listener's attention, so kill that urge to play your two-chord acoustic guitar intro for eight bars. Intros in master recordings average about fifteen seconds.

Well-written structure: The song's structure helps to maintain a good balance between predictability and surprise. (See page 82 for in-depth information on song structure.)

Good sectional contrast: You have a good handle on creating effective contrasts between the sections of your song.

Not enough sectional contrast: Sectional contrast means that the chorus's melody, lyric meter, phrasing, groove or chord changes contrast with that of the verses. The same is true of the pre-chorus and bridge if the song contains them. If you can sing your verse lyric to your chorus melody, chances are you don't have enough lyric meter contrast between verse and chorus (see "Song Dynamics" on page 96).

This is important because the ear goes directly to the place where something changes. Our nervous system is wired that way from prehistoric times. It kept us humanoids alive by making us hear that lion's growl (in contrast to the prairie wind) in time to get away. So in order to hold a listener's interest, a song must continually offer contrasts. This is a crucial strategy for songs geared to radio airplay. Unlike songs for musical theater and dance music for club play, which are used in situations where there is a captive audience, radio music is heard mostly in circumstances where the listener is doing something else (driving, working, etc.). Consequently, radio songs need to have a level of dynamics (changes) that can grab a listener's attention and hold it. I'm not talking about New Age instrumental music that is *intended* to create a mellow ambience, or album-oriented music by your favorite singer/songwriter or band that you listen to on your headset and focus on every word. Chances are you bought that CD because you already like that artist and are ready to accept everything he writes. Because of that, those artists have more creative leeway and aren't depending on a hit single to break through to public awareness. In most of the TAXI listings for songs (as apposed to artist listings), there is an assumption that you know they need hit radio singles, even though they may feel it's not necessary to mention it in the listings.

Could use a bridge: The bridge provides a change and a release from repetition in a song, refocusing the listener. Not all songs need bridges but this is where we let you know if we think the song needs one. (See "Bridge" on page 84.)

Lyric

First line makes me want to hear more: As the first thing you hear from the singer, that first line is very important. It's at that point that a listener begins to decide, consciously or unconsciously, whether or not it's worth continuing to listen to the lyric. This is particularly crucial in ballads, since both lyric and melody get more focus than in up-tempo songs in which listener attention is at least as captivated by the groove and energy of the tracks. However, regardless of tempo or style, the first line is a powerful tool for capturing a listener's attention. (See chapter four, "First Lines," page 64.)

Engaging: Once a lyric is started, does it continue to hold a listener's attention? Does each line build on the one before it and create anticipation for what's going to happen next? The lyrics needs to be balanced with other elements of the song (melody, groove style, performance). There are great lyrics that aren't necessarily engaging but succeed because of the balance of other ingredients.

Cohesive: Is the lyric linear? Does everything hang together, or does it seem like one section or line has nothing to do with the ones that precede or follow it? If the phrases are abstract, do they come together to offer a common thought?

Good use of imagery: Visual imagery is a valuable tool because humans are neurologically wired to remember what we can see or visually imagine much longer than we remember abstractions. Your own way of visually describing something can also show your uniqueness as a writer. It's a valuable tool to use whenever possible, though certainly not a necessity for success in all musical genres (see chapter three, "The Imagination of The Listener" on page 52).

Rhymes well: Rhyme is a powerful memory trigger. Since you want to teach the listener your song as soon as possible, it's risky to ignore this important tool. Be careful of over-rhyming unless you're writing rap or a fun novelty song. Be careful of short rhyming couplets (pairs of rhymed lines: aabb) as they can get a bit too singsong and tend to trap you into writing for the rhyme rather than the content. Better to use abab or abcb schemes, but you'll have to feel it yourself. There are no real rules about that. Try to use a different rhyme scheme in the chorus than in the verse for contrast.

Communicates emotion to the listener: Any emotion will do. We like to be moved whether you can make us cry, laugh, or feel like dancing. Though we like a lyric that generates emotion on its own, let's face it: A very emotional performance of an otherwise boring lyric can make it work. The only problem is that it might get the singer a record deal before the song ever gets picked up—so focus on an emotional lyric.

Lacks focus: There are too many different lyrical elements that seem unrelated to each other. Tell one story or focus on one emotion.

Unique: There are many songs about the same topics and emotions. The challenge is to incorporate unique language and details that make them different than anything else a screener has heard. There are times when we wonder if that's still possible, given all the songs we've heard. But invariably, someone comes up with something that blows us away with its sheer originality and ability to move us. That's what we're looking for.

Too abstract: This usually means that we feel the lyric is too vague or general to be interesting. There are "poetic" lyrics that, though they may not be visual or conversational, still get their point across with style and uniqueness. The "too abstract" box indicates an absence of visual imagery or interesting detail.

I don't understand it: We check this box when we don't have a clue what the song is about. You may know what *you* mean to say but you haven't gotten it across to *us*. It may be that there's a lack of continuity between lines or sections—non-sequiturs. We shouldn't have to ask, "How did you get from here to there?" It may be poor use of grammar or syntax that's confusing. It's always a good test to read the lyric to a friend and ask her to tell you what it's about. If she can't do it, you need a rewrite.

Too predictable: When this box is checked it usually means that you haven't come up with a unique angle on the lyric or story. We've heard it all before in pretty much the same way. This is a frequent criticism, particularly for new writers who aren't familiar with the lyrical history of the genre they're pitching to. There's a tendency to unconsciously "borrow" lyric phrases from the songs you know. There's an old blues line: "She walks like she's walkin' on soft boiled eggs." It says a lot more than "I love the way she walks." And if you're thinking your next line is "I love the way she talks," don't go there!

Too many clichés: This is also about not being original (see chapter four, "Clichés" on page 79).

Awkward phrasing: Among the culprits here are: accents on the wrong syl-**la**-bles or words, "crunched" lyrics (too many syllables for the musical time-frame), unnaturally stretched words or syllables that just feel awkward and seem to distract attention from the meaning of the line.

Vocal does help to sell song: The vocal is adequate to do justice to the song. If in many other respects the song needs work, it probably means that you don't need to spend money on a great demo singer yet.

Vocal does not help to sell song: This is self-explanatory. Though screeners are usually pretty liberal about the quality of the vocals, this box is usually checked if the singer's pitch is a serious problem, or lyrics are difficult to understand because of poor articulation. It's particularly frustrating to hear a great melody and lyric so slurred by the singer that none of it comes across and without a lyric sheet in front of us we'd have no idea what she's singing. It may also be that the singer is the wrong choice for the style—like an angelic, folkie voice trying to tackle a tough-sounding rock lyric.

The numerical ratings: These are sometimes confusing to members. You may receive very high ratings on your song though it still may not be appropriate for the style requested in the listing or it may not be the right lyric for a specific artist. You may also receive lower ratings on some categories and still get forwarded depending on what the listing requires. For example, the arrangements and production value could be excellent and the lyric rating much lower, but it may work great for a specific film, TV, or other listing in which the lyric isn't so important.

6 Writing Music
(by Cat Cohen)

Melody

Writing melodies for commercial songs is an art unto itself. Though there may be some similarity to classical composition, the priorities of pop melody writing are very different. Both traditions carve melodies out of a combination of stepwise scale movement, small leaps, and large leaps; both traditions may use repetitive motives or hooks that help and audience to follow and remember the melody; and both types of melodies tend to resolve from unsettled, dissonant notes to more settled consonant notes. However, the basis of most classical writing is building and varying melodic ideas in depth over an extended period of time, while in pop writing, short melodic ideas are usually repeated and contrasted without much development, and climax in a main chorus or hook section in a much shorter period of time. Also, pop melodies are designed to be sung by the human voice with lyrics, not just played instrumentally.

The starting point of any melody is its *initial idea* or phrase. In 4/4 time, this can be anywhere from a half-measure (two beats) to two measures (eight beats) long. Occasionally, one may find a melodic idea that is four measures long in a slow romantic ballad, but usually this is a feature reserved for art song and classical writing. Short melodic ideas are easier for most people to remember.

Try tapping out one of the short melodic ideas running around in your head. Most songwriters seem to be blessed (or cursed) with these little bursts of inspiration. This is a great place to start, since what often has hooked your unconscious mind will have a tendency to hook others. The challenge of pop melody writing is expanding these ideas into song sections and then into complete songs. You can learn how to do this by using the techniques of *repetition, variation, contrast,* and *development*.

Take a look at a couple of melodic ideas and see how they can be expanded into songs. Here are two examples:

The first example is long, unfocused, and unworkable, while the second one is short and memorable, easy to develop into the kind of catchy, hooky phrases that sell a song. The basic reason that the first melody is unmemorable is a complete lack of repetition in the phrase, either notewise or rhythmically. See how the second melody takes the first three notes of the first measure and repeats them.

Now, take the second idea and see how it can be stretched out into eight effective measures. Start with a one-bar phrase and simply duplicate it.

If it's duplicated four times, though, it might get a little too simpleminded.

Some people confuse being commercial with being mindlessly repetitive. Yes, you need enough repetition to get immediate recognition and familiarity, but Top 40 stations play the same songs over and over, and a song must have enough variety to withstand repeated listening. A better way to expand melodic fragments is to alternate between two melodic ideas.

Actually, the technique of alternating between melodic ideas is nothing new. It was derived from religious services where the priest, preacher, or cantor alternated singing with the choir or congregation. Contemporary gospel music is a great example of this "call and response." The same structure is also found in blues. Up-tempo music—from folk and square dancing to the "Hokey Pokey" to contemporary dance records—has always been based on this foundation, alternating between right and left, front and back steps.

Two ways of using this alternating technique are variation (with repetition) and contrast (with repetition). In variation, the second or "response" phrase is only slightly different from the "call" or original melodic idea. But this difference, no matter how slight, keeps the melody from becoming too predictable.

In contrast, a completely different melody is paired with the original, and the close alternation of the two ideas serves to link them quickly in the listener's mind.

Many pop recordings, especially dance records, are structured almost exclusively this way. Listen to "We Are Family" by Sister Sledge, one of the classic dance recordings of the late seventies, and see how it is composed of variation with repetition (aa'aa').

A more recent example in the opening melody in the verse of Green Day's "Boulevard of Broken Dreams" uses contrast and repetition (abab).

Some pop styles use more complex phrasing than simple alternation. From Burt Bacharach to Michael McDonald to Barry Gibb to Luther Vandross, there is a whole range of more sophisticated approaches to commercial writing. Most of these writers have had some classical background, the kind of instruction that encourages the writer to develop and insert new material. It takes a great deal more craft to develop more melodic ideas, somewhat like juggling with three or four balls instead of just two. It is easy to fall into the trap of taking a melody too far away without enough repetition to keep the listener involved. Inexperienced songwriters have a tendency to lose their audience by trying to say too much—through melody or through lyric—in one song.

A song that gets away with this kind of development is Natalie Imbruglia's "Torn" (written by Phil Thornalley/Scott Cutter/Anne Preven). Another songwriter who writes complicated but memorable melodies is Keith Urban, as in his song "Better Life."

Once you get a handle on duplicating, alternating, contrasting and developing melodic ideas, you can combine them to craft more distinctive song sections that still will be within the commercial ballpark. A song that combines these techniques is Tina Turner's "What's Love Got To Do With It?" (Terry Britten/Graham Lyle). A more recent example is Kelly Clarkson's "Since U Been Gone" (Max Martin/Dr. Luke). There is quite a bit of repetition but not in a predictable way.

Completing Songs

Once you are able to write an effective eight-bar song section, the biggest challenge is then expanding it into a completed song. This is where most songwriters seem to get stuck.

One of the best ways of writing an interesting, complete song is by using *contrasting sections*. Why do you need more than one song section in the first place? With few exceptions (remember "I'm Henry the Eighth, I Am" by Herman's Hermits?), the record-buying public does not respond to simple one-section songs. To keep a listener involved for a full three minutes or more, you must depart from the main melodic material. Coming up with the amount of contrast appropriate to the song is perhaps the most difficult and crucial aspect of effective melody writing.

Here's a good analogy to help you understand how contrast functions: Compare a second song section to a vacation. If you stay at home all the time, life can get a little dull. A trip to another place or environment brings both relief from monotony and the pleasure of returning home. A trip without much contrast (a dash to the supermarket and back) gives neither the enjoyment of leaving nor returning. Similarly, a song with melodic departure and return keeps us involved and interested. A lack of change, and we tune out.

Here are some ideas to help you get more contrast in your song sections:

Change the level of your melodic line. Make the more important section (the hook section) higher in pitch, or use different time values (for instance, change to mostly sixteenth notes instead of eighths and quarters, use long half-notes instead of eighths).

Change the phrase length. If your verse consists of long phrases (two bars or longer), write shorter ones. Or vice versa. Nothing is more boring than a cookie-cutter four-line verse and a similar four-line chorus, all with the same pat phrase along the lines of

> *I think that I shall never see*
>
> *A thing as lovely as a tree*
>
> *La, dee, dah, dee, dah, dee, dah dee*
>
> *La, dee, dah, dee, dah, dee, dah dee . . .*

Change the rhythmic pattern. If the verse has straight-ahead rhythm, make the chorus more syncopated. Or try the opposite. (See chapter five, "Song Dynamics" on page TK).

Define your sections with an appropriate transition. The use of musical "punctuation" is very important to give the listener a clear sense of where the song is. You can accomplish this with a break, stop, build, or musical turnaround. If you try to jump unexpectedly into a hook or second verse, the effect may be arty, but you'll tend to lose your listener. Exceptions to this are album cuts from established artists whose fans look to them for new musical challenges. Top 40 formats don't have the time to let radio audiences figure out what seems puzzling in a song. Unless you are purposely going for an unusual song style, it's better to lead your audience carefully from one song section to the next.

Other considerations important in melody writing are *range* and *scale context*.

Range

Every singer has a vocal range within which he or she can sing consistently and with professional control. Here is a guideline for ranges of different song styles and for different vocal abilities.

Modest: Less than an octave. This is for the less skilled singer, talk singer, or sing-along style performer. Country music and simple rock styles often feature performers whose personality far exceeds their ability to sing. Material written for them should never push them beyond their limited range.

Average: Octave and a third or fourth. Reaching two or three notes above an octave is the typical range for most pop singers and styles. There is room for a few dramatic leaps or high notes, but nothing too demanding for the average performer.

Wide: An octave and a fifth and beyond. This is for divas like Celine Dion or Mariah Carey, or virtuoso singers like Lou Gramm or John Barry. Sometimes groups like Boyz II Men or the Backstreet Boys can handle a song encompassing a wide range.

Scale Context

Another important consideration is scale context. Without getting into an involved theoretical discussion, note that besides the key a song is written in (C major, G minor), the actual scale tones that are used in the melody have a great deal to do with the song's style. Here are a few examples of scale contexts:

MAJOR 7-TONE

"I Will Always Love You"

Written by Dolly Parton; recorded by Whitney Houston, Dolly Parton

"Your Body Is a Wonderland"

Written and recorded by John Mayer

MAJOR 6-TONE

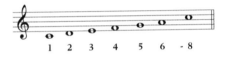

"I Don't Want To Miss A Thing"

Written by Diane Warren; recorded by Aerosmith, Mark Chesnutt

"Complicated"

Written by Lauren Christy, Scott Spock, Avril Lavigne, and Graham Edwards; recorded by Avril Lavigne

"We Belong Together"

Written by Mariah Carey, Jermaine Dupri, Manuel Seal, Johnta Austin, Darnell Bristol, Kenneth Edmonds, Sidney Johnson, Patrick Moten, Bobby Womack, and Sandra Sully; recorded by Mariah Carey

MAJOR 5-TONE (PENTATONIC)

"My Girl"

Written by William "Smokey" Robinson and Ronald White; recorded by The Temptations

"Mississippi Girl"

Written by John Rich and Adam Shoenfeld; recorded by Faith Hill

MINOR 7-TONE (NATURAL)

1   2   ♭3   4   5   ♭6 ♭7   8

"Livin' La Vida Loca"

Written by Desmond Child and Robi Rosa; recorded by Ricky Martin

"Bring Me to Life"

Written by David Hodges, Amy Lee, and Ben Moody; recorded by Evanescence

MINOR 6-TONE

1   2   ♭3   4   5 - ♭7   8

"Billie Jean"

Written and recorded by Michael Jackson

"Bad Girls"

Written by Eddie Swanson Hokenson, Bruce Sudano, Joe Espisito, and Donna Summer; recorded by Donna Summer

MINOR 5-TONE

1 - ♭3   4   5 - ♭7   8

"Witchy Woman"

Written by Don Henley and Glenn Frey; recorded by The Eagles

"Boulevard of Broken Dreams"

Written by Billie Joe Armstrong, Michael Pritchard, and Frank Edwin Wright III; recorded by Green Day

RAGTIME

1   2   ♭3 ♮3 - 5   6 - 8

"Take Me to the Pilot"
Written by Elton John and Bernie Taupin; recorded by Elton John

"The Weight"
Written by Robbie Robertson; recorded by The Band

"Redneck Woman"
Written by John Rich and Gretchen Wilson; recorded by Gretchen Wilson

BLUES

1 - ♭3 4 ♭5 5 ♭7 - 8

"The Sunshine of Your Love"
Written by Peter Brown, Jack Bruce, and Eric Clapton; recorded by Cream

"Fever"
Written by John Davenport (Otis Blackwell) and Eddie Cooley; recorded by Peggy Lee, Little Willie John

MIXOLYDIAN MODE

1 2 3 4 5 6 ♭7 8

"Norwegian Wood (This Bird Has Flown)"
Written by John Lennon and Paul McCartney; recorded by The Beatles

"You Learn"
Written by Alanis Morissette and Glen Ballad; recorded by Alanis Morissette

DORIAN MODE

1 2 ♭3 4 5 6 ♭7 8

"Eleanor Rigby"
Written by John Lennon and Paul McCartney; recorded by The Beatles

"Parsley, Sage, Rosemary and Thyme"
Traditional; arranged and recorded by Simon and Garfunkel

To summarize, pop melody writing is a specialized craft of balancing repetition and contrast. You can do this by duplicating, alternating, and developing melodic ideas. You then craft your ideas into contrasting sections. Writing within a suitable range and scale context helps cater a song to its potential audience. Knowledge of these aspects enables you to write for specific styles and artists, which is what professional songwriting is all about.

Harmony

Knowledge of harmony is very important to a professional songwriter. A completed song includes not only lyric and melody, but a chordal accompaniment as well. Harmony is uniting pleasing musical sounds. The chordal sounds used to accompany and arrange our songs bring out their colors, their emotions. Think of a plain melody and lyric as a black-and-white sketch, a song with harmonization as a full-color painting. Very often, the imaginativeness of its harmonic setting is what gives a song its distinctive appeal.

INTERVALS

In order to understand how chords are constructed, they should be broken down into *intervals*. The basic unit of measuring intervals in Western music is the half-step. You can find a half-step easily on the piano by simply going up or down the keyboard to the next note whether a black key or white key (C-C#-D-D#-E-F-F# etc.). All intervals are measured multiples of half-steps, thus indicating the specific distances between musical pitches.

Here are the intervals inside the major scale, called *diatonic intervals*:

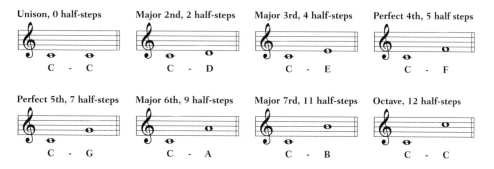

If you examine this chart, you will see that certain intervals have been skipped over. There are gaps in the major scale, tones that are considered to be outside the major scale. These are the minor intervals, colors that are used to form minor and exotic scales and chords.

Here are the intervals outside the major scale—*chromatic intervals*:

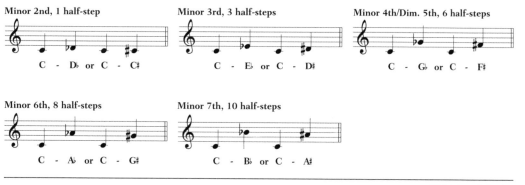

The intervals on the unison, 4th, 5th, and octave are called *perfect* intervals because they rarely change, even when the scales change to minor or modal. The 2nd, 3rd, 6th, and 7th intervals are more coloristic, changing in order to form more interesting scale tone colors.

Three Levels of Chord Construction

When you play three or more pitches simultaneously, you have played an 11 chord, and harmony (or disharmony) is created. You can create a whole variety of chordal colors simply by building chords out of various combinations of intervals. The harmonies you may choose depend on the level of chordal sophistication your song requires. Rock, country, and folk styles use mainly simple *triads* (three-note chords), while jazz-influenced styles are written with more complex chords. Most pop and crossover styles tend to be made up of chords midway between these two extremes.

First Level of Harmony: Triads

The most common triad in pop music is the *major triad*, which has a specific formula of half-steps.

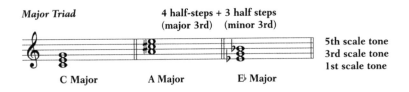

Another triad used in pop music is the *minor triad*, which lowers the middle tone, the 3rd, a half-step.

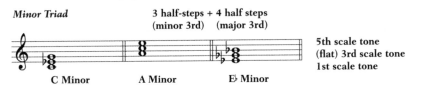

A third type of triad is especially common in rock music, the *suspended triad*, which "suspends" the use of the 3rd and replaces it with a 4th.

Many songs use chord progressions made up of triadic harmony, like Coldplay's "Clocks":

| Eb | Bbm | Bbm | Fm | Eb | Bbm | Bbm | Fm |

122

Another example in a minor key comes from the Eurythmics' "Here Comes the Rain Again":

| verse | | i | | | ♭VI | | | ♭VII | | | i | | | |
| chorus | | ♭VI | | | ♭III | | | IV | | | ♭VII | | | |

Second Level of Harmony: 7ths

For simple styles, triads are all that may be necessary for effective harmonization, but in more middle-of-the spectrum styles such as country-pop, R&B, and MOR, you'll need more sophisticated chords. For most of these styles, adding a 7th tone above the triads may give a fuller, more polished sound and lead the ear to a more interesting resolution.

Dominant 7th   Minor 7th   Major 7th

A dominant 7th chord is a major triad plus a minor 7th, a minor 7th chord is a *minor triad* with a minor 7th added, and a major 7th chord is a *major triad* plus a major 7th.

When harmonizing a melody with 7th chords, it is important to point out that extra 7th tones can give a writer more consonant or resolved spaces for the melody to land or blend in with the chord. However, certain styles of pop melodies are written with 5-tone or 6-tone scales that do not contain the extra 7th chord tones. In blues, one often may even find tones that clash with the harmonies, such as the *flatted 3rd* of blues scale-based melodies against the *major 3rd* of the accompanying 7th chords.

It is common for song passages to be harmonized using suspended triads and 7th chords as illustrated here in a chord progression from Celine Dion's "Because I Loved You" (written by Diane Warren):

| D♭ | G♭ | B♭m7 | A♭sus | Fm7 | G♭maj7 | ....

Alicia Keys's "If I Ain't Got You" (written by Alicia Keys/Kanye West/John Stephens):

| Gmaj7 | Em7 | Am7 | D7 | Gmaj7 |G#dim 7| Am7 | D7

John Legend's "Ordinary People" (written by Will Adams/John Stephens):

| B♭maj7 | E♭maj7 | E♭maj7 | Fmaj7 | B♭maj7 | E♭maj7 | E♭maj7 | Fmaj7

Third Level of Harmony: 9ths, 11ths, and Complex Chords

When you want to write in jazz-influenced harmonies, such as found in R&B-pop, jazz-rock-fusion, Broadway, and pre-1950s pop standards, then even more sophisticated harmonies are called for. These include chords built on 9ths and above, as well as chromatically altered chords (with raised or lowered 5ths, 9ths, 11ths, etc.). This is much too demanding a subject to cover here, but don't be overly concerned. These chords are never used in 90 percent of the music on the charts. They are a specialized sound for a specialized urban audience. If you are interested in studying jazz harmony, there are many excellent books on the subject, such as the John Mehegan *Jazz Pianist* series.

This song passage from Chaka Khan's "Through the Fire" (written by David Foster/Cynthia Weil/Tom Keane) features complex harmonies:

```
                        -13
                        - 9
    | A6 add2 C7 |  Fm7  Ebm7  Ab7  |  Dbmaj7  Cm7  Fm7  |  Bbm7  Eb11  |
```

CREATING CHORD PROGRESSIONS

The true art of harmonization is not just which chords to choose, but also the order in which the chords progress through the song and how they relate to its melodic shape and emotion to determine their effectiveness. To get a better idea of how chords work together, you need to relate them to a scale context. Chords can be built *diatonically* (using only tones inside a scale) or *chromatically* (using tones inside and outside the scale).

Diatonic Chords

Most songs can be harmonized entirely with diatonic chords. Here is how diatonic harmonies are formed inside a C major scale. [1]

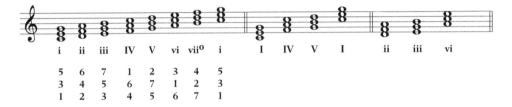

i	ii	iii	IV	V	vi	viiº	i	I	IV	V	I	ii	iii	vi

5	6	7	1	2	3	4	5
3	4	5	6	7	1	2	3
1	2	3	4	5	6	7	1

These diatonic chords fall into two groups, primary chords and secondary chords. The primary chords are the ones most people refer to when describing three-chord rock songs such as "Twist and Shout," country-western classics such as "I Walk the Line," and traditional twelve-bar blues. Secondary chords are minor triads formed within a major scale, and they provide generally darker, more serious shadings of emotion and color. They allow you to give harmonic contrast in a song without having to change keys. Diatonic secondary chords can help achieve a sense of departure for our second song section without having to travel too far

---

[1] Roman numerals are used in analyzing chords to show at a glance which scale tone the chord is built on; whether the chord is major, minor, or altered in some way; whether a 7th or 9th has been added, etc. The numeral corresponds to the scale degree that is the root of the chord. For instance, in the key of C, a iii chord would be an E-minor triad made up of E-G-B. Capital numerals are used for major triads and lowercase numerals for minor triads. For the iii triad in C to be a major chord, the G would have to be raised to a G#. But the IV chord—F-A-C—is a major triad automatically. A iii7 would consist of E-G-B-D. If a chord were built on Eb (an exotic harmony), it would be notated as biii or bIII depending on whether the chord was major or minor. A degree sign (°) is used after the Roman numeral to show a diminished chord—one in which there is less than a perfect fifth between the root and the fifth of the chord. An example in C Major would be the vii°. This triad is made up of B-D-F (while a perfect fifth would be B-F#). The whole system of using Roman numerals can get rather complicated, but this basic knowledge of conventional symbols will suffice for the examples cited here.

---

away harmonically. Diatonic secondary chords are used effectively in song passages like the chorus section of Cher's "Believe":

| I | V | ii | IV | I V | ii | vi |

Toby Keith's "I Love This Bar" (written by Scott Emerick/Toby Keith):

| i | v | iv | i | i | v | iv | i | | vi | v | iv | iv |ii iii|iv v| i | i |

If you get confused as to which primary and secondary chords to use, here are a couple of guidelines:

- **I Chord**: The I or "one" chord is considered to be the "home chord" for any key, and any song section that starts or ends with this chord is rooted and rested at home. A "full harmonic cadence" as this is called in classical music theory ends on a I chord. It functions like a period at the end of a sentence.

- **V Chord**: The V or "five" chord is what I like to call the "home away from home chord" or a place for a pit stop or a brief resolution. It is the ending of a "half cadence" and it functions more like a comma in a sentence—it indicates the end of a phrase, but not the end of the sentence.

- **VI Chord**: The VI or "six" chord is often used as a "deceptive cadence" or false ending (too complicated to go into detail here). Otherwise, all of the remaining chords are "in transit" and do not provide a rest or cadence. Hence, they are rarely used at the end of a song section

If you think of your I and V chords as your basic home chords, and the others as leaving and returning, then you have a basis for creating effective chord progressions.

Minor Diatonic Chords

You can do the same thing to the chords in the minor scale.

| i | ii° | ♭III | iv | v | ♭VI | ♭VII | i | | ii | iv | v | | ♭III | ♭VI | ♭VII |

5	6	7	1	2	3	4	5
3	4	5	6	7	1	2	3
1	2	3	4	5	6	7	1

Many songs make use of minor diatonic harmony as analyzed in the following chord progression from Christina Aguilera's "Genie in a Bottle." This gypsy-like sound is actually a simple four minor diatonic chord loop.

| i ♭VII | ♭VI vm7 |

Chromatic Chords

To get even more contrast and more unusual sounds, you may want to experiment with chords that use tones outside your scale context. Here is a list of chords that are slightly outside, that use only one non-scale tone and do not take you too far out. The Beatles were masters of using one slightly outside chord for temporary shock value in an otherwise straightforward harmonization in their songs.

Major		Minor
II, III, VI, ♭VII, iv		II, ♭II, IV, ii

Song passages using slightly outside harmonies can be found in tunes like Otis Redding's "(Sittin' on) the Dock of the Bay" (written by Otis Redding/Steve Cropper):

| verse | | I | | III | | IV | | II | | I | | III | | IV | | II | |
| chorus | | I | | IV | | I | | VI | | I | | II | | I | | VI | |

Exotic Harmony

For harmonic effects that are even farther out, try using one of these chords. They contain more than one non-scale tone and take a song into strange, unexpected places. However, they have to be used carefully and sparingly or your listener may get confused and lose interest.

| ♭II | ♭III | ♭V | ♭VI | VII | vi |

| ♭V | ♭v | ♭ii | ♭iii |

Chord progressions using these unusual harmonies are not uncommon in songs like Culture Club's "Do You Really Want To Hurt Me?" (written by Roy Hay/Jon Moss/Michael Craig/George O'Dowd):

| | G Bm | Em | G Bm | Em | C G | Am | Bm | B♭ | B♭ | A♭ | A♭ | Gm |
| | | iii | vi | | iii | vi | iv | | ii | iii | ♭II | ♭III | ♭II | ♭II |

VERTICAL OR HORIZONTAL CONSTRUCTION

Now that you've seen how a variety of chords can be used to accompany pop melodies, don't overlook the fact that many pop recordings, especially dance records, do not rely on harmony as an important element. In fact, some contemporary records hardly use chords at all. Instead of the traditional vertical construction of a melody with underlying chords, you will find the horizontal construction of a melody accompanied only with a strong rhythmic background, countermelodic riffs, and bass lines. That's right, no chords, just riffs!

A good example of a song that uses horizontal instead of vertical construction is Ricky Martin's "Livin' La Vida Loca" (written by Desmond Child/Robi Rosa). A more recent one would be Beyoncé's "Naughty Girl" (written by Beyoncé Knowles/Scott Storch/Robert Waller/Angela Beyince).

As you can see in this section, there are many ways to use harmony to make your songs more effective. Think of chords as coloring agents and learn to choose the appropriate simplicity or sophistication of harmonies to match the style of music you're seeking to write. A good way to get a handle on this is to listen to radio stations in your area and see which ones play songs mostly using triads, which ones play 7th chord songs, and which ones play songs using complex 9ths and above. In business, identifying a style of music and targeting the market audience it appeals to is called "demographics." Why don't we coin a phrase and call this "harmonigraphics"? Whatever we call it, you can see that the more you know about chords and how they work together, the more versatility you can achieve in your songwriting.

Groove

Musicians have long referred to groove when describing the basic feel of a song, especially when it feels right. When Duke Ellington wrote "It Don't Mean a Thing (If It Ain't Got That Swing)," or when that infamous dancer on *American Bandstand* said that she thought a particular song was a hit because "It's got a good beat and you can dance to it," they were talking about groove. It is absolutely essential for a songwriter to learn what gives a song the kind of groove or feel that has "hit" written all over it.

RHYTHMIC ELEMENTS

In more technical terms, you can better understand groove by examining its rhythmic elements: pulse, tempo, meter, rhythmic subdivision, syncopation, and texture.

Pulse: A pulse is simply a regular, recurring beat. For instance, a march (*hup*, 2, 3, 4) is based on pulse. In pop music, an obvious example is the bass drum beat (1, 2, 3, 4) of the disco style.

Tempo: The tempo is the speed of the pulse, the number of pulses per minute. You can understand this by comparing any music pulse to your heartbeat. At rest, our hearts beat at 72–80 times a minute. But get us excited (through up-tempo dancing, aerobics, or whatever) and watch our pulse race to 150 times a minute and beyond. Here is a chart showing the relationship of various tempos to pop music function and activity:

Heartbeat = 72 beats per minute: BPM

60 BPM SLOW BALLAD	90 BPM MID-TEMPO	120 BPM UP-TEMPO DANCE	150 BPM HYPER DRIVE
"Yesterday" (The Beatles) "I'll Make Love to You" (Boyz II Men)	"Crazy for You" (Madonna) "No Scrubs" (TLC) "Don't Lie" (The Black Eyed Peas)	"Smooth" (Santana, Rob Thomas) "Independence Day" (Martina McBride)	"Livin' La Vida Loca" (Ricky Martin) "Hey Ya!" (OutKast)

Meter: Meter is the way in which pulses are grouped into measures or bars. Almost all pop music is grouped into 4/4 meter—four pulses (quarter notes) in each measure (or bar). Occasionally, one finds a 3/4 waltz meter with three pulses (quarter notes) in each measure.

Other meters like 2/4, 6/8, 2/2, or more complicated ones like 11/16 or 7/8 exist in classical music and jazz, but are seldom used in pop.

Rhythmic Subdivision: The 4/4 pulse of a pop song is the basis for 95 percent of what we hear on the radio today. What's important is to differentiate the rhythms played on rock stations, country stations, soul stations, and easy listening stations. You may need more technical know-how to learn how rhythmic subdivisions help to define a song's style. A 4/4 measure can be subdivided into any of the following:

March, disco

8th note groove (rock, MOR, new wave)

Santana and Rob Thomas' "Smooth"

Trace Atkins' "Honky Tonk Badonkadonk"

Triplet groove (1950s, blues)

Boyz II Men's "I'll Make Love To You"

Alicia Keys' "Fallin'"

Shuffle groove (1940s, be-bop, country, blues, gospel)

The Beatles' "With a Little Help From My Friends" (written by John Lennon/Paul McCartney)

Gretchen Wilson's "All Jacked Up"

16th groove (funk, R&B, reggae, half-time rock)

Alanis Morissette's "You Learn" (written by Alanis Morissette/Glen Ballad)

Rascal Flatts' "Bless the Broken Road"

Swung 16th groove (Hip-Hop, rap)

1 e + a 2 e + a 3 e + a 4 e + a

Macy Gray's "I Try"

Kanye West's "Gold Digger"

The swung 16th groove is played in a subdivision of six notes to the beat shuffled with the middle 16th of each group of three left out. This is very difficult to read. Consequently, it is usually notated in regular 16ths with an instruction above the first line of music to swing or shuffle the 16ths. It is counted the same way as 16ths but felt with a staggered rhythm, not an even rhythm. There happens to be a nursery rhyme we all know now that is counted in this beat, "One potato, two potato, three potato, four. Five potato, six potato, seven potato more." The phrase "seven potato" fills in the whole triplet of that beat. I often refer to this groove as the potato groove because it can only be done while swinging the 16ths.

Both regular 16ths and swung 16ths are often played on top of a full 8th note feel. This results in two grooves at once, what I call a hybrid groove. Much of the pop music of the 1990s and early 2000s has been played over these hybrid grooves.

8th–16th Hybrid

U2's "Sometimes You Can't Make It On Your Own"

Mariah Carey's "We Belong Together" (written by Mariah Carey/Jermaine Dupri/Manuel Seal/Johnta Austin/Darnell Bristol/Kenneth Edmonds/Sidney Johnson/Patrick Moten/Bobby Womack/Sandra Sully)

8th–Swung 16th Hybrid

Eminem's "Lose Yourself" (written by Jeff Bass/Marshall Mathers/Luis Resto)

Weezer's "Beverly Hills" (written by Rivers Cuomo)

Syncopation: Once you determine the rhythmic subdivision of a groove, the next most important feature that defines style is its syncopation. Syncopation occurs when there are rhythmic accents on the weak inner beats of a groove, *the beats between the pulses.* Dance music is full of syncopated patterns that use one or more of these accents to create rhythmic drive. Syncopated patterns can be found in the rhythm tracks and in the actual melodies of most of today's recorded music.

Examples within each of the four rhythmic subdivisions are listed on the next page:

8th note groove

1 + 2 + + + 1 + 4

Triplet groove

1 + a 2 + a + a 4 a   a 2 + a

Shuffle groove

1 a 2 a a 4 a   a 2 a 4

16th note groove

1 e a 2 e + a e a 4 +   a 2 e + a 4 e

Texture: Once you understand how syncopation creates a danceable groove, you'll want to study the finer points of what makes one dance beat distinctive from another, even if they are made up of the same rhythmic subdivision.

Each groove has its own unique "texture," from sparse to moderate to full. Some rhythm tracks move the beat along with just a few notes while others use many more. Here are examples of sparse and full grooves in 8th-note and 16th-note subdivisions:

Sparse 8th bass line

as in Ricky Martin's "Livin' La Vida Loca" (written by Desmond Child/Robi Rosa)

Full 8th bass line

as in Madonna's "Like a Virgin" (written by Billy Steinberg/Tom Kelly)

Sparse 16th bass line

as in Prince's "Purple Rain"

Full 16th bass line (techno)

as in Blondie's "Heart of Glass"

People in the record industry are looking for songs with the groove already built in. Knowing how to place your song in its best rhythmic setting will give your writing the competitive edge that says "Play me on the radio!"

David "Cat" Cohen enjoys a multi-faceted career as a songwriter, independent producer, keyboard teacher, and author. A songwriter with major credits (Cheryl Lynn, Syreeta, Freddie Hubbard among others), he is a member of ASCAP and NARAS. Cat Cohen is an instructor at UCLA Extension and Musician's Institute in Hollywood. He offers workshops and seminars in songcraft and music theory in the Los Angeles area. He teaches keyboards privately and regularly consults for songwriters. Visit Cat's Web site at www.catcohen.com, where, along with other features, he analyzes hit songs.

---

7 Collaboration

Why Two (Or More) Heads Can Be Better Than One

A substantial percentage of the world's most popular songs are collaborations. Consider the wealth of classic material that's come from teams like Lerner and Loewe; Rodgers and Hammerstein; Kander and Ebb; Bacharach and David; Rodgers and Hart; the Gershwins; Mann and Weil; Holland, Dozier, and Holland; Gamble and Huff; Lennon and McCartney; Goffin and King; Leiber and Stoller; Fleming and Morgan; L.A. Reid and "Babyface" Edmonds; and Jimmy Jam and Terry Lewis, who had long and successful collaborations as well as countless other writers who worked with a variety of co-writers.

In a January 2006 edition of *Billboard* magazine, the Country Chart showed: 52 of 60 songs were co-written, and of the remaining 8, 6 were writer/artists; on the R&B/hip-hop chart, 88 of 100 were co-written, and 7 of those remaining were writer/artists; of the Hot 100, 83 were collaborations, and of the remaining 17, 9 were writer/artists. Today's song market is so competitive that professional writers can't afford to settle for less than the best, so they often elect to team up with other talented writers they enjoy writing with.

Though this chapter is devoted to collaboration, it should be noted here that it isn't *always* the best or the only way to write. Hit writer Randy Goodrum ("You Needed Me," "Bluer Than Blue") has successfully written with and without a collaborator. Here's a quote from an interview I did with Randy:

First of all, I'm not a collaborative writer as a rule. I started off writing for years and years on my own. Most everything that I have ever had that was big was written totally by me until 1987 [Goodrum collaborated with Steve Perry on "Oh Sherrie," "Foolish Heart," and six others on an album]. But there are dangers with collaboration. At least from my experience, it can water down and lose a sense of uniqueness. I was in a seminar one time and somebody said, "Gee, when I heard 'Bluer Than Blue,' I thought, how is he going to rhyme 'closet'?" I said, "feel like it." I rhymed *it*, not *closet*. Well, if I had been co-writing, chances are we would have said, "Let's not use *closet*." We would have thrown it out, yet it's a little bit more unique of a line than other songs that I've co-written. Sometimes the art has to have a little bit of a rough edge in there, in a charismatic sort of sense. There has to be some abandon to it. You just rewrite and rewrite and rewrite and sometimes it's not logical what makes greatness. You know, it's just this little muse that comes along. He doesn't have a business suit on or anything, and it tickles. . . .

So I think with collaboration, it's good to get something that makes you just jump up and down, and if it can be better than what you can do on your own, that's incredible. Or if you can arrive at a place that neither of you can get to by yourselves. . . . I wrote two songs with Michael McDonald for his solo album, and I am proud to say that neither of us has ever written anything like the two songs we came up with. They were totally in another place. So that's a nice way to look at co-writing also.

Though it's not the only way to go, there are several other good reasons why writers collaborate:

• **A writer may have more talent as a lyricist than as a composer, or vice versa.** It's important that you objectively assess your strengths and weaknesses. Obviously, if you're a good lyricist with marginal musical skills, you should look for a composer. Your ego may need to see only your name on the "words and music by" line at the top of the page, or maybe you just want all the royalties yourself. The bottom line, though, is that the song must be as good as it can possibly be, regardless of who did what.

Many talented musicians/arrangers can put the music together but don't feel the lyric is important enough to warrant a collaborator. They risk seriously limiting the artistic and commercial potential of the songs.

• **Writers often tend to get trapped in their own musical and lyrical clichés, and a collaborator can supply fresh ideas.** When you pick up your guitar your fingers automatically go through a familiar and comfortable set of chord changes, picking styles, or rhythm patterns. Out of these established patterns come melodies much like those you've written before. It's easy to get into a creative rut. At that point you need to get a chord book and work out some new chords and progressions, listen to the radio and discover some new grooves, or find a collaborator whose style you like.

Even professional writers aren't always productive and may need the input of other writers. They may write great ballads, but need to team up with someone when it comes to up-tempo songs or another style. In fact, there's always such a demand for up-tempo songs that if you do that well, it should be relatively easy to find co-writers.

• **Writing with someone else disciplines your writing habits.** Many people seem to function better on deadlines and always wait until the last minute, while thinking up all kinds of other projects to avoid the task ("I can't possibly create with a dirty house/broken guitar string/out-of-tune piano"). This avoidance syndrome is a way of signaling and priming the subconscious to start working on the project at hand. At the eleventh hour, when you have to produce, the brain sends a signal to the subconscious that says, "It's time to download all those ideas," and, like magic, they're there.

Many writers will avoid writing altogether if there are no deadlines. Those who function best on that kind of "crisis" basis set up deadlines for themselves. One good way is to find a collaborator and plan on a regular day to get together and write. You know you'll have to come up with some ideas to work on before that deadline, and that subconscious preparation process will operate on an ongoing basis if it knows that every week (or every day) that deadline will arrive.

• **A partner will furnish a constant feedback and critique.** You're stuck for a rhyme and eager to finish the song. You put together the first thing to come into your head and say, "It's okay, I've heard stuff on the radio that rhymes 'rain' with 'again.' Maybe some British guy'll cut it." A conscientious collaborator is there to say, "Wrong! Let's see if we can find something else." Maybe you're a lyricist and your collaborator is a singer and can say, "I'll want to hold this note in the melody, so could we use another word instead of 'garbage'?" This feedback can keep you at your best and help you both grow commercially and artistically. (Though, based on the Goodrum quote on pages 132—133, this could go either way.)

- **The more collaborators on a song, the more people there are networking to get the song recorded.** Let's face it, there's also a political strategy to co-writing. If each writer (and his publisher) has several industry contacts he can play the song for, you'll have that many more opportunities to get the song recorded, and at the same time you'll extend your reputation and your network of writers and industry people.

- **You may be either a better starter or finisher.** When my wife JoAnn, worked for Walt Disney Imagineering, the theme-park think-tank, she created a database for them called the Skills Bank. She interviewed the employees about their skills and preferred work styles. The database helped in creating teams for projects, so an important bit of information was to learn where in the life of a project each employee felt most comfortable and productive. There were those who preferred the front end or conceptual part of the project ("I love to come up with ideas but don't make me have to figure out how to make them work"), while others really enjoyed the challenge of figuring out how to build it and didn't feel comfortable in the concept stage. Still others felt equally at home on both sides, liked the "big picture," and enjoyed seeing the concept through to completion. Those people, as you might imagine, were essential for any team. As JoAnn explained this I kept thinking of how often I'd heard songwriters fell into similar categories: Some were great concept creators, others were great finishers, and still others were equally adept at both. I've met writers with hundreds of titles and ideas but who rarely finish a song. They got bored or couldn't figure out how to finish or were just plain lazy. There are also writers who didn't seem to be as good with concepts but were problem solvers who, when given a concept could see possibilities the originator couldn't see. Those writers need to find each other.

Finding Your Match

Finding the perfect partner can be a difficult process. No matter how you go about it, you' have the same odds of finding the perfect collaborator right away as you' do walking into a singles' bar and finding a marriage partner. The two situations have a lot in common. You're dealing with a whole range of personalities, personal habits, expectations, previous experiences, egos, and lifestyles. With collaborators you can add musical and literary influences, business know-how, and aggressiveness.

But there are a few ways to get started and narrow the odds. Like with a singles bar, you go to a place where other people are looking, too. Put a free ad in a music-oriented periodical like *Music Connection* or the newsletter of your local songwriters organization. Placing an ad in your local newspaper is probably a waste of time because readers don't generally look for co-writers there. A better bet is to make little signs that you can put up on bulletin boards in music and record stores, the Musicians Union, or nightclubs that feature your kind of music. If you're a lyricist, it's also a good idea to put your signs on college music department bulletin boards so composition students can find you. Computer bulletin boards are also a good bet. Search under "song collaboration" or "music collaboration." Since it's possible to collaborate by exchanging audio files on the Internet, distance is no longer much of an obstacle, though it's obviously not as spontaneous as being in the same room.

The ad or message should include the styles with which you're most comfortable, the instruments you play, your favorite lyricists/composers, and your credits, if any. If you're looking for a lyricist and are in a working band, have a production deal, do your own publishing, or have an exclusive publishing deal, mention that too. This tells the lyricists that you have serious prospects for their work.

Another approach is through professional organizations and services. Join Just Plain Folks (www.jpfolks.com), an online community of songwriters, producers, and musicians. It's free to join and you can access their "Lyric Forum" where you can post your lyric for feedback and find co-writers. TAXI's Musicians Junction (www.musiciansjunction.com) is a free service that offers a database of composers, lyricists, and musicians looking to collaborate. If you are in the Nashville area, attend the weekly critique sessions by the Nashville Songwriters Association International (NSAI) or any of the many "writers nights" at local clubs. These are among the best opportunities to screen a writer's work before meeting in person. All workshops, clubs, and showcases offer that opportunity. Joining local or national songwriter organizations or music associations is also a great way to make contacts. (See appendix for lists of songwriters' service Web sites.)

In any of these situations you may hear a singer/songwriter whose music is excellent but whose lyrics are weak, or vice versa. You might diplomatically ask that person if he or she would consider collaboration.

WRITING UP

There's a definite advantage in writing with someone who's out there exposing those songs to the public and the industry. It's also advantageous to your growth to write with those writers you feel are as good as or better than you. This strategy is called "writing up." Having co-written with an established writer provides an entry to other pro-caliber writers and their publishers. One of the best positions to be in as an independent writer is to collaborate with a staff writer at a good publishing company and get a cut of a song you wrote together, particularly if you can keep your own publishing rights.

Try to meet as many people as possible in all areas of the industry. Publishers, though they seldom sign staff lyricists, often like to know of good lyricists that they can hook up with good composers or with other writers on their staff. Producers may be working with bands who could use the services of a strong lyricist. Recording engineers are also good contacts.

Writing With Artists and Producers

A substantial number of successful collaborations today, particularly in pop, R&B, and hip-hop, happen at the source of the project. That encompasses three typical situations: writing with the artist, writing with the producer, or being a writer/producer yourself.

Writing With the Artist

This is a great strategy if you can do it. Assuming you come up with an exceptional song, the artist has a financial interest, as a co-writer, in recording the song. On an artistic level, the process can include talking with the artist about what's going on in his or her life and getting song ideas from the conversation; taking the artist's lyric ideas and helping to structure them and finish them; and initiating your own ideas lyrically or musically.

Jeff Trott, who co-wrote the Sheryl Crow hits "Every Day Is a Winding Road," "If It Makes You Happy" and "My Favorite Mistake," spoke with me in an interview for United Airlines' in-flight entertainment about his collaboration with Crow:

> My relationship with Sheryl is kind of like baseball pitchers: They have a starting pitcher and a closer. I'm really good at instigating ideas but I'm not so good at finishing them. Sheryl's strength is being able to complete an idea. That's very difficult to do. It takes a lot of discipline. That's where our chemistry works. I get the ball rolling and she's the closer.

These collaborations come about from personal relationships with artists, referrals by publishers, producers, managers, and other industry pros as well as other artists.

Writing With Producers

The producer usually has a concept for the artist's sound and the type of material he wants to record. So the producer may look for co-writers who have experience writing a specific type of song. Also if you're a writer/artist, teaming up with a writer/producer is a good strategy. Madonna's successive (and successful) collaborations with writer/producers Stephen Bray, Shep Pettibone, and Patrick Leonard are good examples.

Writing Tracks First

In pop, hip-hop, and contemporary dance styles, it's common for collaborators to start the process by producing *tracks* (basic recordings of primary rhythm instruments, usually on a digital sequencer and occasionally with real instruments) because in those musical styles, grooves are an extremely important factor in their appeal. Note that grooves or *beats* are trendy and innovative sounds are very important. So if you want to write with a track writer, find one who's totally involved in current styles and has the tools to create new sounds. Track writers are usually producers/engineers/mixers. It's all part of the art form.

There are several options for songwriters starting with tracks:

1. The creators of the tracks will look for a singer/songwriter in their specific genre to create the lyric, melody, and performance.

2. They will write the lyric or melody themselves or use someone else on their writing staff.

3. They'll find a lyricist, then give the lyric to a singer to create a melody.

As in any other approach to writing, there are pros and cons. Let's start with the pros:

• The writer of the melody and lyric has a structural roadmap and tempo already laid out for him. When a bass part is included in the track, there is also a tonal structure to assist in creating a melody. (The key can easily be changed in the digital realm.)

• Tracks can make it much easier for a lyricist to create lyric phrases that become totally integrated into the rhythm of the song. You can think of it as a more elaborate version of the process of writing to a beatbox or drum loops.

• Frequently, the tracks are created by a producer, which, from a business viewpoint, means that as a lyric or melody writer, you're already involved in the final production rather than having written a song that you'll have to pitch to another producer.

If you're a writer/producer with a great groove sense, an ear for street trends, and you're an adventurous creator of new sounds, you should be creating tracks.

Now for the cons:

- Some less experienced track producers ignore the structural and dynamic options that make a song commercially viable and rely on a singer to create a vocal performance and a melody and lyric powerful enough to make up for it. A track based on a loop that doesn't change throughout the song can get predictable and monotonous. It may work fine in a dance club environment but will be less successful on mainstream radio. Note that the most successful hip-hop and rap records are those with memorable, contrasting verses, pre-choruses, choruses, and bridges, even if they've sampled them from other songs. This puts a big responsibility on the writer/lyricist to create those dynamic contrasts if they haven't already been created by the track writer. If you're going to have to come up with lyric, melody, and structure on your own, you may as well just write the song and pay a producer to arrange and produce it.

Having said that, there are more examples on the radio today of songs created by savvy producers that *do* use pretty much the same rhythm track loops throughout the song and craft contrasts with background vocal parts, the shift between rap sections and sung vocals, changing densities of instrumentation, and phrasing changeups in lyric meter and lyric density. This provides a hybrid that works as both mass-market R&B/hip-hop and dance music for clubs.

- The business side of working with tracks isn't a negative if you take care of business up front. But this area is frequently contentious so I'll lay out a couple basics. Whether you're a track writer or you're working with one, make sure your co-writer understands the royalty splits. A track writer should get at least a third but one could justify getting half depending on his contributions beyond basic tracks. (That might include further arrangement and production after the melody and lyric are created.) Also, if a track writer asks a singer/melody writer/lyricist to co-write and the co-writer says yes *without agreeing beforehand* to any other split, it will be, by law, 50/50. Work it out, write it down, and copy it for both parties. For a good guide, go to www.johnbraheny.com/bus/colbus.html.

- Don't confuse track writers with demo arranger/producers who charge for their services. They are *not* entitled to any royalties for arranging (creating tracks for) your pre-existing song. Remember that if you agree to pay someone for demo production/arranging services, you are in control and it's up to you to decide whether anyone changes any part of your song in the process of arranging it. There are many individual situations where this gets dicey. Unscrupulous or (giving them the benefit of the doubt) inexperienced, unprofessional demo producers may say *after* the fact, "What I contributed, that great guitar riff or keyboard figure really made this song work and without my contribution nobody would be interested in it." He is trying to intimidate you into giving him a cut of the royalties. Tell him, "I hired you because I expected you to contribute your talent and expertise. Otherwise, I would have hired someone else. If you wanted writer credit for doing what I agreed to pay you for, you should have said so before we started working on it so we could both decide whether it was worth it for you not to get paid and for me to share my copyright."

The future holds increasing opportunities for melody and lyric writers to collaborate with track writer/producers as relatively inexpensive digital composing and recording software allows new producers to practice their art without renting expensive studios. And for groovemeister drummers, writing tracks first can be a natural evolution.

Being a Writer/Producer

If you have the ability to produce artists, that puts you as a songwriter in a great situation. You can write and produce songs, and then shop them to specific artists. There is a distinct advantage to producing master quality tracks: If the artist likes the song and the tracks, there's a good possibility you'll also end up as a producer. That was the case for Steve Kipner, David Frank, and Pamela Sheyne with Christina Aguilera's breakthrough hit "Genie in a Bottle" (as well as 98°'s "The Hardest Thing" and Dream's "He Loves U Not"). I interviewed Steve Kipner about the process of writing "Genie in a Bottle." Though he says he writes differently with different collaborators, this was a process that seems to be pretty common for pop and R&B/hip-hop writers who often start with groove tracks.

"Genie in a Bottle" was a track-driven song. David Frank knew that Pam Sheyne was coming into town, so he got up at 2:00 in the morning, went into his studio, and just started coming up with very strange, interesting music. There's a kick-drum pattern in that song that's a very fast kick-drum. So, he took that eight bars of music and looped it around and around and it just doesn't stop. We let it play and turned it up loud, and all of a sudden we start singing something. So, I'd sing something or Pam would sing something, David would sing something. We weren't really concentrating on anyone else, but just singing stuff—stream of consciousness. We weren't thinking about it. Whatever came out. And someone will say, "What was that?" and we grabbed onto something. So that gave us a little melody and all of a sudden, slowly but surely, everyone started singing relatively the same melody.

There were no words at that point, just a little melody. And then we were walking around and someone said, "If you wanna be with me . . ." and someone else said, "Wow, that's interesting." Someone would grab that and then the next line would come and then someone would say, "I'm a genie. I'm a genie in a bottle." Wow, that's good . . . let's try that. And someone else said, "You gotta rub me the right way." Wow, there you go, there's a new line. So you try it again and it's almost like chiseling stuff away. If something doesn't work, you change it. And you just keep literally knocking things around and molding it until you get an idea of what the song can be about. We had the idea of the right attitude. First of all, when it's an up-tempo, aggressive song, it can't be a namby-pamby lyric. It has to have an attitude that whoever's going to end up singing the song has to have and believe in. It has to be about something that people would want to be bothered with.

Then we'd think, Okay, now what can the verse be about? The verses were more sitting down, looking at the lyrics, and figuring out what this song was about. What was the attitude we wanted to convey? We lived in that little world writing the song, then a couple days went by and we just keep working. It takes a long time; it's not that quick. After that's finished, we started to record and customized it right to the end.

You can also find a great singer, write for (or with) and produce her, then shop her to record companies. You gamble your time and money on the quality of your writing and production, but it's a good strategy. When you shop the artist, you're also shopping your writing and production for future projects.

Can This Marriage Work?

After finding a collaborator who's stylistically compatible, you have the sometimes difficult task of developing a good rapport and business relationship with that person.

One successful songwriter says, "My ego is my biggest problem when I collaborate. I have to keep reminding myself that I'm collaborating with this lyricist because I really respect her work, and when she offers a suggestion or asks me to change part of my melody to accommodate a lyric, I should give it a shot." The ego problem in this example was caused, in part, by the fact that the writer had written both words and music to his songs for years and found it difficult to readjust his habits.

A negative and quarrelsome attitude can destroy any type of partnership, especially with people who are sensitive and involved with such emotional issues as exposing their vulnerable psyches. It's not always easy to deal with someone who tells you your "baby" is ugly. We all want to believe that because the baby comes from us, it's already perfect. Remember that you're both trying to make your song pretty. Even when you're writing alone, the ability to step back and look at your song objectively is a quality of professionalism. When you're working with someone else, that professional attitude becomes doubly important because criticism is a necessary part of the process. A good partner won't let you ignore a flaw. It is, in fact, one of the primary benefits of collaborating.

If you really do feel strongly about a line a co-writer has rejected, a few calm reasons why you think it works may convince your partner to leave it in. If you find yourself fighting too hard for it, it may be more productive to spend the time and energy looking for a new line. Famed lyricists Alan and Marilyn Bergman's rule is: If one collaborator doesn't like the line, it goes. With nearly endless alternatives, they're confident they'll eventually find a line they both like.

The one thing to keep foremost in your mind is that you're both trying to create the best song possible. All criticism and response should be directed toward that goal rather than to protecting your ego. Don't defend something just because you wrote it or because you'll get a bigger percentage if you contribute more—a good argument for a straight 50/50 split of writers' royalties from the beginning (see "Royalty Splits" on page 143).

You'll need to learn not only to accept criticism graciously but also to give it constructively. Critiquing is an art in itself. When you're beginning a relationship, it's crucial that any criticism be given as gently and positively as possible. As your routine develops and you get more comfortable and trusting with each other, you'll probably work out some shorthand to speed up the process. As you communicate better, you'll also get to know which buttons not to push. There's a big difference between saying, "What a dumb line!" and "Let's make that line stronger." The former is an unqualified putdown. The latter acknowledges a line could be better, offers a challenge, and implies faith in you and your partner. It's important that you continuously acknowledge your partner's talent and compliment good ideas. Criticism becomes much easier in an atmosphere of respect. If you find few causes for compliments, you should be writing with someone else.

Approaches to collaboration are as varied as the combinations of individuals involved. It's important to find out right away how your prospective partner likes to work (see "The 'No'-Free Zone" on page 142). Here are some of the variables:

• **Writing lyric or music alone, and getting together later.** Some people are uncomfortable when their partner is in the same room. It disturbs their creative flow. They may be open to criticism and change later, but they need to get something to work from first. Some lyricists would rather write to a finished melody and vice versa. This method is well suited to correspondence. Some who write this way will send a melody or lyric to several writers in succession and say, "Take this lyric (or tune) for a week and see what you can come up with." It gives a writer a chance to hear several versions of his material. And it saves the hassle of waiting endlessly for a collaborator to finish a song—a very common problem.

To make that situation work, however, you should have an agreement in writing ahead of time that it won't be a complete song unless you both agree on the finished product. Otherwise, legally, it is a complete work. I should also mention that it's unethical to give a lyric or music to more than one potential collaborator at the same time *without their knowledge*. They should have the option to agree to that type of speculative situation or not. They may choose to spend their time more productively elsewhere and it's disrespectful of you not to allow them the choice.

For yourself, it's always a good idea to ask if anyone else is working on the same assignment you've been given. Publishers have been known not to volunteer that information and writers rightfully resent it.

• **Writing together in the same room.** Writers who work this way love the give-and-take of instant feedback. They enjoy the excitement and high energy level that can happen when two collaborators really start to groove. It's particularly good for artists who write both lyrics *and* music, so ideas can be stimulated and shared in both areas. With this type of collaboration, your compatibility becomes more important. What is your most creative time of day? Can you work every day or once a week? Do you like each other and not feel intimidated (though a little tension is not necessarily a bad thing)?

Regardless of the approach, you'll need stylistic compatibility and to decide whether you or your partner also want to collaborate with others. It's generally understood that writers may collaborate with many other writers, particularly in Nashville where it's part of the musical culture and business.

COLLABORATION EXERCISE: THE BUMPING UP GAME

Pat and Pete Luboff have written songs recorded by Snoop Dogg ("Trust Me") Patti LaBelle, Bobby Womack, Michael Peterson, and more, as well as "Hometown, USA" from the John Travolta movie, The Experts. *The Luboffs are the authors of* 88 Songwriting Wrongs & How to Right Them *published by Writer's Digest Books, and* 12 Steps to Building Better Songs, *which they self-published. They lead the Sounding Board songwriting think-tank in Nashville every Monday night. For more information, visit www.writesongs.com.*

As part of the workshops we teach on collaboration, we hand out a questionnaire. We ask the writers: What is the most difficult situation you've encountered in collaborating? No matter where we are, the answer is the same: "I wasn't happy with the way the song turned out." This is usually because the writer offered ideas that weren't accepted by his or her collaborator. One or the other ego was more dominant and got to say what ended up in the song. Is this any way to write a song? No!

Here's a game you can play with your collaborator before you get into any struggles with the song. It will give you practice in working together. It's called the "Bumping Up" game. Bumping up the lines means taking the lines you've written and changing some of the ordinary words to more active, emotional, visual, and sensual words. Consider the difference between the phrases "old car," "Model T," "Little Red Corvette," and "VW bus." Can you see how "old car" does not communicate the world of information that each of the others does?

The "Bumping Up" Game

With each one of the sentences or images below, take turns bumping up the line. Remember, bumping up not only changes dry words to juicier words, it adds extra features like inner rhymes and alliteration.

Example: She walked down the street. *Bump 1:* She ambled down 2nd Avenue. (Ambled is an interesting image and has alliteration with avenue.) *Bump 2:* She ran down Broadway. (Running is more active and implies stronger emotion than walking. Broadway is a big street in almost every town in the U.S.) *Bump 3:* Annie sauntered down Easy Street. (Complementary images of sauntered and easy, plus inner rhyme of easy and street.) *Bump 4:* Little Mary skipped down the block to school. ("She" could be anybody. "Little Mary," especially with the line that follows, is definitely a child. Alliteration between skipped and school.)

> He drove to her house.
>
> I want you.
>
> I'm leaving you. (Hey, there must be fifty ways to bump this up!)
>
> Empty house?
>
> She is beautiful.
>
> High in the mountains

COLLABORATION EXERCISE: THE DUMMY MELODY

You can practice collaborating with the world's best writers before you approach your friend next door. How? Take any song that has been a hit or that you simply admire. If you want some lyric writing practice, write new lyrics to the melody. If you want to try out your melody writing, put a new melody to those lyrics. Now, you can take what you've created to another writer without telling her how you did it, and she'll write the new missing part. The advantage of this trick is that while you're writing, you learn about how successful songs are structured, where rhymes go, where the title is placed, how long the song is, how many bars to each section, where the melody rises and falls, and other things we've discussed. And you know your finished product is based on a successful structure.

COLLABORATION PHILOSOPHY: BRAINSTORMING EXERCISE

Multi-platinum songwriter Harold Payne has had over a hundred artists record his songs, including Rod Stewart, Patti LaBelle, the Temptations, Peter, Paul and Mary, Snoop Dogg, the Kingston Trio, and long time collaborator, Bobby Womack.

You can collaborate on an assignment or an organic basis. You should decide at the beginning if you want it to be commercial. If you do, what artist could record it? If you are writing a song that's more production oriented, do you have the facilities among you to make the kind of demo that song needs? If we have a particular assignment to write for an artist, we do research, listen to something like it, and buy the artist's latest album.

If there's no particular assignment, we might work from a title. Both parties must be enthusiastic before looking at each other's ideas. It's chemistry that makes us go on a particular one. You should have a few different ideas, in case your first choice doesn't work, so someone doesn't feel forced to work on something he's not interested in.

Or you can just get together and have a conversation casually. I call that the organic approach. It's for the pleasure of it. It's an opportunity to stretch out a bit and establish *rapport*. Take whatever comes as a result of the interaction, no pressure. If something gets done, that's almost extra. It's also okay if you decide not to write together or not to write that particular idea. You have to be comfortable about saying, "That doesn't turn me on." It has to flow. Meet once a week, don't be afraid if there's no progress. Some obstacles are dislodged by just getting together.

A good way to start the collaboration going is to have a title session. We do this by talking about the world in general, what's happening in the news, what is happening to the way people relate to each other. Then we might decide whether we want to write an up song or a down one. Most of the time, we decide on the "up" side, because we want to be commercial, and positive songs tend to be more commercially acceptable. Then we might decide on a general area, like two people who have gotten back together after being split up. Then, we have to find a unique way of expressing that idea. We might throw around some titles of songs that have already been written on the subject, just to give a clearer idea of where we're heading. Or, we might just throw around titles on various subjects from lists that we've made on our own. Or, we might talk about something that happened in the life of a friend that we feel would make a good story. These conversations over dinner make writing a pleasant social thing, rather than just another task to sit down to after a hard day of earning a living.

The "No"-Free Zone

My friend, Pat Pattison (author of Writing Better Lyrics*), told me about his first co-writing experience with Stan Webb.*

Co-Writing the "No"-Free Zone by Pat Pattison

The best advice I ever got on co-writing was from Stan Webb, my first professional co-writer. When Tom Casey, a V.P. at SESAC in Nashville, set the appointment up for me, he asked Stan to talk to me a bit about the Nashville co-writing process, a process that dominates the songwriting culture there.

I was waiting in the SESAC writer's room with my notes and titles, some complete lyrics, song ideas, and I was feeling nervous. I, after all, am a big-time professor at the biggest-time music school in the world—Berklee—where I teach lyric writing. What if I can't come up with anything? What if he thinks all my ideas are dumb? They don't look too good to me right now either. What if he thinks I'm a fraud? Not only would that humiliate me, but it would put my students' credibility in question too, and it'd be all my fault. Why am I here? Maybe I should leave while there's still time. Couldn't I say I have food poisoning?

Too late. The door opened and there stood Stan Webb, my co-writer for the day, a guy with hits. Stan is a burly guy. He looked a bit shaggy, wearing bib overalls, a tattered t-shirt, and work boots, looking like he'd just come off the farm (which, in fact, he had—he owns one, bought with songwriting royalties). He came in and did something curious: He shut the door, re-opened it, shut it again, and then pushed hard to make sure it was closed. Hmm. Was he worried about folks listening and stealing our good ideas? I was deeply concerned just with having a good idea. I'd be so relieved if I managed to just have one that, as far as I was concerned, the secret listener would be welcome to it.

He sat down opposite me on a couch and seemed to size me up. He grinned and said, "Is that door closed?" Yikes. "Yes it is," I answered carefully, not knowing where he was going with this. Was it a secret initiation? "Good, I'm glad it's closed," he said, "because you can probably tell by looking at me that I'm gonna say some of the dumbest things you've ever heard." I stayed quiet. I was more worried about what he thought of me. He went on, "And if you do your job right today, you're gonna say some of the dumbest thing I ever heard, professor or not." "No doubt there," I thought. He grinned again and said, "But, as long as that door is closed, nobody needs to know how dumb both of us are. I won't tell if you don't."

He told me that he hoped I didn't mind, but Tom had asked him to talk to me about the co-writing process in Nashville, so he wanted to tell me just a couple things before we got going on a song. I told him to take his time.

He said, "*Say everything* that comes to your head. Say it out loud, no matter how dumb it is. Don't censor anything. If you say something really dumb, you might give me an idea that's not quite as dumb. And then I might have a decent one that gives you a better one that gives me a great one. If you'd never said the dumb one, we would never get to the great one.

"So that means that we'll never say 'no' to each other. A co-writing room is a 'NO'-FREE ZONE. If you say something and I don't like it, I just won't say anything. Silence is a request for more, more, more. It says 'just keep throwing stuff out there.' When either one of us likes something, we'll say 'yes' Otherwise, just keep going."

We had a great writing session. I lost my fear of looking like a fool. I came up with a lot of dumb ideas, and my dumbest idea of all led us to the best part of the song. We really did say everything. And the silences were golden. What a great way to ensure that we always get the best out of each other: Nobody has to defend anything, and the only ideas in the song are automatically ones we both love. The "NO" FREE ZONE gets the best out of both writers: there are no arguments, and there never needs to be compromise.

I've always been grateful to Stan for his wise advice that day. It helps me every time I co-write, but also every time I write. My inner critic (most frequent co-writer) has also learned to abide by the "NO" FREE ZONE. And Stan's words still echo in the songwriting classrooms at Berklee College of Music, where literally hundreds of students have worked in the "NO" FREE ZONE and have had great co-writing experiences because of it.

Thanks buddy.

I've added some advice of my own to Stan's, because, in Berklee writing classes, we talk about writing a lot. Lots of process, lots of techniques. And it really helps their writing, learning about what goes into it—what tools are available. My students learn to talk about writing very well. They are good technicians as well as good writers.

Thus, my advice: Never talk about writing in a co-writing room, especially about technique. Telling what you know about writing isn't writing. You're supposed to be writing, not talking about it. Stay inside the song, inside the characters. Don't run away to the intellectual level. Most people are tempted to talk about those wonderful technical effects in their lines—assonance, rhythm, deep thoughts or metaphors—out of fear to cover their bases and try to dress up what they're afraid might be a dumb idea, in academic robes. A dumb professor is still dumb, even with his robes on. Just write. And write fearlessly.

One final thought: in terms of saying everything, I hereby grant you permission to write crap. Lots of it, all the time, the more the better. Remember: Crap makes the best fertilizer.

Collaboration Business

Let's assume that you've found a lyricist or composer whose words or music feel like the magic ingredient you need to write great songs. You find that you can work well together and, first thing you know, you've got a fantastic song. You say, "Great, let's find a publisher!" Your partner says, "Oh, I guess I forgot to tell you, I've got my own publishing company so I'd like to publish the song." At that point the song may be in trouble. You may rightfully ask whether your partner's company is capable of properly promoting the song. Does the company have the connections to get the song recorded? You're better off not having a publisher at all than to have the song tied up with an inadequate one. At least you'd be free to place the song with a good publisher or to actually license it yourself for film or TV and other uses.

If you find yourself in this situation, you might request that if your partner's company doesn't get the song recorded in six months or a year, that he give up his publishing interest and the two of you look for a publisher together. You might also set up your own company and split the publishing, but jointly agree to the time limit. Or you may agree to bring in a third publisher, at which point you both will give an equal share of the publishing (or all of it) to the new party. (See chapter ten, page 191.)

THE ROYALTY SPLITS

You also need to agree on a division of the writer's share of the royalties. Your collaborator may have supplied a title for a song, but you wrote the rest of it. You might feel you did most of the work and should get 90 percent of the money. Your partner may feel that without the title, which supplied the premise, there wouldn't *be* a song. You both may be right, but that kind of bickering could destroy a very promising collaborative effort. It's generally agreed that if you get together with the intention of writing a song or to establish an ongoing writing relationship, you split the writers' royalties 50/50 (three writers in thirds, etc.).

Without an agreement to the contrary, all rights and percentages are split equally. Each writer owns an equal portion of the copyright, and each of the writers is empowered to grant a license to anyone who wants to record it.

If one of you is a lyricist and the other writes music, it's a pretty straightforward arrangement. It tends to get a little touchy if each of you writes music and lyrics or if the contributions are more difficult to quantify. There's more room for argument about who contributed the most. That's why it's always best to agree on equal shares ahead of time.

On some of the John Lennon/Paul McCartney tunes, one of them contributed more than the other but they didn't want to fight over it every time so they divided the royalties equally (in some cases, royalties and credit on songs written by just one of them were still split as a writing team).

Here are some other possible situations you may have to deal with:

• **You've written the song and you take it to someone else to "tighten it up" and that person contributes a new hook or changes the song's direction.** How much writer credit will he get? At the time you bring your song to the writer, try to work it out based on what you want him to contribute. Remember that unless you work out a specific percentage ahead of time, it's 50/50.

• **You take your song to an artist who wants to "personalize" it and changes something.** For this he wants a writer's credit. This is not uncommon and it's a potentially volatile situation, with several factors to weigh:

　　1. Is this an important cut? With an established artist, there's no question about it. But even with a new artist the song could be a major hit or end up on a hit album. Any recording credit may therefore be important enough to you to agree to split.

　　2. How extensive are the changes? "Personalizing" the song by changing a "she" to a "he" does not warrant a writer's credit. If the artist wants more extensive changes and you want to accommodate him, offer to make them yourself. Get as much information as

you can about what the artist is looking for and present several rewrites. If the artist seems unreasonably resistant to your changes, you have to face the reality that you may lose the cut unless you allow him to rewrite or just give him the credit. You can swallow your pride and walk to the bank, walk away with your pride (and your empty pockets), or tell the artist you can't change this song but suggest that you write something together from scratch. If it's just a matter of financial incentive for the artist to record the song, you also have the publisher's share of the royalties to offer if you publish the song yourself. (See chapter eleven, "Negotiating" on page 226.)

3. How badly does the artist want the song? If he thinks it's good enough, he's torn between wanting the writing credit and money and possibly blowing a potential hit. You're in the same position, except that you may also be motivated by anger that someone would have the *nerve* to demand credit for your work.

While many artists wouldn't think of asking for undeserved credit (and royalties), others do it in a New York minute. You ultimately have to decide whether it's worth it to your career to give up a portion of those royalties and credits.

• **A publisher suggests changes and wants a writer's credit.** Generally speaking, it is the publisher's job to suggest changes, and she shouldn't ask for any extra credit as a writer. It would depend, of course, on how substantial the contribution is and it can get a little touchy, but it should be your decision.

• **You decide later that you want a new lyric to a song you've already written with someone.** Is it okay to change? Not without your co-writer's written permission.

• **What if your melody writer or publisher wants a new foreign language lyric?** Do you still get paid? A decision has to be made whether you're going to say, "words and music by _____," or "words by _____ and music by _____." In the former, if a foreign sub-publisher wants to commission a lyric translation, the percentage granted to the translator comes out of both your royalties equally. In the latter, it's deducted from the lyricist's half. In the former, if you're sued for lyric infringement, you both get sued. In that latter, the lyricist gets sued. In the former, if there's a successful instrumental version of the song, both writers get paid; in the latter, the lyricist doesn't. In the former, if a lyric is reprinted, you both get paid; in the latter, only the lyricist. Note that all these are also vice-versa, and know that these questions can be worked out contractually (see paragraph six in "Collaborators' Agreement" on page 148).

All these potential problems point to the need for collaborators to get *all the business straight before they get into the music.* There are few things more frustrating than knowing you've written a winner but can't do anything with it.

Preliminary Business Meeting

K.A. Parker is a professional lyricist, a five-time American Song Festival winner, and former staff writer for Motown's Stone Diamond Music who has taught lyric writing at UCLA, Musician's Institute and throughout the U.S. Her suggestions for conducting a business meeting and a list of considerations for collaborators (which she uses in her classes) is the best I've seen, and, with her permission, I offer them to you minus the more extensive discussions of the ones I've already covered.

CONDUCTING THE BUSINESS MEETING

Setting up a business meeting is like buying fire insurance: You may not think you need it until it's too late. The things that you'll be discussing will only be necessary if and when the songs you write with your collaborator turn out to be good enough to be published, recorded, and released. Of course, there's no way to know this until you actually start working together. But, assuming you believe in your own potential, and in that of your collaborator (and there's no reason to work with another person unless you do), I am going to assume that you agree that a meeting of the minds on business matters is necessary before you begin work on music matters.

Don't fall into the trap of thinking that just because your potential collaborator is "nice," that ironing out the business will be a snap later on. Most of us are "nice" when we are trying to impress others. But greed does amazing things to people, and business is about money, after all. Ego, dreams, and money make a powerful brew. Many successful songwriters have ended up giving their royalty income to the lawyers who were left to sort out the disagreements between two "nice," talented people.

The business meeting has three basic rules:

- **Never conduct a business meeting at the same time as a creative meeting.** You'll need to be organized, closed, and tough to do business. You'll need to be flexible, open, and childlike to be creative. Don't try to be both at the same time—it won't work. Conduct your business in a neutral place, like a coffee shop, on a day when you're not planning to write together. Sharing a meal is a nice idea. It softens the whole affair, limits the time frame (usually not more than an hour), and makes it easy to exit if you see that it's not going well. Of course, if things do go well, it helps to bond the relationship, too.

- **Come prepared.** You may very well end up educating your new partner if she is less informed about the business than you are. Make copies of information you want her to read. Back up your opinion with resources. Take notes or tape the meeting for future reference. Make a checklist or agenda of the items you want to discuss. Be prepared to draw a letter of agreement for signature at a later date, based on the discussion. A business meeting is not a good time to be under the influence of alcohol or drugs of any kind. Have your drink when the meeting is over.

- **Go in with a positive attitude.** Don't enter the meeting with tales about how you got screwed before and you're doing this to protect yourself. Assume good will and go from there. You're building a team and every team needs goals, guidelines, regulations, and direction. Don't be defensive. More than anything, the session should be an information-gathering interview. If you conduct it well, it should save you from any hostile confrontations in the future.

SPECIFICS

Now that you know the rules, what specifics do you discuss? Here's a list. You may want to eliminate some of these points or include some of your own, but all the basics are here:

- **Is your information on your partner current?** Keep your partner's name, address, phone numbers, Social Security number, birth date, and affiliation (ASCAP, BMI, SESAC) in your files to be used when you fill out the copyright forms on your songs. The minute you create a copyright (i.e., a song) together, you must keep up to date on this information. I remember vividly how I felt when a publisher wanted a song of mine badly, but finally passed when my collaborator could not be found. Most publishers will not be interested in publishing half a song. Keep in touch! **Note:** I wait until I know I want to work with someone before I ask for his or her address and Social Security number. Some people may be touchy about giving this info to a new acquaintance.

• **How does your partner feel about publishing?** Does he have his own publishing company? Is it active? Does he want your publishing as well? How does he feel about working with the major publishers if they offer a contract on the tune? Is he interested in working with a small, untried publishing company?

• **Does your partner have aspirations to be a recording artist?** Do you? Will either of you want to keep all the best songs for yourself? This is a source of major conflict with many collaborators and should be thoroughly discussed before the work begins. There is nothing more frustrating than holding back a great song on the chance that your partner might get signed—or seeing all your best songs go to another person, if *you're* the one with artistic aspirations. Be frank about this issue.

• **When is a song completed?** Ideally, it's when *both* of you say so. That's okay if one of you isn't a perfectionist or a procrastinator. Clashes of temperament will be a sore spot here unless you come up with a set of rules about this. What if you disagree? How many times do you rewrite after a critique session? After the demo is complete, will you be willing to go back in and make major changes?

• **How prolific are you? How prolific is your partner?** If one of you writes every day and one of you only writes when you're inspired, that can be very frustrating for the more prolific of the two. Do you or your partner need deadlines? Pressure? How long will you give a lyric or melody to your partner before you expect to see some activity on his part? What do you do when one of you wants the song finished and the other one doesn't want to finish it, or can't?

• **When do you bring in a third party to work on the song?** Who will you bring in? Ideally, it's when you *both* agree you've reached a dead end. Again, in an ideal situation, it should be a mutually agreed-upon third party. But you need to discuss this thoroughly. *Never bring in a third party to work on a song without telling your partner.* You'd be surprised how often this is done, and it usually means the end of the partnership.

• **What about royalty splits?** This is a major bone of contention in many relationships where one party writes both words and music and the other party only writes one or the other. *Professional writers split everything right down the middle, no matter who does what. When a third party is called in, everything is divided into thirds.*

• **What about demos?** Where do you do them? Who decides which songs to do? Who pays for them and how? Who produces, engineers, plays, sings? Generally, the fees are split exactly like the song, 50/50. But what if one partner owns a studio and can play all the instruments, etc.? Does he charge the other partner for the demo costs? This is an individual matter and both parties should agree with whatever arrangement is made, regardless of how they work it out.

• **What connections does each of you have?** Would either of you feel comfortable in using them? Is one of you more aggressive? Do either of you go to Los Angeles, New York, or Nashville on a regular basis? How will you get your songs heard by publishers, producers, or artists? Do either of you belong to professional organizations such as the Nashville Songwriters Association International (NSAI), the Songwriters Guild of America (SGA), or TAXI? Would either of you be willing to join to get professional feedback, pitch songs to producers and publishers and so forth? How do you feel about using online pitching service sites where you can upload songs to be heard by others. Most partnerships without goals die quickly. Once you spend the time and money required to write and demo your songs—then what? Are either of you prepared to move to Los Angeles, Nashville, or New York to better promote your work?

• **How does each of you feel about songwriting competitions?** Who pays the entry fee, and how will the winnings be split?

Creating music successfully with your partner will depend on the flexibility and willingness to work things out that each of you brings to the relationship. If the songs you produce are great, the incentive to work out the snags will be greater. It might help if you adopt the belief that people are more important than songs. If you don't believe that, then maybe you should write alone.

The following is a co-writers' contract with comments to help you tailor it to your own situation:

COLLABORATORS' AGREEMENT

This Agreement is entered into with respect to the following musical composition(s):

The undersigned songwriters have collaborated in the creation of the aforementioned song(s) with the following understanding:

1. No songwriter shall be responsible to any other songwriter for expenses incurred in the preparation or presentation of the song(s) unless agreed upon.

2. All sums received from exploitation of the song(s), as well as all approved expenses incurred, will be divided as follows:

    Writer's name   Percent share

    _____   _____

    _____   _____

    _____   _____

3. _____ wrote all of the lyrics to the song(s);
   _____composed all the music to the song(s).

[NOTE: IF THE WRITERS HAVE MADE VARYING CONTRIBUTIONS TO THE MUSIC AND LYRIC, AND THERE IS NO PRECISE SPLIT IN RESPONSIBILITY FOR EACH, AN ATTEMPT TO IDENTIFY INDIVIDUAL CONTRIBUTION IS OF VIRTUALLY NO USE.]

4. If the song(s) are not [signed to a publishing agreement/commercially recorded/commercially released] by _____ we may each withdraw our respective creative contributions to any song(s) not meeting such requirement, and the other(s) shall have no remaining claim to income from any use then made by the creator thereof. [NOTE: AGAIN, THERE IS LITTLE PURPOSE TO THIS CLAUSE UNLESS THE DIVISION BETWEEN LYRICAL AND MUSICAL CONTRIBUTIONS IS CLEARCUT.]

5. [One or more of the writers] shall have the only right to issue licenses for any use whatsoever of the song(s). [or] All of us shall have equal rights to issue licenses for any use of the song(s), but

---

must pay appropriate shares of any money received as specified in Paragraph 2 above. [or] Any of us may grant licenses for any use of the song(s), but only after obtaining written approval of all of the others.

6. [One of the writers] [All of us] Any of us with approval, etc. may authorize changes to the lyric or melody of the song(s) and may reduce the shares of all of us in equal proportion to compensate any new songwriter(s) adding such creative changes. [NOTE: IF THERE IS A DEFINITE DIVISION BE-TWEEN LYRICAL AND MUSICAL CONTRIBUTIONS AMONG THE ORIGINAL WRITERS, REDUCTIONS FOR CHANGES MAY BE APPROPRIATELY CATEGORIZED BY THE TYPE OF CHANGE AND ASSESSED AGAINST THAT WRITER.]

7. [One of the writers] is hereby granted full power of attorney [or] [*ALL of the writers*] are each granted full power of attorney to assign any rights or grant any licenses respecting the song(s) in the event that the others are unavailable to give their approval for any period in excess of _____ days.

[NOTE: IN SOME CIRCUMSTANCES, WHERE ONE WRITER MAY BE FAR MORE KNOWLEDGEABLE IN MUSIC INDUSTRY MATTERS, OR WHERE ONE WRITER INSISTS ON RESERVING A SONG FOR HIS OR HER PER-FORMING GROUP'S USE ONLY, IT MAY BE APPROPRIATE TO GRANT THAT WRITER THE EXCLUSIVE RIGHT TO GRANT LICENSES AND ASSIGN RIGHTS WITHOUT APPROVAL OF THE OTHERS.]

8. In the event of any dispute between us regarding the song(s) or this Agreement, we will submit the matter to binding arbitration in (the largest nearby city) under the rules of the American Arbitration Association or any local arbitration association upon which we otherwise agree.

Signature_____

Social Security Number_____
Address_____

Phone(s)_____

Note: Although it's not critical, you may wish to have this document notarized. In many states, notarization is required for any power of attorney. Check your state laws as to how a power of attorney is legally granted.

Agreements regarding copyrighted musical compositions may be registered in the Copyright Office in Washington, D.C., if you know the original copyright registration number. This provides "constructive notice" of the agreement to the public, so that anyone dealing with a writer acting in violation of the agreement is deemed to have notice of such a wrongful act. As to companies and individuals who conduct an actual search of copyright office records, a record of the agreement will discourage any transfers or licenses in violation of its terms.

There is a copy of this agreement at www.johnbraheny.com

Writing As a Band—Working It Out

Occasionally you'll pick up a record by a group and see five or six writers (group members) listed after a title. You think, "Do they expect me to believe that all those writers contributed equally to the writing of that song?" There are, in fact, groups in which all members create lyrics and music together, but in most group situations one writer (or two) usually contributes more than the rest. Maybe the lead singer or keyboard player is responsible for the melody or someone else has the lyric concept or writes most of the words. Many bands are formed around a writer/artist or team. There are bands in which several members contribute their own songs or write with another group member.

So why, then, should a group decide to share writing credit with all its members if those members *don't* contribute to lyrics or melodies? There are two main reasons, the first financial, the second artistic.

FINANCIAL CONSIDERATIONS

On the financial side, there are five major areas in which a group member can make money: record royalties, live performances, merchandising, songwriting royalties, and publishing royalties,

Record Royalties: In record royalties, (not writer/publisher royalties), the cold reality is that recording costs, advances, video production and other expenses are recouped by the company from your meager *artist* royalties in major label deals. So most group members never end up receiving any *artist* royalties (from the record company) beyond the original advance unless they're very, very successful. You may receive those royalties much faster in many independent label deals that are structured more like joint ventures.

Live Performances: Regarding live performances, even subsequently successful groups usually take at least two years from the start of a recording contract to begin making any kind of decent money performing. Opening act status and at least two hit singles are needed to bring in enough revenue to do more than pay touring bills unless it's a band that can tour constantly. Having said that, most bands start by building a local and regional following by touring and selling enough CDs independently to attract the attention of record companies.

There are also royalties available for group members for performances in digital media (see chapter nine, "Income From Digital Sources and the Home Recording Act" on page 184).

Merchandising: Merchandising of T-shirts, etc., at concerts can be lucrative but this business also takes time to build and the band may have to sell merchandising rights to get advances to help defray their costs. Concert venues and promoters also get percentages of merchandising. On a smaller scale, it's possible to sell a great variety of one-off items of merchandise online to fans via companies like www.cafepress.com. The advantage is that you don't have to pre-purchase a volume of merchandise and risk the cost of transporting it and possibly not selling it. Many of the indie record deals of today require a percentage of the merchandising income until they recoup their costs.

Songwriting and Publishing Royalties: So, the only relatively reliable sources of income left are from writer royalties or income generated by self-publishing. The songwriting royalties will be earned whether the songs are published by a company outside the group or by a company the group sets up to publish its own songs. The second option, setting up a publishing company for the group and splitting the publishing half of the income with the band members, is a good way to reward non-writing members of the band with mechanical and performance royalties. In that case, an individual or company is hired to administer the group's publishing company for a fee (see chapter eleven, "Administration Deals" on page 234), and the remaining royalties are divided among the group. This, of course, assumes that the band didn't have to give up their publishing as part of the record deal.

ARTISTIC CONSIDERATIONS

On the artistic side, the philosophy is that everyone in the group contributes his own individual talent toward creating the final product and therefore deserves a share of the credit. The final and unique sound of the group is not dictated by the writer/artist/lead singer, etc., but by the interaction of all the members. In other words, if one member left the group, this philosophy says, the sound would be audibly altered.

But, you might ask, "What if the bass player doesn't write lyrics or melodies? How does he justify receiving royalties?" To answer that, we have to ignore our traditional concept of the songwriter. Instead I reiterate that the group may not be writing just a song as we know it, but creating a *sound*, an element frequently as important to the commercial success of a record as lyrics and melodies, particularly in pop, rock, and R&B. So it's not only important what the bass player plays, but how he plays it, what sound modification devices he chooses to use and when. If he's also a singer it's important how his voice sounds, how he uses it, and what parts he creates for the vocal arrangement. He may create an instrumental hook in the form of a bass riff that gives the tune a unique identity or serves as the basis (so to speak) for the whole song. So although he hasn't written a word, or a note of actual melody, his contribution can be extremely important to the success of the record, and ultimately, the group.

It may occur to you that, depending on the situation, all the above musical contributions can be and often are made by others. The studio musician, arranger, or producer are all paid in other ways and are free to solicit work with anyone else. A group member whose first commitment is to the group doesn't always have these options.

Dividing writer royalties doesn't work with everyone and may give rise to jealousy from those who feel their contribution was more important, especially after the big money starts rolling in. So if you're writing with a band, it may be worth considering sharing the credit, especially if you want to attract creative people to your band, and if everyone can perceive each other's contribution as being equally important.

As you can see, collaboration is an option to be seriously considered. It offers many positive advantages, both artistically and commercially. The difficulty in finding a compatible partner and keeping your business straight can be more than compensated for with increased productivity and quality.

PART 2

The Business

8 Protecting Your Songs

The Importance of Taking Care of Business

Now that you've put so much soul and perspiration into writing those great songs, I hope you're not looking at the rest of this book and saying, "Oh, that's just the business stuff. I don't have a business kind of mind, I think I'll skip that part." Or "I'll just get a manager who can take care of all that." Those words have a sad echo for a lot of people I've met over the years whose creativity has been drained and their careers put on hold while they tried to undo by legal means the damage caused by their own ignorance.

There was a time not long ago when there were no books from which someone (who wasn't an attorney) could learn about the business. Now you have no excuse. The following chapters are an introduction to some basics of the music business. It doesn't pretend to teach you everything, but it will give you plenty of streetwise information about the business that you don't have to be a Ph.D. to understand. At the bottom of it all, as you might have suspected, are common sense and human nature. Don't forget that the *music business* is also very creative. You can exercise your creativity every bit as much by figuring out fresh approaches to getting your songs recorded and marketed as you can by writing a song, and succeeding at it can feel just as good.

Your songs and talent are your babies. You want to know that when they go out in the world, they have every advantage. You want them to be protected, to be with people who care about them, to have a chance to do something good in the world, and if they're special, to pay your rent in your old age. Reading the rest of this book is a major payment on an insurance policy you owe to those babies.

I'll show you a lot of options in this half of the book, just in case you thought there were only one or two. There are many different ways to deal with your business, and your personal situation may use a combination of them. Whether you're a self-contained writer/artist/band or solely a writer, the past few years of revolutionary growth in the industry has offered great potential for you to grow as an independent entrepreneur. The Internet and digital technology have ushered in a sea of change when it comes to finding services designed to help you market yourself.

Many wonderful, honest, hard-working people exist in this business who want to see you succeed and who are motivated every bit as much by seeing their creativity pay off for you as they are by the financial rewards they'll receive by helping you do it. They take great pride in their work and go through as much frustration and aggravation in their jobs as you do in yours. Reading the rest of this book will help you find those people and get some idea of what happens on their end of your business. That knowledge will help you make the best kind of business deals, the ones in which everyone is rewarded for his efforts and knows how to work as a team. And it will help you avoid scammers and poor business deals.

This "Business" half of the book will familiarize you with the more traditional side of the music industry that you need to be aware of. However, there are revolutionary changes in progress that affect every area of the industry: copyright, music publishing, the way record companies look for and market talent, technology, and most of all, the opportunities available to take your career into your own hands. I'll try to bring you up to date with the realization that by the time you read this the revolution will be even further along. So I'll offer as many ways as possible to help you keep up with it on your own. It's an exciting time—embrace it!

Your Song Is Your Property

One of the most important business considerations is protecting your songs. While you may be emotionally attached to your "baby," you have to think of it as a product, or commodity—an "intellectual property."

Our government (and most others around the world) has agreed that an artist deserves to retain ownership of his own creations. To encourage creative expression, legislation was enacted so that an artist could expect to be compensated by whoever sought the "right to copy" his work. A creator can assign different rights to different people for different purposes. A sculptor gives a gallery "the right to display." A songwriter can license (or assign) the rights to her song to a music publisher to obtain recordings of her song, reproduce those recordings, and distribute them to the public.

Now we come to the need for a "right to copy," or copyright: How can someone acquire something from you until they are sure it is yours to begin with? Anyone can show me "his" car, even take me for a ride in it, but if there were ever any legal questions regarding that car, we would need to see some proof of ownership.

Countless stories have been told about songwriters who have written some of the most famous and successful songs and either did not know how to register their own works, or depended totally on someone else to give them proper payment as the creators. Years later, as these songwriters became more educated regarding copyright protection procedures, they realized they had blindly signed over all of their rights to earn any income from their songs.

Fortunately, today there are books (like this one), songwriters' organizations, classes, seminars, Web sites, and other learning opportunities available to help people learn about their rights as creative artists. When a songwriter puts so much work, worry, and love into his art, it seems irresponsible not to know how to protect it.

Before I knew better, I had a fantasy about the Copyright Office: When they received my new song, a piano player played it for all the employees just to make sure it was really original. He'd say, "Hey, have you guys ever heard this one before?" I'd break out in a cold sweat as I prayed that I hadn't accidentally written part of something I had heard on the radio or in a club somewhere. One by one, the copyright "experts" (who I knew had heard everything) would shake their heads and somebody would say, "Wait a minute! Play the last two bars of that bridge again. No, I thought it might have been a Beatles tune but it's okay. Let it pass," and I was home free.

If you have that fantasy, you can now wipe it out in favor of cold reality. The Copyright Office processes hundreds of thousands of registrations every year. Needless to say, they don't listen to those songs, but they do check over the forms to make sure you've filled them out correctly. If you haven't, they'll send back your application. They also don't check to see if the song is original, since the copyright registration is only a proof of the *date* of registration.

According to the Copyright Revision Act of 1976, which went into effect on January 1, 1978, *original* (original with the creator of the work) songs are entitled to copyright protection from the time they're "fixed" in a tangible medium of expression. This means on paper (with lyric and music together if it's a song) or "phonorecord," which includes vinyl, tape, or CD. At the time it's written or recorded, it's considered to be *created*. If you sing your song "live" for an audience (before it's in "fixed" form), it is not automatically protected. Technically, it's only considered protected when it's recorded or written. Consequently, it's a good idea to record the song and put the copyright notice on the tape or CD with the date, and even better to obtain a copyright registration before performing it in public. This isn't something you need to stress over. Ordinarily, writer/performers wait until they have a demo produced before they copyright the song. The chances of someone actually stealing your song are extremely remote.

WHAT ARE YOUR RIGHTS UNDER COPYRIGHT LAW?

Copyright is a set of *exclusive rights*. As they pertain to music compositions, they are:

1. The right to reproduce the copyrighted song in copies or phonorecords, including CDs, tapes, and sheet music.

2. The right to prepare derivative works based on the copyrighted work. (See the definition of "derivative works" in chapter nine on page 173.)

3. The right to distribute copies or phonorecords of the copyrighted song to the public via sale, transfer of ownership or by rental, lease or lending. This is different from the right to copy. For example, you can license a CD duplicator to make copies but they don't get the right to distribute them. This is the right that gives you control over the first copy of the work. (See chapter nine, "The Compulsory License" on page 173.)

4. The right to perform the copyrighted work publicly. This includes anywhere. Obviously, you're not going to send the cops to arrest anyone who performs your song at their backyard barbeque, but you will license a performing rights organization (BMI, ASCAP, SESAC) or other organizations to collect your royalties for airplay on radio, TV, Webcasts, jukeboxes, or other situations where your music is played for the public (see the Royalty Flow Chart on page 181).

5. The right to display the copyrighted work publicly. Though this doesn't specifically seem to qualify as a music-related right, it's because of this right that karaoke companies need to get a license to project your lyrics on the screen.

WHAT'S NOT PROTECTED

Ideas/concepts: Consider how many different musical and literary works have been created using the Romeo and Juliet concept.

Titles or short phrases: What if someone could have copyrighted "I Love You" as a title? Short phrases, such as "You're a dream come true," are also not protected.

Chord progressions: What if someone had been able to copyright a twelve-bar blues progression?

Rhythm patterns: None of the great dance rhythms would have ever developed if we had to get permission from someone to write a cha-cha or rumba rhythm. This also means you can't copyright contemporary dance rhythms, though you *can* copyright the *recordings* of the beats.

Copyright protects the *expressions* of the above. In other words, it protects what you *do* with them.

LENGTH OF COPYRIGHT PROTECTION

(Copied from the Copyright Office site. No, it's not illegal to publish government documents—unless they're classified!) The Copyright Office describes the length of copyright protection as follows:

Works Originally Created On or After January 1, 1978

"A work that is created (fixed in tangible form for the first time) on or after January 1, 1978, is automatically protected from the moment of its creation and is ordinarily given a term enduring for the author's life plus an additional seventy years after the author's death. In the case of 'a joint work prepared by two or more authors who did not work for hire,' the term lasts for seventy years after the last surviving author's death. For works made for hire, and for anonymous and pseudonymous works (unless the author's identity is revealed in Copyright Office records), the duration of copyright will be 95 years from publication or 120 years from creation, whichever is shorter."

Works Originally Created Before January 1, 1978, But Not Published or Registered by That Date

"These works have been automatically brought under the statute and are now given federal copyright protection. The duration of copyright in these works will generally be computed in the same way as for works created on or after January 1, 1978: the life-plus-70 or 95/120-year terms will apply to them as well. The law provides that in no case will the term of copyright for works in this category expire before December 31, 2002, and for works published on or before December 31, 2002, the term of copyright will not expire before December 31, 2047."

Works Originally Created and Published or Registered Before January 1, 1978

"Under the law in effect before 1978, copyright was secured either on the date a work was published with a copyright notice or on the date of registration if the work was registered in unpublished form. In either case, the copyright endured for a first term of 28 years from the date it was secured. During the last (28th) year of the first term, the copyright was eligible for renewal. The Copyright Act of 1976 extended the renewal term from 28 to 47 years for copyrights that were subsisting on January 1, 1978, or for pre-1978 copyrights restored under the Uruguay Round Agreements Act (URAA), making these works eligible for a total term of protection of 75 years. Public Law 105-298, enacted on October 27, 1998, further extended the renewal term of copyrights still subsisting on that date by an additional 20 years, providing for a renewal term of 67 years and a total term of protection of 95 years.

Public Law 102-307, enacted on June 26, 1992, amended the 1976 Copyright Act to provide for automatic renewal of the term of copyrights secured between January 1, 1964, and December 31, 1977. Although the renewal term is automatically provided, the Copyright Office does not issue a renewal certificate for these works unless a renewal application and fee are received and registered in the Copyright Office.

Public Law 102-307 makes renewal registration optional. Thus, filing for renewal registration is no longer required in order to extend the original 28-year copyright term to the full 95 years. However, some benefits accrue from making a renewal registration during the 28th year of the original term.

For more detailed information on renewal of copyright and the copyright term, request Circular 15, 'Renewal of Copyright'; Circular 15a, 'Duration of Copyright'; and Circular 15t, 'Extension of Copyright Terms.'"

THE COPYRIGHT NOTICE

Form of Notice for Visually Perceptible Copies

"The notice for visually perceptible copies should contain all the following three elements:

1. The symbol © (the letter C in a circle), or the word 'Copyright,' or the abbreviation 'Copr.'; and

2. The year of first publication of the work. In the case of compilations or derivative works incorporating previously published material, the year date of first publication of the compilation or derivative work is sufficient. The year date may be omitted where a pictorial, graphic, or sculptural work, with accompanying textual matter, if any, is reproduced in or on greeting cards, postcards, stationery, jewelry, dolls, toys, or any useful article; and

3. The name of the owner of copyright in the work, or an abbreviation by which the name can be recognized, or a generally known alternative designation of the owner.

    Example: © 2007 John Doe

The 'C in a circle' notice is used only on 'visually perceptible copies.' Certain kinds of works—for example, musical, dramatic, and literary works—may be fixed not in 'copies' but by means of sound in an audio recording. Since audio recordings such as audio tapes and phonograph disks are 'phonorecords' and not 'copies,' the 'C in a circle' notice is not used to indicate protection of the underlying musical, dramatic, or literary work that is recorded."

FORM OF NOTICE FOR PHONORECORDS OF SOUND RECORDINGS

Sound recordings are defined in the law as "works that result from the fixation of a series of musical, spoken, or other sounds, but not including the sounds accompanying a motion picture or other audiovisual work." Common examples include recordings of music, drama, or lectures. A sound recording is not the same as a phonorecord. A phonorecord is the physical object in which works of authorship are embodied. The word "phonorecord" includes cassette tapes, CDs, vinyl disks, as well as other formats.

"The notice for phonorecords embodying a sound recording should contain all the following three elements:

1. The symbol (the letter P in a circle); and

2. The year of first publication of the sound recording; and

3. The name of the owner of copyright in the sound recording, or an abbreviation by which the name can be recognized, or a generally known alternative designation of the owner. If the producer of the sound recording is named on the phonorecord label or container and if no other name appears in conjunction with the notice, the producer's name shall be considered a part of the notice.

Example: 2007 A.B.C. Records, Inc. Form of Notice for Visually Perceptible Copies"

Copyright Registration

"In general, copyright registration is a legal formality intended to make a public record of the basic facts of a particular copyright. However, registration is not a condition of copyright protection. Even though registration is not a requirement for protection, the copyright law provides several inducements or advantages to encourage copyright owners to make registration. Among these advantages are the following:

- Registration establishes a public record of the copyright claim.

- Before an infringement suit may be filed in court, registration is necessary for works of U.S. origin.

- If made before or within 5 years of publication, registration will establish prima facie evidence in court of the validity of the copyright and of the facts stated in the certificate.

- If registration is made within 3 months after publication of the work or prior to an infringement of the work, statutory damages and attorney's fees will be available to the copyright owner in court actions. Otherwise, only an award of actual damages and profits is available to the copyright owner.

Registration allows the owner of the copyright to record the registration with the U.S. Customs Service for protection against the importation of infringing copies. For additional information, request Publication No. 563 'How to Protect Your Intellectual Property Right,' from: U.S. Customs Service, P.O. Box 7404, Washington, D.C. 20044. See the U.S. Customs Service Web site at www.customs.gov for online publications.

Registration may be made at any time within the life of the copyright. Unlike the law before 1978, when a work has been registered in unpublished form, it is not necessary to make another registration when the work becomes published, although the copyright owner may register the published edition, if desired."

REGISTRATION PROCEDURES

"If you send us a check or money order in payment of Copyright Office services, it will be converted into an electronic funds transfer (EFT). This means we will copy your check and use the account information on it to electronically debit your account for the amount of the check. The debit from your account will usually occur within 24 hours of processing, and will be shown on your regular account statement.

You will not receive your original check back. We will destroy your original check, but we will keep a copy of it. If the EFT cannot be processed for technical reasons, we will reprocess a copy of your original check. If the EFT cannot be completed because of insufficient funds, your service request will not be processed."

WHICH FORM SHOULD YOU USE?

When to Use Form SR (Sound Recordings)

"Use Form SR for registration of published or unpublished sound recordings, that is, for registration of the particular sounds or recorded performance.

Form SR must also be used if you wish to make one registration for both the sound recording and the underlying work (the musical composition, dramatic, or literary work). You may make a single registration only if the copyright claimant is the same for both the sound recording and the underlying work. In this case, the authorship statement in Space 2 should specify that the claim covers both works.

Form SR is also the appropriate form for registration of a multimedia kit that combines two or more kinds of authorship including a sound recording (such as a kit containing a book and an audiocassette)."

WHEN TO USE FORM PA (PERFORMING ARTS)

"For registration purposes, musical compositions and dramatic works that are recorded on disks or cassettes are works of the performing arts and should be registered on Form PA or Short Form PA. Therefore, if you wish to register only the underlying work that is a musical composition or dramatic work, use Form PA even though you may send a disk or cassette.

NOTE: Sounds accompanying a motion picture or other audiovisual work should not be registered on Form SR. The copyright law does not define these sounds as 'sound recordings' but as an integral part of the motion picture or audiovisual work in which they are incorporated. These sounds are classified as works of the performing arts and should be registered on Form PA."

EXAMPLES OF THE PROPER USE OF FORMS PA AND SR

"Jane Smith composes words and music, which she entitles 'Blowing in the Breeze.' Even though she records it, she is not interested in registering the particular recording but only in registering the composition itself. If she decides to submit 'Blowing in the Breeze' for copyright registration, she should use Form PA.

Emily Tree performs and records Jane Smith's "Blowing in the Breeze" after complying with permissions and license procedures. If Emily decides to submit her recording for copyright registration, she should use Form SR.

SHORT FORM OR STANDARD FORM PA—WHICH ONE TO USE

"Use short form PA if:

1. You are the only author and copyright owner of this work, and

2. The work was not made for hire, and

3. The work is completely new (does not contain a substantial amount of material that has been previously published or registered or is in the public domain), and

4. The work is not a motion picture or other audiovisual work. Otherwise, use the standard form PA."

EFFECTIVE DATE OF REGISTRATION

A copyright registration is effective on the date the Copyright Office receives all the required elements in acceptable form, regardless of how long it then takes to process the application and mail the certificate of registration. The time the Copyright Office requires to process an application varies, depending on the amount of material the Office is receiving.

If you apply for copyright registration, you will not receive an acknowledgment that your application has been received, but you can expect:

A letter or a telephone call from a Copyright Office staff member if further information is needed or a certificate of registration indicating that the work has been registered, or if the application cannot be accepted, a letter explaining why it has been rejected.

Requests to have certificates available for pickup in the Public Information Office or to have certificates sent by FedEx or another mail service cannot be honored.

For further instructions on registering your copyright and to download the forms, go to the Copyright Office's Web site (www.copyright.gov) or call the Copyright Office at (202) 707-3000 or write them:

Library of Congress Copyright Office

101 Independence Avenue, S.E.

Washington, D.C. 20559-6000

LOW BUDGET COPYRIGHT REGISTRATION

The least expensive way to register your unpublished songs is to combine them under one title. Here are the guidelines from the Copyright Office:

"Under the following conditions, a work may be registered in unpublished form as a 'collection,' with one application form and one fee:

The elements of the collection are assembled in an orderly form;

The combined elements bear a single title identifying the collection as a whole;

The copyright claimant in all the elements and in the collection as a whole is the same; and

All the elements are by the same author, or, if they are by different authors, at least one of the authors has contributed copyrightable authorship to each element.

An unpublished collection is not indexed under the individual titles of the contents but under the title of the collection."

Caution: The practical application of this last information is that if someone hears your song and wants to initiate a search of the Copyright Office for it, they won't find it under the title of the song if they don't know what you titled the collection since it's not even necessary to include the titles or individual songs. (You can break out individual titles with an additional Corrections and Additions (CA) form later if you want to but it will cost you another $30.) Also, if someone wants to publish the composition/song and you give them the existing copyright number, the number will be for the collection, so be clear on the contract that it's for a *specific* song included in the collection (songs are listed by "title, registration number"). The publisher will register it themselves as the owner of a published work.

Also, and this is *very important:* If your song is *not* registered (and your song cannot be verified as being registered if it's not registered *individually*), you are not eligible to collect compulsory license fees if another artist records it or it's used in an audio/visual production.

THE "POOR MAN'S COPYRIGHT"

Songwriters are always looking for a less expensive way to protect their songs, especially since the cost of registration went up to thirty dollars. The idea of the "Poor Man's Copyright" is an old one though. It's the process of sending yourself your song by registered mail. My emphatic advice is, don't do it!!! It's the least reliable "protection" since it could be argued that, with it in your possession, you could have opened it and altered its contents. Yes, there are ways to do that but I know you don't actually think I'll tell you. Also, if your house burned down, you may have no proof at all that those songs were yours. You may find other services advertised that offer some protection, but there are always more practical reasons why you shouldn't use them.

WHY IT'S BEST TO REGISTER WITH THE COPYRIGHT OFFICE

No matter how reliable or unreliable any of these methods may be, what they don't do is:

• Allow you to sue someone for copyright infringement in federal court if you've registered your song within three months of the date of first publication or before the infringement occurs. Otherwise you'll have to pursue it in civil court. It's tough to prove the date of creation and very expensive and difficult to obtain compensation for damages.

• Allow you to automatically collect statutory damages (if you win) of $200 to $150,000 per work plus attorney fees and court costs, depending on the type and degree of infringement as decided by the court (see "Awarding Damages" on page 164). The court may also award you whatever profit the infringer received from the use of your song, and compensation for your own losses.

• Get you paid a license fee. As mentioned above, unless a potential user of your music can verify that your song is registered, they don't have to pay you a compulsory license fee if they record your song.

So, in the long run, you're much better off dealing with the government on this one.

Copyright Infringement

One of the most common fears of songwriters is that they'll have a song stolen. (Next on the list is that you've inadvertently stolen someone else's!) And while it's been known to happen, infringement is less common than the paranoia would indicate. Publishers would rather publish a song than steal it. They'd rather be in line for your next hit than be in court defending themselves in a copyright infringement case.

The more concrete fear is that another writer will steal an idea. Since neither an idea nor a title can be copyrighted, the possibility is greater that another writer might borrow an idea or title and use it as a basis for a new song. There's no real protection for lyric *ideas*. Throughout the history of literature and music, writers and musicians have borrowed from each other quite blatantly with no apologies for doing it. The originators of musical and literary forms are well documented and the forms are still in use. The storyteller is said to have a choice of thirty-six basic plots. Beyond that, he's dealing with variations. The idea itself is not as important as how he develops it. The language, characterization, and imagery are what make a story, or a song, unique.

If you do come up with a new idea or an unusual variation but don't craft it well, it is unlikely that it will spark interest. There is, however, the chance that another writer will realize you had a good idea but you didn't do it justice. That person may have the craftsmanship and perseverance to make it work and he would have every right to develop the idea in his own way. If the writer took your idea in a totally different direction and used none of your unique language, it would *not* constitute copyright infringement.

When you sign with a publisher or a record company you give *them* some or all of the rights listed on page 155. Copyright infringement is a federal crime that occurs when any of these exclusive rights are violated.

HOW DO YOU PROVE COPYRIGHT INFRINGEMENT?

In order to prove copyright infringement, two things must be established: (1) who has ownership of the copyright, and (2) whether the alleged infringer actually copied the song. A copyright registration number for that song from the Library of Congress can be admitted as evidence that the song belongs to the person filing the suit.

Whether the copyright is registered before or after the infringement will influence the type of damage compensation for which the plaintiff (the one suing) is eligible. The plaintiff also must prove that the song was infringed upon. If a witness cannot testify that he or she saw the defendant actually listening to and copying the song, the plaintiff has to prove (1) access and (2) substantial similarity.

Access. Access is really "the opportunity to have heard" a song or a "reasonable possibility that it was heard" by the defendant. If you prove that a song was widely known, the courts will assume the defendant heard it. "Widely known" is obvious with recorded songs, particularly hits. Where it gets really sticky is in a case where a writer/performer is traveling around the country singing his or her songs. Though no publishing or recording deals are involved, it's possible that the song could be taped or taught to another writer/performer and a chain of listeners created over which the original writer has no control. If you played a concert in the defendant's town, he could have both "opportunity" and "possibility," but it would be tricky to find any kind of proof.

Substantial similarity. Another crucial question is, of course, how similar was the defendant's song to that of the plaintiff? This is where we get into the question of whether it's okay to copy "a few bars" of another work. A popular myth says that more than four bars need to be copied before it constitutes infringement. Not true! On the one hand, there are probably a lot of songs with four-bar passages that are technically the same, but they sound so different that one would not remind you of the other. But there are other songs that are instantly recognizable in just four notes, such as the first four notes of the old *Dragnet* theme, which establish the identity of the song so strongly that using them would constitute a "substantial taking."

The court uses two tests to determine the degree of similarity. Expert witnesses such as musicologists are brought in to testify about whether the actual melodic construction is the same. The other test is for a jury to decide whether, after listening to both songs, they sound alike, or close enough that one could be mistaken for the other, or that the impression to "the reasonable person" is similar. A judge decided George Harrison's "My Sweet Lord" was too similar to the song "He's So

Fine." Though it was decided that Harrison didn't deliberately plagiarize the song, he lost the suit. "I didn't mean to do it" is not a defense.

ILLEGAL FILE SHARING: THE NEW INFRINGERS

The protection of all kinds of intellectual property is an ongoing battle. Challenges generated by ease of communication provided by the Internet are the latest. People who use illegal peer-to-peer file sharing that allows the downloading of songs without compensation to the creators and without their permission are copyright infringers regardless of how they may justify their actions. The rationales go like this:

We're helping to promote the artists. Answer: In some cases, particularly with new indie artists, that has, in fact, proven to be true. "Viral marketing," the concept of one fan turning several others on to the artists and those friends doing the same is a very effective technique. It is also true that record companies' control over distribution and airplay has left few other ways, aside from constant touring, for independent artists to promote themselves. Having said that, the key issue is that it is the right of the creator of the music to determine how his music will be distributed. If that artist intentionally releases an audio file of a song as part of a campaign to promote his CD, that's his prerogative, his right. If not, nobody else has that right.

Record companies are ripping us off. Answer: I find it difficult to be an apologist for major labels. Much of the blame for their losses is due to their failure to drop their traditional marketing paradigm to adapt to Internet opportunities by making legal downloads of their artists' music available early on. Having said that, most music fans know nothing about the economics of the music industry. What they don't see is the money that goes into making them aware of the artists they love and want to download. They want to do it as a result of the labels having done their marketing job effectively. The artists they're successful with are the ones who pay for the 90 percent they lose money on.

The artists are rich and don't mind. Answer: You don't know how much they make or owe. You'd be surprised at how many artists are still in survival mode after selling millions of records. Most music fans are also ignorant of the fact that many artists don't write their own songs and when fans download those artists' recordings, they're depriving *writers* of their royalties regardless of the success of the artists.

Music should all be free. Answer: Only those who have never spent substantial time, effort, and creativity at risk to their well-being, livelihood, and sanity to create and perform their music could make an argument like that. It is only because of commercial success, or the promise of it, that artists and songwriters can afford to continue to create and those in the music business will continue to invest in the gamble. Intellectual property is one of our main exports, valued around the world. When it is no longer able to support artists and songwriters, there may be nothing left that's worth stealing.

The Copyright Office, the Recording Industry Association of America (RIAA), the Songwriters Guild of America (SGA), the Nashville Songwriters Association International (NSAI), National Music Publishers' Association (NMPA), songwriters, and all the other organizations and artists who are fighting illegal distribution of intellectual property will, I believe, prevail enough to stem the tide somewhat, though I don't believe they will ever be able to stop illegal downloading altogether. The Supreme Court decision in June 2005 to hold the software company Grokster Ltd. responsible for promoting illegal downloads was a major victory. There will continue to be challenges like this, however, and songwriters need to support the songwriting organizations engaged in this ongoing battle. If they prevail, everyone who creates music will be able to enjoy the rewards that new distribution technologies are creating.

Public Domain

Often, a defense in an infringement case is that the defendant did not copy the plaintiff's song, but copied part of a "public domain" song that existed long before the plaintiff's song. A song is in the public domain if, like classical works and traditional folk songs, it was composed before copyright laws were established or no one knows who wrote it. It's also in the public domain when its copyright term has expired. Posting your work on the Internet does not put it into the "public domain" and downloading others' work does not constitute fair use.

FAIR USE

Some uses can be made of the works of other writers that don't constitute infringement. These are covered by the doctrine of "fair use." These include criticism (for example, reproducing part of a lyric in a record review), comment, news reporting (using a small portion of another's work as a basis for an editorial comment or a news story that relates to it), scholarship or research (using portions of other works for a thesis or term paper, for instance), and teaching. The latter is the fair use area that most concerns songwriters and composers. Several major music publishing and music educators associations have worked out guidelines for the photocopying of sheet music for classroom use. (See the appendix on page 384.)

Four guidelines help define what constitutes fair use:

1. The purpose and character of the use, including whether it's for commercial or for nonprofit educational purposes.

2. The nature of the copyrighted work itself.

3. The amount and substantiality of the portion used in relation to the work as a whole.

4. The effect of the use on the potential market for, or value of, the copyrighted work.

Parody is a category that can be considered fair use. I say "can be" because it also is subject to the above qualifications and if, for instance, you use too much of the original work you may be on shaky legal ground. "Weird Al" Yankovic has made a career of parodying hits but always obtains permission of the copyright owners for the use of their melodies. It's clearly the safest course of action. In some cases, it amounts to more of a professional courtesy than anything else, but at least you're covered. Parody and other fair use legal disputes are decided by the courts on a case by case basis and it's a gray area of the law because it can also involve, in the case of parody especially, freedom of speech issues. Previous decisions of the courts are often cited as precedents on which to decide cases, and in cases that seem similar, decisions have been arrived at that are quite different.

AWARDING DAMAGES

What can the plaintiff expect to receive if he wins an infringement case? If it can be established how much profit was made by the infringer, or how much monetary damage has been done, it can all be recovered. The plaintiff will probably fare better if it can be proven that the person willfully infringed than it was unintentional.

It's very difficult to prove damages though, so the plaintiff can elect to seek "statutory damages," an amount set by law to encourage copyright registration. (They figured that if they offered a cash reward they could keep you from being your own worst enemy.) The amount can range from between $200 and $100,000. In order to be eligible to collect statutory damages and recover the attorney fees spent on the trial, the copyright registration must have been obtained before or within three months of the date the infringement occurs.

What I've discussed here is a simplification of the subject. If you would like to pursue this further or have other questions answered about copyright, call your local Bar Association and locate a copyright attorney. I also highly recommend *The Musician's Business & Legal Guide* by Mark Halloran, Esq., and *Legal Aspects of the Music Industry* by Richard Schulenberg (see the bibliography for both), or contacting the Copyright Office.

Online Resources

The United States Copyright Office (www.copyright.gov): It's all here: forms, basic info, legislation updates and international copyright info. It also presents updates (in non-legalese) of the ongoing court cases and Copyright Office rulings regarding use of music on the Internet, Webcasting, challenges to copyright laws, and more.

Copyright Website (www.benedict.com): Includes resources, famous court cases, and other fascinating information.

Copyright and Fair Use (http://fairuse.stanford.edu): A Stanford University Library site that's an amazing repository of facts, articles, opinions on copyright, multimedia, intellectual property in general, and cyberspace law.

Avoiding the Songsharks

"Songsharks" are companies and individuals who charge a fee to publish your song or collaborate with you, most commonly to write music to your lyric, which they like to refer to as a "song poem." Others, under the guise of publishing companies, ask you to submit material, then inform you that it just so happens that they've found an album project that your song is perfect for. In fact, what happens is that the "publishing" company sends your song to another branch of their own company that is the "record" company. The latter writes to say that the song is perfect—they just need some money from you first to make sure they can do a good job. You're "double teamed" to make sure the sharks get your money.

Many "songshark" letters have been forwarded to me from songwriters who were concerned about getting ripped off. The most common story is that, out of nowhere, they received a letter asking them to submit material for review. "Where did they find out about me?" is the common question from writers who've received letters out of the blue from a notorious "record company" who wants to record their material. They're always flattered that someone knows about them. Sorry to burst your bubble, but they get your name and address from the Library of Congress where you copyrighted your song (and via the Freedom of Information Act, that copyright information is available to the public).

The next most common story is that the writer responded to an ad in a magazine. In either case they received a letter much like the one that follows, a composite of several I've seen from "record" or "production" companies. Their offers usually contain the same catch phrases. Only the names have been changed. I've highlighted the most common statements and sales pitches:

As a songwriter, **you've probably considered having a song recorded** *at one time or another.* **If you've been disappointed** *and you're about to make that decision to just let that song sit unrecorded, Songshark Music Productions would like you to consider submitting it to us.*

Recording companies need new songs. Without them they would cease to exist. Just think how many new songs you hear on the radio, television, and records. **Some day one of them may be yours! Just compare your efforts with songs on the market today.**

Many writers, perhaps like yourself, produce some really good songs. **Your song may be excellent and worthy of recording.** *We are interested in ALL types of material: Popular, Country Western, Gospel, Rock, Ballads, etc.*

We employ professional arrangers, musicians and vocalists to help you accomplish that commercial production that was, before, out of reach. Best of all, after Songshark Music Productions records your song on a commercial record, **we will ship records to disc jockeys and record stores and pay you a ROYALTY for each record sold.**

Songshark Music Productions will record songs of any style, with or without melody (leadsheet). **If you have lyric only, it will be completed with a commercial tune by our professional arrangers.** *If you have a completed song, rest assured our arrangers will adhere to your lyric and melody as much as possible. If you send a tape, make sure it is accompanied by the lyrics or leadsheet along with a self-addressed stamped envelope for its return.*

Have no fear in sending us your un-copyrighted songs or poems. *Songshark Music Productions is a recording company and is not in the business of stealing songs or poems. However, if you wish to stay on the "safe side," have your material notarized and/or send it* **Registered Mail through the United States Post Office.** *You may have real ability and* **you must act now, today!** *Let us took over your work, so that we may give you* **our honest opinion.** *Don't just let your poem or song sit around.* **Let us help you get it recorded.**

What a great offer! Songshark Music Productions came along just in the nick of time to save your creative life. But take a closer look at this letter and you'll find clues to tip you off to their questionable business practices.

First they use "If you've been disappointed" as an attention-grabber. Who hasn't been disappointed? Sounds like they're going to get your song recorded for you!

Next the pitch gets heavy. The "just compare" line is typical—and effective. There isn't a writer alive who hasn't heard a song on the radio and said, "If that can get on the radio, my song is a cinch!"

Notice that the letter makes no mention of R&B. "Country Western" is a phrase seldom heard anymore. That alone tells you this company is behind the times.

Next they actually promise that *after* they record your song on a *commercial* record (they're already assuming it will be good enough), they'll ship records to DJs and record stores. They'll probably actually do this. They could fulfill this promise by sending it to *two* DJs and *two* record stores. The reality is that they're hoping that *you* will buy the albums, along with all the other writers whose songs are included on it. Songsharks have no real illusions about their ability to get airplay of an unknown artist on a compilation record (containing several different singers). They know that even if a radio station did play one of the cuts from this album and it got good listener response, it would go nowhere because the listeners couldn't buy an *album* of *that* artist. So why should they play it instead of the superstar product from major record labels they're being pushed to play? They wouldn't. If they will play unknown artists, they'd rather play new artists from legitimate independent record companies.

Notice how Songsharks capitalize "ROYALTY" in the letter as though it's an added bonus. As if they want very badly to prove to you that they're really honest and wouldn't think of ripping you off. Receiving royalties for each record sold is a matter of course, and specific percentages are always negotiated upfront.

Many writers are confused by people who tell them that if they can't write musical notation they haven't "written" the melody. Songsharks want you to believe that "melody" means "leadsheet" or the melody written down. In truth, if someone has created a melody in his head and can sing it into a tape recorder he's "written" it. When someone else essentially puts chords to the melody, writes a chord or melody chart, and wants writer credit and half the writers' royalties for it, the first writer must decide if that contribution warrants co-writer credit.

But Songshark isn't looking to share the royalties with you as would a legitimate collaborator who believes her contribution is valuable enough to deserve a royalty split. A legitimate collaborator works on your song because she honestly believes you can make a potential hit together, not because a company pays her to write a melody for "any" lyric she's not otherwise motivated to work with, and for "any" lyricist she's never even taken the trouble to talk to.

The Songshark letter assures you the company is "not in the business of stealing songs or poems." Songsharks often refer to lyrics as "songpoems" knowing that the world is full of frustrated poets who think their poems could be used as song lyrics. They might be quite sincere about not wanting to steal your song, but they're being tremendously irresponsible about it. The worst possible protection is the so-called poor man's copyright, sending your work to yourself registered mail. It's been proven to be legally weak. You notice they didn't suggest you actually obtain a legitimate copyright registration through the Library of Congress. They could just as easily have given you the phone number of the Copyright Office. But they don't care about you. It's in *their* best interest that you don't take time to think about it or check with anyone about this letter.

The last paragraph urges you to hurry and let them help you. This is a prime setup that makes you think this is really an exclusive deal. This actually makes it sound as though you have to be good enough to be able to make use of their services. You're nervous when you send it in, hoping against hope that you have something they'll think worthy to record.

Typically, the next step is that they send you a second letter that says: **"Congratulations!** *Out of all the hundreds of songs we receive, (title) has been chosen to appear on our new (title) album, which will be* **distributed to radio stations around the country. Just send $400** *to cover production costs so that our experienced and creative team of singers, musicians, and producers can record your song with the* **best possible quality for commercial release."**

There's the zinger. You actually think something might happen and you send your $400 (or much more). Another letter arrives to tell you there's yet another album you could get your song on if you send more money. Once you send your first money, they know you're gullible. They know you're not aware that **no legitimate record company would ever charge you to have your song released on their record.** No legitimate publisher, record company, or demo service writes melodies for a fee.

Demo services, by the way, are legitimate businesses (and demo production seems to be a part of the activities of this songshark company).

Some sharks will make a demo of your song under the guise of releasing your song on a record. Demos can usually be done much cheaper elsewhere with your participation, though demo services may legitimately charge for arrangements, lead sheets, or chord charts. However, before dealing with any demo production service, you should hear samples of their work (see chapter twelve, "Demo Production Services" on page 260).

Songsharks are very inventive in coming up with new ways to separate you from your money. They'll "publish," "promote," "record," and charge you large "screening" fees, explaining that screening is a standard practice in the industry. Screening is a standard practice, but charging for it is considered unethical. **In the legitimate music industry, publishers and record companies gamble *their* money on your talent. If you lose, they lose. In the songshark "industry," only you lose. They don't gamble.**

Songsharks usually do operate within the letter of the law. Strictly speaking, they *usually* do what they promise. But everyone in the legitimate music industry considers them *unethical* because what they promise and deliver is not what you think it is. Their carefully worded letters create an illusion that bears little resemblance to how the real world of music publishing works. They prey on ignorant people who don't know how to get good information or who would rather harbor their illusions than deal with hard reality.

The songsharks argue that those people don't *want* to deal with the music industry. Songsharks say they're satisfying a need for people to hear their songs in a "finished" product. If that's the case, then sharks are essentially the equivalent of a "vanity press" for poets and authors, another legitimate business, but one that doesn't pretend to be anything else. If songsharks operated like vanity presses, they'd say it costs X amount to produce a master of your song, X amount to press X number of records, and then *you* do what you want with them. If you want them to actually promote your record, they'd tell you it will cost X amount *if* they thought the record was promotable.

Legitimate promotion is expensive. Major labels regularly spend $100,000 or more on a single. Just sending records to radio stations is *not* promoting a record. Promoting records that you don't believe in is the quickest way to get radio program directors *not* to take your calls and to totally lose your credibility.

When songsharks promise to get your songs played on the radio, they deliver that, too. They buy time on small stations in small markets that typically play your song at 3 A.M. You'll receive no performance royalty because the station can't log the airplay. BMI and ASCAP don't recognize songsharks as legitimate publishers, so songsharks can't put BMI or ASCAP next to the title of your song on their record. You thought that, when they said they'd "get it on the radio," they meant everywhere. *No one can promise that,* even promoters for major artists, unless they're also delivering payola. If they were honest, they'd tell you exactly what they do and how they do it, but songsharks are not in the honesty business.

9 Where Your Money Comes From

One of the most confusing things to new writers is the source of income from their songs. Though it's not important until one of your songs gets recorded, most of us want to know how much money we can make and how we can get it. "How much money" is impossible to predict because there are so many variables. A song may earn nothing or it may earn millions throughout the life of the copyright. How you get paid has, in the past, been quite simple. There are four major income sources from songs: *mechanical, performance, synchronization,* and *print.* The Royalty Flow Chart on page 181 illustrates how these sources relate to the songwriter, and the others who may also get a slice of the pie.

Just to make it a little less simple (and this is what I love about the music business), the industry is currently in a state of uncertainty about the future of royalties, how they will be tracked, and how they'll be divided and distributed. The old established models listed here are being rethought, fought about, and renegotiated, and new concepts are being formulated to better accommodate current and future digital delivery systems. Representatives of music publishers, record companies, songwriters, recording artists, consumer audio manufacturers and consumers, music-oriented Web sites, and online music entrepreneurs all have considerable financial interests at stake.

There are those proposing that the standard Mechanical License be abolished in favor of a single license that combines Mechanical and Performance royalties to make it less difficult for potential users to get permission to use the music. For example, if you want to get legal permission to use a popular song on your Web site, you need a license from the Performing Rights Organization (BMI, ASCAP or SESAC) that represents the copyright owner (usually the publisher) and songwriter, the record company that owns the original master recording, and SoundExchange or Royalty Logic for collecting the new royalties paid to recording artists and record companies for digital uses.

Without an easier way to license songs for a variety of digital uses, it can be financially prohibitive for Web site owners to use those songs. The impasse to a combined license is that each of those organizations is responsible for coming out with the best possible percentage of the pie for their respective members. So they're still fighting it out and may be fighting for some time to come. It's like the example of the monkey that puts his hand in a trap to get the banana and, not being able to get his hand back through the hole with the banana, stays trapped because he won't let go. The result is that nobody gets anything until they figure it out.

For now, here's an explanation of how it works.

Methods of Payment

Mechanical, synchronization, and *print* royalties are collected by the publisher, who takes his share and sends you your share, usually quarterly or semi-annually. The *performance royalties* are collected by the performing rights organizations—BMI, ASCAP, and SESAC. They will send a quarterly check and statement directly to you and one to your publisher, the amounts divided according to the terms of your publishing contract.

For example, if *you have a standard 50/50 writer/publisher split,* the publisher's half of the performance royalties will go directly to him, and your half will go directly to you. If you have a 50/50 co-writer split, half of the *writers' share* (25 percent of the total) will go to you directly, the other half will go to your co-writer. Maybe you're splitting the publishing as well. If *you have a 50/50 co-publishing split* and you're the only writer, the other publisher would get a check for 50 percent of the publishing (25 percent of the total). Your own publishing company would get a check for the other half of the publishing (25 percent of the total). As the writer, you'd get a check for all of the writer's share (50 percent of the total). In the end you end up with two checks comprising 75 percent of the total.

The following diagrams illustrate the way income is divided between publishers and writers, based on contract clauses that may limit what the writers actually earn. Keep in mind that the 50/50 division is traditional and is not an absolute, though the writer should not accept less than 100 percent of the writer's share. I use 200 percent as a basis because the publisher's share is nearly always referred to in terms of 100 percent, i.e., "100 percent of publishing," "50 percent of publishing," etc. The "writer's" share (also based on "100 percent writer's share," etc.) may be divided between any number of writers, and the "publisher's" share may be divided between any number of publishers.

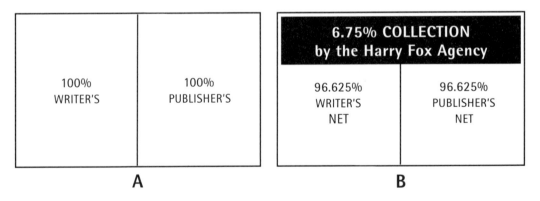

Figure A represents a 50/50 split of gross income. Figure B is the royalty split you get when the contract calls for a 50/50 split of gross income "less costs of collection." The 6.75 percent shown here as an example is the current fee charged by the Harry Fox Agency for collection of mechanical income only. Other mechanical rights organizations charge different fees. It is preferable for the writer if this cost be paid by the publisher (Figure C).

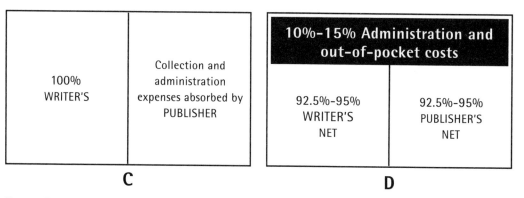

Figure D represents a 50/50 split of gross income less administration and out-of-pocket costs (copyright registration, photocopies, postage, etc.) directly connected to the exploitation of that specific composition. In this example, the writer and publisher share the cost by having it taken off the top before royalties are divided. The writer will want to negotiate for the publisher to absorb those costs, as in Figure C. However, you can't always get what you want!

Split Publishing or Co-Publishing

Figure E shows the division of income for a writer who gets "half the publishing." In this most common situation, the "other publisher" usually absorbs costs of collection and administration. In other cases, such as when two writers with their own publishing companies split the income, an independent administration company may be hired. In such a case, the writers' companies should both share those expenses.

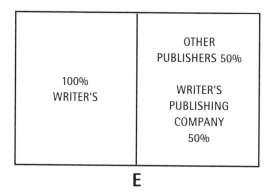

Mechanical Royalties

Mechanical royalties come from the sale of things mechanical—audio records, tapes, CDs, and more recently, DPDs (Digital Phonorecord Distributions) to the general public. The current mechanical rate, called the "statutory rate," set by the Copyright Royalty Tribunal as of January 1, 2006, is 9.1 cents per use for compositions that are five minutes or less; for songs over five minutes, the rate is 1.75 cents per minute or fraction thereof of playing time, whichever is greater (periodically updated). So, if you have ten songs on a CD, the record company owes the publisher 91 cents per CD. (In Canada the standard royalty rate is 8.5 cents or 1.7 cents per minute for more than five minutes and is collected by CMRRA with an added 7 percent Goods and Services Tax.)

At times, you may be able to negotiate a contract for part of the "publishing" (the traditional 50 percent publisher's share in addition to your 50 percent writer's share). This can occur most often if you're a recording artist or a hot writer with a proven success record. A publisher will make that kind of split if he's excited enough about your songs or is in competition with other publishers for your songs, or if you can show him a history of having pitched your songs to producers and artists.

Collecting the money is a very important part of the publisher's job and often a difficult one. Most publishers contract with collection agencies such as Harry Fox who issue mechanical licenses and collect both domestic and certain foreign mechanical royalties for a fee of 6.75 percent of royalties collected. They stopped synchronization licensing services for film and TV in 2002.

They also collect foreign mechanical royalties via affiliated agencies in thirty different countries. Those agencies will take 5–20 percent commissions off the top before forwarding the rest to the Harry Fox Agency.

Because the agencies collect on behalf of many publishers, they have some power, and they audit the record companies regularly to make sure the publishers get all the royalties they've earned. There is a lot of "creative bookkeeping" in record companies *and* publishing companies. Their objective is to hold on to the money for as long as they can so they can make a substantial amount of money from the interest on your royalties.

The major North American mechanical rights organizations that publishers will most often work with are listed here:

NMPA/HARRY FOX AGENCY

711 Third Avenue • New York, NY10017

Tel: (212) 370-5330; Fax: (646) 487-6779 • Web site: www.nmpa.org/hfa.html

In Los Angeles: (323) 466-3861 • In Nashville: (615) 242-4173

CANADIAN MUSICAL REPRODUCTION RIGHTS AGENCY LTD. (CMRRA)

56 Wellesley St. W. #320 • Toronto, Ontario, Canada M5S 2S3

Tel: (416)926-1966; Fax: (416)926-7521 • Web site: www.cmrra.ca

So how do the numbers work out? A little arithmetic shows that one song on a million-seller CD, single, or DPD will bring a total of $91,000. When you have a song as a single, you can figure it will be on the CD album, too. Often a CD single will also contain several re-mixes including different lengths of radio mixes for various formats, dance re-mixes, etc. by star DJs with their own styles. It's a parallel industry. You'll get paid for each of those as well.

If you have a hit single, down the road you may also be involved in "Greatest Hits" and other compilation CDs, record clubs, and TV packages like "The Top Hits of 2006," etc. Producers of these will usually want you to give them a lower "rate," commonly three quarters of the mechanical rate. Their philosophy is that it's an extra market for you—a bonus—and they may sell hundreds of thousands of records after the peak sales period of your original release (see chapter ten, "Reduced Mechanical Royalty Rates" on page 207).

The Cumpulsory License

The first time a composition is recorded, the copyright owner has total control over who records the song and what they're charged. Theoretically, copyright owners could charge even more than the current statutory rate for that first recording but they never do. That first-time control is the reason a producer and artist can be granted a "hold" by a publisher and promise that no one will be allowed to record the song before they do.

After a record of a song has been manufactured and distributed the first time, the copyright allows anyone else to record the song as long as it avoids changing the basic melody or fundamental character of the work. In other words, no one can do an arrangement of your song and get his own copyright on it. Those who record the song after the first recording must obtain a "compulsory license."

Copyright law says: "A compulsory license includes the privilege of making a musical arrangement of the work to the extent necessary to conform it to the style or manner of interpretation of the style and performance involved, but the arrangement shall not change the basic melody or fundamental character of the work and shall not be subject to protection as a derivative work under this title, except with the express consent of the copyright owner." A *derivative work* is a second artistic creation based upon one or more preexisting, copyrighted aspects of an original work, in which that work may be recast, transformed, or adapted. (Sampling, compilations, and songs used in audio-visual media are examples of derivative works.) You need the written permission of the copyright owner to use any of his work in a new creation.

If someone wants to record your work under the compulsory license and it's not a derivative work, they need to find you (the copyright owner), sign a "mechanical license" and agree to pay the current statutory mechanical rate. Failure to obtain a compulsory license constitutes copyright infringement.

In addition, they must file a "notice of intention" with the copyright owner via certified or registered mail before or within thirty days of making the recording and before distributing it. The licensee is required to make payments and accountings by the twentieth of each month for recordings made and distributed during the previous month, and an annual statement of account signed by a CPA. A notice of intention must be filed for each title. If this is not done and not remedied within thirty days, the license is defaulted.

If the licensee can't find you, he needs to file the notice of intent with the Copyright Office. The licensee doesn't have to pay if there is no record of copyright registration filed at the Copyright Office, but once your copyright is registered and he finds you, he needs to start paying. Compulsory licenses are only granted for records, tapes, CDs, and DPDs primarily intended to be distributed to the public for private use.

The U.S. is the only country with a compulsory license.

For further details on the process of filing the letter of intent, go to the Copyright Office's Web site (www.copyright.gov/circs/circ73_amend.html) to see Circular 73, which was amended on July 22, 2004.

Controlled Composition Clauses

If you're a self-contained writer/artist, group, or writer/producer looking for a record deal, you should be aware of the almost universal practice of record companies to demand a reduced mechanical royalty rate on "controlled compositions" (songs and other musical material in which the copyrights are controlled by the artist). The current practice is to ask for 75 percent of the statutory rate or less. Your ability to resist their "take it or leave it" approach is entirely dependent on you or your manager's or attorney's assessment of your bargaining power in that particular situation. New artists are particularly vulnerable and frequently give in with the philosophy that any deal is better than no deal.

Record companies may also tell an artist or producer that even if she chooses "outside material" (songs controlled by a publisher or writer other than themselves), the record company will still pay only 75 percent of the statutory rate and often limit that to ten songs. This forces the artist to negotiate for a lower rate from the other "outside" publisher and writer or make up the difference from his own pocket on those songs, as well as any songs over the ten-song limit. The obvious effect is to reduce the willingness of the producer and artist to record "outside material," possibly reducing the quality of music on the album because the producer or the recording artist must rely on her own material rather than use better-written songs by other writers.

From the record company's point of view, it's expensive to produce, market, and promote a record, particularly if they have to front the money for a video. They want to cut expenses any way they can.

From your point of view, the record company makes their money from selling records. You make yours from that royalty, and without that song there wouldn't be a record! So, though writers and publishers unanimously condemn the practice, it's a reality that you will have to deal with this either as a writer/artist or as an "outside" writer.

Samples

Hip-hop and rap recordings frequently make use of samples (pieces of compositions or sound recordings used from other songs). The artist has to pay the source song's copyright owner *and* record company additional licensing fees to use those samples. Sampling of your work can be an additional source of royalty revenue for you. In the early days of the sampling craze, publisher Jay Warner realized that the songs of his writer, funkster Rick James, were being frequently sampled, and that they could be making royalties from them. So Warner began sending compilations of James' recordings to rap artists, inviting them to sample the songs. He also provided them with forms to fill out listing the cuts they sampled, the length of samples, etc., capitalizing on this new source of income.

If you're a recording artist who wants to sample someone else's recording, you must contact *both* the owner of the copyright on the song (usually the publisher) and the owner of the recording (usually the record company) for permission *before* you release your record. Samples are *not* subject to the compulsory license (see page 173), so you'll have to negotiate based on the length of the sample, how you're using it, the number of times it's used, and the importance of the sample to the potential success of the recording. For example, if you use a whole chorus of someone else's song, it's obviously very important and you'll have to share all royalties with the writer, publisher, and record company, and you will probably also be instructed to credit the writer on the record.

Depending on the criteria above, you may be required to pay a flat fee or a fee plus mechanical royalty. If you wait to seek permission until after your record is released, you're in deep trouble and are in the worst possible negotiating position. The copyright owners could even get an injunction against distribution of your record. So you *must* negotiate for the use of samples before releasing your record, and preferably, at the time you decide you want to use them in a specific song, so that if the price is too high you'll have time to replace it with something else.

There are also recently popularized versions of sampling called bootlegs (boots or booties), mashups, blends, and cut-ups, forms that are used under the collective genre called "bastard pop." They refer to recordings that are made up either partly or entirely of sampled tracks or vocals from other recordings. Though this is an interesting art form, somewhat like collage in the art world, it's as fraught with legal problems as a form of sampling. The biggest problem is that the artists customarily use so many samples that it would be too costly to "clear" them for it to ultimately generate any income. One way around it is the increasing use of a Creative Commons license that allows writer/artists who control their own copyrights and master use rights to grant permission to use limited rights for any non-commercial use, or to grant a license with limitations for a commercial use. Check out the Creative Commons Web site (www.creativecommons.org).

Do I have to pay to use a sample if I go into a studio with musicians and re-record that piece of music I want to use? If you do it that way, you won't have to pay the record company for sampling the original recording, but you will have to negotiate with the copyright owner for the use of the "underlying work"—the song itself.

Performance Royalties: BMI, ASCAP, and SESAC

Performance royalties are a major source of income for a writer. They're not to be confused with the money a performer makes directly from public appearances. Performance royalties are monies the copyright owner(s) and songwriter(s) receive when their song is performed publicly. According to the copyright law, nobody can publicly perform a copyrighted song without permission of the copyright owner. (Don't panic! It doesn't mean if you sing somebody's song in a club you have to find him and ask permission. See page 176.)

The most common uses of music in public performance are familiar to us all: radio, network and local TV, jukeboxes, music services like Muzak, and live performances. When your songs are played in any of these venues, you, as the writer, and the publisher (whoever owns the copyright) are entitled to get paid for its use. The obvious problem is how to go about collecting the money. Do you call the radio and TV stations all over the country to pay you each time they play your song? Do you send a bill to a club owner because you heard someone play your song there? How do you find out how many times they played it? How do you get them to pay? How do you give them permission to play it there in the first place? The mind boggles at the enormousness of the task.

The performing rights organizations, BMI, ASCAP (American Society of Composers, Authors and Publishers) and SESAC (no longer using their original title, Society of European Stage Authors and Composers) are the entities that take care of these problems for you. Through membership in ASCAP or affiliation with BMI or SESAC, you grant them permission to license non-dramatic public performances, "small rights," of your compositions. (Dramatic performances, or "grand rights," are those contained in musical theatre, ballet, operas, operettas, etc., in which the story line of the song is dramatized with sets, costumes, props, and so forth. The licenses are granted directly by the copyright owner.) A writer or publisher may collect from only one of these organizations for the same song.

You may only belong to one organization at a time in the U.S. You can switch from one organization to another depending on the length of your contract period with that organization. You may, however, simultaneously belong to a U.S. and a European organization such as PRS (United Kingdom), SACEM (France) or GEMA (Germany). The advantage is that you'll get paid your foreign royalties faster, though you generally have to be generating a substantial amount of airplay in those countries for it to be worthwhile.

How do these organizations collect the money?

Generally speaking, radio and TV stations and networks pay annual "blanket license" fees negotiated by the performing rights organizations on behalf of their writer and publisher members. Blanket fees give radio and local and network TV permission for unlimited use of the compositions. Fees are based on a percentage of the advertising revenue received by the stations or networks. The philosophy is that if a station has a 50,000 watt clear channel signal, it's reaching millions of people, enabling them to charge top dollar for advertising. (For a list of performance revenue sources see the Royalty Flow Chart on page 181.)

Revenues collected from dance clubs are charged according to their maximum legal room occupancy. Other clubs are charged a fee based on their annual entertainment expenses. Concert halls' charges are based on seating capacity and ticket prices. The American Hotel and Motel Association, The American Symphony Orchestra League, The Amusement Machine Operators of America, and The National Ballroom Operators Association all negotiate for their respective types of licenses. There is an annual fee for every jukebox. That money goes into a fund and is divided between the organizations. The organizations also license cable TV, colleges and universities, airlines, retail stores, and many other music users.

How do they know how many times a song is played?

Each organization has its own method of determining the number of performances, BMI chooses a representative cross section of stations to sample. The stations supply a written record (log) of all music performed during a specific period. The logs are put through an elaborate computer system that multiplies each performance listed by a factor that reflects the ratio of stations logged to the number of stations licensed. They then make a statistical projection that gives them a figure to approximate the number of "plays" on all stations. Different types or classes of stations are weighed in different ways.

ASCAP uses a method involving a combination of station logging and taping selected stations for a given period of time, sending the tapes to a central place where expert listeners pick out the ASCAP songs, tally them, and make the statistical projections.

In addition to their traditional monitoring techniques, both BMI and ASCAP have made strides in incorporating digital technologies that will continue to play a much more important role in accurate tracking of performances.

ASCAP has been using Mediaguide, which they purport to be the world's most comprehensive, accurate, timely, and reliable source for radio airplay information. The proprietary technology electronically monitors nearly 2,500 stations in 150 of the largest markets nationwide, automatically identifies broadcast content, and transforms it into marketing information for the Music, Radio and Advertising industries. At www.mediaguide.com you can see a list of every station that they monitor.

In August, 2005, BMI announced the acquisition of a digital audio recognition technology, to be named BlueArrow(SM), that will greatly expand its ability to measure the performance of music on radio, television and the Internet. The system uses pattern recognition to identify performances from any source containing audio.

The goal of all three PROs is in developing the most cost-effective ways to monitor performances so that more royalties may be distributed to their writer and publisher members. ASCAP and BMI operate on a non-profit basis, distributing to their members all money not used for overhead. Both monitor all network TV performances by direct census from producers' cue sheets. For local TV they use a combination of sampling, cue sheets, and TV Guide type program listings. All organizations distribute foreign performance royalties through reciprocal agreements with foreign performing rights societies. Though there are differences in the way they monitor and determine royalties, the methods of all three organizations are constantly evolving as they each attempt to compete with each other for writer members.

SESAC represents writers and publishers in all styles of music. It's the smallest of the three PROs and a for-profit company. They were the first, in 1993, to directly monitor airplay with Broadcast Data Systems (BDS) computerized tracking system. (Broadcast Data System, Web site: www.bdsonline.com, Phone: 800-688-4634. A visit to this site informs you about how it works. It will give you a list of the reporting stations for specific genres.). SESAC currently generates 100 percent of their airplay monitoring data from BDS (ten million hours annually in all styles of music). SESAC says that because of the immediacy of the BDS system they can pay writers for performances in the quarter after they're monitored as opposed to the other PROs who pay at least two quarters later.

As a private company, SESAC can be very selective about the writers they sign. Because they're smaller, they have much closer relationships with their writer members and will work on their behalf to set them up with co-writers, help find them record deals if they don't have one already, and assist in otherwise promoting their careers. SESAC also has a Latin division called SESAC Latina. For more information about the company, see their website at www.sesac.com.

How much do you make each time it's played?

It varies in both BMI and ASCAP according to the amount of income generated from all sources during the year or the quarter. Each has an equation that gives them an overall per play figure based on the type of station, number of plays, and the overall amount collected from user organizations based on periodic negotiations of blanket licenses. Both ASCAP and BMI have periodically changed their payment formulas for all sources of incomes, including bonuses for certain styles of music. These changes can affect your income for any specific use or style so it's a good idea to visit your PRO's website stay informed about the changes.

For a successful single, performance income for publishers and songwriters (which can continue for many, many years) will generally amount to a great deal more than the money earned from mechanical royalties. All organizations have embraced Internet technology that facilitates licensing, including online filing of cue sheets for film and TV uses.

The performing rights organizations pay quarterly. They send a check to the publisher(s) for the publisher share, and directly to the writer(s) for the writers share based on the percentages you gave them when you registered your works with them.

Do performing rights organizations give advances to writers and publishers?

BMI and ASCAP don't "officially" give advances. but they're known to do so in cases where they're in competition for high profile (or potentially high profile) writer/artists or writer/producers when they're in strong competition with each other for those writer's memberships. They need to know there's pretty much of a certainty that the writers will recoup the advance. It is also possible, in some cases, to have BMI or ASCAP co-sign a loan for you if they know there's already money in the pipepine for a song that's already generating considerable airplay.

How else do the organizations help songwriters?

The more songs licensed by an organization that are receiving airplay, the more money that organization can command in negotiations from the various users. The more money they receive, the more they can distribute to their members. Consequently, the three are in competition with each other for actively productive members. So it's in their interest to try to help you before you need to decide which organization to join. If your material merits being published or produced, whether you're an individual writer, writer/artist or a self-contained group writing your own material, they can help you connect with publishers, producers, or record companies. Their representatives are always looking for great new songwriters, writer/artists, writer/producers and film/TV composers.

All three organizations sponsor local industry showcases, seminars and workshops in most popular music genres that can be very helpful for generating networking opportunities and industry attention. Contact the organizations or go to their Web sites, where they list schedules of their events around the country, FAQs (frequently asked questions) informative articles on the music industry and interviews with their writer and publisher members.

Which is the best?

That's the toughest question to answer because there are so many variables—one of the most important being your own needs. The big question is usually "Who pays more?"—a complicated question that depends somewhat on your unique situation. Talk to them all. Believe me, they'll leave no questions unanswered. But remember: How much they each pay may be the biggest question, but it's not the only one. How do they treat you? Is there someone there you can relate to? Do you feel comfortable calling with a question? Those are the considerations that precede your making money at all. The organization you join is your decision alone. Some publishers will automatically put you in one or the other (if you're not already affiliated) because they feel one or the other is paying more at that time. I've even known publishers to make that choice for you for the mere reason that they prefer filling out one form over another. It's an important decision, however, so don't let anyone else make it for you.

Is there a charge to join?

There are no fees to join any of the organizations.

What else do I need to know?

Be sure to report any new songs that you have published or recorded to the clearance departments of your performing rights organization. If you have a publisher, the publisher should also do this, but make sure it's done, and done with the correct co-writing or co-publishing percentages, if applicable. Also, be sure to notify them if they change your address so they'll always know where to send your check. You can download their forms from their sites.

BMI and ASCAP members may co-write with one another. If the song is licensed by both organizations, each will pay its own writers and publishers. If there is no publisher involved in a song, a BMI writer can collect the full writer and publisher share of performance royalties.

For more in-depth analysis, I recommend Jeffrey Brabec and Todd Brabec's "Music Money and Success" (see bibliography) to help investigate each organization directly.

ASCAP

NEW YORK

One Lincoln Plaza • New York, NY 10023

Tel: (212) 621-6000 •Fax: (212) 724-9064

LOS ANGELES

7920 W. Sunset Boulevard, 3rd fl. • Los Angeles, CA 90046

Tel: (323) 883-1000 • Fax: (323) 883-1049

NASHVILLE

Two Music Square West • Nashville, TN 37203

Tel: (615) 742-5000 • Fax: (615) 742-5020

MIAMI

420 Lincoln Rd., Ste. 385 • Miami Beach, FL 33139

Tel: (305) 673-3446 • Fax: (305) 673-2446

CHICAGO

1608 N Milwaukee, Ste. 1007 • Chicago, IL 60647

Tel: (773) 394-4286 • Fax: (773) 394-5639

ATLANTA

PMB 400, 541 Tenth St. NW • Atlanta, GA 30318

Tel: (404) 351-1224 • Fax: (404) 351-1252

LONDON

8 Cork St. • London W1X1PB

Tel: 011-44-207-439-0909 • Fax: 011-44-207-434-0073

PUERTO RICO

654 Ave. Muñoz Rivera, IBM Plaza, Ste. 1101 B • Hato Rey, PR 00918

Tel: (787) 281-0782 • Fax: (787) 767-2805 • Web site: www.ascap.com

BMI

NEW YORK

320 W. 57th St. • New York, NY 10019-3790

Tel: (212) 586-2000

NASHVILLE

10 Music Square East • Nashville, TN 37203-4399

Tel: (615) 401-2000

LOS ANGELES

8730 Sunset Blvd., 3rd fl. West • West Hollywood, CA 90069-2211

Tel: (310) 659-9109

ATLANTA

3340 Peachtree Rd., NE, Ste. 570 • Atlanta, GA 30326

Tel: (404) 261-5151

MIAMI

5201 Blue Lagoon Dr., Ste. 310 • Miami, FL 33126

Tel: (305) 266-3636

LONDON

84 Harley House, Marylebone Rd. • London NW1 5HN, England

Tel: 011-0044 207486 2036

PUERTO RICO

255 Ponce de Leon, East Wing, Ste. A-262, BankTrust Plaza • Hato Rey, Puerto Rico 00917

Tel: (787) 754-6490 • Web site: www.bmi.com

SESAC

SESAC (HEADQUARTERS)

55 Music Square East • Nashville, TN 37203

Tel: (615) 320-0055 • Fax: (615) 329-9627

NEW YORK

152 West 57th St., 57th fl. • New York, NY 10019

Tel: (212) 586-3450 • Fax: (212) 489-5699

LOS ANGELES

501 Santa Monica Blvd., Ste. 450 • Santa Monica, CA 90401-2430

Tel: (310) 393-9671 • Fax. (310) 393-6497

SESAC INTERNATIONAL

67 Upper Berkeley St. • London W1H 7QX, England

Tel: 0207 616 9284 • Fax: 0207 563 7029 • Web site: www.sesac.com

ROYALTY SOURCES FLOW CHART

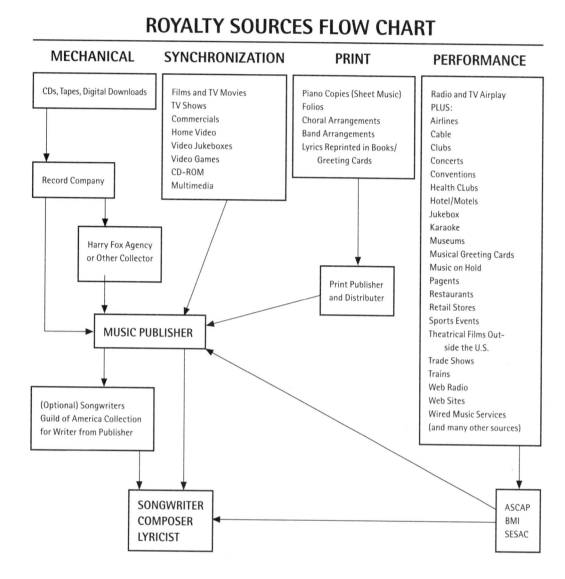

MECHANICAL   SYNCHRONIZATION   PRINT   PERFORMANCE

MECHANICAL

CDs, Tapes, Digital Downloads

Record Company

Harry Fox Agency or Other Collector

SYNCHRONIZATION

Films and TV Movies
TV Shows
Commercials
Home Video
Video Jukeboxes
Video Games
CD-ROM
Multimedia

PRINT

Piano Copies (Sheet Music)
Folios
Choral Arrangements
Band Arrangements
Lyrics Reprinted in Books/
   Greeting Cards

Print Publisher and Distributer

PERFORMANCE

Radio and TV Airplay
PLUS:
Airlines
Cable
Clubs
Concerts
Conventions
Health CLubs
Hotel/Motels
Jukebox
Karaoke
Museums
Musical Greeting Cards
Music on Hold
Pagents
Restaurants
Retail Stores
Sports Events
Theatrical Films Out-
   side the U.S.
Trade Shows
Trains
Web Radio
Web Sites
Wired Music Services
(and many other sources)

MUSIC PUBLISHER

(Optional) Songwriters Guild of America Collection for Writer from Publisher

SONGWRITER COMPOSER LYRICIST

ASCAP BMI SESAC

Synchronization Royalties

An increasingly important area of income for writers and publishers as well as independent artists and bands is the licensing of songs for audio-visual uses, which include film and television productions, commercials, karaoke and video jukeboxes, DVDs, video games—anything that requires synchronization of music with a visual medium.

There is no statutory rate for these uses since they're considered derivative works and require a negotiated up-front payment, a royalty, or both. The producer and music supervisor of the audio-visual work are responsible for negotiating the synchronization and performance license with the copyright owner (usually the publisher). This negotiation to obtain the synchronization rights for the project is called "clearance." There are companies such as The Clearing House in Los Angeles, and similar businesses in New York, Chicago, Vancouver, and other entertainment centers, that represent production companies in this task. If you don't have a publisher to represent you, many independent attorneys with expertise in this area negotiate synchronization rights between film/TV producers and music publishers.

Synchronization for film and television is a booming area for instrumental composers, songwriters, and especially for indie writer/artists and bands that can offer the "synch" rights to their songs and "master use" rights for the use of their recordings all in one package. This is especially valuable to series TV producers and music supervisors who have very little time to negotiate with publishers for the song rights and record companies for the "master use" rights separately.

(Because this is such an important opportunity now, I've expanded on this topic in depth in chapter fourteen.)

Music in Print

Most writers know little about print music. If you write mass-appeal songs, particularly adult contemporary, pop, or country, you'll be able to take advantage of a potentially lucrative print market. With the possible exception of the education print market, though, the songs will have to become very popular records to make all those piano bar singers, cover bands, and other print buyers want them. Ronny Schiff, an independent agent for print projects, has worked for some of the biggest print companies including Warner Bros. Music and Hal Leonard Publishing. Here's her rundown on the types of print music publishing:

Sheet Music: piano/vocal arrangements, often with chord designations for other instruments, and "easy piano" sheet music.

Personality Collection: collections based on a name artist, e.g., "The Songs of . . . ," "The . . . Songbook." These involve an additional contract called a "name and likeness" contract, which allows the print publisher to use the artist's, or writer/artist's name and picture. For example, Carlos Santana could negotiate a "name and likeness" contract if someone wanted to do a personality book that included not only songs he wrote but songs by other writers that he'd popularized. The philosophy is that his picture on the cover will sell that book.

Matching Collection: music matching a particular album or musical theater show. These may also involve a "name and likeness" contract.

Mixed Collection: collections based on concepts like "Easy Piano Tunes," "Greatest Hits of 2005," etc., involving songs from several writers.

Educational: included in this category are arrangements for choruses, marching bands, concert bands, jazz bands, and orchestras. These are obviously sold to schools, churches, drum and bugle corps, etc. This market gives music great exposure beyond actual sales. How many times in school have you heard the same songs being practiced by the band or chorus? Multiply that by the number of listeners in schools or attending sports events, and you get an idea how much exposure is available there. Writers also might receive royalties if their songs are used in a televised event or parade.

The educational print market can be very lucrative, especially for jazz and pop writers; 1,000 copies for a marching band is a big sell. It doesn't sound so big until you realize that arrangements go for $40 to $85 and a song will earn 10 to 12½ percent of the retail price. Choral arrangements of songs can be a good source of revenue, too. Some choral composers can sell 50,000 copies per year of songs that have never even been recorded! It's not unusual for popular choral writers to net $7,000 (10 percent of $1.70 retail units) for a single tune.

There are also freelance opportunities to compose and arrange for concert, jazz, marching bands, and choirs. Schools regularly buy arrangements of original songs as well as hits, but for this you need an understanding of the proficiency levels of different student groups so the parts aren't too difficult for them.

Another area of the educational market is how-to books, DVDs, and online instruction, especially in the areas of guitar, combo, and electronic instruments. This is a market for the songwriter who also has teaching skills. There's also great demand for guitar and bass note-for-note transcription books with tablature. The music print publishers also include specialized software for various music instruments, MIDI and music courses in their purview.

What does the publisher get in print royalties?

Retail prices for print music, like everything else, continue to rise. Currently for sheet music and online sheet music, print publishers will pay your publisher up to 20 percent of the retail price. For music book collections, publishers will pay about 12½ percent of the retail price. In cases where the book contains songs by various writers, this income is pro-rated according to the total number of copyrighted songs.

What does the writer get?

Often, she gets the short end of the stick. There was a practice in "standard" publishing contracts to offer the writer a "penny" value on sheet music sales, currently about six to ten cents per copy. This means that if your publisher can renegotiate his deal with the print company after a new version of your hit becomes popular, you may still be getting pennies a sheet from your old deal while his share goes up.

Try to negotiate 50 percent of all royalties received by your publisher from all your print sales. That way you remain equal partners in all royalties received. The 50 percent is based on a standard writer/publisher split, but should you be able to negotiate one more favorable to you, the print deal should reflect the same split. Publishers have no justification for giving you less than a 50/50 split on your print deal. In some situations, a publisher may have to lay out some legal fees to negotiate a difficult deal with a print publisher, but that's part of the expense of running a publishing company, just like producing demos is yours. If you can't get 50 percent of the publisher's print income, check the Songwriters Guild of America's guidelines for print royalties (see chapter ten, "Negotiable Contract Clauses" on page 200).

Researching Print Music Deals

If you're a self-published writer or a music publisher, you'll need to have some idea of how to go about looking for and sizing up a prospective print publisher. In the early days, selling sheet music and arrangements to the "big bands" and to artists who sang live on radio was the primary avenue of exposure for songs. With the growing popularity of records, sheet music became dependent on the popularity and style of the recording. As music publishers became more involved in the recording industry, they became less interested in print music and began to contract with those equipped to specialize in print marketing and distribution. Print publishers are further specialized in two major areas: pop, which includes sheet music and collections; and educational, which deals with arrangements for chorus, marching bands, orchestras, school jazz groups, and the like.

Ronny Schiff believes the best research method in looking for an effective pop print publisher is to drop in on a few sheet music stores and ask some questions, and you also check their online services:

- **How frequently are they serviced with new hit songs?** You want a print publisher who calls the stores weekly and provides them with a list of the latest acquisitions. (There's heavy competition between print publishers for the rights to new hits.)

- **Does the print company keep sheet music in print** or do they let it lapse after the song has peaked on the charts or do they at least provide it online?

- **Do they use the song in a variety of books online and educational formats?**

- **Do they supply retailers with promotional aids, displays, etc.?**

From an artistic standpoint, you'll want to consider the accuracy of the piano/guitar/vocal copies or guitar tablature copies. Compare them to the record. You'll want to work with a company that is consistently accurate. In negotiating a print deal, try to get a clause that grants you approval of the arrangements, but be reasonable about it. Don't hold up production if you're out of town.

It's possible to negotiate an educational print deal separately from the pop print contract. To research the effectiveness of those educational market specialists, call on some high school and college band and choral directors, and ask them which companies provide the best service and the best arrangements. When you talk to the educational print companies, ask if they do marching band and choral arrangements, and ask to see the promotional packages they send to the schools. You'll want to be sure they'll promote your music aggressively.

A maze of deal points can be negotiated in both pop and educational markets, and all print companies have structured a variety of deals for a variety of situations. It's to your advantage to find an attorney or publisher who's knowledgeable and creative in the print area to help you negotiate your deals.

Income From Digital Sources and the Home Recording Act

One of the upsides of the changes wrought by new digital distribution systems is the possibility of more income for recording artists and record labels (yes, that includes your own indie record label) via new copyright legislation.

Previous to 1995 and the enactment of the Digital Performance Right in Sound Recording Act (DPRSRA) and the Digital Millennium Copyright Act (DMCA) of 1998, only songwriters and publishers got paid a performance royalty for airplay, collected by the performing rights organizations (see "Performance Royalties" on page 175). Artists, singers, and musicians were left out of this royalty stream. They were justifiably upset by this situation since it caused problems within bands (whose writers saw performance royalty income and other members did not). Artists who covered songs they didn't write and were responsible for the great success of those songs were also upset since it's never *just* the song that listeners respond to, but the singers and musicians as well.

With the new law, there was a performance royalty for performing artists and record companies who had been previously left out of the loop (and the loot!), so the new legislation was definitely a positive step. However, non-writing artists, singers, and musicians still could not partake in performance royalties from previous sources (BMI, ASCAP, or SESAC) since those are reserved for writers and publishers only.

The new sources for artist and record company royalties are limited to digital audio transmissions. A "statutory license" royalty is paid by transmission services such as audio-only music channels delivered by digital cable and satellite television transmission systems (e.g., DMX Music, Music Choice), Webcasters (e.g., Yahoo!), satellite music services (e.g., XM radio), and others that qualify for the applicable statutory license. A "voluntary license" royalty may be negotiated with the copyright owner by services that offer interactive (on-demand or personalized) listening/downloading services or those services that do not qualify for an available statutory license.

How are statutory license rates established?

Statutory license rates are established through industry-wide negotiation between transmission services and copyright owner representatives. In the absence of industry-wide settlements, rates are determined through an arbitration proceeding before the Copyright Royalty Board, among those parties who elect to participate in the proceeding. Rates established by the Copyright Royalty Board become applicable to all parties, even to those transmission services and copyright owners that did not participate in the negotiation/arbitration process. The negotiation/arbitration process also establishes key terms and conditions of the statutory licenses that are critical to the fast and efficient distribution of royalties.

How do I get paid?

Performers and labels cannot collect statutory royalties directly from transmission services that utilize sound recordings. Instead, copyright law and regulation require artists and record labels to collect their share of statutory royalties through membership in collectives (called "designated agents") designated and authorized to perform the collection and distribution function. This is similar to the way performance royalties are received by composers and music publishers (i.e., through membership in ASCAP, BMI, or SESAC).

If you are an artist or record company, you receive statutory royalties by becoming an affiliate of one of the collectives. Only two entities have been designated to perform these functions—Royalty Logic and SoundExchange. Each designated agent receives the same statements of account and records of use of sound recordings from the transmission services. An artist may elect to receive royalties through the designated agent of his choice, regardless of which designated agent represents the record label.

If you don't become an affiliate of one of the collectives, copyright office regulations establish a default mechanism for your royalties to be administered by SoundExchange. As a direct result of lobbying by RIAA/SoundExchange, legislation was enacted in 2002 giving SoundExchange the right to recoup its historical licensing, litigation, and other costs, from royalties payable to artists and record companies retroactive to 1995. However, in order to protect the interests of artists and labels that did not want their royalties to be reduced by recoupment of costs that they neither incurred not approved, Congress specifically provided that these costs can't be deducted from artists and labels affiliated with Royalty Logic. So in order to prevent any RIAA/SoundExchange cost recoupment, you must become an affiliate of Royalty Logic. If you do nothing, copyright office regulations provide that you are automatically a "default' distributee of SoundEexchange subject to full cost recoupment.

The designated agents distribute allocated net statutory royalties 50 percent to the copyright owners of the sound recordings, 45 percent to the featured performing artist, 2.5 percent to the independent administrator representing the American Federation of Television and Radio Artists (AFTRA), and 2.5 percent to the independent administrator representing the American Federation of Musicians (AFM). However, where license fees are paid pursuant to voluntary license transactions, federal law ($114(g)(1)) provides that featured recording artists who perform on sound recordings receive payments from the copyright owner of the sound recording in accordance with the terms of the artist's contract. Non-featured recording artists receive payments from the copyright owner of the sound recording in accordance with the terms of the non-featured recording artist's applicable contract or other applicable agreement.

Sound Exchange

In order to facilitate the collection and distribution of Digital Royalties, the RIAA set up the first organization. The RIAA is the lobbying organization for the major labels, and so they established SoundExchange as a non-profit organization to give it an arm's length separation from themselves. As a non-profit, SoundExchange is obligated to represent all qualified artists and record companies. Here's how they describe themselves: ". . . a nonprofit performance rights organization jointly controlled by artists and sound recording copyright owners through an eighteen-member board of directors with nine artist representatives and nine copyright owner representatives. We have been designated by the U.S. Copyright Office to collect and distribute statutory royalties to sound recording copyright owners and featured and non-featured artists. Our board members and staff are dedicated to providing exceptional service and advocacy for artists and copyright owners to ensure the fair compensation for the use of copyrighted sound recordings."

Here is SoundExchange's explanation of how they operate:

Who qualifies to be a member?

"A featured artist, featured recording artist, contract artist, royalty artist, or featured performer means the performing group or, if not a group or ensemble, the individual performer, identified most prominently in print on, or otherwise in connection with, the phonorecord actually being performed. If a sound recording (either musical or spoken word) identifies several featured performers, then the allocation of royalties may be on a pro rata basis among all identified performers. According to the legislative history to the Digital Performance Right in Sound Recordings Act, where both the vocalist or soloist and the group or ensemble are identified as a single entity and with equal prominence (such as Diana Ross and the Supremes), both the individual and the group qualify as the featured recording artist. SoundExchange may also distribute royalties according to any splits agreed to among featured recording artists in private agreements, provided that all of the identified featured recording artists agree in writing to SoundExchange's distribution of royalties according to such splits.

Who or what is a sound recording copyright owner?

"An SRCO is one who owns the sound recording copyright under U.S. Copyright Law to perform publicly by means of a digital audio transmission one or more copyrighted sound recordings or has the right to license the public performance of one or more copyrighted sound recordings by means of a digital audio transmission."

For more information on SoundExchange:

SOUNDEXCHANGE
1330 Connecticut Ave., NW, Ste. 330 • Washington, D.C. 20036

Tel: (202) 828-0120 • Fax: (202) 833-2141
General e-mail: info@soundexchange.com
Web site: www.soundexchange.com

Royalty Logic

The Royalty Logic Web site (www.royaltylogic.com) states: "Royalty Logic is an independent music copyright management organization established to promote the constitutional purposes of copyright by providing a fair return to performing artists and record labels for the licensing of their music in digital media. Royalty Logic is dedicated to providing a simple and efficient way for copyright owners to grant, and for digital music services to obtain, permission to utilize musical copyrights in full compliance with copyright law.

Royalty Logic's management services are open to qualified artists and record labels and include negotiation of 'voluntary' and 'direct' license transactions, as authorized by statute; administration of statutory license fees; and distribution of royalties to artists, record labels, and applicable unions."

> Royalty Logic's President, Ron Gertz, states: "Royalty Logic is a competitive marketplace alternative to the agent established by the RIAA (SoundExchange). We believe that artists and indie labels alike deserve a choice among digital royalty administration services as the best way to insure that royalties are collected and paid in a transparent manner and at the lowest cost. The creators will be the copyright owners—Royalty Logic was established to meet their needs.

For more in-depth information on Royalty Logic:
ROYALTY LOGIC
405 Riverside Dr. • Burbank, CA 91506

Tel: (818) 955-8900 • Fax: (818) 558-3484

Web site: www.royaltylogic.com

How do they know how many times my recording is played?

They get actual track level data. Since it's digital, they don't need to use sampling and projection as the performing rights organizations (PROs) do.

Can I belong to both a PRO and SoundExchange or Royalty Logic?

If you're a songwriter *and* a recording artist you *should*.

Royalties From the Home Recording Act of 1992

THE ALLIANCE OF ARTISTS AND RECORDING COMPANIES (AARC)

In addition to the above organizations, who collect royalties for digital performances, AARC is responsible for collecting the fees levied for the sale of non-commercial home recording devices and media (tapes, CDs, DVDs, etc.) worldwide to compensate for home copying of recordings. It also collects royalties for the rental of sound recordings (rentals are big business in Japan, for example, where they can rent your CD, burn a copy, and return the CD). In case you were wondering, as I was, what happens to that money and how you can get your share, the answer is by joining AARC. Here's how they describe themselves:

"Representing its members, domestically and abroad, AARC ensures they are properly compensated for the home taping and rental of their sound recordings. In existence since 1993, shortly after the passage of the U.S. home taping law, the the Audio Home Recording Act of 1992 AARC is overseen by a board of thirteen artist representatives and thirteen record company representatives. The makeup of its board ensures that AARC provides equal representation to the artist community and recording industry, looking after their mutual interests. AARC currently represents over 65,000 artists and about 6,300 record companies worldwide, including all the major record company labels and many independent labels in the U.S.)."

Every indie artist who releases a recording, whether on CD or digital delivery (iTunes, etc.), should take advantage of this royalty.

ALLIANCE OF ARTISTS AND RECORDING COMPANIES

700 North Fairfax St., Ste. 601 • Alexandria, VA 22314

Tel: (703)535-8101 • Fax: (703)535-8105

General e-mail: contact@aarcroyalties.com

For artist or sound recording copyright owner membership/registration contact:

Deputy Director of Royalties : Bree Dietrich, Ext. 6, bdietrich@aarcroyalties.com

Web site: www.aarcroyalties.com

AFM & AFTRA Intellectual Property Rights Distribution Fund

Can I still receive royalties if I'm a background singer or musician on a recording project and not a "featured artist?"

I've got good news! You can. You need to contact the AFM (American Federation of Musicians) & AFTRA (American Federation of Television and Radio Artists) Intellectual Property Rights Distribution Fund. And you don't have to be a member of either union. Here's how they explain it:

"Why was the AFM & AFTRA Intellectual Property Rights Distribution Fund established?

The AFM & AFTRA Fund was formed for the purpose of distributing royalties from various foreign territories and royalties established by government statute under U.S. Copyright Law.

Where do these royalties come from?

AFTRA and the AFM collectively entered in a variety of negotiations and agreements with organizations including Geidankyo/Center for Performers' Rights Administration (CPRA) in Japan and U.S. government agencies to secure royalties for non-featured performers (e.g., side musicians and background vocalists).

What are the specific sources of revenue currently handled by the AFM & AFTRA Fund?

Currently, the Fund distributes money to non-featured vocalists and non-featured musicians for the rental in Japan of U.S. produced sound recordings, Audio Home Recording Act (AHRA) monies, and statutory license royalties for the digital broadcast of sound recordings in the U.S. pursuant to the DPRSRA (Digital Performance Right in Sound Recordings Act of 1995) and DMCA (Digital Millennium Copyright Act of 1998).

Are there any other projected sources of revenue?

The AFM & AFTRA Fund recently received home taping money from Japan and the Netherlands, and is just now commencing discussions with the applicable organization in Spain for the payment of the home taping remuneration from that country. In addition, rates and fees have been established for Webcasting, and these monies will soon be added to the Digital Performance Royalties (DPR) portion of the distributions.

Are these royalties paid only to union members?

No, distributions of these royalties are made to union and non-union performers alike.

So who do I contact?

First go to their Web site (www.raroyalties.org) and read their FAQ and distribution guidelines:

> **THE AFM & AFTRA INTELLECTUAL PROPERTY RIGHTS DISTRIBUTION FUND**
> Attention: Jo-Anne McGettrick
> 12001 Ventura Place, Ste. 500 • Studio City, CA 91604
>
> Tel: (818) 755-7780 • Fax: (818) 755-7779

Since both the AARC and the AFM & AFTRA Fund collect and distribute income from the same sources, can I belong to both?

Yes, since the AARC only distributes to "featured" artists and record labels, and the AFM & AFTRA Fund distributes to "non-featured vocalists and non-featured musicians." You may be a featured artist on your own self-produced recording and a side musician or singer on someone else's project. Membership in both will assure you get paid regardless of the role you play. AARC, AFM, and AFTRA work closely to ensure that artists' rights are protected in the areas of home taping and rental rights. In fact, a representative of both AFM and AFTRA each serve on the AARC board.

When should I join and what does it cost?

Membership in both organizations is *free* and you should join as soon as you perform on your or anyone else's recording. Once your information is in their system, they'll have it for every recording project you do after that. Just keep updating them with information on your new releases or changes of address.

How do they know how much to pay?

Payments for both are based on data from SoundScan. That makes it very important that you get a barcode from your CD duplicator and register with SoundScan thirty days before the release of the recording. Get the information at www.soundscan.com. (Note that SoundScan defines a record label as having two or more artists.) Distribution of royalties, after deduction of overhead, is based on the formula mandated in the Audio Home Recording Act of 1992. See each of their Web sites for this info.

10 Publishing

The Copyright Law broadly defines "publication," as it refers to songwriting, as the reproduction of a song in the form of any kind of product, printed or recorded, and the offering of those products for sale to the public. The practical concept of music publishing, however, is a lot more complex than any legal definition or theory.

Mention "music publishing" to someone outside the business, and they're likely to associate it with print in the same way they'd think of a book publisher. The business of music publishing in America did, in fact, begin with the manufacture and sale of sheet music copies and piano rolls for player pianos. But through decades of social, economic, and technological changes, the business continues to evolve with the times. Currently, the sale of sheet music is only a small part of music publishing, and its actual manufacture and sale is carried out by a handful of "print publishers" licensed to print and distribute by music companies whose duties, as we'll see, are now much broader.

Leonard Feist's book, *An Introduction to Popular Music Publishing in America*, traces the fascinating history of the business. Feist chronicles the role of the "songplugger" from the early 1900s in New York's "Tin Pan Alley," where most of the music publishers had their offices. In those days they performed the songs for vaudeville troupes that were putting together shows for their tours; for employees of music stores who, in turn, performed the songs for potential sheet music customers; and for anyone else who might influence sales.

Today, songpluggers are still in the front lines, only now, since the business centers mainly on records and films, they're playing demos of songs for managers, record producers, recording artists, record company A&R personnel, and film music supervisors. Today they're called "professional managers" (don't confuse them with "personal managers"), and songplugging is just one of their duties.

It's important to understand all that publishers do, whether you want them to pitch your songs to their contacts, or if you pitch your own songs but want to avail yourself of the other services publishers provide.

What Publishers Do

At its best, publishing demands imagination, creativity, intuition, tenacity, and good business sense. A publisher must be willing to make mistakes and face daily rejection of songs he believes in. Knowledge of how the music industry operates and a familiarity with the work of a great variety of recording artists (both established and new) are also required. It's a special combination of ingredients that makes a great publisher, and few have it all. In your own situation, you may not need all of these services or a publisher with all those qualities. If you're a small indie publisher you may be good at the creative and promotional aspects of the job but farm out the administration tasks to independent administration companies or the administration departments of major publishers.

Many different levels and types of activities come under the label of "publishing," and publishers' activities fall into four categories: *creative*, *promotional*, *business*, and *administrative*.

Creative endeavors include screening new songs, meeting with new writers, attending concerts, going to night clubs and recording studios to hear and make contact with new and established artists, critiquing and working with staff writers and up-and-coming independent writers, reviewing songs already in the catalogue, producing demos, initiating or suggesting collaborations between staff writers or lyricists and producer/writers or artists, and conceiving new uses for songs.

Promotional duties include contacting producers, managers, agents, and A&R reps to learn what songs they need for their artists; reading music, film, and advertising trade magazines, periodicals and tip sheets to discover projects that may need material; mailing demos; conducting casting meetings with professional staffers and writers to determine which songs are appropriate for certain projects; maintaining files on producers, the songs they liked (or didn't), the songs they're "holding" and for how long; making calls to radio stations, record companies, and managers to work out ideas for promotion.

On the **business** side, publishers also hire personnel; establish company policies; negotiate contracts with writers, sub-publishers, music print publishers, and producers, artists, managers or film and TV production companies; initiate and maintain contacts with foreign sub-publishers; make decisions on "holds," and negotiate and grant licenses to users.

Among **administrative** duties, publishers file copyright forms; file notices with BMI, ASCAP, or SESAC for songs released for airplay; file notices with agencies that collect mechanical royalties (for sales of recordings) or make collections from record companies themselves; do general accounting, financial planning, and tax accounting; and compute and pay writers' royalties.

ADDITIONAL ACTIVITIES

There are other tasks that warrant a little more explanation.

Catalogue Evaluation and Purchase

This is the level at which the mega deal-making machinery gets into gear. We've seen much of it in the past several years. Companies merge or one major company buys another. Companies also acquire the catalogues (groups of songs owned by one company) or estates of individual writers. Some catalogues contain "standards" that will probably make money forever. Any time you turn on the radio, you'll hear "oldies" that are obviously still generating lots of performance royalties. Companies that own those songs are always being assessed by experts to determine their future earning power and looked upon as potential investments not only by other publishing companies but also by international financiers.

I'll editorialize here to say that one of the great tragedies involved in catalogue acquisition is that the purchasing company all too often looks at the move as a way to cut expenses by combining staff. In practice, it often means the termination of the staff at the acquired company, the very ones who are most familiar with the history and the songs in that company's catalogue. Seeing the name of a song in a company's database is not the same as having a person on staff who actually remembers the song. New technology is impacting this problem for the better, though. All companies are attempting now to get their songs digitized and into databases that can be searched by a number of criteria, such as style, tempo, lyric content (including the actual lyric), male or female cast, history of past recordings, etc. This makes the songs more accessible to new employees as well as film, television, and commercial producers. It also makes life easier for everybody on the chain to e-mail each other links to the songs for audition purposes. The people involved in mergers and acquisitions aren't generally the ones who are assessing new talent off the street (so you won't have much contact with them), though some "street" experience in evaluating the commercial potential of songs is valuable to those predicting the future value of any catalogue.

Development

Writer/Artist Development

Investing in the production of master recordings and the signing of new writer/artist talent is another level of activity that has become more and more common for those companies who can afford it. The companies look to sign promising writer/artists and self-contained bands. They'll produce masters and shop them to record companies. Obviously, if they get a record deal, they'll own part (usually half) of the publishing on all the songs their artist records, which guarantees them an outlet for the songs and helps them expose the songs to other artists.

In a case like this, a publisher is often acting like a combination manager, producer, publicist, and A&R person all rolled into one. In fact, many publishers have their own A&R representatives since most of the duties described here are the same as those of record company A&R reps. Trying to find the right producer for an artist involves a knowledge of the work of many producers, playing the writer/artist's preliminary tapes for them, scheduling the project, negotiating the contracts and choosing the songs, studio, and musicians if necessary. After the masters are completed, it involves making appointments to play the tapes for key record company A&R people and film music supervisors, putting together press kits, setting up showcases, and following up. It can also involve finding the artist a manager. Writer/artist development deals are most often a strategy limited to major publishers who have the cash flow to be able to afford to gamble.

Development deals usually involve a 50/50 split on the publishing (meaning that you get 100 percent of your writer's royalties plus half of the publisher's royalties which equals 75 percent of the total royalties for you), and the publisher has six months to a year and a half after completion of the masters to get you a record deal.

These publishing/production deals can be a viable alternative for a writer/artist or group, depending on your situation (see chapter thirteen, "Where Do You Start?" on page 269).

Writer/Producer Development

This is another successful strategy for publishers. With the advent of sophisticated and reasonably priced home recording technology, prolific songwriters find it cost-effective to learn to produce and arrange their own demos. In the process, they get valuable production experience. At some point, they may decide to find artists who they can write for or with, a strategy that can pay off massively if they produce a successful artist. Writer/producers are among the world's most successful writers, so naturally, to have a writer who can perpetually get her songs onto a succession of successful albums because she's *inside* those projects, makes it an appealing package for a publisher to invest in. In this case, publishers can act in an A&R capacity to help their writer/producers find hot new artists to produce.

Writer Development

Developing pure songwriters (as opposed to writer/artists or writer/producers) is another important aspect of a publishing company's work. The most common way that publishers do this is to sign writers exclusively to their staffs (for more information, see "Exclusive Staff Writing Positions" on page 210).

Exploring the Possibilities

There are major companies who hire people to do individual tasks, and small independents that must, to some degree, do it all. Still others seem to be publishers in name only and, in effect, serve as "holding companies." This is often the case with managers, producers, or film and TV production companies who use a song once with a particular artist or project and have no staff or time to exploit the song beyond that first use.

Uses of songs are limited only by lack of imagination and perception. The bottom line for any publisher is to make money by finding as many uses as possible for the song. Obviously the big ones are through sales of records, tapes, and CDs, DPDs, synchronization (the use of songs in audio-visual productions), and airplay. If a song is successful in these areas, sheet music can be an additional source of revenue. The song might be suited to a choral or band arrangement for high schools and colleges. It also might have value in advertising, as part of a radio or TV commercial. Manufacturers of autos, audio equipment, and the like compile special CDs to demonstrate auto sound and stereo equipment. They're already starting to install digital music players. Public places such as restaurants, hotels, doctors' offices, elevators, and supermarkets use collections of songs for which royalties are paid. Manufacturers of music boxes, musical toys, video games, and cell phone ringtones and master tones are also licensed to use music. Greeting card manufacturers use song lyrics and electronic melodic devices, and there are more uses on the horizon.

It's not always enough just to be aware of those possibilities. A creative publisher will *initiate* uses for songs already in the company's catalogue and even generate new songs. For instance, the publisher might hear of a new children's book being written, and have his writers or outside writers tailor songs for an album that would be a companion to the book.

New technology has introduced uses for music that were not even dreamed of a short time ago. The cell phone ringtone market exploded in 2003 and has been an immense moneymaker for hit songs in particular. A good publisher will try to stay ahead of all these new uses. It's up to you, with the help of some advice, to assess your needs (they'll differ at various points in your career), and determine which kind of publisher works best for you, or if you should consider self-publishing (see chapter eleven, page 217).

Finding a Publisher

Though finding a publisher who believes in your material can be difficult, your publisher could be your most important music industry contact.

Several organizations are listed in the following section, "Checking Out a Publisher." Beyond that, even outside the major music centers, if you hang out at songwriter organizations and events and college music business seminars, you'll get information from instructors and fellow songwriters. Read the list of publishers of hit songs in trade magazines, such as *Billboard*, *R&R* (*Radio and Records*), and *CMJ* (*College Music Journal*). *Songwriter's Market* (published by Writer's Digest Books, available online and through most book stores) will give you profiles of companies open to listening to new songs, including contact names, what they're looking for, and how to submit demos. As of this writing, most major companies don't have open-door policies, and your best bet is to find small independent publishers who need to find songs and don't have budgets to sign staff writers.

MAJOR PUBLISHERS VS. INDEPENDENTS

In looking for a publisher, the most important elements to consider are the individual's credibility, whether he or she is independent or works for a major publishing company, and your own relationship with that person. Has he earned the respect of producers by consistently bringing them high-quality, appropriate songs for their projects? Does he respect you, love your songs, and believe you'll be successful? Those are the key questions.

Sometimes it's easier for a professional manager (with the emphasis on "professional") to open the doors of producers and artists if she has the name of a major company behind her. A major publisher may also have the cash flow to invest in the development deals mentioned on page 193 if you're a writer/artist/band or writer/producer. The debate over whether to go with a small or large publisher usually gets around to the well-worn axiom that "A small company can give you more individual attention. You'll get lost in a big company." That's not always the case.

Depending on the ratio of professional staff to staff songwriters, you can get individual attention at major companies (if, in fact, you want it). By the same token, a small company may have so much to do that they don't have much time to spend working with you on a personal basis. It all depends on the company and the individuals there.

There are many small but aggressive independent publishers with great contacts and experience. Many independents formerly worked for major companies but wanted the autonomy of making their own business decisions, or got laid off after a corporate merger. They may not have the cash flow to hire staff writers, but can do a great job plugging your songs on a song-by-song basis.

Major publishers are also interested in hearing new songs even though most of their new material comes from their own staff writers or from re-demoing old songs already in their catalogue. They're interested in keeping in touch with the "street" to get a feeling about new trends and to make sure they're not missing out on any hot new writers, writer/artists, or writer/producers, though many count on the networking of their own writers to do that. You may, however, find them less accessible than independents until you've begun to get some success on your own.

Most major publishers are affiliated with record companies, though some have disaffiliated with those companies when others bought them. For example, Motown owned Jobete but then only sold the label, and Rondor Music (Irving/Almo) wasn't sold with A&M Records. But when major labels, like Universal, own their own publishing companies, is this a positive or a negative? Do the publishers hold off pitching songs to artists on other labels in favor of those on the affiliated label? No. Each of those companies has its own financial bottom line. Though the publisher will certainly attempt to get songs to artists on the home label, it's in his best interest to aggressively pitch them to other artists, as well. (There's also no guarantee that an artist on the affiliated label will record the songs, though there are companies who offer bonuses to affiliated producers to record songs in their catalogues.)

Checking Out a Publisher

Let's say you're offered a contract by a publisher. Maybe you've submitted a song by mail. Questions rush through your mind. What if this publisher is a rip off? What if he doesn't do anything with my song? How do I find out about him? Relax! If you want to know what the publisher has done in the past, you have every right to ask. He'll be glad to brag about his success. If he wants your song he should be able to sell you on his abilities.

He may tell you to whom he wants to pitch the song, but sometimes he won't. He's afraid you'll pitch it yourself, or he may not be able to reveal privileged information. Don't necessarily take reluctance as a sign of deviousness. You can negotiate a reversion clause in your contract (see "Negotiable Contract Clauses" on page 200) so that if the publisher is unable to get your song recorded, you'll get it back.

If a publisher is just getting started and doesn't have much of a track record, it doesn't mean he can't do the job. Just ask him why he thinks he can do a good job for you, and get a reversion clause of two years or less. If he has few songs to pitch and is serious about the business, he'll be aggressive and, hopefully, will soon be able to give you a list of projects he's pitched your song to.

If you want to check out a specific publisher, you can call one of the national songwriter organizations or your local organization. Check with Nashville Songwriters Association International (NSAI) in that city, and BMI, ASCAP, SESAC, or the Songwriters Guild of America (SGA) at their respective offices (see the appendix on page 384). There may be someone in those organizations who can give you feedback about individual publishers or companies. There is no "Good Housekeeping Seal of Approval" for publishers, except that songsharks (those who charge to publish your songs, see chapter eight, "Avoiding the Songsharks" on page 165) are not allowed to affiliate with ASCAP, BMI, or SESAC.

You can talk to other songwriters who have worked with the publisher. The problem with seeking someone else's approval, however, is that one writer may trash a publisher for not getting a song recorded, and the next writer may praise the same publisher because her song *did* get recorded. It's hard to sort out these types of subjective evaluations when you don't know all the details. In the end, you have to do as much research as you can, use your own best judgment, and choose a publisher who suits your individual needs. Also, there's a lot to be said for trusting your own intuition, your gut feeling, about somebody. Unless you're just incredibly paranoid about everybody anyway, if it doesn't *feel* right, it probably isn't.

WRITER/PUBLISHER Q&A

Is it good to send songs to a publisher by certified mail?

No, it scares them to death. They feel they're being set up for a lawsuit and they don't feel it's worth it to take a chance on accepting them. It's also inconvenient for both parties.

May I show my song to several publishers at once?

Yes, and you should. It is an ethical and common practice. You have a song you believe in and want everyone to have an opportunity to hear it.

What if more than one publisher says she wants it?

This is a "problem" you hope to have. Get more information from each of them. What are their recent successes? Will they give a reversion clause, pay for a demo, give you an advance? Who do they envision recording the song? Can they get to those artists? Let them know who else is interested. (Don't lie. They may know each other.) If you get satisfactory answers to all your questions but want to check them out further, tell them you want to think it over. If they pressure you to sign a contract immediately, walk away. Call other writers they publish and ask about their reputations.

If I have a publisher, is it okay if I also pitch those songs to producers?

Yes, you should. The publisher will probably appreciate the help. After all, he gets his percentage whether he gets the song recorded or you do. Remember to let him know what you're planning, so you both don't promise the same song to different producers. There may also be a reason why he may not want you to pitch it to a certain producer and he may have a game plan that you'll mess up. The publisher may also be able to help you get in the door or provide useful information about the producer you want to pitch to.

Getting Feedback From Publishers

I often ask writers how they've been received by publishers I know. Though I've heard stories about publishers who were long on ego abuse, in all fairness, that's a rarity. It's not as rare, though, for publishers to avoid offering any feedback or constructive criticism. More often they give a stock answer: "That's not the type of song we're looking for," "I wouldn't know who'd record a song like that," or "I don't think the song is marketable." All those lines, though probably true, don't help you know how to write better or more marketable songs. I decided to ask some publishers why this is the case and got some fairly typical responses.

One publisher said, "I won't give writers a critique anymore unless they're very close to writing hit songs and I know I want to get involved as their publisher. Otherwise, it's more hassle than it's worth. I used to do it all the time because I wanted to help, but I stepped on too many egos and got into arguments. Songwriters don't really want to be criticized. Even when they ask for it, they just argue with me."

On the other hand, he said, "Bob [a writer we both knew] is the kind of writer I will work with. He's come a long way because he listens. The first time I heard his tunes I knew he had a basic grip on how to write a good song. I told him one of the tunes was close but I thought it would be stronger with a bridge. Next day he came back with two different versions of a bridge and we published it and got it recorded. He didn't say, 'What do you mean, it needs a bridge? I wrote it without a bridge and it sounds okay to me!' He just gave it a shot and because he did, we both won."

Another publisher explained, "Hey, if I wanted to spend all my time teaching people how to write songs, I wouldn't have time to deal with the songs I'm already committed to. Besides, most writers don't even want to hear it!"

Len Chandler (my Los Angeles Songwriters Showcase partner) and I once suggested to a writer a change we felt would clarify a particular lyric. The writer couldn't believe his song was being critiqued and replied incredulously, "But I wrote that song in Topanga Canyon!" To that writer, the act of writing the song was akin to receiving a sacred message from the Great Spirit. To suggest any change by himself or someone else was unthinkable.

I'm not going to tell you that it's wrong to feel so personally about your songs, or that you should operate with the attitude that there's something wrong with your songs and all you have to do is find some publisher to tell you what it is. That's destructive to your self-esteem and, in music, you need all the self-esteem you can get. But it's also self-destructive to assume you have nothing to learn from anyone. Nothing will stop your creative and professional growth more surely than that. You need to be able to look at feedback from industry pros as an *opportunity to learn* either or both of two important things: (1) you can learn something valuable about improving that song, about writing in general, or writing more commercially in particular; (2) you can learn about the needs and tastes of that particular person, so even if you decide not to act on the criticism, you'll have learned what to bring or what not to bring that publisher or producer next time.

In any case, you need at least to be *receptive* to criticism and to know that most industry people won't even bother to give it unless they think you have enough talent to begin with. If you're defensive and argumentative, you may have a problem finding a publisher who will want to work with you. There are simply too many other good writers around who *are* open to criticism and are willing to rewrite.

There's another angle to this that should also be brought up. Publishers aren't infallible, and you don't need to believe their every opinion as gospel. In going from one publisher to another you'll definitely find a great diversity of tastes and opinions. Pay attention to the criticism and don't let their experience and willingness to help go to waste. You may learn more from those you disagree with than you will from those who see things the way you do. You need them both. Those who agree will give you support and confidence. Those who challenge you, especially if they're articulate about it, can give you the opportunity to grow.

Uncontracted Songplugging

Writers occasionally ask me how to deal with songplugging without a contract. Most publishers want a contract, at least a letter of intent, before they commit their time and energy to pitching your song. But for those who don't, here's how it works.

A publisher might say, "Just let me run with your song for a month, six months, or whatever you agree to, without a contract, and see what happens. If I can get you a record on it, I get the publishing. If not, you've got the song back." The publisher may suggest this for a variety of reasons:

1. He doesn't want to sign your song, not be able to do anything with it, and have you hounding him forever.

2. He's not sure enough about the song to commit his money or his company's money to do demos, copies, and all the attendant things that go with it.

3. He has a specific artist in mind for the song and if it's rejected he doesn't know anyone else who would cut it.

In any case, he trusts you not to take it to another publisher and will give you the song back if he can't get it recorded. The danger of not having the deal on paper is that one of you may forget the terms of the agreement. Make sure you clarify what happens if an artist or producer puts a *hold* on the song (asks that the publisher not show it to anyone else for a period to give him a chance to cut it or decide if he will cut it). The producer may want to hold the song for longer than you had originally agreed with the publisher. Fairness would dictate that you wait, along with the publisher, until the producer makes up his mind. Since the publisher made the initial contact with the producer, it would be unethical of you to take it to other publishers or publish it yourself. Remember that the music business is like a small town, and word gets around if you abuse the trust people place in you.

It often happens that a publisher won't ask you not to show it to other publishers because he assumes you know the ethics involved and doesn't want to insult you by suggesting your ignorance. But writers who know little about the publisher's job, or the industry in general, may not even consider that there are ethics involved here. They actually may look at the situation as an adversarial relationship rather than a partnership built on mutual respect (see chapter thirteen, "Ethics in the Biz" on page 285). I've run across several writers in the past who told me, quite innocently, that they planned to let several publishers try to market the song, or said "I'll let publisher A run with the tune for a couple of weeks and if he doesn't get anything happening I'll take it to publisher B, who's also interested." The problem was that he hadn't told publisher A that he intended to do that.

Imagine what would happen if both publishers pitched the song for the same project. In other words, they'd both be doing their job as publishers on your behalf, using their hard-earned expertise and credibility. Suppose the producer likes the tune for his artist and wants to cut it immediately. If the producer realizes that both publishers pitched him the tune, he'll probably call both publishers and tell them. They aren't going to be happy about your game, but if you don't have contracts with either, they both might want you to sign one immediately. There's also a good chance that the producer will want to sign the song to his own company.

Who will you choose, and what do you tell the other publisher, who may have worked as hard for you? If you had a contract with A and none with B then A is the winner and B is mad at you for using him unethically. B assumes you knew your contract with A gave A *exclusive* right to publish your song. (He may also decide that he'll never pitch a song again without a contract.) If you're unfortunate enough to have signed contracts with both A and B on the same song, you're in serious legal trouble, because you lied on the contract when you gave exclusivity to two publishers at once. Would you sell your car to two different people? Basically, the rule of thumb is be up front. Let everyone know what's going on. If a publisher wants to plug your song without a contract, agree on a specific period in which no one else will plug the song, and stick to it! (See chapter eleven, "Independent Songpluggers" on page 235.)

Single Song Contracts

Songwriter–publisher contracts covering one song are the ones you'll come in contact with most frequently as a songwriter. I use the plural because there are probably hundreds of different single-song contracts that say "standard" at the top of the page. Publishers obtain these contracts in various ways. Some come right off the rack from music supply stores or buy them via download from companies that sell contracts online. Some publishers will get a contract from their attorney and work out modifications based on that publisher's philosophy of doing business. Well-established companies will have contracts that they've developed over the years. The only things you can count on as "standard" are that, if a publisher hands you a contract, it will be biased to the publisher's advantage, and that it will be negotiable. *Never* believe that because a contract is typeset and says it's "standard," that it can't be changed.

How contracts are worded and how they can be negotiated are very important areas to explore. Paranoia *is* common among songwriters due to a lack of understanding about contract clauses and how to negotiate them. Most of that fear persists because songwriters don't understand the reasons why some of the clauses exist. Many deals have gone out the window because a writer has been told *never* to accept this or that deal point.

Everything is negotiable. You should not attempt to arrange any sort of long-term agreement without the help of someone with experience in dealing objectively with the issues involved in negotiating contracts between writer and publisher.

NEGOTIABLE CONTRACT CLAUSES

The Songwriters Guild of America (SGA) pioneered the ideal single-song contract on behalf of its members many years ago and, while few publishers will substitute it for their own in-house contracts because it disadvantaged *them* in some ways, its basic points are still true today. But since it's not an ideal world, I feel it's useful to use these points as a way to introduce some variables to help you arrive at a compromise. Note that at the SGA Web site (www.songwritersguild.com) you can download the contract and find thorough explanations of each contract clause. I highly recommend that you study them.

These are all great recommendations and most are absolutely essential. Ability to obtain these recommendations depends on the bargaining strength of the writer. I'll add that I'm not an attorney and, not knowing your individual situation, I can't advise you about what clauses would be more or less important in your specific circumstance. I *can* discuss what I feel are the important issues from both sides so you can look at this agreement with some perspective. The best advice is to have a music business attorney look over your contract. Also keep in mind that although a single-song contract is important, unless you think this is the only publishable song you'll ever write, it's not exactly the end of your creative career if you can't get all the clauses recommended here. You need to be flexible.

What makes negotiating so crazy is that it's difficult to get any perspective about your bargaining strength. Even if you've been successful in the past, which definitely gives you an edge, your current material will be judged for its commercial potential in *today's* market. The only thing you can do is try to negotiate these clauses to your own advantage and hope for the best, keeping in mind that the best contract is one in which each party's needs have been addressed and neither party feels he's been had.

Following are SGA's clauses and my comments about them:

1. Work For Hire: When you receive a contract covering just one composition, you should make sure that the phrases "employment for hire" and "exclusive writer agreement" are not included. Also, there should be no options for future songs.

Pretty straight ahead, "exclusive writer agreements" are "staff" deals in which you're not allowed to write for anyone else for a period of time. Those deals usually include "work for hire" agreements, which means that everything you write during that time considers the "employer" (publisher) to be the "author," for copyright purposes. It still means you'll get paid and credited according to your contract, however. There are many other situations, like writing music for commercials, or film scoring, in which you'll be required to sign a "work for hire" contract, but you should be paid very well for it and be able to negotiate for credit and future royalty payments.

2. Performing Rights Affiliation: If you previously signed publishing contracts, you should be affiliated with ASCAP, BMI, or SESAC. All performance royalties must be received directly by you from your performing rights organization and this should be written into your song contract. (The same goes for any third party licensing organization mutually agreed upon.)

Most contracts include this clause to acknowledge that *they* (the publishers) won't be sending your writer's share of performance royalties to you and that you'll receive them directly from your performing rights organization.

3. Reversion Clause: The contract should include a provision that, if the publisher does not secure a release of a commercial sound recording within a specified time (one year, two years, etc.), you can terminate the contract.

The reversion clause in songwriter–publisher contracts was pioneered many years ago by the Songwriters Guild of America in their model writer-oriented contract. Reversion clauses have been a bone of contention with publishers, but nearly all publishers accept them in order to remain competitive. They also keep disgruntled writers off their backs if they're not getting their song cut.

The length of time granted to the publisher is a major negotiating point in this clause. It can be any length you agree on, but it commonly runs as short as six months or as long as three years. Personally, I feel that two years should be adequate. Six months or a year is not always enough time for publishers, for several practical reasons. It frequently happens that an artist may be interested in a song but won't be recording again for another six months. Touring commitments or other circumstances may delay the recording or even the release of the record. If that were to happen, then technically, the writer could get her song back and take the publishing herself after the record was later released, leaving the publisher with no reward for the job done. That fact soured publishers on short reversion periods. Some hits have been pitched multiple times to the same producers before they're recorded.

A producer also may put a hold on the song, asking the publisher to refrain from pitching it to anyone else until a final decision is made. That hold may last weeks or months (see chapter eleven, "Holds" on page 229).

The producer also may have collected fifteen or twenty songs as possibilities for the project, whittled them down to ten, and your song gets whittled out. Or, it actually might get recorded but fail to live up to the expectations of the producer, artist, or label and end up "in the can" (not

201

released), as they say. The record might be released someday, but by that time, the reversion period is up and the publisher has had to return the song to the writer.

So, you see, publishers face problems with short reversion periods. Given that, I feel it would be fair to negotiate a one- or two-year reversion clause with the stipulation that the period be extended for the length of time a producer has the song on hold. (This, of course, would require an agreement in writing between the publisher and producer as well.)

By the time the reversion period is up, the writer should also have had adequate opportunity to assess the amount of activity the publisher has expended on the song. If the writer sees that the publisher has been taking care of business, she could grant the publisher an extended reversion period.

Early in the history of this clause, some publishers would subvert its intent by pressing up a few copies of the demo, sending them to radio stations, and saying, "Okay, I released the song on a record, so that means I can keep the publishing." Currently, the wording goes an extra step by saying the publisher is responsible for the song's being "commercially recorded and released in the recording industry's customary commercial channels."

There are other reasons you can include a reversion clause in a contract besides the inability of the publisher to get a song recorded. The clause can prevent the publisher from reassigning your copyright to another individual or company without your consent. You also can have the song revert back to you if the publisher refuses to allow you, or your representative, to audit his books regarding royalties. I would suggest that you have the contract state that at the end of the reversion period, the song "reverts to you automatically" without requiring you to send a registered letter by a certain time to demand it (which most contracts request). The publisher may count on your forgetting to do that. Here are three sample clauses:

> Within two (2) years from the date hereof, commercial recordings of the musical composition must have been released for either (a) sale to the public on records, tapes, CDs or other recorded products; (b) synchronization in the sound track of a theatrical motion picture released to the public; (c) synchronization in the sound track of a television program broadcast to the public; (d) synchronization in the sound track of a home video program for sale to the public; or (e) other recordings consistent with this agreement that are released and/or sold to the public or the agreement will automatically terminate.
>
> If at the end of two years from the date of this Agreement, a commercial recording has been secured but a commercial release or usage shall not have occurred, Publisher shall have the option to extend the term of this agreement for an additional twelve months (for a total contract term of thirty six months). If none of the foregoing recordings have been released within said thirty-six month time period, this contract shall terminate.
>
> Upon the termination of this agreement, all rights in and to the Composition and in and to any and all copyrights secured thereon shall automatically revest in and become the property of the Writer, and shall be re-assigned to the Writer by Publisher free of any and all encumbrances of any nature whatsoever.

The following example is simpler and doesn't include the option for the publisher to extend the contract, which, as I stated above, is not a bad thing to do. What I like about this is that it also (in section i) qualifies what "released" means and keeps them from getting around it by having their own in-house record label release the song (a common songshark tactic). Of course, if it's Universal Music and their "related" third party is Universal Records this would be fine.

> a. Notwithstanding anything contained in this Agreement, this Agreement shall terminate automatically and any and all rights in and to the Composition shall revert to the Writer, if Publisher shall not secure, within twenty-four (24) months from the date set forth in this Agreement, the following:
>
> > i. A commercial sound recording of the Composition to be recorded and released in the recording industry's customary commercial channels along with a Mechanical License issued for the Composition by an unrelated third party, or;
> >
> > ii. Any other agreement for the exploitation of the Composition which derives an initial agreement fee and/or payment due in excess of the amount of _____ dollars ($_____).

Note that paragraph ii allows you to fill in a minimum amount you'll take for any other use, which will include film synch license, etc. Remember that the "initial agreement fee and/or payment" will be interpreted as a payment to the *publisher*, of which you'll get half. I like this because it can keep the publisher from holding your song for a five-dollar use. You can also specify in the reversion clause that it needs to be released by an artist signed to a major label, an artist with a previous Top 20 hit, or anything else you want to put in.

Here's a new wrinkle you need to consider. If you don't want the publisher to release it directly to a DPD site as a paid digital download in order to get around the reversion clause, you'd better have it in the contract.

> **4. Changes in the Composition:** If the contract includes a provision that the publisher can change the title, lyrics, or music, then this should be amended that only with your previous consent can such changes be made.

Here's a scenario that illustrates the value of this type of clause. You have a contract with a publisher on a song. The publisher pitches the song to an artist. The artist wants a piece of the publishing before he records the song, but the publisher refuses. The artist says, "I basically love the song and I'll record it, but I think the second verse is weak and I'd like to rewrite it. Of course, I'll have to have half of the writer's royalties to do that." The publisher says to himself, "What the hell. I still get all my publishing and the writer should be grateful that he gets co-writing credit with this famous artist. I'll go for it."

Your second verse may not have been bad at all. The artist may write a terrible second verse and destroy the integrity of your song (which you would have to live with), or make it so personalized that no one else would want to record it. If the publisher had refused and had stuck to his guns, the artist might have recorded it anyway. If the artist genuinely felt the second verse was weak and could explain why, you should have been offered the first opportunity to rewrite it. This publisher has just deprived you of half your writer's share of royalties and will come back to you and say, "100 percent of nothing is nothing. I thought you'd be glad to get half of what could be a big writer's royalty." This may be a compromise you're willing to make, but the fact is that without this clause in your contract he has every right to do just what he did *without your permission.*

There have also been cases in which a publisher/writer with greed and a big ego wants his name on your song as co-writer and will put it there on the flimsiest of justifications. He may decide to change your title, or a melody line, or a couple of words here and there, and cut himself in as a co-writer without your permission. The publisher may also insist on unnecessary changes in your song if he's getting flak from his staff writers for signing an "outside" song (from a non-staff writer) and to appease them, he might have one of them "rewrite" the song and take co-writer credit!

Those are some of the situations that do happen. When those types of proposals are made *before* the song is signed to a publisher, you have the choice to forget it or to go along for the sake of your career. The reason to include a "no change" clause is to make sure you still have that choice after the contract is signed. And if a co-writer is still forced on you under any of the above circumstances, there should be at least a clause that provides that no more than 50 percent of your writer's royalties can be split with anyone else.

If a publisher does want to take writer credits himself keep this in mind. It's part of a publisher's job to help inspire, guide, edit, critique, and make suggestions for writers. If you, the writer, feel that the creative contributions of the publisher are substantial enough to warrant inclusion as a co-writer, then you should offer it. There are times, of course, when the publisher does deserve a writer's credit, so if you see a publisher's name on a song, you should reserve your judgment about how it got there until you know the real story.

You might ask why a publisher would not want to give you a "no change" clause if he's such a good guy. Well, here's another scenario. The publisher gets a tip that a major artist is finishing up an album and a couple of her songs didn't turn out so well at the session, or the artist decides the songs weren't right after all. The publisher remembers your song and rushes over. The producer loves it and so does the artist, *except* that (a) she wants the melody to have a little more range to show off her voice, (b) it was written as a man's song so a couple of lines need to be changed, and (c) the title has to be changed to reflect all the other changes. They want to do it *right now*. The publisher calls the last number he had for you and it's disconnected or you're in an ashram in India and can't be reached. The publisher, at that point, has to risk losing the cut and incurring your wrath for it, or risk your taking back the copyright because he allowed the change without your permission. Chances are the publisher will risk the latter and pray that you don't turn out to be an ungrateful person. A publisher could cover himself on this one by stating he'll make his best effort (like a registered letter) to contact you.

Another situation where this applies is when a publisher assigns a writer to create a lyric for your instrumental composition without your consent. It's very seldom that an instrumental becomes a hit, unless it's a movie theme. The commercial viability of the piece may be enhanced appreciably with a great lyric. The right lyric is very important, though. Some great instrumentals could be trivialized and cheapened by any lyric, let alone a bad one. Many dynamic orchestrations can be written for an instrumental without having to be conscious of leaving space for the vocals. Also, without language barriers, an instrumental can be internationally successful. So there are a lot of factors to consider. I believe the original writer, with the input of the publisher, should have the last word on which lyric, if any, should be written for his or her melody (see chapter eleven, "Lyric Translations," on page 232).

5. Royalty Provisions: Basically, you should receive 50 percent of all the publisher's income on all licenses issued. If the publisher prints and sells his own sheet music and folios, your royalty should be 10 percent of the wholesale selling price. The royalty should not be stated in the contract as a flat rate ($.05, $.07, etc.).

We're seeing the development of digital delivery systems we could only imagine for audio and visual creations at the time I wrote the first edition of this book. Vinyl records, except for a small group of die-hard enthusiasts, are obsolete. Audiocassettes, as a medium for distributing music, have followed. CDs prevail and DPDs are on the way up. Some predict they'll rule by 2009. The entire industry is playing catch-up trying to figure out how to track their distribution and collect from users. I don't doubt they *will*, to the extent that they *can*. Publishers are at the forefront of the quest. The bottom line here is that, as a writer, no matter what the new uses they collect for you should get 50 percent of what your publisher collects. It's in your best interest to make sure your contract includes *"any other use now existing or used in the future from which the publisher receives royalties."* Or if they give you a list, add a clause saying *"and all other uses not referred to in this agreement."* Many writers lost out on royalties because their contracts specified tapes, and didn't allow for formats that were developed later. If that clause isn't in there, the publisher doesn't have to pay you for use in a format that's *not listed* in your contract.

> **6. Negotiable Deductions:** Ideally, demos and all other expenses of publication should be paid 100 percent by the publisher. The only allowable fee is the Harry Fox Agency collection fee, whereby the writer pays one half of the amount charged to the publisher. Today's rate charged by the Harry Fox Agency is 4–6½ percent.

Publishers should assume all administration costs except the Harry Fox Agency fee for collection of mechanical royalties. An exception to their assuming all administration costs would be in the case of a co-publishing agreement between the publisher and the publishing company owned by the writer, in which case, those fees could be split. We should also note that, in the day the SGA sample contract was written, almost everybody used the Harry Fox Agency, but that's no longer the case. Often some other organization will do the collecting of mechanical royalties, including legal download sales, and no clause should specifically limit collection to any specific organization.

Regarding demo costs, what's happening now is that writers are approaching publishers with good, appropriate demos, complete and already paid for. In that situation, I think the publisher should pay you up front for all, or at least half, of the demo costs you incurred. Your negotiating position on this point may be weakened if you're also asking for a reversion clause. Most publishers are reluctant to lay out cash on a song if there's a chance they'll have to give the song back to you. They'll have to spend money to promote the song, and they want to minimize their risk. I believe that a reversion clause is more important than front money in general, but that depends on how badly you need the bucks. If you can't get them to pay you for your demo right away *and* give you a reversion, negotiate to have them reimburse you 100 percent or at least not less than 50 percent for your demo when they get the first royalty check.

> **7. Royalty Statements and Audit Provision:** Once the song is recorded and printed, you are entitled to receive royalty statements at least once every six months. In addition, an audit provision with no time restriction should be included in every contract.

This is pretty standard. Many publishers, however, pay quarterly. New royalty accounting software has streamlined this process considerably so it's not such a labor-intensive problem anymore. But the incentive for publishers to prefer semi-annual rather than quarterly payments is that they collect interest on your royalties for three more months. That's not much for a small company, but for the majors it really adds up.

The audit provision with no time restriction is difficult to get. If the publisher doesn't happen to include it, by California statute, you'd have four years to sue him, six years in New York. So he will try to get you to agree to the finality of a royalty statement within a year or two. That means that if you find something wrong with your statement you only have that long to object. Try to get at least three years.

> **8. Writer's Credit:** The publisher should make sure that you receive proper credit on all uses of the composition.

Publishers don't object to this but in some cases it's hard to guarantee. They want it too, but if they're dealing with film and TV synch uses, it's sometimes hard to get unless you have a featured song that plays over the title or end credits or is part of a film that contains many songs and everybody gets credited.

> **9. Arbitration:** In order to avoid large legal fees in case of a dispute with your publisher, the contract should include an arbitration clause.

Here's the Songwriters Guild Contract's arbitration clause:

> Any and all differences, disputes or controversies arising out of or in connection with this contract shall be submitted to arbitration before a sole arbitrator under the then prevailing rules of the American Arbitration Association. The location of the arbitration shall be New York, New York, if the Writer on the date of execution of this contract resides East of the Mississippi River, or in Los Angeles, California, if the Writer on the date of execution of this contract resides West of the Mississippi River. The parties hereby individually and jointly agree to abide by and perform any award rendered in such arbitration. Judgment upon any such award rendered may be entered in any court having jurisdiction thereof.

Pick California or New York and use this if the contract offered doesn't have an arbitration clause.

> **10. Future Uses:** Any use not specifically covered by the contract should be retained by the writer to be negotiated as it comes up. (See # 5 above.)

See the explanation for "Royalty Provisions" on page 204.

SONGWRITERS GUILD OF AMERICA

The Songwriters Guild of America (SGA) offers contract recommendations and, for a small percentage, will check your royalty statement (you have your statements mailed to them directly) and forward it to you immediately. SGA auditors check the statement against your contract, which you send them when you join, and if they find a discrepancy, they call the publisher immediately and try to straighten it out. If they can't, chances are there are other members who are having problems with the same publisher and SGA will audit them on your behalf. Usually, it's an accounting mistake on the part of the publisher and it's easy to remedy. (Hey, we'll give them the benefit of the doubt—the first time!) The problem is that, without someone knowledgeable checking it, you'd never know about it. I suspect that there are a few of you out there who have trouble balancing your checkbook, let alone analyzing a royalty statement. I have several successful writer friends for whom SGA has gone after royalties and have gotten them money they didn't know they had coming, and in one case, *did* know they had coming but couldn't afford to pursue. Essentially, SGA performs the same functions for writers that the Harry Fox Agency performs for publishers in collecting from record companies.

SGA EAST COAST

1560 Broadway West, Ste. 408 • New York, NY 10036

Tel: (917) 309-7869 • E-mail: ny@songwritersguild.com

Web site: www.songwritersguild.com

SGA CENTRAL

209 10th Ave. S, Ste. 534 • Nashville, TN 37203

Tel: (615) 742-9945 Fax: (615) 742-9948 • E-mail: nash@songwritersguild.com

SGA WEST COAST

6430 Sunset Blvd., Ste. 705 Hollywood, CA 90028

Tel: (323) 462-1108 Fax: (323) 462-5430 • E-mail: la@songwritersguild.com

SGA ADMINISTRATION

1500 Harbor Blvd. • Weehawken, NJ 07086

Tel: (201) 867-7603 • Fax: (201) 867-7535

OTHER NEGOTIABLE CONTRACT CLAUSES

Reduced Mechanical Royalty Rates

Try to get this clause: "A publisher may not grant a licensee a rate lower than the current statutory rate without the prior consent of the writer" (see chapter nine, "Mechanical Royalties" on page 171).

It's wise to have such a clause added to the contract. This practice of allowing a company to pay you *less* than the current statutory rate is called "giving a rate." The "rate" refers to the current mechanical rate effective at the time the license is granted to the record company for use of the song.

Here's the problem situation that prompted this clause. Let's say, hypothetically, that your publisher has interested an artist in your song and the record company says, "We'd like Sally Superstar to record the song you brought us, but we don't want to pay the current statutory mechanical rate." The most prevalent reason for that is that Sally, in her recording contract, has a "Controlled Composition Clause" (see chapter nine, "Controlled Composition Clause" on page 173) that requires her to get a "rate" from you if she wants to record your "outside" song. Otherwise, she'd have to pay you out of her own artist royalties. If Sally's record, with your song on it, is a hit, the quarter of the rate given up could add up to a lot of rent money. You can usually trust that your publisher will be reluctant to give up anything less than full statutory rate. Remember he'll be losing money too, unless it would be worthwhile to accept a reduced rate because of a substantial amount of projected sales (e.g., a compilation of hits that can almost guarantee a half a million sales).

One thing about getting your permission that publishers object to is that they may not be able to find you (see the "Changes in the Composition" on page 203). Be sure to notify your publisher and performing rights organization of your new address as soon as you move.

If you can't get the clause, you should at least get one that limits the reduction to a three-quarter rate. The clause should also state that "no less than the full statutory rate should apply to licenses granted to any person or business entity owned, controlled or affiliated, in whole or in part, by or with the publisher," because there's the chance that a publisher might give a very low rate to an affiliated record label.

Sharing in Advances

If your publisher receives an advance, such as for the inclusion of your song in a collection for which he gave a reduced mechanical rate because of the volume of units projected to be sold (a common practice), you should get some of that advance money. Make sure you share in all advances based *specifically on your song*. Publishers will also get advances on their entire catalogue, say, from a foreign sub-publisher, and they can't pay you out of that because they would be hard-pressed to figure out how much of the advance is based on *your* song.

Commercial Exploitation of Demos

Commercial exploitation of your demos should not be allowed without your consent. You've just become a big star and your publisher releases an album of your old demos that you recorded ten years ago when you weren't nearly as wonderful a writer or singer as you are now. You should have had the clause that says, "Publisher shall not commercially exploit any demonstration records embodying the performances of writer without writer's written consent."

CLAUSES AND WORDINGS YOU SHOULD WATCH FOR IN SINGLE-SONG CONTRACTS

1. **"No royalties will be paid for . . .** *copies disposed of as new issues.*" It's common practice in print music to send *new issues* of all new sheet music to dealers to let them check it out. Publishers will get paid for it by the print publishers with whom they sub-contract, but with this clause you, the writer, won't. This clause is usually connected with a clause that mentions not getting paid for *promotional copies* of records, which your publisher *will not* get paid for, so it's all right to leave it in. But make sure *new issues* gets deleted.

2. **"Publisher shall** *reasonably* **pro rate such royalties . . ."** Watch out for vague language. "Reasonable" to the publisher may not be reasonable to you. Pro-ratio formulas should be specifically defined, for example: "In such event, the royalties payable to writer shall be computed by a fraction, the numerator of which shall be one (representing the writer's song) and the denominator of which shall be the total number of copyrighted musical compositions contained in the (folio, book, etc.)."

3. **"A royalty of _____ percent of the** *net* **cash proceeds . . ."** Always make sure that you have spelled out what "net" means. Does it mean after *administrative* costs? If so, forget it. It's the publisher's *job* to administer and those costs should not be deducted off the top from the gross before your writer's royalties are paid. If you're co-publishing the song, though, it's certainly fair to split the costs between your company and theirs. Does "net" mean after demo costs? After promotional costs?

Your Chances for Advances

A royalty advance is, essentially, money paid to you before it's been earned. One of the big questions when you negotiate any contract (whether a single-song contract, a staff writing contract, or recording contract) is "How much of an advance can I get?" A couple of general philosophies operate regarding advance money, which apply more to record deals than single songs because of the huge amounts involved. One is that the more money a company puts out in advances, the more committed they are to recouping it, so naturally they'll work harder—but only to a point. And once a company decides that your project is a loser, another philosophy may kick in, called "don't throw good money after bad." They'll just stop trying. An advance may be the only money you'll see on the deal if they drop your project.

A philosophy you'll hear from small independent publishers is "instead of giving you an advance, I will spend that money doing great demos and other things that will help us both make more money in the long run." He's got a point. In that situation, you have to rely on a most important consideration, that he loves and is committed to your music.

VARIABLES REGARDING ADVANCES

Here are some variables to consider regarding cash advances in a writer/publisher deal. In reality, this is a moot point unless they *really* want your song.

An advance is money paid ahead of time against future royalties, not a payment for the song. The money they give you now comes off the top of any future royalties due you. Despite this fact, I'm surprised at the writers I talk to who are very upset a couple of years down the road when their statement from the publisher doesn't yield them a check. They've conveniently forgotten that the publisher will pay himself back for the advance. The computer doesn't forget!

Advances may also affect getting a reversion clause in your publishing contract. The more money a publisher puts out in front, before actually getting a record cut on the song, the more he gambles. So he is not going to want to give you back the song *and* lose the money if the song doesn't get recorded. Yes, he can just write it off, but of course, he'd rather not. The good part for you is that, if the song never earns money, you're not expected to pay back the advance. So he will probably tell you that he can't give you a reversion clause if he gives you an advance. That's just a good business practice on his part. However, you should try to get both.

Remember that if someone working for a major publishing company offers you an advance, it's not their own money and there's a company budget for those expenses. A small, independent publisher doesn't necessarily get a salary. If he doesn't get songs recorded, he doesn't eat (okay, I exaggerate), and that advance would come directly out of his pocket. He's less likely to give you one for that reason. You may be able to get both an advance and a reversion clause if you agree to return the advance if the song reverts. Some publishers will even want you to pay back their demo expenses on reversion.

Going in with a good demo enhances your chances. Based on the same principle as above, if you go to a publisher with a good, usable demo that saves him the cost of producing it ($500 to over $4,000), you're in a much better position to ask for an advance. You're also in a much better position to ask for a reversion clause but you still may have to decide between the clause and an advance. It's a good idea to ask for at least enough of an advance to cover your demo costs.

If you want to keep a part of the publishing, the publisher is unlikely to want to give you an advance (unless you're already a successful writer and publishers are fighting each other for your songs). Here again, you're reducing the potential income for the publisher because he will now be keeping only a portion of the publishing royalties. In fact, he's likely to ask you to split the demo costs if you want to split the income. Not unreasonable at all, because you'll be business partners.

How much of an advance can you get? Whatever you can negotiate, but $500 for a single song is probably on the top end. Ultimately, everything depends on how badly the publisher wants the song and how much he feels he can afford to give you. The risk for him is that *you'll* take it somewhere else if he doesn't give you what you want. If you need an advance, you should ask for it, but the enthusiasm of the publisher and his willingness to give you a reversion clause are ultimately worth more. The publisher's ability to assess the commercial viability of your song is his game, and if you raise the stakes he loses more if he's wrong. Bear this in mind since the producer is bound to hit a limit at some point. Be prepared to be flexible.

Exclusive Staff Writing Positions

A staff writer may be at one company for several years. During that time, all the songs she writes become the property of the publisher, generally with the standard 50/50 writer/publisher royalty split, though co-publishing deals are also quite common, particularly if you already have a successful track record. The writer is paid weekly (or monthly, quarterly, or annually) advances against future royalties, rather than a salary. The publisher gambles that he'll be able to recoup that money by getting some of those songs cut. If the songs never recoup the investment, the writer doesn't owe the publisher and the publisher loses his investment.

So, why would a publisher gamble like that rather than sign songs off the street? A writer signed to a staff position is likely very talented, dedicated, and prolific. Having a writer under contract for several years makes it worthwhile to invest a considerable amount of time and money in developing that writer's reputation and career. During that time, the publisher hopes that a substantial catalogue of material is developed that will continue to be recorded. That writer's resulting success then attracts other good writers. And having these writers under contract also prevents their songs from going to another company.

CONTRACT ISSUES

You should *never* sign an exclusive long-term staff-writer contract without the counsel of an experienced music industry attorney. However, you can get a general idea beforehand of what the publisher will usually want from you. Here are a few points:

1. The publisher will want to publish all the songs you've already written that aren't already published. He'll want to have (at least) "first refusal." You can argue that any advances in the deal are for future writing services only and that a separate payment should be made for back catalogue, especially if the publisher will be using the demos you paid for yourself.

2. Some publishers will expect a certain quota of songs per month or year (twenty per year is common). Others won't be pushy if you deliver a great song every now and then. You both need to have an understanding of your creative habits. Some writers need deadlines. Some need to be left alone. Sometimes a publisher will set a quota of "acceptable" songs. This is not a good idea for you, especially if the publisher can extend your contract indefinitely until the quota of "acceptable" songs is fulfilled. For purposes of fulfilling your quota, a publisher may consider that two 50/50 co-writes equal one song, or use some other subjective definition of "acceptable.".

3. The publisher will want a one-year contract with at least four one-year options. *His* options. Try to limit it to three. You can build performance clauses into your contract that keep the publisher from picking up the option unless, for instance, he secures a certain amount of recordings during the previous year. You can also negotiate to have your weekly advances increase every time the publisher picks up the option.

4. Advances range from $1,000 to over $4,000 a month, depending on how successful you've been or the publisher *thinks you will be*. Advances of more than half a million dollars have been made for already successful, established, writer/producers. These are "advances" against future royalties. There may be someone out there getting a straight salary (on a standard 50/50 writer/publisher deal) that's not recoupable from future royalties. But if there is, it's extremely rare because, by the time you're a valuable enough writer to command that kind of a deal, you either don't need the money or you're better off just getting an administration deal for your own publishing company.

BENEFITS OF BEING AN EXCLUSIVE STAFF WRITER

The following are benefits that may not be offered by all publishers. They are listed as the benefits you'd find in an ideal situation.

1. You're often provided a work space with instruments and recording equipment. This is great if you don't already have a good setup elsewhere.

2. You're given a weekly "draw," an advance against future royalties so you don't have to worry about the rent.

3. The publisher may pay for all your demos or give you a specific demo budget.

4. You're in an environment where you're encouraged and expected to be productive. Being around other productive writers can help your motivation.

5. You'll receive critical feedback that may help you grow as a writer.

6. You'll be made aware of upcoming recording projects so that you can tailor songs for those artists.

7. Your publisher will hook you up with film and TV assignments, album projects, and collaborators—often artists or producers with projects of their own.

8. If the publisher feels you have artist potential, he may be motivated to find you a producer, a manager, and a record deal.

9. Because of his belief in you and his financial investment, he'll do all he can to promote your career (see "Development" on page 193).

10. Publisher as bank. There are writers, writer/artists, and writer/producers for whom few to none of the above benefits are as important as having their projects financed and getting huge advances.

DRAWBACKS OF BEING A STAFF WRITER

Though the staff writer situation can be wonderful and productive (and certainly has been the best way to go for many hit writers), it's a mistake to assume it's the best situation for everyone. Many staff writers and ex-staffers complain about company policies that they knew about ahead of time but thought that "if the money's good enough, I can deal with it." They later found they couldn't.

211

Some problems could not have been anticipated and were the result of personality conflicts or policy or personnel changes. It's often difficult to fix the blame. but here are a few complaints:

"**My publisher hasn't placed any of my songs. I got all the cuts myself.**" Maybe they signed you because they realized you *could* get your own cuts. If so, maybe you should have split the publishing. Hopefully, you signed with the company because they offered other services beyond securing recordings of your songs. Publishers often can do their most valuable work *after* the song is recorded by securing *additional* covers and uses of the song and by making sure you get paid for all those uses.

"**My publisher demands that the company gets 100 percent of the publishing when I collaborate with another writer, even when that writer has his own publishing company.**" That's one you should know about going in. The bad thing about this policy is that it seriously restricts the number of outstanding writers you can co-write with since the best so often have their own companies and naturally are reluctant to give up their publishing royalties to your company.

Most publishers are more liberal, though, and are willing to do a 50/50 split with the other writer's publisher. The belief is that another strong company involved in the song provides more contacts to get it recorded. You run into problems when you collaborate with a great writer who has his own company and your publisher doesn't think it's worth giving up half to someone who may not be actively pitching the song.

"**The company seems to have lost interest in my songs but they won't let me out of my contract.**" Occasionally the person at the company who was responsible for signing you (and was the most enthusiastic about your material and your potential) leaves. Others at the company are pitching *their* favorite writers' songs because they feel more accountable to the writers they signed. Since you can't force someone to like either you or your material, it's sometimes a losing battle. It usually happens with writers who aren't getting many cuts yet. (Another good reason for you to be pitching the songs yourself.) It's more rare for this situation to develop with a writer who's a consistent money-maker for the company.

Sometimes a company won't let you go because they've invested a lot in you and figure you'll hit with something eventually. What they risk is that you'll stop turning in songs to force them not to pick up your option. This tactic has been used before but it's not a great idea. It's self-destructive to stop creating deliberately for that reason. If you continue to write songs without turning them in to your publisher, you may find yourself in serious legal difficulty later, since they legally own everything you write during the time you're under contract to them. If you're having problems, it's time for a serious heart-to-heart talk.

"**My company is great with my pop and rock songs but doesn't seem to know what to do with my country material (or vice versa).**" It's possible that you're not nearly as good at country writing as you think you are and that's the real reason they're not pitching those songs. It's also possible that your publisher doesn't know a good country song when he hears one. Or maybe he does and sends it to the company's Nashville office where *they* may think your publisher doesn't know what he's talking about.

In general, the major publishers have a pretty good ability to deal with a variety of styles, though, as always, it depends on the contacts and expertise of the *individuals* at the company.

"**My publisher's criticism is destroying my self-confidence and killing my motivation.**" Positive, constructive criticism, given sensitively, with encouragement by someone whose opinions you respect, can help you develop very quickly. There are publishers who can do that. You need to find them if you feel you need a nourishing situation to help you be a better writer. If you don't need that, it's not important. Among publishers, as among the public at large, there is a wide spectrum in individual talents for giving good criticism. Some publishers, though they're very definite about what they like or don't like, don't seem to have the vocabulary or the frame of reference to be specific about why or what you could do to improve your song. For them to say, "It just doesn't get me," won't help you to be a better writer.

Consistently, though not exclusively, the best at critiquing are those who've been writers, musicians, or producers, have *had* good criticism, and have experience in restructuring songs. An inability to critique doesn't make someone a less effective songplugger, but it does make him an ineffective developer of writers.

A publisher can also over-criticize. Hit writer Alan O'Day ("Angie Baby," "Undercover Angel") had a great metaphor for this syndrome: "When you're a hammer, everything looks like a nail."

"There are songs I believe in but my publisher doesn't. I can't stand to see them orphaned." One of the problems with the *basic* staff deal is that they won't want to give you reversion clauses that give you the song back if they don't get it recorded. You *can* negotiate for all the songs to revert back to you that haven't been recorded by a certain number of years after your contract ends. The publisher will attempt to limit this to the catalogue you brought with you when you made the deal, and only ones from that catalogue that haven't been commercially promoted. These deals and contract clauses may be very difficult to negotiate unless you're already a successful writer. Also, if you love the songs, you should always be out there pitching them yourself.

"I wrote fifteen songs last month and they only demoed one. I'm getting discouraged. Why should I keep writing when they don't even demo what I give them?" It may be hard for you to accept that everything you write may not sound like a hit to them. There also may be budget problems. Someone in the company has to decide which songs are worth spending the money on and there may be several other staffers turning out fifteen songs a month. Figure a bare *minimum* of $500 per song and they're into big bucks. One possible remedy for this problem is that, if a certain number of "acceptable" songs have to be turned in each month, you have a clause in your contract that any songs rejected from that quota become your property, free and clear of any interest of the publisher.

I was visiting a publisher friend in Nashville and saw a big box of tapes and CDs next to his desk. I asked, "Are these demos from writers looking for deals?" He said " No man, these are from my staff writers and I haven't even gotten around to listening to them yet." Ouch!

THE INDIE ADVANTAGE

Along with the advantages and disadvantages of being a staff writer, you should consider the following:

1. As an independent songwriter you're free to offer financial incentives to individuals who can help you place your songs (see chapter eleven, "Negotiating" on page 226) that, if you were under contract, your publisher may not be likely to offer unless it's for a major film theme that looks like a good investment.

2. If you can publish the song yourself, you're looking at a lot more potential income.

3. You're never in competition with other writers on the publisher's staff (unless, of course, you're pitching songs to that publisher) as to whose songs are pitched to a particular producer.

4. You can pitch an individual song to any publisher you think can do the best job.

5. You can quickly license your own songs and demos for use in audio/visual productions and keep 100 percent of the royalties.

(For more information, see chapter eleven, "Self-Publishing" on page 217.)

HOW STAFF DEALS HAPPEN

Dreamy-eyed writers who've written ten songs come to me and say they're shopping for a staff-writing deal. Far be it from me to discourage them. In fact, if all (or even some) of those songs sound like hits and the writer also has great artist potential, she is likely to have offers.

More often, songwriters and publishers build a relationship one song at a time. Don't let your dreams keep you from getting a day (or night) job so you can afford to let that process take place in its own time. It's important for you to work with a variety of publishers on a song-by-song basis to find those individuals whose opinions and business practices you respect and who are aggressive about pitching your songs. It's also important for a publisher to have the opportunity to size up your creative output, your willingness and ability to rewrite, your mutual personal chemistry, and obviously, the reaction to your songs from producers. It also can't hurt your negotiating position to have more than one company wanting to sign you. This sizing up process is very important in any long-range partnership. Very few marriages succeed when you go to the altar after knowing each other a week. The mutual personal chemistry aspect was more important than I would have guessed among the reasons publishers sign staff writers, according to the survey below. Remember, though, that the piece below was written in Nashville, where writers come to the publishers' offices to write on a regular basis. In close quarters, the staff likes to be glad to see you.

WHAT PUBLISHERS REALLY WANT

My friend, ASCAP vice president and Nashville hit songwriter Ralph Murphy, along with Mark Ford, assembled an informal survey that polled fourteen Nashville music publishers. (This is an excerpt. Get the whole story at: www.ascap.com/nashville/murphy.html, where Ralph features a wonderfully insightful group of articles. Be sure to read his analysis of a year's worth of number one country songs. It's a road map to the country market.)

Each publisher, within the past twelve months, had placed a hit song on the charts and had signed a new staff writer. The publishers ranked each of the following attributes from one to ten (with one being *least* important and ten being *most* important) based on the last writer they signed, not on any particular "wish list." The scores were tallied (averages for each question appear in brackets) and are listed from least important to most important.

Attributes That Motivate a Publisher

10. Track record [4.9]
9. Persistence pursuing the deal [5.1]
8. Living in or near Nashville [5.3]
7. Record deal/artist potential [6.0]
6. Ability to co-write [6.2] / Ability to perform songs live [6.2]
5. Affordability (amount of draw) [6.3]
4. Ability to write alone [7.5]
3. Ability to write great melodies [8.7]
2. Personality/compatibility with the company [9.0]
1. Ability to write great lyrics [9.6]

Writing on Assignment

Staff writers at publishing companies are often called upon to write on assignment, but even if you're not in that position you'll hear about recording projects you'll want to write for. If you're a "project" writer (see chapter one, "Creativity and Inspiration" on page 14) who works best with specific guidelines, this is a great exercise whether you've been actually given a project or not.

Tailoring songs for a specific artist is a calculated and methodical approach. You may have written down or recorded some great ideas during the heat of inspiration but now, in the light of what you'll learn about your target artist or project, you'll look at the ideas with a whole new perspective. Let's say you have a "prescription" to write. You know that the producer is looking for positive, up-tempo love songs for an artist. If you can, get information from the producer about the artist's vocal range, point of view, attitude and philosophy. If it's not convenient to do that and the artist has previous albums, get them. Make a synopsis of the lyric of each song like, "He left me but I know I'll get over him," "I've had my problems with other women but I know she'll be different," "My friends think I'm crazy to love you but I don't care," "They all want you but I know what you want," etc. (see chapter eleven, "Casting: The Right Song for the Right Artist" on page 221). See if the songs the artist records—particularly the successful ones—fall into a consistent pattern. There are artists who don't like "weak" or "victim" songs that basically say, "You can walk all over me, party with other women, wreck my car, and I don't care. I'll still love you no matter what you do." Other artists have practically built their careers on songs with that attitude. Pay attention to the established image of an artist.

You can often get additional information from reading interviews with the artists in trade or fan magazines. When you hear their records, check out the kind of melodic passages the artist sings well. Does she have a great voice that loves to hold onto long notes and style them? Does the artist not have a great voice, coming off better doing story songs with lots of lyrics and short choppy lines? Does the artist phrase well or have a stylistic trademark that you'd do well to accommodate?

Notice if the artist seems to prefer a particular form. Does he like a form that allows them a minute to jam on the hook during a fade? Does she prefer short, four-line choruses with lots of repetition or four different lines with a strong payoff line? Is the song for a group with more involved vocal parts, needing parallel lyric lines to intermesh? Once you've listened to enough of the artist, you can visualize her singing your lyrics and melodies and it gets much easier to write for the style. A valuable exercise is to try to write a follow-up song to an artist's last hit, taking into consideration all the artistic factors that you feel contributed to its success.

Some writers hate this approach to writing because they feel it's calculated, uninspired hack work. Other writers love it because they welcome the artistic challenge of saying something that comes from them but is tailor-made for someone else. They look at the parameters as an architect would look at building a house for a family's specific needs. Matching form with function is the challenge. If the music that comes from this approach seems uninspired, the writer has no one to blame but himself. All those great, inspired ideas you wrote on all those little scraps of paper or sang or played into a tape recorder should inspire you again.

Norman Gimbel had the phrase "killing me softly" in his notebook long before Lori Lieberman (who he and co-writer Charles Fox were producing) told him about her emotional reaction to experiencing Don McLean ("American Pie," "Vincent") in concert. They used (1) the need to write a song to fit her style, (2) the inspired phrase, and (3) Lori's own experience to put together a fresh and original classic ("Killing Me Softly With His Song") that was later a hit by Roberta Flack and later by Fugees. Many of the successful writers I've interviewed have felt that some of their best work was done under deadline or for a specific project.

For a writer/performer writing primarily for yourself, it can be an artistically liberating experience to write for someone else, as a scriptwriter would, and not be identified with your words, to be able to say something in a way that you wouldn't state it for yourself. It allows you to expand the parameters of your craft, and that can't hurt. For non-performing writers who depend on others to record their songs, tailoring is a valuable discipline to develop.

A possible criticism of this approach is that you may write a song that's *too* tailored to only one artist. If that artist doesn't record it, you may end up with a great song that no other artist could hear themselves singing. I don't agree. I believe that if it really is a great song, you'll find another artist to cut it, even if you have to re-write or re-demo it. A great song is a great song!

11 Self-Publishing

Why Publish Your Own Songs?

In the last chapter, I discussed what a publisher does. Now let's discuss the advantages of having your own publishing company. It's important because the publisher's share of royalties could represent a lot of money.

The information in this chapter is geared to those who want to be your own publisher and actively pitch your own songs and possibly those of other writers. However, there are a lot of situations for which you'd want to self-publish without getting into it that deeply. You may have the occasion to self-publish a few songs. You may get a song recorded and not be asked for the publishing by the producer or artist, or the recording of the song may be released only in the U.S. or with a minor artist for which the collection could be handled easily by an administrator (see "Administration Deals" on page 234). In those cases, only a part of this information may apply to you.

Here are some other reasons why you might want to publish your own songs and some qualities that would help you do a good job for yourself.

• **You are a good commercial songwriter whose tunes are very coverable** (suitable to be recorded by other artists) and you already have a lot of contacts among producers and artists who are interested in your songs. In other words, you're in a position to fulfill one of a publisher's major functions: getting covers. You should be aware, though, that it takes a lot of time, and follow-up is very important.

• **You have the ability to "sell" yourself.** Some people represent others better than themselves. You should be an aggressive self-starter. You should have the ability to be both creator and businessperson. (Yes, it can be done, and yes, it's a myth that creative artists always make poor businesspeople.)

• **You have a great casting sense** that lets you present the right song to the right artist at the right time. Publishers' reputations are built on their credibility.

• **You have your own production company or record company** and you're releasing your own product.

• **You are a recording artist/band who is recording your own songs** and therefore already doing part of a publisher's job.

- **You already have written commercially successful songs** and it is easy for you to get in the doors of producers, record companies, music supervisors, etc.

- **You are writing with someone who does well as his own publisher** and you can negotiate a portion of the rights for your own company. If your co-writer is a staff writer with a major company, this is a great situation for you. However, you may find it very difficult to defend not giving your publishing share to your co-writer's company unless you also have great contacts and are aggressive about pitching your songs. In other words, you would be an equal partner in the promotion of the song.

- **You are a writer/artist or a band whose style is so unique that your songs are unlikely to be recorded by other artists.** You don't need a publisher to get your songs recorded. Be sure not to sell yourself short on the potential for other artists to record your songs, though.

- **You're independently wealthy or have financial backing.** You write coverable tunes and you can afford the alternative of *hiring* someone with experience and contacts to promote your songs.

If you're capable of hustling for yourself, you'll have the satisfaction of knowing that someone with your best interest at heart is on the job. You will not be constantly wondering whether the publisher is sitting on your song, or why he is avoiding your calls. If someone is not on the case, you have only yourself to blame. Can you handle that?

How to Start Your Own Publishing Company

Assuming that, for whatever reason you feel your best plan of action is to start your own company, here's how to proceed:

1. Choose a name for your company. Remember that you cannot have a company with the same name (or very close) as another publishing company. That is because ASCAP, BMI, SESAC, or any of the other organizations that handle your paperwork don't want to confuse your company name with someone else's.

2. You must clear the name you've chosen for your publishing company with BMI, ASCAP, or SESAC. You are eligible to have BMI, ASCAP, or SESAC process your application as a publisher if: (a) a record or DPD (Digital Phonorecord Distribution) is being released containing a performance of the song; (b) a motion picture is being released that includes the song; (c) a television program will be or has been broadcast using the song; or (d) a radio program has been broadcast that played the song.

3. Unless you intend to publish the songs of other writers who may belong to other performing rights organizations, you need only set up a company with the one you are affiliated with as a writer. The reason why you see hyphenated publishing company names (Warner/Chappell, Sony/Tree, etc.) is that one is a BMI-affiliated company and one is an ASCAP affiliated company. If you do want to have a company in each performing rights organization, you need to clear the company names with each. Give them three alternative company names in your order of preference. If your first choice is already being used by someone else, the organization will select the next choice that is not already taken, so be creative and pick something unusual.

If you're a writer representing your own songs, it is a good idea not to use a version of your own name (unless you're already famous) because, if you're pitching to producers and record companies, it signals to them that this is a "hip-pocket" company and not a "real" company and they'll automatically assume the publishing is up for grabs. Not that having a name that doesn't scream "self-publishing" gives you a great edge, but sometimes it's a factor in your favor if they think they'll have to fight for your song. Note that there will be a fee to join the performing rights organizations.

4. Once the name(s) have been cleared, go to your local County Clerk's Office and obtain the forms to register a fictitious business name statement, also known as a d/b/a (doing business as). Then go to your bank and open an account under your new business name. Your County Clerk will refer you to a local publication that will publish a fictitious business name statement that gives the required notice that you are now officially doing business as "Crass Commercial Music" or whatever name you've chosen. The notice must be published once per week for four weeks in a paper of "general circulation" in the county where the business is located. You can use the same d/b/a to list more than one company if you want to add another publishing company, production company, etc. The process and cost of publication varies from city to city and county to county but is generally under $50.

A name using the legal name of the individual owner, as long as the business name does not imply other owners, does not require a d/b/a. "John Braheny Music" would not require any fictitious name registration. "Braheny & Associates Music" or "Braheny & Company Publishing" probably would.

5. Copyright all the songs you wish to have in your company on a performing arts (PA) form assigned to your publishing company (see chapter eight, "Copyright Registration" on page 158).

6. For songs being released on records, or for songs that will be or have been performed in an audio-visual production or radio, fill out both the writer's and publisher's clearance forms from the performing rights organization involved (BMI, ASCAP, or SESAC). These forms notify the organization that a specific song is being released in a specific medium so that, when it's performed on the radio, TV, or online, the organization will know who to pay, what percentage to pay the writer and the publisher, and where to send the checks. Directions are included on the forms and in publisher's manuals provided by the organizations. All are also available online (see Web sites in the appendix on pg. 384). Keep a photocopy or printout of everything related to a particular song in its own file.

7. Matters such as the legal entity under which you should operate your publishing company (e.g., as a corporation, partnership, or sole proprietorship), whether you need to obtain any kind of business license, and whether you need to obtain a federal (or state) employer identification number and report wages and withhold taxes for employees can be complicated issues and are beyond the scope of this book. You should consult an attorney or accountant for this information. Regulations vary from state to state.

8. Organize yourself to be able to keep track of your "song shopping."

Business Expenses and the IRS

You'll incur many expenses in the process of setting up and maintaining your business, both as a songwriter and publisher. Keep records of all your expenses (receipts with date, vendor's name, and amount of purchase, plus sales tax, if applicable), and income records. Use your business checks and arrange for a separate business credit card for those expenses. The IRS will allow you to deduct these expenses for three years without seeing any business-related income. After that, they figure it's just a hobby and won't allow the deductions.

Here is a combined list of both publishing business and songwriting expenses you can deduct.

- **Services of a graphic artist and printing:** Includes the company logo, J-card inserts, labels, and business cards. Costs vary. You'll save a lot in the long run by buying computer programs and a good color printer.

- **Bank account:** Check printing and service charges for business account (+/- $100).

- **Subscriptions:** Trade magazines, books, tip sheets, and online services (between $300 and $1,000+ per year). Also include music subscription services like Rhapsody or Yahoo!.

- **Music business and songwriter organization dues:** Some people belong to several. Costs vary.

- **Postage:** For letters and demos mailed, FedEx, UPS, messenger services. E-mail and a Web site can save you this cost.

- **Photocopies:** Of lyric sheets, cover letters, lead sheets, forms, business correspondence, and anything else you'll need to keep a copy. A printer and well-organized database will save you this in the long run.

- **Stationery:** Letterhead, envelopes, mailing labels, mailing envelopes, card files, and business cards. Good software is available for most of this.

- **Copyright registration:** $30 each and may go up again.

- **Demo recording costs:** About $300 per song minimum, depending on where you are and how elaborate you need it to be and how much of it you can do on your home recording setup.

- **Blank media:** Buy in bulk to save money.

- **Tape and CD duplication:** Costs vary. Save money and invest in a CD burner.

- **Audio-visual equipment:** Cassette/CD/DVD/VCR decks, home and auto systems, iPods or other digital music players, and accessories. Costs include insurance, maintenance, and repair of all of these.

- **Purchase of CDs, downloads, and video rentals:** So you can research artists you want to pitch your songs to. If you're pitching to TV, you need to be familiar with the shows.

- **Entertainment events:** Nightclubs, concerts, movies, and theatre performances. You need to go to clubs to network and check out new artists. You'll need to document this for the IRS. Don't forget to keep your parking and admission receipts.

- **Business meals:** You also need to document these for the IRS.

- **Business gifts:** Up to $25 per person per year. Also gift flowers, greeting cards, holiday, and thank you cards.

- **Promotion and advertising:** Newspaper and magazine ads, fliers.

- **Computer costs:** If you write, keep records and accounting ledgers, and do research on your computer or PDA (personal digital assistant, such as Palm Pilot, you can write off the computers, as well as related equipment including furniture, printer, etc. (Check with your tax service.)

- **Software:** Programs for composing, recording, and mixing your music, and for organizing your networking, accounting, correspondence, and other business.

- **Web site:** Design, hosting, and maintenence.

- **Travel expenses:** For that trip to L.A., Nashville, or New York to meet with publishers, producers, or record companies. Includes airfare, luggage and travel gear, lodging, tips, car rental and gas, laundry, taxi, buses, subways, and upgrades to business class. Keep good records of gas, mileage, food, and lodging.

- **Auto expenses:** Gas, oil, repairs, tires, insurance, DMV, AAA, wash and wax, tolls, parking, and lease payments, can be deducted based on the percentage of work-related travel. Keep mileage and repair records.

- **Home office expenses:** Based on the percent of square footage of your office space relative to the square footage of your home. Includes rent, interest payments, property taxes, insurance, and utilities. Some cities have special regulations and taxes regarding home offices. Check it out.

- **Phones:** Home, cell, pager, DSL, or cable modem. If you're aggressive, these can run $600+ per month. Check out the lower-cost long-distance services. Installing a second phone for business helps tremendously to document those expenses for the IRS.

- **Answering machine:** To make sure you don't miss any calls.

- **Attorney fees:** To put together contracts that reflect your business philosophy and protect your interests, you'll need publisher/writer, single-song, and co-publishing contracts.

- **Accounting fees:** Find an accountant experienced in the music business to make sure you get all the deductions you're entitled to.

- **Business filing fees:** Check with your city or county clerk.

- **Seminars:** Classes, workshops, songwriter-related showcases, and other educational activities (including those on how to run your business better).

- **Web site maintenance:** Building, maintaining, and promoting your site.

- **Musical instruments:** Includes amps, P.A. system, insurance, maintenance, and repairs.

Note: The amount you can deduct for computers, office equipment, sound systems, instruments, etc., can be deducted on a diminishing depreciation scale over several years.

Casting: The Right Song for the Right Artist

"Kelly (or Kenny, Faith, etc.) could sing this song really great!" This statement, and the ignorance behind it, has been the cause of countless unnecessary rejections of songs. Though it's certainly not the only cause, it ranks right up there with poorly crafted songs. But for the sake of this discussion, let's say both the demo and song are excellent. But is it *appropriate*? It's not a question of whether they *could* do it. They could make the phone book sound good. But from the artist's point of view, it's about whether they *need* to record your song.

If you're writing for yourself in a band or solo artist context and don't think this information applies to you, don't stop reading just yet. The history of pop music is filled with songs written by self-contained artists who had no idea their songs could be recorded by other artists. After all, Trent Reznor (Nine Inch Nails) probably never would have dreamed that Johnny Cash would cover "Hurt." Cash covered it because he said it was "the best anti-drug song he ever heard." *Someone* had the skills to recognize that those songs were *right* for those other artists. Wouldn't it be better to develop these skills yourself rather than reward skillful publishers/managers with a substantial percentage of your income for it?

The skill is called "casting," knowing which song is appropriate for which artist. First, there's a process of elimination. Forget about artists who write their own songs. Not that they wouldn't *ever* record a song they didn't write, but generally speaking, they're not motivated financially to record "outside" songs (written by someone other than themselves or their producer). With substantial royalties for sales and airplay on a hit, they'd rather fill their CDs with their own songs, for better or worse. Sometimes worse. Record buyers are getting tired of buying an album with only two or three good songs on it. Though "good" is certainly in the ear of the beholder, things are changing now that in many cases, single tracks can be bought online.

WHO NOT TO PITCH TO—PLAYING THE ODDS

If you're playing the odds, you'll leave self-contained artists until last. First, you'll read the *Billboard* magazine charts to find those artists who record outside songs. How can you tell? You look at the "Hot 100" chart and your favorite genre singles chart: "Hot R&B/Hip-Hop Songs," "Hot Country Songs" or "Hot Latin Songs." (The other charts don't list writers.) You look to the left under the name of the song, and the first name is the producer's, the second (in parentheses) is the name(s) of the songwriter(s). If the same name is in both places, the producer *is* the writer. Then, if you see, in the column to the right, that the artist's name is the same as the writer, you know the odds are bad. You may have a hard time telling who wrote the songs when the artist is a group (although if there are four or more writers listed, you can often assume the group did or they're using samples of other songs). Check it out by going online to their record companies and look up the artists' bios. If they wrote the songs, they'll want everybody to know it.

You'll end up with a list of about 25 percent of the hits on the "Hot 100" on which the artist sings an outside song. About 2/3 of those will be Country. On the "Hot Country" chart about 60–70 percent are outside songs. Check the charts periodically. Tape "countdown" radio or cable TV shows (MTV, VH1, BMT, CMT) of current hits so you can listen more than once and analyze them without having to stay tuned all day. Keep your *Billboard* handy for reference. If you're an Internet user, you can go to Web radio sites like Live365 (www.live365.com) and pick your genre. Last time I looked there were more than two hundred country Web radio stations playing country songs, and those are divided into subgenres.

DOING THE RESEARCH

A critical step in casting is to get all the information possible about the artist to save yourself the embarrassment of pitching something totally wrong. Your best move is to buy the CDs of any artist in your style who records outside songs. Listen to each cut on the album with special emphasis on the successful singles and determine the following:

1. Style. If it's rock, is it influenced by pop, blues, funk, punk, metal, or world music? If country, is it on the rock, traditional, pop, or Texas swing side? You may find different influences in different songs on any given CD, but they'll give you some boundaries of style.

2. Are there any songs the artist *did* write? Pay particular attention to the style of these. Also try to determine the common factors of the outside songs. Chances are the artist or producer had some input into those choices.

3. Lyric message. The shaping of an artist's image is based largely on his philosophies and attitudes about life and love, how he handles disappointments, etc. Those attitudes show up in his song lyrics regardless of who writes them. Read or listen to the lyric of each song and answer the following:

   a. Is the lyric positive or negative, up or down? Do the down songs show some hope in the end? Are the songs in first, second, or third person? Are they about winners or losers?

   b. Does the lyric have a payoff, a final "moral"? Is it based on a high concept such as Tim McGraw's "Live Like You Were Dying" (written by Craig Nichols and Tim Wiseman) or is it just a straight ahead love song?

   c. Is the artist young, naive, inexperienced, and hopeful or mature, experienced, a little world-weary, and sexy? Remember that a successful artist is singing your song and needs to believe the lyric, and that it has to reflect the artist's self-image and personal story. Songs that say, "I'm a terrible human being" don't work unless maybe you're apologizing to someone you've wronged. Remember the prime audience for country is 25- to 40-year-old women (and they *love* to hear a man apologize).

4. Lyrics as vocal platforms. In addition to vocal range, you need to consider whether your lyric allows the artist room to sing. When I see a lyric sheet literally covered with lyric, and hear the words sung so tightly that there's no space for the singer to style the song in his own unique way, I know it's going in the reject pile. Great singers love to hold notes (particularly vowels at the ends of lines) and play with them, embellishing the melody. It may be a wonderful story and brilliant lyric but so much a product of your own unique style that it won't work in their style. A group like Third Eye Blind, for instance, writes unique songs that other artists would have difficulty covering without sounding like them.

5. Who is the artist's audience? Pre-teens and early teens are fans of bright, young pop artists who quickly outgrow the style at the same quick rate as their audience. Listeners in their mid-to-late teens generally become more genre-specific (rock, pop, alternative, rap, hip-hop, or country) and tend to fragment along those styles. You'll need to gear your song and demo to that style or recognize whether or not you write in that style or for that audience.

6. Vocal range. Listen to the song with the highest and lowest notes and you've got the range. Does the artist have a wide vocal range like Celine Dion or Kelly Clarkson? Odds are she'll choose a song that will show it off. If the artist has a limited range, a two-octave stretch won't work. Also, look for a place in the artist's range that she favors because there may be a unique quality or timbre there. It's been referred to as a sweet spot. Make sure the song allows them to use that spot.

7. Structure. Do the artist's successful songs use a repeated chorus, pre-chorus sections, or classic AABA (verse-verse-bridge-verse *a la* "Yesterday")? AABA structures are rarely recorded, except by self-contained artists. It's easier for a listener to learn a song with a repeating chorus, so verse/chorus songs are seen as being more commercial.

Along with analyzing the song, collect articles about and interviews with the artist from fanzines, trade magazines, and the artist's personal and fan Web sites. You can find some great clues to the artist's image

223

and values. Don't send a recovering alcoholic or drug addict your song about the bottle being your best friend. But the song about getting your life together might work. It may help to know that the artist is a parent, donates money to organizations that help kids, just got divorced, is a womanizer, feels women deserve more respect, feels women should stay at home, is a born-again Christian, etc.

Another level of casting expertise involves projecting, based on past success and artist image, where you feel the artist *could* go. This is a common strategy of writer/producer/arrangers and publishers who can conjure a vision of the artist's next step and, in the process, become the artist's producer, at least on the producer's own songs. This requires a thorough knowledge of the artist and, in the best case, the ability to produce tracks that would provide the artist with a fresh sound. There is a point in a very successful career where an artist looks for a stretch away from the too familiar and into adventureland. You can either anticipate that move or help to create it.

Regardless of all the homework you do on an artist, you can still strike out, though the odds will be considerably better if you've done the research. A major benefit is that you now have a great frame of reference when you talk to the manager, record company A&R representative for the artist, or the new producer who may be taking the artist in a different direction. In my experience, those people speak to and listen to demos from so many writers who are clueless about their artists that they welcome a conversation with someone who knows what makes their artist special. It also gives you a level of confidence in that call or meeting that communicates that you should be taken seriously.

Successful Pitching Strategies

The time you spend developing a strategy for pitching a song will eventually save you a lot of rejection and time. Here are some tactics to consider:

Establish priorities. Research the trade charts and tip sheets and compile a list of currently successful artists who record the styles of songs you write, and who record songs by other writers. Choose a particular song and determine which of those artists would be appropriate to send the song to. Make those artists your A list. Make other lists of artists in order of priority. These might include:

> B—new artists with record deals
>
> C—new artists and former hit artists who have production deals with established producers, no record contracts, and are not writing with the producers
>
> D—recording artists with past hits but no recent success, no producer or record deal
>
> E—new artists with new producers and no record deal
>
> F—new artists with no producer and no record deal

Even though this is a logical priority list in terms of playing the odds and spending your time, energy, and money accordingly, the music business isn't known for succeeding on logic. In this case, the situation with any artist on any of those lists could totally change on any given day. A's become D's, D's become A's overnight.

Don't underestimate the value of pitching to new artists. We didn't get a great turnout at the Los Angeles Songwriters Showcase when Arista Records' representatives were looking for songs for a new, unknown artist named Whitney Houston. "Whitney who? Never heard of her. I'm saving my best stuff for superstars." There's a lot to be said for the personal and political rewards of being there when they need you, when nobody else will take the chance. It's also easier to get to new artists, and you're more likely to be heard when they're desperate for hit songs because the major publishers may not be giving them their best material.

Surround the artists with demos. By that, I mean get the song to their manager, attorney, producer, recording engineer, A&R representative, musicians, roadies, hairdresser, chauffeur, secretary, gardener, relatives, lovers, anyone who is a potential contact. But don't do this unless you've done your homework very well and feel confident that this is an outstanding and appropriate song. It will annoy them no end to keep getting the wrong song.

Check the club and concert listings. Look in your local paper and try to find out where the artists are playing. Go to the club early when the artist does a sound check and try to connect with the artist, road manager, or musicians. You should be aware that, for their legal protection, many writer/artists are cautioned by their attorneys not to personally accept any unsolicited demos. With artists who don't write, it's not as much of a problem.

Introduce yourself to some recording engineers at the hot studios in town. Let them hear your songs and offer them financial incentives if they can place songs with acts that record there. You may, in fact, make an offer to any of the above-mentioned contacts. Ten percent of the mechanical royalties on a recording they secure for you is a good place to start, but higher percentages are not necessarily out of line. Use your best judgment and offer whatever feels right (see "Negotiating" on page 226).

Be aware of the successful bands in your area. Maybe there's a great cover band in which none of the members write. They may want a record deal but have no original material. You might be able to co-write with someone in the band. Pay particular attention to the lead singer and keyboard player. It's always a good idea to look for bands that are good enough to have a shot at a record deal. (Look for the qualities described in chapter fifteen, "Getting A Record Deal" on page 364) If they hit with your songs, it may result in a long and lucrative relationship.

Get involved in every musical project you possibly can. This includes student films and video projects, background music for a play, commercial jingles, church choir, anything! In every project, you may meet someone who likes your work and likes working with you, and who will refer you for another project. Networking is one of the best ways to develop a reputation and contacts. When you find good musicians, singers, or writers, refer them to projects. What you give comes back! (Though you can count on the fact that it doesn't always come back from those you'll give it to.)

Think of some creative ways to stand out from the crowd. There are legendary stories about writers and publishers pulling outrageous stunts like dropping tapes from helicopters (a young Kris Kristofferson landed his helicopter in Johnny Cash's yard to deliver a demo tape) or by parachutes or delivering them via strippers or in cakes. A friend of mine sent demos to A&R departments in sealed soup cans with the songs listed as ingredients. Very clever, but he neglected to send along can openers. Some probably still sit unopened in A&R offices as a lasting testament to his ingenuity.

Those are the stories that get passed around in the industry and usually end with, "Yeah, fantastic! If only the *song* had been good!"

The point is that if you can think of an imaginative way to present your material, you'll definitely make a lasting impression, but it's useless to you unless the people who receive your package are also excited about the music.

Make your packaging as professional as your song. Let's assume your music is worth pitching. You need to know what you can do to make an eye-catching professional-looking package. I know a writer whose trademark is hot pink—the color she uses for lyric sheets, cover letter, and cassette J-card insert. Publishers or producers can pick it out of a stack or basket of tapes immediately. Using good graphics with a logo and an artistic layout with possibly a picture on the J-card insert (particularly for performers, but only if your looks and age are an asset!) can strengthen your presentation. There are great graphics software programs available for creating your own as well as graphics you can get for free or for a small fee online that can give you professional results (see chapter twelve, "Presenting Your Demo" on page 264).

A common question comes up regarding logos: If I have my own publishing company, should I send materials out under company letterhead? Not if you're sending songs to publishers, unless you're suggesting a co-publishing agreement in your letter. If the materials are going to record companies, then yes. In sending songs to producers, you have to consider that it might help to get your song through the door, or it might make the producer skittish. A producer usually has his own publishing company and will prefer to record a song he at least partly owns. He may opt to pass on your song if he thinks the publishing rights are not available. However, it all depends on how good the songs are. If he wants to record them and get a piece of the publishing he'll definitely try to negotiate. So, use your company logo and take your chances.

Be prepared. Never leave the house without demos and lyric sheets. If possible, carry a portable player and headset. You never know whom you're going to meet. This is especially important at industry events like South by Southwest (SXSW), the TAXI Road Rally, Folk Alliance, or anywhere fellow writers, bands, and industry are gathering.

Negotiating

A writer I know happened to get to the manager of a major R&B/pop crossover group. The manager loved her song and felt it was so good that the group wanted to record it despite the fact that they usually wrote their own songs. He asked her if the group could have the publishing if they recorded it. She said, "No." He said, "Goodbye." She told me later she was totally unprepared to deal with the situation and had no idea what to say. She was excited that he liked it, but when he wanted the publishing, she thought he was trying to rip her off. Bear in mind that the manager gets a percentage of everything the artist earns, including the publishing income. So he has a vested interest. They may have found yet another song he (on behalf of the group) *could* get the publishing on, so from his point of view he had to go for it.

There are three schools of thought on this situation:

1. "Right, don't let them have the publishing. You did right! You did the job of a publisher by getting it to the group in the first place. Does anyone seriously believe that the manager is going to do anything with that song beyond this group's recording of it?"

2. "My God, do you know that there are writers who'd sell their kids for just an album cut on that group? The writer's royalties alone could be worth a million, especially if it's a single. So what if you do give them the publishing, if you can get a guaranteed release? If you give it to a 'real' publisher, it might never get cut because he's not going to give up *his* piece of the action to that group. Either way, you wouldn't have been able to keep the publishing anyway! It's just one song and it'll help build your career."

3. "Why didn't you negotiate?" She answered, "I don't know, I didn't even think of it. What's to negotiate? Either you give them the publishing or you don't, right?" Wrong!

Let's look at each of these attitudes. The first is certainly defensible and, in fact, it is important to analyze whether this manager (or producer or artist) has an active publishing company with employees who will spend time trying to get other recordings of your song, even after the group has recorded it. If he does, it might be a good situation. If not, you'll know that any subsequent covers of the song will be entirely up to you. And though you'll get your writer's royalty, you won't share any of the publisher's royalties for doing the publisher's work. If he insists on owning the publishing, you could point out that you'll want to be actively pitching this song to other artists after this recording and try to get him to split the publishing with your own company. If that doesn't work, see if he'll give you a portion of the mechanical or performance royalties on any new recordings of the song that *you* are responsible for placing.

Even active publishers (as opposed to holding companies) have different philosophies about splitting the publishing with an artist or producer in order to get a recording. They range from "Under no circumstances will I give up anything. I'm doing the work and I deserve the royalties," to "I'll give up some of what I have to get the tune recorded." It depends a lot on the individual circumstances. How important is this recording? Is this the only artist who could cut the tune? Would this cut be very important in the development of the writer's career in generating interest in the rest of his catalogue? If I give this producer a piece of the action, am I setting a precedent with him that I'll regret later? And always, how badly does he want this song? If you're going to be your own publisher, these are some of the questions that you'll have to consider.

The second attitude is also defensible. This may be a major act and your first recording. One hundred percent of zero is zero. If the manager or producer is adamant about having the publishing and you know it will make you a lot of money for the writer's share of the royalties, it might be best to let him have it. Is this the last or only good song you'll ever write? If he wants it that badly, chances are the song is good enough that you should have more confidence in your own ability. Maybe you won't need to make a deal like that with your next song because you'll be in a better bargaining position if this one turns out to be a winner. There is a danger in being too attached to a song, too protective. It's the classic situation of the bird in hand. If you do decide to give them the publishing and the company is basically a holding company and not an active publisher, *make sure that you have it in writing* that the publishing doesn't get assigned to them officially until the record is actually released. That way, if they decide not to record the song after all, it doesn't end up in limbo because they own it but won't do anything with it.

But don't give it up so fast. There *are* other negotiating positions you can take.

Two major sources of income (mechanical and performance royalties) are negotiable without transferring your ownership of any of the copyright. Generally, when someone says they want "the publishing," they want ownership of the copyright. In the "standard" writer/publisher agreement, you assign the copyright to the publisher in a contract that gives you half the total income as writer, the other half going to the publisher. But the publisher *owns* the song and can sell it to anyone else if he wants to (unless the agreement includes a non-assignment clause). A good businessperson will always want to own the copyright. A copyright's value will increase with the song's degree and length of popularity. So you can't blame him for trying to get as much as he can. He's not trying to rip *you* off. He's just looking out for his own interests. You need to do the same.

"Mechanicals" are the income primarily from the sale of physical recordings (CDs) and DPDs bought online (see chapter nine, "Mechanical Royalties" on page 171). As the writer, you'll take half off the top right away, and from the remainder (referred to as the "publisher's share of mechanicals") you can offer percentages as an incentive for someone to record the song. The advantages of offering a percent of the publisher's share of mechanicals on *that particular recording* is that you still own the copyright and you give them incentive only for their limited use of the song. This is referred to as a "cut in" or a "participation agreement." If someone else later records the song, you still own the copyright so you can make a better deal. You can get *all* the publisher's and writer's royalties for future recordings.

Performance royalties is another negotiable item. The term applies to all the money received through BMI, ASCAP, or SESAC for the performances of your songs on radio, TV, jukeboxes, etc. (see the Royalty Flow Chart, in chapter nine on page 181). Those performing rights organizations pay directly to the publisher *and* the writer. This is a different situation from mechanical royalties that are paid directly to the publisher. If you have a hit song, particularly one that gets played on the radio long after it's been a hit, your performance royalties can amount to considerably more money than your mechanicals.

For the purpose of negotiation, another important difference exists between mechanical and performance income. When you receive your quarterly earnings statement from BMI or ASCAP, they don't note which recording of your song you're receiving royalties from (SESAC does, however). You can't say, "I'll give you X percent of the publisher's share of the performance income on this particular record," since, in some cases, two different versions of the same song (for example, a country and a pop version) have been on the charts at the same time. You *could* say, "I can give you X percent participation in the publisher's share of performance income:

a. for the first _____ quarters in which royalties are received; or

b. until the quarter before the next recording of this song is released."

Another approach is to negotiate a percentage of the mechanical or performance royalties until a *specified maximum dollar figure is reached*. In other words, "I'll give you X percent of the money up to (until you've received) X dollars."

Here are some other points to keep in mind when negotiating with anyone regarding mechanicals and performance income:

1. The percentage or dollar amount you offer is totally negotiable. There are no set rules. You may offer any percentage of the income from the song that you want to offer and still maintain ownership of the copyright.

2. Your performance royalties won't amount to much on an album cut unless your song is a piece that radio DJs take particular interest in. With the exception of the small percentage of stations that specialize in playing albums, radio plays singles. There are times, though, when an album cut unexpectedly gets enough radio excitement going that it forces the company to release it as a single. They may also offer it individually via iTunes or other DPDs and sales there will drive radio interest.

3. On a hot act with good album sales, mechanical royalties on album cuts are worth a great deal. Singles are still worth more because your song will appear on both the single and album and because the single will earn performance royalties if it gets airplay. Remember, too, that each different mix of the same song on a CD single makes the same royalties as the other so you may have

two different radio mixes and two club mixes—four times the mechanical rate—plus the album cut, plus eventually a "greatest hits" CD and other compilations.

4. You'll get the highest mechanical *and* performance royalties on pop records (including R&B/pop) by established artists.

Mechanicals are bit lower on country records because sales are usually not as strong overall, except for country/pop crossover superstars like Faith Hill and Trisha Yearwood and a few other top sellers. But performance (airplay) royalties on a country *single* can be very high because of the great number of country radio stations.

These are generalities to give you a rough estimate of the relative popularity of styles, but the bottom line is determined by the popularity of the individual artist.

5. It may be wise to offer a producer a percentage of royalty participation for an album cut and an additional percentage if the song becomes a single. This may work if the artist or producer you're offering the incentive to can influence the choice of the record as a single. Their increased financial participation if your song is chosen as a single could be a factor in that decision.

6. Make sure the "cut in" or "participation" goes into effect only upon *release* of a specified record by a specified artist on a specified label. If you choose to deal with producers and artists directly and they want some financial incentive, keep in mind that everything is negotiable.

A word of caution in making these deals: If the person to whom you're offering this incentive is employed by a record company and makes this agreement without the permission of the company, your deal may constitute commercial bribery. (And if that ever happened I'd just be shocked!!) But check it out!

Holds

If a producer (or record company or artist) feels your song is right for his recording project, he'll ask for a "hold" on it. It means he'll want to have the first opportunity to record the song. He doesn't want you to pitch it to anyone else in the meantime because he doesn't want to spend the money to produce the song, only to have his release beaten out by another artist.

Producers commonly have exclusive holds on more songs than they need to put on an album. It often happens that even if they get around to recording a song, it may turn out less exciting than they thought.

Aside from that, there are several other reasons why your song may not end up on an album. A writer/artist may have written new songs since yours went on hold and will choose to record those instead of yours. Maybe it was decided that other writers' songs chosen since yours were stronger or better suited to the project. A musical direction or concept for the project may emerge from the material that's gathered and certain songs just don't fit with the others, no matter how good they may be. There aren't enough ballads, or there are too many. The artist, producer, or A&R representative may change his mind about the song at the last minute.

Since any of those things can and do happen, and because selecting the right songs is crucial to an album's success, you can see why a producer wants to hold on to as many songs as possible until the project is finished.

On the other side we have the writer and publisher who may want very much for the producer and artist to record the song. In granting a hold on a song, there is a risk for them that the producer does not share. It can't hurt the producer if he decides not to record the song, but the publisher may be forced to turn down some other equally good, if not better, offers in honoring the hold. In being your own publisher, this is a situation you'll have to deal with, and with great diplomacy.

There are several different attitudes among publishers regarding holds:

1. "If I think the project is worth it, I'll always let them hold it. In the process, I'm building my relationship with the producer."

2. "I never give holds. They all know that if they want the song they'll have to hurry up and record it. I'll stay in touch with the producer and let him know about any other interest in the song as it comes up, and I'll let him know I want him to record it, but I'll keep pitching it."

3. "It depends on my relationship with that producer, how long he wants to keep it, and whether I know if he'll be honest with me about the status of the project—not lead me on by telling me it'll be just a little longer when he knows he'll need a lot more time."

4. "I'll tell them they can have a hold, but if another major project comes along, I'll give it to them, too. I know the odds are that when it gets down to it only one of them will end up wanting to record the song anyway." Be careful with this one. You could burn some bridges if they discover you've given them both holds, particularly if one of them has spent some of his budget to record it. Remember that the music business is like a small town and everybody talks.

If more than one producer wants to hold your song, ask yourself some questions:

Is one of the acts likely to sell more records and get more airplay than the other?

Is the song to be released as a single or an album cut? Do the producers plan for a major artist or a newcomer to record your song? Is it being considered for a country artist (good for performance royalties if it's a single but not as good for mechanical royalties) or for a major crossover artist (good for performance *and* mechanical royalties)?

How long do they each need to hold it?

If one will be able to tell you in two weeks whether he's cutting it and the other needs six months before his act can get into the studio, tell him you'll let him know in two weeks! Stall for time.

Through the years, publishers and songwriters have tried to organize a united front to get record companies and producers to pay "option fees" like screenwriters do for keeping a script out of circulation. It's never worked because screenwriters have a union, while songwriters and publishers don't, so there's no way to enforce it. The only bright spot is that a few major artists have been known to offer many thousands of dollars to hold a song they felt strongly about. Their careers depend on finding great songs and will back up that commitment if they need to. Now if we can only get *that* bit of wisdom to spread . . .

Foreign Sub-Publishing

Foreign sub-publishing has become an important aspect of the publisher's business. It's estimated that 60 percent of the world music market is outside the U.S. The international market for American songs has grown tremendously in the past several years. A publisher with any chart success at all, and a strong catalogue of songs to back it up, won't miss the opportunity to capitalize on it in other countries. Most publishers, including the small independents, have affiliations with foreign publishers in countries where their songs are viable.

In the simplest terms, it works like this: American publisher A contacts foreign publisher F. Publisher A has done research, which shows him that F has had success with songs similar to those in A's catalogue. He's also learned that F is very aggressive about getting cover records, promoting the songs of their U.S. affiliates, and collecting the money.

Publisher A contacts F, often at MIDEM (the international music industry conference held in France each year in the same location as the Cannes Film Festival) or Popkomm (the second largest industry trade show, held in Berlin, Germany) in order to determine if that publisher's style of music activities are relevant to publisher A and whether they are looking for new songs to sign. If so, they will set an appointment to meet for the purpose of exchanging new material (generally a mutual exchange), and to offer the opportunity of playing excerpts of the A catalogue to F (time permitting) and to listen to F's catalogue in order to get a sense of the activities of F's company, their personalities, and their business know-how.

Publisher A needs to feel that F is genuinely interested in reviewing the songs (or A will not hand them over, in lieu of finding another potential associate instead) and discusses the issue of follow-up and what time frame would be appropriate to contact them again following the conference. Publisher A will also seek to determine what other promotional resources F utilizes and whether F also has a label division. It is customary for foreign publishers to do a market feasibility study to first see if the songs are commercially viable (radio/TV, etc.) before they will respond. For example, in Germany, it is not unusual to have over 3,000 new releases in any given month. This makes it very difficult to promote a new release. Therefore, companies in the GSA territories (Germany, Switzerland, Austria) are forging toward new business trends and changing year by year.

Assuming that both publishers are in tune with each other, a contract for a number of years (usually three) is worked out, including an advance from F to A. (This is unless F's commission is low, such as 10 percent, in which case, no advance is paid.) The amount of the advance is based on several factors, including A's track record, current hits, and the strength of the overall catalogue, particularly the number of songs that would be viable in F's territory.

Trends today are seeing more and more companies offering low advances (if any) in favor of using their advance budgets toward the promotion of the song or album release, especially in cases where the publishing company has an in-house label affiliation as well. Also, with the music industry economy going down in certain areas, and online digital distribution and ringtone downloading going up, there is less and less room for the larger advances seen in previous years. Another important reason for A to meet and get to know other international publishers is so that A will be in the loop. If A doesn't know much about F's business practices, sometimes it is a good thing to make discreet inquiries prior to signing any agreement.

The musical tastes of listeners and record-buyers can be very different from one country to the next. Check out the international charts in *Billboard* and you'll see what I mean. Part of the jobs of both publishers may be to come up with a translation of the song for a new artist or a translated version by the original artist. Most major artists produce foreign language versions of their hits.

LYRIC TRANSLATIONS

Often the lyric translator is considered to be an author and F takes part of the copyright ownership of the new version, sometimes with a new title to make the separation of royalties easier. The original writers should always try to get a clause in their contract that gives them approval of translations and agreement that no more than 50 percent of the writer's royalties will be lost to the translated version. The best situation is for the sub-publisher to pay a flat fee to the translator but it's tough to get that. And don't forget to check up on the translation with a separate expert or individual who is fluent in the same language in order to ensure that you don't have an incorrect translation. Some words improperly pronounced can have disastrous definitions!

ROYALTY SPLITS

Royalty splits in self-publishing deals vary from 90/10 to 75/25 for A and F respectively, including both performance royalties from that country's version of BMI or ASCAP and mechanical royalties from local record companies collected by F. That is the case for songs by the original American artist or cover records obtained by A. If F obtains a new cover of the song by an artist in his territory, A and F usually divide the royalties received from that recording anywhere from 70/30 to 60/40. The higher "cover splits" are easier to obtain if the overall deal split is in the higher range. That, by the way, is the reason why you receive a lower royalty from foreign recordings on your writer/publisher contract. You're only getting 50 percent of *what the publisher receives in this country*. Generally a publisher will not be interested in a song if there is 25 percent or less available to them, as there is not enough incentive to work the song. Therefore, third party liabilities are not always a good idea.

It's possible to lose out on an enormous amount of money on an international hit if the foreign sub-publishing deals are not in place or are not good ones. Foreign royalties may be generated that you won't even know about. It's one of the areas that is commonly neglected by writers who retain their own publishing rights and have a big hit. Particularly if you have a hot catalogue, it's well worth the trouble for you or your representative to go to MIDEM, do your research, and choose publishers from Japan, England, Australia, Italy, Scandinavia, Argentina, and other countries where you think your songs are viable. The advances you could receive from the deals you make could more than pay for the trip.

The next best alternative is to contract with another North American publisher or attorney (U.S. and Canadian publishers often work together), who has already set up foreign sub-publishing contracts, to make that trip on your behalf and have them deal with all other countries, excluding the U.S./North America. Don't attempt to negotiate foreign sub-publishing deals without the assistance of an attorney experienced in that area. There are many potential difficulties, such as constantly shifting currency exchanges and taxes that could be negotiated out of your contract with the advice of an expert.

Finding Foreign Publishers

To find foreign publishers on your own, check the international charts in *Billboard* to see which hits are stylistically compatible with yours and in which countries they're popular. You can get lists of publishers in those countries from *Billboard's International Buyers Guide* and the annual *Songwriter's Market*, but there's no substitute for personal recommendations and meetings with prospective sub-publishers.

A creative foreign publisher can be valuable by helping to set up tours and TV exposure for the U.S. writer/artist or group whose songs he represents. The more popular he makes the act and songs in his territory, the more money he makes. He can also arrange interviews on radio, TV, and in newspapers, provide interpreters if necessary, concoct promotions that would work in his own country but maybe not the U.S., find the best lyric translators and adapters, or maybe even facilitate co-writing situations with his own writers.

One of the newer music trends seen today are companies that have been started by experienced former major A&R execs that now offer promotional, marketing, and touring services for labels and artists. There are also companies that offer online distribution services and ask for the publishing to facilitate all aspects of this type of promotion as well. Just make sure you check them out with other companies, by making inquiries with those listed on their Web sites.

Obviously, the agreement works both ways. U.S. publisher A will also become familiar with the songs in F's catalogue and advise him as to what type of songs A could get recorded over here, maybe assisting F in finding an American record deal or producer for one of F's hot local writer/artists. The agreement also gives F the opportunity to sign songs in his country that may not be viable there but that could get recorded in the U.S. It's always important to remember that the whole world loves a great song.

A good way to learn more about performance and mechanical royalties in other countries (where they're usually collected by the same organizations), is to go to the English language Web sites of their performing rights organizations via the National Music Publishers' Association list (www. nmpa.org/links.html#Rights).

My friend Debora Nortman, president of ABACA Entertainment Group (www.abaca-music.com), is a veteran MIDEM dealmaker. She told me this story about MIDEM 2006 that offers a valuable lesson:

I was having a meeting with a publisher from Greece. A woman barges into my booth, slams down this big black three-ringed binder and starts yelling at the guy I'm meeting. In front of everyone she screamed, "You thief! You liar! I am slapping you with a court order. You stole 80,000 Euros [that's equivalent to $96,300 U.S.]. If it takes my dying breath, I will do everything in my power to ensure that you don't get away with this!! You are a liar and a cheat and a thief!!!"

Needless to say, I was out of my chair with all my material in hand in two seconds and over to my associates on the side who were watching the spectacle. Coincidently, I actually had a meeting scheduled with this same publisher from Norway. She has a reputable company and has been of-fering publishing services for years. She was the one who organized the account [a *major* beverage company] and he went directly behind her back, collected the funds and didn't remit to her. His response during the outburst was, "I don't know what you are talking about! You are wrong!"

She ended up following him to each of his meetings and telling the companies how he was doing business. He eventually gave up and left MIDEM altogether. Coincidently again, another member in my booth was aware of this particular deal and told me that she was telling the truth. My case in point here is that *bad news travels fast* so it's a good idea to make as many publishing friends as possible, because we talk. And we did!!!

Yet another example of the music business being a small town, even internationally.

Administration Deals

Let's say you've decided to start your own publishing company for any of the reasons listed at the beginning of the chapter, but mainly because you're a self-contained artist or someone who's looking after the business affairs of a self-contained artist. Maybe you're a manager or a spouse with a good business head. There are lots of things you're good at, but learning the intricacies of managing and protecting copyrights internationally is not one of them. You'll be overjoyed to learn that there are individuals and international companies who love this and have done it for years.

They're called publishing or copyright administrators. You have several choices of administrators. All major music-publishing companies have administration departments to administer the copyrights they own. But they will also administer those of anyone else whose songs are generating a royalty stream that would make it financially worthwhile for them to administer those copyrights even though they don't own them. An example would be that you got a record deal at an affiliated record company but by some miracle you got to keep your publishing rights. They'd certainly come to you (or your manager) and say "You're going to need somebody to do all the legal paperwork to make sure that you collect all the money you're due and make sure your copyrights are protected worldwide." Since they believe you're going to be successful, they may even give you an advance.

Here's another option: There are large international *independent* administration companies that are *primarily* administrators. Bug Music (www.bugmusic.com) is one of the largest. Their niche when they started in Los Angeles in the 1970s and thereafter was bands and artists who wrote their own songs, owned their own publishing, and spent their time touring, recording, and writing. Let's just say their lifestyles and inclinations didn't include what administrators do. But they were selling records and in many cases, others were recording their songs. So they needed administration backup. Bug Music now has offices in Nashville, New York, and London.

Another company that started that way was Music Copyright Solutions (www.mcsmusic.com), based in the U.K. with U.S. offices. They've purchased other administration companies such as Copyright Management Inc. of Nashville. These companies have their own music publishing divisions so they can also pitch songs of the writers they administer. (More about that later.)

Another category is small independent administrators who, in many cases, started their careers as administrators in the major companies. There are also attorneys who, along with their other legal responsibilities, do administration on the side.

What do administrators do?

These tasks, depending on your needs, include the exclusive worldwide right (though you can limit the territories) to act on behalf of the owner of the compositions in licensing and collection of the following: mechanical licenses, synchronization licenses, arrangements, adaptations, grand rights (musical theater), performing rights, print, translation, dramatization, re-transmission, merchandising, and all other uses. Along with the above, you grant them your "power of attorney" to file and renew your copyrights worldwide, and to do your royalty accounting, including writing royalty checks to co-writers, co-publishers, or anyone else associated with the songs by contract. Basically, to take care of everything connected with protecting and exploiting your copyrights.

How do they get paid?

Here's the good part. They don't *own* any part of your publishing (with some exceptions). They get a percentage of the gross income. Anywhere from 10–25 percent depending on what you need them to do. Generally it's about 15 percent. The deal usually lasts from three to five years, with options after the third year. That period might be longer if you ask for a big advance up front, particularly if they haven't recouped it by the end of the term.

Will they pitch the songs?

That's where more variables come in. It's really not part of the basic administration deal. However, they may add on another 10-plus percent beyond the original 15 percent if you want to include that. Those additional duties need to be spelled out carefully in the contract. Administrators may also ask for a percentage of the copyright ownership for whatever exploitation (securing other uses) they secure through their own efforts, particularly if the song becomes a hit. They may be motivated to do that because the more income they generate for you, the more *they* make.

What if I have a co-writer with his own administrator?

Co-administration deals can be worked out, but here's a practical consideration. Let's say someone wants to use your song in a TV show. He needs to get a license immediately and he calls your administrator. He also discovers at that point that there's yet another administrator he needs to deal with. More time, more money. Often he just says "forget it." So you need to either have just one administrator or make sure that either of the administrators can make the deal on behalf of the other. That's why I remind you never get into these deals without representation by an experienced music industry attorney. There are many variables that need to be tailored to the needs of both parties.

Here's another tip. Choose your administrator very carefully and find one whose main job is administration. Now and then an attorney will say, "I can take care of that for you." Maybe and maybe not, depending on your needs; but know that this is a full-time job that needs someone knowledgeable and experienced to handle this constantly changing intellectual property landscape.

To get deeper into this subject, read Richard Schulenberg's *Legal Aspects of the Music Industry* and Donald S. Passman's *All You Need To Know About the Music Business* (see bibliography on page 392).

Independent Songpluggers

For writers who don't want to give up their publishing and can afford to hire someone, hiring an independent songplugger is a viable option. Independent songplugging has also been a good way to enter the music business for someone with good ears and personality, and lots of perseverance. If you're successful at it, you'll most surely get offers from established publishing companies who would rather have you as an employee than a competitor.

If you're pitching your own songs and making good contacts in the industry as a result, you might consider pitching songs of other writers for extra income. You can also keep your contacts fresh by having another reason to periodically call them. If they like your songs and encourage you to come back with more (even if they can't use your songs for the projects at hand), it's a good idea to pitch them songs of other writers you believe in. Nurturing those industry contacts makes you more valuable as a collaborator. You also become more valuable to your industry contacts if they know you'll bring them great songs *regardless* of who wrote them.

Indie songpluggers have been a constant part of the Nashville scene in particular because of the greater percentage of artists who don't write, and consequently record "outside" songs.

Q&A WITH LIZ ROSE

Based on her reputation as one of Nashville's best, I interviewed Liz Rose to shed some light on the subject. Among her many indie top 10 successes are number one singles by Garth Brooks ("She's Gonna Make It") and Faith Hill ("The Way You Love Me"). She's now a staff songwriter for Jody Williams Music/ Sony/Tree.

Who are typical clients of indie songpluggers?

Indie pluggers are usually hired by staff writers from large companies that need more exposure, companies that have catalogues that aren't being worked enough, or writers that don't have deals but have big cuts and want to keep their publishing or have co-pub deals. There is also the writer that has had no success but hires a songplugger so that they can keep the publishing. This is great for the writer if they don't need the draw from the publisher and the money for demos.

How do you establish the credibility to get you through the doors the first time?

Most independent songpluggers like to have a name writer with cuts or a company behind them. Especially for a new songplugger that has no contacts. When I started out I was fortunate enough to have the support of writers like Kent Blazy, Will Robinson, and Jason Blume. Their names helped me get in doors where no one knew who I was. I have worked for companies, hit writers that have their own companies, and new writers that are trying to break in. I've worked with publishers in town and out of town and (pitched) my own catalog, King Lizard Music.

What do you like about plugging?

I love songplugging and being independent. It gives me more freedom as to what I pitch. I am very fortunate to be working with some of the best catalogues and songwriters in the business. I work songs and catalogues that I believe in and feel have a chance of getting cut. The competition is incredible. With all the closings and mergers of publishing companies there seem to be more independents and more creative ways to work catalogues. It's an interesting time to be independent. I love working with songwriters.

What kind of agreements do you have with your clients?

I don't really do single-song deals. I'll work single songs if I believe I can get the song cut and prefer a mutual verbal agreement and trust. I don't like to tie up a writer's songs on single-song contracts. I prefer a year commitment. A year is a good length to see how a song will do, whether you still believe in it, or give up. I have an agreement with my clients to have only a certain number of clients so they are properly exploited.

Are periodic reports a part of the agreement?

I keep a pitch log but I am available any time to discuss pitches. I talk to my clients all the time especially when there is good news!

What are your fees?

My fees are different depending on the catalogue, number of writers, and songs. My bonuses depend on how many records the artist sold the last time, how many they sell on this record, and whether the song is a single and its chart position. I do get a percentage of royalty participation without ownership. In some instances, there is the opportunity for copyright ownership. I own two other catalogues. Most successful songpluggers want a piece of the copyright. After all, it takes a great songplugger to get a song cut these days, and a miracle. Without the songplugger the song would just sit there, and the writer with no publishing contract that owns all his own publishing should work some kind of fair deal with the songplugger. If he signed a publishing contract, he probably couldn't keep *any* of his own (publishing) unless he has major hits behind him.

Do you guarantee a specific number of pitches?

I don't agree to a number of pitches because I don't know what my meetings will be. I exploit the songs I believe I can get cut, no matter the company or the writer, or if it's just a single song. I play what is appropriate at the time of the meeting. The name of the game is not how many copies of songs you throw out there, it's how many you get cut. I usually meet with artists and producers and A&R reps that don't want to go through ten songs a meeting. I usually play one and maybe up to four songs.

How do writers find songpluggers?

Check around town and ask about them. Find out how many and what cuts he has secured, who he has worked with. And if it's a new songplugger, go with your gut about how he reacts to your songs and what contacts he has. Everyone starts somewhere.

Are there any situations writers should be cautious about?

Avoid songpluggers that require a large sum of money and have very little track record, unless it is going to be fairly exclusive and the two parties really feel a great connection.

Liz Rose *is currently a writer with Jody Williams Music in Nashville. Her songs have been recorded by Tim McGraw, Terri Clark, Rebecca Lynn Howard, Lee Ann Womack, Gary Allan and in late 2005 by Bonnie Raitt and Trisha Yearwood. I interviewed Liz when she was representing writers as one of Nashville's most respected and successful independent songpluggers before returning to full-time writing.*

---

12 Demos

Why You Need Demos

Demonstration recordings, called "demos," are used to get publishers, producers, record companies, club owners, and other music industry people to hear your songs. These people will rarely look at a lyric without music, and even the few who can read music won't be able to get the full impact of the song by just looking at a lead sheet (lyrics with musical notation). Since the end product (the recording) is to be heard, they need to evaluate your song by hearing it. So you're left with the options of performing the song for them live or giving them a demo.

Most publishers feel a live audition of a song is impractical and inefficient. To paraphrase what many publishers have said to me, "My major responsibility as a publisher is to devote myself to the songs I've already signed and to the writers on our staff. There's not much time for me to schedule appointments in my workday. The few appointments I make are referrals from people whose 'ears' I respect. I know there are some great tunes just walking around out there looking for a publisher and sometimes I'm too busy to see the writer. So in order to be able to listen to new songs, I need to have CDs. Then I can listen when my head is into it and I'm not distracted. What I'm actually listening for is a song that will be a hit record, so it's easier for me to hear it on CD since I won't be distracted by watching the performer."

Unless you have good contacts in the music business, you probably won't get an appointment to sing your songs "live." So make a demo. Even if you can get a live audition, your contact will want to have a demo to listen to later or play for someone else at the company. With a demo, you also have the time to get the recording just as you want it, and get to avoid the jittery nerves of a live audition.

Publishers prefer demos because they can listen to a lot of songs in a short time—and only as long as they're interested. It's hard for any sensitive person to shut you down thirty seconds into your song while you're looking at him (though it's certainly been known to happen). So handing them a demo is both a time-saver and a convenience for them.

In addition to pitching your demos to the music industry, there are Web sites like www.broadjam.com, www.garageband.com, www.pandora.com, www.myspace.com, and hundreds of others where you can post your digital demos/masters for feedback, networking, or distribution. You can also post your songs on your own Web site.

Creating a demo is an education in itself, whether you're actively producing it or observing someone else putting it together. If you're producing your demos at home, you can learn about the recording process at your own pace. You can experiment and work out arrangements without the pressure of paying for studio time.

The more familiar you become with the finished product, the better perspective you have on the writing process. You can more easily imagine a singer performing the song. You learn more about the use of space and density in your lyric writing, and you also become more conscious of the role that arrangements play in enhancing a song's emotional impact.

One of the great thrills of songwriting is to watch your song bloom into a full-blown musical production, to make it fulfill your vision or surpass it. Your failures as well as your successes are great teachers.

On the business side, demos are efficient. Once you get a good demo of your song, you can make an unlimited number of copies, assured that everyone will hear the same top-quality rendition of your song. That's quality control.

Types of Demos

Different kinds of demos serve different needs.

Basic song demo: A basic guitar/vocal or keyboard/vocal demo with the possible addition of a bass and drum track (depending on the equipment you have available), or, at its simplest, *a cappella* (unaccompanied) vocal demo. Use this as a "dummy-demo" to be critiqued before spending money on a more elaborate version. You can also use it to show the emotional energy and rhythm "feel" of your song as a guide for musicians or demo producers for a bigger production, or to play for publishers or producers who you already *know* will accept simple demos. Often what you play in this "dummy-demo" will actually become part of the finished demo or master.

More elaborate song demo: A studio demo or an elaborate home demo is either produced by the writer to play for publishers or to pitch directly to producers and artists; or produced by the publisher to pitch to producers and artists. This demo usually has a groove (sequenced, looped, or live), bass, guitar or keyboard, lead vocal, and sometimes background vocals. What else goes on the demo is based on the writer or publisher's perception of the style of the artist being pitched to and the personal tastes of the demo's producer. The demo can be mixed in several different ways (strings replaced by steel guitar, for instance) to accommodate different styles.

Artist demo: Used by an artist or band to shop for a record deal, manager, or producer, an artist demo highlights the strengths of the artist—not just the songs, but the arrangements, performances, vocals, instrumental virtuosity of individual members, and the overall style and energy of the group. Even in the case of an individual writer/artist, this demo almost always uses a group in order to show the artist in the musical environment that best suits her style. This is a studio demo, but depending on the style of the group and how well rehearsed they are, it could be done with a minimum of expense.

Master demo: The master demo has the same function as an artist demo, but with the high quality of a studio, engineering, production, and attention to detail that would make it acceptable for release as a record or to be included in a TV or film soundtrack. In terms of sonic quality, current digital recording technology makes these demo/master distinctions based more on arrangements and production, however.

Who Gets What and How Elaborate Does It Need to Be?

In creating your demo, it's important to know what purpose you want it to serve. One way to sort it out is to decide who's going to get it. These are the groups of people to whom you'll be sending demos.

PUBLISHERS

Though it used to be considered part of a publisher's job to produce appropriate demos to pitch to producers (and is still done in Nashville), the reality is that you'll need to produce your own demos well enough for the publishers to use. Even if you have a staff-writing deal, the publisher may deduct at least part of the cost of the demo from your future royalties. So you end up paying for it either way.

One of the advantages in presenting well-produced demos to publishers is the increased ability to negotiate reversion clauses (see chapter ten, "Negotiable Contract Clauses" on page 200). Publishers are reluctant to return songs they've had to lay out money for, and demo costs represent a good share of the initial expense. (Major publishing companies usually have in-house studios for their staff writers to use, but independent companies watch their recording budgets very carefully.) If you give them a high-quality demo, that expense is eliminated (unless, of course, you're asking them in your contract to reimburse you for the demo up front).

Another advantage is that your chances of interesting a publisher in a song based on a simple guitar/vocal or piano/vocal demo are slim. Though some publishers can "hear through" a simple presentation, others need more elaborate production to help them imagine how the finished product might sound. In most cases you won't know ahead of time what a particular publisher needs to hear. Your basic demo is likely to be sandwiched between two or more elaborate demos that sound like masters, and yours will suffer in comparison.

There are exceptions. Country music publishers are still accustomed to hearing guitar or piano/vocal demos. Since the focus of most successful country songs is the lyric, a simple demo will work with a *great* lyric. A word here about country publishers: Though they *say* they'd rather hear a simple demo, the songs *they* pitch to producers are typically produced using the best musicians available (and Nashville overflows with great musicians). After interviewing a few publishers about this apparent contradiction, the best answer I found is that they get tired of hearing spectacularly expensive demos of spectacularly bad songs. They figure they'll hear a great song demoed simply and they'll spend the money on a master demo. But even with mid- to up-tempo songs, it's good to have enough rhythm track to give them the "feel" you want them to hear, particularly as there is more pop influence in country now than in the past.

In another arena, keyboard/vocal demos of pop ballads can work if you have an excellent lyric, melody, keyboard player, and singer. Those are exceptions, though, and no longer the rule. If you have any kind of rock, R&B, or pop rhythm ballad or an up-tempo song, you *need* a basic groove (drums or loops, bass and keyboard, synth or guitar) because the groove and energy are essential ingredients in the song's appeal.

PRODUCERS

Record producers come from a great variety of backgrounds. Some evolve into producers from having been recording engineers and their skills may be focused on how records sound. Others are former studio musicians who may focus mainly on getting the right players and putting together great arrangements. Others, closer to the function of film producers, excel in the overview. Their skill is in putting together the magic elements—the artist, the arranger, the musicians, the engineer, the studio, the money, and most importantly, the songs. Clive Davis is a good example. This kind of producer is often billed as "Executive Producer."

No matter what their backgrounds, their success depends on recognizing great and *appropriate* songs for the artists they produce. As you might guess, their initial impressions when hearing your demo may vary based on their own particular areas of expertise. An engineer/producer may have a negative reaction to a poorly recorded demo (though he'll know how to fix it). A studio musician/producer might cringe at an out-of-tune vocal or guitar, though he *may* be more adept at hearing the arrangement possibilities of a rough or simple demo. The "overview" type of producer may not have the musicians' sophisticated ability to visualize a finished production—he may just know what he likes when he hears it. Obviously, these categories are oversimplified for the sake of illustration, and any individual producer will possess his own unique combination of tastes and skills.

The point is that, in order to deal with that diversity, your best approach is to make sure your demo is technically clean and well arranged. I've heard a successful musician/producer say, "I can hear it from a piano/vocal," and at another time say, "The demo sounded just like the artist—the right key, the musical hooks, and everything was right there. I hardly had to do anything, so we recorded it." One statement doesn't necessarily contradict the other but illustrates the fact that the more you give them, the more *easily* they'll hear it. Of the utmost importance in pitching a song to a producer for a specific artist is that the song is *appropriate* for the artist (see chapter eleven, "Casting: The Right Song for the Right Artist" on page 221). Do your research!

If you're an artist or band looking for someone to produce you, it's most important that the producer hears your best *performance* and your best *material*. He should be able to hear all the voices and instrumental parts clearly. A well-recorded live performance will work just fine if the vocals can be recorded cleanly.

RECORD COMPANIES

In most cases, the person at the record company you'll be pitching tapes to is the A&R representative. A&R stands for "artist and repertoire." In times of old, when almost nobody wrote his own songs, the A&R rep was the one who told the artists what they would record. For better or worse, those days are gone. A&R executives today have a wide variety of tasks to perform and, like producers, come from diverse backgrounds. Different record companies have different philosophies in hiring them.

Each of these philosophies has potential advantages and disadvantages. Some companies want people who know music intimately, such as musicians, producers (in some companies all the A&R executives *are* producers), music journalists, and critics. Producers may become "studio bound" and lose touch with "the street," though they usually have the respect of the artists, managers, and other professionals they deal with and a decent ear for raw talent.

Others subscribe to the "man on the street" theory and hire an opinionated young rock fan to be their rock A&R representative, maybe a kid who works in a record store. That philosophy sees an A&R person as a "general public record buyer." However, the "man on the street" who has been exposed to finished records and masters all his life may have trouble "hearing" less-than-finished product and, because of a lack of music or production experience, may not easily gain the respect of artists or give them cohesive direction. The advantage for the record label is that he's a cool guy who dresses like the artists and shares the same set of cultural references.

Other companies tend to hire from within the company. The former secretary of a producer (who screened all his material anyway) or the guy from the mailroom who used to hang out in the A&R department may be next in line for the job. The advantage is that he pretty much knows how the company operates, and the company knows him. There's no dealing with an outsider who already has his own methods and philosophies, which may clash with the company *status quo* (unless the company *wants* a change).

Each of the above philosophies, by the way, has produced outstanding A&R people.

A&R reps always take a lot of flack for not having "ears," and the "man on the street" variety is probably the most vulnerable to it. If he's the one who signs you, he's brilliant. But if he passed on you, he's deaf. It goes with the territory.

The basic functions of an A&R department today are to find new talent and sign it; and when needed, to find the artist a manager, booking agent, or band members, to supervise and oversee production and budgets of recording projects, and to find suitable hit songs for the artists signed to the label who don't write their own songs. Generally, at major labels, an A&R rep is responsible for several artists.

The legendary president of J Records, Clive Davis, worked with great artists who weren't writers (Whitney Houston, Aretha Franklin, Carlos Santana) and relied heavily on his own ears to find them great songs. That practice is more the rule than the exception for country music, though executives always look for writer/artists like Keith Urban and Alan Jackson. A&R representatives also look for hits for artists on their labels who *do* write, though they may not write enough songs or songs that are commercial enough.

Never waste postage by sending a song to an A&R department "just in case they might have an artist who could do this song." Target a specific artist and know the artist's work, the musical focus of the label, and that the song is right, or don't bother sending it in. If you're pitching the song to a specific artist, write "for Kelly Clarkson" or whomever on the package *and* in a cover letter *and* on the demo CD. They'll either turn it over to the artist's producer without opening it, or listen and decide for themselves whether to pass it to the producer. Or they'll send it back unopened. (More about circumventing that situation in chapter thirteen, "Getting Through the Doors" on page 292.)

If you're pitching yourself or your group to an A&R department as an *artist*, the best way is to go in with two to four finished masters of the best songs you can write or find in your style and a passionate performance. Regardless of the technical quality of the demos, excuses like "I know I can do it better but I had a cold that day," or "Our regular bass player went on the road and this new guy only had one rehearsal," just don't make it. This may be your only shot, and it's better to postpone your session 'til your cold is cured and your bass player is back. You can't expect a record company to sign you if they don't know exactly what they're getting. It's not absolutely necessary, but if possible, include the following with your demo in order of importance: your personal bio or bios of group members (see "Presenting Your Demo" on page 264); photos (if they're really good ones); and a press kit with reviews, list of clubs played, a graphic design or logo and a tape or CD. All this says, "We're ready and we're serious!"

CLUB OWNERS

If you're looking for a live gig in a club, your demo should be live, too. Most club owners won't trust studio demos alone because they've been burned so many times by hearing a great studio tape of a band that sounded very different once they got on stage. It doesn't hurt to include studio cuts, but your demo should contain at least part of a live set with your "between song" rap, audience interaction, applause, etc., intact. Along with the tape, send them photos and bios with a list of clubs previously played, as well as letters from owners of other clubs where you've worked. If it's a "cover" gig where you're playing "the hits" and requests, include a list of the songs you're prepared to play. A live video is much better than a live audio recording, but it's ideal to have both. Your Web site should contain a gig schedule, photos, some song clips, and a video.

What You Can Do at Home

Once you've decided what kind of demo you need and who you're going to submit it to, you have to plan the actual production of the demo itself. It's important to plan ahead because you can waste a lot of time and money going into a recording project cold. Many songwriters cut the expense of demo production by doing their own recording at home.

Recording at home has obvious advantages. Sometimes inspiration for a great lyric or a groove and bass line hits at 2 A.M. when your left brain is winding down and your right brain is starting to talk to you. If your studio is in the next room, you can plug in your headset, crank it up, and catch that idea before it gets away! Within hours you not only have a new song, but you've got the demo done the way you heard it in your head. You didn't have to teach other musicians your song, worry about whether everybody would show up on time for the session, talk the guitar player out of doing a solo, buy lunch for the band at rehearsal, spend your time in the studio watching the clock tick away dollar signs, or worry about what's growing on the coffee cups. These advantages alone may make it worthwhile for you to invest in your own home studio, particularly if you write a lot of songs. For what it would cost you for a few demo sessions in a pro studio, you could buy a good little home studio setup.

You will, of course, be saddled with maintenance of the equipment, and have to suffer the learning curve of getting control of the technology. Then there's the ever-present desire to buy the next piece of state-of-the-art gear to upgrade your setup. No matter how convenient and versatile your equipment, there will always be something you want to be able to do with it that you just can't achieve without one more gadget. Getting hung up in the engineering goes with the territory. Forever fiddling with equipment to get the right sound will actually rob you of spontaneity. There's always a tradeoff. Your individual needs will be the key to your decision to have your own studio.

If you're a musician with even minimal skills, present-day technology (which is increasing at a dazzling rate) can make it possible for you to create very high-quality demos at home. Companies like Yamaha, Korg, Roland, and others make hardware synthesizers, samplers, drum machines, and digital audio recorders, often combined into one piece of gear called a "keyboard workstation." (They also make standalone versions of each.) If you have keyboard skills, this is a great way to get a home studio started. There are a few caveats: This type of machine is not nearly as upgradeable as a computer-based system so it will become obsolete very quickly. This may not matter—as long as it works for you, who cares? Second, you may run into issues of compatibility. If you want to transfer your song from your keyboard workstation to a digital audio workstation (DAW), you may have to jump through some technological hoops. Last, a keyboard workstation is somewhat cumbersome, both to move around and to perform more advanced recording and editing. For example, you won't be able to take your keyboard workstation on a plane and work on your project during the flight.

For that, you'll need a computer-based DAW. The deeper you get into recording, you may have more than one DAW: a laptop for portability and convenience, a desktop computer for sheer power and flexibility. The cool thing is that you can have virtually the same software on both machines. Moving your projects back and forth is a breeze, as is sending a project to other studios or co-writers.

For the computer-based DAW, you'll need:

1. **DAW software.** Choose carefully! If you regularly work with someone who uses Logic (Apple), you should consider using Logic. If your main songwriting partner uses Pro Tools, you should look closely at Pro Tools for yourself. You'll have the benefit of compatibility as well as someone who can help you learn the software. Make no mistake—DAW software is deep! Imagine all of the controls you would find in a well-equipped studio and shrink them down into a computer. Yikes! In addition to recording audio and MIDI, your computer DAW software will either have software instruments (synths, samplers, drum machines, emulations of classics like electric pianos and organs) or allow you to add them from a third party software company. The only piece of hardware you'll need is a MIDI controller to trigger the software instruments.

2. **Audio and MIDI interface.** These are often combined into one unit. Audio interfaces vary widely, but the most basic will include a mic preamp, line input and instrument direct input (DI) and headphone output. The interface will connect to your laptop via USB or FireWire.

3. **Computer.** Not just any computer will do! For example, Logic works only on certain Macintosh machines. The software you choose will have system requirements, indicating what specifications the computer should have. Avoid using a computer with only the minimum specifications—you'll run out of "power" sooner than you like.

4. **Third party software.** Most DAWs include some software-based instruments and effects plug-ins. You will very likely want to add third party software—a sampler, some sounds for it, looping software, the list goes on. There are also specialized tools for correcting vocal tuning, removing noise, and so on. One request: Please don't use pirated software! In addition to the obvious violation of copyright, "kracked" (stripped of copyright protection) software will very likely make your system unstable.

There are also standalone DAWs, but like the keyboard workstations, they have limitations, primarily built-in early obsolescence, and limited capability and compatibility.

If you are new to DAWs, ask friends for guidance or check out magazines, Web sites, and user forums that specialize in modern recording technology. Be aware that magazines rely on advertising revenue from manufacturers, so they are usually gentle when reviewing—only the good news for their clients! Web sites and user forums are a bit more independent, and the result is that you will find plenty of strongly voiced and conflicting opinions.

The end product of your projects will be data, ones and zeros on a computer disk. Data is fragile! Pros use the guideline of "your data doesn't exist until you have three copies." Get an extra hard drive and back up your projects after each session by copying them.

A caveat: Learn to save as often as you are willing to redo. If you don't mind losing an hour's work when your computer crashes (they *all* do sooner or later), then save every hour. Every five minutes might be more practical. I suggest that each day you start work on a project, save the project with a new name (just add a number to the current name—"mysong 1" becomes "mysong 2," etc.). This allows you to get back to where you were last Tuesday when everything was sounding so good.

It's possible to record and make copies of your demo from start to finish in your own home studio. Although many writers choose to record their basic tracks at home, then take what they have to a professional recording studio, transfer it to the studio DAW, and use the studio's microphones and outboard gear (reverb, limiters, compressors, etc.) to record additional instruments and vocals and to mix the tracks. This method can save a lot of money and still produce a high-quality demo. It allows you to spend your creative, experimental time at home without the studio pressure, and to plan the best use of your studio time. Also, with your basic tracks already recorded, you can give your singer a chance to work with them before the vocal session.

Today it's not unusual to create many components of a track in several different studios and then combine them at the studio that will be doing your final mix. The old joke about the studio musicians "phoning in" their parts is now a reality. Many writers, producers and performers are now sending tracks to each other over high-speed DSL, cable, or T1 lines, adding more instrumental parts or vocals, and sending them back with no loss of fidelity. Be sure that you and the engineers involved discuss compatibility—tempo, key, what types of DAWs will be used (Pro Tools, Logic, Digital Performer), what sample rate (44.1kHz, 48kHz, etc.), what bit depth, and what audio file format (.aif, .wav).

For more info on recording techniques, try these free Web sites: www.wikirecording.org, www.studiobuddy.com, and www.homerecording.com, or type "recording tutorial" in an online search engine such as Google (www.google.com).

Choosing a Studio

The big studio of the past is almost gone. Decreasing production budgets and increases in the capabilities of small DAW-based studios have put many large studios out of business. What this means is that you will likely record in a one- or two-room project studio, which should be equipped with a modern DAW and a high quality recording chain—microphone, mic preamp, and compressor. In this situation the skill of the engineer is crucial. He is the liaison between the recording technology and your song.

The way songs are miked, recorded, and mixed is different in each style of music, so no matter what your style, you'll want to find an engineer who's experienced with that type of music, or make sure that the studio would allow you to bring in your own engineer.

Demo or master? The line between demos and masters has narrowed. With today's smaller budgets, it's usually harder to justify spending lots of time on a track—after all, time is money. Also, technology has lifted production quality to the point that in very few hours you can have a track that is ready for release, broadcast, or Webcast.

Don't book too much time in a single block. Sometimes you can get a better deal if you book a large block of studio time, but there's a "burnout factor" that takes place after long periods of tension and concentrated listening, particularly if you're into a time period that runs counter to your "biological clock" (e.g., 4 A.M. if your regular bedtime is 11 P.M.). You may actually waste money by the mistakes you make because your perceptions and high-frequency hearing are not operating efficiently. Avoid the temptation to use drugs to compensate. They only damage your perceptions further and can make you less aware that you're not functioning at your peak. Make sure your engineer is also working at his peak. It's a good idea to take an "ear break" every hour or so. At the end of each session, ask for a rough mix to scrutinize later.

STUDIO DEALS

If you decide to work in a studio, you can make special deals to lower your costs, but you need to be careful not to let your eagerness get you into trouble.

In your search for your next career break, you encounter local studio owner Harry Sessions. He says, "I like your tunes and you're a good performer. I think you've got a shot at getting a record deal. I own a studio and I'd like to take you in and cut some of your tunes just to see what we could come up with."

This is just what you've been waiting to hear. You've been trying to get A&R reps at the record companies to hear your home demos and getting nowhere. Even though they say they can listen to a simple demo, you know they're listening to finished radio-quality masters every day and that those probably have a competitive edge. You've been waiting for a deal like this to come along and say to yourself, "Just do it, don't ask questions."

You finish the four-song project with help from your (or Harry's) musician friends who learned, rehearsed, and recorded the songs with you. You've got no written or verbal contract regarding the ownership of the masters. You figure Harry is a friend helping you out and in some way he'll get paid when you make a deal with the record label. But then he drops the bomb: "Of course, you understand that I get the *publishing* on all these tunes. I assume you're hip enough to know that's the way these deals are done. I get the production points[1] and the publishing."[2]

You're a little shocked but you don't want to appear unhip, and Harry has been so nice to you that you don't want to seem ungrateful. You're behaving exactly the way he wants you to. Now he wants you to sign the contract.

This is a familiar scenario. Periodically someone calls me and asks, "Do I have to give him my publishing? He says he has a right to it because he did the masters." The answer is no, assuming that you made no written or verbal agreement before the sessions regarding the publishing or production points. However, in order to pre-empt Harry from making the claim that he co-wrote the songs with you, be sure to put your songs in some tangible form, whether you write them out or record them, even *a cappella*, before working with Harry.

---

1. A percentage of income earned by the producer paid from your artist royalties. If we assume that your artist royalty is 12 percent of the suggested retail price of the record, 3 to 5 percent of the suggested retail price is the customary producer royalty. The latter is referred to not as percentages, but as "points," to avoid the impression that it's 3 percent of 12 percent. Therefore, 3 points to the producer with an artist royalty of 12 percent actually amounts to 25 percent of the artist's royalty. However, the producer royalty is typically "pro-rated" by the number of tracks the producer contributes to the album in relation to the overall number of tracks on the entire album.

2. Ownership of the copyrights and 50 percent of the income from the songs.

The Craft and Business of Songwriting

Another situation you may run into is when a studio owner offers to produce your demos or masters "on spec." The studio owner "speculates" that the time and sometimes the money that he, as producer, puts in will be recouped when you sell your master to a record label. He hopes he'll end up as (a) the producer of the whole album project, (b) your producer for the life of your record contract, and/or (c) the publisher of all the songs he produces for you. That's Harry Sessions' maximum payoff and he'll need a production and publishing contract with you to achieve it.

Many producers have been burned so often that they've coined the phrase "Spec = (ex)spec(t) not to get paid." At minimum, without a production contract, the producer/studio owner hopes the record company would like you *and* the production enough that they'll buy the masters with enough money for a profit beyond what he put into the recordings. He also hopes he'll get production points and credit on those recordings the label eventually releases. If he does a great job, he deserves that, particularly if he can also make some valuable industry contacts for you, though, to be fair, that's not his responsibility unless you've previously agreed to it. A reputable producer with strong industry contacts may simply want to find new artists to develop and produce rather than wait for the record companies to hire him. He will be more concerned with producer points and his producer advance than profiting from a buyout or publishing.

Unfortunately, for less reputable or unknown producers, if the record company likes you as an artist but doesn't like his production, without a production or publishing contract between you and him, you may get a record deal and he won't get anything. Ironically, it is often the lesser known producers who present the more onerous "spec" contracts in order to avoid getting burned. In fact, because the record company may want you produced by someone *they* choose, you should *never* guarantee that the "spec" producer will be hired by you or the record company to produce any product released in your future record deal. Usually, the agreement should say "I will use my best efforts" to get the producer involved. This also assumes that the recording experience was good for you and was creative and productive, that you felt supported artistically, and that you want to continue this relationship.

Legally, if he doesn't present you with a production contract until after the masters are complete and you don't like the deal he presents you with then, you're under no obligation to accept. If the studio owner hasn't gotten together with you ahead of time and laid out the conditions under which he's speculating his time and facilities, then he's gambling that you'll like his work enough to go along with him or that he can intimidate you like Harry Sessions.

The reality is, though, that if you walk away you won't be able to take your demo or master with you. The producer/studio owner physically owns the recordings. He doesn't have to give you the masters or copies. After all, he figures, why should you be able to use the results of his production expertise and time without his being compensated for it? He can't release the recordings without your permission or sell them to a label without owning the rights to your performances unless you later sign with a label who wishes to buy them from him or unless he has actually paid you to perform on the masters. If you later publish and release those songs, he can't collect any royalties on your publishing without a specific contract to do so. Obviously, without a record out, there aren't any royalties anyway, but writer/artists often worry that some time in the future someone will make a claim based on this studio situation.

In this case, both the studio owner/producer and the writer/artist are responsible for the unpleasant situation because they didn't let it be known in writing what they both expected from the deal before the recording took place.

The preceding example is one I come across more often than I'd like to, but many other studio deals can be made that are fair to both the studio and the writer/performer. With an agreement up front in writing, this could have been one of them. The fact is that you're also speculating that all the hard work and time you put into this project will pay off for you, too. If you're happy with what you accomplished in the studio together and enjoyed working with the producer, you don't want those ugly, unexpected, after-the-fact business realities to damage a promising relationship.

MAKING "SOUND" DEALS

Now that we've got an idea of what can go wrong in negotiating a special studio deal, let's talk more constructively about a better way to approach this situation.

As I said earlier, you have to decide whether you need demos or masters, whether you need a state-of-the-art studio and engineer, or if you can get by with lower quality and less experience for less money. If you can get by with a less expensive demo, you may not need to worry about making a deal.

If you decide that you need a more elaborate demo than you can afford to pay for outright, the next question to ask yourself is, "What do I have to offer that a studio owner/producer or an engineer/producer might want?" The variables are cash, services, or participation. Musicians sometimes barter services in exchange for studio time. Maybe you're a builder or painter, decorator, graphic artist, electrician, secretary, Web site designer or have some other skill that would be of use to a studio owner. You may also own a piece of outboard equipment or a unique instrument you could exchange for studio time.

A producer may ask for participation in exchange for studio time. Participation refers to percentages of the income stream generated by you as an artist or writer and gets a little complex. In the case of an artist, participation means production points (see footnote 1 on page 246). In the case of a writer or writer/artist, it means ownership of your copyrights or receipt of royalties (without ownership) from your songs.If you just need a demo, don't give away percentages of production or publishing. The only exception I can think of is if you're making a deal with a major producer with a great track record who can walk into a record company, play them a demo, and get a budget on the strength of his reputation.

If you're a writer with limited funds, you may encounter studio owners or engineer/producers who will ask for your publishing even for producing a simple song demo. The problem with engineer/ studio owners acting as publishers is that even though they'll sometimes come across opportunities to pitch a tune to a producer in their studio who needs a song, they may not actively be publishers on a daily basis. That's why it would be better to offer them a percentage of the publisher's share of mechanical royalties on any record they secure, but *only on that recording*, without giving them ownership of any percentage of your copyright (see chapter eleven, "Negotiating" on page 226). If their involvement is very limited, such as merely handing your song demo to one person, you may want to ask for a cap on the amount they can receive from your mechanical royalties rather than a perpetual participation.

If you're an artist recording a broadcast-quality master demo, in a studio equipped to give you master quality, you'll need a producer unless you're already a good, experienced producer and have the rare ability to be objective with your own work. It's only fair, in lieu of cash, to offer a producer production points. In fact, he usually gets both. But in a "spec" deal, the cash up front is what he's giving up. A percentage (usually half) of the publishing (owner-ship) on *only* the tunes he produces is also a common deal in lieu of cash. For a full-time publisher/producer, this is called a "development deal." With either of those deals, make sure you settle on a time period—from six to eighteen months (or whatever you agree on) after the masters are completed—in which the copyrights are returned to you and that you have the option to work with another producer if the record deal doesn't happen. The studio or independent engineer will still own the actual master tapes (unless you paid for them), and can get back the investment by selling the master to a record company interested in using a recording you've already made. If the studio insists on owning the masters, you should agree on a buy-out price in the event that you secure a record deal. The studeio may also want to be compensated if the recordings are used to obtain a record deal, even if the record company doesn't buy the masters.

A "spec" or development deal may be separated into its speculative components. For instance, depending on what the studio owner/engineer/producer contributes, you may agree on all or a combination of the following: a pre-set rate or price for use of the studio facilities to be paid out of your advance; best efforts to continue using the producer on the first album under your record deal; a percentage of your advance or "buy out" if the producer shops the masters and helps you secure a record deal; and producer points for those tracks actually used on your first album. Since there are many contingencies to these agreements, you should always have an experienced music industry attorney help you negotiate them.

Be aware, and wary, of exclusive production agreements. These agreements involve providing your exclusive recording services (and often publishing) to a production company and is more similar to a recording contract than a "spec" or development arrangement. Under these agreements, it is anticipated that the production company (not you) will ultimately sign with the record company and furnish your services to the record company. These agreements should only be considered when the person or company is very reputable, and has a proven track record and strong industry ties. The issues to be negotiated can be just as complex as a recording agreement and should only be done with the advice of an experienced music industry attorney.

STUDIO RATES

Whether you're paying cash or bartering services, these are always flexible. When you call a studio for rates, they'll always give you their "book" rate, so dig a little deeper. Here are some of the factors involved in lowering that rate.

Block Booking

The more hours you can guarantee them, the cheaper you usually can get studio time. As I mentioned earlier, though, spending hours in the studio when you're overtired can be counterproductive.

Late Hours and Downtime

You can make a better deal if you can work at the studio's convenience. If you let the owner know that you'll be able to come in on short notice in their downtime (when the studio isn't booked), it helps them by keeping money coming in and they're liable to give you a better rate. Tell them to call you if someone cancels and the notice is too short to book another session at their full rate, or if the studio has to cancel a session because a piece of equipment broke (just make sure you don't need to use that particular piece of equipment). In some of these deals, the studio reserves the right to bump you out when they get a "book rate" session in your time slot. Late night or early morning hours can also be cheaper in some studios

Up front cash will get you better rates. The more you can give the studio in advance of the session, particularly if you've blocked out a large number of guaranteed hours, the better the rates you'll get.

Recording Engineers

The one you choose will have a bearing on your studio costs. Some engineers are still in training and some are well-experienced pros. If you're doing a simple demo, it may be cheaper to hire a beginner (if you can get him to admit it). What you have to weigh is the possibility that a beginner's mistake may cost you time and money.

If you bring along your own favorite independent engineer, it may involve extra time for him to learn the idiosyncrasies of a new studio, though you're saving time by using someone you've established communication with. Another advantage is that he may have a relationship with a studio that will give him a lower rate for bringing in your business.

Make sure when you use any engineer that he hasn't already been working for twelve hours and is too burnt out to react or hear properly. Engineers work more hours under stress than is healthy for human beings anyway. So always find out how long your engineer has worked before your session. If their own staff engineers are unavailable during the hours you want to work, most studios can recommend independent engineers who have worked in their studio before.

Though most seasoned engineers are fairly versatile, some have experience primarily in country music, R&B/hip-hop, heavy metal, or some other style and who will be more familiar with the way instruments and vocals are recorded and mixed in that style. Find one who will understand how to record your style of music.

If you know nothing about production, hire a demo producer who specializes in the type of demo you need. Ideally, you should be at the sessions so that you'll learn how it's done and you can express your opinions *before* recording begins. Being there is especially valuable to help make sure your singer gets your lyric and the vocal phrasing right.

When you're pricing a studio, you may be quoted the studio time rates *without* the engineer, though most demo studios include it. Engineer fees vary from city to city, time of year (January and February are traditionally slow), and even project to project. In other words, the same engineer might charge half his regular record company rate for a January demo. Engineers in L.A. and New York cost more than a similarly skilled engineer does in Kentucky. The range of fees is so wide—from nearly free (what everyone *wants* to pay) to thousands a day plus points—that rather than my quoting figures, it's more important to know the engineer's skills. Can she handle digital editing? How does she interact with musicians and singers (people skills)? Engineering is much more than pushing buttons. The best at all levels will want to keep you happy, since it's easier to keep you as a client than to find new ones.

Make sure you find out exactly what the fees are and figure them into your budget. Independent engineers are usually paid separately, and staff engineers are paid with the same check you pay the studio. Get it straight ahead of time. Talk to the engineer you'll be working with before the session so you both can feel a little more relaxed and confident about what you intend to do.

Pro studios will include a second engineer in your price. These are usually minimum wage employees who do the scut work—notating track sheets, answering the phone, and handling the patch-bay—all things that will save your engineer time.

Many demo studios advertise production assistance, but people are sometimes disappointed by the minimal assistance actually available.

Ask the studio *exactly* what is meant by "production assistance." Is it five minutes with the engineer before the session, or is it playing your songs for someone and discussing a musical direction, musicians, and budget? Regarding the latter, remember that the studio is in business to make money, and therefore may be inclined to offer suggestions that will result in your use of more studio time than you need. Try to determine whether a simple or a full-blown production is appropriate before talking to the studio. The more overdubbing or tracking (adding instruments or vocals to the initial recording) that's done, the more studio time you need. Playing the instruments yourself and building the tracks one by one is most time consuming.

When you work out your budget, decide whether it's cheaper not to pay other musicians and to spend the money on more studio time, or use less time and pay more musicians. The other trade-off is that with good musicians you'll get parts that may be better than what you'd think of or be able to execute.

Equipment

The cost of the studio time is also determined by the equipment you need. If you're doing a piano/vocal you may only need a very basic DAW studio. Cheap! More involved studios will have a more capable DAW (more tracks and plug-ins, better converters, mics, and mic preamps), a second room, some sound treatment, instruments, an espresso machine . . .

Getting all the information before the session will save you money in the end. Knowing what questions to ask ahead of time and knowing what everyone needs to make them happy on the business end are the keys to saving your peace of mind during and after the session.

The Recording Process

Once you've decided on a studio, engineer, and equipment, here are a few things to keep in mind about the recording process:

1. Remember to double your estimated recording time (for listening to playbacks).

2. Test your mixes on your car CD player (if you trust it!) as well as your iPod, computer, portable stereo—as many sources as you can bear. Switch back and forth between your song and the radio or a familiar CD for comparison. Listen for the clarity of instruments and vocals.

3. If you have several days in which to record, in the first session, record your basic drum, guitar, bass, and keyboard tracks first with a temporary "scratch" vocal. That temporary vocal is used so that the musicians can create parts that support but don't get in the way of the vocal. At the end of the first session, "scratch" (eliminate) the vocal and do a rough mix. "Mix" refers to the relative volumes, placement (right, left, or center for stereo), and "EQ "(equalization), the amount of treble, bass, and mid-range emphasis, on each of the instruments. You'll then take home a tape or CD with which the vocalist can rehearse her performance and with which you can work out and rehearse overdubs, additional parts such as instrumental solos and harmony parts, background vocals, and orchestral parts.

During the next session, record the vocals and overdubs and get a rough (quick) mix or two of that session. Take them home and listen to the mixes so you can make decisions about them at your leisure outside the pressure of the studio. It's generally not a good idea to do more than a rough mix at the same session in which you record. It's difficult to have a good perspective on this important process when you and your ears are fatigued.

This is a common approach to the recording process, though not necessarily the best. If you're a well-rehearsed group, and want to preserve a spontaneous sound, you'll consider recording everything "live" at the same time, though it still may be advisable to have a separate mixing session.

You may not have the luxury of recording over a several-day period. If you must do it all at once, prepare very well, rehearse the musicians and singers, and make sure your engineer knows ahead of time what you want to do and how you want to do it. The best idea is to visit the studio first to meet with the engineer.

SAVING MONEY BY BEING PREPARED

The best way to cut down on time, aggravation, and expenses is to have a solid idea of what you want for your demo and a good plan for getting it. In preparing for the session, there are some things to consider that will save you a lot of time and worry.

Choose the right musicians and rehearse ahead of time. One of the most difficult aspects of doing demos is choosing the right musicians. Demos require musicians with an ability to exercise restraint, to control their egos, and to control the desire to show off. Some are too wrapped up in learning their instrument to be able to direct their creativity toward playing something simple that fits and *complements* the whole arrangement or *supports* a vocal.

The ideal in choosing musicians is that you've had an opportunity to work with or listen to a lot of them and can afford to pay $100 or more (varies from city to city) per tune. You may have to pay them extra to overdub other parts. Choose them according to the style of songs you're recording and the way you'll predict that they'll interact with other musicians when left to their own creativity. The goal is that you want to exercise a minimum of direction and get maximum creative contribution from each of the musicians involved. You'll ideally want to find a number of musicians who play together in the same group, or at least have played together often enough that they have their own communication well tuned. A good producer will help you choose musicians he's worked with in the past and know their capabilities, eliminating the need to rehearse.

What if you don't have that much money and you can't afford to be choosy? You should know, then, that there are a lot of musicians around looking for something to get involved in and willing to do sessions for the experience or "on spec" (on the speculation that if and when you get paid, *they* get paid). Make signs explaining your situation and the type of music you're interested in, and put them on bulletin boards in music stores, college music departments, and clubs. Advertise in musicians' magazines. Contact musicians' services that match musicians in your area with opportunities and with other musicians. Musicians Contact Service (www.musicianscontact.com) and TAXI's Musicians Junction (www.musiciansjunction.com) are good ones.

Offer to trade your own services as a musician or singer. You're bound to go through some trial and error to find the right people, but that's what you need to do.

When you find the musicians you want, rehearse with them as much as possible before doing the session. This helps if you're insecure about your arrangements or if you're looking for something out of the ordinary. It'll save you lots of money in studio time. Agree on the fees before the session and pay them promptly. You'll feel much better about directing them if you've taken care of business. Psychologically, you'll eliminate bad vibes and have an eager team working with you.

Prepare master rhythm charts of the songs for each musician before you rehearse, or before the session if there's no rehearsal. Master rhythm charts don't necessarily need to have the melody written out, but should contain a road map of the song: the chord changes and all the directions you've thought of ahead of time, such as when certain instruments enter or exit, or a specific bass line you want to hear. If you don't have the groove written out, bring recorded examples of what you want. Singers who can sight-read music should have a lead sheet that contains the melody line and lyric. They *must* have a neatly typed lyric sheet.

The Nashville Number System is used universally in Nashville (surprise!) and extensively outside of Nashville as a valuable song-charting shorthand. Say you get the singer in the studio and realize at the last minute that his key is wrong. Zap! Transpose the key instantly and all the musicians immediately know the new chord changes. It substitutes numbers for chord letters. It's a universal "language" for studio musicians and very helpful for songwriters. To help you learn, there are a variety of books and software packages available at their Web site (www.nashvillenumbersystem.com). Chas Williams' book, *The Nashville Number System*, will teach you several different styles in use.

Have your musicians check their instruments and amps before the session. This eliminates unwanted hums, buzzes, noisy pedals, or other obnoxious sounds. Listen up-close to the amps where the mics will be placed. This is frequently a problem with musicians who are used to playing live. A slight hum in an amp that might ordinarily go unnoticed in a live situation will make you crazy when it's miked and magnified in the studio. You may end up spending lots of costly time trying to fix a buzzing guitar string or having to call an instrument rental company to send over a new pedal.

Get your "sounds" established on the instruments during rehearsals. Do you want the bass and guitar to be mellow or biting? "Tune" the drums the way you want them for the song or the session. For the studio, producers may or may not prefer the snare to be deadened somewhat with pads of cloth and masking tape near the edge of the head. It depends on the style. They may also deaden the kick drum by removing the front head and pushing a pillow against the inside of the head. This is a matter of personal taste. Those creative decisions should be made as much as possible before the session. You may change your mind later when you hear them over the studio monitors, but at least you'll have a concept to start with. If you're using a drum machine, program it for each song before the session.

It's part of the engineer's job to "get a sound" on the instruments before recording, and you should be prepared to explain the concept you're going for. (Try bringing examples of the drum, bass, or other instrument sounds from CDs you like to show the engineer what you want.) Find out in the initial meeting with the engineer whether this procedure is included in setup time before the clock starts running on your session. Sometimes it is, but usually it's not. Know in advance how much setup time you're allowed. It varies from a half hour to an hour. Make sure your musicians understand this and don't waste time setting up.

Everyone should have spare strings, drum heads, batteries, etc. I don't know a professional musician who hasn't learned that lesson on his first gig, but I thought I'd bring it up anyway, just in case.

Decide the order in which you want to do the songs. Is one song more difficult and another more fun? Find out how the musicians feel about it, assuming you have time to do them all. Be careful to figure realistically how much you can get done. The engineer can help you decide these things when you meet with him before the session.

Make sure the musicians all know exactly where and when the session is, how long it'll take them to get there, and that they all have transportation. If you're using different musicians for different songs, try to schedule as accurately as possible so if they have to wait more than a half hour they don't start looking at their watches and getting progressively more irritated.

CHOOSING THE SONGS

Whether you decide to produce your demos at home or in the studio, before you begin you must choose which of your songs to record.

All the songs you write don't have to be commercial, but the ones you present to publishers and producers must be. Many writers have difficulty determining the commerciality of their songs. How do you know?

You start by asking your friends, most of whom will be so knocked out that you wrote a song that they'll automatically love it (unless your friends are also writers). Tell them to be critical, and don't try to explain the song before playing it.

- Can they sing the chorus back to you?

- Can they tell you what the song is about?

- Did they understand all the words?

- Do they remember any lyrics?

- Can they name the title without your having told them?

- Which of your songs do they like the best?

- Which do they remember? Why?

- Which ones can they sing the melodies to?

Those songs are your best shots.

Get as many opinions as possible. If the critique is negative, thank them and don't get defensive. Keep a cool head and know that they're not attacking you personally. The rewards of their helping you grow and find success in your craft far outweigh the short-term ego damage. Treat criticism like clothing. Try it on and see if it fits.

What if you write a lot of different styles of songs and get good critical response on all of them? Your decision is then based on whether you have the desire or the potential to become a recording artist. You have the best chance at it if you have an easily identifiable voice and style (see chapter fifteen, "Getting a Record Deal" on page 364). If that's your direction, limit your selections to the style you feel most at home with. If you love to sing rhythm and blues-styled tunes, but also write good country songs, stick with R&B for demos to show record companies. It's confusing to them to hear a lot of different styles from one artist and it presents a marketing problem: "Do we market this artist as country or R&B?" Will the people who buy your R&B-styled CD be turned off by hearing a country song on it? It is good, however, to show some variety *within* the style.

For publishers it's different. Though they're happy if you specialize, it's a plus for you to be able to write well in many different styles. So it's okay to present them with your best songs in several different musical genres.

Make sure you have the final version of your song or you'll end up spending money to change it. My friend Hank Linderman (producer, engineer, guitarist, songwriter and author of *Hot Tips for the Home Recording Studio*) tells this story:

I was recording and co-producing a song with a songwriter (Erik Andrews) I had done several demos for. This particular song was a pop ballad, and this version was country, so we decided to hire a singer (Walker Igleheart) with a very clear tenor—perfect for the song. After finding the correct key over the phone with the singer, we constructed a beautiful track, sent out a copy to Walker, and got ready for the vocal session. When that day came, Erik and I were prepared—the mic was set up, the headphone mix was ready, everyone had lyric sheets, pencils, and water. After two hours of work, we had a great vocal. Erik paid Walker, and that was that.

The next morning I got a call from Erik—he had rewritten the second verse. Could we set up another brief vocal session? After reaching an agreement with Walker for a reduced rate, we booked the session.

Once again, we were prepared. Once again, Walker nailed it. Erik paid Walker, and Walker left. Within minutes, Erik was shaking his head—he was concerned with the bridge. He said he'd get back to me.

Once again, after Erik made his changes, we brought Walker in for what hopefully was the final session. When Walker arrived, Erik apologized for the situation and thanked Walker for his good attitude throughout the process. Without skipping a beat, Walker replied, "Erik, we're gonna get this song right if it takes every last dime you've got!"

The final piece of the story is that though the country version was never cut. Erik and I re-recorded the song as an R&B ballad, and Erik got a cut. (It ain't final 'til it's vinyl!)

Arrangements

We'd all like to believe that a great melody and lyric are all that's necessary to make people pay attention to a song. In some cases that may be true, but in most cases the melody becomes more appealing in the context of the harmonies and counter-melodies around it, and the meaning of a lyric can be conveyed more strongly by framing it in the most effective way.

In recording demos or records, you can do several key things to help make lyrics clean and powerful.

Eliminate the conflict between vocal and instrumental tracks. Demos are uncomfortable to listen to if the vocal is buried under the instrument tracks. It sometimes seems that the writer or artist is so insecure about the lyric or vocal that it's intentionally obscured. Or whoever mixed the demo knew the lyric so well, there was no perspective left about whether anyone else could understand it. One of the functions of a producer is to provide the right perspective to the mix. If you don't have a producer, let the engineer do it or call in someone who doesn't know the song when you're close to the final mix. Ask him if he can understand the words. This is the reason so many records are mixed by a separate engineer.

Another good way to avoid this problem is to run a "vocal up" mix in addition to the full mix. You may also want a "no vocal" mix (handy for singing "live" to track), a "backing (background) vocal only" mix and a "no lead vocal" mix (mixed as though there *is* no lead vocal). These mixes give you versatile options, particularly for TV use, or for pitching to production music libraries (see chapter fourteen, "Production Music Libraries" on page 334).

If you're recording a band, letting the whole band (or any one member) mix the tracks will cost you money in studio time because everyone will want his own instrument to be loudest.

The arrangement is also crucial in achieving clean vocals. Some important considerations are:

Melodic movement of instrumental parts relative to the vocal melody. One of the things that makes demos sound busy or cluttered is the conflict of too many melody lines moving at the same time. Our natural tendency as listeners is to focus on the vocal melody. A harmony on that melody (instrumental or vocal) may enhance it, but a different single-line melody on, say, an electric guitar at the same time may be distracting. A slow moving chordal "pad" of strings or synthesizer will work fine because these don't command our attention like a single-line melody. Rhythm instruments and repeated short rhythm parts on the instruments aren't usually a problem because once your brain realizes that they'll keep repeating, you take them for granted. Your body responds automatically, but your mind focuses on the movement of the melody.

Cutting basic tracks or overdubs without being able to hear the vocal phrasing or melody can produce a busy, cluttered sound. That's why it's best to use at least a "scratch" vocal (to be removed later) during a "head" arrangement (not written previously) and during production of both rhythm tracks and overdubs. That way you can tell if your arrangement works and if any of the instrumental parts are competing with the vocal melody. If there are any problems, they can be fixed while the musicians are still there.

Linear placement of instrumental parts relative to the vocals. The idea is to make a window for the vocals, to highlight them and to create expectation and tension. Drum fills perform this function going into a chorus, for instance. Instrumental fills should bracket the vocals, ending when the vocal phrase starts and starting when it ends (see the diagram below). The top line represents the vocal phrase (with accompaniment), the notes represent the ongoing pulse, and the bottom line represents an instrumental fill that picks up where the vocal stops and drops out where the vocal begins again. If, for instance, you have a two-bar, eight-beat phrase and the vocal phrase takes the first five beats, the fill might start as early as that fifth beat. Even if a vocal is holding a single note past that point, a fill will work because the melody line isn't moving.

Vertical placement of the instrumental parts in the audio frequency range relative to the range of the vocals. Again, rhythm instruments and parts aren't usually a problem, but with melody instruments, you can make cleaner tracks and highlight the vocals more by separating the ranges in which the instruments are played. Keyboards and guitars commonly get played in the same midrange area as the vocals. Experiment with moving the parts up or down an octave or two to keep that vocal window uncluttered (see the diagram below of instrument ranges). Other ways to enhance that window are to mix the volume of the instruments lower in that range, to de-emphasize the EQ (equalization, treble/bass/midrange frequencies) in that range, and to pan the instruments (place them apart from each other in the left/right/center spectrum).

If you have a lot of tracks available, there's a tendency to think of ways to fill them. There are always ways to fill empty tracks, but "less is more." Try to have fewer parts and make each one sonically interesting.

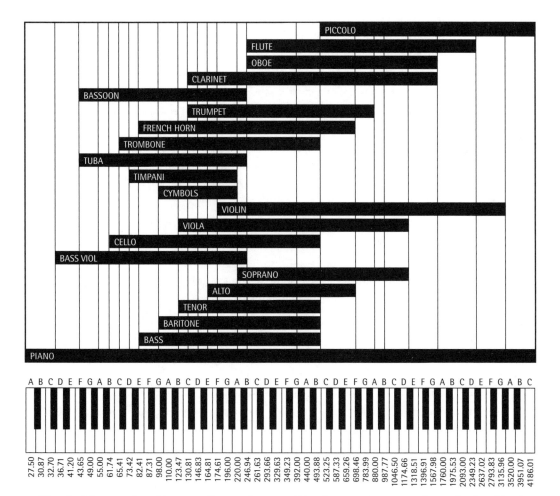

Vocals. The emotional impact of a vocal may well be *the* most important factor in the effectiveness of a demo. Most writers who can sing automatically assume they should be the one to sing on it. Sometimes it's a simple question of economics. You feel it costs too much to hire another singer. Or it could be simple ego. You figure you *know* the song; you *feel* the emotions that went into it. It's part of you. Who could do it better? Even if you're not a great singer, you feel you can at least do it adequately. You may be right. Then again, you may be wrong. You'll never know if the performance of a great singer could have made the difference between acceptance and rejection. Have faith that if the song has emotional impact, a very good singer should be able to put it across with your direction. So the rule of thumb is: *If you know anyone who can sing the song better than you, she should be singing on the demo.*

Make sure that the singer is comfortable with the song's musical style. Classically-trained or musical theater-trained singers may be out of their element doing country or hip-hop, for instance. Stylistically, it must be believable.

The singer should avoid improvising on the melody too much. Stylistic inflections are okay, but vocal gymnastics that tend to obscure the melody are not. What you get is a showcase for the performance and not for the song, making it difficult for an artist to hear what *she* could do with the song without re-creating your demo singer's performance. What you *can* do to highlight both is to have the singer stick to the melody till the last chorus and maybe do a chorus repeat at the end in which the singer improvises to demonstrate some stylistic direction.

If your song could be sung by either sex, do you choose a male or female for the demo? The consensus seems to be that it's much easier for a female artist to hear herself singing a male demoed song than for a male artist to imagine himself singing a song he hears from a female singer. Too bad those sexist attitudes still exist, but your odds are better with a male vocal in these cases. Obviously, if it's practical for you, do both male and female versions.

There's a wide range of fees for demo singers, depending on how good and how fast she is, how well she sight-reads (or how quickly she learns), and how much in demand her services are. Again, if your funds are low, you might suggest barter. Share studio time and assist her to produce her own demo. Remind her that she can put your song on her own performance demo and that you'll be pitching your song, with her vocal, to producers. Many major artists have been discovered through their exposure on demo tapes. You may find a great cover group that needs originals to pitch to record companies. Your songs may be just what they need.

Intros. How you introduce your song on a demo depends on who your audience will be. In *song demos* for publishers or producers, you *must* keep intros short. Get to the vocal/lyric fast. They consider intros a waste of their listening time because they're only listening to the *song*. In *artist demos* to producers and record companies, that's not the case because you're creating a finished product and the creativity of that intro is part of what you're selling.

The length of an intro will vary from song to song. Generally, though, it should be kept under four bars for a ballad because it's more difficult to sustain interest at a slow tempo. An up-tempo dance song that involves a listener's body will generate more excitement simply by increasing the speed of his heartbeat. Consequently, those intros can be longer. Intros in hit songs average about fifteen seconds.

Short or long, an introduction creates an immediate first impression that sets up the listener's expectation for the whole song. It sets the mood, the emotional tone, and ultimately, on a record, becomes the signature that sets it apart from all other songs. When you go to a concert or hear a live recording, you'll hear the audience cheer in recognition of their favorite songs after only a few notes.

So, in producing your demo and writing the song, pay special attention to developing a unique intro. Some writers have a tendency to throw away that opportunity by vamping (repeating the same thing) for four or eight bars between two chords. To bore your audience before even getting into the song is deadly. I've seen publishers angrily push the stop button on their cassette or CD player after eight bars of boredom.

Here are some possibilities to explore:

1. Use a variation or mutation of either your verse or chorus melodic theme as an intro.

2. Work backwards from the first vocal melody to discover a melody or progression that might heighten the impact of the vocal entrance. A big dynamic buildup to a soft, quiet vocal entrance might work well, or maybe a gradual build to a strong vocal entrance.

3. Use an interesting repeating instrumental riff that will be heard later under the verse or chorus (e.g., the Rolling Stones' "(I Can't Get No) Satisfaction," or Stevie Wonder's "Superstition").

4. Explore combining acoustic, synth, and sampled sounds to create a unique signature. It's called "sound design."

5. Introduce a new instrument or part every bar or two to thicken the texture and increase tension. This is fairly common, but if your instrumentation and melody are unique it can be a very effective intro.

6. Develop a groove by starting with the simplest component and adding the other rhythmic parts as you go. Sometimes it's easier to develop the whole groove first with drums, bass, rhythm guitar, and other rhythm parts, then figure out later which of those components to start the intro with. If you've layered them onto separate tracks, experiment by punching various combinations in or out every bar or two. You might start with the bass line, then bring in the drums, then the rhythm guitar, or vice versa, whatever works best. Try all the combinations you can think of.

7. Consider the possibility, particularly in a ballad, of having no instrumental intro at all, just starting with the lead vocal or an interesting background vocal part.

No matter how long it is or what devices you use to create interest, the intro must sustain a listener's attention. Some long ones do and some short ones don't.

EXERCISE

When you listen to the radio, check out the intros. Ask yourself if they keep you interested and note how they are done.

Solos. Solos, like intros, are generally considered by publishers and producers to be a waste of their listening time in *song demos*. If they're judging the song, they don't care if Eric Clapton is playing on your demo. No solos. Just the song, please. Publishers and producers commonly hit the stop button on a demo because of interminably long and self-indulgent intros or just because they know they're going to hear a solo. Most people include long solos only because they don't have enough lyric and want to fill the space, or some friends are helping do the demo and get to show off with a solo as compensation for their time. Don't do it! It doesn't help *you*.

That's not to say that a short solo of a couple of bars that serves a *definite function* as a transition or a dramatic tension-builder can't be very effective in a song demo. Just don't use a whole verse or chorus worth.

If you're cutting masters or *artist demos* to sell a self-contained band to a producer or record company, the above does *not* apply. They *need* to hear the talents of the group, but that long guitar solo better be a killer!

Endings. With endings you have two choices: Work out an ending or fade. The fade is usually done to allow you to keep grooving on an exciting riff or repetitive vocal phrase or the hook, without bringing down the energy level and intensity of the music. On a fade, you only bring down the actual volume. You leave the illusion that the band is just going on down the road and even though, after a while, you can't hear them, you know they're still groovin'. A fade works if you have something great to go out on that feels like it has a natural momentum. Commercially speaking, it's always a good idea for the hook, or chorus, or whatever you want an audience to remember, to be the last thing they hear. With a fade you also give DJs a chance to talk over the ending, which excites *them* as much as talking over the intro (even though it doesn't necessarily excite *us* as listeners). It also lets them do their own fade, which may be considerably shorter than yours. Keep in mind that unless you're playing a dance gig, long, repetitive fades tend to get tedious, so the shorter the better. This is particularly true for demos, presentations to record companies, and showcases.

As for working out endings, it all depends on the song. The only thing I can say is *Please see this as an opportunity to show your originality*. I'll grant you that there are times when the best ending for the song is one that has already been well worn. Just *try* to give it the care you give the rest of your song.

Demo Production Services

Forget all of the above and use a demo production service. If you've decided that all you want to do is write songs, and producing your own demos is way too much of a hassle, never fear! Demo production services have become a major industry. These services advertise in music trade magazines including *Music Connection*, *Billboard*, *American Songwriter*, and *Performing Songwriter*, and the newsletters of songwriters' organizations all over the country. You can also find their Web sites on the Internet where you can immediately hear samples of their work. (Search for "song demo" in an Internet search engine.) Here are some guidelines for dealing with them.

Only deal with demo production services if you can check out their product ahead of time. Some you can hear on their Web sites. Some will send you a CD sample of their work free. Others may charge a nominal fee, but it's worth it to know what you're getting into.

Only deal with those who will tell you exactly what you'll get for your money. They should be able to send you a rate sheet that gives you a choice of options from guitar/vocal to full-scale productions with strings, horn sections, and so forth. Extra rates for lead sheet preparation, copies, and other services should be spelled out—in other words, no surprises. Some companies, on their CDs or Web sites, will give you a choice of singers.

Don't deal with companies who offer to compose music to your lyrics and publish your song for a fee. By the rules of BMI and ASCAP, they are not allowed to be members of those organizations. Therefore, if by some remote chance they actually got airplay on your song, you'd never be able to get paid for it (see chapter eight, "Avoiding the Songsharks" on page 165). You can always call or write your nearest BMI or ASCAP office to check them out or go online to www.bmi.com or www.ascap.com and search their publisher databases for the name of their company.

Regarding the above, Section 17 of BMI's publisher application agreement (with my comments) says:

> 17 – BMI shall have the right, in its sole discretion, to terminate this agreement if:
>
> A. Publisher, its agents, employees, representatives or affiliated companies, directly or indirectly during the term of this agreement:
>
> (1) Solicits or accepts payment from or on behalf of authors for composing music for lyrics, or from or on behalf of composers for writing lyrics to music.

If they're a publisher (rather than just a service) and they write music for your lyrics or vice-versa, they risk being dropped as a publisher.

> (2) Solicits or accepts music and/or lyrics from composers or authors in consideration of any payments to be made by or on behalf of such composers or authors for reviewing, arranging, promotion, publication, recording or any other services connected with the exploitation of any composition.

This is where songsharks who say they're publishers and charge you for the above services get into trouble. Any songs they offer to "publish" won't be honored by BMI. This means you won't get paid if you ever get airplay on your songs.

> (3) Permits publisher's name, or the fact of its affiliation with BMI, to be used .by any other person, firm, corporation or association engaged in any of the practices described in subparagraphs A (1) and A (2) of this paragraph 17.
>
> (4) Submits to BMI, as one of the works to come within this agreement, any musical composition with respect to which any payments described in subparagraphs A (1) and A (2) of this paragraph 17, have been made by or on behalf of a composer or author to any person, firm, corporation or association.

This is the one that's most problematic if you use a service that you pay to co-write your song. It means that if you have your own publishing company registered with BMI via this agreement, they won't allow you to register the song with them. When you submit songs to BMI and you list a company or service as "author" of the music, they can refuse to represent the song or terminate your publishing agreement. They won't pay someone part of the writer's share if that person (or service) has been paid to co-write the song.

This needs a bit more explanation. As a consultant, I have had clients who have used services to create a melody for their lyric as part of a demo production package deal. The songs actually came out sounding pretty good, though there's always a chance they've used the same melody before and you'll never know it. They figure that only a micro-fraction of the songs will ever go anywhere afterward anyway. They assume that if you were a good enough lyricist to get your song recorded by an artist, you're good enough to find a legitimate co-writer and wouldn't need them to write a melody.

One of my clients, however, was pitching the song for film and TV and he was wondering if he'd run into a problem if it got picked up for use. I told him that if he registered a copyright on the song he'd have to say he wrote both lyric and music. And he'd also have to do the same on the BMI (or ASCAP) forms and on the contract with the film or TV production company. He'd also have to "warrant" on that contract that he actually owned both the master recording and the song, so he'd need to have the (demo) service sign a work for hire agreement to show that he owned it in the unlikely event that there was an ownership dispute (more about this in chapter fourteen, "Film and Television" on page 322).

Falsifying the information obviously involves both a moral and legal dilemma. Chances are extremely slim that it would ever generate a lawsuit because any company that runs an established demo service (one would hope) would have work-for-hire contracts with all the singers and musicians who worked on your demos to protect *their company* from legal action. So it's up to you, but my advice is to find a good collaborator you can work with (see chapter seven, "Collaboration" on page 132).

Have I "written" a melody if I can't write the notes? Occasionally there is some confusion among songwriters who think that if they can't write musical notation, they're not "writing" music. If you "think up," "make up," or "compose" a melody that you can sing into a recorder, you have written the music.

If I have written a song—words and music—and ask someone to play it for me for a demo, and he creates an intro and a lead guitar break, does he own the music to the intro and the break? I have tried to explain to this person that that's what's called "arranging" but he insists that he "owns" the music to the intro because it's like a separate song (although it wasn't written until he created it for my song). How do I get it across to this guy that it's part of the "arrangement" of the song? He's a great entertainer and he's not a stupid guy but we have argued about this and he cannot seem to understand that he doesn't own any part of the song. Can you clear up this confusion once and for all?

This is another related question that commonly comes up specifically relating to demos. I'm a mentor for Just Plain Folks (www.jpfolks.com), a free international songwriters networking organization (highly recommended) and was forwarded this question from a member.

This is a common situation that I've dealt with many times as a consultant. If you have written both lyrics and music and go to a demo producer/arranger for their services, that arrangement *is* their service and they deserve to be paid for it. I don't know any legitimate demo production service that asks for writer's credit. If they do, they'll soon be out of business. If you hire a guitar player to play on your session, regardless of what he plays, *he has no ownership of the song.* However, if you say ahead of time, "I want you to help me with this melody and I'll share writer's credit with you," that's a different story. It's all about making agreements and keeping them. If this is his philosophy, he should have told you up front so you would have a choice to reject working with him. To change what is a customary practice in the industry (that demo producers, arrangers, musicians don't share song ownership) *after the fact* is a very bad business practice.

It has traditionally been the policy that if you write words and music, you've written the song. That's not necessarily true any longer. There are those whose specialty is dance music, hip-hop, rap, and R&B who are experts at creating grooves (tracks, beats). Even though they didn't write any actual melody or lyric, they usually receive writing credit. Lest this get too confusing (since part of the arrangement *is* creating grooves), it usually involves creating the groove *first*, then writing the melody and lyric over it. It's a common way for hip-hop writers to create a song or record (see chapter seven, "Writing Tracks First" on page 136). The bottom line is that this agreement is made *before* you write the song.

Let me clarify one more thing. This time it may be on your guitar player's behalf. Musicians and singers on your demo *do* have ownership/copyright interest in their *performance* (though not the song itself). When they play or sing on a demo there is an understanding that it is only to be used for "demonstration" purposes. Consequently, it only becomes a problem when you decide to use it as a master to be sold to consumers or used in a TV show or film, in which you are paid for both the use of the song (synchronization or "synch" fee) and use of the master recording (master use fee). Legally, since it is something that directly creates income for you, you now owe those musicians and singers part of the income you receive (unless they waive that right) from their performances. That's why it's always a good idea to have the musicians/singers sign a work-for-hire agreement that determines how (if at all) you'll pay them in the event that you receive income from your "demo" (see "Work For Hire Agreement" on page 337).

Because demo quality is so good these days, it's likely that, assuming the song is good, you *will* want it to be used for commercial purposes rather than just demonstration, so ask your demo production company to sign a work-for-hire agreement, especially if you'll be pitching the song for audio-visual use.

Some demo production companies offer special services like having lead sheets made for you. A lead sheet looks like printed sheet music. It contains the melody, lyrics, and chord symbols. (Translating your melody into music notation is called doing a "takedown.") It's important to note, however, that lead sheets are *rarely* used to pitch songs to anyone. For those who don't read music, it's too hard to see the song structure.

Takedown or a Nashville Number System chart (for country) is usually included in the demo cost because the demo production company may need to do it anyway in order to get a road map from which to build the arrangement. Arrangement, too, is included in the overall cost of the demo.

Most demo services are mail-order businesses, though many will let you be on the premises. Some will even let you do your own vocals or give you the option of just the tracks without vocals so you can take them elsewhere to record. Most services welcome any creative input you have about how you would like your demo to sound. They thrive on repeat business and pride themselves on giving you what you want. If you like some sound you've heard on somebody's CD and are looking for something like it, send it with your song and it will help them zero in on the sound. It saves them time and gets you closer to what you want.

You should also make sure they include a "tracks only" version of your song. It may be necessary to include it in a pitch for film or TV or you may want to use it in a situation where you'll want to perform your own vocals over it.

CDs vs. Digital Audio Files vs. Cassettes

When you've recorded a demo you're happy with and you're ready to make copies to send out to the pros, be professional yourself. Today's music industry operates mostly on CDs and digital audio files. They're cheaper to mail and easier to handle. Most industry people have CD players in their cars as well as iPods or other digital players that allow them to listen relatively uninterrupted.

Cassettes are rarely used anymore as the audio quality isn't as good and the rewinds are too much of a hassle. The songs submitted by writers serious enough to join TAXI (www.taxi.com) are a pretty good gauge of the relative percentages of media used. TAXI's Michael Laskow told me in early 2006 it was about 70 percent online digital audio files, 25 percent CDs, and 5 percent cassettes, with online submissions gaining on both CDs and cassettes. The songs that TAXI forwards to the industry get transferred from cassette and digital files to CDs.

Check your local phone book for CD duplicating services if you don't have a high-quality copying setup at home. Using studio time to make copies can be very expensive.

Presenting Your Demo

I think it's always enlightening to get a scenario of what happens behind the scenes in the office of a person who listens to demos. Here's a sample from my own experience and that of friends who torture their brains and eardrums in the all-too-often futile search for that killer song or sound.

You should know that if 1 percent of the songs are in the ballpark, they're doing very well. Industry professionals engage in this masochism because they know that when they find that rare song that brings tears to their eyes and makes the hair stand up on the back of their necks, they'll forget about all the bad ones they just listened to. The rejects aren't even all bad. Some have lots of imagination and no craft, and some have lots of craft but little originality. The right combination of ingredients is rare, but they know it's there somewhere. They're anxious to find it as soon as possible. Some listen in the order they receive the demos. Most others don't. What they do is look for the most likely candidates.

First, they look for the names of writers they already know are good. That's where the odds are best to find a great song. Next, they listen to tapes referred to them by other industry people whose tastes (or power) they respect. Next, when faced with a stack of anonymous tapes, they look for a package that is professional, neat, and imaginative. They hope the songs will show those same qualities. The odds still aren't great but they're several points above the lowest. The least likely candidates are the ones that look like the sender doesn't care. The lyric sheets, if any, are scribbled illegibly on the back of a menu and the cover letter with no return address says, "I no thees songs wood bee grate for Garth. Pleez sen them to him." What do you think the odds are that they're going to find a really "'grate'" lyric here? It's not just about bad spelling, but about not caring enough to find someone who can use a spell-checker to check the spelling. It's easy to get the impression that this person doesn't care enough to find out how to write a good song (or a good letter, for that matter).

Though the above scenario is most common, don't get the idea that *all* pros listen in the same way. I've heard stories from A&R reps who were actually intrigued enough by that funky looking package to open it first and have actually found something worthwhile. If you want to play the game with the odds in your favor, however, you'll pay attention to these guidelines.

Here is a checklist that will maximize your chances of getting heard and respect the listener's time:

1. Never send more than three songs unless specifically requested. Demo listeners like watching the "in" pile diminish and the "out" pile grow as quickly as possible. If the listener has a limited time to listen, which is usually the case, the tendency is to listen to a demo they know they can complete. So if you send a demo with ten songs on it and someone else's demo has one song, you can bet that the "out" pile will grow quickly with one-song demos. There's also the psychology that implies, "I've sent you *the* song you need!" This is particularly true in pitching songs to producers for a *specific* artist. Along those same lines, most people resent getting CDs with twenty songs and a letter that says, "I know you'll like at least one of these, so just pick out what you want." They want *you* to do that and send them three songs or less—songs you totally believe in. If you're not far enough along to be able to decide, you're not ready. When sending CDs with more than three songs, highlight three you want the listener to focus on first, and include the *numbers* of the cuts in your cover letter and lyric sheets (so they have a reference while the CD is on their player and they can't see the label). If they like those, they'll listen to the others. And *please*, remove the shrink-wrap!

2. Never send anything you need to have returned. You may never see it again and it's not fair to saddle its recipient with responsibility for it.

3. Place your best and most commercial song first. If you have a strong up-tempo song, it's a good bet to start with that. The first song may be the only shot you get. If you're sending a cassette, put all the songs on the same side and put the label only on the "play" side. Better yet, don't send cassettes at all unless it's for sending to a critique service prior to your spending money for a production. You can also send them to present a rough version of a song to a demo production service.

4. Always cue your demo to the beginning of the first song. If you do send a cassette, you don't want the person to start listening in a bad mood because you just wasted his time making him rewind your tape. When you make your copies, leave four seconds between songs. Most cassette decks have an automatic search feature, which finds the silence between songs, stops the fast-forward, and automatically starts playing the next song. Obviously, this isn't a problem with CDs or digital files. If your CD contains more than the first four you want heard, clearly mark on the CD *and* printed insert which ones you want them to hear.

5. Send a lyric sheet, neatly typed. Letterhead is impressive. It says, "This is my business and I take it seriously." Some don't like to look at lyrics while they listen, but most do. It's a timesaver to be able to see it all at once and to see the structure of the song graphically laid out on the page. Lead sheets are not sent out with demos to publishers or record companies. They're good to have at the point where a producer wants to record your song and you want to be sure he has the correct melody, but since the current copyright law permits tapes or CDs to be sent for copyright registration, their importance has diminished. Lead sheets are bulky to mail, it's too difficult to follow the lyric and visualize the song's form, and many industry pros don't read music anyway. It also pegs you as a songwriter over fifty who has no experience in submitting demos since this practice went out of style about thirty years ago.

When you type out your lyric sheet, separate the sections of the songs with a space and label each one (verse, chorus, bridge) at the upper left side of the section. Do not type your lyrics in prose fashion. Lay them out with the rhymes at the ends of the lines so the structure and rhyme schemes of the song can be seen immediately. Resist the temptation to center the lyric on the page even though it *looks* cool.

6. Make sure there's a copyright notice. (© 2007 I.B. Cool, All Rights Reserved) It should be on the bottom of the lyric sheet and on the tape or CD label. Technically, this isn't necessary but it alerts everyone that your song is protected, whether it's registered or not.

7. Cover letters should be short and to the point. Let the music speak for itself and avoid hype. A professional presentation will do more to impress someone than "I know these are hit songs because they're better than anything I've ever heard on the radio," or "I just know that we can both make a lot of money if you'll publish these songs." Avoid the temptation to tell your life story, and don't explain how you have a terminal disease, you're the sole support of your ten children, and if these songs don't get recorded they'll all be homeless or worse. Don't plead, apologize, or show any hint of desperation. It only gives the message that you have no confidence in the ability of the songs to stand on their own.

Here's what should be in your cover letter:

    a. Address it to a specific person in the company.

    b. State your purpose in sending the demo. Are you looking for a publisher, a producer, a record deal for you as an artist? Do you want the listener to pay special attention to your production, your singing, your band, or just the song? Is the song targeted for a specific artist?

    c. List any significant professional credits that apply to the purpose of your submission. If you want your song published, list other published or recorded songs, contests won, etc. If you're a performer submitting an artist demo, resist the temptation to grab at weak credits: "I played at the same club that (famous star) played." Tell them what drives you, what inspires you. Keep it short. List real sales figures. Don't lie.

    d. Include any casting ideas you might have if you're pitching to other artists. Show them you've done some homework.

    e. Ask for feedback if you want it. Odds are you won't get it, but give it a shot.

    f. List the songs enclosed and writers' names in the order they appear on the demo. (Lyric sheets should also be enclosed in the same order the songs appear on the demo.)

    g. Thank them for their time and attention.

8. The self-addressed stamped envelope (SASE) issue. My advice at this time is not to expect to get anything returned. CDs are cheap and plentiful. Consider them a part of doing business in pursuit of your career. It's too much hassle to ask anyone to deal with returning them to you.

9. Your name, address, and phone number should be on the cover letter, tape, or CD, and every lyric sheet. It seems like such a commonsense request. In fact, it would be embarrassing to even suggest that you might forget to do it if I didn't see it happen constantly. The problem on this end is that, between listening sessions at the office, the car, and home, it's so easy to separate the CD from the box or lyric sheet. Once they've gone to the trouble to find your hit song, not finding *you* is a fate they (and you) don't deserve.

10. Be sure you have adequate postage. Also, don't send your CD in an ordinary stationery envelope. It's risky because rough postal handling could force the edge of the tape box through the envelope. Use a special envelope with an insulated lining. Some people also prefer the soft "bubble" tape box because it doesn't have sharp edges and it's lighter to mail. CDs have an obvious advantage in this respect, as there are lightweight sleeves available for them. Having said that, jewel boxes are preferred because they can stack it on a shelf and read the label on the spine if they decide to keep it.

The main thing to remember is to make your demo submission as easy as possible to deal with.

Using the Internet: Your Demo as Audio File

An increasingly preferred method is sending your demo as an audio file. Obviously, many of the above suggestions don't apply to audio files. All music industry players have high-speed Internet access lines, and more and more of them are open to receiving audio files. Be sure to call before sending them and ask if there's something specific they want to see in your "subject" line that will identify you as "solicited" since they receive hundreds of unsolicited e-mails that will get caught in their spam filters.

The most popular formats are MP3, RealAudio, Windows Media Audio, and QuickTime. The fidelity may not be quite CD quality but still very good. There are a couple different procedures for this.

Send an e-mail with the audio file attached. Follow the suggestions listed on page 266 for a cover letter (include phone number). Also include your Web site address as a link so they can click it and go directly to your site. When they get to your site, they'll hopefully find additional biography material, photos, and lyrics.

There is an explosion of OMD (online music distribution) sites that offer an opportunity for you to post your digital music files and, in turn, enable you to forward links to whomever you want. Since some of you are artists and some are writers only, you'll all have different needs. So I'll recommend a couple of sites that list them with breakdowns of all the services each of them offers. They're constantly changing and being updated. The best list I've found so far is: http://compo10.com/MusicHosts.htm

The site lists over thirty-two different categories of attributes and services for each OMD site including direct links for more information. Among the services listed are whether the service will make, sell, stream, or promote your CDs; sell downloads; offer e-mail on site; build playlists and charts; offer Web radio streaming; and list costs and fees to the artists, number of songs allowed, and much more. They are definitely worth studying. Another Web site with good information and more commentary on each service is www.armydiller.com/musichosting.htm

A very popular site for pitching yourself as a writer/artist is Sonicbids (www.sonicbids.com). It offers their Sonicbids Electronic Press Kit (EPK), a web-based graphic interface that holds the basic information you'll want to make available, including music, lyric, bio, photos, and gig schedule. The EPK can be e-mailed to anyone with a click of the mouse. It's very handy and used by many contests, music conferences, and festivals for their song and artist entries/auditions.

Indie marketing guru and author, Tim Sweeney (www.tsamusic.com) suggests that because of the limited amount of time someone may want to spend at any site and the degree of difficulty her online access speeds may present, it's important to help her decide quickly which of your songs may be of most interest to her. You can help by providing a short description like this one provided on the Web site of Franklin Spicer and Valerie Ford's Pegasus Project (www.pegasusproject.com/

ws/Home.htm), a soft jazz/world music group. Note that the description includes information on the style, what it's about, why it was written and how it was recorded. Their Web site also includes lyrics to all the songs.

ONE PEOPLE

The first song Franklin ever heard from Val was a reggae tune she had recorded called "One People." He really liked the positive message and the infectious chorus. Franklin talked her into doing a rewrite and making it a Pegasus Project tune. They wanted to share a positive message of how we all are part of one global family. This song was shaped from a number of African musical influences, including the Tuku style. The huge chorus backup vocals were done in two days of recording using seven different singers.

Your demo or master recording will introduce you to the eyes and ears of many music industry professionals—and eventually fans. Take this introduction very seriously. It should look good and have something important to say and say it well. There's lots of competition for the ears of industry pros and potential fans. You want to be appealing to both.

Where Do You Start?

Whether your sole goal is to be a songwriter or whether you also have aspirations to be a performer, one of the most common and frustrating problems for a novice is not knowing where to start. Do you approach publishers first, or go right to the record companies? Should you find an independent producer or look for a manager?

The first answer you'll get from anyone is "it all depends." No single approach works the same for everyone. That one step-by-step formula you want so badly just doesn't exist. In this section I'll cover some of the assessments you'll need to make of your own personal situation to help you sort out a direction. The best way to find your path is to get a realistic evaluation of your chances through some professional feedback.

Do you want your songs to be performed by other artists? Are they suitable? You may have developed a songwriting style that's too lyrically personal or musically unique to interest other artists in recording your songs. However, that uniqueness can be a valuable thing if you also perform your own songs. Some of the most exciting artists write so uniquely that it's difficult for another artist to record their songs without sounding like imitators.

The next consideration is to assess your potential as an artist. Do you want to perform your own songs? Do you have the talent record companies require? Do you have a unique vocal identity? Bob Dylan isn't a great singer, but you always know who he is when you hear him. Randy Travis, Macy Gray, Rob Thomas, John Mayer and Björk all have strong vocal identities and very distinctive styles.

Don't kid yourself about whether you have those qualities (see chapter fifteen, "How Record Companies Listen to Your Music" on page 365). *American Idol* makes a fortune at the expense of people with unrealistic ideas about their own talent. Get specific feedback about your abilities. If you don't have that distinctive style or vocal quality, your odds for becoming a major label artist are poor, unless you can create a unique group sound or concept, have fantastic commercial songs, or develop a huge fan-base by touring. (In this last case, you should be starting your own label and publishing company.) To be a successful artist, you need to provide as many ways as possible for the audience to identify, experience, and remember you.

Some people may tell you that you don't have artist potential, and others may tell you that your songs aren't coverable. They may be right, but don't let just one or two different people make that assessment for you.

There are many different publishers with a variety of tastes. Publishers generally want songs that offer a variety of possibilities for recording. If there's only one artist your song appears appropriate for and they fail to get the artist to cut it, they may have a dead song on their hands. Try your songs out on several publishers and others who will give you honest critical feedback about your songs' overall potential.

If you're an intelligent, perceptive writer who's willing to spend some time on your craft, you can learn to write more coverable songs without sacrificing the factors that make your writing unique.

The following are some of the potential routes you can take, depending on your own special combination of talents and aspirations. They are, of course, generalizations. Your situation may fall in the cracks somewhere, but these should give you a rough idea.

THE PUBLISHER OPTION

If you have coverable songs but don't quite fit the bill as an artist or aren't interested in a life on the road, finding a good publisher who will shop your songs to artists may be the best approach. If you want to be your own publisher and contact producers and artists yourself, that's another option (see chapter eleven).

The current reality is that, though very few staff writing positions are available, there are still a lot of independent publishers looking for songs and instrumentals to shop to artists and for audiovisual uses. Indie artists being developed on indie labels also need great songs in all styles.

If the feedback you get is that you're both an excellent singer and writer, find a publisher who is also willing to put up money to record and shop masters of you as an artist. These are called "development deals." If the publisher gets you a deal and he owns half of the publishing rights to your songs (the standard deal) in the bargain, it's gravy for him. He doesn't need to go out and try to get other artists to cover the songs because you've already done it.

If you approach publishers first, you will certainly bargain away a part (if you have the clout), if not all of your publishing rights. But in exchange you'll get (1) someone working on your career (since she has a vested interest), (2) a company who can possibly get you a record deal, and (3) someone who can pitch your songs to other artists (see chapter ten, "Publishing" page 191).

THE RECORD COMPANY OPTION

If publishers don't seem to show much interest in your songs after you've submitted them to several, but most people feel you've got what it takes to be an artist, or if your songs work well for your unique style and you're developing a great live following as a performer, but you aren't writing the kinds of songs publishers think they can place, go for the record companies first.

If your own songs aren't strong enough or you don't have enough potential hit singles to approach a record company, look for great songs from other writers. Though record companies would prefer to sign a totally self-contained artist or band, the next best thing is that you or your producer knows how to pick the right songs. The bottom line is that, one way or another, you have to have material that's considered hit potential by the company. They at least want to feel confident that there's a radio format receptive to the artist's material (see chapter fifteen, "Getting a Record Deal" on page 364).

The reality of the record industry today is that a great major record deal is an unrealistic goal for most, and it may not be worth your time to look for one. That may sound cynical coming from such an optimist and not that long ago I was much more encouraging. Yes, artists and bands *are* still getting record deals and the major labels *are* still signing artists, and every now and then somebody seemingly *does* come out of nowhere and becomes a big star. Those are the ones you hear about but the numbers are very small if you're playing odds. What you really need to do is figure out what you love to do most.

Even though there are many dedicated music lovers who work at major record labels, we have to understand that the people who run them are not in it for the music. They're in it for the money. They're multinational corporations supported by shareholders who demand a return on their investments every quarter. The shareholders are scared enough to hire people successful in other industries unrelated to music to run these record companies because someone convinces the shareholders that these people have some mysterious power to turn a profit—enough to pay them obscene amounts of money to hire them and, it seems, even more when they leave. That money would be enough to start hundreds of indie labels staffed with people who are passionate about the music but are slugging it out trying to stay above water.

How that affects your options is that they want you to be successful already before they decide to sign you because they can then justify to the shareholders that there was a good reason to have signed you—that it wasn't that much of a gamble because you were already "developed" as an artist or band. Never mind that it would cost them more to sign you because of that. It's more important to their bottom line that they reduce their risk.

So, back to deciding what you love to do. If you love to write more than you love to perform, focus your attention on writing and maybe producing. If you're young and full of energy and ambition, and you love to perform, then you should be performing. Make your own recording or find a producer or manager who will work with you. If you have family or day job obligations that keep you from being able to tour but still love to perform, build a local, then a regional following and see where it takes you. There are plenty of options available now to sell your recordings online and at your gigs, and you have the potential to make more money on each recording you sell. Ten thousand CDs or legal downloads sold will get you dropped from a major label—80 percent to 90 percent of major label artists don't sell that many and *are* eventually dropped; however, if you sell that many records *on your own*, you can make a nice living.

Most record companies, including indies, will want to own your publishing. Most major labels will also own your masters, though if you've been successful on your own, you stand a chance to maintain control of your masters or negotiate contract clauses to get them back eventually. You'll have to work every bit as hard as an indie as you will on a major label (did you think a major label would be a free ride?) but *you* will be in control, not the label.

THE PRODUCER OPTION

For a writer/artist, finding an independent producer is another option. There's no point in doing this if you're solely a writer, unless you're collaborating with a writer who *is* an artist. If the producer is putting up the financial backing for demo/masters or an album, he may want half the publishing. It's not uncommon, but restrict it to the songs he records within a time period (six to eighteen months after completion of the masters). Then, if he fails to secure an acceptable record deal within that time, all rights should revert to you. The producer will still own the masters (if he paid for them) and can recoup his money if you get a deal later and the record company wants to use those masters. If he does get you a deal, you're signed to his production company with that producer. A producer respected by the record company and dedicated to your career can work to your advantage.

The record company will need to protect its investment if the production company defaults on your agreement in any way, and the artist *and* the production company will want to be sure that the terms, especially royalty payments, will be the same in the production contract as they are in the record company contract. Their attorney will negotiate for what's called a "flow through" clause that lets them take over your contract obligations if the producer defaults. That clause should also ensure that the royalty percentages will flow through to the highest amount in case the production company gives you a lower percentage than can be negotiated for your record company agreement. In that case, your attorney will make sure that you'll get the higher royalty offered by the label.

If the label that has your product doesn't have strong enthusiasm for it, you're at a severe disadvantage. At a major label you may be competing with more than a hundred other acts for optimum release dates when the company isn't focusing all its publicity and promotion attention on its superstar acts. If that producer/label team doesn't seem to be looking after your best interests, you may be better off trying to get out of your deal so you can pursue another one. Your attorney will include "performance" clauses that nullify your contract if certain sales figures or other terms aren't met and can protect you from some of these problems.

I recommend reading Moses Avalon's books, *Secrets of Negotiating a Record Contract: The Musician's Guide to Understanding and Avoiding Sneaky Lawyer Tricks* and *Confessions of a Record Producer: How to Survive the Scams and Shams of the Music Business*. He runs down a litany of cautions in all these deals. Visit his Web site (www.mosesavalon.com).

THE MANAGEMENT OPTION

If you don't think you have talent as a performer or don't feel it's the career you want, and aren't already a very successful writer or writer/producer, it doesn't make much sense to look for management. You can pay an attorney a fee to negotiate your deals rather than pay a manager 15 percent to 25 percent of your income. As in the case of producers, if you're solely a writer you should approach a manager only if you wish to pitch songs to his artists.

Where to start, as you can see, involves a lot of variables, and it's important to know what they are before getting started. Still, it's a good idea to test the water in all directions before committing to a course of action. Professional feedback is what you'll need to make a good decision. (See chapter fifteen, "Your Manager" on page 370.)

Writers, Writer/Artists, and Writer/Producers in the Marketplace

You'll often hear songs on the radio that you feel are below your standards and wonder how they got there. You feel your own songs should surely have a chance. You may be right, but you may also be misunderstanding a basic fact of life. You're judging your standards as a writer against industry standards of making a record (see chapter three, "A Song Is Not a Record" on page 44).

Some writer/artists have high standards; some don't. But they all have access to the "record-making machinery" that allows them to record their visions and use production and arrangement to compensate for the dynamic factors that writers who aren't artists need to build into their songs. Usually, it's not a question of songwriting standards of excellence, but about the greater degree of creative latitude available to writer/artists and writer/producers who have a much larger canvas, and more colors and brushes with which to paint that final picture. In other words, they have arrangement, sound, and production techniques as further ingredients to help them make an appealing product.

For example, hip-hop records are usually built from the track up and are not necessarily built around a melody or lyric concept, though those elements, particularly lyric, are always important. They're primarily the creations of producers who know their audiences and are masters of creating trendy grooves, fresh sounds, and interwoven vocal arrangements. They're not writing songs in the traditional sense, but instead are writing *productions*.

More and more writers are opening up new creative fields by learning to produce and arrange, finding a singer (if not themselves) as a vehicle, and producing masters or demos that indicate the production possibilities strongly enough to stretch the forms and show them to be workable. The access to inexpensive digital composing and arranging software, instrument software and groove loops is allowing writers a great opportunity to develop as producers, engineers, and mixers, especially when they don't have to watch the clock.

If you're a writer who doesn't have production and arrangement skills, you face the challenge of finding creative ways to paint your ideas on a more limited canvas. To a much greater extent, you need to work within established song structures and to use your creativity to develop well-crafted lyric concepts and exciting, memorable melodies. Whether or not you ever develop arranging or production skills, you'll have the confidence that you can write a great song.

Reading Your Road Map: Researching the Music Industry

If you were making a cross-country drive on a tight timetable and weren't sure about how to get to your destination, would you just start driving in the general direction and hope everything would work out somehow? No way! You'd be studying maps trying to find the best roads, figuring out when and where you'd be sleeping and researching any other information that would make your trip as fast, pleasant, and efficient as possible. (You might even stop to ask somebody for directions!) But it's surprising how many songwriters will make a blind trip into the music industry and spend years just wandering around and going nowhere. They seem to feel that crafting and marketing their songs is one of the few professions in the world that they don't have to know anything about to do successfully. Since you're reading this book, I know you understand the need to learn a lot more about this business and how to improve your odds of success.

It's quite common to hear industry pros say that when they've had an open door policy regarding unsolicited material, over 95 percent of the songs they received were not even in the ballpark for the artist. It was clear that those writers didn't bother to listen to the artist they were pitching to or find out the needs or strengths of the company soliciting the songs. The fact is that there are many easily accessible ways to research the information and learn about the industry. A little effort and time invested in research will put you in that remaining 5 percent.

START WITH THE MUSIC TRADE MAGAZINES

A serious songwriter should read the music trade magazines. They are a music industry education. If you can't afford to subscribe and don't have an Internet connection, go to the public library every week and read them. (Libraries also have Internet access.) If they don't have them, gather a group of others to formally petition the library to subscribe. They may not be getting the music trades because they don't think anyone is interested. Most are weekly magazines and they're very expensive ($250–$300 per year), but if you feel you're ready to begin your assault on the industry, they're one of your best investments.

Billboard (www.billboard.com): You can access lots of info at their Web site without subscribing, including charts, news, and reviews. When you do subscribe, you get complete access to Billboard. Biz, the Web site with all the editorial and charts, plus the daily Billboard Bulletin e-newsletter, archives, Billboard Radio Monitor, and Billboard Chart Alert.

U.S./CANADA

Monthly (U.S./Canada): $24.95

Annual (U.S./Canada): $299

INTERNATIONAL

Annual: U.K./Europe: $450 • Japan: $950

Other: $625

ONLINE ONLY

Monthly (U.S./Canada/International): $19.95

Annual (U.S./Canada/International): $199

Music Connection (www.musicconnection.com): *Music Connection* does not have charts but does offer great industry interviews and features. Every issue also has an up-to-date directory, mostly about the Los Angeles area, but with some national information. Each issue has a special focus (management, songwriting, recording studios, guitar teachers) and the directory focuses on that topic. The magazine also includes weekly demo and live performance reviews. You can get a taste of the directories for free but need to subscribe to get the whole thing. The world's largest free classified section can be accessed for free online. Highly recommended!

Music Row (www.musicrow.com): *Music Row* is dedicated to the Nashville music industry. If you write country, don't be without it. There are monthly and weekly editions.

Country Music Television (www.cmt.com): *CMT* is somewhere between an online trade and a fan magazine (fanzine), but it's still a good research tool. It has charts and other informative features such as "20 Questions" that will familiarize you with country artists, their personalities, and their music.

USE CHARTS FOR RESEARCH

A valuable feature of trade publications is the charts. *Billboard* is the most valuable to writers because their pop, country, and R&B/hip-hop singles charts list the producer, writer, label and release number, distributing label, publisher, performing rights affiliation (BMI, ASCAP, SESAC), and sheet music supplier. Though the other singles, album, airplay, and sales charts don't list writers and producers, they still are a valuable barometer of the popularity of artists, records, and record companies.

Billboard now has more than forty different music and video charts, including Internet, Hot Digital, Hot Ringtones, and Top Independent along with many sub-genres like Bluegrass, Reggae, and Dance Club Play.

Charts are tabulated with SoundScan, that reads the bar codes on every recording sold via reporting retail stores and online retailers. Airplay is monitored with Broadcast Data Systems (BDS) (www.bdsonline.com).

So, what can you learn from all that? First of all, you can get an idea about trends, providing that you're also listening to a lot of radio and are familiar with the songs on the charts. With Internet access, you can also play short clips of the songs on iTunes and most other online sales sites, as well as on the artists' Web sites. You'll see what artists and songs are most popular in their respective styles and which artists and songs cross over between two or more charts. There are also editorial sections relating to those styles, providing analysis and news about artists, labels, and trends. There is more information today on the music industry, music genres, and artists only a click away than at any other time in history.

Veteran record company executive Russ Regan says he studies the charts for the "gaps." If he sees there are a lot of up-tempo dance tunes crowding the charts, he knows it's time for a great ballad, or vice versa. Also, once the public has bought and feels at home with a "sound," when the group who created it drops out for a while, it may be a good time to release a similar sound. Though the time lapse between your writing a song and its being recorded and released probably wouldn't allow you to take advantage of the chart information the way Russ Regan could, it gives you some idea of one of the ways it's used in the business.

There are some other practical applications of that information. The list of the writers' names can tell you if the writer is also the producer or artist, in which case the percentages are *against* your being able to place a song with him. That isn't cut and dry, though. Many writer/artists are open to outside tunes, but your songs would have to be better than those written by the artist or artist/producer. You're also likely to be asked to give up your publishing interest in the song.

The best bets for song placement are obviously with artists who consistently show up on the charts with "outside" material. You can locate the numbers or e-mail addresses of the artist's producers or managers by calling the A&R or artist relations department of the listed record company (or use the research material suggested in this chapter). Then you can pitch your songs to the artist's producers and managers. Though those people may not be open to unsolicited material, your knowledge of their work and ability to discuss it intelligently may get you through otherwise closed doors. It shows them that you're paying attention and you're serious enough to do the research. Consequently, they may guess that you're in that 5 percent that's worth listening to (see chapter eleven, "Casting: The Right Song for the Right Artist" on page 221).

The international music market is so important now that it's always enlightening to check out the international charts for the types of English language songs that are popular in other countries. If you're publishing your own songs and write in a style that is popular in certain countries, you'll know to concentrate on those countries when you look for a foreign sub-publisher (see chapter eleven, "Foreign Sub-Publishing," on page 231).

If you are a writer/artist or group looking for a producer, you can look at the charts for a group that is produced the way *you would* like to hear yourself and find the listed producer. Since he/she has an artist on the charts, it is reasonable to assume that they have pretty good leverage with a label or labels. It's important to know the names and meet the people in the business. This is important if you're actively trying to get something going, either as a writer or a recording artist.

If you're on the outside looking in and you're not hanging out at any of the industry watering holes, it gets very difficult to keep track of who's who, who's what, and where these people are. It's complicated by a musical chairs game unequaled in any other business, except maybe advertising. In some cases, people didn't know they'd been fired until they read it in the trades. Billboard calls its column, "Executive Turntable," Music Connection's column is called "Signings and Assignments." By following these columns, you can see where your favorite A&R person, publisher, etc., is working this month. Another great resource is the Music Business Registry (see "Other Sources" on page 280). Track industry pros online by going to an Internet search engine (Google is my personal favorite) and search under the person's name. If there's been an article written about him somewhere online, it'll show up.

You may have run into an A&R person who liked your band or your songs but couldn't get anything going for you at her previous label. You see in the "Executive Turntable" that she's at (or has started) a new company now, so it's worth another shot. In a new company, she may have more respect, more power, and a renewed motivation to prove herself. Yours might be the act she'll sign or your songs might be better suited to the artists on her new label. It may also be worthwhile to contact the executive who took her place at the old company. Most of the same considerations also apply to executives and professional managers at publishing companies. Again, search online for the name of the company and you'll get the information, even if you missed *Billboard* the week it was announced.

Keep in mind that if you've already signed a publishing contract on a song and you see that the person responsible for signing your song to that company has made an exit, you should call the company and make an appointment with his replacement. If you don't bring your song to his attention, it may get lost in the shuffle of thousands of others the new person has to represent. It also gives you a chance to make a new contact and bring exposure to some of your newer songs. Also call your old contact at his new job, congratulate him, and go to see him at the new company.

Occasionally, a whole company will be restructured by a new president who wants to put together his own team. News of that will be carried in the trades' news columns and likely in a more detailed feature article, where you'll learn about new companies forming or branch offices being set up locally. You may have a situation where people are eager to prove themselves by finding some great new local artists or songs. Call right away to make an appointment.

It's important to develop your critical abilities. You have an opportunity to do that by reading live performance and record reviews in the consumer music trades and online; search the Internet under "CD reviews" and "concert reviews." Listen to the same records they do, go to the same concerts, and do your own reviews. Obviously, opinions differ among reviewers depending on their own personal taste and critical abilities. For your own learning process, though, it's as helpful to disagree as to agree, as long as you've paid careful attention to their critique and given some thought to your own.

The trades, consumer magazines, and artist and record company Web sites contain interviews with music industry people that can be helpful on several levels. You might find an interview with an artist for whom you want to write a song, and you may gain some insight into her likes, dislikes, experiences, and fears that will help you write a song she'll identify with, a song that will "speak" for her.

There are many "right" ways to do almost anything in this business, and it helps to know a number of them. Never be afraid to ask questions of industry people when you have the opportunity. In the interviews

I've done through the years, with few exceptions, music industry people have spoken freely about how they do things and how they feel about what they do. Even as a struggling writer/artist, whenever I expressed a desire to learn about something, there was always someone who would take the time to explain.

TIP SHEETS

Tip sheets are periodicals listing producers, publishers, or record companies who are in need of material for artists. Some are monthly, some biweekly, some weekly. Some are directed to all songwriters in general, and some are restricted to publishers or pro writers with proven track records. This restriction is meant to maintain the tip sheet's credibility with its industry contacts. A tip sheet relies on listings by producers of major artists and other established producers with new artists. If the producers don't want to list their needs, publishers and others won't want to buy the tip sheet. If a tip sheet is sold indiscriminately to amateur songwriters who have no casting sense, don't know how to do their research on the artist, or don't know what the radio format terminology means, they'll end up sending totally inappropriate songs. The producer then calls the tip sheet and says, "Who are you selling this to? I've been getting hundreds of terrible songs and if this keeps up, I'm never listing with you again."

Are tip sheets worth the money? Some list producers who are willing to wade through amateur submissions, and if you've got the right song, they'll hear it. Most of the heavy hitters, though, are going for the restricted lists or the lists that are so expensive that only the very serious can afford them, which is how some of them deal with the problem I just described. Others want proof of your previous recording activity, and others deal with it by canceling your subscription and refunding your money if they get complaints that your submissions are inappropriate or of poor quality.

With tip sheets, remember that you're rarely going to be among the first to know that someone is looking for songs. Any worthwhile publisher will know it before—or at least at the same time as—the tips, because they or their staffs are calling producers daily and the major publishers all have in-house tip sheets. The tip sheet takes some time to collect listings, and print and mail them. By the time you get it, the hot publishers will have their songs on the way to the listed producers. Publishers subscribe to them anyway because they can't afford to miss anything and a new producer may come out of left field that they haven't yet made contact with.

The fact that you're not among the first, however, doesn't necessarily mean you don't have a chance. It's quite possible the producers won't find what they want in the first go-round and will keep looking. It's still important for you to be aggressive about responding to listings.

Every tip sheet will contain its own guidelines for the way you should submit songs. Additional information will also appear on the individual listings like "no ballads," "one song only," or "positive lyrics only." Follow their instructions to help ensure that your demo gets listened to. For further information, reread the sections on "Casting: The Right Song for the Right Artist" (chapter eleven, page 221) and "Presenting Your Demo" (chapter twelve, page 264).

TAXI

Tel: 1-800-458-2111

www.TAXI.com

TAXI is an innovative, and very successful and respected tip sheet and independent A&R service founded in 1992. Members receive 65–100 listings every two weeks by major and independent labels, producers, managers, film and TV music supervisors, and publishers looking for writers, writer/artists, and bands. All those who list are pre-qualified as serious companies. You can get a free informative e-mail every two weeks by getting on their e-mail list for free. That way you can actually see the listings (though they don't give you the submission codes until you join). All submissions are prescreened and critiqued by industry pros, which is the reason TAXI is respected by the industry as a vehicle to the industry. They take all styles including instrumentals. Membership includes a monthly newsletter (past issues are archived on their Web site). The annual TAXI Road Rally conference in Los Angeles (free but restricted to members, plus one guest) has become *the* premiere annual event for songwriters and writer/artists.

TAXI has added TAXI Dispatch for the film and TV industry to facilitate the fast access and delivery of music for their shows by submission of online pitches. The Dispatch membership fee is an additional $149.95 per year and will be prorated for the existing term of your current TAXI membership. To submit music online to TAXI or TAXI Dispatch, you must also join Broadjam (www.broadjam.com).

A one-year subscription for all of TAXI's benefits is $299.95; a two-year membership is $499.95; and a three-year membership is $599.95. There is also a $5 per song submission fee. (Highly recommended.)

SONGLINK INTERNATIONAL

23 Belsize Crescent • London NW3 5QY, England

Tel: +44 (0) 207 794 2540 • Fax: +44 (0) 207 794 7393

www.songlink.com • E-mail: david@songlink.com

David Stark created this international tip sheet in 1993. It lists both new and established artists looking for material and pro writers looking for collaborators and offers 40–50 new leads each month. It also features industry news and extensive links to industry events, sites of classic songwriters, publications, songwriters' resources, portals to European industry sites, organizations, and much more. A class act! A one-year subscription (ten issues) is £240.00/U.S. $395.00/390.00 EUR (includes postage). Three and six month subscriptions are available.

NEW ON THE CHARTS

70 Laurel Place • New Rochelle, NY 10801

Tel: (914) 632-3349 • Fax: (914) 633-7690

www.notc.com • E-mail: lenny@notc.com

Founded in 1976, this tip sheet provides info on who's currently on the charts in all genres, with cross-referenced contact info on the artists, producers, managers, record labels, and booking agents of each hit. It also has the Publisher Leads tip sheet listing artists who need songs; the latest label, publisher, and management signings; the Soundtrack Leads for listings of film and TV music; the Video Spotlight; and the International Deals section. There are different subscription rates for different segments of the services. To subscribe, songwriters must be able to verify at least one nationally released recording of their song. A full subscription (one year or twelve issues) is $365 (plus $45 for international postage).

PARADE OF STARS

Chuck Chellman

P.O. Box 121355 • Nashville, TN 37212-1355

Tel: (615) 352-4848

www.paradeofstars.com • E-mail: paradofstars@home.com

The oldest tip sheet, *Parade of Stars* is a bi-weekly sheet for both professionals and amateurs. There are lots of country listings, but it also lists gospel artists, as well as R&B, pop, and rock artists. Subscriptions are $129 for a year or $80for half a year.

ROW FAX

1231 17th Ave. S. • Nashville, TN 37212

Tel: (615) 321-3617 • Fax: (615) 329-0852

www.musicrow.com

Row Fax is the best country tip sheet. It is published forty-eight times a year by *Music Row* magazine and e-mailed to you every Friday. With your member code you can also access it online. For professionals only. Entries include artist, record label, producer, recording date, and song description details. Address and contact info is not given. (They figure if you're a professional, you'll already know those contact numbers.) Subscriptions are $149 for one year, and $270 for two years.

ONLINE PITCH SERVICES

These services provide a searchable database for songwriters and publishers to make their music available for pre-qualified users (record companies, film/TV music supervisors, ad agencies, schools, etc.). Some take a percentage of any uses generated by the site. Others charge based on the number of songs posted on the site. Still others involve active pitching via the Internet. Some are non-exclusive. Read their contracts carefully.

One of these services, SongCatalog (www.songcatalog.com), began when my friend Steven McClintock, hit songwriter and former staff writer for several publishers, became discouraged when a publisher dropped the ball on a film song license that Steven had initiated, causing him to lose the use. He started thinking about all the songs he'd written that were sitting unused and unpitched at publishing companies as well as all his writer friends in the same situation. He found a financial and tech partner and started SongCatalog to do something about it. Here are a couple of ways his, and similar services, are used.

• A publisher or writer phones up a potential user of his music, saying, "I've got a song I'd like you to check out," and then e-mails to the potential music user with a link to a specific song. The potential user logs on, listens, and decides yes or no.

• A would-be music user needs a song, goes to a writer or publisher's song database, and searches under whatever parameters are needed for the pitch. He gets a list of songs that qualify, looks at lyrics to narrow it down, listens to what looks most promising, contacts the writer or publisher, and negotiates for the use.

The beauty of these services is that you can make a few songs or your entire catalog of songs available. They're as valuable for publishers as for independent songwriters, and they allow you the option of uploading audio file samples and whole songs, lyrics, the song's recording history, contact information, and much more. They're presented in a searchable database in which a potential user can choose the parameters that fit her needs: style, tempo, male or female cast, length, and others. This category of services uses the technology in a way that's timesaving and practical for writers, publishers, and users. Each of the services has its own combination of benefits and costs and is evolving new benefits, so visit their Web sites for up-to-date information. All major music publishers now have in-house online search access to their catalogs and production music libraries. But the following are mostly for independents:

LicenseMusic.com (www.licensemusic.com)

PublishSongs.com (www.publishsongs.com)

Pump Audio (www.pumpaudio.com)

SongCatalog (www.songcatalog.com)

SongScope.com (www.songscope.com)

(See chapter fourteen, "Production Music Libraries" on page 334.)

OTHER SOURCES

Besides the trade magazines and tip sheets, other sources of information are:

THE MUSIC BUSINESS REGISTRY

7510 Sunset Blvd., Ste. 1041 • Los Angeles, CA 90046-3418

Tel: (818) 995-7458 • Fax: (818) 995-7459

www.musicregistry.com • E-mail: ritch@musicregistry.com

This company, headed by former Arista Records A&R rep Ritch Esra, publishes the *A&R Registry*, a comprehensive listing of record company A&R reps, including their stylistic focus, direct phone, fax numbers, e-mails, Web sites, and the names of their assistants. This is the only directory updated every two months. They also publish a *Music Publisher Registry* (semi-annual), *Film and Television Music Guide, Music Producer Registry,* and *The Music Attorney, Legal and Business Affairs Guide.* Single issues are available. Annual prices include continually updated online subscriptions. These are the directories used by most pros.

SONGWRITER'S MARKET, WRITER'S DIGEST BOOKS

4700 East Galbraith Ave. • Cincinnati, OH 45236

Tel: (513) 531-2690 • Fax: (513) 531-2686

www.writersdigest.com • E-mail: songmarket@fwpubs.com

Songwriter's Market is an annual directory that provides listings of industry pros who are open to receiving unsolicited material, how they want the material submitted, and what types of music the company specializes in. The listings are broken down into several sections, including Music Publishers, Record Companies, Record Producers, Managers & Booking Agents, Advertising, Audiovisual & Commercial Music Firms, Play Producers & Publishers, Classical Performing Arts, Contests & Awards,

Organizations, Workshops and Conferences, Retreats and Colonies, State and Provincial Grants, Publications, and Web sites of Interest, along with informative articles on the craft and business of songwriting. *Songwriter's Market* is available in major bookstores and online, or order it direct.

BILLBOARD DIRECTORIES

www.billboard.com

Billboard publishes the *International Talent & Touring Directory*, the *Billboard International Buyer's Guide*, and other directories annually. They list hundreds of artists, their personal managers, booking agents, and other contacts (see the appendix on page 384).

THE INDIE BIBLE

www.indiebible.com

The Indie Bible is a great resource for independent artists. Even their free monthly e-letter gives you fifty new resources a month. *The Indie Bible* gives you 4,200 publications that will review your music, 3,400 radio stations that will play your songs, 600 labels and distributors looking to sign artists, and 500 Web sites where you can upload your music. Each fall they offer an updated supplement issue with the new changes for $10 so you don't have to repurchase the full edition again.

(For more resources see the appendix on page 384.)

281

MORE RESEARCH CENTERS

The *Billboard* SoundScan technology revolutionized the industry by providing accurate retail sales and airplay information. Surprisingly, it showed country music was selling much more than was thought to be true. It's now showing several country artists on the "Hot 100" pop chart. Webcasts have opened a new avenue for exposing and selling music and monitoring systems have been created to track them. The Internet now provides up-to-date research information from the performing rights organizations on their catalogs accessible to anyone with Internet access. New standardized cue-sheet forms for music used in film and television are used by the performing rights organizations and can be filed online. There are now several Internet services available for exposing and selling independent recordings to the online audience. Among them are the biggest, Amazon.com (www.amazon.com), and my personal favorite, CD Baby (www.cdbaby.com). Browsing the music-related Web sites on the Internet will turn up many more. You can keep abreast of these developments by reading the trades regularly.

Record Stores and the Internet

Though brick-and-mortar record retailers seem to be on the endangered species list, until they're actually extinct, there's nothing like them for getting the info you need. Yes, the Internet may be faster if you have a high-speed connection (and easier to walk away from without spending a bundle), but record stores can be great sources of information. Take a notebook or voice recorder with you to get down the info you need. They usually have a list of current hits in your favorite style. Familiarize yourself with them and find the CDs in the bins. Many stores have listening posts where you can spend some time listening to new artists' CDs. Some stores also have information kiosks where you can bring up artist information on a monitor and look up past albums and reviews.

If you're an artist or in a band, check out the CDs of the artists who record your style of music and find out who the record labels are who distribute them, look for the names of the producers—

sometimes a management company name is on the back, too—and the artist or label's Web site. If you're selling your CDs yourself, ask to meet the buyer at the store to find out the requirements for stocking your CDs, especially if you're performing locally.

When you get back to your computer, put those names you've gathered into your Internet search engine and search for the artist, label, producer, and manager. Frankly, you'll find all the info you'll ever need about all the above. This is the age of information and any company, artist, or producer who wants to be visible has (or should have) a Web site with all his info. He'll post reviews, interviews, photos, gig schedules, statistics, lists of previous projects, awards, blogs, podcasts, videocasts, cell phone ringtones, some of which you couldn't care less about. But to be visible in this business, you have to have one place to send people for that info. Go to the record company Web site to see, and maybe hear other artists on the label. If you're in a band, you'll say, "Do we sound like anyone else on this label?" If the answer is "yes," it's a bad thing. If it's "no" but in the general stylistic ballpark, it's a good thing.

If you're a writer (not a performer), there are obviously more advantages in *buying* the CDs. There isn't a better way to familiarize yourself with the style of an artist, and the CD inserts usually contain all the info you need. The lyrics and the names of the writers should be included as well (see chapter eleven, "Casting: The Right Song for the Right Artist" on page 221). Often the management company is listed with an address. You'll also find the names of the producers of that album or of individual songs on it. Of course, the next album may be produced by someone else. But at least you've done some homework and can call the record company, get the A&R or artist relations department, and ask if so-and-so will be working on the next album (if not, who is?) and how to get in touch. If you play it right, they may also give you the manager's office address and phone number.

Organizations and Events—Networking Research

There is a growing list of annual national and international networking and showcasing events for songwriters and bands. Some are small and intimate, and some are huge. For our organization the Los Angeles Songwriters Showcase (1971–1996), Len Chandler and I produced the first national event for songwriters in 1977 called the Songwriters Expo. We produced one each year for twenty years in Los Angeles, plus two in Austin, Texas, in 1994 and 1995. We typically featured about forty pitch and critique sessions and twenty-six panels and workshops for the two-day (later three-day) event. That meant there were about 150 industry pros there for people to meet, and if the attendees were organized and prepared, they could meet a good percentage of them. That's not counting the hundred (two per night, fifty weeks a year) at our weekly songwriters showcases. That experience taught me a few of things that this in-person experience can teach you:

1. These are just people like anyone else. Some of them you like, some you don't. You think some really know what they're talking about; others you just know are faking it. But you *don't* need to be intimidated by them. Most, by far, are personable and very approachable. Many were in your shoes not that long ago.

2. You find out what kind of songs they look for, and what styles and artists appeal to them most. They all have personal tastes that may or may not be in synch with your style, but once you learn about that by hearing them comment on others' songs, you know what to pitch them—or not.

3. They get the opportunity to meet *you*. If you're a very talented writer or artist, they want to meet you; that may be why they are there. They just don't know it yet. Allow me to interject a spiritual notion here. I believe that everything happens for a reason and there are no accidents. Sometimes you meet that one someone you need to meet, and he has been looking for someone with what you have to offer. It was meant to be. And that's when stuff *happens*! Our angels network, too!

4. You learn something every time if you're paying attention. Meeting this person or hearing her speak may not seem important to you—"Oh, I already know about that stuff, I've heard her before"—but that doesn't take into consideration what *she's* learned since you heard her last. Pretty much every time I've made myself attend an event in spite of saying those things to myself, I've been glad I went anyway. I later realized that I'd met a great contact who I never would have met if I hadn't gone—or I learned something valuable despite my feeling that I knew the topic.

Most organizations have regularly scheduled monthly or annual events where they invite music industry professionals to speak and listen to demos. There are major music events in the U.S. and Canada, like Austin's South by Southwest (SXSW). Familiarize yourself with those guests, their histories, and their current needs. The personal contact has much more impact than a cold call. Here's how to make it work for you:

Research the guests before the event. Search their names online and read their bios, articles about them, or interviews with them. Listen to a song they placed or the records they produced. Once you've absorbed that info (take notes for later) you're in a good position to start an intelligent conversation and you never know where it can lead you. "Behind the scenes" people always love when you can talk and ask questions about something they've done that you're familiar with or a fan of. "Hey I loved the guitar sound on that record (you produced). How did you get that?" Don't lie to them though. Be genuine. If you're not, they'll know it right away.

Give them your card and get theirs. Often they won't have them (sometimes on purpose!) and will say, "Just call my office," or tell you to ask the organization host to give it to you. Don't assume that they don't want to be bothered, though. It may be true but you don't want your shyness to stop you if you have confidence in your music. When you get a card from *anyone*, write some notes on the back of the card to help you remember who they are: "We talked about_____"; "Call after first of year"; "Short blonde with great song about_____." Note the date and occasion. You may find the card later and have to rack your brain to remember why you have her card and where you met. Hopefully you've got a database where you can transfer those notes. I use FileMaker Pro and have thousands of those entries. I not only can search by name but by the notes. Who was that attorney I met at the DIY (do it yourself) conference? I put "DIY" in the notes field and several will pop up, narrowing the search. Or I could put both "DIY" *and* "attorney" and narrow it even further.

Demo pitching etiquette at the event. You should always be prepared to give them a demo with lyric sheets or your finished CD. However, it doesn't mean you *should*. It really depends on the event, the person, and frankly, the moment. The people who create the event can tell you if there's a special etiquette for their event. If industry people are there specifically to look for new songs or artists, it may be perfectly okay. If they are there specifically to speak on a panel, it may not be. In that case, it's better etiquette to wait for him to ask you for it. That may not happen until after you've had enough conversation to get comfortable. If it seems okay you may want to ask, "Would you like a copy of my CD to take with you or can I contact you later." It gives him an opportunity to gracefully decline. I've come back from places deluged with CDs I haven't had time to listen to because my business is to consult and critique songs and my priority is to listen to what my clients have paid me to critique. Occasionally I'll get around to listening to others. However, it *is* part of the job of publishers and record companies to listen to them. Give him a card with your photo and Web site address on it. He can remember your face and hear your music on your site.

Meet and talk with as many other writers and artists as possible. Networking with music biz people is very important, but I feel it's equally important to make contact with your fellow writers and musicians. Beyond the obvious focus of finding collaborators and bands to record your songs, it's very important to your *well-being* to *make friends*. You'll find that it's your friends who you can talk to when you're feeling rejected and dejected, people who have been there and understand. It's your friends who you're going to call when you want to celebrate that an artist just recorded your song or that you just finished writing one you're proud of. And you'll be there for them, business or no business. Those aren't the calls you make to the V.P. of A&R at a major label. It'll be your friends who will turn you on to that great new Web site where you can market your songs, or to that great deal on CD duplication, or a lead on a demo producer or that killer bass player.

Whether you're meeting industry people or other musicians and writers, you need to arm yourself with "elevator speech." It's called that because when you get into an elevator you need to maximize your time so you can give someone your pertinent information in about 15 seconds and hopefully have time to get his. Tess Taylor is the queen of networking. She founded two great networking organizations, Los Angeles Music Network (www.lamn.com), which anyone can join, and National Association of Record Industry Professionals (www.narip.com), which only those who have worked in the music industry can join. Her LAMN Sunday brunches where she invites each person to do his "elevator speech" are open to anybody. It allows maybe thirty or forty people to tell their story and hear everyone else's. The ever-gracious Tess will fill in the blanks for someone who forgets to mention a major accomplishment or is being far too modest. She makes sure everybody feels respected. By the time it's over we've all picked out several people with whom we would like to talk further. It's one of the most effective networking strategies I've been part of. Work out and rehearse two or three short speeches without making them sound rehearsed. Think about what you want them to accomplish. "I'm Jim Adams and I'm a singer-songwriter from Chicago. I'm into rock (folk, blues, R&B pop, hip-hop) and I'm here to find a good lyric writer (producer, etc.) to work with. What do you do?" In no time at all you're finding somebody you can get together with later and get a little deeper. So you need to convey a combination of what you do and what you want to accomplish. Always have something ready so you don't waste an opportunity with "Hey, do you think were gonna get some rain?"

Make the most of those events by meeting as many people as possible. They're there to meet you, too.

> Tip: Support the organizations that produce these events with your membership and volunteer time and you'll often be surrounded by opportunities. Organization newsletters frequently provide valuable information about industry events of interest to songwriters. Many of them have free e-mail newsletters for you to subscribe to.

Getting Ready to Face the Industry

Now that you understand how the business operates, you're ready to venture out and start making some contacts. Even when you feel physically prepared, like a soldier going into battle, you need to prepare yourself mentally. No matter which approach you take to get your songs heard and no matter whom you decide to contact, knowing what to expect will give you a lot more confidence. There is a professional way to approach the industry, and the more professionally you present yourself, the more professionally you will be treated.

ETHICS IN THE BIZ

Discussions about ethics in the music business frequently expose a great variety of feelings about it. A business like this that seems so blatant about its powers, pleasures, and extravagance draws many people who are greedy for those most visible things. I always loved that great Hunter S. Thompson quote, "The music business is a cruel and shallow money trench, a long plastic hallway where thieves and pimps run free, and good men die like dogs. There's also a negative side." Now *that's* a cynic! I'm not there yet, but I've come close a time or two.

As a creative industry, it also draws very creative *business* people (for better or worse). Most songwriters and musicians, though they're certainly enticed by the high stakes involved, are much more wrapped up in the music itself and seem to want to keep "The Biz" at a distance. Managers, attorneys, and others on the business end will say, "You shouldn't worry about anything but the music. Leave all the business stuff to us." It's exactly what a lot of musicians want to hear. They'll say, "I don't want to even know about that! Just go ahead and do it!" Both lines are candidates for "famous last words."

I can't count the number of times I've heard musicians and writers say, after a sour business deal, "I should have checked him out before I signed . . ." or "I should have seen an attorney . . ." or "But the vibes really felt right! He told me we'd split the publishing; he'd record masters; he'd get me a record deal; we'd get paid right after the gig; we'd split the advance 50/50 . . ."—and a list of other famous music biz lies. But it wasn't *written* in the contracts.

In many of those cases, I'm sure the businesspeople were quite well intentioned and, at the time, really wanted to do what they promised. (But I'm the kind of guy who'll give anybody the benefit of the doubt at least once.) Others chronically take advantage of people and earn bad reputations. Save yourself a lot of grief by doing some research and talking to others who have dealt with them.

Don't feel obligated to work with the first people who show interest in you. Even when the voice of that poor, trampled part of you says, "Oh, thank you, thank you! I'm *so* glad you like me—show me where to sign." Get a grip on yourself! This may indeed be someone you'll want to work with, but if you go into a deal with that frame of mind, you're begging to be victimized. Calm down, check him out, and don't sign anything without legal advice.

Make sure there's a "performance clause" in the contract. This should state that if the terms of the contract are not fulfilled within X amount of time or in X manner, the contract becomes void. This can quite literally save you years of your creative productivity. Without a performance clause, it's possible for someone to pick up one-year options for five or more years (whatever's in the contract) without doing anything he's supposed to do. Meanwhile, someone else may want to sign you but can't without paying some exorbitant amount of money to buy you out of the deal. According to you, you were ripped off. According to him, he made a good business deal. He recognized good talent, got you to sign, and made some bucks. That's his gig. You may not consider him to be ethical, but you *did* sign the contract.

Remember, they work for you. You don't work for them. Of course, not everyone does business this way. There are lots of straightforward, honest, up-front people in the business who believe that, in the long run, a good reputation will make them more successful than a bad one. No rigid set of ethics governs practices in the music business short of what's actually illegal. Some industry people follow "situational ethics" and follow the credo, "it seemed like the right thing to do at the time." Some subscribe to the basic greed philosophy that "anything goes if it gets me what I want." Others hold the "everybody else is doing it" and "do it unto others before they do it unto you" philosophies. You're likely to run into any of these in *any* business, and the best protection you can have is to get to know enough about the business that you have some idea about whether you're hearing straight talk or jive. If you turn your business over to someone, you should know enough about what he ought to be doing to know whether or not he *is* getting it done.

The type of people you associate with in the industry can have a great effect on your reputation, peace of mind, and creative future. Take it very seriously and find good people to work with. Journalist Paul Lawrence once asked Ken Kravitz of Hit City West recording studio if he felt that "Nice guys finish last." "Maybe nice guys sometimes finish last in the rat race," Ken answered, "but that's not the only race there is."

EGO

Get a grip on your ego and leave it at the door when you go in to show your wares. As you approach industry pros, keep in mind that though your songs may be very personal and expose delicate parts of your being, people in the business must look at them as a *product* or as *content*. They, in turn, must try to sell your product to someone else on the merits of its commercial potential alone. It's understandably difficult for a writer to keep from feeling that it's her who's being rejected, rather than the song. Some of the most powerful songs written are very personal statements and confessional revelations that make the writer's ego vulnerable to destruction when rejected. Don't stop writing those kinds of songs, and don't let your ego get in the way of criticism.

Before you can successfully pitch your songs to the industry, you need to be a good self-critic. Those of you who write songs that you hope will be recorded by other artists will need to be a bit more self-critical than independent artists and bands whose performance and sound are a more important part of the mixture of ingredients that makes for their success. But the quality of your songs is still a major ingredient. There's a point while writing a song where you need to step away from it and try to look at the song as though you were another person—a publisher, a recording artist, a radio program director, or J.Q. Public (see the TAXI feedback sheet in chapter five on page 109). Sometimes, in order to get that perspective, writers put a song away for a few days or weeks so they can later get a fresh look at it. If you're a solo artist or in a band, sometimes an important part of the process is to play the song live a few times.

Ask yourself the same questions that, consciously or unconsciously, others will ask. Is this a song about an event or feeling that many people can relate to? Will the people who most likely relate to the lyric be in a certain age group? Will the music appeal to the same age group? Can the lyrics be understood by everyone? Is there a better, more powerful, more graphic way to say what I've said? Is every line of the song important? Is this a song that can compete with the best songs that I hear on the radio (not the worst songs)?

Doing this kind of self-critique will help you in important ways. It will help you write better songs. It will help you choose from among your songs the ones most commercially viable and therefore the least subject to rejection. It will help you develop that professional detachment to look at your own work more objectively, like someone who makes omelets or clothes or anything else. In accomplishing that, you'll find it easier to approach buyers and to welcome their positive and negative comments. They, in turn, will find it easier to work with you.

Play your songs for friends before approaching the buyers. Even if they can't or won't give you honest criticism, it gives you some instant perspective. I've written songs I was perfectly happy with until I read the lyric or sang the song to someone else and it suddenly sounded trite or unclear. Back to the drawing board!

Get a critique from a music industry professional. This is the next level up from your friends' feedback, and more valuable. A critique from a music industry professional can actually tell you why your song is or isn't working and what you can do to improve it. There are many songwriting coaches and consultants like me who do this for a living and take pride in giving supportive, honest and constructive feedback. Be careful, though, of accepting critiques from those who might have an agenda to sell you recording services by telling you your song is ready to market and it just needs an expensive demo. It's a good idea to learn all you can about improving your song before spending that demo money. Songwriting organizations that offer critique sessions are also a good resource as are a few online sites that offer peer critiques like www.broadjam.com and www.lyricalline.com.

Put yourself in the industry professionals' shoes. It also helps in dealing with rejection if you can sympathize with the publisher or producer's side of the business. It does neither of you any good if he publishes a song he's not enthusiastic about or sees little commercial potential in. He'll have to invest in promoting it and put up with your continued questions about what he's done with your song. He'll have to keep telling you nothing's happened or avoid taking your calls altogether. So if he can't get really excited about your song as a product, he *has* to reject it.

You shouldn't want someone to publish your song unless she's very enthusiastic about it. When *she* gets rejections on your song, you want her to retain enough enthusiasm for the song to continue to pitch it. Several publishers have told me that they had songs in their catalogue that had been rejected over a hundred times! In spite of that, they continued pitching them because they totally believed in those songs.

Sometimes songs or styles are simply ahead of their time. In the late 1970s, for instance, it was common for Los Angeles writers (the Eagles, for example) to get rejections because their "country" songs were "too country" for L.A. and "too pop" for Nashville. There have been black artists whose songs were too rock for R&B airplay (like Prince). Who in Nashville could have predicted Big & Rich? Times and radio formats change but sometimes not until a previously unclassifiable artist becomes a major money-maker.

There are more reasons why you're more likely to be in the wrong place at the wrong time with the wrong song than vice versa. Probably 99 percent of those reasons have nothing to do with you personally, but with the marketplace, your product, and the buyer's ability and inclination to deal with it. Actors say it's like auditioning—"Sorry, you're too: tall/short/ethnic/blonde/etc." and generally, "You just don't have the 'look' we need."

It's a certainty that no matter how good your songs are, they *will* be rejected. If you don't adopt some attitudes that help you to deal with that rejection, you can get too discouraged to persevere, and if you quit, nobody's hurt but you. There will always be more writers out there to take your place.

J. Michael Dolan, co-founder of *Music Connection* magazine, put it in perspective in his inspirational book *Mastering Show Biz . . . From the Heart: 10 Timeless Principles*:

It's common knowledge that rejection is a regular occurrence in Show Biz but that's the risk you take when you hang a "for sale" sign on your talent—you risk no one wanting to buy it. The payoff, however, is worth the risk. The payoff is the world's benefiting from the actions of your Creative Spirit.

Dealing With Rejection

It might comfort you to know that, at all levels, a substantial part of what happens in the music industry involves rejection—rejection of songs, rejection of finished master recordings that people have sunk thousands of dollars into, rejection of record company product by radio stations, and, ultimately, rejection of individual records or styles by consumers.

Every day, for hundreds of different reasons, people in every facet of the industry are facing rejection. They may accept it as inevitable—an everyday occurrence, but it is never easy for anyone to deal with. Egos are bent, reputations are questioned, jobs are lost, and friendships are damaged or ended. There are hundreds of rejection stories of major songs and artists. Elton John was turned down by twenty-two record companies. The Beatles and Billy Joel were each turned down early in their careers by every major record company. Mariah Carey was paid millions of dollars to *leave* her label after a failed film and album but she came back big time. The list goes on and on and continues today. I would venture to say that every major artist has been rejected numerous times before attaining any success. In fact, even after an artist is successful and subsequently goes through an unproductive period, he may again face those rejections. There's even an industry joke about being fortunate to be turned down by certain record execs, because they've rejected so many successful artists that you should worry if they *like you.*

For songwriters it's particularly difficult, though, because you're usually creating in isolation, and it's difficult to find good critical feedback. Often your only artistic validation comes from friends and family who are so excited that you're doing something *they* don't have the talent for that the last thing they' want is to criticize your efforts. They'll be supportive and keep you in that bubble until you smash up against the "real world" of the music business. Songs that your friends liked because they saw you reflected in them (and they like you), songs that audiences seemed to like ("They clapped, didn't they?") are meeting with "Sorry, not strong enough," "not appropriate," "no hook," and other standard lines.

There *are* some ways that you can deal with rejection that will keep you from totally losing your self-esteem.

Cultivate a support group. Yes, there is life outside the music business. Sometimes you can get in a rut, take the whole thing far too seriously, and fail to take comfort in your family and friends who love you whether you're successful in a music career or not. Cultivate friends outside the music business so you can tap into some other worlds and keep yourself from getting too isolated and tunnel-visioned. That cross-fertilization of experiences and ideas is also creatively stimulating. It also helps to hang out with other songwriters who understand what you're going through and can help you get back up when you're down. Stay away from those who will trivialize even your smallest successes or surround you with that "ain't the biz awful" vibe. You don't need negativity.

Develop short-term payoffs. It usually takes a very long time for anything to happen in the music business. So that big reward—the recording, the record deal, the hit, the royalty check, the film score—that's somewhere in the unseen future isn't always enough to make you feel like a valuable human being today. Yes, you should be able to get that by just writing a good song and feeling good about it. But after you've written the song, you're likely to set another goal for it that requires the validation of others and a dependence on a timetable and circumstances you don't have much control over. So it helps to be actively involved in hobbies, sports, another job, volunteering for a cause, or even something as mundane as cleaning the garage or organizing your CDs that gives you a sense of accomplishment and immediate positive payoff.

Don't let rejection stop you from writing. There's a particular song you keep pitching and it keeps getting turned down. You've already rewritten it twice. You're now so totally obsessed with getting it published or produced that you stop writing altogether. A little self-destructive voice inside you says, "This is the best thing I've ever done. If I can't get anything happening with this one, I might as well hang it up because if they don't like this, they won't like anything." So you stop writing "just 'til I get this one cut." Meanwhile, you're forgetting several important things. The next song you write may be much better than this one, or at least more interesting to the industry. You won't become a better writer, or a more successful writer, unless you continue writing. A song you haven't written yet may be just the song that gets everybody interested in everything else you've done. Just the process of writing can make you feel good about yourself. If you're also a performer, work on getting some more gigs. Doing a great show will give you some instant gratification.

Stay healthy. A depressed body begets a depressed mind. There's nothing like a decent diet and a good physical workout to help you get rid of those pent-up frustrations.

Only the "yes" is important. There is an old line that salesmen use to keep themselves going in the face of rejection: It's only another "no" on the way to "yes." The "no"s aren't important.

Honestly assess your strengths and schedule time. This will help you discipline yourself to work on the areas you could improve. A schedule keeps you looking forward and gives you the feeling that you're actually accomplishing something, no matter how small, to keep you moving ahead.

Have additional plans of attack. If you strike out on one, you're ready to try something else right away and you don't have time to feel sorry for yourself. As i mentioned earlier, my wife, JoAnn, worked for several years in Creative Development at Walt Disney Imagineering, Disney's theme park think tank. A common problem among the designers there was a sort of depression after a big project was completed. The company helped to counteract this by giving them information about the next project so they had something to look forward to after the current project ended. Bands often experience that same "down" after a tour.

In-Person Interviews

We get our strongest impressions of people in person. It's helpful for you to be able to size up the people you do business with, and for them to be able to put a face with a name and a song. That's assuming it's a good song and that you usually make a good impression when you meet people.

Appointments for an in-person audition are usually rare without a referral by someone whose taste (or power) an industy pro respects. But there still seem to be unknown writers who just come into town and are able to meet with several publishers in a day. Their success has a lot to do with self-confidence, personality, and timing. Obviously, your best shot is to be able to call ahead of time and say that you're in town for a short while and give them the name of someone who recommended that you see them. But you should call and try to set up an appointment even without a referral, especially if you have any notable credits. Let them know about your success on the initial call. Be nice to the receptionist, secretary, or assistant. If you don't get an appointment, ask if you can drop off a demo and don't be discouraged. It's a long shot anyway. If you do get an appointment, find out approximately how much time the person can give you so you can prepare accordingly, and remember the following:

Be there on time, or ahead of time! If *he's* late, he'll likely be more accommodating out of guilt. If *you're* late, it puts a heavy psychological burden on you. If you're in a strange town, make sure you get good directions from someone and an idea about how long it'll take to get to your appointment. Allow extra time for emergencies.

If something unexpected comes up and you can't be there on time, *call ahead to let him know*. He may have to cancel and reschedule. Personally, I'm extremely reluctant to reschedule if you've set up a meeting with me and didn't call or show up. It shows me that you don't respect my time.

If possible, bring each song on a separate cassette tape or know the numbers of the songs on your CD. This will save time, because it allows you to change the order of your presentation on the spot. If the person says "Play me a ballad," and your ballad is at the end of your tape, you'll have to do a stop-and-start search for that song while you're saying, "No, that's not it. I think it's just a little further on," and on and on. Or "I think it's the next cut (on the CD)." When you have a limited amount of time available, you want him to spend his time listening to your songs, not waiting while you look for them.

Help him maximize his time with you. Before beginning to play your songs, *tell the person conducting the appointment that he's free to turn off your song and go to the next one whenever he likes*.

Be prepared to give him lyric sheets. This way, he can scan your lyric as he listens.

Take extra copies of everything. That way, if he wants to keep something, you can leave it. Be sure that your name, phone number, e-mail address, Web site URL, and street address are on each CD and lyric sheet.

If you want criticism, ask for it. If not, don't. If he gives it to you, thank him for it whether you agree or not. Don't argue! If he likes something enough to ask for a rewrite and you like the person and are interested in forming a working relationship, tell him you'll try it. Do it and get back to him—*the sooner the better*. If you think there's a chance you won't or can't do it, *don't make any rash promises*. It's better to pleasantly surprise him than to let him remember you as a broken promise.

Thank him for his time. When you leave, thank him and his assistant. *Send a "thank you" card or letter that same week*. You'd be amazed at how rarely this happens.

Getting Heard in a "No-Unsolicited-Material" World

Once you've written that great song or completed your writer/artist masters or demos, you face the prospect of getting heard by the music industry. You take off your creative songwriter hat and put on your marketing hat. For some of you, this is an exciting challenge. For others, it runs a close second to major surgery. Like anything else, though, it gets much less daunting when you have some practical information. Let's start by understanding the barriers you may encounter when trying to get through the doors of the music industry.

Why is it so hard to get through the door?

To be able to deal with this problem effectively, we need look at it from the point of view of the publishers, producers, record company A&R representatives, or managers who are your most prominent "targets." They have two major concerns: finding great talent/songs in the most time- and cost-efficient way possible, and protecting themselves from lawsuits.

In the first case, if they have an open-door policy, most companies are deluged with demos. In fact, even with "no unsolicited material" policies, they're still deluged with solicited demos (those referred by other writers or industry people they respect). The biggest problem for those with open-door policies, particularly producers and record companies looking for songs for specific projects, is that most of the songs they receive are wrong for their needs. Consequently, industry listeners already know that more than 95 percent of their time will be wasted. Pretty bad odds for someone who may have only one or two assistants who can screen demos. By the way, that's exactly why they use TAXI (the independent A&R company at www.taxi.com) as a pre-screening service.

Time is another barrier keeping industry professionals from listening to unsolicited demos. Music publishers who may just be looking for great songs or writer/artists for development will have a broader scope of material they're seeking, and it may take more time to evaluate the songs they receive because they're listening for more than whether the song will work for a current project. They're also looking for writers who have potential for future success whom they can work with and develop.

Is the legal barrier also a formidable door-closer?

Most companies' legal departments advise them against accepting unsolicited material for fear of potential copyright infringement suits. A key factor in determining infringement is proof of "access." In other words, if a copyright infringement suit goes to court, the prosecution has to prove that the accused has had the opportunity to hear the material. Proving that someone at the company has opened the package containing your song is, of course, proof of access. You may wonder why an infringement lawsuit can't result from *solicited* material? It can, but the odds are much lower because industry people already know that most infringement suits are brought by writers who are not seriously pursuing a career as a songwriter. These are referred to as "nuisance suits" in which, on scant evidence and understanding of copyright law, a writer says "I wrote a song called 'I Love You' that contains the line 'I love you more than life itself' and that new hit by Joe Rock contained the same line and I can prove I sent it to his publisher/producer/A&R rep last year so I'm suing you." This is an oversimplification, but not by much. The hitch is that Joe Rock could have heard that line in a song while he was still in the womb and in many other songs thereafter. He didn't have to hear it from a demo in his publisher's office. Since a suit has to be dealt with by the company's legal department, it uses up valuable time and resources.

Is this fear of lawsuits why many companies ask you to have an attorney submit a demo for you?

No. Certainly, your attorney could document very definitely the publisher's "access" to your demo. But most industry pros do not believe that submission of a demo by someone with a law degree guarantees its artistic and commercial quality. Not that there aren't entertainment attorneys whose musical tastes are respected, but it isn't the law degree that ensures it. So why is it that they ask you to do it? After pursuing this question for years and asking a lot of questions of a lot of industry people, I've come to one conclusion: *They want to know that you're serious.* On countless occasions I've heard industry people say things like "I don't accept unsolicited material but if someone is really worth hearing, they'll find a way to get to me or I'll hear about them." This is sort of a "survival of the fittest" philosophy that, like it or not, has some merit. They figure that, if you're serious enough to pay a couple of hundred dollars an hour to have an attorney shop your tape or CD, you're serious enough for them to listen to.

Getting Through the Doors

Showing the industry you're serious is the key. One of the most important things you need to do is research. Become aware of the industry people involved in your style of music. Read the credits on the recordings of your favorite artists—find out who produced them, who wrote and published the songs, what record label released it, and possibly even which record company A&R representative worked with that artist. If the A&R rep's name isn't on the package, call the record company's artist relations department or A&R coordinator and get his name. You can also get the phone and fax numbers of the artist's producer and manager. Also, study the artist in order to "cast" the right song so you can be reasonably confident it will be appropriate (see chapter eleven, "Casting: The Right Song for the Right Artist" on page 221). Whenever possible, try to find out from the artist's producer, manager, or record company if there's a change in the artist's direction. If you're pitching for a new artist, get information from those same sources or find a tip sheet (see "Tip Sheets" on page 277).

Use what you've researched. Now you have the names of companies, producers, managers, and A&R reps who know how to market the artists and groups in your musical style and you're ready to make those industry phone calls.

Here's a hypothetical example: In *Billboard* you see Bonnie Newcomer's name on the charts with a new single. You don't have any of her CDs yet (you'll buy them today) but you've heard her on the radio and think you might have something for her. You've also read an article about her in which she talks about the songs on her new project, where she got them, who wrote them, and about working with her new producers. Though you've seen their names listed as writers under the song title on the chart, you've also noticed other writers' names so you know she's open to "outside" songs. You learn that she's on Hot Stuff Records, so you call Hot Stuff and ask for the A&R coordinator. "Hi! This is so-and-so at This and That Music. Will the same producers be working on Bonnie Newcomer's next album? Do you have a number for their companies? Who's doing A&R on the project?" Get those names down quick. If you ask them to spell it for you, you're already another step away from credibility with them. They figure that if you're the pro you seem to be, you'll already be familiar with the names. Look to directories such as the Music Business Registry's *A&R Registry* to help you out (see "Other Sources" on page 280).

Once you have the name of the A&R person at Hot Stuff or someone in the producers' offices, call him directly and ask about the musical direction of Bonnie's next album and how to go about submitting songs for it. It's a good idea to ask if there's a code you should use on the package. If you can send him an e-mail with links to the songs you want him to hear, ask what you should put in the "subject" line to get it through the spam filter and what e-mail address to use.

All the trade magazines publish special-focus issues that will contain a treasure of information on special-ized areas of the industry. Among them are children's music, classical, heavy metal, alternative, folk, music publishing, Latin, Celtic, and film music. They may focus on cities and countries that are emerging as music centers such as Minneapolis, Seattle, Atlanta, Ireland, and Germany. You'll get information on the movers and shakers in those genres or places, the record labels, publishers, producers, managers, radio stations, booking agents, and artists, along with stories about who signed whom and their career strategies.

Making the Calls

Initiating industry calls is always tough if you're not used to it. But if you realize up front that industry people are deluged by calls from writers and artists who haven't done their homework, you have a distinct advantage if you put in the research time before you call. It lets you call with a certain amount of confidence in your voice. Don't come off as arrogant, but do project confidence. If you can let them know you're serious and have done your research, the "gatekeepers" will be afraid to shut you down too quickly because, for all they know, you may be someone important to their boss. The boss is also more likely to take you seriously. Don't beg for a chance to be heard! This is very unprofessional. Though you may not actually say it, the subtext of your conversation should be, "I have great songs that I know are appropriate for this artist. They deserve to be heard."

Regardless of the "we're not listening" policies and the reasons behind them, most publishers and A&R people still do listen to new songs and artists, but very selectively. They want to weed out the writers who haven't learned anything about how the business works, or the hobbyists with two or three songs who take a quick shot at it, and then retreat. The pros size up a writer and her attitude and presentation, from the first contact, and then decide whether to spend time listening or not. They know that even with all of a writer or artist's positive attributes, the odds are still minimal that they'll find something they can publish or an artist they can sign with genius-level talent. That's why it's important to them to set up a tough screening process.

MAKE FRIENDS WITH THE "GATEKEEPERS"

On the front lines of that process are receptionists, secretaries, and assistants. Unless you have the name of a specific person at the company, your phone call won't get past that point. Even if you do have a name, you'll be referred to that person's secretary or assistant. He will say something like, "May I tell her what this is about?" or "He's not in right now. May I help you?" The worst thing you can say is, "Sorry, but you can't help me. I need to talk to the main man." That person's job is to save the main man's (or woman's) time. How you present yourself to a secretary or receptionist may determine whether or not your demo gets heard.

Here's a scenario:

> **Writer:** Hi, I'm a songwriter and I've got a hit for Mariah Carey and another one that would be great for Shania Twain. Actually, I've written over twenty songs. Could somebody there listen to them?
>
> **Receptionist:** Could you please drop off a demo? (You'd be very lucky to get this request.)
>
> **Writer:** No, I won't leave a demo. How do I know you won't steal my songs?
>
> **Receptionist:** Who referred you to us?
>
> **Writer:** I got your name out of the phone book. Could you connect me to the man in charge?

I'm exaggerating here to make a point, but it's not really *that* much of an exaggeration, as any industry gatekeeper would tell you. What do you think are the odds that the caller will get through? An important part of a secretary's (and often a receptionist's) job is to screen out this type of call from songwriters. If she recognizes your name or you've been referred by someone whose name they know and whose reputation she respects, your chances of getting through the door are much better. In other cases, it's pretty much up to her discretion who to accept demos from or whose call to put through to their bosses. Consequently, the first encounter you have with the front desk is vital. If you present yourself as a rank amateur, she'll assume your writing is just as amateur and that their chances of finding a great song from you are zilch.

Every secretary or receptionist has his own criteria for figuring the odds in favor of the boss. Let's look at the call again. Only an amateur who has done no research will be ignorant of the fact that Mariah Carey and Shania Twain aren't likely to do outside songs. If you've written only twenty songs, you're obviously a beginner. You can't be on the scene long and not know you're going to have to leave demos. Get them protected first so you won't have to worry about songs being stolen (though that's a *very* remote possibility). You also haven't done your research if you don't have the name of a person at the company and have to resort to the phone book for the company name. If you don't know the name of "the man in charge" you just might be insulting the *woman* in charge. Do your homework (see "Reading Your Road Map: Researching the Music Industry" on page 273).

I asked the receptionist at a major publishing company how she screens unsolicited calls. She said she tells writers that the company is not listening to demos now. If they ask when the company will be listening (and they seldom ask), she tells them to call back in a month. If she *does* get a call back from that writer, she accepts his or her demo. It shows her that writer is persistent, professional, and organized enough to follow up the call. She figures you're serious!

I've gained a lot of insight into this process by going from being a struggling songwriter to the other side of the desk as a screener. It's taught me some important lessons that have been pretty much corroborated by my "other side of the desk" peers.

We always respect persistence, even though we may at times find it annoying and guilt-provoking. We know that no matter how talented you are, you need persistence to succeed. The hardest part of being persistent is continuing to be pleasant about it and not allowing yourself to become bitter or desperate from the rejection you'll experience. It turns people off when they sense that desperation in you.

A secretary I talked with said, "It's a real turn-off to have someone spill her guts out to me that this is her last chance or she needs to pay her doctor bills or whatever. I don't want to subject my boss to that either. It's very unprofessional."

There's also a thin line between confidence and arrogance. We like to feel that you believe in yourself and are confident about your talent and abilities even though you're open to criticism and direction. If you come off as arrogant with the attitude, "I'm God's gift to the music world and if you can't recognize it, you're a Neanderthal," it will be difficult for you to find people to work with you.

No matter whom you're trying to reach, be nice to assistants and secretaries. Treat them with respect. There's a better than average chance that they *are* the ones who will initially be listening to your demo. In fact, you may acknowledge that possibility ahead of time by asking for *their* opinion on your songs. Also, by the next time you call, *she* may be the boss and the relationship you developed on the phone gets you into her office. If you're serious enough to want a career as a writer or artist, you need to think years ahead and build bridges now.

Always request permission to submit demos. For the reasons I described earlier, you must get permission to submit your demo. It's always preferable do this by phone, but you won't have much time to "sell" yourself. You can attempt to e-mail a request but the chances of it getting caught in their spam filter along with hundreds of others make it pretty much a futile gesture.

FOLLOW UP!

If you do get through the door, consider it a great accomplishment but only the first of a series. Don't figure that all you have to do now is just wait around for him to call you back and tell you how great your song is. Know that he's very busy and you may have to remind him that he has your demo. Two weeks is an adequate amount of time to follow up once you know he has it. That doesn't necessarily mean he should have listened to it in that time. He may have hundreds of CDs to hear, and listening to them is not a *major* part of his job in most cases. Don't get upset and demand your demo back. He'll be only too glad to get rid of it. Leaving a demo somewhere indefinitely means, at worst, you lose the small cost of the CD. At best, a producer or publisher goes through a box of demos in a couple of years, finds yours and calls you. Don't think it hasn't happened. Obviously you can save a lot of that time and trouble by asking if you can e-mail a link to your Web site or to specific songs at a site where he can stream or download them. (If you do, ask what you should put in the "subject" line that will get you through the spam filter). For those who would rather send a CD or have been requested to send one, here is how you follow up:

After calling to make sure she has received it, always ask her to give you a date or timeframe to check back. You might say, "Look, I know you're busy and I don't want to make a pest of myself so I'd appreciate it if you could give me some guideline about when to check back." Make sure you get a name, so when you do call back you don't feel like a pest because you can say, "_____ suggested I call back in a couple of weeks." Don't be shy about calling back several times. Nobody in the music business will ever fault you for persistence. Though it will be frustrating, don't let it affect your professional attitude on the phone.

Stay in touch. "The squeaky wheel gets the grease" is a cliché that remains true. When someone calls me looking for a singer for a project "right now," if I have no time to research and get to my lists and you're a good singer I know whom I just talked to a couple days ago, your name will jump out of my mouth. If I haven't heard from you in a year, it won't. The lesson here is that no matter how positively someone has responded to you and your music, never assume that she will remember you and what you're doing if you don't remind her periodically. Putting her on your e-mail list every time you get a gig isn't quite the same. It really gets to be "Oh, it's *that* band again." He knows it's a mass mailing and unless he's really into you already, it's just one more spam message. That's why snail-mail still works. Once e-mails were unusual; now they're not.

Say "thank you." If someone (a boss or gatekeeper) has given you his time, advice, or help in any way, take the time to drop him a "thank you" card. It's another positive way to make contact, to acknowledge the value of his contribution, and to let him know that you're appreciative, organized, and taking care of business. If you knew how seldom it's done, you'd realize what an impact it has. Yes, you could e-mail him—and that's appreciated too—but a card . . . That shows some class!

OTHER AVENUES

If you plan to pitch your songs directly to record companies, managers, producers, and artists, you're acting as a publisher. You'll get through their doors easier if you have your own company, logo, and letterhead. Don't choose a name for your company that reflects your own (JoJac for Joe Jackson), or it will be obvious to them that you're a "hip-pocket" publisher (a writer only representing your own material) rather than a company who has invested in a writer it believes in. Yes, I know you believe in yourself, but it doesn't give you that business edge here. If you decide to pitch your songs to publishers, don't send it on your publishing company letterhead. They'll wonder why another publisher is sending *them* a song (see chapter eleven, "Self-Publishing" on page 217).

You *can* send your letterhead packages to record companies, producers, and managers. The manager should not be overlooked since, as "captain" of the artist's team, he is usually very close to the decision process on selection of songs, direction of the artist, and choice of producers and may not be as deluged as record company A&R reps and producers.

Make sure you keep a demo and lyric sheets with you at all times. You never know when you'll get an unexpected opportunity to give it to someone. That someone could be the artist's hairdresser, limo driver, recording engineer, road manager, touring musician, friend, or anyone else who has access to the artist or the artist's official team. You can even offer them a sales incentive of a percentage of the income on whatever song any of those people are responsible for helping you place (see chapter eleven, "Negotiating" on page 226).

Always remember that this is a "people" business. As in most other businesses, maintaining your personal relationships, networking for new contacts, taking advantage of your memberships in organizations that can put you in touch with the industry, doing favors for your colleagues, researching the trade magazines, and being ready immediately to take advantage of opportunities are all things that will contribute to your success.

Survival

Getting through the door involves continuously and consistently making contacts and being able to support yourself while you're doing it. If you're a writer who isn't working as a performer, don't assume you'll be making it "any day now" and borrow from friends and family to survive until your big break comes.

Get a day job so you can spend your evenings writing with others who have day jobs, and attend industry events, workshops, and clubs. And just as important, get a day job so you'll be able to afford to eat and pay rent, and to embark on a songwriting career. You'll need money for demos and other songwriting expenses, as well.

Try to get a job in some aspect of the industry. It's tough because everyone else wants those jobs, too. Don't be afraid or too proud to start on the bottom rung. If you have good typing or other office skills, get work with temporary employment agencies that specialize in the entertainment industry.

In Dan Kimpel's insightful book, Networking in the Music Business (see the bibliography on page 392), he offers:

Six Ways To Get A Job In The Music Business

1. Be an intern for a label.

2. Develop computer skills; you'll find your employee potential is greatly enhanced.

3. Apply for a mailroom position.

4. Meet promotional representatives from the labels on the local and regional level who can provide a bridge to their companies.

5. Write articles about bands for magazines and newspapers in your area. You'll meet the publicity department, and they'll soon have clips of your writing.

6. Promotional jobs at record labels have a high turnover rate. If you're optimistic, energetic, and great on the phone, apply to this department.

I'll add another one: If you're cyber-savvy, there's a lot of work for you. Companies look for people who can contribute to their online marketing plans, Web site design or maintenance, and research. Members of *Film Music* magazine's Film Music Network (www.filmmusicworld.com), and Tess Taylor's Los Angeles Music Network (www.lamn.com) often get announcements about music industry intern jobs.

Also, volunteer! Do volunteer work for songwriter or other industry organizations that put you in action centers where you can keep in touch with what's going on. Volunteer to work in recording studios in exchange for studio time. If you're a dedicated, hard-working volunteer for a music company or songwriter organization, when a paid position comes up, you just might be considered first because the boss already knows you and likes your work. Whether you get a job in the industry or not, the security of a regular paycheck will keep you from desperation and taking the first deal that comes along. There's definitely an advantage to negotiating a deal knowing that you don't need the money.

The Options of an Out-of-Towner

The best advice if you're serious about a career as a songwriter is to move to a major music center: New York, Nashville, or Los Angeles. The next best advice is to move to a not-so-major but active music center. Periodically, places like Austin, Seattle, Minneapolis/St. Paul, Boston, Chicago, and San Francisco get a burst of heat when a local act or two break nationally. Even when they're not hot, these cities seem to support a thriving live music community. The recording scenes there tend to evolve around local producers and studios that have spawned successful acts. The area may also have a characteristic music style based on what those particular producers have had success with. Obviously, you need to find out who those producers are and get their attention if you migrate to or live in one of those areas.

I have a philosophy about what takes place to bring music industry attention to a city. Networking and mutual support between local bands will always bring more industry attention to a scene than competition between bands. I've noticed through the years that the scenes that always seem to explode are ones whose musicians share their contacts and resources and help to promote each other. What is at work there from an industry standpoint is record companies seeing a cluster of activity. Somebody makes an industry contact and maybe that A&R rep, for example, is interested in a band, comes out from Los Angeles to check the band out, and the band he came to see says "You gotta see my friend's band, they're great!" What begins to happen (assuming the other band is good, too) is that the A&R rep starts to feel the "buzz," the energy in the place, and says to himself and his company, "Hey, there's a real 'scene' here and we'd better get on it because this place is going to explode. There's a bunch of great bands here and if we don't sign somebody here, everybody else is going to hear about it too and start signing them." Seattle in the late 1980s and early 1990s was a scene like that in great part due to the wisdom and community building of Sub Pop Records in Seattle who nurtured Nirvana, Soundgarden, and other bands. When bands have a "small town" mentality of competition, it signals that there's not enough success to spread around to everybody and they need to keep information to themselves or they'll lose an advantage. It's deadly!

Hasn't the Internet made music and finding music and networking a global situation?

Yes, it has. So is it still an advantage to live in a music town? Yes and it's an unprecedented time to network and market online. But here's the difference. I live in Los Angeles and in just the past week there have been two occasions when I've run into music industry people I know in my local Whole Foods Market. We got to talk longer there than we ever did on the phone. That happens to me in Nashville at the Pancake Pantry or Noshville, two popular restaurants where musicians hang out. That's the real beauty of it, but I realize that not everyone can do that.

If you stay in your own town, find out if there are any local recording studios, producers, publishers, booking agents, radio programmers, or DJs. Make it a point to meet them and let them know what you're doing. Aside from specific programs that feature local talent, the radio people won't give you airplay unless you have a record deal (exceptions: college stations, Web radio, and public radio stations). But they may refer you to local record promoters who will, in turn, refer you to the record companies they represent. This is a good way to network from your local scene to industry people in the major recording centers. If you're not a performer, have a hot local act record your demos and pitch them to the above. If your musical style is at odds with the local focus, give it a shot anyway. You may be the breath of fresh air they've been looking for. If not, start packing your bags for a reconnaissance trip to greener pastures.

"But," you say, "I have a good day job, a wife (or husband), and five kids, so relocating is not exactly a practical solution. What's the next best thing?" Actually, joining TAXI (www.taxi.com) and establishing a good Web site is the *next* best thing (see "Your Home on the Web" on page 310).

But it's still important to try to make personal contact, too. Try a vacation trip first. Do some online research, use the resources provided here, or get some information from your local songwriters association, if you have one. Write, call, or e-mail some publishers at your destination. If you're a member of ASCAP or BMI and you're going to a city where they have an office, try to set up an appointment for when you'll be in town (see "In-Person Interviews" on page 289). If you can't accomplish that, at least get their permission to send them some songs. Publishing staffs are down to bare bones these days so it may be difficult. If there's someone who can refer you, that's always an advantage. Send them links to your songs so they can hear something first at their leisure (if they have any left). The point in trying to meet with them is that they'll remember you better when you contact them from home later. Those solid, in-person contacts will make it much easier to continue your long-distance relationship.

Another thing that works for you as an out-of-towner is that industry people seem to be more accommodating if you call ahead and say you'll be in town for only a few days and would like to schedule an appointment. They may be impressed by your commitment to make the trip.

Over the years, I've seen many writers set up long-term business relationships with industry people in this way. On the other hand, I've also seen in-towners get complacent and not nurture those relationships because they feel as though they can do it any time. Hit country writer Steve Seskin ("Don't Laugh at Me") lives in the San Francisco area. I asked him once how he managed to succeed in Nashville when everybody says you have to live there to make it work. He said he went there often enough and made sure he saw lots of people when he was there that after a while he figured people thought he actually lived there. Let's face it, no matter where you are, it's all down to how much you want success and how persistent you are about working for it.

Marketing Your Lyrics

The situation for lyricists in the marketplace has its positives and negatives. On the plus side, it's necessary for you to collaborate to have a suitable melody for your words. I know that doesn't really sound like a plus, but if you're a prolific lyricist, finding several collaborators represents an opportunity to produce a great number of finished songs. Those who insist on writing both lyrics and music, in my experience, are rarely so prolific. As a lyricist, you can develop your lyric skills in a variety of styles without needing to restrict yourself for marketing purposes, as many writer/performers do.

On the minus side, it's very difficult for you to get a staff-writing deal. You really have to be an extraordinary lyricist with some commercial success under your belt to get an exclusive staff-writing situation. And it's virtually impossible to make a single-song deal on a lyric with no melody. There are audio-visual firms that commission lyricists to write material for them. Check with local firms to see what their needs are, and find additional contacts listed in *Songwriter's Market*.

So, outside of that, what can a lyricist do? Find collaborators. Along with the methods listed in chapter seven (chapter seven, "Collaboration" on page 132), pay particular attention to political strategy. Find co-writers who are further ahead in their careers than you and still moving forward. Among collaborators to consider are new bands that are getting some industry attention or at least drawing great audiences locally. Good lead singers and keyboard players are usually worth considering because they're more likely to write exciting melodies that may need equally exciting lyrics. Find other writers who are starting to get their songs recorded or those who are already on staff at a publishing company. Find writers in strong positions to make contacts with artists, such as studio musicians and recording engineers. With all the above you have the advantage of writing with people who could get good demos made at a reasonable cost—a big plus for you.

If those situations are just not available to you, look for skilled musicians in bands, college music departments, churches, theaters, and other logical places.

If you speak another language fluently, gather samples of your song translations from, and into, the language. Contact publishers both here and in the countries where the language is spoken. They can be found in directories like *Songwriter's Market* and *Billboard International Buyer's Guide*. The Spanish-speaking market, for example, is enormous. I have a client who's written several English lyrics for a wonderful South American composer.

Make contact with as many potential co-writers as possible and enter lyric writing contests. *American Songwriter* magazine (www.americansongwriter.com) has a lyric contest every two months and they publish the winners in the magazine. Put notices in music stores, schools, and magazines and music Web sites. I'm proud to be a mentor for Just Plain Folks (www.jpfolks.com), is a major online music community with over 50,000 members. It's free to join. They have a songwriters' forum where members can post notices that they're looking for collaborators and post a sample of their lyrics. Let everyone know what you're looking for, and you'll find that your opportunities will grow quickly.

Caution: Do not send your lyrics to companies that advertise for "song poems" and ask you to pay a fee to have them write melodies to your lyrics (see chapter eight, "Avoiding the Songsharks" on page 165).

Organize Your Song Shopping

If you plan to actively "plug" your own songs, it's important to keep track of what's going on. You'll want to be as professional as the successful music publishers who are out there pitching their writers' songs to some of your same contacts (see chapter eleven, "Successful Pitching Strategies" on page 224 and "Casting: The Right Song for the Right Artist" on page 221). You'll need to develop a list of producers and recording artists for whom your songs may be appropriate. Keep a good database. Print a hard copy file on everything in case you forget to back up your computer and lose your database. Every time you make contact, you can note who he's producing, what type of material he needs for the upcoming LP, where he's recording, what kind of demos he prefers, whether he usually asks for a percentage of publishing, and so on. If you're also shopping for publishers, keep a similar file for them.

Here are good computer programs available for keeping track of songs, writers, contacts, casting, contracts, forms, and more. Go to their Web sites and check them out in detail. The inefficiency of file card systems doesn't quite make sense anymore when computers can run software that gives you the kind of comprehensive control over your business that these programs do.

SONGTRACKER

Working Solutionz Software
111 Main St. • Simi Valley, CA 93065

Tel: (805) 522-2170 • Fax: (805) 527-7787

www.bizbasics.net • E-mail: sales@bizbasics.net

The original, started in 1975 and still going strong. SongTracker 3.0 manages the business side of your songwriting or music-industry company with an economical and easy-to-use office database system, designed in FileMaker Pro 6 (version 8 in the works) for Macintosh (OSX compatible) and Windows. SongTracker is a comprehensive contact manager that automates and prepares copyrights, ASCAP/BMI registration forms, DAT/CD/cassette inserts, contracts, songplugging correspondence, and more. Digital sounds may easily be stored or played with a mouse click. An optional "PRO" version offers your network of coworkers a set of sophisticated management/tracking modules for the contract, licensing, administration, and royalty aspects of your publishing or record company needs. Over 130 reports provide powerful music industry information. SongTracker 3.0 is $249; SongTracker PRO 3.0 is $798.

MUSIC PUBLISHER

YEAH! Solutions
P.O. Box 163507 • Austin, TX 78716

Tel: (512) 347-9324 or (800) 593-9324 • Fax: (512) 347-9325

www.yeahsolutions.com

The high-end Music Publisher software suite is for Windows only. It has features for A&R, business affairs, copyright, licensing, royalties, and sub-publishing, all for approximately $2,000 (with support packages it would be about $3,000).

THE MUSIC REVIEW

Network Marketing, Inc.

P.O. Box 41635 • Nashville, TN 37204-1635

Tel: (615) 599-5793

www.musreview.com/musicdata.html

"The Music Industry Search Engine." If you want to promote your CD project, here's a series of databases that that you can download to your system. They say they update daily. Radio Station Data Base has over 15,000 stations for $139.95; Distributors has 1,500 plus distributors for $79.95; Retailers, Book Stores is $89.95; Booking Agents has 2,000 plus listings for $79.95; and access to All Data Bases is $269.95. Explore this site. It's good for research.

SETTING UP YOUR DATABASE

Your database should have plenty of information on artists, producers, managers, and collaborators—whatever will help you to better work for them, pitch to them, or write for them.

The information you keep on an artist should include vocal range, what style he or she prefers, and personal idiosyncrasies like "hates sexist songs" or "positive lyrics only." This information can be obtained from the producer, consumer and trade magazines, tip sheets, radio and TV interviews, or, if you're one of the more fortunate ones, from the artist personally.

It's smart to keep a record in the "notes" field of your database of personal items about the producer (or anyone else), such as "plays golf," "anti-nuke activist," "just had a baby," "going to England in August," and so forth. This type of information is useful in all businesses where personal contact is important. It allows you an instant recap when you call someone or set up a meeting. It gives you an idea for opening a conversation to break the ice, and it lets him know that you're concerned about him as a person. It doesn't take the place of having good songs, though, since many producers have little time for "small talk" and are best served by a brief presentation of your material. However, it can create a better climate for you to get feedback on your songs and help you develop as both a writer and publisher.

After every meeting or phone call, make notes regarding the outcome. Write things like "Loved 'Don't Take That Away,' doesn't feel it's right for (artist's name) but wants to keep demo for future reference—remind him," "Didn't like 'Do It Again' but maybe if the hook were stronger, rewrite," or "Will be producing (artist's name) in September—start writing."

Set up file folders. (Yes, it *is* a good idea to keep hard copies, even if you have a database that you back up frequently.) Include the name of each song you're working on, one song per folder (alphabetical by title, if you have several songs). Each folder will contain:

- **The lyric sheets and lead sheets for that song.** If you keep your rough drafts and rewrites, mark them accordingly, so you don't send out the unfinished versions by mistake!

- **The names, phone numbers, and addresses of each co-writer** on that song *and* their performing rights affiliation (BMI, ASCAP, or SESAC).

- **The names, addresses, and phone numbers of any co-publishers on that song for reference.**

- **Photocopies or printouts of any correspondence that pertain to that song.** If a letter you receive mentions more than one of your songs, make a photocopy for each respective file.

- **Photocopies or printouts of any contracts or legal documents that pertain to that song,** for example, a co-writer's agreement, a co-publisher's agreement, or an assignment of copyright agreement. You don't want any unpleasant surprises looming over your future about anyone who has ties to your song without your knowledge.

- **The copyright registration certificate** (or the letter saying you've sent for it), or any forms from other song protection services.

- **The performing rights clearance forms** (BMI, ASCAP, or SESAC) and any correspondence with them.

- **Any correspondence or forms from the Harry Fox Agency** or other agency collecting your mechanical royalties (or reports from the record company about these).

The value of these files will become apparent after you've called about thirty producers and are preparing for another call or visit when you discover you can't remember whether it was producer X or Y who already "passed" on the song you want to present.

Aside from the obvious value in being able to keep track of what you have or haven't done with a song, this organizational process is psychologically valuable in helping you view your songs as products in the marketplace. It takes a little of the edge off rejection by keeping you constantly involved in pitching your songs to many industry people on an ongoing basis.

Keep your CD copies well labeled with the song titles on each. Once more, don't forget to put your name, address, and phone number on the CD, the insert, and your lyric sheets. Have everything ready so you don't need to delay if someone asks you for a copy.

It's also a good idea to keep a small notebook with you (or a PDA handheld such as Palm Pilot, Handspring, or BlackBerry) at all times so you can jot down any info you pick up "on the street." The notebook is better than little scraps of paper or matchbook covers because they don't get lost. The street information you pick up is usually about who's recording now, a new producer with an unknown act who might give you the opportunity to get in on the ground floor, or a valuable Web site or service.

Showcasing

Performing your own songs on live showcases, either alone or with a band, is yet another way to expose them for various purposes:

1. For feedback from an audience.

2. For other songwriters as a way to network and find collaborators.

3. To audition for record companies or other industry people (producers, managers, publishers).

4. To audition for booking agents and club owners to get live performing gigs.

Most cities, regardless how small, have a club where you can play a few original songs. Though most professional club gigs require that you play predominantly contemporary hits or standards, depending on the audience, you can usually get by with throwing in a few of your own over the course of an evening. This is a good way to gauge audience reaction to your songs. You don't always get it right away, but after they hear them a few times, you'll see which ones start to get requests.

In most big cities there are "writers' nights" somewhere that are fairly loose. They are informal gatherings where you just show up and play, or organized events that you may have to audition for in advance. Talk to whoever's in charge of organizing the talent and get the real story so you don't sign up late and end up showcasing for two drunks and a bartender at 3 A.M.

If money is tight for you, you may have to weigh the value of taking part in these showcases. You will rarely, if ever, be paid for writers' night showcases. Occasionally, a club owner might split part of the admissions collected at the door with the performers, but don't count on it. If you're in a working band and you have to give up a paying gig somewhere to showcase without pay, you're going to want some assurance that someone will be listening who will be worth showcasing for. If you do it just for fun and performing experience, that may be enough. The deciding factor is the degree of benefit you get out of it.

Established, well-publicized showcases in major music centers that regularly draw industry people are always worth playing at (and attending regularly, even if you don't play). Networking is the most important benefit of these showcases. You not only have a chance to meet and be heard by industry pros, but meeting, hearing, and being heard by other writers and artists can lead to an amazing number of career opportunities. For example:

- Someone likes the way you sing and wants you to play on a demo or master session—or you want her to play on yours.

- Someone likes your songs, lyrics, or music and wants you to collaborate with him—or vice versa.

- You make new friends and become part of a mutual support group.

- You find out about resources, organizations, and services that can further your career.

- You get the gossip about local artists' recording sessions and other projects needing material.

- You are inspired and motivated by being around other creative people who are being inspired and motivated.

The more people you meet, the more possibilities can open up for you. One person introduces you to a few more who, in turn, introduce you to others. All these contacts increase your odds of finding whatever you're looking for.

If you're auditioning for record companies, it's imperative that you perform primarily original material. A&R people are not interested in the way you play the hits unless you do them in a totally unique way. If you're working a "cover" gig, make sure to check with the owner to see if you can throw in a set of predominantly originals to play when you know the company reps will be there. Make sure the companies know what time you'll be doing your original set. Hopefully by then, you'll have developed a snail-mail or e-mail list of appropriate music industry people who should be invited.

Get flyers printed. If you're working a regular gig at the club, try to get the owner to help pay for them (good luck!). Tell him you'll distribute them. Note that fliers on telephone poles, trees, and windshields are *not* effective. Hand them out in person along with a CD with a couple of songs on it. Hopefully, you're working at a club that has a mailing list or e-list. (If not, try to get the club owner to put one together by having his patrons sign a list.) Better yet, don't depend on the club owner. Take your own sign-up sheet and post someone at the door with it. Another option is to put a card at each table for people to write their e-mail address and comments. Before your set ends, ask them to sign your list—make sure they print! Send an e-mail notice when you're playing there again. E-mail lists are golden!

Consultant and author Tim Sweeney (www.tsamusic.com) suggests that you have a rubber stamp made with your Web site address on it. Give it to the doorperson at the club to use (instead of the one he usually uses) to stamp people's hands as they enter. It reminds people to check out your Web site once they get home.

15 WAYS TO MAKE YOUR SHOWCASE A SUCCESS

If you're doing a one-shot, one-night showcase at a club you haven't played before:

1. **Make sure your appearance is listed on their mailer, or e-list, if the club has one.** If it's a regularly scheduled "showcase night" that promotes itself generically it may not mention specific acts.

2. **Check with the people who run the showcase for any tips that will help you come off well in their club.** Remember, they've seen lots of acts win or lose in their place, and that perspective can be very valuable to you.

3. **If you have a band, make sure the stage is big enough.** It must be able to accommodate your instruments, amps, etc., with enough room for whatever stage movement you need to show yourself to best advantage. If there isn't enough room, look for another club.

4. **If there is a house PA system, talk to whoever runs it.** Generally, if you have a sound person you work with regularly and the house system is adequate, it's better for him to work with the club's sound person to get the best sound out of the room. If the club's sound system isn't adequate and you bring in your own, the procedure is riskier. Your sound person should be someone who can tailor the sound output to the acoustic properties of the room with the right EQ (treble/bass adjustments) and speaker placement, and who is willing to accept advice from the club's sound person. I've seen some good groups empty the house because they wouldn't listen to advice and played too loudly for the room. Volume must be tailored according to the size and shape of the room and whether the walls are reflective or absorbent. If you're doing a record company showcase, being able to hear clean vocals is important, so start there and mix around it.

5. **Make sure you have a sound check.** This will help you work out all the problems and set your instrument levels.

6. **Show up on time for sound checks and performances**.

7. **Make sure the lighting is adequate.** Will someone be running the lights? Make sure he's aware of any lighting cues you might need. Write them down.

8. **See if they have a place to display your photos.**

9. **Know ahead of time exactly how much time you can have for your set and stick to it.**

10. **If you need a piano, make sure it's in tune.**

11. **Be cooperative with everyone at the club,** including the waitresses. It's the difference between your coming back to the club or not, and between having the employees tell everyone to come and see you or telling everyone you're losers.

12. **Talk with the owner about guest lists and guest policies beforehand.** This way you'll know what arrangements to make for them. This will avoid a bad scene at the door involving guests whom you want to be in a receptive state of mind toward your group.

13. **Dress with some conscious thought about how you look individually or as a group on stage.** No matter what you decide to wear, make it a calculated choice rather than looking like you didn't give it any thought. You want to be visually memorable.

14. **Plan your sets carefully, considering the length of the set, pacing, and where you should place your strongest material.** Generally, if you have a potential hit single, or other very commercial material, begin and end with it. If you're going to be the last set, put strong material at the beginning of your performance. Record people frequently have other places to go and are in a hurry to leave. If you play a couple of less commercial tunes to open with and think you'll "finish strong," you'll find that when you hit your blockbuster your guests have already gone.

15. **Make sure all information concerning the showcase is conveyed to the *whole* group.**

If you're auditioning for a club gig, most of the above list will also apply, but here are some additional questions to ask that will help you tailor your performance to the needs of the club: What does the club owner want—classic rock and R&B, all Top 40 stuff, Top 40 with some originals? Who will be in the club's audience—under 18, a singles' bar drinking crowd?

Pick a club that wants the kind of music you enjoy playing or you're wasting your time. The audience won't like you and the gig will get old very fast. The attitude "we'll make them dig what we do" is admirably ambitious but chances are the owner knows the audience better than you do unless you're bringing your own fans.

ONLINE DIY BOOKING AND MANAGEMENT SERVICES AND SOFTWARE

The best online booking service I know of is through Onlinegigs (www.onlinegigs.com). This software offers support, tips, advice, and directories of clubs, colleges, and music events, As well as automated Web updates, press releases, contracts, riders, and itinerary planning. Onlinegigs is totally professional.

Also excellent and very affordable is Charlie Cheney's Indie Band Manager (www.indiebandmanager.com). The software runs on Macintosh or Windows and costs $39.95. The PRO version costs $199.95.

Contests

Contests provide songwriters, singers, and bands with an opportunity for validation and acknowledgment of their talent—as well as an opportunity to win prizes.

Contests are created for many different reasons, and it's important to be able to assess whether or not you're wasting your money to submit material at all. Most contests are created to make money, though there are always contests that spring up for other reasons, for example, to find a theme song for an organization or a city. There have been several competitions for a new national anthem, for instance. Many non-profit songwriting and music organizations use competitions to raise operating funds. These contests are usually open to writers from all over the world.

The loftier reason, aside from making money, is to find and expose new talent. Seldom do contests translate *directly* into commercially successful record deals or hit songs. But there is a wide range of potential benefits, depending on the scope of the contest.

The long-defunct American Song Festival and Music City Song Festivals offered great benefits for songwriters by virtue of their judging procedures. Not only were the song entries heard by many judges, but judges could turn in the code numbers of songs they particularly liked, and after the contest was over, they would be provided with lists of the writers they requested along with their addresses and phone numbers so the judges could request additional material on their own. This benefit helped open a lot of doors for many writers to establish ongoing relationships with the music publisher and producer judges. Today's contests do the same. I judge several and have referred many of my favorite songs to other industry folks. My favorites, by the way, aren't always the winners.

Beyond prizes and validation, the contest winners also received publicity for winning—something that also helped open doors. This could, in turn, be included in query letters or e-mails to industry professionals requesting permission to send CDs.

SUBMISSION PROCEDURES

Each competition will give you its own submission requirements on the entry form. Most contests now have downloadable forms, but the following are common to all.

An entry form must accompany each song submitted in each category. (This applies only if there is more than one category.) Be sure to fill out each form completely as though it were the only one submitted. In nearly all cases, it is acceptable to make copies of the original form. To save yourself some work, fill out the basic name/address/phone information on the original before making the copies so all you have to add is song titles, writers (if different), and categories.

A fee is required for each entry submitted in **each category.** (This is not true for the Just Plain Folks contest, which is free). Fees range up to $30 per song per category. Entry fees are certainly justifiable. It is not cheap to promote and organize a contest of any kind. Advertising is expensive and necessary despite the luxury of free online promotion. Contest producers have discovered that it's not enough just to announce that the deadlines are rolling around and assume that those songwriters who entered last year will automatically enter again. Each year they have to go after a whole new group of writers because last year's entrants who didn't at least receive an honorable mention are likely to believe that, if someone didn't recognize their hit, the contest is a rip-off and the judges don't know anything. The last thing they'll allow themselves to believe is that their song just wasn't good enough.

In addition to advertising, contests must hire people to process entries, book, coordinate and supervise judges and judging sessions, keep financial records, answer phone inquiries, and many other tasks. In some cases, judges are also paid.

Some critics have actually advised writers not to pay a fee for submission to contests, particularly if they get a critique because "you should never pay for a critique." Nonsense! That philosophy originated as a way to protect writers from songsharks who would ask a writer to pay a small fee for a critique, then give her song a rave review as a way to set her up for a publishing contract for which they would unscrupulously ask for an additional fee.

A lyric sheet is usually requested to speed the judging process. A judge can listen to and judge a song by listening to a verse and chorus of the song while scanning the remainder of the lyric. Lyric sheets should always look as professional as possible and be neatly typed with sections (verse/chorus/bridge) separated so the judge can clearly see the song's structure.

RULES AND REGULATIONS

Some competitions request that your name not appear on the tape/CD or lyric sheet to avoid the possibility of favoritism should the judge recognize the name of a writer. It is especially important, in those cases, for the writer or performer to completely fill out the submission form so that the person initially processing the tape can code the submission form, the lyric sheet and tape/CD. Don't be too concerned about it, though. If you don't eliminate your name, the contest employees will black it out themselves. In fact, it's always a good idea to have a proper copyright notice (© year, copyright owner) on each lyric sheet no matter where you send it or for what purpose.

STYLISTIC CATEGORIES

Amateur songwriters often have difficulty distinguishing pop from R&B or rock, country from folk, etc. They either enter the same songs in several categories just to be safe, or risk entering one song in an inappropriate category and having it eliminated, not because it's not a quality song but because of a poor category choice. The best approach is to play it safe by entering more than one category, if you can afford it, after getting as much feedback as you can from fellow writers and friends on the most appropriate category.

Some of the criteria to consider in making the choice of songs to enter involve a process of elimination, which is involved in the judging as well. So it may be instructive to come from the viewpoint of a judge who knows that certain factors will preclude a song being a winner even though it may receive an honorable mention. Here are a few:

1. A song without a chorus
2. The title doesn't appear in the chorus or first or last line of the verse
3. Clichéd lyrics
4. Little or no melodic contrast between verses, chorus, and bridge

(See the TAXI feedback sheet in chapter five on page 109.)

While the previous factors will immediately eliminate a song from competition, a well-produced demo will enhance its chances of staying in the race. Though most song contests will ask judges to focus on the song itself, production can't help at least subliminally affecting a judge's decision, particularly with styles like R&B, hip-hop, straight ahead rock, and up-tempo pop/rock. This doesn't always mean spending $1,000 in a state-of-the-art studio. A good sounding demo recorded on a digital audio workstation (DAW) can be more than adequate. But make sure you have a great singer. There's no other factor more important other than the song itself. Don't sing it yourself if you're not the best singer for it.

PRIZES

You will partially base your decision whether or not to enter a competition on the lure of the money, hardware, software, and memberships offered to winners. Customarily, a grand prize is awarded to an overall winner and first, second, third and more prizes awarded in each stylistic category. In addition, honorable mention certificates may be awarded to songs that judges felt deserved special consideration but didn't make the finals.

CAUTIONS

A history of take-the-money-and-run contests makes it important to be on the lookout for some distinguishing factors that help you recognize the legitimate ones. Here are some things to look for:

1. If a contest has been in operation for more than a year, they should be willing to provide you with a list of previous winners.

2. If they offer you merchandise prizes, they should be able to prove to you that they have purchased them or, with an affidavit from the manufacturer, that the merchandise has been donated. Note: Most manufacturers no longer directly donate equipment, but they may work in conjunction with a local or online music store to make it available to the contest in consideration of publicity. Don't worry too much about this one, though. Contests that have been around for a while can't handle the bad PR generated on the Internet by winners who were denied their prizes.

3. If the contest offers a cash prize, they should be able to offer proof that the money is in an escrow account that may only be distributed to winners. A common downfall of contests is to promise prize money with the honest hope that money received from entries will exceed the prize amount by enough to cover all expenses and profit. This is a very risky gamble because it is expensive to get enough publicity to ensure *that* many entries, and once a contest fails to provide prizes on time, its reputation has been destroyed. It's the same as not having merchandise prizes—bad Internet PR.

4. The individuals responsible for the contest should be listed in the advertising or on a Web site, and there should be an e-mail address, street address, and phone number where they can be reached.

5. The contest officers, owners, representatives, judges, and their families should be ineligible to enter the contest.

6. Prize schedules and amounts, entry deadlines, and deadlines for notification of winners and awarding of prizes should be clearly listed on the application and the contest's Web site. If a deadline becomes impossible to meet, a pre-determined process for notifying contestants should be implemented. New deadlines must be clearly stated.

7. Judges of the contest should ideally be music industry professionals with proven experience in judging and critiquing songs and in a position to further your career. There are also many peer-judged contests online and you just have to decide if it's worth it for you. The Compo-10 International Song Contest (http://compo10.com) is a good example, but in that case it's free.

8. Don't enter contests in which your entry becomes the property of the contest. Look for a phrase that specifically says that it doesn't. However, the contest should have the right to play the song,

print it, or use your name and photo for promotional purposes. Your career benefits directly from that publicity and is one of the unstated "prizes" for a winner.

There is another caution related to ownership of your entry or winning song. Every year there are at least two or three people who want to get into the music publishing business and think that a great new way to find songs and finance their businesses is to have a contest and offer the winner a publishing contract. Sometimes they'll form a record company and their first recording artist will sing your song. Savvy writers don't enter these contests for two main reasons:

a. If you believe in the commercial potential of your songs, the worst "prize" you can imagine is that your song will be owned by an inexperienced and unconnected new publisher whose only means of financing a company and finding songs is to hold a contest.

b. Legitimate publishers never charge you to screen your songs. It is part of the business of a music publisher to find material and convince the writer that he can represent your song better than anyone else. So to set himself up as someone who you "automatically" would want to publish your songs, without a track record or connections, is arrogant, to say the least. Frankly, under certain circumstances there may be writers who should not even sign with well-established *major publishers* because, in their individual circumstances, it may not be in their best interest.

FINDING CONTESTS

Sonicbids

Sonicbids (www.sonicbids.com) has become the submission vehicle of choice for not only contest entries but festivals and conferences in which bands audition to be showcased. Sonicbids is a reputable and very effective service and online music community with forums in which members can share personal stories about the relative merits of festivals and contests (among many other topics). Their core product is the EPK (Electronic Press Kit) that's like a mini Web site that contains some of your digitized songs, lyrics, photos, bio, videos, press reviews, set list, contract requirements, and gig calendar. You can send it anywhere with one click. It's one of the best values on the Web. Use it to enter most contests. My first judging experience with it was the ROCKRGRL magazine contest (www.rockrgrl.com). It's very easy to judge with the EPK. There are too many other features to list, but check it out.

The Muse's Muse

Founded by Jodi Krangle, The Muse's Muse (www.musesmuse.com) is the pioneer of the songwriters community resource site and songwriters e-mail newsletter. At the Muse's Muse Web site you can get a list of all the contests with comments and info on each. She also encloses info on at least one in each newsletter.

Songwriter's Market

Songwriter's Market has a complete section of contest listings with details about submission requirements and prizes. The book is available in major bookstores or online.

There are new contests being created on a regular basis. It's difficult to keep up with and futile to try to list them all, but periodically check the above sites, and join them, in the case of Sonicbids, or subscribe to the free newsletters. Also, use your online search engine to search "song contests."

Among the established and reputable contests are:

Billboard Song Contest (www.billboard.com/songcontest)

The Great American Song Contest (www.greatamericansong.com)

International Songwriting Competition (www.songwritingcompetition.com)

The John Lennon Songwriting Contest (www.jlsc.com)

Just Plain Folks Music Awards (members only, but membership and contest are free) (www.jpfolks.com)

Mid-Atlantic Song Contest (www.crosstownarts.com/saw/masc.asp)

SongPrize.com International Songwriting Competition (www.songprize.com)

Unisong International Songwriting Contest (www.unisong.com)

The U.S.A. Songwriting Competition (www.songwriting.net)

Your Home on the Web

In the second edition, I explained some pros and cons to creating a Web site for yourself, particularly if you're a songwriter and not promoting yourself as an artist. My, how quickly times change! Now that list of cons is *very* short. There's only one downside you need to consider. It involves your commitment to writing and promoting yourself. You may be a hobbyist and are perfectly happy just writing songs for yourself and your friends and have no ambition whatsoever to go beyond that simple pleasure. No problem. The downside is that unless your other hobby is building and maintaining a Web site, it may be way too much trouble and you'll spend a lot of time feeling guilty for not updating it. If you already have enough guilt in your life, just leave it alone.

For me, I always understood the value of it but my wife and friends had to keep pestering me for way too long to actually make the commitment. Also, that was a few years ago when there weren't nearly as many user-friendly tools available. Since I made that commitment though, I don't know what I'd do without it.

I'm not going to get very deep into this here because it's so much a part of the culture now that it's impossible to go online or to any bookstore and *not* find a wealth of material on how to build and maintain a Web site and use it to promote yourself and your music.

But I will give you a list of ways you can use your Web site to help you as a songwriter, just in case I can push you over the fence on this.

You put your Web site on your business card and you can direct people to your site. When they say, "Oh, you're a songwriter? I'd like to hear some of your songs," they can just go there, listen, and read your bio. No burning CDs for them, no need to spend time getting together to play them some songs—unless you *want* to.

If you're a lyric writer looking for a collaborator you can post some lyrics on your site. This allows potential collaborators can see them. Tell them what you're looking for stylistically and list your favorite artists.

Ask your singers to add a link from their sites to yours. This is only necessary if you have great singers doing your demos. Generating more interested traffic to your site will expand your contacts and maybe interest someone in recording your songs or collaborating.

A Web site can create an incentive to write. If you need deadlines to give you a push, promise to have a new song posted on your site every week or every other week. Failure will produce incredible pangs of guilt, which, depending on your upbringing, can be a great motivator.

Artists will be able to find you from all over the world. So if you have songs that are interesting, unusual, or commercially viable (or not) on your site, they can be found by artists looking for material or looking to use them in special compilations. For example, I know three songwriters who have written songs about dogs that have attracted dog-loving artists and just plain dog lovers who want to buy them, do CD compilations to offer as premiums for dog food companies and on and on. Check out my friend Freebo's site (www.freebo.com) and you'll find his CD *Dog People*. Or search for "dog songs" online and see how many sites you turn up. See what I mean? Search engines can find whatever interesting topics you write about for people who are looking for that topic.

If you compose instrumental music and can describe it on your site in terms of style, mood, and instrumentation, it will give anyone looking for it with those terms an opportunity to find it. It's important to place those descriptions near the top of your homepage so search engines that scan that page can find it.

Can I accomplish the same things without committing to a Web site of my own?

Yes; there are many online services that that offer a Web site-like presence within the host site like MySpace.com (www.myspace.com) and Indie911 (www.indie911.com), but ultimately it's like a hotel where you always like to stay when you're in another town. It's okay, but you're just putting some of your stuff there temporarily, and you have to accommodate to *their* layout and it's not quite home. Your own Web site is your home, and you can make it look however you want. You can change the furniture whenever you want. Like your home, it's a representation of who *you* are, reflecting your unique personality. There are other sites like Broadjam (www.broadjam.com) that are very helpful in networking with other musicians, but your profile and music are only available to other Broadjam members unless you specifically send someone there.

COSTS AND MAINTENANCE

It'll cost about $15 per year at www.directnic.com to register your URL (Web address). If you're good at graphic design, and want to invest in the software to build it yourself, go for it. Otherwise, you'll need to hire someone to build and maintain the site. If you're good at learning from manuals, you can, without a lot of difficulty, learn to write HTML (HyperText Markup Language) and maintain your own site. There are software programs like Macromedia's Dreamweaver and others that will make it fairly easy for you to design and maintain your site. There are many others that will help you buy pre-fab kinds of sites with a choice of their graphics.

The least expensive are ones that come combined with hosting, which you'll need to pay for regardless. That means they maintain the servers, the computers where your information lives and is routed to and from. You can get hosting services for under $10 per month on up. The cost factors are based on how much computer memory you'll consume and how much activity you generate. It depends on how many pages, the amount of graphics and audio files you want (both big memory hogs), how many e-mail accounts and how much activity (how many people will be visiting your site).

Another factor to consider is customer service. If there's a problem, you need to know if somebody will be there to call 24/7 when your server goes down.

Before you decide to give it up though, here are a couple of complete design and hosting services specifically for songwriters and musicians that might just put you over the edge when you see how easy they are and how much they offer. There are many more, but I can vouch for these.

Hostbaby (www.hostbaby.com) Yet another great service of CD Baby's Derek Sivers, programmer extraordinaire. Some of my favorite artists are using this.

ASCAP Web Tools (www.ascapwebtools.com) Your Web page is provided by Nimbit from $11 to $19 per month, depending on how many services you need. For ASCAP members only. Good reports by users.

THE HARD WORK PART

This involves periodically updating your Web site, uploading samples of your songs and lyrics and any personal info you want to add, and to the extent it's important to you, promoting it by actively linking to other compatible sites and making sure it's searchable by all the search engines.

Just because you build it doesn't mean anyone will automatically want to visit. It just doesn't work that way. Most of the people who will visit are those you'll personally send to it unless you have the time to invest in a promotional campaign to let people know you're there, and to have a good enough experience to make them want to come back.

To make it more interesting, whenever you post a new song, write a piece to go with it explaining why and how you wrote it. Make it a kind of songwriter's diary or blog (Web log) where you talk about what's going on in your life, what you do to promote your songs, and what songs of other writers you like. My favorite sites of songwriters contain this kind of diary information.

If you're a writer/artist or band, there are many more benefits.

1. Fans can keep track of when and where you're performing.

2. You can post samples of your recordings, interviews, both text and audio, video clips, photos of the band in action, and bios of band members.

3. You can communicate with your fans via e-mail through your Web site. Send mailings to your entire list about upcoming gigs and news of your accomplishments. This communication could be one of your biggest assets in building your fan base.

4. You can sell your records and merchandise (t-shirts, etc.) through an online retail section.

5. You can pomote contests and events, and offer free recordings for special fans.

The challenges for artists include all those mentioned above for songwriters. It takes time and hard work to make it pay off for you and take advantage of all the benefits it provides. Regardless of all that, I feel that if you're serious about your career those benefits can more than make up for the work.

I feel it's beyond the scope of this book to get into how to build and promote your Web site, and there are a lot of great books and other Web sites out there that can do the topic much more justice than I could. The technology advances so quickly that the Internet itself becomes the most expedient way to research the latest books and sites about the topic. The changing technology also makes possible new and efficient services to help you market your music, like some of those mentioned in this chapter. Visit my Web site (www.johnbraheny.com) to keep up to date.

There are some new tools that can help considerably with your marketing efforts, whether you're solely a writer or you're a writer/artist: blogging and podcasting.

Blogs

IF YOU CAN WRITE, YOU CAN BLOG

Since my last edition, there's been a major addition to your arsenal of marketing and creative tools. A blog, short for "Web log," is a powerful way to stay in touch with and grow your audience. Undoubtedly, you've been exposed to blogs unless you literally have been living in a cave on an extended radio, television, newspaper, and Internet fast. Hey, I've actually considered doing one myself. The media *can* be overwhelming! So, if you've considered starting a blog, like with the Web site decision, you may need some info to help you decide. Should everyone have a blog? Absolutely not. You may not have any inclination or time to do one. Like a Web site, it does require a commitment. If it's out of the question, just stop reading this part. But if you're wondering if you could do it, here are some things to think about.

The best way to practice your songwriting craft is to write—not just songs, but anything. The beauty of blogging is that you're free to write anything you want, restricted only by what you want it to do. You can make it a diary (for your fans). If you're more of a journalist/researcher/information junkie, then you can provide your songwriting community with resources. You can explore your personal creative process, write about where your ideas come from, post questions you may have about your craft and business and how you go about finding the answers, find online articles about songwriting that you can introduce to your readers—all things that would be of interest to other songwriters. You might also open up for others to dialogue in the way of a "forum." A good example of that is on the Just Plain Folks site (www.jpfolks.com).

So if you can join the dialogue on the forums, why would you want to write a blog? Forums are limited to a dialogue between writers on each forum. From a marketing standpoint you want to increase the traffic to your Web site so you need the visibility you can only get by networking on your own. When you become known as a source of interesting writing and helpful information, you'll draw people to your Web site where they'll find your music or anything else you want to sell them.

In response to her students' and friends' requests for more creativity exercises, my wife, JoAnn, who is a career counselor for artists, developed her own blog called "Goosing Your Muse." It's located on my Web site (www.johnbraheny.com/joann). She loves to write and explore the Internet anyway, and once she started, she found it to be a free and easy method (using minimal tech skills) to provide her audience with up-to-the-minute articles, event announcements, helpful book recommendations, and much more—all on the topic of creativity. The items (or posts) are archived and remain accessible and are totally searchable. Maintaining the blog encourages her to write on a regular basis, plus people get the benefit of a digest.

Douglas E. Welch (www.welchwrite.com), master blogger and podcaster (see "Podcasting" below), writes three blogs around his interests and profession. One is a column on high-tech careers "Career Opportunities: The High-Tech Career Handbook." Another is "My Word," a more personal blog about things he learns, experiences, or thinks about. And "A Gardener's Notebook," compiles info and tips for gardeners. His site is good to explore for the many things that are possible to do with blogs, including his frequent podcasts and micro-movies.

To set up your own blog, go to any of many, many blog hosting sites that will take you through a few easy steps to have you up and running in a very short time.

Here are a couple of excellent sites:

Blogger (www.blogger.com)

TypePad (www.typepad.com)

More info on types of blogs and blog history can be found at http://en.wikipedia.org/wiki/Blogs.

A UNIQUE WAY TO PRESENT YOUR MUSIC AND CONNECT WITH FANS BY DOUG WELCH

Douglas E. Welch is a freelance computer consultant based in Los Angeles, California. He also writes Career Opportunities: The High-Tech Career Handbook, a weekly column now in its 10th year, for ComputorEdge magazine.Douglas was among the first 20 podcasters when podcasting was introduced in September 2004 and his Career Opportunities podcast is approaching its 200th show and 2nd anniversary as of 6/06.

Imagine being able to get your music into the ears of thousands of people who really want to hear it. Imagine being able to engage in a conversation with your fans, no matter where they might be in the world. Imagine creating a radio station where you control the schedule, the playlist and the content. There is no need to imagine any more. Podcasting makes these fantasies a reality . . . today.

Podcasts are best described as niche-based, radio-like shows that are delivered via the Internet rather than over the airwaves. They are delivered as MP3 files which are downloaded directly to a listener's computer, giving them the ability to listen whenever they have the time. They can be created once a day or once a month. They can be downloaded directly from a standard Web site, or listeners can "subscribe" to an RSS feed and receive each new "show" on their computer or MP3 player as soon as it is released. And, like radio shows, they can be about anything from cars to gardening to science. But when it comes to music, they offer a unique opportunity to showcase your talents for a broader audience than the local coffeehouse.

One important note—despite its name, creating or listening to podcasts does not require an Apple iPod. You can use any MP3 player, or listen to podcasts directly on your computer, or burn them to CD.

Despite its recent notoriety, podcasting really isn't anything new. Its constituent parts—the Internet, MP3 audio files, the World Wide Web, portable MP3 players and RSS feeds have been around for quite some time. What is new, though, is the combination of all these parts into an extremely useful whole. This combination allows you to easily distribute your music, or other content, without relying on the traditional middlemen of radio, television, and record companies or waiting for a talent scout or agent to "discover" you.

The Four Podcasting Pieces

There are four basic elements that make up a podcast. Depending on how many of these items you already have at your disposal, you can be delivering your first podcast to the world in just a few hours.

Content: Your content might be music recorded in the studio, live show recordings, interviews with fellow musicians, fully produced radio shows, videos, and more. Anything that can be stored as an MP3 audio file or MPEG video file can be delivered as a podcast. This can be existing content, such as tracks off your latest CD or any other type of content that you can imagine. Creating audio and video content is easy in today's high-tech world. Every PC on the market has the ability to record audio and video. Commercial and free software is readily available to turn your computer into a fully equipped, multi-track recording environment. You can develop the equivalent of your own radio station studio if you wish, but with nothing more than a few CD tracks and an inexpensive microphone, you can get started today. First, you need someplace to hold this content so your listeners can find and download it.

Web Site: A Web site provides a place to store your content and deliver it to your listeners. Most artists and bands today have some form of Web site. Most existing sites can be used for podcasting with only a few small additions. For those that haven't made the leap onto the Web yet, a complete Web hosting arrangement can be arranged for as low as $5 a month from a variety of companies. This cost usually includes the hosting of a domain name, such as johnbraheny.com, as well as providing a large amount of hard disk space to hold your files. Setting up a Web site, either on your own or with the help of knowledgeable friends, is a relatively simple task.

Once you have your content and a place to store it, you are podcasting at the most basic level. Users can visit your Web site, click on a link to the MP3 content, and either download the file to their computer for later listening or play the file from within their Web browser. You might even be doing this today. If you provide songs from your Web site you are already 99 percent of the way to a podcast. To meet the textbook definition of a podcast, though, you need to provide one more element, an RSS feed.

RSS Feed: A Really Simple Syndication (RSS) feed provides the final step in the podcasting process—subscriptions. Using an RSS feed, which is nothing more than a specially formatted text file, your listeners can "subscribe" to your podcast using any number of "podcatching" software programs. This software runs on a listener's computer and regularly checks your RSS feed to see if anything new has been added. If the software finds new content, it automatically downloads the file to their computer and adds it to a list of new shows on their computer or MP3 player. Apple Computer's iTunes software is one example of a podcatcher. Along with all its other functions, it allows listeners to easily locate, subscribe and listen to podcasts on their computer or their iPod music player.

You can create an RSS feed from scratch if you wish, but there are a number of free services that will generate an RSS feed automatically each time you add content to your Web site. One of the simplest methods of adding new podcasting content is by creating a Web log (also called a blog). A Web log allows you to easily add information to your Web site without manually editing HTML Web pages. It also provides the additional benefit of automatically creating the RSS feed files that allow listeners to subscribe to your podcast. This can be done using free services, such as Google's Blogger (www.blogger.com) or using free software such as WordPress (http://wordpress.org/) installed directly on your Web site.

Directories and Promotion

Once your content is accessible, and listeners can subscribe, you only need to let them know that your podcast exists. If you already have a mailing list, you can send out an announcement to get things rolling. Then, you can start listing your podcast in the numerous podcasting directories on the Internet. Podcasting directories are free services that provide a searchable index broken down by genre and description. One of the most important directories is maintained by Apple Computer and is accessible via their free iTunes software (**www.itunes.com**).

Other podcasting directories include:
Podcast Alley (**www.podcastalley.com**)
Podcast Pickle (**www.podcastpickle.com**)
LearnOutLoud.com (**www.learnoutloud.com**)
Yahoo! Podcasts (**http://podcasts.yahoo.com**)

To find more anytime just search for "Podcast directory."

Adding your podcast to a directory is usually as simple as visiting a Web site and completing a form with the appropriate information. This usually includes the name and description of your podcast, the location of your Web site (i.e., www.johnbraheny.com) and RSS feed, and the category where your podcast should be placed. With a minimum of effort you can easily list your new podcast with ten to fifteen different directories in a few hours.

Podcasting is a unique new way to present your music and your thoughts on music to listeners throughout the world. Podcasting can be your journal, your nightclub, your stage or your radio station. Its uses are only limited by your imagination.

What benefits do I receive from fans hitting both current and archived podcasts? Commercials? Sponsorship?

I believe in keeping everything available. Who knows what someone might find interesting from a podcast that is three years old? Why leave the song in a desk drawer if someone might at least stumble upon it on the net? The nature of podcasts is such that the "feed" only contains the last X number of shows, so new subscribers will only see that much, but the older shows will still be locatable via Google and other search engines. Google ads still work even if the content is old. Commercials and sponsorships might have expired, so the advertiser gets a free ad. I think it all comes out in the wash, unless you have an ugly breakup with a particular sponsor and don't want their name on anything.

What kind of promotional opportunity is valuable for sponsors of the band? Can they have a commercial message from the bands sponsor on each podcast or videocast?

Yes. Easily done. "This podcast brought to you by . . . Miller Beer. Live the High Life. millerbeer.com."

Can people steal your tracks or songs? Can you mix the tracks with commentaries under the song so they won't get the whole song without, say, getting directions to the artist's site?

Podcasting is not about stealing. If you put an MP3 out via podcast, every single subscriber has a digital copy forever. **Don't put anything out you don't want circulated.** This isn't streaming. These are real MP3 files traveling the Internet. If you don't want to give away the whole song, play excerpts during a fan podcast, put together a sample compilation of excerpts or something else, but if you aren't playing the whole song, make sure there is plenty of "value add" in the other material. Really, I foresee that you wouldn't be sending out songs raw anyway. There should always be an *intro* explaining if it were a live show and where it took place, and an *outro* how to get to your Web site. It is of the highest importance that every MP3 includes good MP3 tags showing title, artist, etc., with artwork (like you see on my podcasts) and Web site and e-mail addresses included in the comments field. Too many MP3s I see have no identifying information at all. What a waste!

NOTE: MP3 tags are added when you convert your podcast to an MP3 file. If you're using iTunes you're offered an opportunity to fill out info in an ID3 tag containing the fields above so that anyone who receives it can identify it, and you. If you're using a software program that doesn't offer this feature, you can get find one at VersionTracker (**www.versiontracker.com**) or Download.com (**www.download.com**). When you get there, type "ID3 tag" in the search window and you'll find a list with ratings for each. Pick one and download it.

Uses for Podcasts

Doug and I brainstormed a few more uses, most of which are already being used (or should be!).

Writers can feature their own songs. They can also include information about writing them, talk about their bio (just the interesting parts), post interviews, and communicate with fans. Artists can cultivate a more intimate relationship with their fans than ever before. Fans can send back audio feedback and questions, and the band can establish a mailing list or forums that allow interaction between the fans and the band.

Once they've bought your CD, they get access to the bands rehearsal recordings. This may be a recording of the band or an artist actually writing a song as a podcast. It is more work technology-wise, but you can open certain forums or download areas for those fans that have "earned" the privilege by purchasing your CD or other merchandise from your site or sending a receipt from another site.

If you want, you can restrict RSS feeds to just your fans. They must log in by signing your mailing list and getting password access.

Record your world—discussions with your friends about music, life, and philosophy. List your recommend books, movies, and Web sites. Introduce them to other bands by playing their music. It makes your podcasts more multi-dimensional. The more the fans get to know about the artist or band, the more they are likely to follow their music and careers.

Get in the van after gigs and talk about the gigs. Robert Fripp and King Crimson have written fascinating tour diaries on their Web site (**www.dgmlive.com**) for years. You could do it live and actually phone in your podcast. You have to visualize somebody driving to work or school in the morning listening to your podcast about last night's gig, and sharing it with friends. Make your fans part of your life. They are anyway.

Interview fans after shows. Edit for great comments to show others who your audience is. **With videocasts, or Vcasts, videotape parts of your shows** for A&R reps, managers, and fans, who can get regular updates.

Use podcasts to pitch concepts to potential investors in your band or new record label. Post interviews with principals discussing goals and philosophies of the company and play your music, and that of artists you're thinking about signing or have signed.

To see and hear some good examples of songwriting blogs and podcasts go to www.google.com/blogsearch and enter "songwriting."

Podcasting Software

GarageBand (www.apple.com/ilife/garageband): Version 3 (and later editions, I'm sure) has a special setup for podcasting. It's free with new Macs. Or purchase in iLife Suite.

Wiretap Pro (www.ambrosiasw.com/utilities/wiretap/): Ambrosia's program is compatible with Mac OS 10.4+ and is very inexpensive.

Audacity (http://audacity.sourceforge.net): It's free and works with PC, Mac, and Linux.

For more high-end, software check out:

Adobe Audition (www.adobe.com/products/audition): PC only.

Apple Soundtrack Pro (www.apple.com/finalcutstudio/soundtrackpro): Mac only.

Legal Questions About Podcasts

Along with Doug Welch's comments about posting your songs on the Internet, there are some other considerations.

Be careful of using cover songs. You're safe when you use songs for which you own the copyright to both the song and the master recording. However, you need to go through a process of obtaining permissions when you use songs and masters owned by others. For a good breakdown on the steps to get permissions, there's a great description of the process on CD Baby's marketing Web site, "How To Legally Sell Downloads of Cover Songs" (www.cdbaby.net/dd-covers).

At the time of this writing, there are no licenses required for podcasting music you own. ASCAP, BMI and SESAC all require licensing for use of songs and masters owned by anyone else. It is likely in the future that they'll be working out ways to not only track podcasts but to require ratings for sexual content and language. For now, they're still arguing about it and who knows when they'll come to a decision. Check with the Copyright Office, (www.copyright.gov), or Google "podcast legal issues" and make sure the information is current.

If you're doing interviews it's always a good idea to get a release form from them at the time of the interview just to cover yourself for this and future uses.

I posed the following questions for entertainment attorneys, Ben McLane and Steve Winogradsky (www.winogradsky.com) regarding legal issues about Webcasting and podcasting.

Does sending a complete song over the Internet via a podcast or Webcast, posting a song for others to hear/download for free on the writer or artist's site or another site legally constitute "publishing" or only if it's offered for sale?

BM: The general definition of "publishing" is making available for sale or distribution to the public. Primarily, the intent would be for profit but this is not always the case, so I would argue that sending a complete song over the Internet via a podcast or Webcast, or posting a song for others to hear/download for free on the writer or artist's site or another site, would legally constitute being "published" in most cases as these are mediums that are now being recognized and licensed by the performance rights societies."

SW: Does streaming via Webcast constitute distribution, or does distribution require a copy to be made available, as in a podcast that is generally downloaded to a device?

I believe that streaming is distribution under the publishing definition, although see comments below.

Does it constitute a "first use" relative to the compulsory license?

BM: The general definition of "first use" is the first recorded and released version of a new song once it has been "released" to the general public under a valid license or with the permission of the copyright holder.

SW: If the party "X-casting" the recording is the owner, or supplied the recording to the X-caster with that intent, that would qualify as a valid license. See comment to #1, above. I don't think that streaming constitutes a first use under the statute, only downloading or distribution of physical product. So an artist allowing others to stream their music only may reserve their first use rights. But since many podcasts are downloaded, the copyright owner may be waiving first use exclusivity without realizing it. If the artist is not the copyright owner of the composition, he may have violated the owner's rights.

Are there any cautions writers or writer/artists need to be aware of in sending digital files or making them available via link to a site like Broadjam, Garage Band, MySpace or making them available for streaming or downloads from those sites?

BM: To me the purpose of music is to be heard, and this will lead to money-making opportunities if the public reacts positively. Hence, all of the above-named sites are a great place to make one's music available to be heard, as they have high traffic consisting of music lovers. Of course there is always the risk that someone might "steal" or "bootleg" one's music no matter what format or medium it is in, but I think the worries here are minor compared to the promotional value.

SW: Again, if the artist is not the writer, the copyright owner's rights may be violated by not having a mechanical license.

Free Music Marketing Advice and Newsletters

There are some individuals who have distinguished themselves as writers and researchers on indie music marketing techniques, on and off the Internet. This doesn't pretend to be a complete list but these people are those I've found to be helpful resources and they'll turn you on to others.

BOB BAKER, TheBuzzFactor.com (www.bob-baker.com/buzz)

Bob's been a champion of indie marketing since 1995. Interaction with indie artists continues to inform his already considerable knowledge base. He shares it in his free marketing tips ezine, his Indie Music Promotion Blog, *Artist Empowerment Radio* show, many articles on his Web site, and several marketing books. Visit the site.

BOBBY BORG (www.bobbyborg.com)

Bobby is the author of the excellent *The Musician's Handbook* (see Bibliography) and a great teacher. I've co-taught with him and been a guest in his UCLA classes many times. His Web site is full of excellent articles. He also has contributed to the TAXI newsletters and has a forum on his site for Q&A from indie artists.

CHRISTOPHER KNAB (http://musicbizacademy.com/knab)

A Seattle consultant with Four Front Media & Music, prolific journalist, and educator about the music business and indie music marketing, Chris has partnered with Music Biz Academy.com to provide marketing expertise. He also has more than seventy articles on Music Dish (www.musicdish.com), another great source of indie marketing info.

MICHAEL LASKOW (www.taxi.com)

Michael's creation is TAXI—the world's leading independent A&R company. Though I mention TAXI throughout this book because in my opinion they offer the best way for songwriters to get to connect with the industry, I mention them here because their Web site and Michael's free bi-weekly newsletter (no need to join to get it) are packed with great articles, industry interviews, and very helpful marketing tips.

DEREK SIVERS, CD BABY

Pioneer, founder, and main dude at CD Baby, the best distributor of indie CDs and downloads. There are three sites within the CD Baby family: CD sales (www.cdbaby.com); news, views, philosophies, marketing advice, forums (www.cdbaby.org); and lots of valuable advice on marketing on and off the net (www.cdbaby.net). All three are full of great articles. Derek is relentlessly dedicated to providing the best and least expensive services for his members.

PETER SPELLMAN, MUSIC BUSINESS SOLUTIONS (www.mbsolutions.com)

Peter wrote *The Musician's Internet: Online Strategies for Success in the Music Industry* , *The Self-Promoting Musician: Strategies for Independent Music Success*, and several other music business development guides. These guides are used by music entrepreneurs in over twenty countries around the world. Peter is also Director of Career Development at Berklee College of Music in Boston. Get his bi-monthly newsletter, *Music Biz Insight* (www.mbsolutions.com/biz).

BRIAN AUSTIN WHITNEY, JUST PLAIN FOLKS (www.jpfolks.com)

Brian created Just Plain Folks as a community site for writers and writer artists with free membership branches around the world that have their own local meetings. The forums on the site explore a great diversity of topics and offer peer information and support. Brian also seeks out music industry people (like me) as mentors to help him answer members' questions. He sends a free newsletter to all members—about 50,000 by the time this book is released. The annual Music Awards Show turns up phenomenal indie talent.

OMDS (ONLINE MUSIC DISTRIBUTORS) AND MUSIC HOSTS

In March 2006, iTunes sold their billionth legal song download. They hit the halfway mark in July 2005, which gives you some idea of the growth rate of this distribution system. And that's just iTunes. There are more sites being created every day. By the time you read this, online sales may have overtaken the sales figures of brick-and-mortar stores.

As more and more artists want to market their songs as online downloads, more online "stores," or OMDs, are being created. Very few, however, are limited to sales and most provide a great variety of services. They're called "music host" sites. Some of the services are free, and others charge for various levels of services, numbers of songs posted, etc. Among the services are:

- Exposure on multiple Web sites
- Posting various numbers of songs—numbers and fees vary accordingly
- Direct feedback from artists
- Direct promotion to consumers

- Feature articles and front-page features
- Forums
- Events page
- Charts
- Possibility to sell downloads
- Possibility to make CDs
- Possibility to sell CDs
- Posting of music videos
- E-mail on site
  - Streaming on a variety of players
  - Customization with HTML or JavaScript
  - FM radio distribution
  - Podcasting/iPod download

The question naturally arises about how to find out who they are and assess their relative merits and services. There's a great Web site (www.compo10.com/MusicHosts.htm) that's continually updated by the services themselves and the site's proprietor, Compo-10. They provide links to the individual OMDs and music host sites, and a grid that allows you to make comparisons of their services. In addition, they provide an extensive list of music-related Web sites and services. It's the best resource I've found yet—a researchers dream!

SELLING YOUR MUSIC OFFLINE AND ONLINE

The two most popular sites for physical CD sales in the U.S.:

AMAZON.COM www.amazon.com

The popularity of the Amazon.com site for sales of practically everything makes it a customer magnet. Get the info you need about how to get your CD sold there by going to the site and finding their Amazon.com Advantage program for music. There's a $30 charge to set it up, and they take 55 percent.

CD BABY www.cdbaby.net

By far the favorite choice for indie artists is CD Baby. This is the most successful seller of indie CDs due to the personal customer service and dedication of founder Derek Sivers and the wide variety of individual services and marketing information CD Baby makes available to members. There's a $35 setup fee. They take $4 for each sale regardless of what you charge for your CD and pay you weekly. They will also submit your music to a variety of download sales sites and take 9 percent of each sale. Can't beat it. Visit the site to see why.

(See the appendix for a further list of great songwriter's information books and Web sites.)

14 Additional Markets

Though most writers seem to think primarily in terms of commercial radio, your skills can be used in a variety of lucrative ways. Each of these paths requires its own skill-sets, tools, learning curves, income streams, marketing strategies, and legal intricacies. However, the same high degree of creativity, craftsmanship, and perseverance that would serve you in pursuing a hit song or a career as a writer/artist or band will guide your journey into any of these growing markets.

In this chapter, I'll look at a several of those markets. I'll give you a good overview, some specific detail, and words of wisdom from experts, but there are excellent books available to take you much more in-depth in each topic. Check the bibliography for recommended books and visit my Web site (www.johnbraheny.com) for up-to-date articles and resources in all these areas.

Writing for Audio-Visual Media

FILM AND TELEVISION

Film and television, though always important users of music, have become even more important in recent years. The success of TV shows featuring popular contemporary music, and youth market films that spawn million-seller soundtrack albums have combined to leave no doubt among film and television producers of the commercial power of contemporary music. That awareness has prompted them to hire, or contract on a project basis, music coordinators and music supervisors with record company and music publishing experience to make sure they get the best contemporary composers, songwriters, and bands for their projects. The explosion of well-produced and readily available recordings by independent artists has allowed audio-visual production companies to easily license both *synchronization* rights (for the song itself) and *master use* rights (for use of the master recording).

In addition, the proliferation of relatively inexpensive digital video cameras and editing software is fueling a new generation of amateur video producers getting practical experience making independent videos, and all those new filmmakers need music. Whether you start at that level or you feel you're far enough along to start tackling bigger projects, there are some things you'll need to know.

The Craft and Business of Songwriting

Skills

If your goal is to do instrumental scoring and themes, you're ahead of the game if you know how to arrange and orchestrate. It also pays to have a good working knowledge of current synthesizer, MIDI, music composing and sequencing software, and recording technology. If you have a good digital audio workstation (DAW) and know how to use it, as well as some experience working with and recording live musicians, it's a real plus. Sound-design skills are also important. It's an asset to have an arsenal of techniques for combining sounds and coming up with unique stuff nobody's ever heard before. Obviously that takes a sense of adventure, curiosity, and a good imagination, all traits of great film-TV composers. Nobody wants to hear the same old overused sounds. Your knowledge of a variety of musical styles will also work in your favor.

Film and TV composers come from a variety of backgrounds. Some start as rock artists, session musicians, pop music arrangers, or record producers. Some come from classical backgrounds as composers and arrangers. Consequently, they're called on to score certain projects specifically *because* of those backgrounds.

Film and TV producers want a finished product (composed, performed, produced) for as little money as possible. That means that, when you're starting out you'll be competing with other wannabe composers who can (and will) do it for practically nothing. Those who can do it with the least manpower in the fastest time can quote them the best prices. The best paying but most demanding of all the jobs in this area are the weekly TV series, which require technical skill, discipline, and speed. Also important are "people skills." You need to be a good networker to generate work. You'll also need to be a diplomat to be able to work with the egomaniacs and control freaks among the producers and directors who will be hiring you. So your diplomatic skills will be put to good use.

Learning

Colleges and universities with film and television departments offer the best opportunities to learn the craft of scoring because you can get actual experience working with those departments as well as having access to live orchestras and smaller live ensembles. In the major film and TV centers (Los Angeles in particular), there are excellent classes taught by professional film and TV composers, such as at USC and UCLA Extension. On the East Coast, Berklee College of Music has a great course in film scoring. Traditional music schools that emphasize the *art* of composition, while very useful from a musical standpoint, aren't going to get you jobs in scoring film and TV. Academic credits aren't important to those who would hire you. Actual scoring credits are the most important because the skills involved are so specialized. Listen to and analyze great film scores. Get the DVDs and study them.

If you're looking to gain experience with a minimum of pressure, there are also opportunities to score industrial, educational, and student films, as well as local cable shows if you're competent and aggressive. Pursue student film projects by finding your closest college or university film department and posting your credits, skills, and availability on the department bulletin board. For *cable shows,* make a visit to your local cable TV station and find out if you can submit your music for consideration on any local programs that use music on their shows, or new shows being produced that may need themes. They usually use music from "production music libraries" (see "Production Music Libraries" on page 334) but you may be able to prevail on them to let you write something custom-made for them.

Cable "public access" shows are low budget shows created by local entrepreneurs using production interns. They satisfy the cable companies' agreements to provide community access. They're usually the worst produced shows on cable because they're so low budget and really set up to be learning opportunities. Why not use them to help *you* learn?

These days there are throngs of young wannabe filmmakers out there making mostly really bad videos. (They have to start *somewhere*!) It might be a good idea to do some research by going to Web sites that feature amateur and occasionally way better than amateur video producers. Sites like YouTube (www.youtube.com), blinkx (www.blinkx.com), and Brightcove (www.brightcove.com) and video.yahoo.com feature showcases of short videos.

MySpace.com (www.myspace.com) has a section called MySpace Film that's a great place to meet new film and video directors, stream their videos, and contact them about submitting them samples of your work. You might post some low-fi samples on your MySpace site. They also have a "classified" section where composers can advertise their services. If you're a songwriter or band you'll spend most of your time in MySpace at MySpace Music, but you can broaden your reach into the audio-visual world by specifically networking with filmmakers.

You'll find that many are little more than home movies, but occasionally one stands out. Find something you like and contact the director (there's usually a contact e-mail address) and offer to do a score for her next project. There will likely be no money in it, but at the beginning you need to just start working on something for the experience.

Read everything you can find about scoring and stay abreast of technical developments. If you're really serious, you'll join the Film Music Network (www.filmmusicworld.com). They have live Webcasts of their many panels and workshops for members that focus on various aspects of writing for audio-visual media, and a bookstore with some very practical books for those trying to break into the industry. Anyone can tune into their Film Music Radio, podcasts of shows that feature the best in film music and discussions with the composers. If you live in Los Angeles, San Francisco, or New York, you can attend their meetings and network with other members. They also feature job listings for members. Another important organization to join is the Society of Composers & Lyricists (www.thescl.com), which has good educational and networking opportunities.

Finding Work

Hopefully, you will have been able to do enough entry-level projects and do them well enough to have given you a good selection of cues (pieces of music) to put together a professional demo of impeccably recorded pieces.

Your Demo

Your demo should feature film-style music (not jazz or pop *songs*) that feature memorable melodies in a variety of moods and musical styles. Not too cluttered—keep it simple and focused. Show a different aspect of your talent with each one. Not too repetitive. No long loops with nothing interesting going on. No long sections or long intros. Put your best up front. Use live players whenever possible and don't rely *too* much on digital tracks. If you're pitching for a specific project, make sure there is something on the demo that sounds like what they want. (Ask what they're looking for.)

You may also win friends and admirers along the way who will turn you on to yet more lucrative jobs. Those who become successful enough to score several series often hire assistants who are orchestrators, arrangers, copyists, and engineers, so if you have those skills, working for a pro is a great way to get "hands-on" experience. Most professionals work in their own studios and can be found through the TV network on which the show is broadcast. Each show has its own office, so always ask for that specific show.

As soon as you've acquired enough credits to interest a film and TV music agent, you move into another strata where it gets easier to gain access to bigger opportunities, but even then it remains very competitive.

Each of the major film and TV studios has a music executive who is the liaison with music supervisors and film composers. Most prefer to deal with established writers, agents, music publishers, or record companies but "open door" policies exist at some companies. Independent music supervisors and song placement companies who deal with film projects are generally more accessible, but you can't afford not to try them all (see "Presenting Your Songs to Music Supervisors and Song Placement Companies" on page 327).

Reading *Variety* and *The Hollywood Reporter* (see Bibliography) will give you leads on what films are casting, in pre-production, and currently shooting. There are also several tip sheets available for audio-visual productions. Visit their Web sites for full information. Most are for professionals only and list requests for both songs and scores.

> **TuneData/Music Reports** (www.tunedata.com): A division of Breakdown Services, Ltd., n Los Angeles.
>
> **Production Weekly** (www.productionweekly.com): Hollywood and international.
>
> **Mandy's Film and TV Production Directory** (www.mandy.com): Look for "composer" listings under "Post-Production."
>
> **In Hollywood** (www.inhollywood.com):_For the U.S.
>
> **CueSheet** (www.cuesheet.net): U.S. and Europe.
>
> **Television/Film Production Information & Jobs** (www.crimsonuk.com): U.K. listings.

Songs in Film

Songs have always played a role in the success of films—particularly in films directed at the youth market. They've been great vehicles for launching and assisting the careers of many artists going way back to *Blackboard Jungle*'s Bill Haley and His Comets hit "Rock Around the Clock" in 1955. Today film songs and soundtracks are an integral part of the marketing of new artists, and the concept of musical artists as actors with scripts built around their music (e.g., Eminem in 8 *Mile*) is becoming more commonplace for better or worse—mostly worse! However, it underscores (no pun intended) the recognition of the power of the combination of songs in film and the potential marketing value for both.

One of the most common strategies of film producers in obtaining soundtrack songs is to find a major recording artist to sing (or write *and* sing) at least the title song. A hit song in a film can be a major marketing tool for both the record and the film. The album with songs from *Saturday Night Fever* in 1977 was the first film in which the success of the Bee Gees hit "Stayin' Alive" *preceded* the release of the film and drove the marketing of the film. It represented a new marketing paradigm in which filmmakers started to pay more attention to getting hit artists on the charts before the film's release so they could cross-market. Part of what's involved there is for the record company to get to release the soundtrack CD. It can be a lucrative situation, especially if it's a song-oriented soundtrack that can also help introduce some of the label's newer artists.

But several things can go wrong. The artist or record company may reject the offer because they may not feel that the film will help the artist's career, the release schedule of the film may conflict with the release of other products from the artist, or, in the end, the film company can't afford the artist. The film company can be running out of time and budget without finding that major song and major artist to sing it. This opens up possibilities for less established songwriters and bands to get in on the action.

The temp track strategy is a back-door approach that involves presenting your songs to the music editors, producers, and directors of specific films so they can use them as "temp tracks" (i.e., songs temporarily used in scenes to establish a mood or set a dance tempo before making a final decision on songs). If they use a song of yours that has the right tempo, groove, and vibe, they may ultimately want to replace it with a current hit but, in the end, may not be able to negotiate the rights to use the hit in the film and end up using yours.

With the "temp track" approach, after hearing your song used repeatedly, the music editor and director may begin to feel as though it belongs there, and if other strategies fall through you're already in position. Note that more often they will pick the hit as the temp track, and when they realize they can't afford it they'll look for something "kind of like it." The above scenario happens predominantly in mid- to low-budget films. Major big-budget film producers don't like to leave as much to chance and there are so few great film vehicles compared to TV that publishers will even split the copyright to a song with the film company as an investment in what a successful film could generate in royalties. (Tip: It helps to make friends with music editors!)

It's important to be aware that the decision-making politics in filmmaking is, in most cases, extremely erratic. Financial backers, producers, directors, stars, agents, and others vie for decision power. These are most often people with no musical background who "know what they like" or "have a nephew who's a songwriter," a situation that can be both a blessing and a curse. One day you've got a song in a film, the next day it's out. Or vice versa. If your song is good and is perceived that day to be appropriate (or you *are* the nephew), you've got a shot.

There are occasionally opportunities with big budget films to put together compilations of songs "inspired by" the films. These are usually the result of the director receiving too many great songs written for and pitched to the film company often by writers who were sent a script or invited to early screenings of the film to inspire them to write songs for it. All or them wouldn't be appropriate in the end, but they're related enough to the story to form a separate project.

Note also that in these cases and certainly in the case of songs appearing in the film, the film company will want to own the publishing on the song whether or not they actually hired the writer to create it.

If you want to pitch songs for TV, look for TV series that use lots of new, unknown songs. You have the luxury of "researching" while you watch TV since the credits list the production company and music supervisor. Turn on the VCR for the credits since you really need to be a speed-reader to catch them alongside the intros to the next shows. Barring that, just go to the Web site of the show to get the credits. Often, they'll even give you the names of songs and artists.

Indie artists and songs have generated so much interest on those shows that a new Web site named Tunefind.com (www.tunefind.com) is tracking them and listing them under the shows (and films) that feature them. Click on a song and it takes you to the iTunes store where you can play a short clip of the song and learn more about the artist and maybe buy the CD. Your research questions are: What styles of songs or bands does that show tend to use? What kind of lyrics and moods? How are they used?

Much of the focus of the "Craft" part of this book is on creating song dynamics that work primarily live and on audio media. The real beauty of submitting songs for film and TV is that, in most cases, they're used in visual media in a totally different way. Songs play a role that supports the story, provides an emotional and lyrical subtext, and does not have to be constructed to hold a listener's attention for three to four minutes. In most cases, a long piece of a song in a TV series is sixty seconds. It doesn't have to sound like a hit at all. They only use the parts of the song that best serve the scene.

PRESENTING YOUR SONGS TO MUSIC SUPERVISORS AND SONG PLACEMENT COMPANIES

The best resource I can give you is to go to a series of interviews with music supervisors and music editors along with other very valuable information by Skip Adams (www.globalgraffiti.com/EM.htm).

Skip Adams is a music publisher who specializes in custom placement for film and TV at Global Graffiti Music (www.globalgraffiti.com). The following is part of his interview with Madonna Wade-Reed whose music supervision credits include *Boston Public*, *Alias*, and *Smallville*. I especially like her candor in describing what she does.

SA: What, if anything, is different about the process of finding music these days as opposed to when you first started? For instance, everyone knows that the Internet has changed the world, but has it changed your world as a Music Supervisor?

MWR: You know I was asked this question when I did a panel for the Nashville Film Festival. It varies, I'm sure, from supervisor to supervisor, but about the only thing the Internet does for me is if I'm in a big hurry I can send an MP3 of a song to somebody. People send you music sometimes with links, and this is what I said in Nashville, "Do you really want me to hear your song through six little pinholes in my computer? You want your song heard?" It does no writer any justice to have his music heard over a computer. Yes, it can give somebody a hint of what he wants, but then he's asking me to listen twice, when I might only have to listen once.

I have my seven rules of submitting music. I have a list. I type it and I keep it right here by my computer, because when I'm in a big rush and someone calls and wants to submit music, I forget stuff, but I've learned over the years exactly what I need to receive in order to consider someone's music.

SA: **Would you mind sharing it with the readers?**

MWR: Sure, it's short.
1. **Use a proper CD case**. I hate envelopes. I don't like clamshells. I don't like slim cases because when you put them on a shelf, you will never find them again, which leads into . . .
2. **Label your spine.** If you want us to find it on the shelf among all the other CDs, that is.
3. **Put your track list on the jewel case cover**, not just on the CD, because once I put the CD into the machine to listen to it, and I like a song, I only know it by a track number if you haven't given me a track list. Very annoying.
4. **Put your contact information on the cover and the sticky label.** I've gotten many CDs with no contact information. We can't license your song if we don't know whom to contact.
5. **If you have co-writers, give me writing and publishing information.** Do you control your publishing, or does someone else control it? I have an hour to clear a song. So, I need to know this information.
6. **Same with the master.** Who owns it? Who controls it? How do we reach them?
7. **Don't call us. We'll call you.**

I say this last one with the greatest amount of sympathy. Chances are, if you called and asked me my address, and I've given it to you, then I'm getting your CD. If I stopped and spoke to every person who called to follow-up, which is the right thing to do—it's a real catch-22. Jennifer and I each must get about fifty packages a day. How are we going to talk to everyone who sent something? Nobody who calls just wants to hear me say, "Yes, I got the package"; they want to talk about it. If you've put your contact information on the CD and we like it, we'll call you and say, "We really like this. Do you have more songs? Can I pitch it? Would you license it for this fee because I'm in a bind? This is how much money I have, and how much time I have to clear it." It's the hardest part of my job, the submissions.

There are music supervisors who are hired by TV series and as well as independents who are hired for individual films and made-for-TV movies. Major film production companies have in-house film music executives who may hire supervisors for individual films.

In searching for songs for their productions, filmmakers and television producers and directors rely heavily on music supervisors for a variety of creative and business duties. They work very closely with the directors and music editors to determine the kinds of songs and instrumental music segments they need for each show and prepare music budget estimates based on choices such as whether the show needs mostly underscore, mostly songs, or a combination.

For an ongoing TV series it becomes a pretty well oiled machine once the overall preferences of the director and the musical tone of the show are set. Though it's always subject to changes based on new characters and situations, the communication process gets ironed out quickly as their frame of references get ironed out. ("Is this what you mean by an 'emo' artist? This is what *I* call hard rock. What artists do *you* mean when you say 'Alternative'?") For each episode the script is presented as soon as possible and it's decided with the music editor where songs or specific kinds of music need to be used. At that point the supervisor will start looking for the right music for those scenes. Time is critical and the supervisor may have only twenty-four to forty-eight hours to find the right songs and "clear" them because a weekly production schedule is a grueling process.

Clearance is the term for negotiating with the copyright owners for the use of the composition and use of the master recording. Once that process is finished, the music editor mixes the music into the soundtrack.

The music supervisor has a database and a library of songs/artists/bands in various styles both on CD and online that she can quickly access. She also has to review new songs and bands that are sent to her by song placement companies, music publishers and others, like TAXI Dispatch, whom she trusts to send her appropriate material. She needs to deal with as few people as possible because time is so tight, making it tough for individual writers and bands to get through to them. So songwriters and bands often find it a better option to pitch their music to intermediaries such as placement companies and music libraries who can pitch and negotiate quickly and knowledgably on their behalf because they usually have long-standing relationships with music supervisors.

Film and TV song placement companies and music libraries often operate within the same company but function in different ways. They both operate as "feeder systems" (for lack of a better word) for music supervisors. They are trusted sources of good quality and appropriate material to fit the needs of the project. The supervisor sends them an e-mail describing what she needs, usually with a scene description that contains information about style, mood, tempo, type of voice, instrumentation, and anything else that's relevant. Placement and library reps respond as soon as possible with a link to the music on an online site or to a specific track on an actual CD library of theirs that she may already have. With her own in-house database, CDs, or online access to music provided by production music libraries, as well as her own memory of songs or artists the supervisor may have used in the past, she may also find something quickly on her own.

The next important job is to clear the material. The supervisor has to obtain two licenses: a *synchronization* (a.k.a. *synch*) license for the use of the "underlying work" (the song or music itself) and a *"master use"* license to use the master recording. It's common practice today, particularly in series TV where a quick turnaround is necessary, to use a license that combines them both.

If the project needs a song that's been a hit in which the copyright owner and artist are different, they need to obtain the synch and master use licenses from different holders. Let's say they wanted to use Ray Charles singing "Georgia on My Mind." They'd have to go to writers' Hoagy Carmichael and Stuart Gorrell's publisher, peermusic, which owns the publishing, to get the synch license. It would have to be negotiated because film/TV is a "derivative use" (see chapter nine, "Where Your Money Comes From" on page 169). Then they'd have to go to Ray Charles' record company to negotiate permission to use the master recording. Both of those fees may add up to a considerable amount of money. In some cases, particularly with a song that's used frequently, the publisher and record company might get together ahead of time and agree on terms for various uses so the publisher could grant both licenses, making it easier to facilitate a quick clearance

The sometimes time-consuming difficulty of clearing those past hit songs has its own set of problems for feature films and made-for-TV movies, but there's more lead time. In series television, the need for speed has actually opened the door for indie bands and artists who own their own copyrights and are free to quickly grant those combination licenses.

Film and TV music placement companies specialize in representing the songs of artists and bands who own their own songs and masters. Writer/artist/bands give the placement companies permission to represent them in negotiating licenses with music supervisors. The placement companies establish relationships with the supervisors that allow both parties to negotiate the licenses quickly. Since it makes the supervisor's job easier, she's more likely to use the music the companies represent. Most placement companies take 30–40 percent of the synch and master use fees paid for placements, and some take part or all of the publishing ownership. Deals can vary considerably from company to company.

How You Get Paid and What You Can Earn

The pay in film and TV ranges from ridiculously bad to incredibly good based, as usual, on your bargaining power and the budgets of the projects. Your bargaining power for film comes from your talent, skill, speed, and past credits.

For pre-existing songs, synchronization licenses are granted to the film or television production company by the copyright owner (publisher) and are totally negotiable. But usually film producers want to own the publishing rights to your song unless they can't afford to pay you a good up-front synch fee.

For songs or score written specifically for the project, they want it to be a "work for hire" so they'll own it outright. Either way, you'll probably get a creative fee, retain 50 percent of the performance royalties from airplay, 50 percent of the mechanicals if it gets into a soundtrack album, and hopefully writer credit on screen.

For TV, the biggest income comes from themes and scores for series that play every week, or even better, every night. You'll receive performance royalties from BMI or ASCAP every time they're shown. You'll hope the shows go into syndication so you'll continue to be paid. Be sure to check with your performing rights organization regarding proper reporting procedures (see "No Cue Sheet, No Pay" on page 332). The performing rights organizations do not pay royalties on American theatrical performances for films, but will collect from their foreign counterparts for theatrical performances in those countries. In the U.S., performance royalties are paid if the film is shown on television. The best income is from the networks (more people watching) and cable and local television pay much less.

If you're offered a contract to have a song in a film or to score a film, get the advice of an entertainment attorney who specializes in film and TV, as this is a very complex area. If you have a publisher, they'll negotiate with the production company, and if you self-publish, you'll hopefully have an administrator or an independent clearance organization who will do it. (Find them in the Music Business Registry's [www.musicregistry.com] *Film and Television Music Guide*.)

In "Motion Picture Soundtrack Songwriting and Performing" from *The Musician's Business & Legal Guide* (see bibliography), Mark Halloran (a founding partner at Erickson & Halloran law firm and former Vice President of Feature Business Affairs at Universal Pictures) and Thomas A. White (a business affairs advisor in the record and music publishing industries) give the following picture of writer royalties for a chart-oriented single from a film by a writer/artist/producer. The information was gathered in 2001.

Let's assume you make a deal at a major film studio. You are a writer/performer/producer who writes a title song and records a title song master. You are paid $25,000 for the song and $25,000 to record. You retain the writer's share but the studio retains the publisher's share. You receive a royalty of 12 percent of 130 percent of the wholesale priced in the U.S., pro-rated on CDs. Depending on the record company, you might be paid on less than all of units sold (e.g., 85 percent), but we have not assumed that here. Your master is three minutes long. The picture is a blockbuster. Your recording hits number one on *Billboard*'s Hot 100 Pop Chart. The soundtrack CD, on which you have one of the ten cuts, sells 500,000 copies in the United States and 375,000 copies overseas. Exhibit 3 gives you an idea of what your earnings might be.

EXHIBIT 3: ROUGH INCOME SUMMARY

The following rough income summary is designed to alert you to sources of income rather than to provide exact figures (although we have done our best to be accurate).

A. WRITER

1. Writing Fee (non-recoupable)..$25,000

2. Song Synchronization License For Film...0

3. Performance Income (worldwide)

(a) From Film in Theaters

```
        (i) United States..................................................................................0

        (ii) Foreign .............................................................................$20,000

    (b) Radio Performances.............................................................. $100,000

    (c) Home Video..........................................................................0

    (d) Pay TV ...............................................................................$3,000

    (e) Free TV

        (i) U.S. Network TV (two runs).............................................$4,000

        (ii) U.S. Syndicated TV (two runs, 150 stations).....................$1,500

        (iii) Foreign............................................................................$5,000

    4. Sheet Music (40,000 copies at 10 cents/copy) ......................$4,000

    5. Mechanicals

    (a) United States (3/4 statutory)

        (i) CD (500,000 x 6.825 cents) .............................................$17,062

    (b) Foreign

        (i) CD (375,000 x 10.00 cents)..............................................$37,500
    _____

    Total ....................................................................................$217,062


    B. RECORDING ARTIST

    1. Recording Fee (non-recoupable) ............................................$25,000

    2. Master License For Film .........................................................0

    3. United States Record Sales

        (a) CDs (500,000 copies)........................................................$49,401

    4. Foreign Record Sales

        (a) CDs (375,000 copies)........................................................$27,225

    Less Soundtrack Conversion Costs ............................................($3,000)
    _____

    Total ....................................................................................$146,438
```

I highly recommend reading *The Musician's Business & Legal Guide* from which the above summary is excerpted (new edition due in early 2007). In the book, attorneys present and analyze a great variety of contracts, not only for film/TV but also for a variety of songwriter and recording artist contracts. For additional in-depth information including current fees, read Todd Brabec and Jeffrey Brabec's book, *Music Money and Success* (new edition in June 2006).

No Cue Sheet, No Pay

Beyond the initial synch fee for the use of your song, you're likely to earn most of your royalties from your performing rights organization (ASCAP, BMI, SESAC) for continued U.S. and foreign broadcasts of the show. The way those royalties are determined is based solely on the show's producer filing a cue sheet with those organizations. It's usually the show's music editor or music supervisor who fills it out because she's the closest to being directly involved with the information needed.

Cue sheets contain series/film title, series/film episode title, episode number, air date, length, music length, production company information, song/cue title, composer, publisher, performing rights organization, timing, and usage. The music's "usage" information is critical to how much you get paid and is often the subject of some confusion.

Carl Sealove, an L.A.-based composer, bassist, and film editor, gave the best explanation I've found in an article he wrote for the *Editors Guild Magazine*—it's addressed to other music editors. With his permission, here's part of that article. (The rest is information I've already explained.)

As a songwriter, I have been fortunate to have quite a few songs used in different ways in many different television series, TV movies and feature films. I learned very well that the music cue sheet was the defining factor in how my performance royalties were calculated. Because the dollar amount for royalties is derived from how the music is used in the show, the key issue is the usage category that the music editor assigns to each piece of music. The list of usage categories for music in a film or television show is:

VV   **Visual Vocal:** On-camera vocal performance.

VI   **Visual Instrumental:** On-camera instrumental performance.

VD   **Visual Dance**—On-camera dance.

OT   **Opening Theme:** Opening title theme.

CT   **Closing Theme:** End title theme Only one song can be categorized as CT. If there's more than one song in the crawl, the others must be BI or BV.

FV   **Featured Vocal:** Music with vocal that plays with a visual montage, for example.

FI   **Featured Instrumental:** An instrumental cue featured in some specific way other than visual. (This is a rarely utilized usage category.) If an instrumental composition is well known, and its title or recognition factor strongly relates to the scene, it might be argued that this is a featured usage of an instrumental cue—if the Ventures song "Pipeline" plays during a surfing scene, for instance.

BI   **Background Instrumental:** Underscore and non-visual (off-camera) source.

BV   **Background Vocal:** Underscore with vocal or non-visual vocal source.

The first seven categories (Visual Vocal, Visual Instrumental, Visual Dance, Opening Theme, Closing Theme, Featured Vocal, and Featured Instrumental) are considered "featured performances," during which music is the prime focus of the scene.

Featured performances generate much higher royalties than background performances. BMI royalties for a feature performance of 45 seconds or more on network primetime can be as much as $2,400, which is divided between the composer and publisher. (Featured performances less than 45 seconds are prorated.) BMI background performance royalties on network primetime are

---

much less—approximately $340 per minute, which is again shared between the composer and publisher. ASCAP rates are slightly different, but comparable.

Sometimes a cue may start out as a featured performance and then become background as the scene progresses. In this case, it may be appropriate to list the composition as two separate cues that reflect the actual usage and associated times.

There are also some situations where the music editor must make a judgment call on whether a music cue should be considered to be a featured performance. In a montage where there is no dialogue, vocal music could be considered to be featured—for example, in a scene where a couple walks romantically on a beach and Roberta Flack's "The First Time Ever I Saw Your Face" is heard. Instrumental music is generally not considered "featured" unless the performer can be seen on camera. If an instrumental composition is well known, and its title or recognition factor strongly relates to the scene, it might be argued that this is a featured usage of an instrumental cue—if the Ventures song "Pipeline" plays during a surfing scene, for instance.

Source music, which is music that the characters themselves are able to hear, can be either featured or background. It is considered featured when it is the heart of the scene. Often, even if we hear music and see a music-producing device such as a radio or CD player on camera it may not be considered a featured performance. Sometimes we see people dancing to music in the background of a scene without any on-camera indication of the source of the music. In a strict sense, these are not featured performances because the music is not considered the prime focus of the scene. Another special case is the Visual Dance category, which is usually reserved for choreographed dance routines such as ballets or cheerleading displays. Someone shaking her booty does not usually qualify as a choreographed routine.

Before you fill out that cue sheet, be sure to consider the ramifications of your usage category choices. When in doubt, it may be worthwhile to place a call to an advisor at ASCAP or BMI. The composer and the publisher (often the production company or producer of the show that you worked on) will be grateful for your accuracy.

Cue sheets need to be filed within three months of the first airing so your performing rights organization can pay you (they pay quarterly) for that use. Production companies have been known to not fill out the cue sheet properly so it's not a bad idea to follow up on it.

SAMPLE MUSIC CUE SHEET (COURTESY OF BMI)

Series/Film Name:	Weekly World Of Music	Series/Film AKA: World Of Music	
Episode Name:	Rock and Roll Episode AKA:	Rock N Roll	
Prod. #: WWM 101	Episode #: 101	Show Duration:	30:00
Original Airdate:	May 12, 2006	Total Music Length:	05:28

Production Co./Contact Name: Music Music Music Productions

Ms. Ima Worker

3422 Music Place

This City, CA 31234-1768

(USAGE CODES) **BI**: Background Instrumental **VI**: Visual Instrumental **EE**: Logo
BV: Background Vocal **VV**: Visual Vocal **TO**: Theme Open **TC**: Theme Close

CUE # TITLE	(W) COMPOSER	%	SOCIETY USAGE
	(P) PUBLISHER		TIMING

001	Weekly World Opening Theme	TO	:32	
W		Sam Writer	50%	BMI
W		Joe Lyric	50%	ASCAP
P		My Publishing Co.	50%	BMI
P		JoLyr Music	50%	ASCAP
002	Weekly World Bumper	BI	:15	
W		Sam Writer	50%	BMI
W		Joe Lyric	50%	ASCAP
P		My Publishing Co.	50%	BMI
P		JoLyr Music	50%	ASCAP
003	Pop Song	VV	3:43	
W		Swen Composer	60%	PRS
W		Galen Lyricist	40%	PRS
P		SwenSongs Inc.	0%	PRS
P		SwenSongs USA	100%	BMI*
004	Weekly World Bumper	BI	:18	
W		Sam Writer	50%	BMI
W		Joe Lyric	50%	ASCAP
P		My Publishing Co.	50%	BMI
P		JoLyr Music	50%	ASCAP
005	Weekly World Closing Theme	TC	:35	
W		Sam Writer	50%	BMI
W		Joe Lyric	25%	ASCAP
W		Sara Artist	25%	SESAC
P		My Publishing Co.	50%	BMI
P		JoLyr Music	25%	ASCAP
P		Sara's Music	25%	SESAC
006	Music Music Music Productions Logo	EE	:05	
W		Sally Logo Writer	100%	BMI
P		Music Music Music Publishing	100%	BMI

• Note: SwenSongs USA (BMI) administrating for SwenSongs Inc. (PRS) in U.S.

Production Music Libraries

As I mentioned above, production music libraries are a major source of songs and underscore for film and TV productions, multi-media projects, video games, commercials, music between TV and radio programs and commercials, station IDs, station and show promos, direct-to-DVD/video productions, and many other uses where producers need quick access to pre-cleared, inexpensive music. There's been an explosion of production music libraries in the past few years that parallels the growth of new digital cable channels, satellite, and Web radio broadcasts.

If you're an unknown writer or band who doesn't have the clout to get your songs into big budget productions and don't have the time to constantly research all the new low-budget shows that may be in production and in need of underscore music or songs, music libraries represent a major opportunity for you. These companies secure the rights to broadcast quality songs and instrumental underscore compositions submitted to them that they feel they can place in audio-visual productions. They then assemble and reproduce "libraries" of these collections on CDs or online and make them available to production companies.

They're indexed by musical style, mood, instrumentation, length, tempo, male, female or group vocal, and any other attributes that allow an audio-visual producer to quickly target the type of music they need. They find the piece, use it, and fill out a cue sheet (see sample on page 335) for the music library and your performing rights organization (ASCAP, BMI, SESAC) that includes information on how the song is used, how long it is, the name of the piece, the composers, and the owner of the copyright.

Some of the bigger libraries hire their own in-house composers to create music for them but will also sign individual songs and complete new libraries from indie composers. That's where you have your best opportunity.

What does "broadcast quality" really mean? Don't feel you have to spend a bundle on studio masters. Any good digital audio workstation (DAW) setup or a good live recording can give you the quality you need if you know what you're doing (see chapter twelve, "Demos" on page 238). Apple's GarageBand 3 is currently available, and they'll certainly have yet another upgrade to take even more advantage of the new screamin' Intel Core Duo processor by the time you read this. The trick is to study and experiment with it (or any other software or operating system you use) to maximize the quality of your recordings. *Recording, the Magazine for the Recording Musician* (www.musicmakerpub.com) is a great resource. In fact, in 2005 they published a whole issue including an interactive CD devoted to GarageBand. If you're submitting instrumental pieces, they should be well arranged. Stay away from using stock sounds that come packaged with your keyboard or software. Use live musicians whenever possible, particularly for rock and country. They hate keyboard triggered samples that emulate steel or acoustic guitars, saxes, etc. Try to create fresh sounds. Generating a mood is important. They'll use pieces with strong melodic themes but will also use underscoring that just enhances a mood. It's also a good idea to produce mixes with and without lead instruments.

Songs are used in many different ways. Sometimes the lyric is important. Sometimes it's irrelevant, and your song will be barely audible in a bar scene behind a conversation. It may be more important that the *style* is authentic and appropriate for the era in which the story is set.

EXERCISE:

Tape TV shows (try a drama and a comedy) with just an audio recorder. Play them back and make lists of all the "cues" (pieces of music used) with info about mood, number of instruments, style, length, use of songs vs. underscore, and how many are under the dialogue. Are they using different mixes of the same track for different cues? There are actually cases of entire shows being scored using a single five-minute piece of music that's dissected and used in different configurations for each cue: only drums and bass in one, just the string pad of part of the piece in another. Use this information as a guide to the cues you'll submit as demos.

The comments in the above section about composing for film or TV are also relevant for pitching to music libraries, so let's get to the issue of how you go about connecting.

Demo presentation for instrumental segments should be sixty seconds each. If they like it they'll ask you for five, ten, thirty-second, or longer versions. For songs, send the complete song. Prepare them as you would for music supervisor Madonna Wade-Reed on page 327.

Advances are rare. They know that you know you'll make most of your income on the "back end" from your performing rights organizations after it's broadcast. In most of the situations listed above you'd get an advance for synch and master use licenses when pitching *directly* to music supervisors for specific shows or a percentage of the advance when pitching via song placement companies. That's not the case with music libraries.

Contracts vary from library to library, *so read them very carefully*. Some are actually publishing agreements in which they own the copyright just like any other publishing contract. You get your 50 percent writer's share. I've also seen *exclusive* publishing deals in which the library exempts a maximum amount of CD sales—5,000 or 10,000, for example (this is undoubtedly negotiable)—that the group is allowed to sell without the publisher taking publishing royalties.

Ideally you'd want a non-exclusive deal in which you're free to use the song in your own CD and sell as many as you want—or place it in film TV on your own. A trade-out on that situation is that they'll often want not only the publisher's share of income but 50 percent of the writer's share, leaving you with 25 percent overall. Though splitting the writer's share goes against everything holy to me, you have to decide how important it is to you to have a non-exclusive contract. You need to consider that carefully, especially if you have a co-writer, which means that you'd now be looking at 12.5 percent.

Speaking of co-writers, it's important that you have a written agreement that neither of you can make any kind of deal other than a compulsory license without the other's consent (see chapter nine, "The Compulsory License" on page 173). That would certainly include the above situation.

Reversion clauses can sometimes be negotiated. These give you back the rights to the song within two or three years if it hasn't been placed.

THE LEGAL BACKUP YOU'LL NEED

For the master recording, a license must be granted to the audio-visual producer that states that you control all the rights to the performances on the recording. Each musician or singer who contributes a performance to your recording has a copyright interest in his performance and you *must* cover yourself with a "work for hire" release agreement with your musicians/singer(s). Though you may not have to show these releases to the production music library or the audio-visual producer, you'll have to "warrant" in the contract that you *have* done it so your singer doesn't sue them when she hears herself on that TV show.

If you pay your musicians and singers for the sessions and get the releases, you have no obligation to pay them more later and it's cleaner that way. However, a situation in which you might consider it would be if you have a band or a dedicated group of musicians/singers you work well with and can always count on to give you great performances. Sometimes it's tough to find a crew like that and you want to keep them happy by sharing a percentage of the "master use" half of the income. As an indie self-published writer you—and any co-writers—get the "synch" portion. A caution in making the decision to give your musicians a piece of the action is that it could compromise or preclude your ability later to make a deal with the publisher or others who placed your song, with whom you would need to share all or part of the master-use fee.

Note: If you hire a demo service to produce your demos, do not forget to have them sign a work for hire agreement. Before you even commit to hiring them be sure to let them know that you *require* it. Most demo services today do broadcast-quality work that will easily qualify for broadcast use.

WORK-FOR-HIRE AGREEMENT

Note: This is a sample agreement and may not apply to your specific situation. Always have an experienced music attorney check your agreements before using them.

This agreement is entered into as of this _____ day of _____, 20____, by and between _____ (hereinafter referred to as "Artist") and_____ (hereinafter referred to as "Musician"). The parties hereby agree as follows:

1. Artist hereby engages Musician's services and Musician hereby accepts such engagement to perform, without limitation, at rehearsal sessions and phonograph recording sessions for the purpose of creating the following master/demo recordings:

Musician agrees to diligently, competently and to the best of Musician's ability experience and talent perform to Artist's satisfaction all of the services required of Musician hereunder.

2. Conditioned upon Musician's full and faithful performance of all the terms and provisions hereof, Artist shall pay Musician the sum of $_____ per [track/session/hour] as full and complete consideration for Musician's services hereunder. Musician acknowledges that this agreement (and your services and the services of anyone else hereunder) is not subject to any collective bargaining agreements since Artist is not a party to any collective bargaining agreements that might be applicable to the type of services provided herein.

3. Musician agrees that his/her performances shall be considered as works made for hire as contemplated and defined in Section 101 of the United States Copyright Act of 1976. Musician hereby grants to Artist all rights of every kind and nature in and to the results and proceeds of Musician's services and performances rendered hereunder, including, without limitation, the complete, unconditional and exclusive worldwide ownership in perpetuity of any and all recordings and audiovisual reproductions embodying Musician's performances hereunder. Artist shall accordingly have the sole and exclusive right to copyright any such recordings or audiovisual reproductions embodying Musician's performances under Artist's name as the sole owner and author thereof.

4. Musician hereby grants to Artist the worldwide right in perpetuity to use and publish and to permit others to use and publish Musician's name, likeness, voice and other biographical material in connection with Musician's services and performances hereunder.

5. Artist shall use best efforts to credit Musician as performing on the recordings herein in the event such recordings are released for sale to the public and shall place Musician's name on the cover, sleeve, jacket or insert of the recording as part of any list of musical works. No casual or inadvertent failure by Artist and no failure by or of any third party to accord the requisite credit herein shall be deemed a breach of this agreement.

6. Musician hereby warrants, represents, and agrees that Musician is not under any disability, restriction, or prohibition, whether contractual or otherwise with respect to Musician's right to execute this contract, to grant the rights granted hereunder, to perform each and every term and provision required to be performed by Musician hereunder. No materials, ideas or other properties furnished by Musician and utilized by Artist will violate or infringe upon any common law or statutory right of any person, firm, corporation, including without limitation contractual rights, copyrights and rights of privacy and/or publicity. Musician shall hold Artist harmless and hereby agrees to indemnify Artist for all costs in connection with any breach of the above warranties and representations.

7. Musician fully understands that Artist would not have employed Musician without an agreement on Musician's part to give, grant, release and assign to it all rights of every kind in and to the work performed by Musician for Artist, together with all results thereof and incidental thereto.

8. Musician acknowledges and agrees that nothing in this agreement shall obligate Artist to employ or otherwise engage Musician's services in connection with any other recording agreement.

9. Musician acknowledges and agrees that if she provides musical equipment or other property of any nature in connection with services required hereunder, Artist shall not be liable for any loss or damage to such equipment or property.

10. This agreement sets forth the entire understanding of the parties hereto relating to the subject matter hereof and supersedes all prior and contemporaneous negotiations, understandings and discussions. No modification, amendment, waiver, termination or discharge of this agreement or any of its terms or provisions shall be binding upon either party if not confirmed by a written instrument signed by Artist and Musician.

11. Any and all disputes between the parties arising under and/or relating to this agreement shall be determined in accordance with the laws and the courts of the State of California.

IN WITNESS WHEREOF, the parties have executed this agreement on the date first written above.

(Artist) _____

(Musician)_____

The following are two additional optional clauses in case someone actually wants to split some percentages from the Master use half with their musicians or singers.

2a. Not withstanding the foregoing, in the event that the recording embodying Musician's performance is licensed for synchronization with an audiovisual production for which Artist receives a fee for Master Use, Musician will receive _____ percent of 50% of the total of combined Synchronization and Master Use fee received by the Artist or _____ percent of 100% of the Master Use fee (if paid separately) received by Artist.

2b. Furthermore, if Artist signs a contract with a major recording company and the recording embodying Musician's performance is released by that company pursuant to the recording agreement, and the provisions of paragraph 2, above, notwithstanding, Artist shall use best efforts to cause the company to pay Musician the difference between what Musician has already been paid and the American Federation of Musicians session scale.

RE-TITLING

A common practice for music libraries is to limit their involvement only to audio-visual uses. The benefit for the writers is that they're free to use the songs on their own CDs, for example, without having to pay royalties to the music library for a song they played no role in exploiting. The benefit to the library is that they're able to offer a non-exclusive license to the writer and it gives them competitive access to better material from bands that wouldn't go for an exclusive contract.

Actually, re-titling as been working pretty well so far despite the fact that, according to some attorneys and publishers, this is problematic because the rights given to the music library are *actually* for the same song since nothing is really changed but the title. Music business attorney Andrea Brauer has much experience with these deals and offers this advice about some things to watch for in the contracts.

> The practice these days with music libraries is to acquire the rights for a "derivative work" of the original song, thereby allowing the songwriter to retain ownership of the composition and at the same time allowing the music library to license and thereafter collect its proper income on placements of the composition. Of course to create this derivative work, the library simply takes the original work, as is, and re-names it. Unfortunately, this re-titling of songs clashes head on with copyright law, which will not recognize the existence of a separate work unless the new work has been fundamentally changed in terms of its lyrics or melody. Nevertheless, music libraries are not likely to change their practice until confronted by the Copyright Office, so here's some advice about what should be contained in those contracts.
>
> First of all, the whole point from the songwriter's perspective is to protect her rights in the original song. Therefore, the contract must specifically acknowledge the existence of the original song and its title; it must acknowledge that the rights being granted are for a derivative of the original song and it must state the proposed new title of the "derivative work." There must be a clause reserving all rights in the original song to the songwriter and a clause stating that the music library has no rights to the original song. This may all seem self-evident but you'd be surprised at how many poorly written contracts fail to mention any titles at all and, as a consequence, the library gets credited with the wrong title.
>
> Two final points: If the library seeks the right to authorize a true derivative work (i.e., to bring in a new songwriter to alter the lyrics or melody) it must not be allowed to do so without the original writer's permission. Otherwise the original writer will quickly lose control over who gets to use the song. And last but not least, make sure there is an audit clause in the contract so that if the accounting looks suspicious, it can be challenged.

Music libraries offer a great opportunity for writers of both songs and instrumental tracks to potentially earn a substantial income from the use of their music in film, television, games, and a variety of other audio-visual uses. It does take time, dedication, and patience because you need to grow it song by song and placement by placement. Nothing happens overnight.

RESOURCES

The Music Business Registry (www.musicregistry.com): To find music libraries, get the Music Business Registry's *Film and Television Music Guide*.

Music Library Association
(www.cftech.com/BrainBank/COMMUNICATIONS/MusLibSrc.html)

ProductionHUB.com (www.productionhub.com/directory): Go to "Post Production" then "Sound Library/Libraries—Music."

Google (www.google.com): Search Google under "Production Music Libraries."

Children's Music

In early 2006, articles in *Billboard* and *The New York Times* pointed out the growing success of kids' audio in the U.S. According to *Billboard*, sales are up 55 percent year to date (March 2006) over 2005. Kids' CDs are topping the *Billboard* 200 chart, with Jack Johnson and Friends' *Sing-A-Longs and Lullabies for the Film Curious George* debuting at number 1, while Laurie Berkner entered *Billboard*'s Music Video DVD chart at number 1 with her first DVD, *We are . . . The Laurie Berkner Band*.

This may be a temporary spike but despite its periodic ups and downs, one of the many good things about writing and recording music for children is that it's a stable market. Unlike the pop record business where, if the planets or cards (or whatever you believe in) are aligned right, you can make a lot of money in a relatively short time, the children's market is slow but sure, and doesn't burn out overnight. Walt Disney Productions, for instance, will consistently sell well (many times over a million copies) on just about every audio or video project it releases because everyone trusts Disney to have consistently good products. In many cases, parents are buying the same records for their kids that they themselves grew up with.

If you establish yourself with a body of work in this market, you can sell a million records over several years. You'll never make the *Billboard* charts, but chances are that if you're genuinely interested in this market, it won't matter to you.

Styles of children's music range from the same contemporary pop, rock, hip-hop, and country that kids hear on the radio, to more traditional folk music, classical, and show and novelty tunes. Lyrics, however, are directed toward kids. There is a strong push for nonsexist, nonviolent, non-racially-stereotyped messages that promote positive self-images. There's also the feeling that children should not be "talked down to" but should be treated as intelligent individuals.

MARKET STRUCTURE

The children's music market is generally divided into the home entertainment and the educational music markets even though there are obvious crossovers.

Home Entertainment

The home entertainment market is made up of the major companies involved in children's music for entertainment purposes though some (such as *Sesame Street*) cross over into the educational market to some degree. These include Disney; Disney-Pixar (*Toy Story, Finding Nemo, The Incredibles, Ratatouille*); The Jim Henson Company (the Muppets); Children's Television Workshop (*Sesame Street*, Elmo); Hanna-Barbera (now Cartoon Network Studios—the Flintstones, Yogi Bear, the Jetsons, Scooby-Doo); Warner Bros. (Bugs Bunny, Road Runner, Porky Pig, Daffy Duck); and Music For Little People. These companies continue to develop new characters and frequently produce albums based on those characters.

Also included in this category would be live performers who specialize in original songs and stage shows. These performers include the list of artists below who write their own material, but there may be others who are open to recording songs by other writers.

Do research by going to a local record store featuring children's CDs, large toy stores, or your local library (best bet because you can read the liner notes without having to purchase anything). Check to see if there are songs not written by the artist. If there are, copy the contact info, including Web site and e-mail address. Then write for information about submitting material.

The Educational Market

Educational companies specialize in products that have a direct educational value for developing children's language, motor, and social skills in addition to having entertainment value. The greatest share of business in this category is done by mail-order sales. The records and videos are sold through ads in parent's and teacher's magazines, education conventions, and Web sites. They're used in workshops, day care centers, parks and recreation departments, public and private schools, and preschools.

Educational music, though it may sound deceptively simple, is not easier to write than other kinds of music. You must have some experience and understanding of age-specific teaching methods, child psychology, and learning processes to be an effective writer in this genre. Often, these recordings include activity suggestions. A good sense of humor is also valuable, since, after all, nothing communicates quite as powerfully to a child as a good laugh.

You could do your research by going to the periodical section of the library and researching magazines for parents and teachers for ads of companies that supply these products. All the companies now have Web sites where you can order them. Buy a few and study them.

There is also a part of this market that deals primarily with printed music and includes easy choral pieces (two or three part) for grade school and junior high, children's musicals, vaudeville/variety shows, and children's educational computer games.

To research the Educational Market check out:

Children's Technology Review (www.childrenssoftware.com) for reviews of the latest products.

Kidsongs.com (www.kidsongs.com) has an excellent line of audios and videos for kids.

Noggin (www.noggin.com) is an innovative and popular site. It's an interactive pre-school education/entertainment online portal to Noggin's digital cable and satellite programming. One of their musical features is *Jack's Big Music Show* that presents videos of children's artists, a hint at what's ahead in children's "edutainment."

Writing for children's theater is of particular interest to community and professional theaters. There is a good list of resource links at Community Theater Green Room (www.communitytheater.org) and a wealth of information of local and regional theater companies online. Just type "Children's Musical Theater" and add your state name in your search engine.

Often, touring shows come to schools and provide children with their first exposure to live music and theater. Packages for the latter usually come with suggestions for costumes, props, staging, background music, and the like. Educational touring shows come with study guides to stimulate class discussion and theater appreciation.

MORE CHILDREN'S MUSIC RESOURCES:

The Children's Music Web (www.childrensmusic.org)

The Children's Music Network (www.cmnonline.org)

Kidsentertainment.com (www.kidsentertainment.com)

National Association for the Education of Young Children (www.naeyc.org)

The Children's Music Portal (http://childrens-music.org/index.htm)

Allegro Music (www.allegro-music.com/childrens.asp): For sales of kids' music.

Below is a list of children's music writer/performers who have had long and successful careers. There are certainly many more, but these are artists I know personally or are friends. If you're interested in being a children's performer, as opposed to being solely a children's writer, these artist's sites will give you a good sense of the breadth of activities that are involved.

Peter Alsop (www.kiddomusic.com/AlsopPeter.html)

Joanie Bartels (www.joaniebartels.com)

Tom Chapin (http://members.aol.com/chapinfo/tc/)

Dan Crow (www.dancrow.com)

Katherine Dines (www.hunktabunkta.com)

Dave Kinnoin (www.songwizard.com)

Hap Palmer (www.happalmer.com)

Parachute Express (www.parachuteexpress.com)

Raffi (www.raffinews.com)/

Sharon, Lois, and Bram (www.casablancakids.com)

Stefan Shepherd (http://zooglobble.blogspot.com)

CAREERS IN CHILDREN'S MUSIC

There are two main paths for those who want to pursue a career in children's music.

Children's Writer/Performers

Most of the artists listed above are primarily writer/performers. They all believe that what children learn about life has a major influence on their later lives, and they take their roles as teachers very seriously. They have also found that there are few things in life that give them more joy than making kids laugh. Their careers have lasted a long time. All of those listed have been entertaining kids for at least twenty years, have released many albums, and have enjoyed great success. They've all been awarded Parents' Choice Awards and some have received Grammy Awards or nominations. Some have sold more than a million albums. They're primarily DIY indie artists. Some have managers or assistants to help with their booking and business, though most are still very hands-on.

They all started small and locally and expanded from there to build followings of kids that are now parents who are buying these artist's old and new albums for their own kids. Nobody tells them they're too old to be a performer and when you see them in action you know why. Kids don't care.

Income for these artists comes from a variety of sources: record and video/DVD sales, school concerts and standalone kids' concerts, early childhood educational clinics for teachers and parents, and merchandising.

There are a number of reasons why you may not see yourself pursuing a career as a performer. You have a great day job you love or need and it's just not in the cards to give it up. You don't really enjoy performing very much or realize you're just not very good at it. Despite the reasons, you still like to write kids' songs. Your imaginative, adventurous, silly and innocent "inner kid" is still very much alive and wants to get out and be heard.

Your options are to just let that kid out now and then to write a song just for fun or to entertain your own kids. Another option is to write for kids' TV shows and characters.

Writing for Film and TV Characters

To do this you need to have just as much skill and imagination but need to work within tight guidelines. You'll write for specific personalities, much as a scriptwriter would write a part for a character in a drama or sitcom. The producer gives you a "bible" that lays out all the specific personality traits of the character, including language (what he would or wouldn't say and how he would say it), and the character's strengths and weaknesses.

Writer/artist/producer and consultant Robin Frederick used to write songs for Winnie the Pooh and told me to remind you that the songs will be sung in the character's voice and range (Pooh had a four-note range).

Some of the children's writer/artists listed above, like Dave Kinnoin, straddle both worlds. Based in Los Angeles, Dave loves to perform and tour but has also written more than 200 songs for Disney, Jim Henson, Sesame Workshop, Sony Wonder, Simon & Schuster Interactive, and other entertainment and educational companies.

He says, "I love the challenge of having strict parameters. Give me an eleven-second assignment about a porcupine who needs a friend and I'm into it. Beyond needing to tell the story and say what the character needs to say within a time limit, I have a lot of creative freedom. I'm rarely told what musical style to write and I like to surprise them. I've written songs in odd time signatures and a variety of styles but I always have a singable and memorable melody that carries it."

Though he plays both guitar and keyboards, he prefers to write in his head-first and go to instruments later. "I work with great musicians," says Kinnoin, "who can give me any feel I want or come up with something I wouldn't have thought of myself. I get to express my personal philosophies in my non-children's songs so I always have an outlet for that, but writing on assignment for children's projects has long been my bread-and-butter gig and I've always loved it."

What does it pay?

Writing for characters is usually done on a per-song basis. The producers will pay a demo budget of around $300 per song and there's a range from company to company of anywhere between $700 and $3,000 as a creative fee for each song depending on the budgets for each show and success of the company and show. Often you'll be working on a show as part of a team of writers who each work at home and turn in two or three songs a week. Even though many of the shows eventually go to video distribution, writers rarely get paid on video sales. A buy-out for those rights is usually included in the deal for each song. On the plus side is that you'll always receive your performance rights income from your performing rights organization (ASCAP, BMI, SESAC) every time the show airs, and for many of these shows there are multiple repeats.

Connecting With Projects

Go to your *TV Guide*, look up the kids' shows and tape them. Make notes about the different characters in each show who sing—personalities, styles, subject matter, vocal range, etc., as well as other non-character songs that may be included in the show. Also check to see if they credit songwriters either on the show credits or the Web site. At the end of the show get the name of the production company and music supervisor. If there's no contact information for them, go to their Web site and find it there. Also see if they credit writers.

Dave Kinnoin adds this sage advice on presenting your work and gentle persistence:

Burn a custom CD containing only songs that have the same target age as the show's target age, and make personal contact with someone at the company to obtain permission to send your demo first. You will likely have to address the envelope a certain way to ensure its arrival and opening and (we can dream, can't we?) listening. Companies ordinarily throw unsolicited mail in the trash. They're not trying to be mean or disrespectful; it's just that the stream of unsolicited material is endless, and music supervisors and other song-users simply don't have time for it. Also, there may be legal reasons why they cannot open unsolicited mail. In many cases, you'll have to be creative in finding an open door.

One of my most effective techniques is to put each potential client on what my wife calls a "tickler file." That is, I contact them again at certain intervals. For some, it may be every six months—for others, every month. At no time do I ever risk bugging them. If I think a certain call or e-mail or letter might possibly constitute "bugging them," I send some chocolate chip cookies or a news clipping about some industry business they might appreciate or something else to make them feel gently towards me.

Always be polite.

Don't irritate anyone. There's a fine line between persistence and stalking. And don't tell potential clients where you went to college or what disabled person you saved from ruin. All clients care about is what comes out of the speakers. Always include a neatly typed lyric sheet for each song, and always put your copyright and contact information on all parts of your submission.

If you send a DVD, be sure to indicate that's what it is, as audio CDs and DVDs look alike. Once someone loves your material, there is time for getting to know each other as a person, but don't be insulted if all they ever want is just great songs, one after another after another, with no small talk. This is business, folks. And don't dare be even one day late. Stay up all night and hire a replacement horn player at 1:00 A.M. if you have to.

Music for Video Games

Recent technological innovations have given rise to many new uses for expertise in scoring and songwriting. Software-based entertainment has become a major component in the spectrum of global media. Pay a visit to any game arcade and you'll find games that have originated from comic books, feature films, television series and rock artists. The market for game hardware and software has become a $10 billion-plus market as of 2006 and though the market has slumped a bit as the next level of Sony and Microsoft game platforms has been delayed, there's no reason to believe that the interest in games will diminish.

Games, for both home use and arcades as well as multiplayer online games in a great variety of hardware and software platforms, are becoming increasingly sophisticated, and music plays an integral part in generating the excitement needed for their success. There is a cult following for music featured in games. Popular pieces can end up on compilations marketed both online and offline that earn money for the writers, though there is also plenty of unauthorized trading of favorite titles over the Internet.

Composing music for games is not my area of expertise, but my friend Jeannie Novak is an expert in this field. She's an Internet pioneer with one of the first music sites on the net, Kaleidospace, for independent artists, now called Indiespace (www.indiespace.com).

Her hosting of our Los Angeles Songwriters Showcase magazine, Songwriters Musepaper, in the early 1990s made us the first music magazine on the Internet. She's a composer, pianist, author, teacher, and journalist. Her latest book is Game Development Essentials: Game Story & Character Development. Find out more about her at www.jeannie.com. I asked Jeannie to give us an introduction to composing game music.

MUSIC FOR GAMES BY JEANNIE NOVAK

In order to compose music for games, you need to think like a game designer. You must understand the intersection between non-linear storytelling and gameplay mechanics. A game composer doesn't necessarily create just one cue (piece of music) for each section of the game, but must often create several cues based on what the player might do to respond to a particular situation. A game essentially consists of a series of challenges, and each challenge can be addressed by the player via any number of strategies. For example, you might be confronted by an enemy (the challenge) and must decide how to handle the situation. Depending on how sophisticated the game is, you might fight the enemy directly, "trick" the enemy through indirect combat, or cooperate with the enemy by negotiating. For each of these strategies, you might have a different cue that is triggered by the player's decision. Each of these three cues must work in conjunction with whatever cue was initially used to underscore the beginning of the challenge. This is just a simple example of how non-linear storytelling and player choice can affect the scoring of a game. Music written in this way is known as "adaptive" (formerly "interactive") music.

Another interesting feature of scoring for games involves the lack of a "spotting" session. Composers do not "watch" the game after it has been completed. This is another feature of non-linear storytelling and gameplay mechanics. Composers are often given cue assignments without even seeing what the game looks like. Otherwise, composers would have to play through the game as players—using every possible strategy to respond to every challenge. This would understandably be a very inefficient way to compose. Instead, composers should take a subset of situations and score three possible cues for them, just to get a better idea of how the game is played.

The ability to think in a non-linear fashion and understand how gameplay works is essential for a game composer. In the "music for games" courses that I teach, I actually train composers to be game designers so that they fully understand the core mechanics of game development. I do the same with traditional screenwriters who are trying to migrate to the game industry. These writers are used to writing scenes in a linear fashion, never considering that players might make any number of choices when presented with a challenge. In a way, players become co-authors of the game, and the player characters must be written "loosely" so that players can truly make decisions.

A background in scoring for film or television is helpful, but not absolutely necessary. What's more important is to have an open mind and versatility so that you feel comfortable composing "musical options" that naturally extend from a core musical motif. You'll need to be familiar with various "adaptive music" software programs such as DirectMusic Producer. Other tools used by many game composers are Pro Tools, GigaStudio, Logic, Reason, and SoundMAX.

Sound design and dialogue are two other important areas of game audio. Just like game music, there are often several different versions of sound effects and dialogue—again, depending on the decisions made by the player. If a player encounters the same door twice (even if the player makes the same decision to open it), the door may sound a little different the second time around. The same goes for dialogue: If a player encounters the same non-player character (such as a merchant) again, that character should not give the player the same speech as if the character never saw the player before!

Often, the game is at a fairly late stage before music is added. However, sometimes music can affect the design of a game. During the testing phase of a game project, it isn't uncommon to create several versions ("builds") of a game based on tester recommendations. Sometimes these builds do change depending on the music, which is almost always added toward the end of the development process.

Pitching your music. The best (and still unique) way to impress a prospective employer in the game industry is to participate in a game project such as one that you might see on Gamasutra (www.gamasutra.com)—or even build your own "mod" (modification) of a pre-existing game using your original music. It's important for industry professionals to hear your music in context, especially if they can actually play a game that utilizes it. A simpler way to handle this is to play a "scene" in a game three times, using three different strategies. Record all three versions of the scene and write a different score to each. Make sure you begin with your basic score and create a variation from the point at which you (the player) utilizes a strategy. I have students do this in my "music for games" course. It's also good to have a Web site available containing any cues, mods, or even audio samples. Contact prospective employers via e-mail so that they can easily click on a link and check out your material. Follow up with a phone call.

Play as many games as you can. I can't stress this point enough. Don't enter into an industry that you know nothing about. Can you imagine composing music for film without ever seeing a film? Find out what type of player you are, and what your favorite genres are. Focus on approaching companies (development studios or publishers) that put out the games that you personally enjoy.

If you are going to put together a demo containing music scored to games that already exist, choose games that you enjoy and improve upon their music scores. Approach the companies that put out those particular games. Go to the Game Developers Conference (March in San Jose) and Electronic Entertainment Expo (May in Los Angeles), and network with companies and fellow composers on the show floor and at after-show parties!

Jeannie Novak: Founder, Indiespace (www.indiespace.com)
Personal Web site: Jeannie.com (www.jeannie.com)

Jeannie Novak is lead author and series editor of Game Development Essentials *and an instructor and subject matter expert at Art Institute Online (game art and design), Westwood College Online (game software development, game art and design), DeVry University (game programming and simulation), UCLA Extension, Art Center College of Design, Santa Monica College Academy of Entertainment & Technology.*

Despite the rare superstar composers for game music doing full orchestral scores for six-figure budgets, there's a major difference between the revenues of film and TV composers and those of game music composers. In the latter, there's typically no "back end" royalty stream since there are no broadcasts to receive performance royalties from. Most game composition is done on a work-for-hire basis and "buy outs" in which there's a set fee and no per game sales income after that. It can work a bit differently for existing songs (not composed specifically for the game) that are used in video games.

Negotiations can include the possibility of receiving royalties for the increasing popularity of CDs and broadcasts of the most popular game music soundtracks, as well as potential digital download sales. Because of the variety of new uses for game music outside the context of the original games, contracts are continually evolving. But here is Jeffrey and Todd Brabec's look at the variable deal points in a license agreement for use of an existing song in a video game:

LICENSING SONGS FOR VIDEO GAMES
BY JEFFREY AND TODD BRABEC

When a producer wants to use a pre-existing song in a video game, the license normally covers the following areas:

Game description: The request for the composition or master will describe the overall nature of the game and then will detail how music is actually used. In some cases, the description is very detailed (e.g., being played from an in-car stereo or a brief portion of music being heard when a game character passes an open window on the street), and other times the description may be somewhat general.

Music: There will be a description of the composition being used, including information on the title, songwriter, publisher, and percentage controlled. There should also be a description as to how the song is used in the game. The actual timed length may be stated or the language may say "up to the entire length of the composition." The contract may also state that there can be more than one rotation. In addition, some agreements provide for use in cross-sell trailers in the other games or as part of promotional broadcast features such as "making of" programs.

Game title: The exact title of the game will be mentioned.

Description of the configuration: Some descriptions are very broad, and others are very specific. For example, some agreements include language covering all software programs or other electronic products in any format or platform that is designed for use with computers. Others refer to any existing electronic devices as well as any which may be developed in the future. Many also indicate the type of distribution medium on which the game may be distributed. For example, the contract may actually mention DVD, CD-ROM, console arcades, handheld devices, magnetic diskettes, and optical disks as permitted distribution media. Others will be less specific or mention the previous media but provide that distribution of the game will not be limited to only the areas mentioned.

Online versions: If the game is available online, the agreement will have language which permits the transmission of the game over telephone lines, cable television systems, cellular telephones, satellites and wireless broadcast, as well as other ways of transmission which are in existence or which may be developed in the future.

Fees: Some agreements provide for an actual royalty but most provide for a one-time buy-out fee per composition regardless of the number of games actually sold or how many times the game is played. Per-game royalties range from eight cents to fifteen cents per composition and buyouts range from $2,500 to over $10,000, but can be more than $20,000. As in many other areas, royalties and fees depend upon the value of the composition, the prior history or anticipated sales of the game, bargaining power of the parties, and the needs of the video game producer, music publisher, and songwriter.

Term: Some agreements have a set term (such as five years, seven years, ten years, etc.) during which the song can be used in the video game. If there is a set term, the video manufacturer will many times have the right to sell off its inventory of games for a period of time once the term is over. Other licenses last for as long as the video game is in distribution. For example, the term might be "life of the game (this second version only)," or it might be "commercial life of the game." And others state that the term is for the life of copyright of the composition.

Territory: The territory of distribution is usually the world.

Companion products: Many game producers receive the right to release the compositions used in the video game in companion products such as an audio CD or separate DVD release of the game. Sometimes fees are actually set in the agreement (for example, 100 percent or 75 percent reduced statutory rate for a CD) and other times there is a good-faith negotiation provision as to the ultimate fee that will be charged for the applicable companion product.

Collateral materials: Many agreements provide that the video distributor can use the composition in its advertising, promotional, and marketing materials related to the video game. This may include internal and external sales meetings, conferences and seminars, in-store promotions and demonstrations, DVD trailers and even advertising over closed-network college campuses, as long as the use is in context. Such promotional usage does not include out-of-context uses or other types of advertising campaigns such as network, cable or satellite television, radio, or theatrical.

Credit: Most contracts provide that credit for the composition is given on the inside of the video game packaging. Credit may also be placed in the manual for the game or actually in the digital format of the game. If there is a master recording also licensed, the notice will usually contain the name of the record company and the name of the recording artist in addition to the composition information.

Web site of a game: A number of game producers will feature the music used in the game on the official Web site with appropriate credits. In some cases, there might be a streaming music player or jukebox that will allow the user to listen to a thirty-second clip of the song. Many times there is also information on where to purchase the music either online or from a physical location and, in some cases, the download can occur directly from the site. There may also be links to the artist's Web site, as well as album cover displays and information on the artist. Many of these items may also be featured on the video producer's site.

Other provisions: Notice, applicable law, audit, warranty, and indemnification provisions are similar to most other license agreements

---

This information is excerpted from the 5th edition of the book Music, Money, and Success: The Insider's Guide to Making Money in the Music Business *written by Jeffrey Brabec and Todd Brabec (published by Schirmer Trade Books/Music Sales). By permission © 2006 Jeff Brabec, Todd Brabec. Also see www.musicandmoney.com.*

After reading many articles on music for games, I see an exciting future for the medium. Here are some things to look forward to: more interactivity, more surround sound, more music use, more sophisticated consoles, and less MIDI. Music "expansion packs" are a new way for game players to expand the amount of music they can hear in a game, which will have an obvious effect on the amount of songs licensed for games. With the expansion pack model, players will get a possible four more hours of music they can download, and it will integrate into the gamers' current music tracks. When you consider the fact that avid gamers will spend hundreds of hours listening to the scores and songs in the games, you can imagine how this innovation alone can affect the market for new music.

Good resources for projects, jobs, and industry knowledge:

Gamasutra (www.gamasutra.com)
Music 4 Games (wwwmMusic4games.net)
Game Audio Network Guild (www.audiogang.org)
VGM: Video Game Music (www.vgm.com)
Blue's News (www.bluesnews.com)
GameSpot (www.gamespot.com)
GameSpy (www.gamespy.com)
Game Music Radio (www.filmmusicworld.com)

Search Amazon.com for *The Complete Guide To Game Audio: For Composers, Musicians, Sound Designers, and Game Developers* by Aaron Marks. It's touted as a great introduction to the field.

Another great resource is the dmoz Open Directory Project (www.dmoz.org). Go to "music," then "video games," and you'll get a good idea of the scope of this area with a multitude of useful links.

If you're interested in this field, chances are you already have high-speed Internet access. Search the net under "video game music" or "multimedia music."

Cell Phone Ringtones and Master Tones

Sales of cell phone ringtones are outselling legal CD downloads and CDs. Ringtones are basically MIDI monophonic sounds, just the melody (almost extinct). Polyphonic ringtones and master tones (sometimes called realtones) are a sampling of a short piece (usually thirty to forty-five seconds) of the actual recording. It's interesting to note that with the original monophonic ringtones, only the music publisher was involved. All royalties went to the publisher as the owner of the copyright to the *song*. Once actual master recordings were used, royalties had to be split between publishers and the record companies who owned the right to license the *master recording*. At that point, a turf battle ensued over who should get the biggest percentage of the royalties when licensing them to the cell phone companies. Publishers argued that without the song there would be nothing to sell. Record companies argued that without the production and promotion money they spent, no one would be familiar enough with the artists to make people want to buy them. That's because ringtones are largely *fashion* items and represent the current tastes of most young users who tend to change them frequently. This is enhanced by the ease of downloading them and paying via their cell phone bills.

This is an example of the kind of infighting that keeps these markets from expanding even more quickly in the U.S. than they do in Europe and Asia. Some believe that, as MP3 and iTunes downloads and fans' own CD music collections can be edited and converted to ringtones, the market may diminish somewhat, but as new technology develops it will still remain a source of income for all.

In my research, I ran across an article by Los Angeles music business attorney Dina LaPolt (www.lapoltlaw.com) that contained some good information on the state of the cell phone ringtone boom and the income it generates for songwriters and publishers. The following is an excerpt from her article on Music Biz Academy.com (www.musicbizacademy.com) that she was kind enough to let me reprint. Keep in mind that this area is evolving as quickly as the technology and since this article was written, master tones have become much more popular in the U.S. You've undoubtedly heard them while you were waiting in the checkout line at the supermarket, and if it was *your* song you heard you wouldn't have been nearly as annoyed. You'd just think, "Ka-ching!"

RINGTONE DEALS IN THE U.S. BY DINA LAPOLT, ESQ.

Usually, these agreements are made between a cell phone aggregator (i.e., distributor) and music publishers and/or songwriters for the re-creation (i.e., "replay") of a song either monophonically (archaic) or polyphonically (preferred). The terms of these agreements are short, ranging from one to three years. Although most of the deals are worldwide, the music publisher most often will try to limit the deal to the U.S. and Canada. The way in which the aggregators pay royalties to the owners and controllers of musical compositions in the U.S. is usually the greater of ten cents ($0.10) or ten percent (10%) of the ringtone price paid by the consumer. Accordingly, there is always a floor of ten cents ($0.10) per ringtone, which is a step up from what songwriters and publishers are used to being paid on sales of record albums, pursuant to the statutory rates set by the U.S. Copyright Office. (The current minimum statutory rate for record albums is $0.091 cents for under five minutes of playing time.) Accordingly, if a ringtone sells for $3.00, then the royalty paid to the owners and controllers of that particular musical composition would be $0.30 cents.

In addition, most agreements have a "most favored nations" clause in them, which states that if another music publisher (or songwriter) receives a higher royalty rate for its share of the copyright relating to the ringtone, then the same higher rate shall apply to all. The "most favored nations" clause will usually apply to all the provisions of the agreement (i.e., term, territory, advances, etc.), not just the royalty rate. Many ringtone agreements are contingent on the company's also obtaining licenses from the respective public performance organization (i.e., ASCAP, BMI, or SESAC) and those monies will flow to the publisher and songwriter as well.

Although the technology in the U.S. is not quite as advanced as the technology available in Asia and the rest of Europe, the U.S. is catching up fast. In Japan, iMode is one of the leading cell phone aggregators and they boast that they have over 47 millions subscribers. In Europe, Vodafone is the biggest cell phone aggregator, boasting that they have over 146 million subscribers (this would mean that approximately one out of every four cell phone users in Europe signed up with Vodafone).

Using 3G technology, iMode and Vodafone provide customized cell phones which can offer a number of personalized services, such as music shops, music video channels, buying tickets to concerts through mobile ticketing, visual radio, personalized content (such as wallpaper and imaging featuring your favorite artist), and editorial content.

Taken from lectures presented by the Mobile Music Forum at the MIDEM music business conference in Cannes, France, in January 2005, the Forum reported that studies show a person takes the following three items each time they leave their house: keys, a purse (or a wallet), and a cell phone. Accordingly, it is only a matter of time before the cell phone becomes the ultimate multimedia device, which will incorporate technology used by other devices such as the iPod and be able to receive streaming services. The ability to receive streaming services on portable devices like cell phones may make devices containing fixed music, like the iPod, unnecessary. In fact, Asia and Europe have been utilizing these types of customized cell phones for several years already.

However, most of what we have in the United States are still only monophonic and polyphonic ringtones, whereby the actual song is recreated through a series of tones, most of them through MIDI (i.e., musical instrument digital interface). According to lectures taken from the Mobile Music Forum at MIDEM, monophonic and polyphonic ringtones generated an estimated $4 billon in 2004. Currently, with the use of the relatively new 3G technology, a consumer in the U.S. can now download the actual master recording to a cell phone, as opposed to downloading a monophonic or polyphonic ringtone. These new types of tones are being referred to in the industry as "truetone masters" or "master tones."

In some Asian countries where cell phone technology is more advanced than in the U.S., revenues from the secondary usage of master recordings (e.g. master tones, ringtones and ringbacks) have already surpassed revenues from the primary market of recordings.

Dina LaPolt is a music lawyer in Los Angeles at LaPolt Law P.C. (www.LaPoltLaw.com). Her clients include the estate of Tupac Shakur and other clients in the music, television, merchandising, and book publishing industries.

Music for Commercials

The marketplace for music in commercials has undergone a major change in just the past few years and a sea of change from when I had my own commercial jingle company in the 1970s. The philosophy then was that no self-respecting artist would ever consider selling out to corporate sponsors by allowing his music to be used in commercials. There were special clauses they demanded in their contracts that prevented it, and their managers realized the artists could lose a major part of their fan-base if they were presented in this way. Now, despite holdouts among revered artists like Bruce Springsteen, Tom Waits, Neil Young, and the Doors (well, Jim Morrison anyway, even though the band had vowed to stick together), others including Led Zeppelin, the Rolling Stones, Paul McCartney, and Bob Dylan went for it. Who knows why—did they really need the money? My attitude in those cases, after the initial shock, was, "I think they've earned the right to do whatever they want. If I don't like it, that's *my* problem."

Unknown indie bands and artists slogging it out on the road with families to feed can get a lot more pragmatic, and it's not hard to see why they'd go for a good paycheck. Young idealistic fans often get disillusioned by that move, though, so it can be a risky proposition for some bands, even when they see the possibilities of mass exposure. The risk is softened in many cases by some of the ways current commercials use music:

1. **Hit song with a hook that becomes a perfect fit for an ad slogan**: Bob Seger's "Like a Rock" for Chevy, Billy Steinberg and Tom Kelly's "True Colors" for Kodak.

2. **Song that crafts a message specifically written for the product**: Squeak E. Clean's "Hello Tomorrow" for Adidas.

3. **Song creates a mood, much as it's used in TV or film**: Gorillaz's "Feel Good Inc." for Apple's iPod, Sting's "Desert Rose" for Jaguar. All of the tracks from Moby's *Play* album are used in a variety of commercials.

4. **Lifestyle background music, a presentation of what someone in the ad might be listening to**: Volkswagen ads by Stereolab and Spiritualized.

The last two categories are ones that some bands and artists feel more comfortable with since they seem less like an endorsement of the product and more like the music *they* listen to.

For artists who have yet to experience mass exposure, commercials can be a career boost. The Sony PlayStation Portable ad introduced Franz Ferdinand to a mass audience with "Take Me Out." Same thing with the Concretes' "Say Something New" for Target.

PROS AND CONS

Artists with major hits who are approached to use them in commercials need to carefully consider the effect of using their songs in commercials before deciding to do it.

Will it negatively affect the future market of the song? Sometimes overexposure can make people not want to hear it anymore. Or it can actually corrupt the "nostalgia factor" by too much association with the product. High blood pressure pills being advertised by the song you fell in love to in high school might be a bad idea. On the upside, if a listener hasn't heard the song in years it could rekindle the "nostalgia factor" in a positive way—again, depending on the product.

Another positive effect might be that once people in film, TV, video games, and ringtones hear the song again, they may want to use it in their own media. This is a common effect for unknown bands, too.

Positive or negative, big money talks and huge corporations have it to spend on advertising. For established hits on a year-long ad campaign, selling to a commercial can be worth over $1 million.

THE APPEAL OF THE INDIE ARTIST TO AD AGENCIES

It's all about smarter marketing and economics. Ad agencies who create the campaigns and individual commercials realized that, for certain youth-oriented products, using contemporary music was a more effective and less expensive approach. It helps their clients become, in effect, part of the *tribe* they're selling the product to. The thirty-something creative staff of the ad agencies is part of that musical culture, so when they think of music to use in their ads they think about music *they* like. It conveniently happens that some of their favorite bands and artists are independent artists or signed to small record labels that make their livings primarily by touring and sales of merchandise and CDs. From the agencies' point of view, they give the bands national exposure—and at a fraction of what it usually cost their clients for music in commercials.

So, the lines are blurring between the shame of selling out and the hipness of buying in. Not that there aren't still artists who feel they'll lose their fan base, autonomy, and dignity by doing commercials—just a lot fewer of them.

If you're a band or solo artist who writes your own music and owns all the rights to it (you haven't assigned your publishing rights to another publisher), and you also own your own masters (you haven't signed a record deal in which the record company owns your master recordings), you make it easy for an agency to license your song for use in a commercial. (Obviously, you need to be a very good band!) You'll get a few hundred to a few thousand dollars depending on the budget of the client, whether the ad is local or national, on radio or TV, and how long they want to use it. If it's renewed past the original contract period, you get an additional payment. You'll get most of the income from the up-front synchronization fee and master-use fee. You'll get some, but not much, from your performing rights organization as they all pay just a fraction for commercials of what you'd get for use in film or TV shows.

MAKING IT HAPPEN

To pursue the scenario, get in touch with song placement companies or services like TAXI (www.taxi.com) or SongCatalog (www.songcatalog.com), or some of the online pitch services mentioned in chapter thirteen (on page 279).

Call major ad agencies, tell them your situation, and ask if there are placement services that they work with that you can contact. This gives them a way to politely turn you away knowing that if you're worth hearing there's someone they trust who will prescreen. Just in case they're intrigued though, it also helps if you have a Web site to refer them to, or another place they can hear your music online.

They also use music libraries (see "Production Music Libraries," in this chapter, on pg. 334) to supply them with underscore music if they don't want to hire someone to create custom tracks for them.

YOUR OWN JINGLE PRODUCTION COMPANY

You may already be producing film and TV music or library music and want to branch out. If you decide you want to start your own jingle company, you'll need to have very good production skills or to partner with someone who does. You need to own or have access to excellent recording facilities, musicians, engineers, arrangers, and an attorney. Because most ad agencies are signatories to American Federation of Musicians (AFM), American Federation of Television and Radio Artists for singers and actors (AFTRA), and Screen Actors Guild (SAG), your company should also be a signatory to their agreements. This allows you, as a union member, to play on your own sessions and for you and the other musicians and singers to collect residual payments for every thirteen-week period the ad is used after the initial period. Check with your local union to set that up and learn how to do the reports or the union reps can refer you to someone who can do it for you. Go to AFM (www.afm.org), AFTRA (www.aftra.org) and SAG (www.sag.org) and search for "commercials." A thirty-second commercial can bring you $5,000 to $50,000 for the combined production costs and creative fee depending on whether it's local or national and how long it is used.

The agency will always want this to be a work for hire and will want to own all rights to what you create for them. If possible, try to retain rights to receive performance royalties from your performing rights organization (ASCAP, BMI or SESAC), or if it's a song, to receive any writer's share of royalties that might come from other uses: film, TV series, or ringtones. Chances are you won't be able to negotiate that, but it's worth a shot.

DEALING WITH AD AGENCIES

Large ad agencies may have multi-million dollar accounts and with the stakes so high, they can't afford to gamble. If they choose music that sounds less than professional and appropriate, they risk losing an account and their jobs. So a composer not only needs to understand the advertising medium and be thoroughly professional, but must be a kind of psychologist, instilling confidence in his abilities and making agency personnel feel secure in their musical choices.

They'll usually want to hire you because of something else they heard from you. If not and you're just pitching them your music cold, you'll need to develop a musical and personal rapport with the creative exec you'll be working with. You'll need a musical frame of reference, much like a music supervisor does with a film or TV director described earlier (see "Writing for Audio-Visual Media" on page 322), since the agency people may not have a technical knowledge of music. Good communication will save you lots of time and error.

When you start a project, they'll have a storyboard already worked out—a series of drawings or a simple animation depicting the way they see the commercial from beginning to end. Each section is timed with a script that shows where the voiceover (VO) goes.

They may want you to create the lyric yourself or more likely give you a lyric or slogan to work from. (If you're lucky, the lyric is actually singable!)

You and several other producers will usually be asked to come up with demos to play for the client. They may give a minimal budget to cover demo costs, but occasionally you'll be asked to do the demos on spec (your money). Digital demos are usually not hard to put together for a maximum sixty-second spot and not hard to adapt and change quickly. It's a good idea to come up with more than one to give them a choice. If you get something they like, you can ultimately just embellish the tracks you have or arrange it for live musicians.

Ad agencies prefer to do business with music producers with whom they have good rapport, who are professional, who understand their needs, and who deliver the goods at an equal or better price than anyone else. They also like to deal with people who are personable and even charismatic, because they can depend on them to impress their clients. It won't do to have the client come to your session and have the ad executive who hired you have to apologize for your bad attitude. That's not the way business is done at that level. He wants the client to have confidence in you and compliment him on his good taste. A great personality will never substitute for competence in this business, but in this case at least it can provide a competitive edge.

NEGOTIATING YOUR CREATIVE FEE

Just as it is in any other business, negotiating your fee depends on clout and chutzpah. It takes a lot of nerve to ask for twice what you think you can get and negotiate from there. At any rate, figuring out what to ask for is one of the most difficult parts of the business. You don't want to downgrade yourself by asking too little or price yourself out of business by asking too much. Get all the information you can ahead of time about the client's needs, the target demographic, and whether it's a national or regional campaign. A union representative may be able to give you guidance on what other producers charge as creative fees. They'll also be helpful in planning your recording budget if you're using live musicians. There are some general principles to remember that I learned by trial and error.

I once bid against two competitors on a job that was to be a series of thirty-second spots, variations on a basic theme. My bid was based on my figuring out a low-cost way to do the variations. (This was in the dark ages before digital software.) I lost the bid, and it wasn't until two years later that the agency representative would tell me why. The spots had gone for nearly twice my figure, he said, because the other two bids were in the same neighborhood and the client decided that if my competitors, both well-known pros, were charging that much, he didn't see how I could possibly deliver for half that amount. The agency exec, for whom I'd done other projects, tried to convince the client, but the psychology of "If it costs more, it must be better" worked against me. After that I changed my negotiating tactics.

Bid high, and let them tell you it's too steep. You can then say, "Well, let me see if I can figure out some shortcuts without compromising the quality." Then get back to them with something like, "I made a good deal with a new studio so I can knock off a couple hundred," or "I can use three singers instead of six." If you have a solid relationship with the ad agency, they may hint at what sort of ballpark figure they're thinking about, but they'd rather not. Obviously, if you're talking about Coca-Cola, you're dealing with a company that annually spends billions on advertising, as opposed to a local jewelry store that spends thousands.

THE AUDITION DEMO

Because this field is very competitive, having a first-rate demo that shows your skill and versatility is essential. Collect up to ten pieces (no more) in no more than five minutes of music. If you've already got legitimate credits, include them. If not, don't be intimidated. The agencies are always looking for new talent because some composers, after a few years, get too expensive or their style gets old. Agencies look for fresh ideas and very contemporary styles, particularly for youth market products. Put a sample of whatever you do best first on the demo. Do a piece of atmospheric background on it. Create some jingles for imaginary products. Show them some different moods in both vocal jingles and instrumental underscore in different styles.

Many commercials only identify the product on screen and not in the jingle. Create a couple of evocative jingles with lyrics that express some emotional comment on life in general. Print a label and CD insert with your logo so you'll look like a pro. Print some credits or other self-promotion on the insert, don't forget your address, phone number, e-mail address, and Web site. If you have a site devoted to your business with samples of other commercials you've done, you're ahead of the game, but you also want them to have an actual CD (or a DVD with a video collection of past work) and résumé that they can keep on file and put their hands on quickly.

MAKING CONTACT

Try to make personal contact by setting up a meeting, especially if you tend to make a good impression in person. If you have an impressive studio, try to get them there for the meeting. When you get a meeting at their office, take copies of your audio-visuals. After the meeting, send a card to thank them for their time. On a file card or database, keep track of your meetings, listing:

1. Their contact information

2. Their clients (always subject to change)

3. Who you met there

4. Their comments on your presentation

5. The names of their secretaries and assistants

6. A date and time to call back (ask them before you leave the meeting)

You'll probably make several calls before you talk to your main contact, but you'll make friends with the secretary or assistants who also will be able to give you valuable information on upcoming projects. Continue to update your data file every time you call, noting the date. All this is important because after your first twenty appointments (or sooner), you'll start to lose track of who's where.

Most major jingle activity is in New York, Chicago, Dallas, and Los Angeles, so if you don't live near those cities you need to pursue some other options. Among those options is to establish an Internet presence with a great looking Web site. Make that your online office. Since audio files can be sent anywhere and since any ad agency worth approaching these days has a high-speed Internet connection, you can do a lot of business that way.

Here are some other suggestions for finding work as an independent jingle producer:

- Place ads in advertising and production trade magazines such as:

    Adweek (www.adweek.com)

    Advertising Age (www.adage.com)

Millimeter (www.digitalcontentproducer.com): More on the video/film post-production tech side.

Adtunes.com (www.adtunes.com): Just for fun and to update yourself on popular music used in commercials.

- Contact your state film commission and try to get listed as a music resource in the catalogue they send to companies to solicit film projects in your state. These catalogues are also sent to companies within the state. Search the Internet under "film commission."

- It may cost you $1,000 for the CD-ROM edition but the Advertising Redbooks (www.redbooks. com) have all the information on major ad agencies, their personnel, contact information and client lists. Before you spend the money though, call your local library and see if they have a reference copy.

- Most major cities have an ad club whose members include ad agencies, media professionals, clients, and music producers in that region. They also have newsletters in which you can advertise. The American Advertising Federation is a national organization for advertising professionals. They have periodic conventions in various cities that provide valuable opportunities to show your wares and make contacts. Get information on membership and schedules from:

AMERICAN ADVERTISING FEDERATION

1101 Vermont Ave., NW, Ste. 500 • Washington, D.C. 20005-6306

Tel: (202) 898-0089 • Fax: (202) 898-0159

Web site: www.aaf.org • E-mail: aaf@aaf.org

WESTERN REGION OFFICE

251 Post St., Ste. 302 • San Francisco, CA 94108

Tel: (415) 421-6867 • Fax: (415) 421-0512

PURSUING SMALL LOCAL AD ACCOUNTS

Yet another possibility is to form your own small-scale ad agency and music production company dealing with small local accounts. It's a good idea to start small. It's possible to build a business on small local accounts and progress into bigger accounts. This works best if you live in a small town outside large metro areas where you don't have as much competition and know people on a more personal basis. Take advantage of the fact that you know business people from school, church, and work. It requires less research when you already know your potential clients. But even in big cities there are lots of potential customers. Check out local restaurants, clubs, hotels, tourist attractions, car dealerships, and similar businesses to see if they already do or will do radio ads. If you have a good home studio, put together a catchy jingle for some of them. Write a sample script, get a voiceover actor to read it, and present your potential clients with a thirty-second version of the whole thing. If it sounds professional, you'll be surprised at how positively people react to hearing their very own commercial jingle. They may even want to do the voiceovers for their own commercials (an approach that can either be wonderful or a disaster!).

Research the various businesses to see how they're promoting themselves currently—local radio spots without music or stock library music underscore, print ads only, etc. Record several styles of music for various businesses—Latin for Mexican restaurants, country for a western clothing store, some solid pop or rock tracks for any kind of business. Spend some creative time coming up with something special after you've made note of their business slogans or whatever means they've used to distinguish themselves in their market.

Your competition for local radio ads are the radio stations themselves, whose salesmen sell businesses package deals that include their staff announcers writing and reading the ad copy. A good plan is to form alliances with the ad salespeople at the stations and help them put together those packages. Your advantage is that you can provide the client with an original jingle and likely can do it cheaper than a jingle house, which has more overhead. You would sell the jingle to the client and have the station's announcer write and read additional copy.

A drawback to this approach is that, in order to give the client an inexpensive deal, you'd pretty much have to do it without union help. When you do non-union spots and play on them yourself, you do not receive residuals. You charge a one-time "buyout" fee that includes your creative fee and covers your production cost. You hope to create a lasting relationship with the client and periodically create new jingles for him.

Check out Jingle Course (www.jinglebiz.com). They have a list of resources and offer a reasonably priced course in starting your own jingle business.

All of the above can be applied to television ads as well. Find a video production company to partner with and come up with some creative concepts together.

WORKING FOR A JINGLE PRODUCTION COMPANY

If you're not interested in being in business for yourself, another alternative is to hook up with a jingle music production company or "jingle house." These are established businesses that usually represent several composers. You may not have the potential to make as much money if you choose this route, but you wouldn't have as many expenses and headaches, either. Find them in the Yellow Pages and on the Internet, usually under "music arrangers and composers," "music producers," "jingle production," or "commercial music production." Also, check out the local recording studios and find out if any jingle production is done there and who is doing it. Compile a demo of your best work and play it for them.

What if you have a jingle idea for a major product?

If you think up an outstanding jingle or concept for a particular product, can you sell it to an agency? Your odds are not good. Remember, ad agencies who represent those products pay a lot of money to copywriters in their company to come up with those ideas. There's a good chance they don't want to hear yours. If they do, you risk that they'll borrow your idea or some important aspects of it without paying you. Ideas are not copyrightable. What you *can* copyright is an actual slogan or jingle (song), but unless it's compatible with the product image already planned by the agency, the odds are against the company using it no matter how clever the idea. Having said that, if you believe enough in your idea you should give it a shot anyway. Your best strategy is to find out which ad agency represents the product, present them a finished product, get your ego out of the way and allow one of the creative execs at the company to take credit for it. Always consider that, in this kind of situation, you need to join power, not fight it.

Musical Theater

Musical theater is a wonderful collaborative art form combining music, drama, dance, design, costuming, sometimes film, and who knows what else in the future.

For a musical to succeed, it requires the collaborative efforts of a composer and lyricist working closely with a *librettist* (book-story-script writer) to spot songs within text and maintain emotional clarity as to what is required in each musical moment. Once the musical is written (or you *think* it's written.) and moves into presentations or a production, the collaborative team expands to include the director, choreographer and music director, all of whom will point out problems, discrepancies and needs from their particular perspective. Another important member of the team is a *dramaturg*. The function of a dramaturg varies with theater companies and individual productions. It can encompass auditioning librettos or source materials for possible expansion into musical theater productions, creating development teams, and being a sounding board and coach during all phases of writing and production.

Songwriters crossing into musical theater find that it demands great discipline, craftsmanship, and patience, since it will inevitably require constant rewrites to accommodate running time, pacing, choreography, and the personalities of the characters and the actors who portray them. Even the best writers discover that songs and musical scenes they'd visualized won't work on stage quite the way they were envisioned and require quick rewrites.

Though some of the most memorable recorded hits to come from musicals have been ballads, stage musicals depend heavily on fast pacing and choreographed up-tempo numbers to generate the visual and auditory excitement that reaches to the last rows of the theater. The vast majority of the songs written for shows are specific to characters and plot points, and are not required to "step out" of the show (a somewhat counter-intuitive approach for hit-oriented songwriters) though within context they can provide thrilling theatrical moments.

Launching a major musical theater production is a tremendous undertaking. The weight of selling the show is on the shoulders of you and your partners. Once the show is written—a process that can take several years—a key step is to interest a producing theater or independent producer in your project. Until they come in to support and promote the show, the financial burden of launching the show is yours. This includes all expenses of recording and copying the demo recording, sending out libretto and CD to potential producers, and putting together a presentation/backers' audition of your material. For this, you will need to hire a director, singers, and possibly a musical director and accompanist, lease a hall, negotiate contracts, and invite potential financial backers.

I've attended many backers' auditions. In the most common means of putting one together, a narrator tells the story and describes the action while actor/singers read the dialogue leading into the major musical numbers. Sometimes the music for those numbers is pre-recorded and sometimes musicians are hired, depending on your budget. Union contracts permitting, these presentations may be videotaped so the material can be shown again to anyone who couldn't attend. Be aware, however, that theater on video carries only a fraction of the impact of a live performance. Be prepared to edit the video down to highlight its strong points and eliminate whatever doesn't sparkle. As an alternative to sending a video, it is standard practice to submit a synopsis and audio sampler from the show.

Another approach is to create a Web site for the show. It gives you the advantage of presenting, well-produced demos of the music, script reading, and story synopsis. You might also include graphics or photos of proposed set design and costuming, resumes of the librettist, composer and lyricist and any other relevant information all in one place. While it doesn't have quite the magic of a live performance or the important live networking potential, it *does* have the advantage that a potential backer can audition it anytime, anywhere in the world. For that reason, however, wait until it's *really* ready and copyrighted and be aware that you *can* set it up so you can only grant access to those you authorize to see it. Regarding recording and videotaping, you may run into union restrictions if you're working with union artists. Be sure to check that out before you hire a video crew.

For an example, the Web site for Bob Christianson and Cappy Capossela's rock opera *The Grail* (www.the-grail.net), contains well-produced music for the show, a synopsis, some of the lyrics, and the names and photos of the performers, as well as a way to buy the cast CD.

TRAINING

Most writers I know who write for musical theater are those who have always loved it and know all the musical scores. They've been "going to school" in musical theater for a long time, even if they have no formal training. It's definitely an asset to be a fan. The public library and the Internet, as always, are great places to do research. The Samuel French bookstores in New York and Los Angeles have many librettos for sale. Read every libretto you can find and see as many new musicals as possible: readings, workshops, small theater, community or high school productions, dinner theater, and major touring productions. Don't just attend shows that you think you'll like, or that are well reviewed. There is often more to learn from an unproduced or undeveloped musical than from a hit.

The key to writing a successful musical lies in the strength, emotional complexity, and clarity of the libretto. You can be the best songwriter in the world, but if the book (script) of your show doesn't work, the show will inevitably fail. Without a strong book, you might as well be writing a musical revue, a collection of songs with perhaps a connective theme, but without a coherent story line. While revues may contain marvelous songs, theatrically they do not pack the emotional punch of a full book show. In addition, they tend to be a harder sell to producing theaters and rarely have the extended runs and years of viability that book shows do.

The theater world is filled with stories of shows that had wonderful scores but died because the book tanked. Book writing for a musical is a highly under-appreciated talent, one that is practiced by few scriptwriters in these cinema-obsessed days. If you find a librettist who understands your musical vision and whose dramatic vision matches your own, nurture the working relationship and consider yourself very fortunate. Traditionally, the book writer supplies songwriters with structure, script, dialogue, and descriptions of what is needed within an emotional moment before the song is written. That way, the music and script fit with each other to embellish character and plot—one of the goals of a fully integrated book musical.

While New York has been the home of musical theater, an increasing amount of development is happening in Los Angeles, much of which is centered on the organization The Academy for New Musical Theatre in the NoHo (North Hollywood) theater district (see page 363). ASCAP sponsors a musical theater workshop in Los Angeles and New York. BMI currently sponsors the Lehman Engel Musical Theater Workshop in New York. Other organizations involved in new musicals and/or helping new musical theater writers include Theatre Building Chicago and Musical Theatre Works in New York. Contact information on these organizations follows.

For more information on workshops, contact BMI and ASCAP in New York and Los Angeles and the other organizations listed below. The annual *Songwriter's Market* publishes a list of play producers and publishers looking for original musicals.

Take part in any aspect of university, community, or dinner theater, and summer stock musical theater productions and write for as many original projects as possible. These are great places to try out your ideas. There's no better way to learn.

THE MONEY

Between the Broadway and road performances, musical theater shows generated $1.4 billion in the 2004–2005 season. Costs of financing a show on Broadway are $5–$15 million. They need to take in $400,000 to $600,000 per week to cover costs of writers' royalties, cast, crew, advertising, and rent. The income for composers and lyricists can be substantial whether the show is a hit or not. They include pre-show options and advances from the show's producers and investors, pre-Broadway performances (most shows are launched in other cities to keep initial costs down, test all aspects of the production and generate good pre-Broadway press). There's income during the Broadway run and from touring companies during and after the Broadway run. (Road versions can be substantially lucrative and last a lot longer.) Other sources of income are the same as those covered in chapter nine Where Your Money Comes From: radio, TV broadcasts, sales of singles, soundtrack albums, videotapes and DVDs, film and made-for-TV versions, and "The Making of . . ." specials. Songs that have great appeal beyond the show will be covered by other artists on their own CDs and on and on.

There are a variety of payment options available for all participants. Once you've decided you'd like to pursue this more seriously, I recommend that you buy the most current edition of Jeffrey and Todd Brabec's book, *Music, Money, and Success*. It breaks down all your options, percentages, and numbers, including typical weekly show expenses for Broadway and road productions, that will be an authoritative resource if you're creating a business plan for presentation to backers. It also includes up-to-date royalty terms for Dramatists Guild and non-Dramatists Guild contracts as well as analyses of all after-Broadway income streams.

The Dramatists Guild, the world's strongest protective organization for writers, provides model contracts for musical theater writers at every level of production.

WRITING FOR MUSICAL THEATER

To get some information for you on the realities of writing for musical theater as a career, I interviewed an old friend, **Michael Silversher**, whose work has encompassed many facets of this genre. He says most people immediately think of Broadway but there are a lot of different projects you can get involved in closer to home, wherever that might be.

Michael and Patricia Silversher earned the 1999 Grammy Award for Best Children's Recording for *The Adventures of Elmo in Grouchland* and co-wrote more than one hundred songs for Disney companies. Michael was the founding/resident composer, musical director, and resource artist for Robert Redford's Sundance Playwrights' Lab and Sundance Children's Theatre for many years, and co-wrote seven children's stage musicals. He says writing for TV is easier and more lucrative but not nearly as much fun. More info at www.michaelsilversher.com.

You've developed and presented shows for schools. How does that work?

Generally the funding comes from corporate sponsors and there's naturally an educational focus. One series I do for the schools is funded by Kaiser Permanente and is for kindergarten through high school. We do three different schools a day. Each show is forty-five minutes long. We call it "bell to bell" theater, and there are usually four of us—three actors/singers and a stage manager. There's also an education guide for teachers and a curriculum developed with it so teachers can maximize the educational benefits both before and after the show.

The schools let us know what topics they need to deal with and, for the appropriate grade levels, we've done topics including nutrition, conflict resolution, dealing with bullies and strangers, and AIDS education. The object is to show relatable characters and situations. The songs also need to incorporate mnemonic devices to help the information stick in kids' heads.

When I do shows at schools I'm also aware that I may not only be giving them their first theatrical experience and helping to create audiences for theater, but I feel I actually may be creating theater itself when somebody in the audience says, "Hey, I'd love to do that! How do I do that?" It gets them curious about doing something that's not like television, playing games or like the movies, not like anything else in their experience. It feels so much more real.

You got your start in the famed Palo Alto Youth Community Workshop near San Francisco (now called Theatre Works [www.theatreworks.org]).

Stanford University founder Leland Stanford created the city charter for Palo Alto and mandated that 1 percent of the utility bills would go to fund arts programs. The Palo Alto Youth Community Workshop was one of them. I met my wife and a lot of my musical theater friends there and got just an unbelievable education. Starting in 1970, I wrote eleven full musicals through them and learned how to do everything wrong. Lehman Engel said that everybody needs a place to fail and this was a great place to fail because it was outside the eyes of everyone. I learned how to write out of range, out of style, out of character—but because of that I learned how to write in range, style, and character.

It shows the kind of influence a local project like that can have on a whole industry

Yeah, when you consider that some of my fellow students at the time were Rob Minkoff who went on to direct Disney's *The Lion King* film that spawned a whole industry in itself, Kirk Wise who directed *Beauty and the Beast,* and a bunch of other great actors, directors, and writers. Most Broadway theater starts in local and regional workshops.

If someone wants to write a musical theater piece, what's a good kind of project to get your feet wet on?

It's always better to pick a story in the public domain like a fairy tale or Shakespeare or something that you don't have to worry about getting the rights to.

If there's a novel or short story or play you do need to get rights to, how do you do it?

Here's an example. I read a great book by Lois Lowry called *Gathering Blue*, about a society that enslaves its artists. I and my librettist, Richard Hellesen, wanted to develop it into a musical theater piece. You can either get amateur or professional rights. Amateur rights are cheaper. Our agent in New York negotiated for the rights from Lowry's publisher for $2,500 for eighteen months. During that time no other amateur rights can be granted. It has to be done in a non-profit theater but if the show works you can then get a license for the professional rights, which costs a lot more.

We got a $15,000 grant from South Coast Repertory and did our first reading in (2005) and we're continuing to develop it.

Note: Michael has been Composer in Residence for the Educational Theatre Program at South Coast Repertory (www.scr.org) since 1989. It's one of the top five theaters in the U.S. for developing award-winning Broadway plays and musicals.

I see a lot of pop songwriters who want to get into musical theater. What's the difference between the two disciplines?

What the song needs to do is show you what the character is *feeling*, or a discussion about something important between the characters, not to do exposition or narration. Too often they'll be singing about something they should be showing you. A pop song is only responsible to itself and in theater it's responsible for so much more. It should show you the motivation of the characters. Pop songwriters also tend to write to current musical trends. It's important to write to your time and sensibility but don't write to current trends because by the time they get into production the musical trend is gone and it sounds dated. You need to write timeless songs.

Organizations

THE DRAMATISTS GUILD OF AMERICA

234 W. 44 St. • New York, NY 10036

Tel: (212) 398-9366 • Fax: (213) 944-0420

Web site: www.dramatistsguild.com

Associate, student and professional memberships available with a number of educational craft and business resources and a bi-monthly journal, *The Dramatist*.

ASCAP

Michael Kerker, director of Musical Theater division

One Lincoln Plaza   New York, NY 10023

Tel: (212) 621-6000 • Fax: (212) 724-9064

Web site: www.ascap.com

BMI - LEHMAN ENGEL MUSICAL THEATRE WORKSHOP

Jean Banks, Senior Director of Musical Theatre for BMI and Dicrector of the Lehman Engel Musical Theatre Workshop

320 W. 57th St. • New York, NY 10019

Tel: (212) 830-2508 (Workshop) • Fax: (212) 262-2824

Tel: (212) 586-2000 (BMI)

Web site: www.bmi.com

Sponsored by BMI, this is one of the oldest and most respected workshops for developing musical theater projects.

ACADEMY FOR NEW MUSICAL THEATRE (ANMT)

John Sparks, Artistic Director; Scott Guy, Executive Director

5628 Vineland Ave. • North Hollywood, CA 91601

Tel: (818) 506-8500

Web site: www.anmt.org • E-mail: academy@anmt.org

The Academy for New Musical Theatre has very impressive education and development programs. It supports workshops, readings, studio productions and collaboration opportunities for writers, composers, actors, directors, and producers. John Sparks is also Artistic Director of Theatre Building Chicago (www.theatrebuildingchicago.org), which presents excellent educational and development programs, as well.

VALUABLE WEB SITES

- Artslynx (www.artslynx.org): The best arts info portal online. International arts resource links to theater (including musical theater), dance, music, poetry, and more.

- Musicals101.com (www.musicals101.com): A great educational site that's a must for anyone wanting to learn about musical theater.

- National Alliance for Musical Theatre (www.namt.org): An alliance of musical theater organizations with a list of membership organizations searchable by state.

- Writing Musical Theatre (www.writingmusicaltheatre.com) is an online course presented by the Academy for New Musical Theatre for those who want to write for this medium.

- *Playbill* (www.playbill.com): News, reviews, auditions, and job listings. It's mainly Broadway-centric but worth checking out. Free membership.

BOOKS

- *The Songwriter's Market*, published annually by Writer's Digest Books
- *Words With Music: Creating Broadway Musical Libretto* by Lehman Engel
- *Writing the Broadway Musical* by Aaron Frankel
- *Making Music: The Guide to Writing, Performing & Recording* by George Martin

15 Getting a Record Deal

For the performer or songwriter/performer, obtaining a recording contract is a major step toward mass public exposure. Remember, however, that the real goal is not the record deal—that's only the *means* of manufacturing and marketing your artistry. The recording contract is far from a guarantee of fame and fortune. At its best it represents the legal basis for a cooperative marketing effort in which a team of experts exposes a product (you) to an audience who will translate their appreciation of your music into purchase of your music. The record deal is only part of a larger effort by your own personal team to promote your career in as many ways as they can and to earn you (and them) as much income as possible so you can keep doing what you love to do.

When approaching this or any other career decision, it's important to get as much information as possible about the circumstances, needs, and responsibilities of the other parties involved. In this chapter, I'll explore the information you need from the point of view of the record company. You'll learn how a record company looks at you as an artist, at your songs, and at your professional team. And since a deal with an established record company is not something every artist can count on (there was a time when most major artists couldn't get a deal), we'll look at the very viable, and sometimes preferable do-it-yourself option.

The Artist vs. The Writer/Artist

Exceptional writer/artists have always been around. Most popular songs on the radio were not performed by the song's writers until the 1950s and 1960s, with the increasing exposure of country and black music, and the birth of rock and roll. With the phenomenal success of the Beatles, who wrote their own songs, record companies began to realize that they could get publishing rights to the songs the artists were writing and thus be able to keep the potentially enormous publishing income along with the recording profits. The self-contained act was an attractive package because, though in most cases they would pay writers one of the two cents (the old rate) in mechanical royalties per side per unit sold, by also owning the publishing rights they could keep that other penny "in house." They could also participate in the publisher's half of the performance royalties collected from BMI and ASCAP.

RECORD COMPANIES, PUBLISHING, AND THE SELF-CONTAINED ARTIST

Today, virtually every record company has a publishing affiliate. Although the business affairs departments of the major record companies and their publishing companies will aggressively pursue the publishing rights of new artists signed by the company, if they want the artists badly enough, there's always a compromise that can be made. The publishing affiliates operate independently and also have income from other projects, so they are not dependent on their affiliated labels for their bottom line. That relationship is strongly encouraged, though.

Small, independent record companies, however, don't sell as many records. The royalties they receive from the ownership of the publishing rights, along with money from record sales, can help to offset their overhead. This makes the publishing a very important consideration in the deal. In that situation, being a self-contained act with publishing rights to offer is an asset.

For both the major labels and independents, a big advantage of the self-contained artist or group is that it eliminates the need to come up with outside material. That's because, even though the record company A&R staff is constantly on the lookout for songs for their artists who are not self-contained, they don't always have enough time to screen songs as well as to deal with their responsibilities to the many other acts on their rosters. So, the trend has been to give that responsibility to the producers or writer/producers (sometimes several for the same album) to write or find and produce songs for the project. Though that's generally a better gamble, I know of many projects that have been doomed by writer/producers who have insisted on writing all the material themselves and ended up with no hits. Having said that, major labels would still rather bet on the skills and promotional potential of attaching a well-known producer to the project, particularly for a new artist.

One of the most exciting attributes of the self-contained artist is the potential to create a consistent fusion of style and material that is quite unique and that offers fans the opportunity to get to know the writer/artist in a personal way. With a non-writing artist, though he or she may have a consistent vocal identity and style, it's much more difficult to achieve a consistency with the material. The most common way has been in the long-term relationships between writer/producers and artists.

One challenge non-writing artists face is the never-ending search for hit material that they and their record companies can agree on. The flip side of that problem is that those artists have access to the best songwriters in the world.

So, though the self-contained artist will most likely be the first choice of a record company, each situation is unique, and many different factors will be weighed in the decision to sign an act. The following sections will delineate those factors. Remember, these are all presented as ideal situations and the likelihood of a record company finding an act that "has it all" is almost nonexistent. The reality is that they take the best combination of ingredients they can find, and then try to compensate somehow for what's missing and roll the dice.

How Record Companies Listen to Your Music

The A&R rep gets to the office at ten. Last night he was at a gig of a band he's been courting for months and didn't get to bed 'til three. He has an East Coast call list to follow up on and the manager of one of his acts wants to talk about some extra tour support. This means he has to talk to several people at the company about this. He's stressed because he's got a deadline to finish an album project on another band for a Christmas release and the band just got a couple gigs they *had* to do and they are pushing the deadline. Another of his artists has fifteen new songs she's written for her next project. She wants to meet to talk about them. Let's make a leap and fantasize that after that meeting he actually has time to listen to your CD. This is assuming that someone on his staff has already pre-screened it.

If you can imagine this A&R scenario, stay with it and imagine him putting your CD on his player while he's answering some e-mail. This may be the pivotal moment in your career. What will he hear and how will he hear it?

Let's even say it wasn't pre-screened but the A&R rep has gotten a request or hears a buzz that makes him want to check out your Web site or MySpace page or your electronic press kit (EPK). He might be more focused at that point, but the process will be pretty much the same, and the considerations will be, too.

What takes place at that moment is a series of well-honed responses that are unique to each person listening, not even counting their state of mind at that moment. They range from the listener who is looking for a specific sound or style, and anything that doesn't fill the bill gets rejected automatically, to those who listen to the music in the background, and if anything jumps out at them they start to pay attention, to those who actually take time to focus totally on your music on the first listen.

The record company representative has several considerations to weigh when listening to your demo. Their main goal is to expose this song to as many people as possible. Depending on the focus of their label, the best way to do that is through the radio and word of mouth, which are dependent on first, a hit single, and second, a good marketing plan. They may be committing up to a million dollars of the company's money with close to a 90 percent chance they'll be wrong about the song and their job and new BMW are in serious jeopardy. So, they know, whether they're consciously aware of it or not, the common ingredients both artistic and business related that have to be there in the demo for them to get interested.

What are those ingredients? I can give you an answer based on my experience of having listened to thousands of songs in this way and having listened to and interviewed hundreds of publishers, producers, and record company A&R executives about this at countless seminars and at the Los Angeles Songwriters Showcase for many years.

The identity factor: When A&R executives listen to artists and bands, they're interested in a combination of factors beyond the songs. They look for a sound, style, or vocal quality they've never heard before, although they like to say it's *sort of* like (insert name of currently popular artist) because it helps to know there's already an established market for this genre of music, which makes the odds better for their investment. Given that, the song also needs to be different, unique, and totally identifiable. Once a listener hears this artist/band on the radio, she would never forget it and would always be able to identify it. It's a variation of brand recognition, which big-time product marketers know they must establish to be successful. Think about your favorite artists, and you'll know this is true.

If the artist is low on "brand recognition," the *song* becomes the most important factor. It can be a sliding scale. With a more recognizable sound, the songs may not be the most important aspect (except in country music) or the songs can afford to be more unorthodox, unusual, and unique. Ideally though, the execs want to hear both well-crafted songs *and* a unique sound.

Songs: Quality songs are crucial. When execs hear demos, they're listening for songs that have hit potential or that represent a consistent, identifiable sound. They want to know that you have a command of your craft and that the quality of the songs you write (or co-write) will be as good on the next CD as the ones they're hearing now. Just for insurance, they want to know that you're willing to record an *outside* song (written by someone else) assuming that it fits your style, or that you'll seriously consider collaborating with other writers. This won't be important if you're a self-contained band or artist and your appeal is based on your unique sound and your unique point of view and style in your writing. In that case, though, execs want to know that you have high standards for your writing and take it very seriously. They also hope that you're prolific and can write even in adverse situations, like a lengthy tour. They'll keep in mind that iTunes and other online sales sites are selling single downloads, so they might want to know if you've got an album full of songs so good that fans will want to buy them individually

Beyond what they hear on your demo, there are several other important factors they have to weigh before they get close to committing.

Live performance: This is incredibly important, since your ability to win an audience (along with airplay) is the best promotion tool they have. Word of mouth, particularly if you're not an artist with mass-appeal radio hits, is still the best way to build an audience of potential album buyers. Live performances can lead to reviews in the press and help to keep your name out in front for the public while giving local DJs and fans something to talk about. They can also provide contact with your audience so you'll know what they like about you. And performing live gives *you* a kind of high that can't be duplicated.

If he's interested enough in your demo to want to see you perform, the A&R rep will want to see another set of factors: confidence, good musicianship, and camaraderie. He'll want to see you interacting with each other, enjoying being on stage, and communicating with your audience, not standing there like robots, each in your own little world. That doesn't mean you have to do the splits, moonwalk, or choreograph dance steps if that's not your style. He'll also be checking out your choice of songs and their placement in the set, your arrangements, and the way you dress.

If you look great, or at least have an interesting and memorable look, it's a major plus. Now is a time when visual media is a major component in exposing you to potential fans.

You should talk to the audience. If that doesn't come naturally, prepare something you're going to say on stage before you get out there. Regardless of how great your music is, the audience wants to feel that you care about them. This is as important as your music, and a vital part of what they'll remember about you. There are a lot of good singers out there, not many great entertainers. The A&R rep wants to know that if there's one person in the audience, you're giving that person all you've got.

If you spent a few years as a live performer, that impresses an A&R rep. Show him some great reviews of your performances, preferably by recognized critics (your high school or college newspaper won't quite do). But most of all, he wants you to excite a tough audience, not one where all your friends are stacking the house. Let him see you perform in a club or in concert. But if you pull off a powerful performance inhis office for him and his critical and cynical staff, he will be impressed. By the way, the first time Christina Aguilera came to Ron Fair's office at RCA he told me he just had her sing *a cappella* in front of him. The rest, as they say, is history.

Move and speak confidently: Remember that we retain more information with our eyes than our ears, which is one reason we can sell a lot of records to people who attend your concerts and see your videos. Do you have a good sense of your personal identity? The A&R rep wants the audience to go away from your performance with a feeling that they know who you are and like you, or that you've given them enough pieces of yourself in your musical visual presentation to create an intriguing mystery that makes them want to know who you are.

Performance quality: Can you reproduce your demo sound in person? The A&R rep wants to know that the things he likes on your demo can be reproduced live. He doesn't expect to see an orchestra, but the basics have to be there. For example, if a significant degree of your appeal to me is based on your group vocal sound, he'd better hear it in your live performance. Though it's technically possible to pull off lip-synched vocals and to get a technically perfect vocal through the magic of AutoTune and other studio technology, he needs to know that some reviewer won't trash you for lip-synching vocals in concert or having a backing track malfunction while performing on *The Tonight Show*.

Sacrifice: Are you willing to sacrifice? Though it may take a couple of years of money-losing opening-act status, touring can eventually provide a major source of income (as can concert merchandising of T-shirts and other items), particularly for group members who don't receive songwriter's royalties.

CONNECTING WITH A&R ONLINE

Music Connection magazine's Scott Perham interviewed (in '06) Doc McGhee, a personal manager whose clientele has included Motley Crue, Bon Jovi, Skid Row and continues to represent Kiss, Ted Nugent and country artist Chris Cagle. When asked about scouting new talent, he said:

"Because of MySpace and sites like that, we can look at an artist without ever getting a package. Part of our checklist is that these people are innovative in a way that they get things to you, and that they're working hard and contacting their fans and being part of a culture. So we get mostly digital packages now. Or artists just send us a link to MySpace and we can see them and hear three or four songs. We listen to stuff every single day."

In another of Scott's *Music Connection* interviews in '06, Steve Lillywhite, (Sr. VP of A&R at Columbia Records whose production credits include Dave Matthews Band, The Rolling Stones and U2) says:

"The Internet is a great way of discovering music. I've had my eye on MySpace for about a year or so and I love it. If someone e-mails me a link, I can go there straightaway and hear their music. I will admit that some things pass me by, but if I don't hear it the first time it doesn't necessarily mean it's not good for me. I'll normally give it a second listen and sometimes after a while it will start growing on me."

Note: Steve is a unique individual. Most don't get a second chance. Also note that both of these pros check out MySpace.

Marketability

Now, if an A&R rep signs you, he has to assess how he's going to make people aware of you. What you need is PR potential!

Use your "story" as a hook to grab people's attention. Maybe you're the brother or sister, or son or daughter of somebody famous—though after the curiosity of the first album wears off, you'd better be able to deliver something substantial and very much your own. It also helps if you have famous friends who would like to sing or play on your record. That in itself doesn't get you signed, but it does give an exec something of an incentive to consider you.

Maybe you have been in the background as a musician, a backup singer, or a writer and are now coming up front to make your own music. There may be quite a few people out there who remember you when you were doing whatever you were doing in the background. If not, then maybe they can arouse their curiosity by association. People might think, "Oh, yeah, if he played with that artist, who I really like, he must be something like him. I'd probably love his stuff." Maybe you wrote a well known hit on one of the artist's albums.

What's interesting about your life? Jewel grew up in Alaska and lived in her car in San Diego while trying to get gigs in clubs. Christina Aguilera and Britney Spears got their start on the *Mickey Mouse Club*. Sheryl Crow was a schoolteacher who got her start at the Tuesday Night Music Club. Did you make a living playing in the New York subways? Did you live in the park while you played for tips in Santa Monica? Did you get your start driving a cab, collecting trash, waiting tables, or writing songs in jail? Do you have an interesting and flamboyant personality or hang out in social circles that automatically attract attention from the media?

What were the turning points in your music, in your personal outlook on life, your philosophy, your inspired decisions? What incidents or experiences changed your whole life?

People want to know things about you personally that enhance the mystique, that reveal you as a human being of substance, strangeness, virtue, or character, or all of the above.

Can you speak well and confidently? Do you have something interesting or funny to say? If not, the exec will make sure Letterman and Leno *don't* invite you to talk to them after you sing and that you *don't* do interviews. If you have strong and well-articulated opinions, on the other hand, you might be good on Bill Maher's show. Are you willing to do radio and TV interviews and in-store appearances?

More important than those hooks, though, is the marketability of your music itself. It's important that the music has a unity of style so that, when you do find the audience, you're the same artist from album to album, but still show artistic growth and change within your general style.

Writer/artists frequently ask if record companies like to hear stylistic variety. "I can write country, Hip-Hop, pop, rock, anything! Why don't I give them a little of each and see what they pick up on?" That's commendable if you want to be a staff songwriter, but a record company will no doubt ask, "But who are you, really?" If country music is what you write and perform best and enjoy most, what's the point in trying to market you as an R&B artist and release an R&B single on you? If it takes off, are they going to be trying to sell half an album of country tunes to a rock or R&B audience, or vice versa? So it's a marketing problem. Of course, they don't want all your music to sound the same and they do want you to grow; they just need for you to have developed your style to the point where you're the same identifiable artist from one album to the next. You should know who you are and how you want to be presented to the public. Maybe you've found a way to blend your stylistic influences into something totally unique and identifiable.

PERSONAL FACTORS

Considering the tremendous investment the company will make in your career, it's important for them to know that they're not going to be flushing it down the drain due to your lack of commitment or other personal factors beyond their control. These are important factors that they have to weigh.

Everyone else on your team doesn't want to worry that you're a heavy drug user and that you'll die of an overdose, or that you'll spend your advance on drugs, or that the drugs will ruin your health and relationships with your group. They like to know you're responsible enough to show up for gigs and interviews.

They want to know that you have a reasonably stable domestic situation, that your wife/husband/live-in can deal with your being on the road or that family problems won't interfere in any other way with your career.

Do you network? Do you like to meet new people? Maybe you enjoy hanging out with other artists and musicians. Maybe you systematically network, making and keeping industry contacts.

Ideally, the A&R rep likes you, since you may be spending a lot of time together. I personally like to enjoy my work and don't look forward to putting my neck on the line for someone I don't like and respect. Life's too short!

If you're a band, show that you've established a strong bond between band members and that each knows and accepts his function within the group. There may be strong egos involved and if they get out of hand, they can ruin the band. Money changes everything and if you're successful and doing a lot of touring, the pressures of both can do more to break up the group (and lose our investment) than anything else. So, a rep needs to get a sense of who you are as individuals and how you interact with each other.

You need to have a level of commitment that will get you through the really hard work and pressure that *starts* when you get a deal, go on the road, are away from your family, have no lasting relationships, answer your millionth "How did you get started?" question, and aren't seeing any songwriting royalties because everybody downloaded your album for free.

As I said earlier, this is the ideal situation. All of these elements will not necessarily be in one artist, but record companies will always look for them.

The Professional Team

Now we get to a subject that is very important for a record company executive to consider: the people on your team.

Your team should be made up of professional people who believe in you, and whose work the A&R rep respects. If you come to his attention through the efforts of your manager, producer, and attorney, who have been generating energy and momentum on your behalf, it will tell him that if he signs you, his company will have lots of competent aid from your team to ensure your success, and that if he doesn't sign you, someone else probably will. Another element that will tip the scales in your favor is having a competent manager and producer.

YOUR MANAGER

A manager, among other things, should be able to initiate publishing, record company, and production deals, and know what clubs or concerts you should play and what radio and TV shows you should do and when. She should oversee or coordinate the activities of your booking agent, road manager, publicist, accountant, attorney, business manager, publisher, and producer and be your official contact with the record company. She is the buffer between you and the business. She's your advisor and alter ego, and the captain of your team. Your manager should be excited about you and your talent and dedicated to helping you become a successful artist. She should be a manager with a record of successes, one who has managed other successful artists, one who knows the record business and understands the functions of all the component parts of the talent machine and the need for coordination and teamwork. Your manager knows your strengths and limitations, and has a plan for the long-range development of your career.

What if your manager does not have a stellar track record and is not knowledgeable about the record business? Unless she is willing to learn and take direction, she's going to have lots of problems. Enough arguments erupt between record companies and managers who *do* know the business. It's particularly crazy to try to deal with someone who has no way of knowing when an executive is making important concessions to her or suggesting a course of action that from his experience is advisable, but one that the manager does not understand.

Inexperienced managers may assume adversary roles to cover their ignorance, rather than finding ways to work with the company. It's a plus if you have a manager with whom the rep already has a good working relationship because their problems may have already been worked out, or at least they've learned how to argue with each other. He might even sign an artist he's not totally sold on if he believes in the abilities of the manager.

So, if you have an inexperienced manager, try to hook her up in a co-management situation with a successful manager so that she can learn and you won't have to suffer from her inexperience. Otherwise, it's better you didn't have one, so the rep can help you find a good one. Another option is a fresh, young manager who already works for a superstar management company. Often she may have acquired that job because she already brought a new artist to the company.

General Information

Managers get paid between 15–20 percent (sometimes 25 percent) of your gross income, rarely of your net because net is too hard to figure out. That includes songwriting, publishing, record royalties, touring, everything. It's possible, however, to exclude areas of income from management percentages. For example, you could exclude income from songwriting and publishing royalties and maybe give the manager a higher percentage on everything else. Usually, however, the manager feels that without her efforts in other areas, those songwriting royalties wouldn't be worth as much. That's a valid point, unless you've already got a substantial career as a writer. Management deals can be complex. I recommend you do your homework: *Musician's Business & Legal Guide* by Mark Halloran and *All You Need to Know About the Music Business* by Donald S. Passman are good sources. And, at the risk of being redundant, *never* sign a management agreement without an experienced entertainment attorney to negotiate for your interests!

It's difficult, but not impossible, to get a good, experienced manager unless you already have a record deal. The best managers don't have to take on the burden of building a career totally from scratch, since they can afford to be choosy. But it's not an impossible situation. There's no accounting for human chemistry and a manager's basic gambler's instinct. If she thinks you've got star quality, she just knows she can get you a deal!

Some artists need a manager they can relate to on a very personal basis. Others just need a manager to take care of their business and stay out of their personal life. You should know which type you need before you start looking. Let managers know what you're looking for right away. Having said that, it's extremely important that you like each other, know each other well, and respect each other, as your manager is really an alter ego for you and your representative and ambassador to the industry. Your manager works for *you*! I've known managers who thought otherwise.

One of the things a manager will ask you to do is give her "power of attorney" so she can make deals and sign contracts, cash your checks, and hire and fire your crew, all on your behalf. There will be occasions in which it's physically impossible for you to sign every live performance contract, so granting her power of attorney might be valuable. You should be sure about the scope of this power, though. It's a good idea to limit that power to certain types of contracts and specific dollar amounts and only if you are not there to do it yourself. Anything beyond those limits, you have to approve in writing which is easy to do via e-mail. This is one of those areas that can ruin you if it gets out of your control. Horror stories abound. Billy Joel and Leonard Cohen are just two examples.

Find an established manager by looking at the credits on CDs of artists who are in your genre of music (though some managers like to diversify). *Billboard* annually publishes a list of artists, and their managers and booking agents. Your local songwriters organization or music association may also have a list. If possible, try to contact an artist who the company manages (though they might see you as competition) or who the company *used to* manage (you'll hear the worst but you'll be forewarned).

The California Manager's Dilemma

In California and, to a lesser extent, in New York, labor law prohibits a manager from offering, promising, procuring, or attempting to procure employment for her clients (see California AB 884 and 2860, and New York Art and Cultural Affairs Law § 37.07). The exception to this is that your manager can shop a record deal for you. The effect of this law can be devastating to managers. An all too common scenario is that a manager, in an attempt to find work for his client, sets up showcases ("attempting to procure") and gigs ("procuring"). After much diligent work, the manager finally gets his client to the point where he gets offered a record deal. The record company has a manager in mind that they think is better and maybe have already established a personal and business relationship with, and talks the artist into dumping the first manager by invoking the law that negates the manager/artist contract. So if your manager doesn't want to try to get you gigs you know why. Loyalty under these circumstances is hard to come by, and managers are extremely vulnerable.

YOUR PRODUCER

If your demo is a finished master recording ready for the radio and produced by someone with a successful track record, it gives the record company another way to hype you to radio and the press. It also ensures that the rest of the product will be competently produced. Your producer should know your strengths and weaknesses and have a plan for how he will produce you to make you as commercially viable as possible. With a successful producer as part of the package, it isn't even necessary to bring the company finished masters, just demos of exceptional songs and performances.

If you bring demos produced by yourself or an unproven producer, there is no way of knowing that the finished product will be well produced. The record company may make a judgment call on whether to sign you that depends on the strength of the various ingredients in that particular situation. It's possible that they'll want to hear a finished master before they decide or they'll want to find you a producer who they *know* can deliver a great record. Another option is to find a great mixer, who can take what you have and tweak it to be airworthy. One of the problems is that a producer (whether it's you or someone else) can sometimes lose objectivity and can benefit from a fresh set of ears to mix the record.

If you've produced your own masters, the record company doesn't have to worry about you having problems with your producer, but the potential for you to be less objective in your choice of material will make them keep a close eye on it.

If you're already signed to producer A, who the rep believes to be incompetent or inappropriate, then he will have to buy out your contract with that producer, convince him to allow another producer (B) to work on the project through A's company, or not sign you at all. If the exec is impressed enough with you, he'll buy out the contract.

General Information

Producers have a dual responsibility: to deliver to the record company a record it can sell and to get the best performance from the artist or band. Part of this includes choosing the best components needed for that particular project, which may mean songs, studios, musicians, arranger, engineers, and recording equipment. The producer bears the responsibility for both the technical and artistic quality of the record.

The worst way to find a producer is to send your demos randomly to producers whose work you don't know. The best way is to buy records of artists in your general style of music and listen to the sound of the record. If you like it, research what other projects that producer has worked on and listen to them. Often the production company's address is listed on the CD. If not, call the record company A&R or artist relations department and ask for it. Also, *Billboard* lists the producers of hit records on its charts in all styles of music, and *New on the Charts* (see Appendix) gives you their contact info. If you read *Billboard* on a regular basis (you can read much of it for free at www.billboard.com), you'll get to know who's producing your favorite records. You can always just search for his name on an Internet search engine. He probably has a Web site.

Beyond the question of liking their work is the question of compatibility. Some producers have their own characteristic style no matter who they produce. If you need a stylistic direction look for one whose style feels right for you. Others work to enhance the unique qualities of the artist or group, and a producer with that philosophy may suit you better.

Producers come from a variety of backgrounds. Some are engineer/producers who went to "producer school" by engineering hundreds or thousands of sessions in which they've observed and participated in the work styles of many different producers. If you're a writer/artist/arranger with a unique sound based on your arrangement ideas, your vision may be enhanced more by an engineer/producer than by an arranger/producer.

Arranger/producers with experience as studio musicians go to that same "producer school" and benefit from the same exposure but from the other side of the glass. They'll excel in creating the musical dynamics and hooks that may have already helped launch some hits. If you're a singer or singer/songwriter who needs the most assistance in creating an instrumental sound, check out the musician/arranger/producer. Many of them are also songwriters who like to co-write with the artist. This could also be advantageous if you need material and like to collaborate. Those producers will also be attracted by the additional royalties they'd receive by writing with you.

Regardless of his background, a producer needs to be able to choose the best songs for a project, whether by choosing from among your own or by finding appropriate songs from other writers.

Some are better than others at this, and if finding or writing strong commercial songs is a problem area for you, it'll be necessary to have an expert working with you. As you can see, an assessment of your own strengths and weaknesses is essential to be able to find a producer who can make up for your weaknesses and enhance your strengths.

As an artist without a record deal, your chances of getting a major, established producer to work with you are slim. They usually have projects booked far into the future. Though you shouldn't abandon that approach, you should also check the charts for new producers who have recently had their first hit. It's more likely that they're not booked so far ahead and may be looking for their next project. It's not impossible, though, to find an excellent producer or production team who will work with you on spec, particularly if they own their own studio and if you're flexible enough to work at times their studio isn't booked.

Producers get paid a fee per track and a royalty as percentage points based on record sales. It amounts to roughly about a third of what your artist royalty is, give or take one or two percentage points. That also depends on how much in demand they are. There are very successful hip-hop producers, for example, who get $100,000 per song once they've had some hits.

ATTORNEYS

Attorneys representing artists with demos or masters frequently approach record company executives. Since attorneys are negotiating many contracts with record companies, they have made good contacts at the labels and find themselves in a position to know if and when a company is looking for a certain type of artist. Since they have an inside track, it's easier for them to shop your masters (and *you*) than, for instance, an out-of-town manager or a new one who doesn't know his way around yet. The record company wants to deal with an entertainment attorney, in particular, a record business attorney. When he comes to the company attorney to negotiate a deal, he must speak the language and have up-to-date knowledge of current record industry practices. If not, they will end up engaged in needless hours of fruitless negotiations and the record company will have educated your attorney at your expense.

Let's say you're presented with a production or record contract and you call your lawyer uncle, whose specialty is suing auto manufacturers. He *should* refer you to an entertainment specialist, but maybe business is slow this month, or he knows there are lots of bucks in the music business, or he has visions of his nephew being a big rock star, or he thinks it would be great to get involved in a more glamorous business, and he figures, "What the hell, how hard could it be to negotiate a record contract?" He gets the contract and the first thing he objects to is the fact that this big record company wants all recording costs recouped off the top from your royalties. He thinks it's terrible (it actually is terrible, but he may be unaware that it's a firmly established practice in the industry) and decides he should try to negotiate that point, thereby exposing his ignorance. The record company attorneys will either not want to negotiate with him at all or eat him for breakfast.

Needless to say, none of this helps you at all. Entertainment law is very complex, and just knowing law academically is not enough to make someone a good attorney in that field. Personal experience, good contacts, and knowledge of current industry practices and of the needs, personnel, policies, and contracts of specific record companies are equally important. The record company wants to deal with an attorney whose philosophy is that the best deal is one that comes closest to being fair for both parties. Obviously, the company attorneys will negotiate for the company's advantage, but if that means it's unfair to you, they know they are going to have problems with you later and you won't be happy with the deal (though if you're successful, they know you'll be renegotiating). So, as you can see, it's very important to choose this team member well.

General Information

In relationships with attorneys, fees are always a major concern. Attorneys in this field are expensive, and fees range from $125 (not many) to $500 per hour. They'll log all the time spent on your behalf on the telephone and in meetings with you, with the record company, or whatever, and bill you for that time and for materials used on your behalf. Some attorneys, in lieu of an hourly rate, will offer to shop your demos or masters and negotiate your deal for 5 percent of your income from that contract for the life of the deal (though sometimes it's just from the advance). Make sure you're very clear about the parameters of this deal. Some may also want to include other types of income in the deal, including touring and merchandising, which would in a sense operate as if it were a management commission. On the surface, this may seem like a good deal, particularly if you're broke, but you should consider that maybe in a couple of months you'll become disenchanted with your relationship and want to get another attorney. You'll then be paying two attorneys, and that original 5 percent is part of your income that you might find a better use for.

An attorney working on a percentage may also be tempted to "front load" a deal. Here's a simplified scenario for the sake of illustration: In negotiations, the attorney has an opportunity to obtain maybe a $500,000 advance from the record company for you, the artist, by trading it off for a 10 percent artist royalty instead of 12 percent. Let's say that for 12 percent there would only have been a $350,000 advance. If the attorney is getting 5 percent of that advance (because he gets 5 percent of all your income from the deal he negotiated for you), he may have a quick fantasy about $7,500 with wings on it, flying out of his pocket if he gets you the higher royalty and lower advance. If he decides to act on that fantasy, he can go back to you and say "Great news! I got you a $500,000 advance" and never tell you about the extra 2 percent artist royalty he gave up for it, which down the road could mean a substantial amount of money. If he's ethical, he'll give you the pros and cons and let you make that decision. This is the kind of thing that could happen. I don't want to totally freak you out with it, just scare you enough to make you pay attention. You should ask (and they should inform you) about the pros and cons of their negotiations.

Attorneys will sometimes work on spec or "deferment," which means that they'll keep track of their time spent on your project but defer payment until they've made a deal for you and then collect their accumulated fees from the front money. They are most likely to do this if a producer or record company has shown enough interest in you to present you with a contract, or if they have good ears and feel you've got a favorable shot at a deal. It is a very high risk for them though, because they could conceivably spend a lot of time, the deal doesn't happen, and they'd risk not getting paid.

Another way they can work is an hourly fee against a monthly retainer covering everything they do. That may be part of an overall fee for the project depending on what they'll be required to do, then deduct what you've already paid from the final overall project fee. They'll give you an estimate up front and let you know when it looks like they'll have to go past it.

Here are some additional tips on dealing with attorneys:

Never sign a contract without some legal advice. I'm sure you've heard this before, but I'm still appalled by the number of unfortunate situations I come across in which people who knew better ignored the advice. They say something like, "The people were so nice . . ." or "They said they would . . ." But, unfortunately, what they said they would do wasn't written into their contract and consequently, they don't have to do what they merely said.

If you and your manager are discussing your deal with a company, take notes on the verbal points they're offering you. Relay this information to your attorney so he can incorporate it into the contract in case the company selectively forgets. (Your attorney will clarify this immediately, though, since A&R reps will often talk about deals in broad strokes, or "deal memos" that they're pretty sure you don't quite understand.) Most companies already have their own contracts that they've worked out over the years from their own legal battles and those of associates, reflecting industry practices as well as innovating their own terms. A good reason for hiring an experienced music industry attorney is that he's had to negotiate with a great variety of companies and is familiar with the negotiating practices and contract terms of most of them. If your attorney has already negotiated deals with a particular company, that experience could save a lot of the attorney's time and your money.

Don't ask the company with whom you're negotiating to recommend an attorney. Never go to an attorney for advice who also represents those who are offering you a contract. To avoid conflict of interest, your attorney should have no connection with your manager, producer, record company, or anyone else with whom you are doing business. An ethical attorney will always let you know that, but ask anyway. If there is a known conflict, like you and the record company live in a town where there's only one experienced music business attorney, the attorney will ask you to sign a document that states that you're aware of the conflict of interest but you want him to represent you anyway. This can be a real dilemma for an attorney who makes most of his income from that record company.

Always ask an attorney what his fees are and try to get some sort of estimate of how much the service you need could cost. It will sometimes be hard to tell you exactly, but you should at least have a ballpark figure. That way you can determine whether it's out of your league.

Your conversation and business with your attorney is confidential. That is, unless you consent to "leak" information as a business tactic (such as the amount of money another company is offering you).

If you "discharge" your attorney and decide to get a new one, the new attorney has the right, with your authorization, to copy your files from the previous attorney. They're your files.

Communicate in writing whenever you can. It documents and dates your requests and comments, and avoids communication breakdown due to lapses of memory and human error. If you're using e-mail, send PDF files of anything you don't want them to change.

Keep a photocopy of all correspondence with anyone you do business with. This includes a copy of every contract presented to and signed by you, *before* you return it. You do this because it is possible to add a clause to a contract after you sign it and you'd otherwise not be able to prove that you didn't consent to the added clause.

Ask an attorney what he's done lately. If you're looking for an attorney to represent you in negotiating a record deal, you'll want to find one who has had *recent* experience in negotiating that kind of contract and uses up-to-date contracts.

Shop for an attorney with expertise in the area in which you need help. There are many specialists among entertainment attorneys as well as veterans who've done it all. You may want different attorneys to negotiate management, publishing, production, film music, or recording contracts. Ask them what they specialize in.

BOOKING AGENTS

Even though it's essentially your manager's job to find the right booking agency for you, a record company executive may be able to help, since the record company has ongoing relationships with many of them. Sometimes booking agents help companies "discover" new artists and send in demos of hot new artists because artists are constantly approaching them looking for work. They may also be booking artists in parts of the country that the company doesn't have much regular access to for scouting talent. If you already have a good agency and you're working regularly, it's a plus for the record company because you may already have a strong following of potential record buyers.

If you're an artist who loves to perform, the booking agent is an important part of the team. The decisions you and your manager make with her about where and when you play could be very important to the success of an album. In the coordination of album releases and touring schedules, timing is critical.

General Information

Booking agents (also referred to as talent managers, as opposed to personal managers) are those who secure work, negotiate contracts, and collect your money for live performance gigs, film work, and so on. Though major agencies occasionally work with unknown artists without record deals, it's rare. If you're a new artist/band, you're better off finding a small or medium-sized agency that deals with unsigned or newly signed artists because they regularly deal with clubs and small concert venues that feature talent at your level of development.

Booking agents with a career development plan in mind can do a lot to advance your career. Major agents can assist by bringing you to the attention of record companies that they deal with on behalf of other major clients. Their approach, if they can get you close to a record deal, is to try to get the label to agree to let them represent you as an agent; however, it's ultimately your call since you sign the contract.

It's also to the advantage of smaller agencies that you get a record deal even with a small independent label, because they can then charge more for your appearances. Acts that are on the road constantly and making $5,000 or $6,000 or more a week may find that their agents balk at the time off the act may need to produce an album. For every week you don't work, your agent doesn't make (at 10 percent) $500 or $600 or more. Those agents truly concerned with your growth will not obstruct your career. In the long run, the additional fees the agent will be able to charge once you have a record out will more than make up the temporary loss.

One of the best ways to locate a reputable agent is through the American Federation of Musicians (www.afm.org), American Federation of Television and Radio Artists (www.aftra.org), or Screen Actors Guild (www.sag.org) who keep an up-to-date list of those agents who they've licensed and who comply with their regulations. Another way to find a booking agent is through other musicians who seem to work regularly. Finding an agent who deals with college concerts is a good way to go if you just want to play primarily original material. (Club gigs, in general, discourage a predominance of originals in favor of a cover tunes or "standards" repertoire.) You can find such agents by calling some college student activities directors and asking which agents they like to deal with.

Agents charge 10 percent of the gross receipts from the jobs they secure for you. If you sign exclusively with an agent, he'll want that percentage on all the gigs you get for a period of one to more than three years, regardless of whether you or he secures the job. If you have already formed your own relationships with clubs or colleges where you've performed in the past, you may want to exclude these venues from the list of clubs where the agent can collect a percentage so that he isn't earning money on gigs you secured and relationships you've developed before your contract. If you can get the agent to agree to this, you'll need to put it in your contract with a specific list of excluded clubs. On the other hand, the more you limit the situations he can get his percentage from, the less enthusiastic he'll be, since it will deprive him of his percentage on those gigs. Note that all contracts sanctioned by the unions have clauses that get you out of the contract if the agent doesn't get you work within specified time periods.

Booking agents look for a combination of musical talent and the desire and ability to entertain in the acts they consider representing. Some agents specialize in specific musical styles. Some are "full service" agencies for those who also have the talent to expand their careers into acting, modeling, writing, and other directions. Some also represent composers for film and TV music. If you have a manager, as captain of your team, she'll be primarily responsible for dealing with your booking agent.

Are there agents just for songwriter? Except for talent agencies who specialize in film and TV and represent *very* successful writers (and composers) whose songs or songwriting ability they promote for film and TV themes, the answer is no. Music publishers and independent songpluggers come closest to filling that bill, though (see chapter eleven, "Independent Songpluggers" on page 235) .

The Campaign

If you want a record deal, you can't afford to wait for it to find you. You and your representatives need to plan an effective campaign to make sure you get heard by those companies in which you're interested.

A&R people at record companies seldom go to clubs at random to see artists they've never heard before. They'll respond to a buzz, talk on the street or in the industry about a hot, new band. They'll also go to see a band whose songs and sound they liked on a demo they've heard. Except for the most aggressive A&R reps, they have little time to see an artist otherwise. They'll always try to improve their odds of finding a great band and waste as little time as possible in the process. So, if there's such a thing as a standard campaign (and there isn't) that makes the most efficient use of your time and theirs, it's close to this:

1. Put together your package with masters or high-quality demos, press kit, photos, reviews, and bios. Don't forget to include your name, address, phone number, e-mail address, and Web site on all materials.

2. Send or deliver your demos, preferably via an attorney, manager, or agent, to whomever that person knows in the record company A&R department who is appropriate for your style of music. It's not necessary to see the vice president of A&R unless you or your representative knows him. Staff A&R representatives may be much more accessible. This requires some explanation. A&R execs

at a VP level at major labels have the power to sign you and are happy to take the credit even if a subordinate finds, courts, and champions you to the company. If you are pitched to the company from a friend of the VP or higher, that's a great situation. If you don't know anybody there, an A&R representative below VP level can still be effective. Label politics is one of those minefields that a well-connected entertainment attorney should be a big help with.

3. Schedule a showcase about three or four weeks after delivery of the demos. If possible, announce the showcase in the package you present and e-mail reminders. If you're releasing an indie CD, the release party combined with a showcase is the ideal situation. Try to get some press before and after the showcase.

4. About two weeks before your showcase (or release party), send out a special invitation to the people who have your package, the press, booking agents, producers, or anyone else you'd like to be there. Again, an e-mail message will do.

5. Follow up a few days later with phone calls to find out (a) if they have heard the demo/new CD, (b) if they like it, (c) if they got the invitation, (d) if they're coming to the showcase. If so, tell them you will put their names on the guest list. If not, ask if they'd like to be notified of future appearances. (Keep your mailing list current with their present job and e-mail addresses and phone numbers.)

6. If they attend the showcase, follow up immediately with a "thank you" card and a phone call to find out what they thought.

7. If all that fails, cut some new demos and try it all again. Persist!

You can either do this project yourself or have a friend, producer, spouse, or a combination represent you. Know that this seldom works the first time. You will have to continue, so don't be discouraged. There is value in just getting your name in front of them periodically. Generally speaking, in the case of rock groups, most A&R reps would rather hear *about* your great performance and the buzz you created, and pursue you themselves. So concentrate on getting reviewers there to contribute to the buzz. Note: Don't do *any* of this until you *know* you're ready. A *bad* buzz can sink your ship before it sails.

Your Web Site Is a Critical Factor

Sometimes it's more effective to invite them via e-mail to your Web site or MySpace.com (www.myspace.com) or another site where you can let them hear your music, see where you're playing next, and read the reviews. Keep them on your e-mail list and keep your Web site updated. Make sure you attach a link to your Web site and list phone number in every e-mail (see "Your Home on the Web" on page 310).

Why a Major Label Deal May Not Be Best for You

Though it's been possible for writer/artists to release independent recordings for many years, the more recent availability and affordability of great digital recording equipment and the marketing potential of the Internet have done a lot to level the playing field for indie artists. Though the four major labels (Universal Music Group, Sony BMG Music Entertainment, BMI Group, Warner Brothers Music) and their subsidiaries still control most of the expertise and capital to market, influence airplay, and fill shelf space at record retailers, they're no longer the only game in town. It's possible, with a lot of work, for an artist or band to develop and expand their own audience without airplay. Many artists are gaining the attention of the majors *because* they have already accomplished it. At that point, they may be making a good enough living to hire their own team, control their own careers, and keep the profits themselves, rather than risk the following problems of signing with a major.

1. Your odds of being successful are about one in ten or less. Statistics show that only 5 percent of records released sell over 500,000 copies (gold record), and less than 10 percent recoup the production and marketing costs.

2. The allegiances of major labels are primarily to their shareholders, and to artists only to the extent that they contribute to the bottom line. That is not to say that there aren't employees of those labels who are passionate about the music and the artists they sign. It's just that they're forced to perform a kind of triage on a regular basis that makes them prioritize in favor of the most likely to succeed at the moment and take their attention from those who aren't, despite what may be their best efforts. It's just the nature of the beast. A friend of mine who was a major label tour publicist quit his job in frustration at having too many artists to deal with and having a limited window of time to deal with each. It seemed that with just a bit more work with an artist he'd be able to see a breakthrough, but was required to turn his full attention to another before he could make it happen. He ended up working for artists on his own time because he believed in them. He finally couldn't handle it anymore and started his own PR company. This is not an unusual story.

The music industry is full of horror stories from that 90 percent of artists who placed all their dreams into the hands of major labels and felt betrayed by them. To be fair, some of them weren't prepared for those deals to begin with.

3. In "standard" label deals, the company recoups—*from your artist royalties*—the costs of your advance and producing the records (in "all-in" deals, production costs are covered in the advance). They also partially or totally recoup video costs and costs of tour support, and anything they can list in the contract that's not negotiated away. They don't ordinarily recoup manufacturing, advertising, marketing, and shipping.

You understand, though, that if you market yourself, *you'll* be paying those costs, although you won't be spending as much, and you'll be getting all the profits after recouping your own costs of recording, marketing, and distribution.

4. Though maximum contract terms are seven years, many contracts also contain clauses that require a specific number of albums delivered and artists are rarely allowed to deliver the required number of albums within the time period, nor can they record for anyone else until those requirements are met regardless of the time period. Some companies have recently backed off on this.

5. Until the requirements are met, the artist's contract can be assigned to any other company regardless of the wishes of the artist. So the artist may end up on a different label than the one she wanted to sign with, often without anyone at the new label who has an interest in her career. This can effectively keep the artist out of the marketplace for many years. This can be negotiated from your contract by a good attorney who can make sure there is a "key man" clause that says that if

the person who believed in you enough to sign you leaves the company, you can leave too. Or if the company is sold to another, you have the right to get out of your deal if you want to.

Should You Do It Yourself?

For many years, as it's been increasingly difficult for acts to get signed to major record labels, a grassroots movement of independent artist-owned labels have emerged. You're a good candidate for this approach if you fall into these categories:

- In the process of pitching yourself to major labels you constantly hear, "I really like it personally, but the company doesn't see it as something they can sell," meaning that they don't see you as a "mass market" artist, or "This is really good, but I don't know what radio stations would play it," meaning they don't think you have a radio hit.

- You find yourself difficult to categorize stylistically and so do others. You sort of "fall into the cracks" now, though what you do might be very hip in two or three years. Innovative artists are usually ahead of the marketplace.

- You're an excellent live performer with a strong, enthusiastic following. This is very important if you're going to make your own recording because, if you don't get radio or video play or create a style of music with an established marketing network, you must rely on live performances for people to sample your wares. Yes, you can give them a free download or offer a short sample for them to hear on iTunes, but you have to get them to know you're there and live performances are among the best ways to do that. The press is very important, but they can't review your performance if you're not playing somewhere.

- You're an ambitious artist with a good business head who's not afraid of hard work, is good at delegating, and has good people skills.

It's my firm belief that there is an audience out there for anything that's done well. The problem of the major labels is that the cost of their star-making machinery, including their offices, personnel, and especially executive salaries dictate that it takes half a million to a million dollars to record and market a new artist's album to the public and promote it to radio. They have to sell a lot of records to recoup that investment, and since less than 10 percent of the albums released ever do recoup, it makes major labels very cautious to sign only artists that appear to have a clearly defined market and fit an existing radio format.

However, a sort of "farm team" approach has developed within the record industry and many small independent labels that have managed to find their own markets successfully have made distribution agreements and a variety of other arrangements with major labels. There's a great breakdown of those various deals by industry consultant Christopher Knab at Music Biz Academy. com (www.musicbizacademy.com), and in Mark Halloran's *The Musician's Business & Legal Guide* (see bibliography).

Apart from that development, new networks and avenues of exposure and distribution have developed, particularly for niche genres such as children's music, new age, blues, reggae, and other non-mainstream genres that are already served by a network of fans, clubs, magazines, Web sites, and specialty radio shows and college radio stations. Through these networks, independent labels have become increasingly sophisticated in finding their audiences.

Mail-order forms shipped with CDs; astute ad placement; exposure at conventions and music festivals; Web site links between similar artists; Web rings, blogs, and podcasts to fans; Internet downloads and street distribution of free samples of their artists work; building fan e-mail lists; promotional "street teams" of fans; and exposure and viral marketing via online social networks all contribute to marketing plans for independent labels.

Obviously, having a good indie label behind you gives you a lot more time to create, record, and tour while their time is devoted to marketing you. You can and should use those same techniques to jumpstart your own career and sell your CDs at, say, CD Baby and through their online download network. You may be able to recoup your investment after sales of as few as 1,000 to 3,000 CDs (depending on how low you keep your recording costs and what you charge for CDs). In fact, it's quite likely that your odds are better to make a profit marketing your own recording. Your success in doing that yourself is what will make you more attractive to *any* label.

(For some excellent books on marketing your own recordings, see the bibliography.)

The Future of the Music Revolution

The recording industry is in a state of rapid change (as if I had to remind you). For example, mergers of traditional record companies with Internet services as well as new Internet marketing divisions within the international entertainment conglomerates themselves, threaten their longstanding symbiotic relationships with traditional brick-and-mortar retail stores. The capability of delivering music via the Internet and communications companies directly to computers, digital music players, combination cell phone/music players, and other means yet to be developed are in the process of cutting traditional "record stores" completely out of the picture. Now you can buy CDs and downloads from Starbucks with your coffee and Garth Brooks can make a deal directly with Wal-Mart and avoid a record label altogether. For the next few years, brick-and-mortar retailers will still provide a service for customers who want to handle the physical merchandise, though a new generation of fans (and a growing number of older fans) will be increasingly comfortable learning about and buying new music online. There's little debate, though, that in a few years CDs will be obsolete and our music will all be digitally delivered and even more portable.

Creators of music and visual entertainment will have access to more tools and services that will enable them to create and market their music in new and exciting ways. But despite those innovations, there are some things that will never change. One is the magic of a great live performance; another is the bond between artists and fans that's been enhanced by e-mail, video, and social networking sites. Viral marketing will remain one of the artist's best marketing tools. If you have exciting music to offer, more fans will discover you sooner and in greater numbers than at anytime in history, and it will grow exponentially. Another constant is that no matter how many tools and services are invented to make your life as an artist easier, you'll still have to work hard, study, read, keep learning, practice, be disciplined, maintain faith in yourself, and persevere in the face of considerable odds if you want to succeed.

For writer/artists and bands, this revolution offers new opportunities to take charge of your own careers. Online labels are proliferating, and many new hybrids of major and indie labels are being formed to take advantage of the strengths of both. In the future, it looks to me like there will be a new wave of companies that will be marketing services tailored to the needs of individual artists rather than the old model of controlling artists to benefit the companies. In the past several years even the major labels have begun changing some of the more oppressive aspects of their old deals and are now offering much more flexible options. Meanwhile, both major and independent labels have something to offer to artists and somewhere there's a situation that's best for you.

These developments are happening so quickly that anything I could offer at this point would be old news by the time you read this. So, rather than go deeply into this area, I suggest you subscribe to music industry newsletters and read current articles online and off and new book releases recommended throughout this book and in the following pages. There's never been a time when there's been as much helpful information available to artists.

In any revolution, things change that take a while to shake out. Though the future looks bright, music creators need to be constantly vigilant because there are continuing challenges to your rights and your potential income from those whose businesses depend on the "content" that you create. They would like to use it with as little expense to their businesses as possible. They have powerful lobbies to support legislation that will serve their interests and work against yours if fair checks and balances are not established. This is the nature of free enterprise. Innovative technology companies have revolutionized the music industry in a very positive way and their continued contributions are essential to expanding the accessibility of your music in increasingly consumer-friendly ways. We need them, and they need us.

I believe it's possible to arrive at a compromise that encourages the inventors and manufacturers of new technology and, in the process, assures that the creators of music, video, film, and other forms of entertainment are fairly compensated in a way that enables them to continue to create it. To make that happen, songwriters and musicians need to take an active interest by joining and staying in touch with the unions and organizations that are representing *your* interests in Washington. Learn the issues and don't hesitate to write your representatives to express your views. In every state, legislators are well aware of the hardware and software commerce that contributes to their economy but rarely do they hear the voices of the creators of the music that fuels it.

We need to also be vigilant about the motives and conflicts *within* our industry. There are issues for which industry organizations need to be allies and those for which we'll be adversaries, but I'm always an optimist. In the words of Lennon and McCartney, "We can work it out."

Appendix: Songwriter's Resources

For Industry Contacts

RECORDING INDUSTRY SOURCEBOOK

http://www.isourcebook.com

More than 15,000 listings in 60 categories. Listings include names, titles, phone, fax, styles of music and whether unsolicited material is accepted. Producer listings include rates, credits and specialties. CD/ROM available with book purchase.

BILLBOARD DIRECTORIES

www.billboard.biz/bb/biz/directories/
index.jsp
(800) 449-1402

These comprehensive Billboard directories of business-to-business listings include Billboard International Buyers Guide, Billboard International Talent & Touring Directory, Billboard Record Retailing Directory, Billboard Tape/Disc Directory, The Radio Power Book, Billboard International Latin Music Buyer's Guide, The Nashville 615/Country Music Sourcebook, Music & Media/Billboard EUROFILE, Musicians Guide to Touring & Promotion. For many of these, specialized mailing labels and data extracts are also available.

MUSIC BUSINESS REGISTRY

www.musicregistry.com
(800) 377-7411 or (818) 995-7458
7510 Sunset Blvd. #1041
Los Angeles, CA 90046-3400 USA

This company, headed by former Arista Records A&R rep, Ritch Esra, publishes the A&R Registry, a comprehensive listing of record company A&R reps including their stylistic focus, direct phone and fax #s and the names of their assistants. The only directory updated every two months. They also publish an annual Music Publisher Registry, Film and Television Music Guide (includes music supervisors, clearance companies, music editors and much more), Music Attorney, Legal & Business Affairs Registry, Producer and Engineer Directory (Full contact info and credits for 1600 producers and engineers.) Online subscriptions also available.

THE MUSICIAN'S ATLAS

www.musiciansatlas.com

Annual print edition and online versions available. More than 24,000 U.S. and International music contacts in 28 categories including clubs, studios, showcases, tape/disc manufacturers, record stores, record distributors, major and indie label A&R,

producers, film/TV music supervisors, publishers, music journalists, managers, agents and attorneys, commercial & college radio, national and regional press, conferences, creative services, promotion companies, publicists, Web sites, schools, Canadian college radio and booking.

THE NASHVILLE MUSIC BUSINESS DIRECTORY AND ENTERTAINMENT GUIDE

www.nashvilleconnection.com
Phone & Fax 615-826-4141
9 Music Square South Suite 210
Nashville TN 37203

A complete directory of the Nashville music and entertainment industry. Over 3,000 music business listings and inside contacts

INDIE BIBLE

www.indiebible.com/icb
(800) 306-8167 N. America. (613) 596-4996
Outside N. America Fax: (613) 596-2294
PO Box 6043, Ottawa J, Ontario K2A 1T1
Canada

A highly regarded directory that lists 4,200 publications that review music, 3,400 radio stations, 600 labels and distributors, 500 Web sites for uploading music and more than 50 helpful articles. They also offer a free monthly newsletter with 50 new listings in each. Go to the site to sign up.

Pollstar

www.pollstar.com
(559) 271-7900   Fax (559) 271-7979

For more than 25 years, Pollstar has provided music business professionals with a reliable and accurate source of worldwide concert tour schedules, ticket sales results, music industry contact directories, trade news and unique specialized data services. In addition to publishing the concert industry's leading weekly trade publication, Pollstar also maintains the world's largest database of international concert tour information. Their Contact directories include a bi-annual Agency

Roster for over 10,000 artists and their booking agencies; bi-annual Record Company Rosters including a list of major label executives; bi-annual Talent Buyer Directory listing concert promoters, clubs, fairs, colleges, festivals and theme parks; also Concert Venue Directory, Concert Support Services Directory, and ConneXions, an annual directory of 10,000 music industry company listings. Though they don't list it on their Web site they also publish a semi-annual Manager Directory of artists and their managers.

For Getting Your Demos Directly to Music Industry Pros No Matter Where You Live

TAXI

http://www.taxi.com
(800) 458-2111

An innovative tip-sheet/independent A&R service. Members receive listings every two weeks by major and independent labels, producers managers, film and TV music supervisors and publishers looking for writers, writer/artists, bands. All submissions prescreened and critiqued by industry pros. They also offer Taxi Dispatch for an additional membership fee. It allows you to pitch online to audio-visual projects, particularly series television. All styles including instrumentals. Many members feel that their annual Taxi Road Rally songwriters conference (free to members) alone is worth the price of membership. (Highly recommended.)

Online Pitch Services

These services provide opportunities for songwriters and publishers to make their music available for users (record companies, film/TV music supervisors, ad agencies, schools etc.) via a searchable database. Some take a percentage of any uses generated by the site. Others charge based on the number of songs posted on the site. Most are non-exclusive, some actively pitch, others facilitate your own pitching. Well worth visiting their sites. Read their contracts carefully.

Licensemusic.com www.licensemusic.com

PublishSongs.com www.publishsongs.com/

Pump Audio www.pumpaudio.com

SongCatalog.com www.songcatalog.com/

Songscope.com www.songscope.com

Local Organizations

Throughout the U.S. there are more than 100 local songwriters organizations that provide a variety of services, including showcases and workshops featuring music industry guests. Rather than list them all, I'll mention the national organizations.

You can find a list of others on the Internet at www.MusesMuse.com or www.Songwriter Universe.com. *American Songwriter* magazine also maintains a list. Some of the largest local orgs are:

ARIZONA SONGWRITERS ASSN. (PHOENIX)

(602) 973-1988 www.azsongwriters.com.

L.A. SONGWRITERS NETWORK (LOS ANGELES)

www.songnet.org

SONGWRITERS ASSN. OF WASHINGTON (DC)

(301) 654-8434 www.saw.org

WEST COAST SONGWRITERS (FORMERLY NORTHERN CALIFORNIA SONGWRITERS ASSN.)

(415) 654-3966,
www.westcoastsongwriters.org

National Organizations

JUST PLAIN FOLKS

www.JPFolks.com

With close to 50,000 members (as of 6/06), this organization serves an international songwriter and writer/artist community with mutual support and networking via the JPNotes online newsletter, regional and local showcases coordinated by local volunteer chapters, the world's largest music awards program, online music industry mentors to answer questions and post articles and an opportunity to promote yourself. Very active member forums on all topics. Free.

NASHVILLE SONGWRITERS ASSOCIATION INTERNATIONAL (NSAI)

www.nashvillesongwriters.com
(615) 256-3354

Founded in 1967, it's primarily, though not exclusively, focused on country music. It maintains nearly 100 local workshops throughout the country. Check to see if there's one near you or for info on starting one. Professional and general memberships. Produces many excellent educational events throughout the year.

SONGSALIVE!

www.songsalive.org
In N. America (310) 238-0359 In Australia
New Zealand + 61 (02) 9294 2415

With 20 chapters throughout the world, Songsalive! is a non-profit organization dedicated to the nurturing, support and promotion of songwriters and composers worldwide. Founded in 1997 by Gilli Moon Aliotti and Roxanne Kiely, in Sydney Australia, Songsalive! is run by songwriters for songwriters. They provide opportunities for collaboration, promotion, education and industry networking through workshops, showcases, CD samplers, songcamps & retreats, live events and showcases, songwriter critique workshops, songleads and industry pitches.

SONGWRITERS GUILD OF AMERICA (SGA)

www.songwritersguild.com
New York: (201) 867-7603 Nashville: (615) 742-9945 Los Angeles: (323) 462-1108

The oldest songwriters organization (1931), the Guild pioneered the ideal song contract for writers and is the only organization officially sanctioned to lobby on behalf of songwriters in the many legislative issues that face them. It will assist writers in collecting proper royalties from publishers. It administers (optional service) the publishing catalogs of its writer/publisher members among other services. Its non-profit division, The Songwriters Guild Foundation, offers consultation, seminars, workshops and critique sessions to its members.

SONGWRITERS ASSOCIATION OF CANADA (SAC)

www.songwriters.ca/
In Toronto: Phone: 416-961-1588 Fax: 416-961-2040 Toll Free: 1-866-456-7664

They are "an association led by active professional and amateur songwriters, committed to the development and recognition of Canadian composers, lyricists and songwriters by pursuing: their right to benefit from, and receive fair compensation for, the use of their work; the advancement of the craft and enterprise of songwriting through educational programs, networking opportunities, dissemination of business knowledge and other services; a more favourable environment through the provision of a united national voice when dealing with government, the music industry and the general public; and the development of activities which allow members to reach out and enjoy the sense of community shared by songwriters." They offer song assessment and song registration services among others. They have a new Regional Writers Group program to set up chapters throughout Canada.

Local Newsletters

All local and national organizations listed here have regular newsletters for members and others who have expressed an interest in the organizations. In addition, there are some noteworthy individuals who have taken it upon themselves to create newsletters to promote all local events:

DOAK TURNER

Doak is one of the great networkers in Nashville. Go to his site, www.nashvillemuse.com and subscribe to the Nashville Muse (He e-mails to 10,000 each Monday) or e-mail him at Doak@comcast.net. Be sure to do this before going to Nashville so you won't miss anything important, like his regular networking parties the 3rd Sunday of the month. Tell him I sent you.

JIMI YAMAGISHI

Co-founded and runs the L.A. Songwriters Network. The group maintains a newsletter of events that's updated almost daily by members, so the local events planners post their info there. Go to www.songnet.org and sign up. Join the organization (it's free), participate in their events and tap into other L.A. area events and opportunities.

Performing Rights Organizations: BMI, ASCAP, and SESAC

See chapter nine, page 179, for worldwide contact info. Their basic responsibility is logging and collecting royalties for the public performance (radio, TV, clubs, restaurants and concert venues) of music for distribution to their writer and publisher members. Beyond that, they present showcases for new talent, offer grants and scholarships and support many helpful organizations and events in the music community. They also, along with other songwriting and publishing organizations, fight the battles to protect the royalty income of music creators and publishers.

Via their Web sites, you can get information on copyright legislation, showcases and educational events around the country, grant and scholarship applications and search their catalogs for songs, writers and their publishers (where you obtain licenses to use their songs). They also provide on-line clearance forms and cue-sheets for TV and film uses.

Online Songwriters Resources

Whether you're looking for used gear, a songwriters organization to help you get oriented to the industry in a new town, information on copyright, a book explaining publishing or record deals, hearing a new group, or to talk with someone with similar interests, the Internet is your new community. There are thousands of music-related Web sites out there now and growing exponentially. Once you get into it, it can be a bottomless time pit, so I've put together several of my favorite information sites relating to songwriting in particular. Several of them are valuable as starting points because of their links to other good info sites.

CHRISTIAN SONGWRIT-ERS NETWORK

www.wordpress.christiansongwriters.org
Tel: (850) 624-3867 (leave message) Fax: (707) 549-4436

A great info portal for all aspects of Christian songwriting: articles, forums, resource lists.

THE COPYRIGHT OFFICE

www.copyright.gov
Tel: (202) 707-5959 8:30am-5pm Eastern time, M-F.

If you want straight answers to your copyright questions (No, it's not okay if you only copy two bars!) and free downloads of all the forms you need to protect yourself, go to the source.

INDEPENDENT SONGWRITER WEB MAGAZINE

www.independentsongwriter.com

An online magazine featuring the same variety of craft and business articles, classifieds and interviews as most print magazines plus a Web radio show and their monthly Indie Minute TVshow. Free newsletter too. Good stuff.

LI'L HANKS GUIDE FOR SONGWRITERS

www.halsguide.com

Hal Cohen has put together a great service with his Open Mic and Showcase Guide for singers and bands wanting to find exposure in the L.A. area, including feedback from those who've played the clubs as well as his Schmoozarama Message Board inviting info from other cities around the country. Also songwriting, legal and biz articles and stories from industry vets and great links.

LYRICAL LINE

www.lyricalline.com

An excellent gathering of articles and columns on song craft as well as lists of resources, forum, audio showcase, newsletter, peer critiques. "I Write the Songs Internet Radio Show" hosted by Mary Dawson and Sharon Braxton is very good with many archived shows on site.

THE MUSES MUSE

www.musesmuse.com

A great site! The pioneer of songwriting Web sites. A comprehensive and helpful resource maintained by Canadian, Jodi Krangle. Features lists of songwriters' and Music Industry organizations, useful web links, articles on songwriting, chat room, classifieds, contests, book and artist reviews, e-zine.

THE RECORDING ACADEMY (NARAS)

www.grammy.com

The GRAMMY organization. Check on NARAS educational and cultural events throughout the country, networking opportunities, band competitions, grants, membership and other activities in your area. Interviews with industry experts on hot current topics. Polls, news and events.

SONGWRITERS, COMPOSERS, AND LYRICISTS ASSN. INC. (SCALA)

www.scala.org.au

Proving the international scope of cyberspace, this South Australian site features songwriting articles from SCALA news as well as links to other organizations and services worldwide.

SONGWRITER 101

www.songwriter101.com

Excellent site that includes interviews, news, forums, with a stellar faculty comprised of hit songwriters and industry pros.

SONGJOURNEY.COM

www.songjourney.com

Nashville hit songwriters Kye Fleming and Mark Cawley created this interactive site as a way to give back their talent and success by helping educate writers about the business, find them collaborators and get them published. Very personal and hands-on.

SONGWRITER UNIVERSE

www.songwriteruniverse.com

Successful publishing executive and consultant Dale Kawashima created a site that combines a formidable list of resources with interviews with recording artists and hit songwriters, chat rooms and forums. He's also added Singeruniverse.com for singers.

SONGWRITERS HALL OF FAME

www.songwritershalloffame.org

A virtual museum of songwriting history. Educate yourself about the great writers of the past and present who have been inducted. Read their bios and listen to their songs. The National Academy of

Popular Music in New York is an activity of SHOF that produces showcases and workshops in that area. Check out this site and get their newsletter even if you don't live in New York.

Music Industry Information Sites

THE VELVET ROPE

www.velvetrope.com

The primo music bulletin board. Lots of topics, including inside gossip about major labels, industry pros, hirings, firings, mergers, disgruntled artists. Juicy stuff. Also valuable industry insights from the pros.

MUSIC DISH

www.musicdish.com/

An intelligent and deeply examined flow of articles and interviews from music industry observers and participants in addition to practical career tips for artists and entrepreneurs. They can also subscribe to their e-journal.

MUSIC INDUSTRY NEWS NETWORK

www.mi2n.com

This site aggregates music related stories from a variety of sources and you can subscribe to their newsletters based on your interest area (Business, Indie, Radio and Your Top News).

Tipsheets

INDEPENDENT MUSIC SALES AND DISTRIBUTION SITES

If you have good audio on your computer, you can make use of some great new music showcase and sales sites to stay current with new artists or to showcase your own music. There are many of these, but here are three majors and a portal for the rest:

COMPO10

http://compo10.com/MusicHosts.htm

Not a sales and distribution site, but an information site where you can compare more than 50 attributes of 80 sites for hosting and distributing music.

CDBABY

www.CDBaby.com

Not only the best venue for selling your physical and downloadable CDs but a stellar site for marketing info on their www.CDBaby.net and www.CDBaby.org sites.

AMAZON.COM

www.Amazon.com

You already know about Amazon if you've bought anything online. As an indie artist it's a viable option mostly because it's so visible to those who may be new to finding unknown artists. Not the best deal though, so don't let it be your only avenue.

THE ORCHARD

www.theorchard.com

The Orchard is as well-respected as the leading digital distributor, promoter and marketer for independent record labels. They represent thousands of labels and artists spanning 73 countries and every music genre.

Also see page 319 for a list of my favorite indie marketing people and info sites.

The Trade Magazines

See page 274 for details.

BILLBOARD.

(800) 745-8922 www.billboard.com

COLLEGE MUSIC JOURNAL

www.cmj.com

MUSIC ROW

(615) 321-3617 www.musicrow.com

MUSIC CONNECTION MAGAZINE

(818) 995-0101 www.musicconnection.com

RADIO AND RECORDS

(310) 553-4330 www.radioandrecords.com

Songwriters Print Periodicals

I highly recommend you subscribe to both of these:

AMERICAN SONGWRITER

www.americansongwriter.com
(615) 321-6096

PERFORMING SONGWRITER

www.performingsongwriter.com
(800) 883-7664

Film and TV Trades

These resources will help you research films in pre-production or production that may be looking for songs/composers or learn about the field.

BACKSTAGE.COM

N.Y (646) 654-5700 L.A. (323) 525-2356
www.backstage.com

Mostly for performers/actors etc. but some film music and Broadway musical coverage.

DAILY VARIETY

www.variety.com
(323) 857-6600

WEEKLY VARIETY

www.variety.com (800) 323-4345

The venerable veteran of entertainment news of all kinds, including music biz.

FILM MUSIC MAGAZINE

www.filmmusicworld.com 1-800-774-3700
or (310) 645-9000 Fax: (310) 496-0917

"The Professional Voice of Music for Film and Television." Great magazine and website. Their organization, the Film Music Network is also excellent with monthly meetings in New York, L.A. and San Francisco for professional networking, guest speakers and panel discussions. They also have an online Film Music Directory and a Film Music Store offering some outstanding books, CDs and resources to help you do business. Now featuring "Film Music Radio" on-site with film composer interviews.

FILM SCORE MONTHLY

www.filmscoremonthly.com
(310) 461-2240

"The Online Magazine of Motion Picture and Television Music Appreciation" has lots of great articles, interviews and a personable approach. A valuable resource for film music fans.

HOLLYWOOD REPORTER

www.hollywoodreporter.com
(323) 525-2000

Go to "Production Listings" to research lists of films in various stages of development and production. Combined print and online subscriptions available. Check website for rates.

SOUNDTRACK.NET

www.soundtrack.net
(Must e-mail for phone number)

"The Art of Film and Television Music." Great online source of research, interviews, stats, resources, reviews, current news. Now featuring podcasts.

Audio-Visual Media Tip Sheets

These publications tell you which audio-visual productions need music, what they need, and how to get it to them. All are pricey subscriptions but necessary if you're serious about writing music for audio/visual media.

WWW.TUNEDATA.COM

TuneData/Music Report. A division of Breakdown Services Ltd. In L.A.

WWW.PRODUCTIONWEEKLY.COM

Hollywood and International

WWW.MANDY.COM

Look for "composer" listings under "Post-Production"

WWW.INHOLLYWOOD.COM

For the U.S.

WWW.CUESHEET.NET

US and Europe

WWW.CRIMSONUK.COM

UK listings

SOCIETY OF COMPOSERS AND LYRICISTS (WWW.THESCL.COM)

with good educational and networking opportunities.

Bibliography

Amabile, Teresa M., et al. *Creativity in Context: Update to the Social Psychology of Creativity.* New York: Westview Press, 1996.

Growing Up Creative: Nurturing a Lifetime of Creativity. New York: Creative Education Foundation, 2nd ed., 1992.

Billboard's International Buyer's Guide. Annual. New York: Billboard Books.

Brabec, Jeffrey, and Todd Brabec. *Music Money & Success.* New York: Schirmer Books, 5th ed., 2006.

Cameron, Julia. *The Artist's Way: A Spiritual Path to Higher Creativity.* Los Angeles: Jeremy P. Tarcher/Perigee, 2002.

Chapman, Robert L., and Barbara Ann Kipfer, eds. *The Dictionary of American Slang.* Harper Collins, 3rd ed., 1998.

Davis, Sheila. *The Songwriters Idea Book: 40 Strategies to Excite Your Imagination. Help You Design Distinctive Songs, and Keep Your Creative Flow.* Cincinnati: Writer's Digest Books, 1996.

Dolan, Michael J. *Mastering Show Biz . . . From the Heart: 10 Timeless Principles.* Mulholland Pacific, 1998.

Gamez, George. *Creativity: How to Catch Lightning in a Bottle.* Peak Publications, 1996.

Halloran, Mark, ed. *The Musician's Business and Legal Guide.* Beverly Hills Bar Association Committee for the Arts, Englewood Cliffs, N.J.: Prentice-Hall, 3rd ed., 2001.

Kimpel, Dan. *Networking Strategies for the New Music Business.* Vallejo, CA. Artistpro, 2005.

Lees, Gene. *The Modern Rhyming Dictionary.* Cherry Lane Music, revised edition, 1987.

McGraw Hill's Dictionary Of American Slang And Colloquial Usage. McGraw-Hill, 4th ed., 2005

Mitchell, Kevin. *Hip-Hop Rhyming Dictionary.* Alfred Publishing Company, Inc., 2003.

Passman, Donald S. *All You Need to Know About the Music Business.* Free Press, 5th Ed. 2003.

Pattison, Pat. *Songwriting Essential Guide to Rhyming.* Milwaukee, Wisc.: Hal Leonard Publishing Corp., 1992.

Pattison, Pat. *Writing Better Lyrics.* Cincinnati: Writer's Digest Books, 2001.

Schulenberg, Richard. *Legal Aspects of the Music Industry: An Insider's View.* Billboard Books, 2005

Songwriter's Market. Annual. Cincinnati: Writer's Digest Books.

Spears, Richard A. *NTC's American Idioms Dictionary: The Most Practical References for the Everyday Expressions of Contemporary American English.* McGraw-Hill, 3rd Edition, 2000.

Wood, Clement, ed. *The Complete Rhyming Dictionary.* Laurel, rev. ed., 1992.

Additional Recommended Books

Beyond the above books referenced in the text and in the related chapters, there are others I'd like to recommend. There are obviously many additional books, literally too many to mention here, that are worth reading. I suggest you go to Amazon.com, read the reviews, consult songwriters organizations and publications, and visit my Web site at www.johnbraheny.com, where I have a lot more space. Until then, try my following list of recommendations (not necessarily in order of preference):

CREATIVITY

Bayles, David and Ted Orland. *Art and Fear.* Image Continuum Press, 2001.

Goldberg, Natalie. *Writing Down the Bones: Freeing the Writer Within.* Boston: Shambhala Publications, Expanded edition, 2006.

Michalko, Michael. *Cracking Creativity: The Secrets of Creative Genius.* Ten Speed Press, 2001.

SONGWRITING

Blume, Jason. *6 Steps to Songwriting Success: A Comprehensive Guide to Writing and Marketing Hit Songs.* Watson-Guptill Publications, 1999.

Luboff, Pat, and Pete. *88 Songwriting Wrongs & How to Right Them: Concrete Ways to Improve Your Songwriting and Make Your Songs More Marketable.* Cincinnati: Writer's Digest Books, 1992.

Tucker, Susan, and Strother, Linda Lee. *The Soul of a Writer: Intimate Interviews with Successful Songwriters.* Journey Publishing Company, 1996.

Webb, Jimmy. *Tunesmith: Inside the Art of Songwriting.* Hyperion, 1999.

Zollo, Paul. *Songwriters on Songwriting.* Da Capo Press, 4th edition, 2003.

LYRIC WRITING

Davis, Sheila. *The Craft of Lyric Writing.* Cincinnati: Writer's Digest Books, 1985.

Davis, Sheila. *Successful Lyric Writing.* Cincinnati: Writer's Digest Books, 1988.

Lewin, Esther, and Albert E. Lewin. *The Thesaurus of Slang.* Wordsworth Editions, 1998.

Oland, Pamela Phillips. *The Art of Writing Great Lyrics.* Allworth Press, 2001.

MELODY WRITING

Josefs, Jai. *Writing Music for Hit Songs: Including New Songs from the '90s.* Music Sales Corp., 2nd ed., 2000.

Perricone, Jack. *Melody in Songwriting: Tools and Techniques for Writing Hit Songs.* Milwaukee, Wisc.: Hal Leonard Publishing Corp., 2000.

Rooksby, Rikky. *How to Write Songs on Guitar: A Guitar-Playing and Songwriting Course.* Backbeat Books, 2000.

SONGWRITING IDEA JUMP-STARTERS

Aschmann, Lisa. *750 Songwriting Ideas: For Brave and Passionate People.* Hal Leonard Publishing Corporation, 2003.

Jordan, Barbara L. *Songwriters Playground: Innovative Exercises in Creative Songwriting.* Creative Music Marketing, 1997.

Rooksby, Rikki. *The Songwriting Sourcebook: How to Turn Chords Into Great Songs.* Backbeat Books, 2003.

Scott, Richard J. *Money Chords: A Songwriter's Sourcebook of Popular Chord Progressions.* Writer's Club Press, 2000.

MISCELLANEOUS

Bond, Sherry. *The Songwriter's and Musician's Guide to Nashville.* Allworth Press, 3rd edition, 2004.

Carter, Walter. *The Songwriter's Guide to Collaboration.* Mix Books, 2nd ed., 1997.

MUSIC BUSINESS

Avalon, Moses. *Confessions of a Record Producer: How to Survive the Scams and Shams of the Music Business.* Backbeat Books, 3rd ed., 2006.

Avalon, Moses. *Secrets of Negotiating a Record Contract: The Musician's Guide to Understanding and Avoiding Sneaky Lawyer Tricks.* Backbeat Books, 2001.

Blume, Jason. *This Business of Songwriting.* Billboard Books, 2006.

Borg, Bobby. *The Musician's Handbook: A Practical Guide to Understanding the Music Business.* Watson-Guptill Publications, 2003.

Kohn, Al, and Bob Kohn. *Kohn on Music Licensing.* Aspen Publishers. 3rd Bk&Cdr edition, 2002 (with update supplements).

Krasilovsky, M. William, and Sidney Shemel. *This Business of Music: The Definitive Guide to the Music Industry.* Billboard Books. 9th Ed, 2003.

Schulenberg, Richard. *Legal Aspects of the Music Industry: An Insider's View of the Legal and Practical Aspects of the Music Business.* Watson-Guptil Publications, 2005.

INTRODUCTION TO MUSIC BUSINESS

Aczon, Michael, Esq. *The Professional Musician's Legal Companion.* Artistpro, 2005.

Rapaport, Diane Sward. *Music Business Primer.* Prentice Hall, 2002.

MUSIC PUBLISHING

Beall, Eric. *Making Music Make Money: An Insider's Guide to Becoming Your Own Music Publisher.* Berklee Press, 2003.

Poe, Randy. *New Songwriter's Guide to Music Publishing: Everything You Need to Know to Make the Best Publishing Deals for Your Songs.* F & W Publications, 3rd edition, 2005.

Whitsett, Tim, and James Stroud. *Music Publishing: The Real Road to Music Business Success.* Mix Books, 5th ed., 2001.

Wixen, Randall. *The Plain and Simple Guide to Music Publishing.* Hal Leonard, 2005.

FILM AND TV

Churchill, Sharal. *The Indie Guidebook to Music Supervision for Films.* Filmic Press, 2000.

Davis, Richard. *Complete Guide to Film Scoring: The Art and Business of Writing Music for Movies and TV.* Berklee Press Publications, 2000.

Fisher, Jeffrey P. *Cash Tracks: Compose, Produce, and Sell Your Original Soundtrack Music and Jingles.* Artistpro, 2nd edition, 2005.

Kompanic, Sonny. *From Score To Screen: Sequencers, Scores, And Second Thoughts: The New Film Scoring Process.* Schirmer Books, 2004.

Miller, Lisa Anne, and Mark Northam. *Film and Television Composer's Resource Guide: The Complete Guide to Organizing and Building Your Business.* Milwaukee, Wisc. Hal Leonard Publishing Corp., 1998.

Rona, Jeff. *The Reel World: Scoring for Pictures.* Backbeat Books, 2000.

SELF-PROMOTION AND PUBLICITY

Fisher, Jeffrey P. *Ruthless Self-Promotion in the Music Industry.* Artistpro, 2nd edition, 2005.

Lathrop, Tad, *This Business of Music Marketing and Promotion.* Billboard Books, Revised and updated edition, 2003.

Spellman, Peter. *The Self-Promoting Musician: Strategies for Independent Music Success.* Berklee Press Publications, 2000.

MUSICAL THEATER

Frankel, Aaron. *Writing the Broadway Musical.* Da Capo Press, 2000.

Green, Stanley. *The World of Musical Comedy* (4th Edition, Revised and Enlarged). Da Capo Press, 1980.

Jones, Tom. *Making Musicals: An Informal Introduction to the World of Musical Theatre.* Limelight Editions, 1998.

INDEPENDENT RECORD PRODUCTION AND MARKETING

Baker, Bob. *Guerrilla Music Marketing Handbook.* Spotlight Publications, 2005.

Rapaport, Diane Sward. *How to Make and Sell Your Own Recording.* Prentice-Hall, 5th ed., 1999.

Schwartz, Daylle Deanna. *Start and Run Your Own Record Label.* Billboard Books, Revised and expanded Edition, 2003.

Spellman, Peter. *Indie Marketing Power: The Resource Guide For Maximizing Your Music Marketing.* Music Business Solutions, 2006.

Spellman, Peter and Bennett, Dan. *CD Marketing Plan.* Music Business Solutions, 2005.

INTERNET MARKETING

Baker, Bob. *MySpace Music Marketing: How To Promote & Sell Your Music on the Worlds Biggest Networking Site.* (PDF download from www.thebuzzfactor.com) 2006.

Nevue, David. *How To Promote Your Music Successfully On The Internet.* The Music Biz Academy, (Avail. as updated PDF download from www.musicbizacademy.com).

Novak, Jeannie, and Pete Markiewicz. *Creating Internet Entertainment.* John Wiley & Sons, 1997.

Sweeney, Tim, and John Dawes. *Using Email Effectively as an Artist or Songwriter (Audio CD).* Taco Truffles Media, 2004.

HOME RECORDING

Coryat, Karl. *Guerrilla Home Recording: How to Get Great Sound from Any Studio (no matter how weird and cheap your gear is).* Backbeat Books, 2005.

Mills-Huber, David and Philip Williams. *Professional Microphone Techniques.* Artistpro, 1999.

Volanski, John. *Sound Recording Advice.* Pacific Beach Publishing, 2002.